The End

IAN KERSHAW

The End

The Defiance and Destruction of
Hitler's Germany, 1944–45

THE PENGUIN PRESS
New York
2011

THE PENGUIN PRESS
Published by the Penguin Group
Penguin Group (USA) Inc., 375 Hudson Street, New York, New York 10014,
U.S.A. · Penguin Group (Canada), 90 Eglinton Avenue East, Suite 700,
Toronto, Ontario, Canada M4P 2Y3 (a division of Pearson Penguin
Canada Inc.) · Penguin Books Ltd, 80 Strand, London WC2R 0RL,
England · Penguin Ireland, 25 St. Stephen's Green, Dublin 2, Ireland
(a division of Penguin Books Ltd) · Penguin Books Australia Ltd,
250 Camberwell Road, Camberwell, Victoria 3124, Australia (a division
of Pearson Australia Group Pty Ltd) · Penguin Books India Pvt Ltd,
11 Community Centre, Panchsheel Park, New Delhi – 110 017, India ·
Penguin Group (NZ), 67 Apollo Drive, Rosedale, Auckland 0632,
New Zealand (a division of Pearson New Zealand Ltd) ·
Penguin Books (South Africa) (Pty) Ltd, 24 Sturdee Avenue,
Rosebank, Johannesburg 2196, South Africa

Penguin Books Ltd, Registered Offices:
80 Strand, London WC2R 0RL, England

First published in 2011 by The Penguin Press,
a member of Penguin Group (USA) Inc.

Illustration credits appear on pages vii–ix.

LIBRARY OF CONGRESS CATALOGING IN PUBLICATION DATA
Kershaw, Ian.
The end : the defiance and destruction of Hitler's Germany, 1944–1945 / Ian
Kershaw.
p.   cm.
Includes bibliographical references and index.
ISBN 978-1-59420-314-5 (hardback)
1. World War, 1939–1945—Germany.   2. Sociology, Military—Germany—
History—20th century.   3. Hitler, Adolf, 1889–1945—Military leadership.
4. Hitler, Adolf, 1889–1945—Public opinion.   I. Title.
D757.K38 2011
940.53'43—dc23   2011020135

Printed in the United States of America

1   3   5   7   9   10   8   6   4   2

Contents

List of Illustrations

List of Maps

Acknowledgements

One of the most pleasant parts of finishing a book is to thank those who, in different ways, have contributed to the making of it.

My thanks first of all to the British Academy for a grant which helped me to undertake the initial, exploratory research. I am also grateful to the archivists and staff of the various record repositories where I have worked: the Bundesarchiv in Berlin/Lichterfelde, the Bundesarchiv/ Militärarchiv in Freiburg, the Bibliothek für Zeitgeschichte in Stuttgart, the Bayerisches Hauptstaatsarchiv and Staatsarchiv München, the Staatsarchiv Augsburg, the International Tracing Service, Bad Arolsen, the National Archives in London, the Imperial War Museum at Duxford, and the Liddell Hart Centre for Military Archives in King's College, London. At the Bibliothek für Zeitgeschichte in Stuttgart, part of the Württembergische Landesbibliothek, I had every reason to be most grateful for the help and advice of the library's director and good friend of mine, Professor Gerhard Hirschfeld, and the head of its archival collections, Dr Irina Renz. Dr Susanne Urban was most helpful in guiding me through the extensive sources related to the death marches – only recently opened to researchers – at the International Tracing Service in Bad Arolsen, where I would also like to express my thanks to the director, M. Jean-Luc Blondel. At Duxford, I benefited greatly from Dr Stephen Walton's expert assistance in consulting the valuable holdings of German documents. I started, and finished, the research for the book in the incomparable Institut für Zeitgeschichte in Munich, where I have had the good fortune to be a welcome guest for many years, and I would like to express my warmest thanks to the director, Professor Horst Möller, and his colleagues, especially the library and archives staff, who as always dealt with my many requests with unfailing courtesy and friendliness.

Professor Otto Dov Kulka (Jerusalem), a highly esteemed colleague and friend with whom I have shared a lengthy and fruitful correspondence over many years, first pointed me in the direction of the records at Bad Arolsen. Beyond that, as ever I have been extremely grateful for his interest in my work, and for his valuable suggestions. Laurence Rees, good friend and brilliant producer of television documentaries, was kind enough to make available to me relevant transcripts of interviews, kept in the BBC Archives in London, from one of the series on which we collaborated, offered excellent advice, and was as always stimulating company, cheerfully helpful and most encouraging.

Numerous other friends and colleagues also helped, sometimes perhaps without being aware of how helpful they had been. Among them, I owe thanks to Professor Daniel Blatman (Jerusalem), for answering a number of queries about the death marches, and for related material which he kindly sent me. Dr Andreas Kunz, of the Bundesarchiv/ Militärarchiv in Freiburg, gave me some valuable tips on relevant archival holdings on my first visit there in connection with this project. Dr Heinrich Schwendemann of the University of Freiburg most generously went to great lengths to send me documents related to the French occupation of south-west Germany in 1945 and other relevant material that was not easy for me to access. Other colleagues who also supplied me with documents, papers or other materials, provided answers to my questions, or made me think more clearly about what I was attempting include Professor John Breuilly, Dr Michael Buddrus, Mr George Burton, Dr Simone Erpel, Dr Wolfgang Holl, Dr Holger Impekoven, Professor Tim Kirk, Dr Michael Kloft, Dr Alexander Korb, Mr Michael D. Miller, Professor Bob Moore (who went to undue trouble to send me a batch of documents on a specific point related to the Netherlands, his chief area of expertise), Professor Jonathan Steinberg, Dr Klaus Wiegrefe and Dr Benjamin Ziemann. I am glad of the opportunity to extend my warm thanks to all and apologize to anyone whom I have inadvertently omitted.

As I was feeling my way into the project, I benefited enormously, as always, from lengthy discussions with long-standing German friends, Professor Hans Mommsen (Feldafing), Professor Norbert Frei (Jena), Dr Hermann Graml and Dr Elke Fröhlich (Munich), all of whom helped me greatly in shaping my ideas. I am most grateful to each of them.

Two scholars and friends I want to thank especially. Dr Jürgen Förster, a fine historian and notable expert on the Wehrmacht at the

Bundesarchiv/Militärarchiv in Freiburg, answered numerous queries, directed me to important records, and, not least, read and commented on the completed typescript. Dr Nick Stargardt, Magdalen College, Oxford, who is currently working on what will be an important study of German society during the war, has been full of penetrating insights throughout. He also took the time and trouble to read the entire typescript and make numerous valuable suggestions. I am most grateful to both. Of course it needs to be added, as always, that responsibility for any remaining errors is my own.

An important debt of gratitude for their valuable suggestions on the typescript is also owing to splendid editors at Penguin – Simon Winder in London, and Laura Stickney in New York – while Andrew Wylie has been, as before, a wonderfully supportive agent. I would also like to thank all at Penguin who have helped to produce the book, Elizabeth Stratford for her excellent copy-editing and Cecilia Mackay for researching the photographs.

Finally, there are the personal debts of gratitude. Traude and Uli Spät have, as on so many occasions in the past, been extraordinarily generous in their hospitality during my stays in Munich, and taken a keen interest in my work over many years. Throughout this project Beverley Eaton, my long-serving secretary, has continued to provide excellent support, even now that I have left the University of Sheffield, and I am particularly grateful to her for undertaking so efficiently the laborious task of compiling the List of Works Cited. Last of all, my family remain the foundation on which all is built. My thanks and love to Betty, to David, Katie, Joe and Ella, and to Stephen, Becky, Sophie, Olivia and now Henry – the latest wonderful addition to the family roster.

Ian Kershaw
Manchester, November 2010

Preface

As disastrous defeat loomed in early 1945, Germans were sometimes heard to say they would prefer 'an end with horror, to a horror without end'. An 'end with horror' was certainly what they experienced, in ways and dimensions unprecedented in history. The end brought destruction and human loss on an immense scale. Much of this could have been avoided had Germany been prepared to bow to Allied terms. The refusal to contemplate capitulation before May 1945 was, therefore, for the Reich and the Nazi regime not just destructive, but also self-destructive.

A country defeated in war almost always at some point seeks terms. Self-destruction by continuing to fight on to the last, down to almost total devastation and complete enemy occupation, is extremely rare. Yet that is what the Germans did in 1945. Why? It is tempting to give a simple answer: their leader, Hitler, persistently refused to entertain any thought of surrender, so there was no option but to fight on. But this simply poses other questions. Why were Hitler's self-destructive orders still obeyed? What mechanisms of rule enabled him to determine Germany's fate when it was obvious to all with eyes to see that the war was lost and the country was being utterly laid waste? How far were Germans prepared to support Hitler to the end, even though they knew he was driving the country to destruction? Were they in fact still giving him their willing backing? Or were they merely terrorized into doing so? How and why did the armed forces continue fighting and the government machine keep on functioning to the end? What alternatives did Germans, civilians and soldiers, have in the last phase of the war? These and other questions soon arise, then, from what seems at first to be a straightforward query inviting a simple answer. They can only be tackled by examining structures of rule and mentalities as the catastrophe inexorably engulfed Germany in 1944–5. That is what this book seeks to do.

I first thought of writing such a book because, to my surprise, I couldn't think of another book which had tried to do what I had in mind. There are, of course, libraries of books about the end of the war, written from different perspectives, and widely varying in quality. There are important studies of the top Nazi leaders and, increasingly, of some of the regional chieftains, the Gauleiter.[1] Biographies exist also for many of the leading military figures.[2] There are literally thousands of accounts of events in the final climactic weeks of the Third Reich, both at the front and, it sometimes seems, for practically every town and village in Germany. Many local studies give graphic – often horrific – descriptions of the fate of individual townships as the unstoppable advance of the Allied and Soviet military juggernauts enveloped them.[3] Memoirs of experiences at the front or in the homeland, in cities pounded by Allied bombs, or facing the ordeals of flight and homelessness, abound. Detailed, often localized, military histories or accounts of specific Wehrmacht units or major battles are also commonplace, while the battle for Berlin, in particular, has naturally been the focus of numerous works.[4] The sixth volume of the German Democratic Republic's official history of the war, produced in the 1980s, despite its obvious ideological slant, provides a valuable attempt at a comprehensive military history, not confined to events on the front.[5] And more recently, the last volumes of the Federal Republic's own outstanding official military history series offer excellent detailed studies of the Wehrmacht, often stretching far beyond operational history.[6] Even so, these and other fine works on military history[7] touch on only some – if important – aspects of what I thought was necessary to answer the questions I wanted to tackle.

My initial intention had been to approach the problem through exploring the structures of rule in Nazi Germany in this last phase. It seemed to me that the major structural histories of the Third Reich tended to peter out largely by late 1944, dealing quite superficially with the final months of the regime.[8] This applies also to studies of the Nazi Party and its affiliates.[9] It rapidly became plain to me, however, that a mere structural analysis would not be enough, and that my examination had to be extended to the mentalities – at different levels – that underpinned the continued functioning of the regime. A comprehensive study of German mentalities in the last months has not yet been attempted.[10] Reconstructing them has to be done, therefore, from fragments.

I have tried to take into account the mentalities of rulers and ruled, of Nazi leaders and lowly members of the civilian population, of generals and ordinary soldiers, and on both the eastern and the western fronts. It is a wide canvas and I have to paint with a broad brush. I can, of course, present only selective examples to illustrate the spectrum of attitudes. For not least of the problems in trying to generalize about mentalities is that during its final months, and at a highly accelerated pace in its last weeks, the Nazi regime was splintering as well as shrinking. Germany was a big country and while, obviously, the extreme pressures of war afflicted all of its regions, they did not do so at the same time, or in exactly the same ways. Experiences of the civilian population in the different parts of the country and those of soldiers in different theatres of war naturally varied. I have tried to mirror the differing mentalities rather than resort to superficial generalizations.

The book mainly relates to what we might call the majority German population. There were, however, others whose experiences, themselves not reducible to easy generalization, were quite separate from those of most Germans since they did not and could not belong to mainstream German society. The fate of the horribly persecuted pariah groups in the clutches of the Nazis forms a further important part of the story of the continued functioning of the Nazi regime, amid the inexorable collapse and gathering doom. For, unenviable in the extreme as the situation was for most Germans, for the regime's racial and political enemies, ever more exposed to vicious retribution as it imploded, the murderous last months were a time of barely imaginable horror. Even when it was faltering and failing in every other respect, the Nazi regime managed to terrorize, kill and destroy to the last.

The history of the Nazi regime in its final months is a history of disintegration. In trying to tackle the questions I posed to myself, the main problem of method that I faced was the daunting one of trying to blend the varied facets of the fall of the Third Reich into a single history. It amounts to trying to write an integrated history of disintegration.

The only convincing way to attempt this, in my view, had to be through a narrative approach – though thematically structured within each chapter – that covered the last months of the regime. One logical place to begin would have been in June 1944, as Germany was militarily beset in the west by the consolidation of the successful Allied landings in Normandy, and in the east by the devastating breakthrough of the Red Army. However, I chose to start with the aftermath of the attempt on Hitler's life in July 1944, because this marked a significant *internal* caesura for the Nazi regime. From there I look in successive chapters at the German reactions to the Wehrmacht's collapse in the west in September, the first incursion of the Red Army onto German soil the following month, the hopes raised then promptly dashed by the Ardennes offensive in December, the catastrophe in the eastern provinces as they fell to the Soviets in January, the sharp escalation of terror at home in February, the crumbling of the regime in March, the last desperate attempts to hold out – accompanied by uncontrolled violence towards German citizens and, especially, perceived enemies of the regime – in April, and the efforts of the Dönitz regime even in early May to fight on until troops in the east could be brought westwards. The book ends at the German capitulation on 8 May 1945 and the subsequent arrest of members of the Dönitz administration.

Only through a narrative approach, I felt, could the dynamic – and the drama – of the dying phase of the regime be captured, as it inexorably fell apart in the wake of gathering military defeat. Only this way, too, I thought, was it possible to witness the ever despairing, but nevertheless for months partially effective, attempts to stave off the inevitable, the improvisation and scraping of the barrel that allowed the system to continue to function, the escalating brutality that ultimately ran amok, and the imploding self-destructiveness of Nazi actions. Some important elements of the story necessarily recur in more than one chapter. Bombing of cities, desertion of soldiers, death marches of concentration camp prisoners, the evacuation of civilian populations, collapsing morale, the ramping up of internal repression, the increasingly desperate propaganda ploys, are, for example, not confined to a single episode. But the narrative structure is important in showing how devastation and horror, if present throughout, intensified over the passage of time in these months. I have tried, consequently, to pay close attention to chronology and built up the picture essentially through going back to archival sources, including plentiful use of contemporary diaries and letters.

It is important to emphasize what this book is *not*. It is not a military history, so I don't describe what took place on the battlefield in any detail and provide only a brief overview of developments on the fronts as a backcloth to the questions that are central to the book. Nor does my book attempt to provide a history of Allied planning, or of the stages of the Allied conquest.[11] Rather, it views the war solely through German eyes in the attempt to understand better how and why the Nazi regime could hold out for so long. Finally, the book does not deal with the important question of continuities beyond the capitulation and into the occupation period, or the behaviour of the German population once a territory was occupied before the end of the war.[12]

It is impossible to recapture the reality of what it must have been like in those awful months, how ordinary people survived through extraordinary – and horrifying – circumstances. And, though I have worked on the Third Reich for many years, I found it hard, as well, to grasp fully the sheer extent of the suffering and death in this climax of the war. Suffering should not and cannot be reduced to bare numbers of casualties. Even so, simply the thought that the losses (dead, wounded, missing and captured) in the Wehrmacht – not counting those of the western Allies and the Red Army – ran at about 350,000 men per month in the last phase of the war itself gives a sense of the absolute slaughter on the fronts, far in excess of that of the First World War. Within Germany, too, death was omnipresent. Most of the half a million or so civilian victims of Allied bombing were caused by air raids on German cities in the very last months of the war. In these same months, hundreds of thousands of refugees lost their lives fleeing from the path of the Red Army. Not least, the terrible death marches of concentration camp internees, most of them taking place between January and April 1945, and accompanying atrocities left an estimated quarter of a million dead through exposure, malnutrition, exhaustion and random slaughter. The extent to which Germany had become an immense charnel-house in the last months of the Third Reich is barely imaginable.

At least by the end of writing the book, I did think, however, that I had come closer to an answer to the question I had set myself: how and why, given the scale of the mounting calamity, Hitler's regime could function – if, naturally, with diminishing effectiveness – for so long. If others think that after reading this book they, too, understand that better, I shall be well satisfied.

Dramatis Personae

The following list includes only those German political and military leaders who figure prominently in the text in some way, and is confined to indicating their positions or ranks in the months covered in the book, July 1944–May 1945.

POLITICAL LEADERSHIP
Reich

BORMANN, MARTIN (1900–1945): head of the Party Chancellery; Secretary to Hitler.

GOEBBELS, JOSEPH (1897–1945): Reich Minister of People's Enlightenment and Propaganda; Reich Plenipotentiary for Total War from July 1944.

GÖRING, HERMANN, Reich Marshal (1893–1946): designated successor to Hitler; head of the Four-Year Plan; Chairman of the Reich Defence Council; Commander-in-Chief of the Luftwaffe.

HIMMLER, HEINRICH (1900–1945): Reichsführer-SS; head of the German Police; Reich Commissar for the Strengthening of German Nationhood; Reich Minister of the Interior and Plenipotentiary for Reich Administration; Commander-in-Chief of the Replacement Army from July 1944.

HITLER, ADOLF (1889–1945): Leader; head of state; head of the Reich government; head of the Nazi Party; supreme commander of the Wehrmacht; Commander-in-Chief of the Army.

KALTENBRUNNER, ERNST (1903–46): SS-Obergruppenführer; head of the Security Police and the Security Service.

KRITZINGER, WILHELM (1890–1947): State Secretary in the Reich Chancellery.

LAMMERS, HANS-HEINRICH (1879–1962): Reich Minister and head of the Reich Chancellery.

LEY, ROBERT (1890–1945): Reich Organization Leader of the Nazi Party; leader of the German Labour Front.

RIBBENTROP, JOACHIM VON (1893–1946): Reich Foreign Minister.

SCHWERIN VON KROSIGK, LUTZ GRAF (1887–1977): Reich Finance Minister; First Minister and Reich Foreign Minister in the Dönitz government.

SEYß-INQUART, ARTHUR (1892–1946): Reich Commissar for the Occupied Territories of the Netherlands.

SPEER, ALBERT (1905–81): Reich Minister for Armaments and War Production; Reich Minister of Industry and Production in the Dönitz government.

STUCKART, WILHELM (1902–53): SS-Obergruppenführer; State Secretary in the Reich Ministry of the Interior; Reich Minister of the Interior in the Dönitz government.

Provincial

GIESLER, PAUL (1895–1945): Gauleiter of Munich-Upper Bavaria.

GREISER, ARTHUR (1897–1946): Gauleiter of Reichsgau Wartheland.

GROHÉ, JOSEF (1902–88): Gauleiter of Cologne-Aachen.

HANKE, KARL (1903–45): Gauleiter of Lower Silesia.

HOFER, FRANZ (1902–75): Gauleiter of the Tyrol.

HOLZ, KARL (1895–1945): Gauleiter of Franconia.

KOCH, ERICH (1896–1986): Gauleiter of East Prussia.

RUCKDESCHEL, LUDWIG (1907–86): Gauleiter of Bayreuth, April–May 1945.

WÄCHTLER, FRITZ (1891–1945): Gauleiter of Bayreuth until April 1945.

WAHL, KARL (1892–1981): Gauleiter of Swabia.

MILITARY LEADERSHIP

BLASKOWITZ, JOHANNES, Colonel-General (1883–1948): Commander-in-Chief of Army Group G, May–September 1944, then December 1944–January 1945; Commander-in-Chief of Army Group H, January–April 1945.

DIETRICH, SEPP, SS-Oberstgruppenführer and Colonel-General of the Waffen-SS (1892–1966): Commander of the 6th SS-Panzer Army, October 1944–May 1945.

DÖNITZ, KARL, Grand-Admiral (1891–1980): Commander-in-Chief of the Navy; Reich President following Hitler's death.

GUDERIAN, HEINZ, Colonel-General (1888–1954): Chief of the Army General Staff, July 1944–March 1945

HARPE, JOSEF, Colonel-General (1887–1968): Commander-in-Chief of Army Group A, September 1944–January 1945; Commander of the 5th Panzer Army, March–April 1945.

HAUSSER, PAUL, SS-Oberstgruppenführer and Colonel-General of the Waffen-SS (1880–1972): Commander-in-Chief of Army Group G, January–April 1945.

HEINRICI, GOTTHARD, Colonel-General (1886–1971): Commander of the 1st Panzer Army, August 1944–March 1945; Commander-in-Chief of Army Group Vistula, March–April 1945.

HOßBACH, FRIEDRICH, General (1894–1980): Commander of the 4th Army, July 1944–January 1945.

JODL, ALFRED, Colonel-General (1890–1946): Chief of the Wehrmacht Operations Staff in the High Command of the Wehrmacht.

KEITEL, WILHELM, Field-Marshal (1882–1946): head of the High Command of the Wehrmacht.

KESSELRING, ALBERT, Field-Marshal (1885–1960): Commander-in-Chief South to March 1945; Commander-in-Chief West, March–April 1945.

MANTEUFFEL, HASSO VON, General of the Panzer Troops (1897–1978): Commander of the 5th Panzer Army, September 1944–March 1945; Commander of the 3rd Panzer Army, March–May 1945.

MODEL, WALTER, Field-Marshal (1891–1945): Commander-in-Chief Army Group Centre, June–August 1944; Commander-in-Chief West, August–September 1944; Commander-in-Chief of Army Group B, September 1944–April 1945.

REINHARDT, GEORG-HANS, Colonel-General (1887–1963): Commander-in-Chief Army Group Centre, August 1944–January 1945.

RENDULIĆ, LOTHAR, Colonel-General (1887–1971): Commander-in-Chief Army Group Courland, January 1945, March–April 1945; Commander-in-Chief Army Group North, January–March 1945; Commander-in-Chief Army Group South (renamed 'Ostmark' at end of April), April–May 1945.

RUNDSTEDT, GERD VON, Field-Marshal (1875–1953): Commander-in-Chief West, September 1944–March 1945.

SCHÖRNER, FERDINAND, Colonel-General, from 5 April 1945 Field-Marshal (1892–1973): Commander-in-Chief Army Group North, July 1944–January 1945; Commander-in-Chief Army Group Centre January–May 1945.

VIETINGHOFF-SCHEEL, HEINRICH VON, Colonel-General (1887–1952): Commander-in-Chief Army Group Courland, January–March 1945; Commander-in-Chief South, March–May 1945.

WOLFF, KARL, SS-Obergruppenführer, General of the Waffen-SS (1900–84): from July 1944 Plenipotentiary General of the German Wehrmacht in Italy.

The End

Introduction:
Going Down in Flames

Wednesday, 18 April 1945: American troops are at the gates of the town of Ansbach, administrative capital of Central Franconia. The Nazi District Leader has fled during the night, most German soldiers have been moved to the south, the citizens have been camped out in air-raid shelters for days. Any rational thinking signals surrender. But the military commandant of the town, Dr Ernst Meyer – a fifty-year-old colonel of the Luftwaffe, with a doctorate in physics – is a fanatical Nazi, insistent on fighting to the end. A nineteen-year-old theology student, unfit for military service, Robert Limpert, decides to act, to prevent his town being destroyed in a senseless last-ditch battle.

Limpert had witnessed the complete devastation through Allied bombs of the beautiful city of Würzburg the previous month. This had prompted him to the dangerous venture of distributing leaflets earlier in April pleading for the surrender of Ansbach, its picturesque baroque and rococo buildings still intact, without a fight. He now takes an even bigger risk. Around 11.00 a.m. on that lovely spring morning he cuts the telephone wires which he thinks connect the commandant's base with the Wehrmacht unit outside the town – a futile attempt at sabotage, in fact, since unbeknown to him the base had just moved. He is spotted doing so by two boys, members of the Hitler Youth. They report what they have seen, and the matter is urgently taken up by the local constabulary. A policeman is sent to Limpert's home, who finds the young man in possession of a pistol and incriminating evidence, and arrests him.

The local police report the arrest to the head of the remaining civil administration in Ansbach, who telephones the military commandant, currently out of town. Predictably enraged by what he hears, the commandant hastens to the police station and peremptorily establishes a

3

three-man tribunal consisting of the head of the constabulary, his deputy and the commandant's own assistant. After a farcical 'trial' lasting a mere couple of minutes, in which the accused is not allowed to speak, the commandant pronounces him sentenced to death, the sentence to be carried out immediately.

As a noose is placed round his neck at the town hall gate, Limpert manages to struggle free and make a run for it, but within a hundred metres is caught by police, kicked and pulled by the hair before being hauled back screaming. No one in the assembled crowd stirs to help him. Some in fact also punch and kick him. Even now his misery is not over. The noose is again put round his neck and he is hanged. But the rope breaks, and he falls to the ground. The noose is once more put round his neck, and he is finally hoisted to his death in the town hall square. The commandant orders the body to be left hanging 'until it stinks'. Shortly afterwards he apparently requisitions a bicycle and immediately flees the town. Four hours later, the Americans enter Ansbach without a shot being fired and cut down the body of Robert Limpert.[1]

As this grim episode shows, in its terroristic repression the Nazi regime functioned to the last. But it was not only a matter of the rabid Nazi military commandant, Colonel of the Luftwaffe Dr Meyer, ruthlessly dispatching a perceived traitor and saboteur, an agent of the regime imposing his will through superior force. Even faced with such fanaticism, the policemen, aware that the Americans were on the verge of entering the town, might have acted to save themselves future trouble with the occupying force by dragging out the arrest and interrogation of Limpert. Instead, they chose to follow regulations and carry out their duty as they saw it as expeditiously as possible, continuing to function as minor custodians of a law that, as they later claimed to have seen at the time, was now no more than the expression of the commandant's arbitrary will.

The same could be said for the head of the local civilian administration. He, too, could have used his experience and awareness of the imminent end of the fighting to procrastinate. Instead, he chose to do what he could to hasten proceedings and cooperate with the commandant. The townsfolk who had found their way into the town hall square and saw Limpert escape could have rallied to his aid at such a juncture. Instead, some of them even helped the police to drag the struggling young man back to his execution place. At every level, then, in these extreme circumstances and in these final moments of the war, as far as Ansbach was concerned, those wielding power continued to work in the interests of the regime – and in doing so were not devoid of public support.

Incidents as harrowing as this case, where local inhabitants attempted to prevent futile destruction at the very end and encountered savage reprisals, while others were still prepared to back the repression of the regime's functionaries, were no rarity in these final stages of the most terrible war in history. Dozens of other cases could be chosen as illustration of the continued functioning of the regime's terror – now, in the last months of the conflict, levelled at its own citizens as well as at foreign workers, prisoners, Jews and others long regarded as its enemies.[2]

It was not just in the ever wilder displays of terror by fanatics and desperadoes that the regime kept going to the last. Most important of all was the behaviour of the military. If the Wehrmacht had ceased to function, then the regime would have collapsed. The signs of dissolution and disintegration in the Wehrmacht were manifold in the later states of the war, most obviously so in the west. Soldiers deserted, despite the threat of brutal punishment. By early 1945, certainly in the west, most felt that to continue the struggle was senseless, and yearned only to be back with their families. Yet the Wehrmacht continued the fight. Generals and field commanders still issued their orders, even in the most hopeless of circumstances. And the orders were obeyed.

Beneath the hail of bombs, in the mayhem of destruction of towns and cities as the Reich collapsed to immensely superior force in east and west, a semblance of 'normality' in the mounting chaos was sustained as bureaucracy strained every sinew to continue functioning. Of course, the Reich was shrinking by the day, channels of communication were collapsing, the transport network was as good as at an end, basic utilities like gas, electricity and water were no longer available to millions of homes, and bureaucratic administration faced any number of huge practical problems. But where Germany had not yet fallen under occupied rule, there was no descent into anarchy. Civil administration continued, however ineffectively in the face of extreme adversity and immense dislocation. Military as well as civilian courts continued to hand out ever more severe sentences. Wages and salaries were still being paid in April 1945.[3] Grants awarded by a leading academic body in

Berlin were made down to the last weeks of the war to foreign students, even now regarded as an investment for continued German influence in the 'new Europe'.[4]

Despite mounting handicaps, distribution of the ever more restricted food rations was maintained with difficulty and, increasingly by improvised means, post continued after a fashion to struggle through. Limited forms of entertainment still somehow functioned as a conscious device to sustain morale and distract attention for a short while from the unfolding disaster. A last concert by the Berlin Philharmonic took place on 12 April, four days before the Soviet assault on the Reich capital was launched. The finale from Richard Wagner's *Götterdämmerung* was, of course, on the programme.[5] Some cinemas remained open. Only a week before Stuttgart capitulated on 22 April its citizens could find momentary distraction from their trauma through a visit to the cinema to see *The Woman of my Dreams*.[6] Even football matches were still played. The last game of the war took place as late as 23 April 1945, when FC Bayern Munich, 'Gaumeister' of 1945, beat their local rivals TSV 1860 Munich 3-2.[7] Truncated newspapers still appeared. The main Nazi paper, the *Völkischer Beobachter*, was published in the unoccupied part of southern Germany to the very end. Its last edition, on 28 April 1945, two days before Hitler's suicide in the Berlin bunker, carried the headline: 'Fortress Bavaria'.

The reasons for Germany's collapse are evident, and well known. Why and how Hitler's Reich kept on functioning till the bitter end is less obvious. That is what this book seeks to explain.

The fact that the regime *did* hold out to the end – and that the war ended only when Germany was militarily battered into submission, its economy destroyed, its cities in ruins, the country occupied by foreign powers – is historically an extreme rarity. Wars between states in the modern era have usually ended in some kind of negotiated settlement. The ruling elites of a state facing military defeat have generally sued for peace at some point, and eventually, under some duress, reached a territorial agreement, however disadvantageous. The end of the First World War fitted this pattern. The end of the Second was completely different. The rulers of Germany in 1945, knowing the war was lost and complete destruction beckoned, were nevertheless prepared to fight on until their country was practically obliterated.

Authoritarian regimes facing defeat in unpopular wars and seen to be heading for disaster do not usually survive to preside over outright catastrophe. Some in the past have been overthrown by revolution from below, as in Russia in 1917 and Germany in 1918 (in the latter case after the military elite had already taken steps to end a lost war). Others – a more usual development – are toppled by a coup from within, by elites unwilling to be taken down with the failing regime and wanting to salvage something. The deposition of Mussolini by his own Fascist Grand Council in 1943 is a prime example. In Germany, by contrast, the regime, though universally recognized, not just by ordinary people but by those in positions of power, civilian and military, to be heading for the buffers, fought on until it was completely destroyed and, unlike 1918, under foreign occupation.[8] Approximate parallels come to mind only in the cases of Japan in 1945 (which, however, surrendered while the country was still unoccupied) and more recently – and in this case very faintly (given the very short-lived and militarily one-sided war) – in Saddam Hussein's Iraq.

The contrast between 1918 and 1945 in Germany again raises the question: how and why was Hitler's Germany able to fight on to the bitter end? Was no other conclusion to the terrible conflict possible? And if not, why not? 'The real puzzle', it has been aptly remarked, 'is why people who wanted to survive fought and killed so desperately and so ferociously almost to the last moments of the war.'[9]

Of course, in the First World War there had been no Allied demand for 'unconditional surrender'. The formula produced by US President Franklin D. Roosevelt at the Casablanca Conference in January 1943, and agreed by the British Prime Minister, Winston Churchill, was the first time that a sovereign state had been formally offered no terms short of total and unconditional capitulation.[10] This was often seized upon in the early post-war years, particularly by German generals, as the sole and adequate explanation for Germany's prolonged fight, since, it was claimed, the demand for 'unconditional surrender' ruled out any alternative.[11] Some former soldiers long after the war ended still insisted that it had helped to motivate them to keep on fighting.[12] It is certainly possible to argue that the demand was counter-productive, and that it simply played into the hands of Nazi propaganda. As such, it contributed, at least initially, to strengthening the will to hold out, but it is doubtful whether attributing blame to the Allies for a mistaken policy of 'unconditional surrender' amounts to any more than what one scholar has called a 'flimsy excuse'.[13] According to General Walter Warlimont, Deputy Chief of Operations in the OKW, 'hardly any notice was taken of it' in the High Command of the Wehrmacht and 'there was no examination by the OKW Operations Staff of its military consequences'.[14] In other words, it made no difference to the strategy – or lack of one – adopted by the German military leadership in the last phase of the war. Answers to the question of why Germany fought on have consequently to be sought less in the Allied demand, whatever its merits or failings, than in the structures of the German regime in its dying phase and the mentalities that shaped its actions.

Why, unlike in 1918, did the German people not rise up against a regime so obviously taking them to perdition? In the early post-war era, for the German people just starting to pick up their lives again after the trauma of such death and destruction, and not anxious to dwell upon any deeper causes of the catastrophe that had beset their country, it seemed unnecessary to look much further for explanation than the terroristic nature of the Nazi regime. It was easy, and in some ways reassuring, for Germans to see themselves as the hapless victims of ruthless oppression by their brutal rulers, stifled in any scope for action by a totalitarian police state. The feelings were understandable and, as subsequent chapters will show, certainly not without justification. Of course, there was an undeniably apologetic strain to the way such an explanation could be, and was, used in post-war Germany to exculpate almost the whole society from the crimes placed at the door of Hitler, the all-powerful Dictator, and a clique of criminally ruthless Nazi leaders. But scholarly interpretation, too, in the post-war era placed the overwhelming emphasis upon terror and repression in the 'totalitarianism' theorem that dominated so much historical and political science literature at that time (though without direct focus on the last phase of the war).[15] A society coerced into acquiescence, unable to act because of the comprehensive coercion of the highly repressive 'totalitarian state', provided, it seemed, sufficient explanation.

Terror is unquestionably critical to the question of how and why the regime continued to function to the end. As we shall see, the level of terroristic repression, which now boomeranged back from the treatment of conquered peoples to be directed at the German people themselves as well as perceived 'racial enemies', does indeed go a long way towards explaining why there was no revolution from below, why an organized mass uprising was not possible. Given the level of repression, together with the immense dislocation in the last months, a revolution from below, as at the end of the First World War, was an impossibility. But terror cannot completely explain the regime's capacity to fight on. It was not terror that drove on the regime's elites. Terror does not explain the behaviour of the regime's 'paladins' – both those who shared Hitler's *Götterdämmerung* mentality and were ready to see Germany go down in flames, and the far greater number of those seeking to save their own skins. It does not explain the continued functioning of a government bureaucracy, both at central and local levels. Not least, it does not explain the Wehrmacht's readiness – at any rate the readiness of the Wehrmacht leadership – to continue the fight. Nor, finally, does terror explain the behaviour of those in the regime at different levels prepared to *use* terror to the very last, even when it served no further rational purpose.

Although after the end of the Cold War the 'totalitarianism' theorem underwent something of a renaissance,[16] its emphasis upon terror and repression in controlling the 'total society' has never regained the ground it held in the early post-war era as an interpretation of the behaviour of ordinary Germans during the Third Reich. On the contrary: recent research has increasingly tended to place the emphasis upon the enthusiastic support of the German people for the Nazi regime, and their willing collaboration and complicity in policies that led to war and genocide.[17] 'One question remains,' a German writer remarked. 'What was it actually that drove us to follow [Hitler] into the abyss like the children in the story of the Pied Piper? The puzzle is not Adolf Hitler. We are the puzzle.'[18] Such a comment, leaving aside the suggestion of bamboozlement, presumes an essential unity, down to the end, between leader and led.

Whereas the emphasis used to be placed on society and regime in conflict[19] – essentially presuming a tyranny *over* a mainly reluctant but coerced people – this has shifted to a society in harness with the aims of the regime, largely in tune with and supportive of its racist and expansionist policies, fully behind its war effort. Relentless Nazi propaganda had done its job; it was 'the war that Hitler won', according to an interpretation advanced many years ago.[20] The Nazis were successful, it is now frequently claimed, in inculcating in people the sense that they were part of an inclusive national-racist 'people's community', integrated by the exclusion of Jews and others deemed inferior and unfit to belong to it, unified by the need to defend the nation against the powerful enemies surrounding it and threatening its very existence.[21] 'Notwithstanding the disillusionment and bitterness of large parts of the German population in the last war years, the "people's community" remained intact to the bitter end', one scholar has asserted.[22] Moreover, Hitler's regime had 'bought off' the German population, securing loyalty through a standard of living sustained by plundering the occupied territories.[23] Though it is usually acknowledged that this 'people's community' was starting to crumble in the face of impending defeat, lasting support for Nazism – bound together through knowledge of terrible German crimes – is still advanced as a significant reason why Hitler's regime was able to hold out to the end.[24] 'The basic legitimacy of the Third Reich remained intact', another historian has claimed, 'because Germans could not envision a desirable alternative to National Socialism', demonstrating 'remarkable commitment to National Socialism in the war'. Their subsequent sense of betrayal by Nazism 'rested on a strong identification with the Third Reich right up to the moment of abandonment'.[25] In perhaps the apogee of this approach, it has been suggested that 'the great majority of the German people soon became devoted to Hitler and they supported him to the bitter end in 1945'. 'Some', it is acknowledged, hinting at a tiny minority, 'had had enough', but the consensus that had underpinned the dictatorship from the outset, the argument runs, held up to the end.[26]

The chapters which follow will provide a good deal of evidence to cast doubt upon this intepretation. They will question whether either the scale of terror or the extent of support for the regime can provide an adequate explanation for its ability to hold out until Germany was smashed to smithereens. Yet if neither terror nor support fully explains it, what does?

A number of questions immediately arise. Beyond the significance of the Allied demand for 'unconditional surrender', one could ask how far Allied mistakes in strategy and tactics, which certainly occurred, weakened their own efforts to bring the war to an early end and temporarily boosted the confidence of the German defenders. But whatever significance might accrue to such factors, the determining reasons for Germany's continued fight have surely to be explained internally, from within the Third Reich, rather than externally, through Allied policy. What weight, for instance, should we attach to the feeling of Nazi leaders that they had nothing to lose by fighting on, since they had in any case 'burnt their boats'? How significant, indeed, was the greatly expanded scope of the Nazi Party's powers in the final phase, as it sought to revitalize itself by evoking the spirit of the 'period of struggle' before 1933? In what ways did a highly qualified and able state bureaucracy contribute, despite increasing and ultimately overwhelming administrative disorder, to the capacity to hold out? How important was the fear of the Red Army in sustaining the fight to the end? Why were German officers, especially the generals in crucial command posts, prepared to fight on even when they recognized the futility of the struggle and the absurdity of the orders they were being given? And what role was played by the leading Nazis beneath Hitler – in particular the crucial quadrumvirate of Bormann, Himmler, Goebbels and Speer – and the provincial viceroys, the Gauleiter, in ensuring that the war effort could be sustained despite mounting, then overwhelming, odds until the regime had destroyed itself in the maelstrom of total military defeat? In particular, how indispensable was the role of Speer in continuing to defy enormous obstacles to provide armaments for the Wehrmacht? Finally, though far from least, there is the part played by Hitler himself and the lasting allegiance to him within the German power elites.

A simple – though self-evidently inadequate – answer to the question of how and why Germany held out to the bitter end is, in fact, that Hitler adamantly and at all times refused to contemplate capitulation, so that there was no alternative to fighting on. Even catacombed in his bunker, the borders of fantasy and reality increasingly blurred, Hitler's hold on power was not over until his suicide on 30 April 1945. A central tenet of his 'career' had been revenge for the national humiliation of 1918; the '1918 syndrome' was deeply embedded in his psyche.[27] There would, he frequently and insistently declared, be no repeat of 1918, no new version of the 'cowardly' capitulation at the end of the First World War. Destruction with honour intact through fighting to the end, upholding the almost mythical military code of battling till the last bullet, creating a legend of valour for posterity out of the despair of defeat, and above all enshrining in history his own unique, self-perceived heroic legacy, was in his mind infinitely preferable to negotiating a 'disgraceful' surrender. Since he personally had no future after defeat, a suicidal approach was not hard to adopt. But it was not just personally self-destructive. It meant also condemning his own people and country to destruction. The German people, in his eyes, had failed him, had not proved worthy of his leadership. They were expendable. Without him, in fact, his monstrous ego told him, everything was expendable. In his crudely dualist way of thinking, it had always been victory or destruction. He unwaveringly followed his own logic.

Hitler's own central part in Germany's self-destructive urges as the Reich collapsed is obvious. Above all, his continued power provided a barrier to any possibility, which his paladins were keen to explore, of negotiating a way out of the escalating death and destruction. But this only brings us back to the question: why was he able to do this? Why did his writ continue to run when it was obvious to all around him that he was dragging them down with him and taking his country to perdition? Accepting that Hitler was a self-destructive individual, why did the ruling elites below him – military, Party, government – allow him to block all rational exit routes? Why was no further attempt made, after the failed coup of July 1944, to impede Hitler's determination to continue the war? Why were subordinate Nazi leaders and military commanders prepared to follow him down to the complete destruction of the Reich? It was not that they wanted to follow him to personal oblivion. As soon as Hitler was dead, they did what they could to avoid the abyss. Almost all Nazi leaders fled, anxious not to follow Hitler's example of self-immolation. Military commanders were now prepared to offer their partial capitulations in rapid succession, fighting on only to get as many of their men as possible into the western zones and away from the Red Army. Some harboured fantasies of being of future service to the western Allies.

Total capitulation followed in just over a week from the final act of the drama in the bunker. The mopping-up of Nazis on the run, now with nothing left to fight for, swiftly ensued. The occupation began its job of sorting out the mayhem and trying to set up new forms and standards of government. So Hitler was without question crucial to the last. But his lingering power was sustained only because others upheld it, because they were unwilling, or unable, to challenge it.

The issue stretches, therefore, beyond Hitler's own intractable personality and his unbending adherence to the absurdly polarized dogma of total victory or total downfall. It goes to the very nature of Hitler's rule, and to the structures and mentalities that upheld it, most of all within the power elite.

The character of Hitler's dictatorship is most appropriately depicted as a form of 'charismatic rule'.[28] Structurally, it resembled in some ways a modern form of absolutist monarchy. Like an absolute monarch, Hitler was surrounded by fawning courtiers (even if his 'court' lacked the splendour of Versailles or Sanssouci); he depended upon satraps and provincial grandees, bound to him through personal loyalty, to implement directives and see that his writ ran; and he relied upon trusted field-marshals (handsomely rewarded with large donations of money and property) to run his wars. The analogy rapidly fades, however, when crucial components of the modern state – an elaborate bureaucracy and mechanisms (here chiefly in the hands of a monopoly Party) to orchestrate popular support and control – are included. For an important part of the edifice, crucially bolstering Hitler's authority and creating for him untouchable, almost deified status, towering above all the institutions of the Nazi state, was the mass plebiscitary backing that a combination of propaganda and repression helped to produce. However manufactured the image was, there can be no doubt of Hitler's genuine and immense popularity among the great mass of the German people down to the middle of the war. From the first Russian winter of 1941, nevertheless, everything points to the fact that this popularity was sagging. From the following winter – the winter of the Stalingrad debacle, for which he was directly held responsible – it was in steep decline. In terms of mass appeal, therefore, Hitler's 'charisma' was terminally undermined as the war turned sour and the defeats mounted.

Structurally, however, his 'charismatic rule' was far from at an end. Even compared with other authoritarian regimes, Hitler's was personalized in the extreme, and had been from the outset, back in 1933. No politburo, war council, cabinet (since 1938), military junta, senate or gathering of ministers existed to mediate or check his rule. Nothing approximated, for instance, to the Fascist Grand Council which triggered Mussolini's deposition in 1943. A vital hallmark of this personalized 'charismatic rule' had been, from the start, the erosion and fragmentation of government. By mid-1944, when this book begins – at a point of intense shock and internal restructuring in the immediate aftermath of the failed bomb plot of 20 July 1944 – the process of fragmentation had become greatly expanded and magnified. No unified body posed a challenge to Hitler. Put another way, the structures and mentalities of 'charismatic rule' continued even when Hitler's popular appeal was collapsing. They were sustained in the main not by blind faith in Hitler. More important, for arch-Nazis, was the feeling that they had no future without Hitler. This provided a powerful negative bond: their fates were inextricably linked. It was the loyalty of those who had burnt their boats together and now had no way out. For many of those who by this time were lukewarm if not outrightly hostile to Nazism, it was often as good as impossible to separate support for Hitler and his regime from the patriotic determination to avoid defeat and foreign occupation. Hitler represented, after all, the fanatical defence of the Reich. Removing Hitler (as was attempted in July 1944) could be, and was, seen by many, in a rehashing of the 1918 myth, as a 'stab in the back'. Not least, as everyone was aware, the Dictator still had a ruthless apparatus of enforcement and repression at his disposal. Fear (or at least extreme caution) played an obvious part in the behaviour of most. Even the highest in the land knew they needed to tread warily. Whatever the range of motives, the effect was the same: Hitler's power was sustained to the very end.

As the end neared, and central government fragmented almost completely, life-and-death decisions passed ever further down the hierarchy to the regional, district and local levels to the point that individuals like the military commandant in Ansbach acquired arbitrary and lethal executive power. But this radicalization at the grass roots, crucial though it was to the mounting irrationality of the final phase, would have been impossible without the encouragement, authorization and 'legitimation' provided from above, from the leadership of a regime in its death-throes facing no internal challenge.

Perhaps the most fundamental element in trying to find answers to the question of how and why the regime held out to the point of total destruction revolves, therefore, around the structures and mentalities of 'charismatic rule'. Linking such an approach to a differentiated assessment of the ways in which ordinary Germans responded to the rapidly gathering Armageddon offers the potential to reach a nuanced assessment of why Nazi rule could continue to function to the end.

The chapters that follow proceed chronologically, beginning with the aftermath of the failed bomb plot of 20 July 1944 – a caesura in the governmental structures of the Third Reich – and extending to the capitulation on 8 May 1945. By combining structural history and the history of mentalities, and dealing with German society from above and below, the narrative approach has the virtue of being able to depict in precise fashion the dramatic stages of the regime's collapse, but at the same time its astonishing resilience and desperate defiance in sustaining an increasingly obvious lost cause. The focus throughout is exclusively on Germany: what the Allies, often puzzled themselves by the German willingness to carry on fighting under hopeless circumstances, were thinking, planning and doing forms no part of the analysis. Of course, this was scarcely unimportant for the course of the war, and what happened on the battlefield in the various theatres of war was ultimately decisive. But this is no military history, and the relevant stages of the Allied advance on Germany, east and west, are tersely summarized, primarily in order to provide a framework for the subsequent assessment.

Since we know the end of the story, it is hard not to ask why contemporaries did not see as obviously as we do in retrospective: that the war was plainly lost, at the absolute latest by the time the western Allies had consolidated their landings in France and the Red Army had advanced deep into Poland in the summer of 1944. But, until surprisingly late, that was not how they did see it. Certainly, they knew that the great vistas of 1941–2 could not be realized. But the German leadership, not just Hitler, thought there was still something to be gained from the war. Strength of will and radical mobilization, they thought, could prolong the conflict until new 'miracle weapons' came along. The war effort would be sustained so far that the Allies would look for a negotiated way out of mounting losses as advances were blocked or reversed. A split between east and west would materialize, and Germany would still be able to hold on to some territorial gains and, eventually with western aid, turn against the common enemy of Soviet Communism. Such hopes and illusions, if harboured by a rapidly dwindling number of Germans (especially once the Red Army reached the Oder in late January 1945), lingered almost to the end. So even in the final, terrible phase of death and devastation, faced with insuperable odds, the fight went on amid a mounting series of regional collapses, driven by increasingly irrational but self-sustaining destructive energy.

Trying to explain how this could be so – how the regime, torn apart on all sides, could continue to operate until the Red Army was at the portals of the Reich Chancellery – is the purpose of this book.

I

Shock to the System

It takes a bomb under his arse to make Hitler see reason.
Joseph Goebbels, 23 July 1944[1]

I

It was the beginning of the end for the Third Reich. By late July 1944, the D-Day landings of the western Allies that had taken place in Normandy on 6 June 1944 had been consolidated. Troops and arms were being shipped over to the Continent in ever greater numbers. Direct ground attack on the Reich itself was now in prospect. On the eastern front, the Red Army, in its massive offensive 'Operation Bagration', launched just over a fortnight after D-Day, had smashed through the defences of the Wehrmacht's Army Group Centre (an immense formation of 48 divisions, in four armies, and pivotally placed over a 700-kilometre stretch of the enormous front), inflicting huge losses, and had advanced more than 300 kilometres. To the south, Rome had fallen to the Allies and German troops were engaged in fierce rearguard fighting near Florence. Meanwhile, ever more German towns and cities were exposed to relentless devastation from the air. With resources and manpower stretched to the limit and hugely inferior to the combined might of the enemy, now forcing back the Wehrmacht from the east, west and south, the writing was on the wall for the Hitler regime.

At least, that was how the western Allies saw it. They were confident that the war would be over by Christmas.[2] Viewed from Germany, it was a different matter. Here, attitudes about the state of the war and Germany's prospects varied widely, whether at the elite level, among the civilian and military Reich leadership, or among the public on the 'home

front' and the millions of men under arms. Defeatism, reluctant acceptance that the war was lost, realistic acknowledgement of overwhelming
enemy strength, waning belief in Hitler, and fears for the future were more
evident by the day. On the other hand, support for the regime, not just
among Nazi fanatics, was still widespread. And many in high places and
low still refused to contemplate the prospect of defeat. Their thinking ran
along the following lines. The enemy – the unholy coalition of the western
democracies and the Communist Soviet Union – could still be repulsed if
the war effort could be revitalized; in the event of a serious reverse, the
enemy could split apart; new, devastating weapons were on the way and
would bring a sharp turn in war fortunes; and, if subjected to significant
military setbacks, the Allies would be forced to entertain a settlement,
leaving Germany some of her territorial gains and peace with honour.
Such thoughts were by no means moribund in the summer of 1944.

Among the mass of the population, however, the predominant feeling
in mid-July 1944 was one of mounting worry and anxiety. Whatever
their carefully couched criticisms of the regime's leaders (including
Hitler himself) and, in particular, of the Nazi Party and its representatives, the great majority of ordinary citizens were still unhesitatingly
loyal in their support for the war effort. The mood was anxious, not
rebellious. There was no trace of anything similar to the growing unrest
that eventually burst into open revolution in 1918, despite Hitler's
pathological fixation with the internal collapse of that year. There were
contingency plans to cope with the possibility of an uprising by foreign
workers (numbering by this time, together with prisoners of war, more
than 7 million). But there was no serious expectation of revolution by
the German population.

Regional reports of the SD (*Sicherheitsdienst*; Security Service)
indicated an increasingly apprehensive mood, falling to 'zero point',
producing 'deep depression', and amounting to an 'anxiety psychosis'
and 'creeping panic', in the light of the Red Army's advance in the east.
There was intense worry about the likely fate of East Prussia. People
feared that, once on German soil, the Russians would never be forced
out. Women in particular were profoundly apprehensive. 'The eastern
front will probably soon collapse,' ran one reported comment. 'If the
Bolsheviks get in, we might as well all hang ourselves, with our children.
The Führer should make peace with England and America. The war can
no longer be won.' It was not an isolated sentiment.

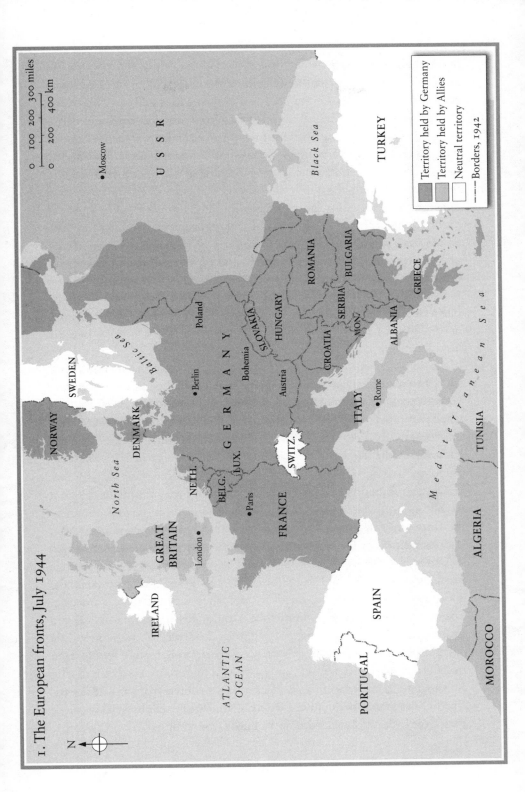

1. The European fronts, July 1944

N

GREAT BRITAIN
London •

IRELAND

ATLANTIC OCEAN

PORTUGAL

SPAIN

MOROCCO

ALGERIA

TUNISIA

Mediterranean Sea

NORWAY

SWEDEN

DENMARK

North Sea

Baltic Sea

NETH.
BELG.
LUX.
FRANCE
Paris •

SWITZ.

GERMANY
Berlin •

Bohemia

Austria

ITALY
Rome •

SLOVAKIA

Poland

HUNGARY

CROATIA

SERBIA

MON.

ALBANIA

ROMANIA

BULGARIA

GREECE

U S S R

Moscow •

Black Sea

TURKEY

Territory held by Germany
Territory held by Allies
Neutral territory
Borders, 1942

0 100 200 300 miles
0   200   400 km

Though overshadowed by events in the east, attitudes towards the western front were also gloomy, with widespread acknowledgement of the enemy's overwhelming superiority in men and resources. There were still hopes of the promised 'miracle weapons', though earlier exaggerated expectations of the impact of the V1 missile in air raids on London had left disappointment and scepticism about propaganda claims. And the inability of the Luftwaffe to offer protection against the 'terror raids' which were taking place in broad daylight offered a constant source of anger, as well as constant and mounting anxiety. The collapse of the Wehrmacht in the east left many searching for both explanations and scapegoats. Reports from soldiers on leave of the morale of the troops, alleging their lack of belief in victory, and of the inability of their officers, used to material comfort in their rear positions, to provide proper defence, also had a negative impact on mood. And more and more families were receiving the dreaded visit from the local Party leader with the news that their loved one had fallen at the front. 'How long can we still hold out?' was a question frequently asked.[3]

At the other end of the opinion spectrum, among the regime's elite, such views were unspoken, whether tacitly entertained or not. Leading Nazis continued to give their full support and loyalty to Hitler, not least since their own power was solely dependent upon his. But there were frustrations, as well as the continuous jockeying for position that was endemic to the Third Reich. Hermann Göring was still Hitler's designated successor. His earlier popularity had, however, vanished, and, within the Nazi elite, his star had been waning for months in the light of the Luftwaffe's failings. Hitler fell into repeated paroxysms of rage at the impotence of the Commander-in-Chief of the Luftwaffe to prevent the destruction of Germany's cities. Characteristically, however, he was unwilling to dismiss Göring, conscious as usual of the loss of prestige this would constitute and the gift it would provide to enemy propaganda. Another who had lost his earlier prominence was the once influential Foreign Minister, Joachim von Ribbentrop, whose every prediction and initiative had proved catastrophically mistaken. He, too, was now little called upon – not least since there was, in effect, no longer any foreign policy to conduct.

As some Nazi paladins lost face, others profited from the adversity. Martin Bormann, head of the Party Chancellery, could exploit more than ever his constant proximity to Hitler, controlling the portals to the

Dictator's presence and serving as his master's mouthpiece. Bormann, born in 1900, an unpretentious figure in his ill-fitting Party uniform, short, squat, bull-necked, with thin, receding hair, was hated and feared in equal measure by leading Nazis, well aware of his ruthlessness, capacity for intrigue, and his opportunities to influence Hitler. He had long been Hitler's indispensable man behind the scenes, for years managing his private financial affairs and in the mid-1930s organizing the building of the Berghof, the Dictator's palatial retreat on the Obersalzberg, near Berchtesgaden. His absolute trustworthiness in Hitler's eyes was his prize asset. Bormann had risen almost unnoticed in the Party's central office in Munich, where, through tireless energy and efficiency, along with the necessary 'elbow power', he attained mastery of the Party's bureaucratic apparatus. He was, however, no simple functionary. He had been involved in anti-Semitic and paramilitary organizations in the 1920s before he found his way to Hitler, and had served time in prison for his involvement in a political murder. His ideological fanaticism never wavered to the end.

In 1929 he had married Gerda, herself a fanatical Nazi and daughter of the head of the Party Court (which adjudicated on matters of Party discipline), Walter Buch. Together they had ten children (nine of whom survived, all but one of them after the war becoming Catholics, one even a priest, despite – or because of – their parents' radical detestation of the Church). The Bormanns appear, from their surviving letters, to have been devoted to each other. Yet the marriage was far from conventional. Gerda positively welcomed Martin's news in January 1944 that he had succeeded in seducing the actress Manja Behrens, hoped that she would bear him a child, and even went so far as to draft a proposed law to legalize bigamy.

By this time Bormann was one of the most powerful men in Germany. In the immediate aftermath of Rudolf Hess's flight to Britain in May 1941, he had been the obvious choice to take over the running of the Party and, once Hitler made him head of the Party Chancellery, rapidly consolidated his control over its bureaucracy. His role as Hitler's trusted factotum finally gained its formal recognition when in April 1943 he was granted the title of 'Secretary of the Führer'. As Germany's fortunes declined, Bormann used his command of the Party's central administration, backed by the fanatical Robert Ley, the Reich Organization Leader (and head of the German Labour Front), to reinvigorate the Party and extend its reach, underpinning his second source of power and making him a figure of crucial importance.[4]

There were limits, nevertheless, to Bormann's power. He could not prevent other leading figures in the regime having direct access to Hitler and exerting their own influence on him. And even within the Party organization, he faced constraints. He was not wholly successful in extending his power over the forty or so regional Party bosses, the Gauleiter. Though nominally his subordinates, some of the Gauleiter, trusted 'old fighters' who had proved their worth since the early days of the Party, in many cases had a direct line to Hitler which limited Bormann's control. One Gauleiter who epitomized the difficulties in imposing any centralized control – or any control at all, for that matter, even from the Wehrmacht authorities in his region – was Erich Koch, who ran his domain in East Prussia as if it were his personal fiefdom.[5] Like most other Gauleiter, Koch had been appointed a Reich Defence Commissar, giving him extensive powers in the organization of civil defence and the possibility, therefore, which he readily exploited, to interfere in non-Party matters in his province. Already in mid-July 1944 Koch was using his direct access to Hitler to block a proposal by Goebbels, which the Propaganda Minister and Gauleiter of Berlin had negotiated with the railway authorities, to evacuate from the endangered East Prussia around 170,000 Berliners who had taken refuge there from the bombing in the capital city. Koch gained Hitler's approval to restrict the evacuation to 55,000 women and children from a small number of districts most threatened by Soviet air raids. It was the first of a number of interventions by Koch to prevent evacuation from his region, causing administrative confusion and, more importantly, with fateful consequences for East Prussians.[6]

The massive accretion of power by Heinrich Himmler (head of the SS, Chief of the German Police, Reich Commissar for the Strengthening of German Nationhood, and Reich Minister of the Interior) had given him mastery of the regime's entire elaborate repressive apparatus throughout occupied Europe. The sinister figure wielding such immense power was still only in his early forties, a strange, cranky individual – but also a fanatical ideologue. He was unimpressive in appearance, no more than medium height, slender in build, his pale face dominated by his trimmed moustache, rimless glasses, receding chin and extreme variant of the short-back-and-sides haircut. He treated his SS leaders with fussy paternalism and urged upon them the virtues of 'decency' at the same time as presiding over the orchestrated murder of millions of Jews in the 'Final Solution'. As the most feared Nazi leader beneath Hitler, Himmler had even expanded his power within Germany itself when he replaced Wilhelm Frick as Reich Minister of the Interior in August 1943. This move had rendered redundant his aim to create a Reich Ministry of Security, detaching the police from the Ministry of the Interior and placing them under his leadership.[7] In July 1944, the power-hungry Reichsführer-SS was edging towards new important extensions of his empire, this time in the sphere of the Wehrmacht. Rivalry with the Wehrmacht had always held in check the growth of Himmler's own military wing, the Waffen-SS. But on 15 July, Hitler gave Himmler responsibility for the indoctrination in Nazi ideals and control over military discipline of fifteen planned new army divisions.[8] It was a significant inroad into the domain of the Wehrmacht.[9]

Joseph Goebbels (Reich Minister of Propaganda, and head of the Party's propaganda organization), and Albert Speer (Reich Minister for Armaments and War Production) had utilized the needs of the war to emphasize their own indispensability to Hitler. Losses at the front had left troop numbers severely depleted.[10] Destruction of equipment urgently required a concentrated armaments drive. Labour had to be combed from all possible sources for Wehrmacht recruitment as well as for armaments work. Not least, new efforts in propaganda were vital to mobilize the population, compelling them to recognize the need for utmost self-sacrifice in the interests of the war. Yet here the frustrations with Hitler's leadership, within a framework of unquestioned loyalty, were evident. They centred on Hitler's unwillingness to move to the requirements of all-out 'total war', meaning much more drastic measures to maximize recruitment to the Wehrmacht and war production.

Goebbels – a diminutive figure in his late forties with a pronounced limp in his right foot (a deformity of which he was very self-conscious), one of the most intelligent Nazi leaders, possessed of a cruel wit, ruthless and dynamic, organizationally able, a fervent Hitler acolyte who in his mastery of propaganda managed to combine utter cynicism with extreme, brutal ideological fanaticism – had been pressing for a move to 'total war' (to maximize every conceivable resource of hitherto unused manpower and drastically curtail any activity not essential to the war economy) since February 1943, in the immediate aftermath of the disastrous defeat at Stalingrad. Speer had joined him at that time in urging a reorganization and revitalization of the war effort at home. Goebbels most of all aspired to take over the running of the home front, leaving Hitler to concentrate on military matters. But Hitler had commissioned little beyond token steps and total war had remained largely a propaganda slogan. In a long private meeting with Hitler on 21 June 1944, just before the Soviet breakthrough on the eastern front, but with the successful Allied landings in northern France plainly constituting a major threat, Goebbels once more vehemently pressed the case for total war and a drastic overhaul of the political and military command structure. Again Hitler demurred. He wanted, he said, to proceed for the time being 'along the evolutionary, not revolutionary, way'.[11]

The depletion of labour resources as a consequence of the enemy inroads from the west and the east had prompted Albert Speer temporarily to join forces with Goebbels in July in the attempt to persuade Hitler to adopt total-war measures aimed at dredging out remaining reserves of manpower. Speer, only thirty-nine years of age, good-looking, cultured and highly intelligent, a superb manager and organizer, and from the outset intensely ambitious, had rapidly established himself in the 1930s as a 'court favourite' by exploiting Hitler's passion for grandiose building projects. Before he was thirty he gained Hitler's commission to design the Reich Party Rally stadium at Nuremberg. In 1937 he was given responsibility for turning Berlin into a capital befitting a master-race. In the last year of peace he delivered, on time and at breakneck speed, Hitler's imposing new Reich Chancellery. Hitler saw in Speer the architect of genius he himself had wanted to become. Speer for his part revered Hitler; and he was intoxicated by the power that the favour of the Dictator brought.

When Fritz Todt, in charge of weapon and munitions production, mysteriously died in an air crash in February 1942, Hitler, somewhat surprisingly, appointed Speer to be his new Armaments Minister, endowed with extensive powers. Since then, Speer had masterminded an astonishing rise in armaments production. But he knew the limits had been reached. He could not compete with Allied superiority.[12] In a memorandum written to Hitler on 12 July, Speer purported to accept the Dictator's claim that the current crisis could be overcome within some four months through new weapons, notably the A4 rocket (soon to be renamed the V2). And he agreed that, despite all difficulties, new recruits were potentially available from different sectors of the economy, including armaments, to replenish the Wehrmacht. At the same time, Speer argued, everything had to be done to strengthen the workforce in the armaments industry, and not simply through more foreign workers conscripted from across the Nazi empire. It was essential to make total-war demands on the population. People were ready to make the necessary sacrifices to their daily lives, he stated – a point that internal SD opinion reports seemed to back up.[13] He suggested that women could be freed up for work in great numbers and that organizational improvements could produce new labour supplies. He recommended tough measures to 'revolutionize' living conditions. A proclamation on the mobilizing of last reserves would produce enthusiasm of a kind not experienced since the Wars of Liberation from Napoleon in the early nineteenth century, he thought.[14]

Hitler finally gave an indication that he accepted the need for action. The somewhat colourless head of the Reich Chancellery, Hans-Heinrich Lammers, gave notice on 17 July that Hitler wanted a meeting of ministerial representatives most directly concerned about 'a further strengthened deployment of men and women for defence of the Reich' to take place four days later.[15]

Leaving no stone unturned in the pressure for total-war measures, Goebbels took up the charge on 18 July, following Speer's lead, in a manoeuvre plainly coordinated with the Armaments Minister, and pushing in the same direction.[16] In his memorandum to Hitler, Goebbels urged wide-ranging powers to be invested in one man (meaning himself, of course), who would work through the Gauleiter at regional level to galvanize action. He claimed that through the rigorous measures he had in mind he could produce fifty new divisions for the Wehrmacht in under four months.[17]

Speer then added his own second memorandum just over a week after the first, providing figures on current manpower in armaments, administration and business, pointing out the organizational mistakes that had allowed large-scale unproductive hoarding of labour, and indicating potential sources of recruitment to strengthen the Wehrmacht. He estimated (though the figures were hotly contested by those who would have to yield manpower) that as many as 4.3 million extra men could be found for the Wehrmacht through an efficiency drive. Though there was a need to protect the skilled workforce in armaments – a self-interested plea – he was adamant that the manpower problem for the needs of the front could be solved, but only if responsibility were given to a 'personality', endowed with plenipotentiary powers, and prepared to work with energy and dynamism to overcome vested interests and coordinate the necessary organizational changes in the Wehrmacht and Reich bureaucracy to allow for a rigorous exploitation of available human resources.[18]

Speer was making a scarcely veiled request to be handed control over the coordination of armaments and personnel within all sections of the Wehrmacht to add to his existing powers over the production of arms. Had this ambition been fulfilled, Speer would, through his armaments empire, have become the supremo of the total-war drive.[19] What impact this memorandum might have had on Hitler, and on the meeting planned for 21 July to discuss total war, at precisely this juncture cannot be known. For there was no time to present this second memorandum to Hitler before events on the very day it had been composed, 20 July 1944, concentrated the Dictator's mind.[20]

II

What hopes Germans still harboured as they reeled from the events on the western then the eastern front in summer 1944 crystallized in what had emerged as the last remaining war aim: defence of the Reich. The grand, utopian ideas of German rule stretching from the Atlantic to the Urals had long since been forgotten, except by lingering fantasists. Gradually, almost imperceptibly, and almost surreptitiously, the once heady vistas of a glorious 'final victory', however inchoate they had been, had yielded to bitter reality and to a limited and defensive object-ive: keeping the enemy from German soil. The time of the devastating blitzkrieg offensives, when the Wehrmacht would cut through weaker enemies like a knife through butter, was long past. In a war that had become a protracted rearguard against powerful enemies with immense resources, Hitler's limitations as a warlord became ever clearer. At the same time, what he saw as the aim of the war, or how it might end, had become utterly opaque.

He symbolized, of course, an indomitable will to hold onto every inch of territory, never to capitulate. And he could still enthuse those in his presence with the strength of his own will, and with his unquench-able optimism. Hardened military commanders could begin an audience with Hitler sceptically and come out of it reinvigorated. Others, how-ever, were struck by the absence of clear thinking on strategy and tactics. When General Friedrich Hoßbach met Hitler on the evening of 19 July 1944, to be given command of the 4th Army, he saw the Dictator, whose Wehrmacht adjutant he had once been, as 'bent and prematurely aged', unable to offer any far-reaching strategic goal and highly superficial in his comments on the tactical position. Hoßbach simply accepted the commission, told Hitler he would act on his judgement when he assessed the situation, and would do his utmost to recover a position lost in the destruction of Army Group Centre.[21]

Numerous military commanders had by this time contested Hitler's decisions to no avail. It was impossible to sustain a reasoned counter-argument in his domineering presence. As supreme leader, he would brook no opposition. His right of command was accepted by all. And those in positions of authority continued to try to implement his orders. But heady rhetoric, and sacking generals for failing to achieve the unachievable, hardly amounted to a strategy, let alone a clearly defined set of aims. In particular, and crucially, he had no exit strategy from the war in which he had embroiled his country. Repelling the Allied invasion, he had once told his military advisers, would be decisive for the war.[22] When the invasion proved successful, however, he drew no conclusions, other than to fight on. Outright victory was no longer attainable. Even Hitler could see that. But negotiating with the enemy from a position of weakness could not be entertained for a second. That left fighting on and hoping something would turn up. And that meant playing for time.

Hitler's military right hand and mouthpiece, General Alfred Jodl, head of the Wehrmacht Operations Staff, reflected the absence of clear strategic goals in addressing his staff on 3 July 1944:

> Our own war leadership, on all fronts: focuses now on gaining time. A few months can prove simply decisive for saving the Fatherland. . . . Our own armaments justify great expectations. . . . Everything is being prepared, with results in the foreseeable future. So the demand is for fighting, defending, holding, psychological strengthening of troops and leadership. Nail down the front where it now stands.[23]

There were many in high positions in the Wehrmacht who shared such a stance. Shoring up stretched defences, holding on, keeping the enemy at bay, rebuilding lines while feverish attempts were made to maximize armaments production, find troop reinforcements and produce new weapons, became ends in themselves, rather than stages on the way to a accomplishment of a preconceived military and political strategy. Colonel-General Heinz Guderian, the redoubtable tank commander, now Inspector-General of Panzer Troops, thus approvingly remarked that, in replacing Field-Marshal Ernst Busch (an ultra-loyalist, but made the scapegoat for grave mistakes in the disaster that had befallen Army Group Centre) by the tough Field-Marshal Walter Model, Hitler had found 'the best possible man to perform the fantastically difficult task of reconstructing a line in the centre of the Eastern Front'.[24] This was, however, not a strategic goal, but merely a 'fire-fighting' operation by the man who, for the number of difficult positions he was asked to rescue, became known as 'Hitler's fireman'. Most military commanders, whatever their varied level of enthusiasm for Hitler's regime, acted similarly to Model in doing their utmost to carry out their duties professionally, and with iron discipline, to the limits of their ability and, at least publicly, to ask no questions about political objectives. Those bold enough to voice any views that, however realistic, did not fit the prescribed optimism demanded by Hitler found themselves replaced, as did the highly experienced Commander-in-Chief West, Field-Marshal Gerd von Rundstedt, and the able Commander of Panzer Group West, General Geyr von Schweppenburg, at the beginning of July.

In private, leading Wehrmacht officers were divided in their views on war prospects. Alongside the loyalists, and the front commanders who seldom had the time for lengthy contemplation and, in any case, had little perspective on the overall position, were those whose views on Germany's military and political prospects were far from rosy. Hitler himself had, for years, castigated the allegedly defeatist and negative attitudes that, in his jaundiced opinion, characterized the General Staff of the Army, responsible for overall operational planning in the east. His mounting and bitter disagreements with the Chief of the General Staff, Franz Halder, had led to the latter's replacement in September 1942 by the energetic and dynamic Kurt Zeitzler. But, worn out by the constant conflict with Hitler that had reached its climax with the destruction of Army Group Centre, Zeitzler suffered a nervous breakdown at the end of June 1944. He had just told Hitler that the war was militarily lost and that 'something had to be done to end it'.[25]

Zeitzler was expressing a sentiment then widespread within the General Staff, according to a letter composed in his defence by his adjutant, Oberstleutnant Günther Smend, on 1 August 1944. Smend had been arrested for his connection with the Stauffenberg plot and would be sentenced to death on 14 August and executed on 8 September. His letter may well have been preceded by torture and somewhat exaggerated the subversive feeling at General Staff Headquarters. It gives, nevertheless, a clear insight into the mood. Facing almost certain execution, Smend had no obvious reason to dissemble. Doubts about a final victory had mounted, wrote Smend, since the catastrophic defeat at Stalingrad in February 1943. The widening gulf between the recommendations of the General Staff and Hitler's decisions had given rise to strong criticism of the Führer, notably in the Operations Section, and this had not been dampened by senior officers. Indeed, the head of the section, General Adolf Heusinger, had himself been party to the condemnation of Hitler's war leadership.[26] There was no longer any firm belief in Hitler. The mood in the entire General Staff was one of despair, prompted especially by the disasters in the east but also by the bad news on all fronts, leading to the conclusion that the war was lost. Critical mistakes had been made, and Hitler was seen as a military liability. On the day of his breakdown, Zeitzler had, according to Smend, been blunt in his assessment of the situation in speaking to Hitler. He had recommended the appointment of Himmler as a 'homeland dictator' to drive through the total-war effort that had been propagated but not implemented with the necessary rigour. Thereafter, with Zeitzler out of action and the General Staff effectively leaderless for almost a month, the mood grew that 'the Führer can't do it'. Opinion hardened that 'it's all madness'. Young officers, especially, held Hitler responsible. It was common knowledge, wrote Smend, that ideas of eliminating Hitler were in circulation.[27]

On 20 July 1944 such ideas – engendered, adumbrated and elaborated in a conspiracy involving prominent figures in the armed forces, military intelligence, the Foreign Ministry, and other sectors of the regime's leadership – culminated in the attempt on Hitler's life undertaken by Count Claus Schenk Graf von Stauffenberg and the subsequent failed *coup d'état* launched from the headquarters of the Replacement

Army in Berlin. Stauffenberg had placed a bomb under Hitler's table at a military briefing just after noon that day at Führer Headquarters in East Prussia. The bomb had exploded, killing or badly injuring most of those present in the wooden barrack-hut. But Hitler had survived with only minor injuries. Once it had been plainly established that Hitler was alive, support had drained away from the coup planned to follow his presumed death, which collapsed in the course of the evening. Stauffenberg and three other close collaborators were shot by a firing squad late that night. The other plotters were soon rounded up. Most were tortured, subjected to appalling show trials, and then barbarously executed.

Stauffenberg's assassination attempt marked an internal shift in the history of the Third Reich.[28] With the failure of the plot came not only the fearful reprisals against those involved but also a sharp radicalization of the regime, both in repression and in mobilization. The aftermath of the failed plot had a significant impact on the governmental structures of the regime, on the mentalities of the civilian and military elite (to some extent, too, on the ordinary public), and on remaining possibilities both for 'regime change' and for ending the war.

III

Looking back during his post-war interrogations in May 1945, Göring thought it had been impossible to organize an effective anti-Hitler movement at the time of the bomb plot.[29] So, in the same month, did General Hoßbach, Hitler's one-time Wehrmacht adjutant. According to Hoßbach, the attempt on Hitler's life had no basis of support in the mass of the people or the Wehrmacht. 'Despite all setbacks, Hitler still enjoyed high popularity in 1944,' he adjudged. The association of Hitler with patriotic support for the country at war was a strong bond, making it extremely difficult 'to topple the god'.[30] Indeed, those engaged in the plot to kill Hitler knew only too well that their actions lacked popular backing.[31] Stauffenberg himself accepted that he would 'go down in German history as a traitor'.[32] The immediate reactions to the events of 20 July lend credence to such views.

Among ordinary Germans, there was a widespread sense of deep shock and consternation at the news of the failed assassination. Effusive outpourings of loyalty and support for the Führer were immediately registered in all quarters, alongside furious outrage at the 'tiny clique' of 'criminal' officers (as Hitler had labelled them) who had perpetrated such a vile deed, and rank disbelief that such base treachery could have been possible. It would, of course, have been near suicidal to voice regrets in public that Hitler had survived – though certainly that was the private feeling of a good many people. So the recorded expressions of support inevitably provide a distorted impression of attitudes. This was even more the case with the extremes of pro-Hitler fervour emanating from the big 'loyalty rallies' staged within days all over Germany by a revitalized Nazi Party straining every sinew to mobilize the population by orchestrating 'spontaneous' demonstrations of joy at the Führer's survival and outrage at the monstrous attempt to assassinate him.[33] Even so, all the indications are that there was an upsurge of genuine pro-Hitler feeling in the immediate aftermath of the attack on his life.

The SD took immediate soundings of opinion on the day after the assassination attempt. 'All reports agree that the announcement of the attempt has produced the strongest feelings of shock, dismay, anger and rage,' ran the summary of initial reactions. Women were said to have broken into tears of joy in shops or on the open streets in Königsberg and Berlin at Hitler's survival. 'Thank God the Führer is alive,' was a common expression of relief. 'What would we have done without the Führer?' people asked. Hitler was seen as the only possible bulwark against Bolshevism. Many thought his death would have meant the loss of the Reich. It was at first surmised that the strike against Hitler was the work of enemy agents, though this presumption soon gave way to recognition that it had been treachery from within, and fury at the fact that this had come from German officers.[34]

Reports from the regional propaganda offices across the country told the same story. People were shaken by what had happened, but it had strengthened trust in the Führer. Some officers, it was said, felt the reputation of the army to have been so besmirched by the treachery that they wanted to transfer to the Waffen-SS. There was much speculation about how the attack could have happened: the Wehrmacht had been given too much freedom, and the Führer kept uninformed about what was happening. He had been too lenient towards his generals, simply dismissing rather than executing them when they had failed in their duties. It was taken for granted that a 'new wind' would now blow. There was a demand for severe reprisals against the 'traitors' and for them to be publicly named. Wild rumours circulated implying the involvement of a number of leading military figures, including the former Commander-in-Chief of the Army, Walther von Brauchitsch, Field-Marshal Gerd von Rundstedt, who had recently been replaced as Commander-in-Chief West, and even Field-Marshal Wilhelm Keitel, the head of the High Command of the Wehrmacht.[35] People could not understand how such a plot could have gone unnoticed. They were disturbed that at the very heart of the army there had been those working against the Führer's intentions and actions.[36] It was not long before sabotage from within came to be seen as the obvious reason for the recent disastrous collapse of Army Group Centre.[37]

Coloured though such reports were, they nevertheless represented strands of genuine opinion. People sent in money in thanksgiving for Hitler's survival. Substantial amounts were collected and passed to the NSV to provide for children orphaned by the war.[38] One woman, the wife of a worker and mother of several children, accompanied her gift of 40 Reich Marks to the Red Cross with a note to her local Party office, stating that her donation was 'Out of great love of the Führer, because nothing happened to him.' She was happy, she wrote, 'that our Führer has been preserved for us. May he live long yet and lead us to victory.'[39] A corporal apologized to his wife for being unable to send any money home at the beginning of August since he had donated it all to a Wehrmacht collection to show gratitude for the Führer. Many, he said, had given much more. However obliged they might have felt to contribute to the collection, the level of generosity was beyond what was necessary.[40]

Many letters and contemporary entries in private diaries reflect unforced pro-Hitler feelings. 'I don't think I'm wrong when I say in such a sad hour for all of us: "Germany stands or falls in this struggle with the person of Adolf Hitler,"' ran one diary entry for 21 July from a young pro-Nazi, a prisoner of war in Texas. 'If this attack on Adolf Hitler had been successful, I am convinced that our homeland would now be in chaos.'[41] This was no exception. More than two-thirds of prisoners of war in American captivity indicated their belief in Hitler in the weeks after the assassination attempt, a rise on levels prior to the bomb plot.[42] Faith in the Führer was also still strong among serving frontline soldiers. 'The high number of joyful expressions about the salvation of the Führer' in letters home from soldiers at the front was remarked upon by the censor.[43] It was as well to be extremely careful in expressing any negative views in letters that might be picked up by the censor. But there was no need for effusive pro-Hitler comments. Similar sentiments could be read in the letters that soldiers received. 'I cannot imagine how things would have developed without the Führer in view of the present situation in our country,' wrote one woman in Munich to her husband.[44] A major in the supply unit of an infantry division behind the lines headed his diary entry for 20 July: 'Evening. Bad news. Attack on the Führer', noting next day, after hearing Hitler's late-night broadcast, that it was only a small clique of officers, and that a purge would follow. 'It's a crying shame', he added, that this should take place, and with the Russians 'at the gates'.[45] Another officer, on the western front, and evidently sceptical about the course of the war, next day revised his initial view that it had been merely a small officers' clique and saw the attack as 'an entire plot against A[dolf] H[itler]', denoting a split in the Wehrmacht between loyalists and opponents. He recalled someone who had known Stauffenberg speaking of him as an excellent officer and courageous soldier. But he was 'evidently politically stupid', he added.[46]

In the upper ranks of the army, too, the response was highly supportive of the regime.[47] There was immediate dismay and condemnation of Stauffenberg's strike at the head of the armed forces in the midst of a world war.[48] The reaction of Colonel-General Georg-Hans Reinhardt provides a telling example. He was an experienced and capable commander who remained a Hitler loyalist despite having to comply with the absurd orders from the Führer in late June 1944 that prevented the retreat of his 3rd Panzer Army, resulting in its destruction by the Soviets. He was distraught at the news of the attempt on Hitler's life.[49] 'Thank God he is saved,' was his immediate reaction, in consternation and disbelief that such a thing had been possible. 'Completely broken', he added next day. 'Incomprehensible! What has this done to our officer class? We can only feel deepest shame.'[50] His belief in Hitler remained intact, as did his sense of duty at fulfilling the will of the Führer. 'Duty calls. I will go where the Führer commands,' he wrote on taking over command of the remnants of Army Group Centre a month later. 'It's a matter of justifying his trust.'[51] General Hermann Balck, a teak-hard tank commander and seasoned campaigner on the eastern front, a strong loyalist and highly regarded by Hitler for his dynamic leadership of armoured formations, had known and admired Stauffenberg, but was forthright in his condemnation of him as a 'criminal'. His act, which Balck regarded as comparable with the killing of Caesar by Brutus, had made Germany's difficult situation worse. He saw the causes in a long-standing inability within the officer corps to place 'oath and honour' above all else. The 'General Staff's revolt' was 'shameful' for the officer corps. But it appeared to be a 'cleansing storm' at just the right time. Now there would have to be a merciless purge of all conspirators, a *tabula rasa*. 'For us it means attaining victory despite everything under the banner of the Führer,' he concluded.[52]

Officers who were far from outright Nazis in their sentiments still faced the perceived dilemma that, even in the plight that had befallen Germany, killing Hitler appeared an intensely unpatriotic act which undermined the fighting front, was morally wrong in itself and constituted a betrayal of the oath of loyalty to the Führer. Such attitudes, whatever the doubts about Hitler's leadership qualities, made Germany's military leaders for the most part instinctive loyalists. Proxy for many who felt this way was General Hoßbach, later to be sacked by Hitler as commander of the 4th Army during the last battles for East Prussia in early 1945. Reflecting on the bomb plot less than a fortnight after Germany's capitulation in May that year, and in full recognition of the calamitous losses and colossal destruction of the last months of the war, Hoßbach offered no realistic alternative to what had taken place. He accepted the patriotic need for the armed forces to 'redeem Germany from the domination of a criminal clique'. But how this might be achieved he left uncertain. He condemned the attempt to overthrow Hitler's regime by assassination and *coup d'état* as 'immoral and un-Christian', a 'stab in the back', and the 'most disgraceful treason against our army'.[53] In rejecting force, however, his only alternative seemed to presuppose a collective challenge to Hitler's disastrous leadership by the generals. Since he acknowledged that the bonds with Hitler, both within the Wehrmacht and among the people generally, were still very strong in 1944, it is not clear how he imagined that such a collective challenge might have been possible.

The revival of support for Hitler personally and the corresponding shrill demand for severe reprisals against the 'traitors' and a drastic cleansing of those allegedly sabotaging the war effort crucially gave the regime a new lease of life at a most critical juncture. It offered the opportunity, which Nazi leaders were only too keen to grasp, for a thoroughgoing radicalization of every aspect of regime and society, aimed at imbuing in a country with its back to the wall the true National Socialist ideals and fighting spirit necessary to fend off rapacious enemies.

IV

The days immediately following the failed assassination attempt saw extended power pass to Himmler, Goebbels and Bormann. Speer, the fourth big baron, found himself squeezed in the contest dominated by this trio. Even so, his own position, in charge of armaments, still left him irreplaceable and retaining formidable influence. Between them, these four men controlled most of the avenues of power and did much to direct the course of the regime in its final months. They did so, however, within the framework of Hitler's own supreme authority, which none sought to challenge. On the contrary, their own individual power-bases were derived directly from it. In this way, the bonds with the Führer, which had been a decisive element of his charismatic authority from the early days of the Nazi movement and had become a constituent element of the regime after 1933, remained intact and prevented any internal collapse. The corrosive impact of charismatic authority on the structures of government was also undiminished. Still, now as before, there was no unified government beneath Hitler. The quadrumvirate, far from acting as a coherent body, were to the last effectively at war with each other, trying to use access to Hitler to jockey for power and compete with each other for resources and expanded areas of competence.

Hitler took the first major step in radicalization within hours of surviving the bomb blast in his East Prussian headquarters in appointing Himmler to replace General Friedrich Fromm as Commander-in-Chief of the Replacement Army.[54] The headquarters of the Replacement Army had been the epicentre of the plans for the intended *coup d'état*, and, despite his endeavours to prove his loyalty – once he knew Hitler had survived – by turning on the plotters and having Stauffenberg and three of his co-conspirators shot by a firing squad late in the evening of 20 July, Fromm was himself soon arrested and, some months later, executed.[55] The Replacement Army was viewed as the Augean Stables that had to be cleansed. In Himmler, the man was at hand to take on this task.

Himmler had, in reality, failed as head of security in the Reich to protect Hitler from the assassination attempt or to uncover the plot that lay behind it. Hitler either ignored or overlooked these omissions in turning now to Himmler to place his stamp on a central office of the Wehrmacht. Himmler, as we noted, had already a foot in the door of the Replacement Army's sphere of competence on gaining responsibility for ideological 'education' on 15 July. His influence was now, however, substantially extended as he brought under his aegis one of the most important positions within the Wehrmacht, on taking charge of armaments, army discipline, prisoners of war, reserve personnel and training. With the Replacement Army, almost 2 million men in conventional military service were placed under Himmler's control.[56] It was a significant addition to his already enormous range of powers.

Himmler's impact was soon felt. He immediately countermanded Fromm's orders of 20 July and started to fill the key positions in his new domain with trusted SS lieutenants, making the head of the SS operations head office (*SS-Führungshauptamt*), Hans Jüttner, his deputy in running the Replacement Army.[57] He then embarked upon a series of pep-talks for army officers. While short on specifics, these speeches gave a clear impression of the changed climate.

As early as 21 July, Himmler addressed officers under his command as Chief of Army Armaments, an area which had now fallen within his own imperium. In 1918, he began, the revolt of the soldiers' councils had cost Germany victory. This time, there was no danger of anything similar happening. The mass of the people, in bombed-out cities and factories, were of unprecedented 'decency' (one of Himmler's favourite words) in their behaviour. But now, for the first time in history, a German colonel had broken his oath and struck at his supreme warlord. He knew it would come to this one day, he said, vaguely glossing over what he might have been expected to have gleaned of the background to the plot. The attempt to kill the Führer and overthrow the regime had been suppressed. But it had been a grave danger. It had been more like Honduras or South America than Germany. The previous afternoon, he had received the mandate from the Führer to restore order and take over the Home Army. He had accepted 'as an unconditional follower of the Führer' who had 'never in my life been guilty of disloyalty and never will be'. He had taken on the task as a German soldier and not as the commander-in-chief of a rival organization, the Waffen-SS. He now had to clean up. He would, he went on, restore trust and bring about a return to values of loyalty, obedience and comradeship. It was sometimes necessary to go through hell, he declared, but the supreme leadership had strong nerves and knew how to act brutally when necessary. He ended by outlining the meaning of the war: confirmation of Germany as a world power; the creation of a Germanic Reich to grow to 120 millions; and a new order within that Reich. An 'invasion from Asia' would recur every fifty, hundred or two hundred years. But there would not always be an Adolf Hitler to help repel it. The necessity, therefore, was to prepare a bulwark against future attacks by colonizing the east through German settlement. 'We shall learn to rule foreign peoples,' he stated. 'We would have to be deeply ashamed if we were now to become too weak.'[58]

Two further speeches by Himmler to officers in the next few days had much the same tenor: the recourse to the baleful precedent of 1918, the fulfilment of duty this time by the people and almost all the army but the shame 'a colonel' had brought on the officers corps, the lack of loyalty of some officers, and the need for ruthless action against those guilty of cowardice. The emphasis was once more on the war aims that could not be given up – including, now, mastery over the Continent to afford protection in future wars through the extension of defence frontiers.[59] The unbounded ruthlessness that was more than ever to become the Reichsführer-SS's trademark in subsequent months was evident in his message to his liaison officer in Hitler's headquarters, Hermann Fegelein, that at the sign of any disintegration among divisions serving in the east (which he put down to sedition spread by Communist infiltration) 'reception detachments' (*Auffangkommandos*) of 'the most brutal commanders' were to shoot 'anyone opening his mouth'.[60]

Himmler's authority to intervene in what had hitherto been army matters was widened still further by another Führer decree on 2 August, giving the Reichsführer-SS powers, through radical restructuring, to inspect and 'simplify' (meaning reduce in size, producing savings in manpower) 'the entire organizational and administrative basis of the army, the Waffen-SS, the police and the *Organisation Todt*' to produce more manpower for the army.[61] The last of these bodies, the OT, was the huge construction complex, whose massive workforce Speer had now agreed to expose to the Reichsführer-SS's new powers for labour saving.[62] Cuts in what he saw as a bloated army administration had been part of Himmler's intention from the start, and he was able through his excisions to raise another 500,000 troops for the front and create fifteen *Volksgrenadier* (People's Grenadiers) divisions from new recruits.[63] With this new authority, Himmler was now a party to the power-struggle at the top of the regime for control of the new total-war drive.

Goebbels was a second key winner from the events of 20 July. The crucial role that he had played in crushing the uprising in Berlin was acknowledged by Hitler. Under the impact of the attack on his life, and the shock to the system that this represented, Hitler was now at last prepared to grant to his Propaganda Minister the position that Goebbels had been seeking for well over a year, and finally make him Reich Plenipotentiary for the Total War Effort.

The meeting of ministers or their representatives chaired by Lammers that took place on 22 July, a day later than had originally been arranged, amounted practically to a ritual acclamation of Goebbels as the new total-war supremo.[64] At the very outset of the meeting, Lammers – safe in the knowledge that the Reich Chancellery, over which he presided, had been exempted by Hitler from any inroads into its personnel – proposed the Propaganda Minister for the task of mobilizing the civilian sector. Keitel, Bormann and all others present supported the proposition. Goebbels spoke for an hour, portraying the issue as threefold: providing new manpower through cutting back on Wehrmacht administration, drastically reducing the state bureaucracy, and a vaguely couched 'reform of public life'. The Party, Goebbels acknowledged, did not fall within his purview. That was Bormann's domain, for him alone to handle. Combing out the military sector was also ruled out of the proposed operations. This was set aside for the new Commander-in-Chief of the Replacement Army, Heinrich Himmler.

Speer, who had tried hard in mid-July to press for total war, found himself now largely on the sidelines. His memorandum of 12 July, received, on Hitler's instructions, only little attention to prevent the meeting becoming immersed in detail. When Speer spoke, in fact, the figures he gave for potential savings from state bureaucracy were immediately contradicted by Lammers and the State Secretary in the Reich Ministry of the Interior, Wilhelm Stuckart. Vested interests came into play straight away as Stuckart emphasized how little spare capacity for manpower savings existed in the state bureaucracy. Goebbels steered the meeting away from a likely descent into detail and back to the general issue. For the Propaganda Minister, as he plainly stated, total war was 'not only a material, but especially a psychological problem', and he acknowledged that some of the measures taken would 'in part have merely optical character'. Ideological mobilization was, as ever, his chief concern. The meeting ended, predictably, with Lammers agreeing to propose Goebbels for the position as Plenipotentiary next day, when most of those present would gather again to report to Hitler at his East Prussian headquarters.[65]

Goebbels was happy. 'All those taking part', he jotted in his diary,

> are of the opinion that the Führer must provide the most extensive pleni-potentiary powers, on the one hand for the Wehrmacht, on the other for the state and public life. Himmler is proposed for the Wehrmacht, I, myself, for the state and public life. Bormann is to get corresponding full powers to engage the Party in this great totalizing process, and Speer has already received the powers to intensify the armaments process.[66]

When the meeting reassembled in Hitler's presence the following afternoon, Göring and Himmler were also in attendance. Göring protested in vain at yet a further diminution of his power in handing Himmler responsibility for matters which should properly, he claimed, be those of the commanders-in-chief of the Wehrmacht. Hitler intervened to back Himmler. The resulting experience could then be utilized by Göring and Grand-Admiral Karl Dönitz, who, as Commanders-in-Chief of the Luftwaffe and Navy, continued to be responsible for their own domains. The compromise was accepted. For the rest, Hitler, who had evidently carefully read Goebbels' memorandum of 18 July, backed the Propaganda Minister and the proposal for drastic new measures in the total-war effort. 'The Führer declares that there is no further use in debating specific points,' Goebbels recorded. 'Something fundamental has to be done or we can't win this war.' Hitler's position, he noted, was 'very radical and incisive'. In what would become a cliché in the last months, Hitler spoke of the new radicalization as a return to the Party's roots. Characteristically, too, he played on the populist assumption 'that the people wanted a total war in the most comprehensive fashion and that we cannot contradict the will of the people in the long run'. Goebbels was delighted at the outcome, and at Hitler's changed approach. 'It is interesting to observe', he commented, 'how the Führer has changed since my last talk with him on the Obersalzberg [on 21 June]. Events, especially on the day of the assassination attempt and those on the eastern front, have brought him to the clarity of the decisions.'[67]

Two days later, on 25 July, Hitler signed the decree making Goebbels Plenipotentiary for Total War.[68] Goebbels was elated over his triumph – a far greater success, he claimed, than he had imagined. His press secretary, Wilfred von Oven, thought he was now 'the first man in the Third Reich after Hitler'.[69] Three times in his diary the Propaganda Minister himself spoke of 'an internal war dictatorship', implying that this, his coveted goal, would now be in his hands.[70] It was a fine conceit, but Goebbels was aware that he would remain, if with strengthened authority, only one, not the sole, source of power beneath Hitler and that, as ever, this power would be wielded in competition, not unison. The very wording of the decree, as he recognized, limited the scope of his powers. He could issue directives to the 'highest Reich authorities', but any decrees of implementation that arose had to be negotiated with Lammers, Bormann and Himmler (in his capacity as General Plenipotentiary for Reich Administration, which had fallen to him when he became Minister of the Interior). He was dependent upon Bormann's support for measures involving the Party. And in the case of unresolvable conflict arising from his orders, Hitler reserved his own authority to make any necessary decision. Some exemptions were made on Hitler's express authority. The personnel of the Reich, Presidial and Party chancelleries, the Führer's motor vehicle staff, and those involved in planning the rebuilding of Berlin, Munich and Linz were excluded.[71] And a major area, the army, had, of course, from the beginning been carved off and given over to Himmler.

Undeterred, Goebbels presided over a veritable torrent of activity in subsequent weeks, dispatching instructions to all Gauleiter in a telephone conference each midday.[72] He had to contend with numerous obstacles and vested interests, which he did not always surmount. And, however drastic his interventions, there were in fact fewer slack areas of the economy able to provide extra manpower than he had anticipated, while some of his 'rationalizations' proved to be inefficient. In some cases, Hitler himself intervened to limit the cuts that Goebbels sought to impose. Through Bormann, he requested that the Propaganda Minister consider in each case whether the ends justified the means, if this entailed significant disturbance to public services such as postal deliveries.[73] Even so, Goebbels raised nearly half a million extra men for the Wehrmacht by October, and around a million by the end of the year.[74] Many were, in fact, far from fit for military service and were in any case outweighed by German losses at the front over the same period.

As a means of countering the massive Allied superiority in numbers, it is obvious that Goebbels' total-war effort, scraping the bottom of the barrel, was doomed. But in terms of prolonging the war, and enabling Germany to fight on when beset by disaster on all fronts, the total-war mobilization that flowed from Goebbels' new powers certainly played its part. Through his measures, the German population were more dragooned, corralled and controlled than ever. Few people were inwardly enthused for long. Most, where they could gain no exemption, had little choice but to fall in with the new demands. Dislocation, atomization and resignation usually followed. Though the appetite for the ever more desperate struggle was diminishing, there was scant room for any alternative.

Martin Bormann, head of the Party's administration, was the third big winner from the military disasters of the summer and, especially, of the radicalization of the regime that followed the shock of the attempt on Hitler's life. He exploited the new crisis atmosphere to reinvigorate the Party and massively expand its power and his own power and influence in the process.[75] Even before the assassination attempt, he had started to sift through the Party organization to make manpower available for the Wehrmacht or the armaments industry.[76] Goebbels' total-war initiative was, therefore, both timely for him and could be used to his own advantage. Goebbels set up a relatively small coordinating staff in Berlin, but envisaged the crucial work of the total-war effort being carried out through the Party agencies at regional level. This was grist to the mill for Bormann. He could utilize the changed climate to bolster the power of the Gauleiter in the regions at the expense of the state bureaucracy.

As Reich Defence Commissars (*Reichsverteidigungskommissare*, RVKs), the Gauleiter already possessed the scope to interfere in matters deemed to pertain to the defence of the Reich in their regions. This had been widened, a week before the assassination attempt, by a decree from Hitler stipulating what would prove to be unclear guidelines for collaboration of Wehrmacht and Party in military operational zones within the Reich. The decree opened the door to future interference by the RVKs in crucial issues within the operational zones such as the evacuation of the civilian population and immobilization or destruction of industry.[77] Bormann was now able to extend their power substantially in what was in effect a permanent crisis subsumed under the mantle of total war, authorizing them to issue directives to the state administration in areas which had previously been beyond their remit.[78] The Gauleiter, each of whom had acquired his position through readiness to use 'elbow power', were only too happy to comply with the invitation to throw their weight around more than ever.[79]

The decentralization of power that this implies was, however, only one strand of what has been dubbed, slightly awkwardly, a policy of 'partification'.[80] While backing the Gauleiter against the state authorities, Bormann was keen to extend the control of the Party Chancellery over the regional chieftains and to hold all reins of authority in crucial policy areas in his own hands. The dominance of the Party, which was happening with his backing in the regions, also took place in central administration: increasingly the Party Chancellery pushed the Reich Chancellery, under Lammers, out of key areas of policy. Lammers' office as head of the Reich Chancellery, once so important as the link between the Reich ministers and Hitler, now lost all significance, serving from now on as little more than a postbox and distribution agency for orders laid down by Bormann. Lammers, completely sidelined, was to see Hitler for the last time in September.[81] In despair, he would from the following March be incapable of work and driven to a near nervous breakdown.[82] But in the second half of 1944, there was already no central government, in any conventional sense of the term. Bormann had usurped the Reich administration, combining his control over the Party with his proximity to Hitler to create an enhanced powerhouse in Führer Headquarters.

Even so, it was, however important, not the only powerhouse. 'Partification' at the expense of state bureaucracy created neither a streamlined administration nor an alternative central government as the Reich started to fragment. What it did do, however, was to enhance the organizational capacity of the Party and, above all, to strengthen massively the grip of the Party over government and society.[83]

The key positions in the Nazi movement of Himmler, Goebbels and Bormann enabled them to take advantage of the climate of crisis, amid the shrill cries of treachery and thirst for revenge after the Stauffenberg plot, to promote their own power. Speer, in contrast, enjoyed no position or special standing within the Party. He lacked both a populist touch, such as Goebbels instinctively had, and the organizational base of Himmler or Bormann. There was much more of the technocrat of power than Party activist about him. He had joined forces with Goebbels in the attempt to persuade Hitler to introduce radical measures for total war. But that was before Stauffenberg's bomb had gone off. His hopes of gaining control over the entire arena of army armaments were immediately dashed when Himmler was made head of the Replacement Army. Speer even had to contend with suspicions, in the immediate aftermath of the assassination attempt, that he himself had been implicated.[84] And, in the swift moves to create a Plenipotentiary for Total War, Goebbels' populism and élan caught Hitler's mood while Speer's drier assessment of the needs of the armaments industry took a back seat. Bormann's control of the Party machinery and his conscious push to widen the remit of the Gauleiter, as RVKs, also weakened Speer since his own armaments drive invariably encountered the rooted interests of the provincial Party bosses and their frequent interventions at regional level.

Moreover, once the total-war push was under way, Speer quickly found himself up against his former ally Goebbels and the new alliance that the Propaganda Minister had forged with Bormann, who could usually engineer Hitler's backing. The obvious question of demands on the scarce manpower located by the various 'rationalization' measures, whether this should be allocated to the Wehrmacht or to armaments production, had been characteristically avoided during the time of the short-lived Goebbels–Speer axis. As soon as the issue of power over the total-war effort had been resolved and the question of labour allocation became acute, Speer found himself on the defensive.[85] He had made powerful enemies in fighting for his own domain. Goebbels' laconic comment on the Armaments Minister immediately after winning the battle was: 'I think we have let this young man become somewhat too big.'[86]

Speer's standing with Hitler had also weakened. Not only was he no longer so obviously Hitler's favourite; he had to struggle against the increased influence of his own ambitious subordinate, Karl Otto Saur, head of the technical office in Speer's ministry who earlier in the year had been placed by Hitler in charge of air defence. It would be as well, nevertheless, not to interpret Speer's relative loss of power in the top echelons of the regime – which the former Armaments Minister was keen to emphasize for posterity – as meaning that he had been ousted from all significant spheres of influence. He continued, in fact, to occupy a decisive position at the intersection between the military and industry. The military needed the weaponry he made available. Industry needed his driving force to produce the weapons, in the face of severe and mounting difficulties. No amount of propaganda or repression by the Party's populists and enforcers could supply the army with weapons.

On 1 August Speer was, moreover, able to extend his already sprawling empire when Göring was compelled to hand over to him control of the Luftwaffe's armaments production.[87] Whatever the internal struggles he had to undertake in the power jungle of the Third Reich during the phase of its inexorable decline, Speer remained indispensable to Hitler and the regime. Writing to Hitler near the end of the war, he claimed: 'Without my work the war would perhaps have been lost in 1942–3.'[88] He was surely right. His achievements constitute an important element in the answer to the question of how Germany held out so long.[89] To this extent, Speer, notwithstanding a weakening of his internal position, was a crucial – possibly even the most important – member of the quadrumvirate that directed Germany's path into the abyss in the Third Reich's last months.

V

The combined efforts of the quadrumvirate would have served little purpose had the armed forces shown signs of disaffection and wavered in their backing for the regime. We already saw, however, that, amid the shocked response at Stauffenberg's assassination attempt, military leaders were keener than ever to demonstrate their loyalty to Hitler and dissociate themselves from the uprising against the regime. The arch-loyalist Jodl, his head bandaged after being slightly wounded in the bomb blast and in deep shock at what had happened, set the tone. He told Goebbels that the loyal generals who worked closely with Hitler would help him 'ruthlessly hunt down the defeatists, putschists and assassination instigators'.[90] So outraged was he at the 'treachery' from within that he favoured disbanding the General Staff altogether.[91] 'The 20th of July', he told officers of the Wehrmacht Operations Staff, was the 'blackest day in German history', worse even than 9 November 1918, 'unique in its monstrosity'. Now there would be pitiless reprisals against those reponsible. When 'everything rotten has been weeded out', there would be a new unity. 'Even if luck should be against us, we must be determined to gather round the Führer at the last, so that we may be justified before posterity.'[92] Jodl sought a personal show of loyalty from the officers present who were to seal their commitment to sharing their destiny with the Führer by a handshake.[93]

Fear of any connection with the plotters, and the dire consequences such a discovery would entail, naturally played a significant part in the new rush to demonstrate loyalty beyond question. But the support for Hitler and denunciation of treachery by the army against their supreme commander and head of state was for the most part spontaneous and genuine. Even so, Hitler and the regime leadership were leaving nothing to chance. The upsurge of bile vented at the officer corps by Party fanatics, which Bormann even had to dampen down, now offered the perfect atmosphere in which new controls could be introduced and new efforts made to improve the ideological indoctrination of the army. The introduction (initiated by the commanders-in-chief of the armed forces, not by Hitler) on 23 July of the 'Heil Hitler' greeting instead of the military salute provided an external sign of the reinforced bonds with the Führer.[94]

Hitler's immediate step, within hours of the assassination attempt, was to restore order in what he had regarded, long before the plot, as the army's most critical weak spot. For three weeks since Zeitzler's breakdown at the beginning of July the army had in effect lacked a Chief of the General Staff. With the imminent danger of the Red Army breaking through into East Prussia, a new chief was a vital necessity. And since, in Hitler's eyes, the source of the cancer that had led to the attempted uprising lay in this key centre of army operational planning, a reliable new chief was essential to make the General Staff both militarily effective and politically sound. Hitler's intended choice, General Walter Buhle, had been injured in the assassination attempt. He turned, therefore, to the highly experienced and well-respected tank specialist Heinz Guderian, since early 1943 Inspector-General of Panzer Troops. A fervent nationalist and anti-Communist, a personality of great drive and dynamism, extremely forceful in his views, and a daring strategist, Guderian had played a notable part in persuading Hitler, whom in earlier years he had greatly admired, of the tactical value in modern warfare of concentrated and swift panzer attack. He had gained plaudits for the great panzer thrust through the Ardennes in 1940 that had played a major part in the spectacular collapse of Allied forces in France. A year later, his panzer forces had spearheaded the initially notable advances in Russia. Conflict with the Commander-in-Chief of Army Group Centre, Field-Marshal Hans Günther von Kluge, over tactics, and Guderian's fiery temperament had brought his dismissal in the winter crisis of 1941, but he had been recalled by Hitler in February 1943, in the wake of another crisis, the catastrophe at Stalingrad. Though increasingly sceptical about Hitler's conduct of the war, and despite being approached by the conspirators, Guderian had the following year kept his hands clean in the plot, and still condemned Stauffenberg's attempt after the war. He certainly had Goebbels' imprimatur. The Propaganda Minister described him as 'insurpassable in loyalty to the Führer'.[95] In his dealings with Hitler, Guderian would learn in the months to come that loyalty and sound military judgement seldom went hand in hand. But following his appointment on 21 July, he was keen to display his credentials as a loyalist and establish unconditional loyalty in an almost entirely reconstructed General Staff, which had seen so many of its former officers arrested under suspicion of complicity in the plot. He rapidly denounced what he depicted as the defeatism and cowardice that had led to the disgrace of the General Staff, and guaranteed an officer corps now completely loyal to the Führer. One of the early steps he took was to ensure that not merely the high level of ability associated with the General Staff, the 'intellectual elite' of the army, but ideological commitment to Nazi ideals was now required. On 29 July he issued the order that every General Staff officer should be a National Socialist Leadership Officer (*Nationalsozialistischer Führungsoffizier*, NSFO), that 'he must demonstrate and prove, as well as in tactics and strategy, through an exemplary stance in political questions, through active direction and instruction of younger comrades in the intentions of the Führer, that he belongs to the "selection of the best"'.[96] The General Staff, having failed disastrously and criminally in the eyes of the regime's leaders, was now particularly exposed to Nazification. No further disaffection could be expected from that quarter.

Hitler had established a corps of NSFOs within the High Command of the Wehrmacht in December 1943 and placed it under the charge of

General Hermann Reinecke. Its task was to instil the Nazi spirit into troops who, he feared, were being affected by subversive Soviet propaganda. For Hitler and the regime's leadership, breathing fanaticism into the troops was the road to victory.[97] There was little liking for the new institution among the officer corps, and the NSFOs had a hard time gaining acceptance. The failed uprising of July 1944 drastically changed the situation.[98] It was not that the NSFOs were now greeted with open arms by most soldiers, or that their message was warmly welcomed and taken to heart. On the contrary: their presence often remained resented, and their pep-talks frequently still fell on deaf ears. Even so, much of the Wehrmacht's mass base was still potentially receptive to Nazi ideals, since around a third of ordinary soldiers were or had been members of some Party affiliate.[99]

In any case, the new circumstances meant that there was now no protection against the extended deployment of these military missionaries of Nazi ideology. Their chief, General Reinecke, indicated the possibilities in August: 'With the traitors wiped out, the last opponents of a decisive politicization of the Wehrmacht have been eliminated. There must be no more obstacles in the way of National Socialist leadership work.'[100] By the end of 1944 there were more than a thousand full-time and as many as 47,000 part-time NSFOs, most of them members of the Party, working in the Wehrmacht. The task accorded them was to 'educate' the soldiers to an 'unconstrained will to destroy and to hate'.[101]

'Guidelines for the NS-Leadership', distributed on 22 July, offer a glimpse of this doctrinal intrusion. The troops were to be fully informed of the 'cowardly murderous strike against the Führer' and the events of 20 July. The addresses that evening by Hitler, Göring and Dönitz were to be read out. Every soldier was to be clear that any sign of insubordination would be punished by death. It was the duty of any soldier of honour, conscious of his duty, to intervene as strongly as possible against 'symptoms of unsoldierly and dishonourable behaviour'. National Socialist Germany would know how to prevent a repeat of the 'stab in the back' of 1918 or anything similar to the 'pitiful treason' in Italy (at the toppling of Mussolini in July 1943). Only the united strength of all Germans could fend off the threat to the whole of Europe from the Reich's enemies. One man alone could save Germany from Bolshevism and destruction: 'our Führer, Adolf Hitler'. The message was, therefore, to stand all the more solidly and fervently behind the Führer, and to fight still more fanatically.[102]

A fateful, lasting consequence of the bomb plot was the elimination of any possibility of the armed forces constituting an agent of regime change in the last months of the Third Reich. At the pinnacle of the military system in the High Command of the Wehrmacht, Keitel and Jodl remained totally behind Hitler, emotionally committed to him in a way that surpassed their functional positions. Wilhelm Keitel, tall and well built, an officer during the First World War and excellent organizer with long experience of army administration, had been deeply impressed by Hitler from the time he had first encountered him back in 1933. At the complete reorganization of the Wehrmacht leadership in early 1938, Hitler, on establishing the OKW, had made Keitel its administrative head. Thereafter Keitel, in whom obedience to the will of the ruler had long been ingrained, was wholly in thrall to Hitler – so much so that he was widely lampooned as being simply his lackey. Alfred Jodl, a tall, balding Bavarian, had also served as an officer in the First World War and, like Keitel, in the small German army during the Weimar Republic. Well versed in operational planning, he had been appointed Chief of the Wehrmacht Operations Staff just before the invasion of Poland in 1939, and had impressed Hitler a few months later with his part in planning the invasion of Scandinavia, then the major western offensive, in spring 1940. Jodl himself had been full of admiration for Hitler's leadership during the great victory over France. He thought Hitler was a genius – and, despite later disagreements with him on tactical matters, did not change his mind.

Beyond the OKW, the Army General Staff, under Guderian, could no longer incubate any source of disaffection. Nothing but ultra-loyalty could be expected of the Luftwaffe, under Göring's command. And the navy was headed by the radically pro-Nazi Grand-Admiral Dönitz. With the Replacement Army under Himmler's tight control and the General Staff purged and brought into line, any new moves to resist the self-destructive course of the Nazi leadership from the two areas most closely associated with the assassination attempt were ruled out for the duration. And no insurrection could be expected from top generals, the frontline commanders-in-chief or their subordinate officers.

The chief waverer among Army Group commanders, Field-Marshal von Kluge, Commander-in-Chief West, had blown hot and cold on the resistance movement, eventually turning his back on the conspirators, but falling nonetheless under deep suspicion in Hitler's headquarters.

He was to kill himself, still protesting his loyalty to the Führer, some weeks later. Dissident officers in Paris, Vienna and Prague had fallen victim to the purge that followed the quashed uprising.[103] The other Army Group commanders and leading generals, whatever their disagreements with Hitler's orders, were outright loyalists, and remained so. Field-Marshal von Rundstedt and Colonel-General Guderian served – the latter, he subsequently claimed, with great reluctance – on the 'Court of Honour' which dismissed from the army officers implicated in the bomb plot, throwing them onto the tender mercies of the 'People's Court' and its notorious presiding judge, Roland Freisler.

Field-Marshal Walter Model, Commander-in-Chief at different times of three Army Groups in the east, an excellent tactician, good organizer and stern disciplinarian who had stood up to Hitler on a number of occasions but remained high in the Dictator's favour, saw himself as purely a military professional, standing aside from politics. But whatever the self-image of the unpolitical soldier – a delusion he shared with other generals – he of course acted politically in a system that made it impossible to do otherwise. He refused to believe the plotters' claim on 20 July that Hitler was dead, he was the first military leader to send a declaration of loyalty to the Dictator on hearing of his survival, and he never wavered in his support.[104] At the end of July, he sought through a combination of renewed trust in Hitler and straightforward fear to restore wavering morale and discipline in the devastated Army Group Centre, which had lost 350,000 men killed or captured. 'The enemy stands at East Prussia's borders,' his proclamation to his troops ran. But his own men still held a position enabling them 'to defend the holy soil of the Fatherland' and repel the danger of 'murder, fire and plundering of German villages and towns', as the Führer, people and comrades fighting on other fronts expected. 'Cowards have no place in our ranks,' he went on. 'Any waverer has forfeited his life. It's about our homeland, our wives and children.' Intense concentration of all forces could combat the temporary superiority of the enemy in numbers and *matériel*. The new responsibilities given to Himmler and Goebbels had provided all the necessary prerequisites for this. 'No soldier in the world is better than we soldiers of our Führer, Adolf Hitler! Heil to our beloved Führer!' he ended.[105]

If each of these examples illustrates the corruption of military professionalism in the Third Reich, the last is of a commander, Colonel-General

Ferdinand Schörner, of a different type, a fanatical loyalist from ingrained Nazi conviction, a believer in 'triumph of the will' and the need for a revolution of the spirit in the army.[106] An indicator of Schörner's acknowledged fanaticism was that he had served for a brief spell in March 1944 as 'Chief of the NS-Leadership Staff of the Army', responsible for coordinating relations between the military and the Party.[107] He brought to Army Group North on his transfer there on 23 July an unprecedented level of ferocious internal discipline that produced, as in his other commands, countless executions for 'cowardice', 'defeatism' and desertion. He made it plain at the outset that the slightest show of disobedience would be mercilessly punished. In an early declaration to his generals, he expounded his belief that the war was 'not to be won by tactical measures alone'. Belief, loyalty and fanaticism were increasingly necessary as the enemy neared German borders. Everyone had to realize that the aim of Bolshevism was 'the destruction of our people'. It was a 'struggle for existence' in which the only alternatives were 'victory or downfall'. To stop the 'Asiatic flood-wave', as he described the Soviet advance, faith in victory was 'the strongest life force'. He ended his communiqué: 'Heil to the Führer'.[108] Ten years after the war, an officer who had served under him described Schörner as trying 'to replace energy through brutality, operational flexibility through inflexible principles of defence, a sense of responsibility through lack of conscience'.[109] With such ruthless leadership, the slightest sign of insubordination, let alone any hint of mutiny, was tantamount to suicide.

Quite apart from their personal loyalty to Hitler, and whatever the individual variation in their views on his conduct of the war, or Germany's prospects, these and other leading generals saw their unconditional duty as doing all they could to defend the Reich against enemy inroads. Nazi values intermingled, often subliminally, with old-fashioned patriotism. As the pressure on the fronts, east, west and south, mounted inexorably, field commanders had little time for other than urgent military matters. Had they been of a single mind, and even dreamt of staging another putsch to end the looming catastrophe, organizing one would have proved impossible. So would confronting Hitler with an ultimatum to stand down or negotiate peace terms. In practice, however, such thoughts never entered the heads of the military elite. Jodl summarized the stance at the top of the military establishment: 'fortunately the Allied demand for unconditional surrender [laid down at the

Casablanca Conference in January 1943] has blocked the way for all those "cowards" who are trying to find a political way of escape.'[110] Doing what was humanly possible to prevent the destruction of the Reich was seen as the unquestioned imperative. In adhering to such a goal, of course, the generals ensured that precisely this destruction would happen.

VI

At a time when Germany was rocked by disastrous military defeat, amid soaring anxieties over the superiority of enemy forces, Hitler's war leadership and the prospects for Germany's future, the assassination attempt and uprising had the effect of strengthening the regime – at least in the short term. In the aftermath, mentalities, structures of control and possibilities for action were all changed.

Attitudes were adjusted – to some extent reshaped. Hitler himself was changed. His paranoia had never been far from the surface. Now it knew no bounds. He sensed treachery on all sides. Treachery gave him the explanation of military failure and of any trace of what he saw as weakness in those around him. It prevented any need for the narcissistic personality to contemplate his own part in the catastrophe. 'Anyone who speaks to me of peace without victory will lose his head, no matter who he is or what his position,' he was later claimed to have repeatedly threatened those in his vicinity as the fronts were collapsing.[111] Such a mentality at the head of the regime percolated outwards and downwards. Blind fury, not just at the conspirators, but at the officer corps as a whole, fuelled by a hate-filled tirade by Robert Ley, head of the Labour Front and Organization Leader of the Nazi Party, which advocated the extermination of the aristocracy (described as degenerate, idiotic 'filth') – many of the plotters had aristocratic backgrounds – ran in the veins of Party fanatics in these days, but spilled over, too, into the wider public.[112] Bormann even had to contain it in the interests of retaining his own control rather than pour oil onto the flames.[113] Wise and cautious voices kept quiet. Signs of anything that could be interpreted as defeatism now invited fearful reprisals.

Within the armed forces, leading officers of Schörner's kind needed no encouragement. But the change in mentalities went beyond soldier fanatics. Belief in victory, commitment to the last reserves of will to hold out, rejection of anything that smacked of the slightest doubt in the struggle, became more than ever incontrovertible tenets of all public parlance, constantly reinforced by the more widely deployed NSFOs. Private doubts were best not aired. At whatever rank, anyone voicing criticism of the war effort was taking a risk. Even close circles of friends and comrades had to take care lest any comment that could be seen as subversive should reach prying ears. From the top downwards in every division, every battalion, every company, officers felt the need to demonstrate loyalty and clamp down on the slightest sign of dissent. It was little wonder that the numbers of executions in the military, as in the civilian sphere, started to soar.

The failed uprising also brought the changes we have examined to the structures of rule. Some of these changes had already been initiated, in the light of the intensified pressures of the war, when Stauffenberg's bomb went off.[114] The extended role of the RVKs, and, with that, the increased scope for intervention by the Party into state bureaucracy and spheres of military responsibility offers one example. Goebbels saw this as a further sharp incision into the power of the generals.[115] But even where developments were already in train, the events of 20 July and their aftermath served as a sharp accelerator. Radicalization along the line acutely intensified. It was as if the dam had broken and now, finally, a revolutionary war could be fought, on truly National Socialist lines.[116]

The pillars of the regime had been shaken by the events of 20 July, but were left not only standing, but buttressed. Hitler's charismatic appeal had long since been weakened, but had been temporarily revived by the attempt on his life. More importantly, his hold over the regime was undiluted. The major wielders of power were divided among themselves but united in their dependence upon Hitler's favour. Each general of the Wehrmacht, too, knew his command lasted only until Hitler took it away. Beneath Hitler, the regime's grip had been strengthened. The key controls of the regime were in the hands of Nazi leaders with nothing to lose: they knew, and had participated in, its crimes against humanity, most obviously the extermination of the Jews.

Himmler's empire extended into the Wehrmacht itself. His ruthless repression, now increasingly against members of the 'people's community', as well as conquered 'Untermenschen' and 'racial enemies', plumbed new depths. Mobilization for total war underwent a frenzied phase of activity under Goebbels, who at the same time cranked up the propaganda machine into overdrive for the backs-to-the-wall effort. Bormann revitalized the Party, finally offering it the prospect of the social and political revolution its fanatical activist core had always sought. And Speer defied adversity in new exploits of mobilizing the armaments industry.

Military power, too, had been consolidated in the hands of loyalists. As fortunes on the battlefield worsened, the military leadership had bound itself to Hitler more tightly than ever. In the process, it had cut off any possibility of extricating itself from those bonds. It had committed itself to the very dualism that Hitler himself embodied: victory or downfall. Since victory was increasingly out of the question, and Hitler invariably and repeatedly ruled out any attempt at a negotiated settlement, that left downfall. Possibilities had changed. There was now no exit route.

From the comfortable distance of imprisonment just outside London, the recently captured Luftwaffe officer Lieutenant Freiherr von Richthofen said in early August in a conversation secretly bugged by British intelligence that he was glad the assassination attempt on Hitler had failed. If it had succeeded, he claimed, there would have been a 'stab-in-the-back' legend such as had bedevilled German politics after 1918. This time, he added, it was politically necessary for the nation to go down the road to the bitter end.[117] This assessment was to leave out of the equation the millions of lives that would have been saved had the bomb plot succeeded and the war been rapidly ended. But it was surely correct in its assumption that a new 'stab-in-the-back' legend would have arisen, posing a threat to any post-Hitler settlement. And it was undoubtedly correct in its assumption that the failure of the attempt to topple Hitler from within in July 1944 meant that the regime could from now on be overthrown only by total military defeat. Just how the regime might sustain its war effort until that point – as it turned out, still over eight months away – was a question, however, that Richthofen did not pose.

2

Collapse in the West

We want to build a new Europe, we, the young people facing the old! But what are we? Famished, exhausted, and drained by madmen. Poor and tired, worn out and nerve-ridden. No, no, no! It's not on any more.

An officer on the western front, September 1944

'Victory must be ours. . . . One does one's duty and it would be cowardice not to fight to the end.' 'We don't give up hope. It is all up to the leaders. Something quite different will happen from what everybody expects.' 'If we don't win, Germany ceases. Therefore we shall win.'

Views of captured German soldiers on the western front,
September 1944

I

At the time of the attempted uprising on 20 July, the progress of the American and British armies in Normandy had, from an Allied view-point, remained disappointingly slow and arduous. They had still not broken out of a relatively constricted area of north-western France. From the German perspective, it still looked in mid-July as if the Allies could be held at bay. By winning time, new possibilities could open up. All was far from lost.

The landing in early June had by now been fully consolidated. The Americans had pushed westwards that month to take the important port of Cherbourg, but it had taken twenty-three, not the expected fif-teen, days and they found the harbour so wrecked that it was six weeks before it could be opened up to Allied cargoes. The city of Caen had been a D-Day objective but its environs were fully secured by the Allies, in the teeth of fierce German resistance, only in mid-July. Then as the British pushed southwards towards Falaise, they became embroiled in further heavy fighting before their advance in the ill-fated 'Operation Goodwood' was called off, amid torrential rain and heavy losses of men and tanks, on the very day that Stauffenberg's bomb had exploded in Hitler's headquarters. Five days later, the big offensive 'Operation Cobra', starting with a huge carpet-bombing assault on German lines, aimed at a strong thrust by American troops to punch through numerically inferior German defences, further pulverized from the air, south-westwards to Avranches, near the French coast. By 30 July the offensive had succeeded. Late that night Avranches was in Allied hands.[1] A major breakthrough was now possible. The road westward to the coastal ports of Brittany lay exposed (though it was to be weeks before stiff German resistance was overcome and the ports captured). To the south lay the Loire. Eastwards, towards Paris itself, only weakened German forces now stood in the way of the Allies.

Hitler's thinking so far had been to play for time. He had reckoned that further dogged German resistance would ensure that the Allies continued to make only slow progress. His priority in the west was to hold the U-boat bases on the French coast, essential for the war in the Atlantic on which so much still hinged, in his view, and fanatical defence of the harbours to deny the Allies the possibility of large-scale troop reinforcements. Containing the Allies in north-western France and gaining time would allow defences to be strengthened and preparations made for a major German offensive, an idea already germinating in Hitler's mind. Inflicting a defeat on the western Allies and halting their presumed march to victory would then force them into armistice negotiations.[2]

He was now faced, however, with the implications of the Allied capture of Avranches. It was an ominous development. Characteristically, he chose not to respond by withdrawing German troops to new lines to the east. Instead, he commissioned Field-Marshal Hans Günther von Kluge – whose idea it had originally been – to launch a quick counter-offensive westwards through Mortain, aimed at retaking Avranches, splitting the American forces and re-establishing the German lines. Kluge's attack took place in the early hours of 7 August, but was effectively over after a single day. German troops did succeed in regaining

Mortain and advancing about 11 kilometres. But, subjected to ceaseless bombardment, they could get no further. By insisting on Kluge continuing the attack long after wisdom dictated swift withdrawal, Hitler invited disaster. Since Kluge faced increasing danger of encirclement by American forces, Hitler eventually allowed a retreat from the Mortain area on 11 August, but as late as 15 August refused Kluge's entreaty to withdraw 100,000 troops in great peril near Falaise.

Hitler's suspicions of his field-marshal boiled over when he could not reach him by radio that day, and he peremptorily dismissed him from his command, replacing him by the trusted troubleshooter, the tough and unyielding Field-Marshal Model. Soon afterwards, correctly fearful that he would be put on trial before the dreaded People's Court for his connection with the conspiracy against Hitler (even though he had been careful not to join the plot), Kluge committed suicide. Model eventually extricated around 50,000 men from the rapidly tightening 'Falaise pocket'. But roughly the same number were captured and another 10,000 men killed, while huge quantities of armaments and equipment had to be abandoned. During August, the German army in western Europe had in all lost over 200,000 men killed, injured or captured.[3]

It had been a disaster. A full-scale German retreat turned into little short of a rout. It could even have been worse had the Allies pressed home their advantage, closed the pocket enveloping the German troops, and prevented so many hardened warriors and seasoned officers from escaping to fight again another day. Even so, the Allies could now race northwards and eastwards. German morale seemed on the verge of collapse.[4] When Paris fell on 25 August, it was without a fight. Withdrawal was also under way from parts of Belgium and Luxemburg. By the end of August, some 2 million Allied soldiers were already in France, others rapidly adding to that number. To the north, the Allies could drive on to the Channel ports. The Allied push into Belgium brought the liberation of Brussels on 3 September and, next day, the capture of Antwerp. Meanwhile, American and French troops had landed on the coast of southern France on 15 August. By late that month they had taken Marseilles and advanced on Lyons. It was little wonder, then, that Allied optimism peaked around this time. The Germans, it seemed, could not last through the winter. The war was approaching its final stages. It would all soon be over.

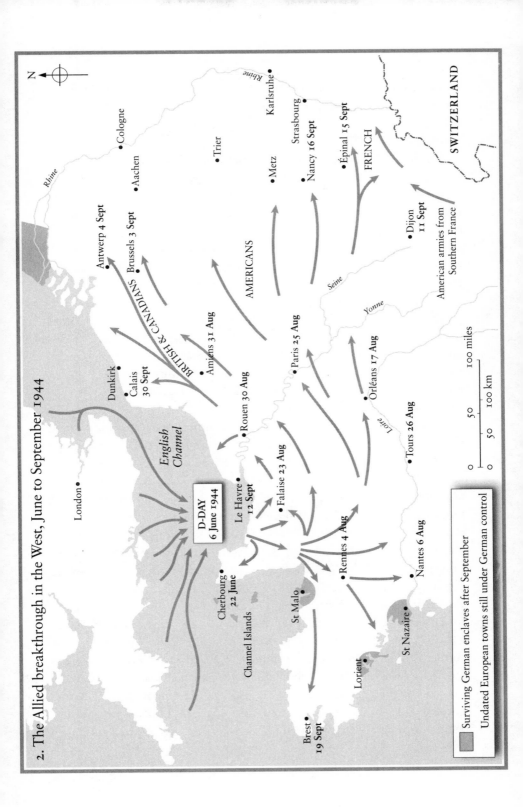

2. The Allied breakthrough in the West, June to September 1944

Unexpectedly, however, the Allied advance stalled. The aim evinced at the beginning of September by the Allies' supreme commander, General Dwight D. Eisenhower, of pressing forward to the Reich borders on a broad front before German defences could be consolidated soon proved an impossibility.

The Allies fared worst in the northern sector. Serious tactical errors brought the advance there to a halt. The arrogant British commander, Field-Marshal Bernard Montgomery, impatient to exploit the German disarray and press boldly ahead into the Ruhr and on to Berlin, made costly mistakes that vitiated his aims – headstrong and immensely risky as these would have been anyway. The conflict of strategy and personality between Montgomery and Eisenhower was unquestionably damaging to the Allies at this vital time. Montgomery's failure to exploit the important capture of the undestroyed Antwerp port by pressing forward to secure the Scheldt estuary left the crucial port unusable until the end of November and allowed large numbers of German troops who could have been cut off in the area to escape. This was compounded by the disaster at Arnhem, where Montgomery's insistence on a daring airborne assault to cross the Rhine resulted in high British losses. The risky offensive 'Market Garden' began on 17 September but was in effect already over three days later. From then on, hopes of a rapid advance across the Rhine and into Germany's industrial heartland, the Ruhr, had to be abandoned.

On the southern sector of the front, the US Third Army under General George Patton had sped eastwards during the second half of August, crossed the Meuse and reached the Mosel. Patton was optimistic that he could drive on into Germany, and that the war could be rapidly won. The first step was to press over the Mosel into Lorraine. The important industrial belt of the Saar beckoned thereafter. But in early September Patton's advance slowed almost to a halt. His supply line to Cherbourg was almost 650 kilometres long. His tanks were simply running out of fuel. And Eisenhower had given priority for the time being to Montgomery's intended drive into the Ruhr. A furious Patton was held back. As his rapid advance became almost immobilized, German defences facing his attacking forces were urgently strengthened and placed under the command of the redoubtable General Hermann Balck, battle-hardened from the eastern front and high in Hitler's favour. The momentum had been lost. It would be a further two months and much hard fighting before fierce German resistance at Metz, the fortress heartland of Lorraine, would be overcome.[5]

The best prospects lay in the central sector of the front. The US First Army, under General Courtney Hodges, advancing north-eastwards from the Paris area in late August, had destroyed several German panzer divisions, taking 25,000 prisoners, before reaching Mons, in Belgium. Part of the army, the V US Corps, then turned south-east to advance through Luxemburg and almost to the German border near Trier by 11 September, while the VII US Corps drove directly eastwards towards Aachen. Around 6 p.m. on 11 September, the first American troops set foot on German soil, just south of Aachen, a city by now largely free of defending troops and with a panic-stricken population. But the Americans pressed their advance over too wide an area. German forces regrouped and, through tenacious fighting, blocked the larger and stronger American forces. Within five days, reinforced German units had succeeded in repulsing the American attack. German authorities were able – for the time being – to restore their control over Aachen and prevent any American breakthrough in the direction of Cologne. Another chance had been missed. It would take a further five weeks of bitter fighting before Aachen became the first German city to fall into Allied hands, on 21 October. And it would be nearly six months before Cologne, only 90 kilometres or so away, was taken.

Meanwhile, Rundstedt had been recalled as Commander-in-Chief West (in overall command of the army in that theatre) on 5 September, leaving Model, a brilliant defence strategist, to take charge of Army Group B (one of two Army Groups on the western front; the other, Army Group G, was commanded by Colonel-General Johannes Blaskowitz). Under Model's command, the German defences, helped by shortened supply lines and hardened reinforcements, both salvaged from Normandy and brought across from the eastern front, had been strengthened. By mid-September the Allies stood close to the German border over a long stretch of the front from Belgium almost to Switzerland. But it was now clear that expectations which the Allies had held for months, drawing on the experiences of the First World War, of the sort of German collapse that had happened in 1918 were misplaced.[6] The war was set to drag on.[7]

The Allies had shown hesitation and made costly errors at crucial junctures. But the Germans had made their own major contribution to prolonging the war. For Germany, despite fierce and courageous fighting by the outnumbered forces of the Wehrmacht, the collapse in France had come as a dreadful shock. Within a little over three months, the Allies had liberated France and reached Germany's borders. Soon, it was evident, the war would be fought on German soil. Under Model's able command, however, they had survived the critical, but not fatal, defeat near Falaise. Since then, they had surprised the Allies with the tenacity, even fanaticism, of their fighting. Though outnumbered, they had shown energy and initiative. And they had some technically superior weaponry and tanks – if in insufficient quantities. The main weakness was not on the ground, but in the air, where the Luftwaffe was increasingly paralysed and Allied superiority immense.[8] Even so, German defence was stubborn, and not easy to break down. Unlike the Russian army in 1917, the German army the following year, the Italian army in 1943, or other instances where heavy defeats had produced a collapse in morale with devastating political consequences, the German armed forces in late summer and autumn of 1944 were far removed from the point at which they were unwilling to fight on any further. What lay behind the extraordinary tenacity of the fighting front in the west?

II

Had the Allies seen reports that were reaching the German leadership at this time on the demoralization among the German civilian population on the western borders of the Reich and within the Wehrmacht produced by the disastrous military collapse in the west, they might have been encouraged in their 'collapse theory' based upon the events of 1918.[9] Such reports certainly did not give the impression that Germany was capable of fighting on for a further eight months.

A sense of relief in Germany that the eastern front appeared to be stabilized was said to have been dissipated in mid-August through the depressing news of the Allied breakthrough in the west, for which the population had been completely unprepared.[10] Optimists suggesting that the war could yet be won with a supreme effort had a hard time in the gathering gloom of opinion about the huge superiority of enemy forces, scepticism about the promised new 'wonder weapons', and feelings that the total-war effort, though generally welcome, had come too late and would, in any case, not be evenly spread in its burdens. Letters from loved ones at the front, and even official news bulletins from France, were cited as indicators that Germany could not compete with the Allied supremacy in men and weaponry. 'I don't believe we'll be able to stop the storm of the enemy,' one quoted letter home ran. 'Their superiority is far too great, in the air and above all with tanks, tanks and still more tanks.' 'Where are the great reserves that have always been talked about?' people were asking. In the depressed mood, the desire for an early end to the war was all the stronger, and with it the view that the consequences of defeat would be less dreadful than claimed. Scepticism and defeatism were becoming inseparable.[11]

By early September reports from propaganda offices across the country were indicating that the mood of the people had reached its lowest point during the entire war. Since the general tenor of such reports – more so than those of the SD – was to emphasize the pro-Nazi sentiments of the population, the clear indication of depression and hopelessness conveyed at this time is all the more striking. A sense of insecurity was widespread. Those with 'negative' attitudes were gaining in numbers and undermining morale through defeatist comments and 'concealed criticism of the leadership'. Many were asking why the Allied landing had not been halted, why total war had not been proclaimed earlier, and why the 'poison' that had produced the uprising of 20 July had not been spotted earlier and destroyed. The criticism was aimed at the Führer himself, even if people were too wary to mention him directly.

Those holding such views could see no way to improve the situation and repel the enemy. The wounded soldiers and refugees streaming in from the west only bolstered their pessimism. Ordinary soldiers and the 'homeland' were not to blame, they were saying, if it all went wrong and Germany were to lose the war. It was not a matter of fate. The ability of the generals was called into question; and the leadership had not done everything necessary. Above all, the sense of powerlessness in the face of immense enemy superiority in numbers and equipment was dispiriting. Women with children were especially prone to anxiety about the future, it was said. Thoughts of suicide were increasingly common. Hopes in the new weapons were fading, particularly since it was felt that everything had been done too late to make a difference. People were saying that if Lorraine and the Saarland could not be held, the loss of centres of vital armaments production would force Germany to surrender. Few thought that the *Westwall* – the huge line of German fortifications that had been built in 1938, known to the western Allies as the 'Siegfried Line' – would hold up the enemy advance any more than the French 'Maginot Line' had stopped the Wehrmacht's march into France in 1940. With the enemy at the borders of the Reich, the desertion of Germany's allies – Romania had sued for peace and joined the war against Germany on 25 August, Finland was on the verge of breaking off relations with Germany, other countries were about to follow suit – and exposure with no defence to intensified 'terror from the skies', it was difficult to avoid pessimism.[12]

Refugees from Rombach in Lorraine contributed to a worsening of the mood in factories in the border area with rumours that they had been shot at during their evacuation by train, that enemy parachutists had dropped near Metz, and that the German retreat had been a rout, with officers leaving their soldiers in the lurch as they fled eastwards in whatever vehicles they could find. On top of that, they were saying, the V1 was no longer being fired. Predictably, the report was dismissed in Berlin as mere exaggeration. That did not diminish, however, the damage that was being done by such rumours.[13] A similar story was provided to Reichsführer-SS Heinrich Himmler by his friend from schooldays and now head of the SS sanatorium in Hohenlychen, north of Berlin, Professor Karl Gebhardt, during a visit to the western front in early September. The population of Trier, he reported, had been disturbed by the numerous rumours in circulation and by the 'unpleasant sight' of Wehrmacht vehicles streaming in from Aachen. The ordered evacuation of Eupen-Malmédy – a former enclave of Belgium, annexed by Germany in 1940 – had turned into a panic flight of the German population, in the company of Party functionaries who evidently had no intention of returning.[14]

The Party's evacuation of Aachen (the first major German city in Allied sight) and adjacent areas close to the *Westwall* on the approach of the Americans had been nothing less than a shambles. Evacuation plans had been laid, and on 11 September Hitler's approval had been given. The evacuation began around midday on 12 September. It had scarcely begun, however, when, as it seemed amid the start of heavy artillery attacks and repeated air raids that the fall of the city was imminent, panic had broken out among the population. It was impossible, amid gathering chaos, to carry out an ordered evacuation. By mid-evening, some 10,000 frightened civilians were crowded onto Aachen's stations, desperate to get away but with transport made extremely difficult by the bombs raining down on adjacent tracks. Thousands took matters into their own hands, rushing eastwards from the city on foot in long columns, jamming nearby roads. The Nazi authorities themselves estimated shortly afterwards that some 25,000 had managed to leave between 11 and 13 September, to add to the 20,000 who had left the previous week.

Soon afterwards on the late evening of 12 September, Party officials, Gestapo, police and fire-service joined the panic and fled, leaving the people of the city leaderless. Precisely at this juncture, the divisional staff of the 116th Panzer Division arrived, under the command of General Gerd Graf von Schwerin. In the absence of Party leaders, Schwerin took responsibility on 13 September for restoring order, not least to allow for troop movements. 'Wild' evacuation was halted. Citizens were directed into bunkers. Reckoning that the Americans were about to arrive, Schwerin left a note, written in English, informing the commanding officer of the US forces that he had stopped 'the stupid evacuation' of the population. At the time there were still between 20,000 and 30,000 people in the city, most of whom were in fact evacuated in the following days.

When German forces, unexpectedly, proved able for the time being to repel the American attack and prevent the occupation, the Nazi authorities seized upon Schwerin's note, which had come into their hands, to cover their own lamentable failings. The matter was taken as far as Hitler himself. Schwerin was promptly dismissed, and Hitler ordered the utmost radicalism in the defence of the city. An investigation found, however, that Schwerin had acted properly within his responsibilities, and that the failure had plainly lain with the Party authorities. Schwerin was converted in fickle post-war memory into 'the saviour of Aachen'. In fact, there had been no defiance of orders or humanitarian action on Schwerin's part. He had undertaken no act of resistance. In crisis conditions he was simply carrying out to the best of his ability what he saw as his duty in line with the military demands of the regime.[15]

Goebbels noted 'extraordinary difficulties' in the evacuation of the territories close to the *Westwall* and the population of the border districts being 'thrown here and there', but saw this as unavoidable at such a time of crisis.[16] A few days later, acknowledging that the situation in

Aachen had become 'critical', he advocated the principle of 'scorched earth' in the question of evacuation. With the future of the nation at stake, little consideration could be given to the people of the area.[17] Goebbels was put fully in the picture – if in a scarcely unbiased account – about the 'desolate situation' and the evacuation of Aachen by the Gauleiter of Cologne-Aachen, Josef Grohé (whose authority had been badly damaged by the flight of his subordinates). Party and Wehrmacht had stood at loggerheads. The Party had left the city. A general chaos had ensued. 'Unprecedented scenes' had taken place on the roads east-wards from Aachen. The situation there and in Trier – whose centre (including the great hall of Emperor Constantine dating from the early fourth century) had been badly damaged by bombs in mid-August, and which in the night of 13/14 September was under sustained artillery attack – had to be regarded as 'extremely serious'.[18]

Speer, returning from a visit to the region, where he had been driven through the masses streaming away, echoed the accounts of the 'debacle'.[19] The troops he had seen were exhausted. The newly estab-lished *Volksgrenadier* divisions contained many older recruits who could not cope with the physical demands. There was a big drop in the effective strength of the fighting forces and a growing crisis of con-fidence. Party functionaries labelled officers in general 'criminals of 20 July' and blamed them for the military setbacks in both east and west; soldiers themselves dubbed officers 'saboteurs of the war' and accused them of lack of fighting spirit. The troops had been badly affected by the mishandling of the evacuation of Aachen. The trains had been stopped without any notice and women, children and old people had been forced to leave on foot. Columns of refugees were to be seen everywhere, sleeping in the open air and blocking roads. There was a chronic shortage of munitions, weapons and fuel.[20] In the report he sent to Hitler, Speer noted the contrast between soldiers in shabby and tat-tered uniforms and Party functionaries in their gold-braided peacetime uniforms, the sarcastically dubbed 'Golden Pheasants' (*Goldfasane*), who had not been visible in organizing the evacuation of Aachen's inhab-itants or helping to reduce the misery of the refugees.[21]

Xaver Dorsch, one of Speer's leading subordinates, in charge of fort-ifications, and offering his own impressions of a visit to the area on 12–13 September, commented on the damaging impression left by the botched evacuation, and how striking it had been that so few Party functionaries had bothered about the refugees. The unnecessary evacuation could, he thought, lead to a catastrophe if the Allied advance continued during subsequent days. He feared disintegration in the army through the anger stirred up by Party officials blaming Wehrmacht officers for the retreat in France.[22]

Ernst Kaltenbrunner, head of the Security Police, left Himmler in no doubt about the disastrous situation when he wrote at length in mid-September about the mood of the population during the evacuation and occupation of the western border regions. The evacuation in Luxemburg – annexed to the Reich in August 1942 and attached to the domain of the Gauleiter of Koblenz-Trier, Gustav Simon – had been carried out in an atmosphere of total panic. The Gauleiter's measures had been overhasty, and the civilian administration had broken down. Following Simon's order to evacuate, fortification work on the *Westwall* had ceased and the workers had left. The mood of these workers had in any case been poor. They had been badly organized by the Party officials, who had then set the worst kind of example by merely supervising but not working themselves. The failings of the Gau administration were evident in the evacuation of 14,500 citizens in the Saarburg district, where there was panic and chaos. The transport laid on was hopelessly insufficient. The lucky ones left by special train, some of the women, children and sick by bus. But most trudged away by foot, in long, wretched columns who occupied the roads for days, their possessions trailing along in horse-drawn wagons. Clothing, shoes and blankets for the evacuees were in short supply.

As a result of the chaos, there was a good deal of anger directed at the Party. Many people refused to follow the Party's orders to leave (which were often confused and contradictory); others could not find accommodation and came back. In Aachen, where thousands of citizens had defied the evacuation orders, pictures of the Führer had been taken down and white bedsheets hung from windows in gestures of surrender. The Party had lost face through the flight of its functionaries. Organization was poor; women and children became separated in the evacuation. And there had been little sign of anything resembling a 'people's community'. Those with access to cars sped away, unconcerned for anyone else. It was every man for himself.[23]

Kaltenbrunner listed some prominent individuals who had left Luxemburg and Trier prematurely to bring their families to safety. The

Gauleiter himself and the District Leader (*Kreisleiter*) of Metz were among those noted as deserting their posts in a separate report to Himmler about the uncontrolled refugee movements in Lorraine, endangering troop movements. The railways had stopped running because the German personnel had fled, and the civilian administration had detonated essential installations before pulling out so there were electricity and water shortages and the telephones did not function. Russian prisoners of war had been left free to roam the countryside, posing a threat to security.[24]

One officer, Lieutenant Julius Dufner, stationed at Kyllburg, a small spa town in the Eifel, in the Bitburg area just north of Trier, jotted his own first-hand account of the desolate conditions in his diary. 'The war is lost!' he stated baldly on 1 September. In Trier itself, he observed a day later, there was nothing more to be had. Fuel was in such short supply that vehicles would soon be unable to move. 'We want to build a new Europe,' he wrote, 'we, the young people facing the old! But what are we? Famished, exhausted, and drained by madmen. Poor and tired, worn out and nerve-ridden. No, no, no! It's not on any more.' When reproachful citizens asked soldiers why they were retreating, they answered that they, too, wanted to go 'home to the Reich'. It had all been a bluff, he wrote, alluding to the 'miracle weapons'. That was what happened when an advertising boss – he meant Hitler – became supreme commander of the Wehrmacht. Files and papers were being destroyed in huge quantities. 'Everything that seemed at one time indispensable is today valueless and nothing at all.' Who was to blame for it all, the diarist asked. Not those in lowly places, was his answer, those who simply did not want to fight and die for a lost cause. Everything had become crystal clear. All that talk of the new Europe, of young and decrepit peoples, of Germanic leadership, of revolutionary zeal: it was 'baloney', a 'swindle'. He would not have said such things out loud.

As enemy artillery started firing on Trier on the evening of 13 September, and the evacuation of the inhabitants began next day, hundreds of emergency workers – 'a column of wretched looking, careworn old men and also young lads from the Hitler Youth' – traipsed into the city through the rain to dig fortification ditches. These might have fended off Huns and Mongols, Dufner mused, but it seemed doubtful that they could hold up modern tanks. Few of the workers had anywhere to sleep. But there was no complaining, just resigned acceptance. It looked as if the last reserves were being summoned up. As Bitburg itself came under fire, officers still managed to celebrate the birthday of one of their comrades with fine Saar wine and Sekt.[25] It was a case of drink today; there might be no tomorrow.

Such partying with the enemy on the doorstep would have confirmed the widespread prejudice among Nazi functionaries, much of the civilian population and many frontline soldiers about the *Etappengeist* – the 'spirit of the rear lines' – the weak and decadent lifestyle of officers still able to enjoy the good things in life while others were dying for their country. This was the alleged cause of the collapse in France.[26] Behind the front were the lines of communication, the bases for provisioning, administration, transport, field hospitals and for the planning staffs of the fighting army. This all constituted the *Etappe*, an essential element in the structure of any military machine, but, as in the First World War, one much derided by the ordinary front soldiers at the dirty end of the fighting, all too ready to spread to their loved ones back home scurrilous rumours of officers enjoying creature comforts and high living away from the bitter warfare.

'That our rear-line jackasses flood back in such wild panic', Goebbels commented, 'can only be put down to their lack of proper discipline and that they have been more taken up during their long period of occupation in France with champagne and French women than military exercises.' He blamed lack of leadership by the generals for the 'debacle'.[27] The Gau office in Baden reported to the Party Chancellery in early September that the attitude of the retreating units 'breathed the worst sort of rear-lines air, disorderly uniforms, a lot of drunken good-time girls and soldiers hanging together in the worst and most dubious groups, lorries loaded with the most various goods, fittings from apartments, beds, etc. These images reminded war veterans of the conditions of 1918.'[28] In the immediate wake of the collapse of the German army in the Allied breakthrough at Falaise, Himmler had issued orders to the Higher SS and Police Leaders – his main agents in security issues – in western areas, through cooperation with military commanders to abolish once and for all 'the repulsive German rear lines in France', and send those involved to the front or put them to work.[29] A few days later, Martin Bormann passed on to Himmler a letter he had received from Karl Holz, the acting Gauleiter of Franconia, containing reports of 'ill-discipline, subversion and lack of responsibility' in the rear lines in France. Holz suggested sending in 'general inspectors', comprised of 'energetic and brutal National Socialists', to clear up the malaise, though Himmler found it impossible to oblige unless he were given details.[30]

A description of the military failings that had led to the Allied break-through at Avranches – 'the most serious event of the summer' – found its scapegoat in the alleged cowardly behaviour in the rear lines, while praising German efforts that had prevented a worse catastrophe.[31] A report by the *Geheime Feldpolizei* (secret military police) reached a similar conclusion. The failure of officers during the retreat in the west had shaped the mood, reflecting the alleged distrust of officers since 20 July. Instances were adduced from soldiers' accounts of poor behaviour of officers – similar, according to one, to that of 9 November 1918 – and indicating signs of disintegration in the army.[32] Among the strongest denunciations was one from the office of General Reinecke, head of the National Socialist Leadership Staff of the Army, based upon a visit to the western front in late September and early October to assess the work of the NSFOs. These, it was said, were working well. Conditions earlier in the rear lines in France had been 'scandalous'. For four years, those behind the rear lines had lived in a 'land of milk and honey'. The retreat in 1918 at the time of the revolution had been like the proud march of a guard regiment compared with this 'fleeing troop rabble'.[33]

For all their obvious bias in the need to find scapegoats for the disastrous collapse in the west, such reports give a plain indication of low morale and signs of disintegration in the retreating German army. Added to the chaos produced by the evacuations in the border region, the panic among the population and the contempt for the Party that the flight of its functionaries had sharpened, the potential for a growing, full-scale collapse similar to 1918 could not altogether be ruled out. The slowing down of the Allied advance and the accompanying strengthening of German defences did much to ensure that this did not happen. So did the political measures undertaken to stiffen the resolve to fight on and prevent any undermining of either the fighting or the home front. But these in turn rested on attitudes that were sunk in resignation, not burning with rebellion, and were persuaded at least in part by the cause for which they were told Germany was fighting, and ready, therefore, to comply, however unenthusiastically, with the ever tighter regulation of their lives and the demands of the war effort.

III

The most crucial step was to shore up the crumbling western front. Model had to do the best he could to regroup a broken army in the immediate aftermath of Falaise. The size of the field army in the west had dropped from 892,000 men at the beginning of July to 543,000 on 1 September. The command structures had, however, been left intact. They now served as the basis for the organization of new units. Supply lines were shortened, fortifications strengthened (particularly along the *Westwall*) and minefields laid. Most importantly, desperately needed reinforcements were rushed to the west. The new divisions created were, to be sure, improvised units, lacking the best equipment and weaponry.[34] They were strengthened, however, in September when hundreds of tanks and other armoured vehicles were sent west from the hard-pressed eastern front. New levels of uncompromising enforcement were also introduced on the western front, including rigorous measures to round up 'stragglers' and assign them to new units. At the same time, some two hundred NSFOs were dispatched into the western defence districts to prop up faltering morale. The NSFOs, military police and Party agencies provided backing for the army in imposing a network of controls along the front to stiffen the shaky discipline.

On 10 September Field-Marshal Keitel, head of the High Command of the Wehrmacht, advocated 'extreme ruthlessness' to stamp out any signs of subversion of morale. Less than a fortnight later, citing Hitler's express instructions, he issued directives to counter the 'signs of dissolution in the troops' through 'extreme severity', including the use of summary courts with immediate executions in view of the troops to serve as a deterrent.[35] More than a hundred soldiers were shot by SS units while fleeing from the front during the following weeks. On 14 September, Field-Marshal von Rundstedt, newly reinstated as Commander-in-Chief West, ordered the *Westwall* to be held 'down to the last bullet and complete destruction'. Two days later, Hitler amplified the command. The war in the west, he declared, had reached German soil. The war effort had to be 'fanaticized' and prosecuted with maximum severity. 'Every bunker, every block of houses in a German town, every German village, must become a fortification in which the enemy

bleeds to death or the occupiers are entombed in man-to-man fighting,'
he ordered.[36]

The combination of emergency means – through organization, supplies, recruitment and enforcement – succeeded for the time being in
bolstering a desperate situation. Towards the end of September, the outlook was, if not rosy, at least much better than it had been a month earlier.

Just how effective the orders by Hitler and Rundstedt for a 'do or die'
spirit of last-ditch resistance were in practice is not easy to judge. Feelings of helplessness in face of the might of the enemy, resignation,
pessimism, defeatism, and blind fear as battle approached, were not
easily dispelled, however urgent the appeals to fight to the last, however
remorseless the control mechanisms to 'encourage' total commitment,
however ferocious the threats for attitudes less than fanatical, however
severe the punishment for perceived failure of duty. War-weariness was
widespread, as it was among the civilian population. Most soldiers on
the western front were preoccupied with survival rather than fighting to
the last bullet. Colonel Gerhard Wilck, the commander at Aachen, forcefully reminded by Rundstedt 'to hold this ancient German town to the
last man and if necessary to be buried in its ruins', repeatedly professed
his intention of fighting to the final grenade. His actions did not follow
his words. Instead, he made preparations to surrender.[37] Soon after the
city's capitulation on 21 October, Wilck found himself in British captivity. Speaking to his fellow officers, unaware that his conversation was
bugged by his captors, he criticized the last-ditch mentality of the Wehrmacht High Command. Among his troops, the feeling was that the
sacrifice of the 3,000 men forced to surrender at Aachen 'merely to
defend a heap of rubble for two or three days longer' was 'a useless
waste'.[38]

Attitudes were, nevertheless, not uniform. The forces on the western
front in mid-September included armoured and infantry divisions of the
Waffen-SS, known for their fanatical fighting and imbued with Nazi
values.[39] Towards the end of 1944, the Waffen-SS overall comprised
910,000 men, and had some of the best-equipped panzer divisions.[40] But
fervent Nazis were by no means confined to the Waffen-SS. They were
also found in the branches of the much larger conventional armed
forces. Some SS men even served there, and not in the Waffen-SS.[41]

Alongside critical letters back home from the front (which ran the danger of being picked up by the censors, with drastic consequences) were letters with a strongly pro-Nazi tone.[42] Around a third of the Wehrmacht's soldiers had experienced some 'socialization' in the Nazi Party or its affiliates (often greatly enhanced by wartime experience itself). Anyone born after 1913 and serving in the armed forces had been exposed to a degree of Nazified 'education', if only in the Reich Labour Service or compulsory military service (introduced in 1935).[43] It was not surprising, therefore, to find that Nazi mentalities still found expression.

An Allied report from 4 September on morale, based on the questioning of captured soldiers, painted a varied picture of attitudes. It found unmistakable signs of low morale among infantrymen. It nevertheless pointed to high morale among paratroopers, junior officers and SS men. Some representative comments were cited. 'Victory must be ours. . . . One does one's duty and it would be cowardice not to fight to the end.' 'We don't give up hope. It is all up to the leaders. Something quite different will happen from what everybody expects.' 'If we don't win, Germany ceases. Therefore we shall win.' 'Spirit against material. It has never yet happened that mere technology has conquered spirit.' 'I have done my part and have given my Führer, Adolf Hitler, that which can only be given once,' ran one soldier's last letter to his wife. 'The Führer will do it, that I know. . . . I have fallen as a soldier of Adolf Hitler.' Faith in German victory, the report concluded, was most strongly correlated with 'devotion to Hitler personally, identification with National Socialist doctrine, [and] exoneration of Germany from war guilt'.[44]

Another report, a week later, drew conclusions on the ideological sources of continued Wehrmacht fighting morale from observations during about a thousand interrogations carried out during August. Most prominent were: fear of return to a Germany dominated by Russia; conviction in the rightness of the German cause and belief that the Allies had attacked Germany rather than grant her just and necessary concessions; devotion to Hitler, who had only the welfare of Germany at heart; and feeling that the 'unconditional surrender' policy of the Allies meant that the German people could not expect the western powers to help in postwar reconstruction. About 15 per cent of captured soldiers, it was said, held such beliefs 'with fanatical conviction', and had an influence on doubters, while up to 50 per cent were 'still devoted to Hitler'. There was a good deal of admiration among combat soldiers for the fighting capacity of the Waffen-SS.[45]

As with soldiers at the front, the stance of ordinary citizens towards the war and the regime varied widely. Germany, despite more than a decade of Nazi rule, had remained, beneath the veneer of uniformity, in some senses a pluralistic society. Beliefs that were a deeply ingrained product of earlier socialist and communist subcultures could find no expression. But they were suppressed, not eradicated. Fervent Christian beliefs and traditions, institutionally underpinned within the Protestant and, especially, the Catholic Church, persisted despite relentless Nazi ideological pressure. On the other hand, the years of indoctrination and compulsion to conform had not failed to leave a mark. And the ever more pressing external threat to the country affected, in one way or another, all Germans and provided its own impulse to conformity. The panic at the approach of the Americans had been confined to the regions in the vicinity of the front. Even there, some had endeavoured, Canute-like, to hold back the rising tide of alienation from the regime. Away from the border provinces, there was no indication of collapse. Nothing suggested that the widespread pessimism about the war was likely to result in a popular uprising. Despite the gathering gloom it had described, the weekly propaganda report on 4 September concluded that the people were ready for any sacrifice to avoid destruction or enslavement. They would not 'throw in the towel'.[46] The Nazi leadership itself distinguished between 'mood' and 'attitude', accepting that people were hardly likely to be of sunny disposition if their houses were being blown to bits and their lives upturned by the war, but praising the forbearance and readiness to fight which marked their underlying determination to overcome the hardships and attain victory.[47] This was, of course, a useful internal rationalization of the population's reaction to incessant bad news, and a way of shaping the propaganda of total war. But it was not altogether misleading. For among the pessimists were still many, if a minority impossible to estimate in size with anything approaching precision and certainly diminishing sharply, who – outwardly at least – upheld the positive lines of propaganda, were loyally supportive of the regime, and expressed sentiments redolent of years of exposure to Nazi doctrine.

Some, without question, still thought that Hitler would find a way out of the crisis, and wanted him to speak to the people to provide reassurance.[48] Goebbels was in receipt of a hefty postbag of letters exuding, among 'genuine National Socialists', deep confidence that the crisis would be mastered.[49] There was still hope, if rapidly dwindling, in parts of the population that the promised new 'wonder weapons' would reverse war fortunes.[50] Attitudes towards those not seen to be sharing the burdens and wholly committed to the war effort, and especially to anyone perceived in some way to be 'subversive', were uncompromisingly hostile and often aggressive in demanding recrimination. The ferocious reprisals against the 'traitors' of 20 July were reportedly greeted with satisfaction by many.[51] Despite the widespread worry and anxiety about the war, the slightest hint of opposition still invited terrible retribution, which the police could enforce only through help from ordinary citizens. Listening to foreign broadcasts, increasingly common despite the dangers, frequently led to trouble. Anyone bold enough to make openly defeatist remarks or criticize Hitler's leadership outright was still likely to be denounced to the authorities by zealous loyalists.[52] And the more radical Goebbels' total-war measures appeared to be, especially if targeted at the better-off and privileged, the more approval they apparently found. More than 50,000 letters had been received by the Propaganda Ministry by the end of August, most of them from workers, the middle classes and soldiers, approving in strong terms the total-war measures adopted, but often wanting to go further in their radicalism.[53] Whatever the growing popular fears, anxieties and depression about the state of the war, the SD adjudged, with some reason, that the will to resist was still there, though people were doubting whether resistance would be worthwhile.[54]

That extensive reserves of loyalist backing continued to exist in the face of increasingly extreme adversity is no surprise. The Nazi Party, making strenuous efforts to counter the losses in its ranks of those killed during service in the Wehrmacht, had around 8 million members – about a tenth of the population (a significantly higher proportion of adults) – in 1944.[55] Not all members, of course, were fervent activists or devoted followers. Increased pressure, for example on Hitler Youth groups, to join the Party as war fortunes went into steep descent was not guaranteed to produce fanatics for the cause. Even so, members, however they had come to join, had at least superficially shown some commitment to Hitler and the regime and, once in the Party, were more exposed than the rest of the population to demands to conform. The

Party's organizational tentacles stretched far into community life. The 42 regions ('Gaue'), 808 districts, 28,376 local groups, 89,378 'cells' and 397,040 'blocks' into which Germany was divided by the Party's administration ensured that not only members were subjected to invasive controls and routine surveillance. Besides the passive membership, there were the functionaries, who, even if they wanted to, could barely escape regular doses of indoctrination during their work for the Party. In July 1944, functionaries in full-time employment by the Party and its affiliates numbered 37,192 men and as many as 140,000 women, around 60,000 of those in the Nazi welfare organization, the NSV (*Nationalsozialistische Volkswohlfahrt*, National Socialist People's Welfare). An estimated 3 million citizens served the Party in some unpaid capacity.[56]

This army of apparatchiks constituted a major instrument of social and political control, usually working in close cooperation with the police and other forces of repression, so that for ordinary citizens the space to organize any form of oppositional behaviour was simply not available. Beyond that, however, the Party functionaries formed a still significant basis of the 'charismatic community' attached to Hitler's leadership. Though Hitler's popular appeal was in steep decline, the functionaries, who had in better times provided the core of Führer worshippers, were still less likely than most to break all allegiance. Beyond any lingering, if by now often diluted, devotion, the functionaries had long since pinned their colours to the mast. The Party had given them careers, social standing, privileges, financial advantages, and often – in varying degrees – some kind of power, if only at the local level, over their fellow citizens. Not a few felt they had no option but to stand or fall with the Party, and with Hitler, on account of their actions in earlier years. Some undoubtedly had bad consciences or at least qualms at possible post-war 'revenge' for their involvement in past events. Many had justified fears for a future without Hitler, for what might happen to them when their Party positions dissolved and what fate might hold for them should the enemy succeed in defeating and occupying the country. The higher the position, the greater the zealotry they had shown, the dirtier their hands, the more cause they had to worry. This meant in turn that they had little or nothing to lose as the end approached.

For the present, however, other than in the perimeter regions touching on the fighting zone, the Party showed no outward signs of crumbling. In fact, its revitalization by Martin Bormann in the second half of 1944 meant that it played a significant role in bolstering the home front. Its activities formed part of an increasingly frenzied effort by the regime to overcome huge and mounting difficulties. And, for the time being, the effort had some success in staving off complete military catastrophe and keeping Germany fighting – at enormous cost in death and destruction.

I V

The impetus behind the appointment of Goebbels as Plenipotentiary for Total War, triggered by the failed bomb plot, had been the destruction of Army Group Centre in the Red Army's offensive in late June and July. No sooner had the programme been initiated than the additional grave losses through the collapse of the western front in August added massively to the demands for huge labour savings, already targeted, to provide men for the front. Goebbels had provided 300,000 men by 1 September. But Hitler now wanted another 450,000 men during the following month.[57] The new circumstances brought the breakdown in the earlier coalition of interests between Goebbels and Speer which had prompted Hitler to agree to the total-war effort. From late August onwards, as the implications of the disaster on the western front became plain, Goebbels and Speer were increasingly at loggerheads.

Goebbels had thrown himself with his customary enormous energy into his new role as Plenipotentiary for Total War. The planning committee he established, headed by Werner Naumann, his State Secretary in the Propaganda Ministry, had swiftly prepared a raft of measures aimed at manpower savings to provide soldiers for the Wehrmacht. Speed of action and an image of dynamism were objectives in themselves for Goebbels, and the haste and improvisation frequently created rather than solved difficulties. But whatever the doubts about the effectiveness of the measures introduced, they made deep incisions into public life. Postal services were cut back, theatres closed, the number of orchestras reduced, film production pared down, university study for all but a few working in disciplines essential to the war or incapable of war service halted,[58] publishing houses shut down, newspapers limited to a few pages only or discontinued. The age for labour conscription for women was extended from forty-five to fifty. By late August, men were required to work sixty and women forty-eight hours per week.[59]

Goebbels was careful to keep Hitler abreast of the measures he introduced, and cleverly played to the Dictator's mood.[60] But he did not always have his own way. He eventually succeeded in overcoming Hitler's initial resistance to increasing further the age for women's labour duty to fifty-five,[61] and particularly to the closure of theatres and variety shows, as well as the abolition of some magazines that he liked. Hitler drew the line, however, at Goebbels' plans to stop the production of beer and sweets. Even the Bolsheviks had never halted sweet production, Hitler stated, and thought they were necessary not only for citizens at home, but also for soldiers at the front. And, as regards beer, he feared above all 'severe psychological repercussions in Bavaria', and thought the move could provoke popular resentment.[62] Hitler's instinct, much more pronounced than that of Goebbels, for avoiding popular discontent remained undiminished, and was again demonstrated in mid-August in the directive he gave to finance the provision of 190,000 bottles of egg-flip to be handed by the NSV to those in the west suffering from bomb-damage (though why anyone bombed out of house and home would have welcomed the repulsive liqueur is another question).[63]

Cuts in administration in government offices also proved less easy to implement than Goebbels had imagined. The Reich Defence Commissars were instructed, for instance, in early September, with recourse to Hitler's instructions, that they should desist from commandeering personnel in ministerial offices or the administrative departments in the *Länder* for service in the newly established divisions of the Wehrmacht.[64] And while the Prussian Finance Ministry was finally abolished – a move of little significance, first mooted the previous year – the equally redundant bureau of the Prussian Minister President (one of Göring's panoply of offices) was retained.[65] The 'combing-out' process did produce substantial gains in some areas. More than 250,000 men were let go by the Post Office and more than 50,000 from the railways, among other significant reductions. But overall, the reductions in staff fell short of expectations.[66] And those released were, predictably, often too old or too unfit for active military service. In fact, able-bodied men were to be found in large numbers only in exempted occupations in the armaments industry, an area in which it made scant sense to lose skilled and experienced workers to have them replaced by less well-trained men.[67]

The obvious tension between providing men for the Wehrmacht and retaining them for armaments production was bound to lead to conflict between the erstwhile allies, Goebbels and Speer. As the need mounted for men to compensate for the losses on the western front, and at the same time the pressures on Speer grew to provide the munitions and weaponry to address the deficiencies created by abandoned *matériel*, the conflict was not long in coming.

Until the collapse in the west, Speer had publicly at least professed optimism.[68] He was, in fact, still telling Goebbels in early September that the armaments industry would be adequately provisioned until the beginning of 1946, even if all the occupied territories were lost.[69] And he had initially been accommodating towards Goebbels' requests for manpower. At the beginning of August he had offered 50,000 men from armaments production for the total-war effort.[70] On the evening of 9 August, he had quickly reached agreement with Goebbels, and indicated his readiness to make 47,000 hitherto exempted employees in the less critical sectors of the armaments and related industries available, with the assurance that replacements would be found.[71] At this point he was still optimistic of obtaining the necessary labour for his own domain from the total-war effort. But the harmony was soon to end. Control over the entire war economy was at stake.[72] By the beginning of September, Goebbels had come to count himself among Speer's most bitter opponents.[73]

Goebbels did not mind whose toes he trod on to reach by one means or another the extravagant savings in manpower he had promised Hitler. And the Gauleiter predictably competed with each other to make the highest savings. Speer found himself on the receiving end of high-handed actions which he saw as extremely damaging to armaments production.[74] At the beginning of September, Goebbels was still expecting Speer to find the promised 50,000 men that month. But the tug of war between the two of them had started, and the conflict deepened as the month progressed.[75] Without a base of support within the Party, and seen as unreasonably insistent on protecting his own domain from the sacrifices other areas had been forced to make, Speer faced a losing battle. He had to contend with powerful enemies. Not just Goebbels and Bormann, but also Himmler and Robert Ley, were among his critics. Attacks by the Party, and interference at the regional level by the Gauleiter, grew.[76] He did his own cause little good when he admitted to

Goebbels at the beginning of September that production was holding up well despite the loss of men in exempted positions that he had been compelled to provide for the Wehrmacht.[77]

Speer felt his only recourse was to appeal directly to Hitler. He did so in a lengthy memorandum on 20 September defending himself against strong allegations from Goebbels and Bormann that his ministry was a 'collection of reactionary economic leaders' and 'hostile to the Party'. Claiming that his task was 'non-political', he objected to the Party's intervention in his sphere of responsibility and wanted the Gauleiter made responsible to him, not Bormann, in armaments matters.[78] But Hitler was never going to transfer any control over the Gauleiter from the Party to Speer's hands. Bormann told the Armaments Minister in no uncertain terms that, as regards the total-war effort, he was subordinate to Goebbels.[79] In any case, Speer no longer had the influence with the Dictator that he had enjoyed in earlier years. His repeated argument that this war was a technical one, and that more and better weaponry would decide it,[80] rather than simply supplying more men to the Wehrmacht, fell on deaf ears, when Hitler and Goebbels both insisted on the obvious counter-argument that increased supplies of both men *and* weapons were a necessity. Goebbels, constantly supplying Hitler with progress reports on the success of his total-war effort, seemed bound to end up the winner in the conflict.

Speer again addressed Hitler directly in rejecting Goebbels' demands for 100,000 armaments workers to be recruited for the September quota of total-war recruits (beyond the 200,000 he had provided since 25 July). These could not be delivered, he claimed, without impairing armaments production. He needed time to prepare for the large inroads into his workforce, and with difficulty could only manage to offer 60,000 from 25 October, then the remaining 40,000 by 15 November. To his frustration, he then found, on returning from a visit to the western front at the end of September, that Hitler had decided that most of the 60,000 were to be sent to the army earlier than he had stipulated, something he described as 'an extraordinarily serious and drastic measure'.[81]

He nonetheless infuriated Goebbels by his obstinacy in resisting further demands to surrender exempted workers from the armaments sector. And as the autumn drew on, and Hitler recognized the achievements of Speer – 'an organizer of genius' – in surmounting extraordinary difficulties to maintain armaments production, the latter's bargaining hand became stronger.[82] His efforts had reinstated him in Hitler's favour. Try as he might, Goebbels failed to persuade Hitler to come to a decision to compel Speer to release a further 180,000 exempted workers from the armaments industry.[83] Speer's attritional, and time-consuming, battle with Goebbels over the retention of his workers had led in the end, therefore, to something approaching stalemate. Hitler had, as so often, proved reluctant to reach a decision in a dispute of significance between two of his leading paladins. The infighting between the heavy-weight ministers could, however, find no resolution if Hitler was not prepared to offer one.

The long-running dispute over scarce manpower was regarded by Speer as a major drain on his energy and resources. Despite this, he made extraordinary efforts in the wake of the setbacks in the west to enable Germany to fight on.

The high point of armaments production for the entire war had been reached in July 1944. The level attained, however, flattered to deceive. It has aptly been described as being like the last sprint of the marathon runner before he sags, energy expended.[84] During the autumn, all spheres of production fell sharply. The main reason was the huge increase in Allied bombing – 60 per cent of all bombs dropped over Germany fell after July 1944. Following the Allied breakthrough in France, September brought a crucial acceleration in the devastating air raids. With Allied aircraft now able to use bases closer to the German borders, and the Luftwaffe more and more paralysed through destruction and through lack of fuel, sustained attacks on industrial installations and transport networks had become far easier. Raw materials production fell by almost two-fifths in the autumn months. Allied attacks on seven mineral-oil works on the same day, 24 August 1944, resulted in a drop of two-thirds in production of aircraft fuel in September, contributing greatly to the ineffectiveness of remaining air defences. Massive damage was caused to the industrial infrastructure as power stations were put out of action. Gas and electricity supplies were badly affected. Gas output in October was a quarter down on what it had been in March. Repeated attacks on the rail network of the Deutsche Reichsbahn, on the lines, locomotives, other rolling stock, bridges and marshalling yards, as well as waterways and Rhine shipping, caused massive disruption to transport arteries with huge knock-on effects in supplies to industry, not least coal provision from the Ruhr. At least, as yet, the coal mines themselves in the west remained largely unscathed. The decline in output of vital weaponry was not to be stopped, despite levels of production attained still outstripping those of 1942.[85]

What remains little less than astounding, however, is not why armaments production fell drastically, but how, given the extent and well-nigh insuperable nature of the problems, Speer was able to keep it at such a relatively high level.

Speer's rapid grasp not just of problems, but their possible solutions or at least amelioration, his enormous energy coupled with unquestioned talent for organization, and the authorization he had to push through changes, thanks to his manipulation of his frequent armaments briefings with Hitler, all contributed to his ability in autumn 1944 to paper over the widening cracks. He was preoccupied with doing all he could to maximize fuel supplies (badly affected by air strikes against the hydrogenation plants in central Germany since the spring), to build up air defences through increased fighter production, to keep transport moving and to save all that was possible for industry in the evacuation of border areas.[86] In pressing the demands of the armaments industry, he strived constantly to protect his own domain from the other 'big beasts' in the Nazi jungle, to prevent the Party from undermining the 'self-responsibility of industry', and to avoid deliberate 'home-made' destruction to industrial installations as German troops retreated, to add to that of the enemy.

Speer paid two visits to the western border regions in September, the first, from 10 to 14 September, taking in Karlsruhe, Saarbrücken, the vicinity of Metz, the *Westwall* to Trier, then Aachen to Venlo. He identified significant weaknesses in munitions and fuel supplies, and serious problems as territories were evacuated. He established, for instance, that the quartermaster-generals of the armies in the west had too little contact with business agencies and were failing to make use of the experience of the latter in the western regions to help, for example, master transport problems. He pointed, as a way forward, to how Hermann Röchling, the steel magnate, had liaised daily with military leaders in the Saar to ascertain their munitions requirements and organize deliveries accordingly. He recommended setting up an office attached to the headquarters of the Commander-in-Chief West which could directly incorporate business in producing and delivering the equipment needed by the troops. A simple measure to improve supplies was to use the columns of lorries deployed in bringing back important salvaged equipment from the front and returning empty, to carry supplies for the frontline troops the other way. And clarifying organizational lines to make maximum use of the industrial area close to the border in supplying the western front directly would, he indicated, save wasteful journeys by lengthy transport routes used for carrying armaments from other parts of Germany. His main concern was 'that production would continue in the endangered areas to the last minute' and he opposed, therefore, what he saw as premature evacuation. Even under artillery fire, munitions production could go on just behind the front to a very late stage.[87] He sent a series of orders to the western Gauleiter in September, instructing them to see that production was not curtailed prematurely, and that – given the possibility of recovering the territories vacated (mere rhetoric to placate Hitler, to judge from Speer's later account[88]) – the evacuation of industry eastwards should follow only the disabling, not destruction, of industrial plant. Speer's report to Hitler also stressed the shortage of weapons, repeating a point in his running dispute with Goebbels that troops without heavy weaponry were pointless and that 'in this war, which is a technical war, a levée en masse is not decisive'.[89]

Speer's second journey to the western front, from 26 September to 1 October – carried out at such a tempo that his travel companions found it difficult to keep up with him – emphasized the urgent need to shore up the border zone west of the Rhine, and his anxiety about the threat to the Rhineland-Westphalian industrial area, which provided half of German armaments. 'If significant losses of territory occur here through enemy operations,' he warned, 'it would be far more serious than all the losses in the other theatres of war.' His report to Hitler was a further advertisement for his own achievements. The troops were enthusiastic, he commented, about the improved model of the Tiger tank that had been produced. The supplies of new weapons had contributed greatly to restoring morale after the retreat from France, and there was now confidence that a new line of resistance could be held, underlining the importance of delivering more weapons and munitions to the front line. This could not be done, he pointed out, if, as had happened previously, valuable skilled workers were taken out of tank production, something which tank commanders themselves did not want to happen. His conclusion was effectively, then, a further plea to make no more withdrawals from the armaments industry to provide recruits for the Wehrmacht.[90]

In fact, to a limited extent at least, he was prepared to see manpower go the other way. Desperate to mobilize all labour resources to sustain armaments production, he complained to Himmler at the end of October that full use of concentration camp prisoners was being hindered through shortage of guards, and suggested – probably to little effect – that a contingent of suitable Wehrmacht soldiers could be transferred to the SS to take on guard-duty.[91]

Without Speer's extraordinarily strenuous efforts to sustain armaments production and organize the repeated rapid repair of railway lines and bridges destroyed in bombing, the war would have surely been over earlier. He later gave the impression that he viewed the continuation of the war as senseless from the time of the Allied invasion, and that by September it was a 'hopeless situation'.[92] In recognition of this, everything he did, according to his subsequent account, was directed at preventing the destruction of German industry. Doubtless, this was indeed one objective. Speer had at least one eye on a Germany after Hitler (in which, probably, he hoped to play some significant part). Germany would need her industry, and in his emphasis on immobilization rather than destruction, Speer was naturally working in full agreement with leading industrialists, who, unsurprisingly, combined an all-out effort to manufacture armaments with thoughts, not to be aired in public, of survival after defeat.[93] But contemporary records from his ministry do not suggest that this was the sole, or even the dominant, aim. Rather, it seems, Speer was genuinely doing everything in his power to enable Germany's war effort to continue. The extremes of energy and endeavour he deployed are not consonant with someone who thought fighting on was senseless and the situation hopeless. He could have done less without endangering himself. It would have brought the end, which he claimed to see as inevitable, closer. Without doubt, he recognized by this time that 'final victory' was out of the question. Did he also believe, at this point, that total defeat was the only alternative? He appears to have been far from ready to admit that the Reich was doomed. For some months yet, he thought it possible that Germany could avoid the worst. Had he done less to prolong the war, the worst might indeed have been avoided for millions.

Of course, it was far from Speer alone. He presided over a huge empire, run by an immense bureaucratic machine – 70,000-strong in early 1943.[94] He had highly able heads of his ministerial departments and ruthless lieutenants in Xaver Dorsch and Karl Otto Saur (increasingly his arch-rival for Hitler's favour). Saur himself, said after the war to have ruled by fear and to have treated his staff – as well as his workforce – brutally, was not yet at the point where he accepted the war was lost.[95] At the intersection of the military and industry, Speer had the closest connections with Germany's leading industrialists, keen to preserve their factories, but also still to maximize production for the war effort. And he was backed by the enforcement agencies of the Party, the police, the prison service and justice administration – tens of thousands of prisoners had by now been put to work in armaments[96] – as well as being supplied by Fritz Sauckel, the crude and brutal Reich Plenipotentiary for Labour, with the legions of foreign workers who slaved in armaments factories in near indescribable conditions.[97] But Speer's initiative, dynamism and drive were the indispensable component that made the ramshackle armaments empire function as well as it did. His personal ambition and determination not to lose his own power-base meant that he was personally not ready to capitulate. He remained prepared to use his remarkable energies to fend off attempted inroads into his empire by Goebbels, Bormann and the Gauleiter, playing on the support from Hitler that he never entirely lost. And, of course, he showed no scruples in the utterly inhumane treatment of hundreds of thousands of foreign workers, forced to slave to enable the Reich to continue fighting long after reason dictated that the war should be ended.

V

The German people – even more so the 'enemies of the people' in the regime's grasp – were subjected to far more rigorous controls as the enemies encroached closer towards the borders of the Reich. Coercion now became an omnipresent element of daily life. Alongside the restrictions of Goebbels' total-war measures, and inroads into the workplace through recruitment to the front, went increasingly long hours on the shopfloor. Any worker suspected of slacking was threatened with being treated in the same way as deserters. Foreign workers – now constituting around a fifth of the labour force in Germany – were particularly vulnerable to police round-ups, and investigations of the existence of any subversive material, that could result in their being sent to concentration camps, or worse.[98]

For Germans, orders for evacuation in areas close to the front could come at an hour's notice. In bombed towns and cities, people had to comply with commands barked out by local Party officials, and by the police and military authorities. Surveillance had become intensified. The regime's suspicions of the population it controlled mounted as memories and fears of a repeat of 1918 revived. Communist cells were penetrated and broken up, their members and other suspected opponents of the regime arrested and often subjected to torture.[99] The police were alerted to the threat of internal unrest and instructed to take immediate measures to nip in the bud any signs of disturbance to public order. The Higher SS and Police Leaders were given powers by Himmler to put down with all means at their disposal any unrest in their areas and immediately to deal with those threatening security and order.[100] Party officials were handed extra weapons to deal with 'internal unrest or other extraordinary circumstances'.[101] Germany was increasingly an atomized, dragooned society run on the basis of fear. It was also by this stage an entirely militarized society.

In his new capacity as Commander-in-Chief of the Replacement Army, Himmler was able to extend his policing powers to the military sphere. Hitler gave him full authority to 'establish order' in the areas behind the fighting zone and sent him, at the beginning of September, to the western border region to put a halt to the retreat of the 'rear-lines' troops. Within twenty-four hours, according to Goebbels, he had stopped the 'flood' of retreating soldiers, and the images of panic that accompanied them.[102] The Gauleiter were instructed that all returning members of the Wehrmacht, Waffen-SS, police, OT and Reich Labour Service, as well as 'stragglers', were to be picked up and turned over to the Replacement Army by 9 September. Local Party leaders were to report to their District Leaders by 7 p.m. the previous evening the numbers of stragglers in their area, and they in turn would pass the information to the Gauleiter within two hours, who would then immediately inform the commander of the Defence District.[103] Himmler was proud of his achievement in arresting the disintegration in the west, and recommended 'brutal action' to deal with manifestations of 'rear-lines' poor morale.[104] By the middle of September, 160,000 'stragglers' had been rounded up and sent back to the front.[105]

Himmler's decisive action was rewarded by Hitler by a further remit. It arose from a combination of the increased concern for inner security together with the need felt to provide border protection, especially in the east, following the Red Army's inroads in the summer. Since early in the war, the Wehrmacht had been ready to conscript civilians in an emergency to support local defence operations. The police were also involved in earlier planning for militias. Himmler had in 1942 set up a 'Countryside Watch', later followed by an 'Urban Watch', made up mainly of members of Nazi affiliates not called up to the Wehrmacht, to help local police in searching for escaped prisoners of war and repressing any potential unrest from foreign workers. By the end of 1943, the 'Urban' and 'Countryside' Watches comprised in all around a million men. Some Gauleiter had then in 1943 and 1944 taken steps to form their own 'Homeland Protection Troops', reaching beyond Party members to include all men aged eighteen to sixty-five. These did not, however, at this stage find favour with Hitler, who sensed they would have a negative impact on popular morale.

Even so, as war fortunes deteriorated, the Wehrmacht also prepared plans for larger, more formalized militias. With the Red Army approaching the Reich's eastern frontier, General Heinz Guderian, the recently appointed Chief of the General Staff, proposed what he called a *Landsturm* (taking its name from the Prussian militias which fought against Napoleon's army in 1813), to be composed of men exempted for whatever reason from military service, who would help to strengthen border protection in the east. Guderian recommended the deployment of alarm units which would carry out guerrilla-like warfare in their own localities. Every officer would act 'as if the Führer were present'. Guderian advocated the use of cunning, deception and fantasy, claiming that Red Indian-style action could be successful in fighting for streets, gardens and houses and that the Karl May stories about cowboys and Indians in the Wild West – much liked by Hitler – had proved useful as training manuals.[106]

Guderian's fanciful schemes never materialized. They were overtaken by plans for the creation of a nationwide organization under Party, not Wehrmacht, control. Some Gauleiter, encouraged by Bormann, had already in August created militias in their own regions. The leader of the

SA, the Nazi stormtrooper organization, Wilhelm Schepmann, and Robert Ley, head of the enormous Labour Front, separately contemplated in early September the construction of a *Landsturm* for national defence, each imagining he would lead it.[107] Hitler's view, as the conflict between Schepmann and Ley surfaced, was that Himmler was the only person capable of building the envisaged *Landsturm*. Goebbels agreed, as usual, with Hitler. Schepmann would rapidly succumb to 'the lethargy of the SA', while if the task were given to Ley, 'only pure idiocy would come of it'.[108]

Quietly, however, from behind the scenes, another Nazi leader scented a chance to extend his power. With the enemy close to Germany's borders, east and west, and a perceived possibility of internal unrest, the way was open for Martin Bormann, working together with Himmler, to devise proposals for a national militia and persuade Hitler that its organization and control had to be placed in the hands of the Party rather than be given to the 'untrustworthy' army, thereby ensuring that it would be subjected to the necessary Nazi fanaticism. By the middle of September, Bormann had worked out drafts, approved by Himmler, for a decree by Hitler on the establishment of a 'People's Defence' (*Volkswehr*).[109] Within a few days, the name had been changed to the more stirring 'People's Storm' (*Volkssturm*). Himmler told Defence District commanders on 21 September that 'if the enemy should break in somewhere, he will encounter such a fanatical people, fighting like mad to the end, that he will certainly not get through'.[110]

Hitler's decree on the establishment of the *Deutscher Volkssturm*, dated 25 September though actually signed next day and reserved for publication until mid-October, stipulated that the new militia was to be formed of all men between sixteen and sixty who were capable of bearing arms. The Gauleiter, under Bormann's direction, were given responsibility for summoning the men, forming them into companies and battalions, and all attendant organizational matters. The political aspects of the new militia were left to Bormann, acting on Hitler's behalf. This gave Bormann enormous scope for defining his remit. Himmler, as Commander-in-Chief of the Replacement Army (not as head of the SS and police), was placed in charge of the 'military organization, the training, weaponry and armaments' of the *Volkssturm*. Its military deployment, under Hitler's directive, was in his hands, though he delegated its running to the head of the SS Central Office and General of the Waffen-SS, Obergruppenführer Gottlob Berger.[111] The very division of controls outlined in the decree guaranteed in a fashion characteristic of the Third Reich, that there would be continuing disputes about responsibility and control. But, powerful though Himmler and the SS were, the victor in conflicts over control of the *Volkssturm* turned out to be Martin Bormann. His constant proximity to Hitler enabled him to fend off attempts to reduce his dominance in this new domain by playing on the unique position of the Party to imbue the 'people's community' with the fanatical spirit of National Socialism in the defence of the Reich.[112]

Militarily, the value of the *Volkssturm* turned out over subsequent months to be predictably low. The loss of the many men – too old, too young, or too unfit for military service – who would die in *Volkssturm* service would be utterly futile. The creation of the *Volkssturm* certainly amounted to a desperate move to dredge up the last manpower reserves of the Reich. But it was far from an admission by the regime that the war was lost. In the eyes of the Nazi leadership, the *Volkssturm* would hold up the enemy, should the war enter Reich territory, and help Germany win time. New weapons, they presumed, were on the way. The enemy coalition was fragile. The more losses could be inflicted on the enemy, particularly on the western Allies, the more likely it was that this coalition would crumble. A settlement, at least in the west, would then be possible. Seen in this way, time gave Germany a chance. Moreover, the *Volkssturm* would achieve this goal through the inculcation of genuine National Socialist spirit. It would embody the true Nazi revolution as a classless organization, where social rank and standing had no place, and through fanatical commitment, loyalty, obedience and sacrifice.[113] It would also, it was imagined, help to raise popular morale.[114] In reality, these Nazi ideals were far from the minds of the vast majority of those who would trudge unwillingly and fearfully into *Volkssturm* service, minimally armed but expected to help repel a mighty enemy. A minority, impossible to quantify precisely but including many *Volkssturm* leaders, were, even so, convinced Nazis, some of them fanatical. Even in the dying days of the regime, *Volkssturm* members would be involved in police 'actions' and atrocities against other German citizens seen to be cowards or defeatists. So whatever its obvious deficiencies as a fighting force, the *Volkssturm* – a huge organization envisaged as comprising 6 million men[115] – served as a further vehicle of Nazi mobilization, organization and regimentation. As such, it played its own part in preventing any internal collapse and ensuring that a war, rationally lost, would not be ended for some months yet.

VI

Germans without weapons in their hands were by late summer 1944 likely to be holding spades instead. As the enemy approached Germany's frontiers, conscription – also for women – to dig fortifications, trenches, bunkers, tank traps and roadblocks was introduced. Bormann, here too, orchestrated operations from the centre. His agents, the Gauleiter in their capacity as RVKs, organized the work at regional level. The Party's District, then Local, Leaders ensured that it was done. Party affiliates like the Hitler Youth assisted in the mobilization and deployment. The police were once more on hand to force waverers into line. Again, as the prospect of fighting on Reich soil loomed ever larger, the impositions of the regime on its citizens and the level of controls to which they were subjected on a daily basis intensified sharply.

The frantic fortification-building through conscription of the local population had started in the east in July, following the Red Army's breakthrough, when Gauleiter Koch persuaded Hitler to commission the construction of an extensive 'Eastern Wall' as a bulwark against Soviet inroads.[116] The collapse in the west in August then rapidly necessitated the adoption of similar methods to reinforce defences, particularly along the *Westwall*, whose pre-war array of 14,000 bunkers over a length of 630 kilometres was in urgent need of strengthening. On 20 August Hitler ordered a people's levy, under the leadership of four western Gauleiter, for the construction of western fortifications. At the end of the month, he empowered additional Gauleiter to enlist civilian workers to strengthen northern coastal defences as a protection against invasion and to levy the population for work on the *Westwall*. Extra labour, where necessary, had to be provided by neighbouring Gaue.[117] The entire border of the *Westwall* on the German side was now to be placed in defence readiness. The RVKs were responsible for arranging the accommodation and feeding of hundreds of thousands of workers, and taking steps to evacuate the population in a strip of about two kilometres depth behind the *Westwall*.[118]

As with the *Volkssturm*, Robert Ley had ambitions of taking charge of the nationwide command of fortification work. Ley, who had a doctorate in chemistry, was among the most fanatical Nazis, possessed of an almost mystical belief in Hitler. At the end of 1932, Hitler had made him head of the Party's organization and a few months later boss of the mammoth German Labour Front. The ambitious Ley was always looking to extend his own empire, early in the war taking over responsibility for housing in Germany. But his arbitrary and arrogant exploitation of his power, and his public reputation for drunkenness, made him enemies in high places. And in trying to take control of fortification work, to the pleasure of Goebbels, who held Ley's organizational capabilities in scant regard, he was to be disappointed.[119] Once more, Martin Bormann, close to Hitler and possessing his confidence, was in a position to gain exclusive control of the new range of powers. On 1 September Hitler gave Bormann sole authority to instruct the Gauleiter, in his name, on all measures relating to fortifications. No other Party agencies had any rights to intervene. Bormann would name commissioners, directly responsible to him, who could commandeer Party members where necessary to assist in carrying out the work – through supervision and controls, that is, not through actually digging themselves. Robert Ley, as Reich Organization Leader of the Party, was at Bormann's disposal in providing such members – a clear victory for the head of the Party Chancellery over one of his rivals.[120]

The work began without delay, and with great urgency. On 3 September the Essen *National-Zeitung* spoke of the 'entire frontier population' being involved in extending defences on the western borders, and the men and women of the Gaue in the west starting 'with spades and shovels' to work 'to ensure the freedom of our homeland'.[121] By 10 September, 211,000 women, youths, and men too old for military service, along with 137 units of the Reich Labour Front and Hitler Youth formations were engaged in heavy labour on the *Westwall*. The minimum period for conscription was stipulated as six weeks. After that, Germans, though not foreign workers, could be replaced by others.[122] Bormann reminded the Gauleiter at the beginning of October of the urgency of completing entrenchments before the onset of the cold and wet autumn weather when women, girls and youths could be deployed only to a limited extent and when illness among men was sure to increase and be exacerbated through shortage of equipment, clothing and accommodation.[123]

By this time, the Gauleiter had been given widened powers by Hitler in the event of the war encroaching onto German territory. Amending his decree of 13 July through further decrees on 19 and 20 September, Hitler accorded the Gauleiter, as RVKs, executive power in civilian matters in operational areas with rights to issue legally binding decrees and directives to all agencies of the state administration. With this, Bormann's own centralized authority was bolstered still further, though Hitler yet again muddied the waters, providing for conflict and demarcation disputes, since his decree stipulated that coordination of the measures determined by the RVKs rested with Himmler.[124]

Bormann was by this time at the height of his powers. Through his presence at Führer Headquarters, his ability to control access to Hitler to a large extent and to influence his thinking, his exploitation of his position to outmanoeuvre other bigwigs in the Third Reich's constant power-struggles, his control of the elaborate Party machine, and his capacity for sheer hard work – as his frequent letters to his wife, Gerda, indicate, he was working almost round the clock – Bormann had become perhaps the most pivotal figure after Hitler himself in the top Nazi echelons. And he was still an absolutely committed true believer. Unlike Himmler or Speer, he appears to have had no alternative personal agenda in mind for a world without Hitler. And unlike Himmler, Goebbels, Göring and Ribbentrop, he seems never at any moment to have contemplated any form of negotiation with the enemy as a way of ending the war. He was content to be Hitler's mouthpiece, with all the power that gave him. Acknowledging to his wife in late August that it was hard to see a silver lining as the fronts closed in on Germany, he nonetheless added: 'In spite of it all, our faith in the Führer and in victory is completely unshaken, which is truly necessary, for in this situation very many people begin to soften up understandably.'[125] A few weeks later, he even found it possible to look back upon the catastrophic months of 1944 with some satisfaction because, despite military collapse in east and west, 'the national community has stood its test, and we are so far able to overcome the thousand difficulties which the enemy's domination of the air creates for us'.[126] His optimism probably arose from necessity. Like the other leading Nazis, he knew he had no future after Hitler.

During 1944 the Party Chancellery that Bormann ran – sarcastically dubbed by Goebbels on one occasion the 'Paper Chancellery' because of the streams of directives flooding out of it – issued 1,372 circulars, announcements or orders, alongside numerous other instructions and Führer orders.[127] State bureaucracy still functioned, though increasingly as an administrative organ for directives and intitiatives emanating from the Party. Civil defence in all its ramifications, organization of mass conscription for entrenchment work, mobilizing non-servicemen for the *Volkssturm*, providing welfare for evacuees, and implementing the myriad orders for total war, were all in the hands of the Party that now controlled Germany as never before.

For ordinary Germans, there was scarcely any avenue of life free from the intrusions of the Party and its affiliates. In the armed forces, too, the scope for escaping Nazification had diminished. The repercussions of the failed bomb plot, the need to demonstrate loyalist credentials, extended deployment of NSFOs, increased surveillance and fear of falling into the clutches of Himmler (who now possessed greater room for intervention in the military sphere) left their mark on both officers and men. Whether at the front or in the civilian population, as the war had come close to home, and the popular base of the regime had shrunk, compliance with ever more invasive controls had come increasingly to dominate daily life.

The regime had appeared during the summer to teeter close to the edge. It had survived an internal uprising, but its armed forces had been pummelled in east and west. As summer had turned into autumn, it had stabilized the military situation and redoubled its energies at home to galvanize an often reluctant or truculent population into action to shore up defences and provide manpower for the front and the armaments industry.

In mid-October, Aachen – by now a ruined shell, its remaining inhabitants cowering in cellars – became the first German city to fall into enemy hands. But by this time, attention had switched to the east. There, in East Prussia, the population was already gaining a horrific foretaste of what Soviet conquest would bring.

3

Foretaste of Horror

Hatred ... fills us since we have seen how the Bolsheviks have wrought havoc in the area that we have retaken, south of Gumbinnen. There can be no other aim for us than to hold out and to protect our homeland.

Colonel-General Georg-Hans Reinhardt to his wife after visiting the scene of Soviet atrocities near Nemmersdorf, in East Prussia, 26 October 1944

I

The disastrous collapse of Army Group Centre, steamrollered by the Red Army as its gigantic summer offensive, 'Operation Bagration', drove back the Wehrmacht, then the smashing of the Army Groups North Ukraine and South Ukraine, and the cutting off in the Baltic of Army Group North left the German east precariously exposed. The scale of the calamity from the German perspective could scarcely be exaggerated. In 150 days, the German army in the east lost more than a million men, dead, wounded or missing – 700,000 of them since August. Put another way, more than 5,000 men a day were dying. Only around a third of the losses could be made good. On 1 October 1944 the overall strength of the Wehrmacht was just over 10 million men. Of the 13 million who had served since the war began, 3 million were lost.[1]

The disaster on the eastern front in summer 1944 was in terms of human loss by far the worst military catastrophe in German history, worse than the First World War slaughterhouse at Verdun, way beyond the losses at Stalingrad.[2] Army Group Centre, its operative strength of around half a million men grossly inferior to that of the Soviet forces, was like a house of cards waiting to be knocked over. In the first phase of the offensive, 25 divisions with more than 250,000 men of Army Group Centre were destroyed.[3] By the end of July the Red Army had swept through Belorussia, recovering all the territory lost since 1941, and through eastern Poland to the Vistula. On the northern flank of the advance, the Red Army had also overrun much of Lithuania, including the main cities of Vilnius and Kovno. The borders of East Prussia, the farthest eastern frontier of the Reich, now lay perilously close. In a short-lived incursion on 17 August, Soviet troops did, in fact, cross the East Prussian border near Schirwindt, entering the Reich for the first time, though on this occasion they were quickly repulsed.[4]

To the south of Army Group Centre, further disaster rapidly unfolded. Army Group North Ukraine (the former Army Group South, renamed earlier in the year) suffered huge losses in intense combat as the Red Army drove into Galicia, in southern Poland, taking Lemberg (Lvov) and forcing a German retreat of nearly 200 kilometres over a 400-kilometre-wide area. Of the 56 divisions of Army Group North Ukraine (including some Hungarian divisions), 40 were partially or totally destroyed. As Soviet troops on the northern flank pressed on north-westwards to the Vistula and the approaches to Warsaw, the southern flank pushed German forces back towards the Carpathians. The desperate German attempt to defend Galicia was a recognition of the strategic and economic importance of the region. By mid-August almost the whole of the Ukraine and most of eastern Poland were in Soviet hands, while the basis had been laid for attacking the crucial Upper Silesian industrial belt, 200 kilometres to the west.[5] Meanwhile, on 1 August, Warsaw's martyrdom had begun with the rising of the Polish Home Army. As the Red Army stood inactive in the vicinity, unwilling to assist the rebels, the SS moved in to destroy the rising and pulverize the Polish capital.[6] In the unfolding tragedy over the following two months, the city was turned into a ruined shell, with some 90 per cent of its buildings destroyed and 200,000 civilians left dead amid the terrible German reprisals.[7]

In the Balkans, too, where Romanian oil, Hungarian bauxite and Yugoslav copper were crucial to Germany's war economy, the Wehrmacht suffered crippling defeats, leading to the defection of its allies in the region. The position of the German Army Group South Ukraine, around half of it composed of war-weary Romanian units, was already weakened by mid-August through the withdrawal of 11 out of 47 divisions to help shore up the battered Army Groups Centre and North Ukraine. When a major Soviet offensive began on 20 August, many Romanian units, with no further stomach for the fight, deserted. Three days later, following an internal coup, Romania sued for peace and changed sides. During the next few days, Army Group South Ukraine was demolished. The German 6th Army, reconstituted after Stalingrad, was again encircled and destroyed. In all, 18 divisions of the Army Group ceased to exist; the rest were forced into headlong retreat to the west and north-west. Within a fortnight, more than 350,000 German and Romanian troops had been killed or wounded, or had entered captivity.[8] Huge quantities of armaments were also lost, as were the Ploesti oilfields, vital for the German war effort, on which Hitler had always placed such a premium. Bulgaria soon followed Romania's example, switching sides and declaring war on Germany on 8 September. German occupation of Greece and Yugoslavia was now no longer viable. Control over the Balkans was as good as at an end. And for the Red Army, the approaches to Slovakia and Hungary lay open, and behind them the Czech lands and Austria.[9]

At the opposite end of the eastern front, on the Baltic, Army Group North fought throughout the summer in a desperate attempt to avoid being cut off. The Soviet advance had opened up a huge gap between Army Group North and what was left of Army Group Centre. Entreaties to Hitler, already in early July and later, to allow Army Group North to withdraw to a more defensible line to the west were predictably rejected. The Baltic could not be surrendered, since Swedish steel, Finnish nickel and oil shale (used by the navy) from Estonia were vital for the war effort. But Hitler was also influenced by the need to retain the Baltic harbours for trials of the new generation of U-boats, which, Grand-Admiral Dönitz had impressed upon him, still offered a chance for Germany to turn the fortunes of war in her favour by throttling supplies to Britain and cutting off Allied shipment of men and *matériel* to the Continent.[10] Bitter fighting continued throughout July and August as Army Group North was forced to retreat some 200 kilometres to the north-west and evacuate parts of Estonia, Latvia and Lithuania, though it was able for the time being to prevent the Red Army from breaking through to the Baltic. What contribution, if any, to Army Group North's resilience was made by the fanatical and ferocious leadership of its

Commander-in-Chief, Colonel-General Schörner – one of Hitler's outright favourites – is hard to say. Schörner, the most brutal of Hitler's commanders, was unremitting in his demands for ruthless and fanatical fighting spirit, and in his merciless punishment of any that he deemed to be falling short of his demands.[11] His tactical errors, however, accentuated the plight of the Army Group.[12] Almost a quarter of a million strong, comprising three armies, its situation remained precarious, facing Soviet forces on three sides and mainly dependent upon supplies by sea across the Baltic. Meanwhile, by 2 September Germany's important northern ally, Finland, had pulled out of the struggle and was soon to sign an armistice with the Soviet Union.

After a brief lull in the fighting, the Red Army opened a big northern offensive on 14 September. By the end of the month, the Wehrmacht had pulled out of Estonia and most of Latvia with great losses of men and equipment. The main forces had managed to withdraw, however, and were concentrated on a shorter front. A Soviet breakthrough in the area of Riga was held off – though not for long. In early October the Red Army forced its way through to the Baltic coast, just north of Memel. With that, the main forces of Army Group North were cut off from East Prussia. The German retreat from Riga was by then under way and the city fell to the Soviets in the middle of the month. By the end of October, intense German efforts to re-establish links with Army Group North had irredeemably failed. The Army Group's defences were by now stabilized. But its 33 divisions were completely cut off on the Courland, the peninsula north-west of Riga. Apart from 3 divisions that were promptly evacuated and a further 10 divisions brought out by sea in early 1945, its main forces, comprising around a quarter of a million frontline troops, so badly needed elsewhere, would remain there, isolated and of little further strategic relevance, until the capitulation in May 1945.[13]

From the Baltic to the Balkans, Germans armies had reeled at the ferocious onslaught of the Red Army in the summer months of 1944. In those months, the magnitude of the losses and the secession of crucial allies meant that Germany's hopes of a victorious outcome to the war in the east had vanished. Goebbels was among those in the Nazi leadership who plainly recognized this. In September, he took up a Japanese suggestion for separate peace soundings with the Soviet Union and put the proposal to Hitler in a lengthy letter.[14] Hitler took no notice of it. Whether there was the remotest chance of Stalin showing an interest in coming to terms with Germany when his forces were so rampantly in the ascendancy might well be doubted. But the issue could not be put to the test. Hitler's silent veto was sufficient to rule out any possibility of an approach. The structures of Nazi rule ensured that there was no platform of any kind where Hitler's adamant refusal to contemplate a negotiated end to the war, east or west, could be deliberated, let alone challenged.

In the Soviet Union, as with the Americans and British, the scale of Germany's defeats raised expectations that the war might be almost over. It could have been, too, had Stalin and his military advisers, like the western Allies, not made strategic errors in their operational planning. Mighty though 'Bagration' was, the attack on four fronts was less decisive than the attack that the Germans had feared most: a huge, concentrated surge through southern Poland to Warsaw and from there to the Baltic coast, east of Danzig, cutting off two entire Army Groups (Centre and North) and opening the route to Berlin.[15] The colossal battering the Wehrmacht had taken in the summer fell short, crippling though the losses were, of the decisive death blow that such a manoeuvre could have inflicted. The armies of the east, as in the west, could be patched up to fight on. Rapidly dwindling reserves of manpower and weaponry were dredged up. It was a mere plaster on a gaping wound. But it allowed the war to continue for several more months of mounting horror and bloodshed.

II

Behind the capacity to keep on fighting lay, as in the west, attitudes in the Wehrmacht which were not uniform in nature, but essentially resilient, and structures of government and administration, crisis-ridden but still intact. For the civilian population there was little choice but to grit their teeth and carry on. In conditions of perpetual emergency, the regime put people under extreme pressure to conform and collaborate. Private space to avoid such pressure dwindled almost to zero point. Ad hoc, piecemeal measures to attempt to hold off the inroads of the Red Army could, therefore, be implemented by a workforce now embracing almost the entire adult (and youthful) population, seldom (other than within parts of the Hitler Youth) enthusiastic, sometimes willing, often

3. The Red Army's advance, June to August 1944

grudging, but scarcely ever rebellious. At the root of the readiness to comply, however reluctantly, a sentiment prevailed that was far more searing and penetrating than in the west: fear.

In East Prussia, the most exposed of Germany's eastern provinces, the fear was palpable. Older citizens still had memories of the incursion of the Russians in the opening phase of the First World War before the Germans finally beat them back in February 1915. Some 350,000 people had fled in hasty evacuations as the Russians approached in August and September 1914. By the time the Russian troops had been forced out of East Prussia, according to German reports (though there is no reason to doubt their essential veracity), towns and villages had been ransacked, more than 40,000 buildings destroyed, several thousand inhabitants deported to Russia, and around 1,500 civilians killed.[16] Thirty years later, the fear rested not just on old memories. The anti-Bolshevik propaganda, relentlessly pumped into the population by the Nazis, had seemed less abstract in this region than in western outposts of Germany. And for three years, soldiers had been passing through East Prussia backwards and forwards to the eastern front. Those with ears to hear had heard stories – not just vague rumours, but often concrete detail – of disturbing happenings in the east. Not only tales of the intense bitterness of the fighting, but news of atrocities perpetrated against the civilian Russian population and massacres of Jews had filtered back. The war against the partisans, it was well known, had been brutal. It had been no holds barred. As long as the war had been going well, what German soldiers had been doing to Russians and Jews had been of little concern. Many, influenced by propaganda, had no doubt approved. But now the tables had been turned: the Soviets were in the ascendancy, crushing German forces, pressing on the borders and threatening to break into East Prussia.

Elsewhere in the eastern provinces, the danger of Soviet occupation was not so imminent. But the fears were little different from those of the people of East Prussia. The Nazi Party had gained some of its greatest electoral successes before 1933 in the eastern regions of Germany – largely, apart from the Silesian industrial belt, Protestant and rural. Border issues, resentment at the territorial losses in the Versailles Treaty, and revanchist feelings had contributed to making these regions disproportionately stalwart in their backing for Hitler's regime after 1933. The early war years, sheltered by German occupation of Poland and the

Nazi–Soviet Pact of 1939, had been relatively calm for eastern Germany. But the start of the war against the Soviet Union in June 1941 brought the regions far closer to the fighting front. Some compensation derived from the new military importance of the eastern provinces; the location of government and army bases close to Hitler's headquarters in East Prussia, for instance, produced some economic benefits for the region. Following the rapid conquests by the Wehrmacht, the reality of war, even in the east, seemed at first far away. The area was also free from the heavy bombing – East Prussia suffered from some light Soviet bombing sorties in June 1941, but little more – that increasingly beset the western parts of Germany from 1942 onwards. In fact, one of its main roles was as a reception area, forced to take in large numbers of evacuees sent from the bomb-threatened towns and cities of western Germany. By early 1944 about 825,000 evacuees were housed in eastern regions.[17] They were often seen as a burden, providing a real test for the solidarity of the much-vaunted 'people's community'. The presence of the refugees, in such numbers, was a clear sign that the war was close to home. The east had so far been spared the worst. That was now to alter rapidly.

Unsurprisingly, panic had spread like a bush fire through the east in the wake of the Wehrmacht's collapse.[18] As the Red Army's advance then slowed and the German front gained some semblance of stability, the initial panic had subsided. But the population remained subdued, depressed and acutely worried. A general nervousness prevailed. Any negative news had a pronounced impact on people. 'The unfavourable and dangerous military situation in the east has such a depressing effect on the mood of the great proportion of the population', the SD reported in early August, 'that the same anxious fears about the further development of the war can be heard in all strata.'[19] Influenced by letters home from the front, and from the stories of evacuees from formerly occupied parts of Poland, people were sceptical about the capacity of the German forces to halt the Soviet advance completely and were not convinced that the danger for East Prussia had subsided.[20] The fears were that the Soviets would eventually succeed. And everyone, it was said, was aware of the threat of Bolshevism. What that meant in concrete terms was left unstated.[21] But the implications of dire consequences should the Soviets break through were plain enough. By early October, following the defection of Germany's eastern allies, the destruction of the 6th Army in

Romania and the penning in of Army Group North in the Courland, the mood in the German east sank to 'zero point'.[22]

Fear was also a prime motivating factor for many frontline soldiers. Aware, at least in general terms if not always specifically, of at least some of what German troops had done in the occupied Soviet Union, fear of falling into the hands of the Red Army was intense, and highly understandable. Whatever the feelings towards the British and American enemies in the west, nothing there equated to this. Alongside it went the fear of being one of the growing, countless victims of the eastern war. While fear of dying and hopes of survival were common to all soldiers, of whatever army, on whatever front, the reported casualties and intensity of the battles in the east sent a special shiver of anxiety down the backs of those learning that they had been called up to serve on the eastern front. Not surprisingly, though official reports were loath to admit it, there was growing anxiety about the call-up.[23] And anyone summoned to serve fervently hoped it would be in the west, not in the east.

As in the west, the attitudes of soldiers actually fighting at the front varied. Army reports in August and September indicated the predictable negative impact of the retreats and recognition of the great superiority of the enemy in men and heavy weapons. Young replacements and older men produced through the 'combing out' of the total-war recruitment actions were said to be particularly affected by the nerve-wracking intense fighting with such heavy losses. They feared another major Soviet offensive, and their powers to resist were said to be shaken. Anxiety and war-weariness were seen as the cause. 'Serious, but nevertheless confident' was, however, the somewhat unlikely gloss put on the mood in general. 'Unconditional trust in the Führer' was, of course, ritualistically asserted. But from Army Group North, cut off in the Baltic, it was reported that the known 'Bolshevist conditions' and the fear of never seeing the homeland again if the war were lost served to strengthen fighting morale. And those soldiers whose fighting spirit fell below expectations were subjected to increasingly ferocious discipline. Worries about the threat to East Prussia and their families were recorded from soldiers with homes in the eastern regions.

A more positive mood among the troops of the 4th Army in East Prussia at the beginning of October was said to have arisen from the stabilization of the front and better conditions for soldiers in the area. A summary of the attitude of soldiers on the Italian front the previous month almost certainly applied, too, to the troops in the east. Frontline soldiers, the report indicated, had little time for reflection. Individual events came and went in a blur. Only the general impression remained. The physical and psychological pressures of battle demanded of the soldier that he do his duty to the limits of the possible. Whatever the input of the NSFOs, their impact was short-lived. Very soon, daily worries and cares took over again. Ideals and grand causes were not at stake, the report implied. The soldier 'fights because he is ordered to do so, and for his naked life'.[24]

As this lapidary comment implies, for soldiers, but also for the civilian population, compulsion and duty were main reasons why people kept going. And what alternative was there? In addition came fear, and the strong feeling that the homeland – meaning, in concrete terms, families and property – had to be defended. Such sentiments could easily be exploited by the regime. But behind the propaganda, the rhetoric, the exhortations and the hectoring, belief in National Socialism, in the Party and even in the Führer was dwindling fast, impossible though it is to be precise about the levels of remaining support.

Whatever people thought, however, the omnipresence of the Party and its affiliates was sufficient to keep them in line, all the more so given the urgency of the defence measures that were implemented with all speed and pressure in the eastern regions in the wake of the Red Army's rapid advance. A first priority was to build a network of defence fortifications and entrenchments along the eastern borders of the Reich and strengthen those already in existence. The principle of deeming specified towns or cities 'fortresses' to be held to the last – a tactic unsuccessful in Russia as the Red Army swept around them – was now introduced in eastern Germany as the Wehrmacht retreated. More than twenty such 'fortresses', including the most important and strategically valuable towns, were established in Germany and the occupied parts of Poland, with eventual disastrous consequences for the inhabitants of most of them. In addition, the organization of a huge programme of fortification work thoughout eastern Germany at breakneck speed now fell to the Party under the direction of the Gauleiter, as Reich Defence Commissars (RVKs). Over the course of the summer, before the work started to recede in the autumn, ceasing at the end of November,[25] around half a million Germans (many of them youths, older men, and women) and foreign workers were conscripted to do long, back-breaking daily work in East Prussia, Pomerania, Silesia and Brandenburg in building what became generally known as 'Eastern Wall' (the *Ostwall*), to complement that in the west. An estimated 200,000 were deployed in East Prussia alone. In German occupied parts of Poland (Danzig-West Prussia, the Warthegau and what was left of the General Government, the central region of Nazi-occupied Poland) the work was undertaken by Polish forced labourers.[26]

Frontier defences in the east had been erected before the First World War. New fortifications were then constructed during the Weimar Republic, when Poland was seen as a major military threat. The pre-war years of the Third Reich had seen these extended and new defences built. Despite rapid acceleration of construction work, and one stretch of almost 80 kilometres along the Oder–Warthe rivers that was more heavily fortified than the *Westwall*, the defensive line was far from complete by the time war broke out. For five years thereafter, with German occupation pushed so far to the east, a heavily fortified line within the Reich frontiers seemed unnecessary. At any rate, it remained largely neglected until the collapse of Army Group Centre in summer 1944, at which point no worthwhile defences stood between the Red Army and East Prussia.[27] The attempt was now made to remedy this deficiency within a matter of weeks through conscripted labour and rapidly improvised organization.

On 28 July 1944, transmitting Hitler's decree of the previous day for the construction of fortifications in the east, Guderian, the newly appointed Chief of the Army General Staff, declared that 'the whole of eastern Germany must immediately become a single deep-echeloned fortress'. The State Secretary in the Reich Ministry of the Interior, Wilhelm Stuckart, amplified the order, laying out details for implementation of the construction work to the eastern Gauleiter and Hans Frank, boss of the General Government. The fortification workers would need spades, pickaxes, blankets, eating utensils and marching rations. Their overseers were to have pistols and other weapons – a hint of the possible need for harsh action to stamp their authority on a recalcitrant workforce. The Reich Transport Ministry and railway authorities would organize transport. Building materials and equipment would come from OT offices. Horses and carts were to be used as far as possible for carrying the building materials. Rations would be allocated through provincial food offices or, in the case of the General Government, through deep inroads into the provisions of the region.[28]

At the beginning of September, Hitler made it clear that command over the fortification work was exclusively in the hands of the Party, to be deployed by the RKVs under Bormann's direction.[29] In reality, the Gauleiter, as RKVs, had a good deal of independence in the way they ran affairs in their provinces. Erich Koch, the brutal Gauleiter of East Prussia, one of Hitler's favourite provincial chieftains, led the way in dragooning the population of his province into compulsory labour service. Already on 13 July he had decreed that the entire male population of specified districts between the ages of fifteen and sixty-five were to be conscripted with immediate effect for fortification work. Anyone defying the order would be subject to punishment by military court. Shops and businesses not absolutely necessary for the war effort were closed and their owners and workers sent to dig. Trains leaving the East Prussian border were controlled, and men taken off them and brought back for construction work.[30] Koch's example was followed by the other eastern Gauleiter. A report from Königsberg in East Prussia, noted by British intelligence authorities, indicates the effect of the conscription on daily life in the province.

> Great simplifications have been introduced in the everyday life of the population. In restaurants guests must go to the kitchen with their plate, so that all waiters and male kitchen staff can dig. The newspapers no longer publish regional editions but only one standard edition. Thus editors, compositors and printers are released for digging. Every business which is not of importance to the war has been closed. Every East Prussian fit for military service has been called up. The large gates of Königsberg University have been closed. The students and all men employed at the University are digging.

Even harvest workers were taken away at the most crucial point of the agricultural year to dig, though in separate waves so that the garnering of the harvest was not impaired.[31]

Anxiety probably underpinned an early readiness to help in the digging operations, notably in East Prussia, closest to the front line. Certainly, there was a positive initial response to appeals to take part as the local population, most readily members of the Hitler Youth, rallied round in an emergency, though propaganda about the enthusiasm of the diggers should be taken with a sizeable pinch of salt.[32] The Party itself, though claiming there was a good deal of understanding for the necessity of the digging action, was aware of the extensive criticism of its poor organization of the entrenchment work and lack of conviction that the fortifications had any military value.[33] Practical difficulties – poor accommodation and food, transport difficulties, even a shortage of spades – and the very nature of such cripplingly hard toil, digging the baked ground hour on hour in the heat of summer, soon withered whatever good spirits had prevailed at the outset. Women in Pomerania wrote to Goebbels complaining that they had received no medical inspection before deployment, that they had to sleep on straw mats in primitive communal quarters, and that food and sanitary arrangements were lamentable. For foreign workers and prisoners of war, needless to say, the conditions were far worse.[34]

The behaviour of Party officials and overseers often did not help. There were reports of Party officials drinking, skiving, siphoning off food and drink meant for diggers, of their high-handed behaviour and dereliction of duty setting the worst example to the conscript workers. Driving up to the columns of diggers in a car, inspecting the ranks without picking up a shovel, and bawling at elderly men and women actually doing the work was not guaranteed to encourage enthusiastic commitment to the task or endear the Party to the conscripts. Unsurprisingly, there were attempts to evade the work. Even veterans of the First World War, it was reported in East Prussia, had absconded, less than enamoured by the work they were being compelled to carry out, and worried that the front was so close. They had to be hauled back by the police.[35]

The weeks of grinding toil by hundreds of thousands of men and women were militarily as good as worthless. Even Goebbels saw that the East Prussian fortifications erected by Koch were pointless unless troops and weaponry were poured in to hold them.[36] On paper, the achievements looked considerable: 400 kilometres of defences erected in Pomerania, for instance, and a 120-kilometre ring to hold five armed divisions around the newly designated fortress of Breslau.[37] Much was made by propaganda once the Russians had been forced back about the value of the entrenchments, eulogizing about the usefulness of all the hard work that had gone into them. But in reality, the kilometres of earthworks, entrenchments and hastily constructed, inadequately manned, fortifications were never going to stop, or even hold up, the Red Army for long. Their worth had been severely limited. And of the designated 'fortresses', Königsberg, it is true, only fell in April 1945, and

Breslau held out until 6 May. All this meant was that the futile loss of life of civilians, let alone of front soldiers, was magnified.

If the digging marathon in the east served any purpose, it was in large part as a propaganda exercise, demonstrating the continued will to hold out. How effective the propaganda function was is difficult to assess. It has been claimed that the endeavour shown in the fortification work bolstered the patriotism of the east German population and their resolve to defend the homeland; that the communal work served as an inspiration elsewhere in Germany, underpinned faith in the Party, and boosted military morale through showing the troops that, in contrast to 1918, they had the undiluted backing of the 'home front'. Such claims are impossible to test accurately, but almost certainly greatly exaggerated.[38]

It would be a mistake to presume that the brash propaganda trumpeting of the fortification effort had no effect at all. Conceivably, it did help to solidify patriotic feeling in eastern Germany. And it conveyed a sense that the actions of ordinary Germans mattered in the fight to hold off the Red Army. But at most it boosted a readiness – from fear, if nothing else – to defend the homeland that was already present. Outside the eastern regions, and perhaps within them, too, people were as likely to see the frenetic entrenchments less as a heroic achievement than as a panic move, a sign that the situation was indeed extremely grave.[39] As for faith in the Party, this was so sharply on the wane in the summer and autumn of 1944 – whatever the lingering reserves of hope in Hitler himself – that it was as good as impossible for the fortifications programme to alter the trend, apart, perhaps, from impressing a few gullible waverers in the eastern regions by the energetic actions of Koch and other Gauleiter. Finally, while soldiers were doubtless gratified to hear of solidarity at home, it is questionable whether their fighting morale drew much inspiration from news of a huge digging programme carried out by the young, the old, and female labour on fortifications about whose defensive qualities against the might of the Red Army a level of scepticism was only too understandable.

Whatever the dubious propaganda value of the fortification drive, it was overshadowed by its objective function in providing a further vehicle for control of the population. This is not to say that many of the workers were not idealistic patriots, and not a few of them enthusiastic backers of the Party's efforts to mobilize all that remained of the population for the task. But after the first, short-lived surge of enthusiasm, not many, it could with some justification be surmised, were true volunteers who would have come forward without being conscripted. The digging programme quite literally wore the population out, ground them down into compliance, showed them again that there was no alternative, that the Party controlled all facets of civilian life. It was a further means of trying to inculcate into the population the spirit of the 'last stand' – with the classic Hitlerian choice of 'hold out' or 'go under'. Reluctant compliance rather than a readiness to swallow such imperatives was the stance of most ordinary citizens. Few were prepared to go under. But as the threat to the eastern frontiers of the Reich mounted, they had little choice but to fall in line with the diktats of those in power who were determining their fate.

This was the case, too, with service in the *Volkssturm*, launched in a fanfare of publicity on 18 October by a speech given by Himmler at Bartenstein in East Prussia and broadcast to the nation. Keitel, Guderian and Koch were present as Himmler addressed thirteen assembled companies of *Volkssturm* men. The date had been carefully chosen as the anniversary of the highly symbolic 'Battle of the Nations' in Leipzig in 1813, the clash which had brought Napoleon's defeat on Prussian soil. The date was a crucial one in propaganda depictions, resonating in German history and evoking the legendary defence of the homeland by the *Landsturm*, as, faced with slavery at the hands of the French, an entire people rose up to repel the invaders. Reading out Hitler's proclamation of the *Volkssturm* and reminding his audience of the significance of the anniversary, Himmler announced that the Führer had called on the people to defend the soil of their homeland. 'We have heard from their own mouths', he declared, 'that we have to expect from our enemies the destruction of our country, the cutting down of our woods, the break-up of our economy, the destruction of our towns, the burning down of our villages and the extirpation of our people.' Of course, the Jews were as ever portrayed as the root of the intended horror. Men of the *Volkssturm*, stated Himmler, pointing out that East Prussians had formed its first battalions, must therefore never capitulate.[40]

There was for the most part a sceptical response, to judge from reports on the reception of propaganda. There was a growing feeling that 'we are being pressed into a hopeless defence', and the announcement of the *Volkssturm* was often interpreted as confirmation of the exhaustion of

Germany's forces.[41] Any early enthusiasm swiftly evaporated as doubts were raised about the military value of the *Volkssturm* and anxieties voiced that those serving would not be covered under the international conventions on the treatment of prisoners of war, but would be viewed as partisans.[42] There were fears that they would be summarily executed on capture, and the enemy would take reprisals against the civilian population – views betraying knowledge of how the Germans had themselves behaved in the occupied territories.[43] The regime sought to allay the anxieties and define the duties of the *Volkssturm* within the Hague Convention of 1907. The fears were not baseless, however, as the treatment of captured *Volkssturm* men by the Red Army would highlight.[44] In any case, the frequent reluctance to serve in the *Volkssturm* was in vain. Over the next weeks, the Party's organizational tentacles would reach far into German civilian life to drag into service hundreds of thousands of mainly middle-aged men, badly armed and poorly equipped. Few were fired by the fanaticism demanded by the regime's leaders. However, they could rarely avoid service. Exemptions were hard to attain. And the *Volkssturm*'s commanders – many of whom had some background in the military and in the Party or its affiliates – were generally far more committed than the men they led to the ideals of the organization, however limited they were in ability and competence.[45] So detachment from Nazi ideals and fanaticism was not easy in this mammoth organization in the hands of the Party with a strength of 6 million men by the end of November and potentially embracing twice as many.[46] If only a fraction of this number was actually involved in combat, the further militarization and regimentation of civilian society was massive.

The military futility and pointless heavy loss of life among *Volkssturm* men in action would be fully laid bare in the first months of 1945. But in East Prussia, where Koch had proposed local militias as early as July, the *Volkssturm* would have an earlier baptism of fire. More than a week before Himmler's announcement of its existence, the *Volkssturm* had its first taste of action in the outer suburbs of the fortified Baltic port of Memel (north of East Prussia, annexed by Germany in 1939). Two lightly armed companies of *Volkssturm* men in civilian clothes with only green armbands to distinguish them took heavy casualties as they helped to stave off weak Soviet attempts to break the defensive perimeter until regular troops could arrive to stabilize the position.[47]

Little over a week later, the *Volkssturm* was in action again. This time it was within the borders of East Prussia. For on 16 October the Red Army crossed the German frontier into its easternmost region. It was the start of eleven days that would leave a searing mark on the mentalities of Germans in the eastern regions of the Reich – and not just there.

III

On 5 October Soviet troops launched their attack in Memel and five days later were on the Baltic, surrounding the town. The 3rd Panzer Army, weakened though it had been, managed to hold out in the siege until reinforcements arrived, with the help, as we noted, of much battered *Volkssturm* units. Two days before the Red Army's attack, local civilians were still frantically digging trenches and anti-tank ditches. The Wehrmacht wanted the area evacuated.[48] But only on 7 October were evacuation orders belatedly issued by the Party authorities. Anyone not obeying was to be treated as a traitor. Panic and chaos resulted, all the more so when the local District Leader of the Party countermanded the order and decreed that people should for the time being stay where they were. The confusion was all the greater since there had already been an earlier partial evacuation of Memel and surrounding districts in early August, but the population had returned when the danger had receded. There was initially some sense, therefore, that this, too, would prove to be a false alarm. But when the order to leave was finally given, on 9 October, it was for many already too late. Thousands were left behind, cut off by the rapidly advancing front. Many were reluctant to leave their farms unprotected against what they saw as a 'roaming mob' of prisoners of war and Polish workers. They missed the chance to escape. Most who could – predominantly women, children, the elderly and infirm, since men were generally held back for service in the *Volkssturm* and other duties – took to the road in horse-carts, or on foot, carrying with them a few possessions hastily thrown together. Rumours that the Red Army was in the immediate vicinity caused renewed panic. A sense of terror was widespread.

Explosions and fear of air raids sometimes caused the refugees to take cover where they could, in the fields away from the road. Women fell on their knees to pray. It was a race against time as main highways

N

Baltic Sea

Memel •

Kurisches Haff

Cranz •

Tilsit • *Memel*

Pillau • •Königsberg

Insterburg • Ebenrode

Wehlau • Gumbinnen •

Danzig •Heiligenbeil Nemmersdorf •

Friedland • Gerdauen • •Angerapp

Braunsberg

DANZIG-
WEST
PRUSSIA •Elbing •Bartenstein Goldap •

•Heilsberg Rastenburg

Marienburg E A S T P R U S S I A •Lötzen

•Marienwerder •Allenstein Lyck •

Deutsch-Eylau •Osterode

Johannisburg •

•Tannenberg •Ortelsburg

Neidenburg

• Soldau

•Łomza

•Włoclawek

Vistula • Płock *Bug*

0   10   20   30   40   50 miles

4. East Prussia   0 10 20 30 40 50 km

Warsaw •

became cut off by Soviet troops. Abandoned wagons and household goods littered the roadside. The lucky ones, after an anxiety-ridden wait on the shores, finally crammed into a fleet of little boats that ferried them, though without their livestock and most of their possessions, to temporary safety over the abutting saltwater inlet, the Kurisches Haff, to improvised billets in parts of East Prussia. Some sought to swim across, and were drowned. The last most of those fleeing saw of Memel was a red glow in the night sky. An estimated third of the population fell into Soviet hands. There were stories of plunder, rape and murder by Red Army soldiers.[49]

The fate of Memel marked the start of more than two weeks of dread and horror for the population close to the East Prussian border. Worse was yet to come. As General Guderian later commented, 'what happened in East Prussia was an indication to the inhabitants of the rest of Germany of their fate in the event of a Russian victory.'[50]

On 16 October, the Red Army began its assault on East Prussia itself amid a barrage of artillery fire over a 40-kilometre stretch of the front and intensive air raids on border towns. There was as good as no defence offered by the Luftwaffe, and the German 4th Army, severely weakened in the collapse of Army Group Centre in the summer, was forced to pull back westwards. On 18 October Soviet troops advanced across the German frontier. Within three days they had penetrated German lines and forced their way some 60 kilometres into the Reich across a front of around 150 kilometres. The border towns of Eydtkau, Ebenrode and Goldap fell into Soviet hands, while Gumbinnen and Angerapp narrowly escaped that fate, though the former was heavily damaged through air attacks and Soviet troops reached the outskirts. The Soviets reached as far as the village of Nemmersdorf in the early morning of 21 October where, despite their finding a key bridge over the river Angerapp intact, the offensive halted.

The leadership of Army Group Centre had expected that the Soviet attack, when it came, would be the prelude to a huge offensive that might break through into Germany's heartlands. As it was, the Soviets' pause in Nemmersdorf gave the 4th Army the opportunity to regroup, muster its strength and, with panzer reinforcements, attempt a daring and successful encirclement manoeuvre against superior forces that took the attackers completely by surprise and inflicted heavy losses. Soviet commanders, impressed by the Wehrmacht's counter-offensive, immediately went on the defensive and pulled back their troops. By 27 October their offensive was abandoned. On 3 November German troops freed Goldap – reduced to ruins and plundered by Red Army soldiers – and two days later the 'first battle of East Prussia' was over, at a cost of extremely high losses on both sides. A highly damaging Soviet breakthrough to the East Prussian capital of Königsberg had been prevented. German soldiers – especially those who came from the eastern regions – despite often limited training and inadequate weaponry, had fought furiously to fend off the invaders. Even so, a border strip of East Prussia, 100 kilometres broad and up to 27 deep, stayed in Soviet occupation. The front in this area stayed stable until January.[51] But East Prussians were from now on a highly endangered species.

The reason why the Soviet attack had halted after occupying a good position on reaching Nemmersdorf became plain when German troops were able to retake the village on 23 October, barely forty-eight hours after it had fallen to the Red Army. What the German soldiers found awaiting them was a scene of horror. The name of Nemmersdorf soon became familiar to most Germans. It told them what they might expect if the Red Army were to conquer the Reich.

The fate that would overtake Nemmersdorf and the inhabitants of neighbouring districts was compounded by the lamentable failure of the Nazi authorities – repeated with even graver consequences a few months later – to evacuate the population in good time.[52] Evacuation in the whole imperilled area was chaotic. Koch was the paradigm example of power draining from the centre to the provincial Party chieftains, a development that would intensify generally in early 1945. Abetted by his deputy, Paul Dargel, he had complete control over evacuation measures. Supported by Hitler, Koch refused to countenance early evacuation because of the fears that it would begin a stampede out of the province, and would send defeatist signals to the rest of the Reich. The population were to remain as long as possible as a sign of unwavering morale and determination. The Wehrmacht's own wishes to have the area cleared were ignored.[53] The Commander-in-Chief of Army Group Centre, Colonel-General Reinhardt, was himself reduced to paroxysms of futile rage at Koch's high-handed behaviour in the region.[54] When evacuation orders were finally given, they were predictably chaotic in their execution. Dargel and other Party functionaries could not be located for hours. A District Leader briefly emerged, only to disappear into a local pub and drink himself into a stupor. A lorry commandeered to help with the evacuation did not turn up; it had allegedly been sequestered by a Party office to carry off stores of food and drink. At the most critical time, Party functionaries – the only people who could give orders – had failed miserably in their duties.[55]

Nemmersdorf, the most westerly point of the Soviet incursion, was heavily involved in the belated, chaotic evacuation. As Soviet troops approached, inhabitants of nearby towns and villages fled in panic, and at the last minute. Horse-drawn covered wagons from all around queued to cross Nemmersdorf's crucial bridge. People took what few possessions they could and fled for their lives. Helped by the cover of thick autumnal mists, most in fact managed to get across the bridge to safety further westwards even in the final hours before the Red Army arrived. But for some, inhabitants both of Nemmersdorf and of other nearby townships, it was too late. They woke in the early hours of 21 October to find Soviet soldiers already in their villages.[56]

The battle-hardened soldiers of the Red Army had fought their way westwards out of their own country, through Poland and now, for the first time, into the country of the hated enemy. As they had advanced through wastelands of death and destruction, they had witnessed the legacy of the savage brutality of German conquest and subjugation and the scorched-earth devastation of a once imperious army in headlong retreat. They saw the unmistakable signs of the terrible suffering of their own people. Soviet propaganda directly encouraged drastic retribution. 'Take merciless revenge on the fascist child murderers and executioners, pay them back for the blood and tears of Soviet mothers and children,' ran one typical proclamation in October 1944.[57] 'Kill. There is nothing which the Germans aren't guilty of' was the exhortation of another.[58] Reaching German soil, and encountering for the first time a civilian enemy population, pent-up hatreds exploded in violent revenge. As German troops moved into villages and townships retaken by the Wehrmacht after days of Soviet occupation, they came across the corpses of murdered civilians, grim indicators of the atrocities that had taken place. The worst had taken place in Nemmersdorf itself, which came to symbolize these early atrocities of the Red Army.

Details of what exactly happened in Nemmersdorf, however, remain murky. From the outset, fact became difficult to separate from propaganda. Some testimony, given a few years afterwards, which left a lasting

mark on the gruesome imagery of events, is of doubtful veracity. According to the most vivid account, provided some nine years later, a
Volkssturm man whose company had been ordered to assist in the clearing up of Nemmersdorf after the attack spoke of finding several naked
women nailed up through their hands to barn doors in crucifix positions, of an old woman whose head had been split in two by an axe or
spade, and of seventy-two women and children bestially murdered by
the Red Army. All the women had allegedly been raped. The bodies had
been exhumed and the findings established, he claimed, by an international commission of doctors.[59]

A report compiled by the *Geheime Feldpolizei* (secret military police),
dispatched on 25 October, two days after the Soviet troops had left the
village, to interrogate any witnesses and discover what had happened,
paints, however, a somewhat different picture – though one which was
grim enough. There had been plundering, the report registered, and two
women had been raped. The corpses of twenty-six persons, mainly elderly men and women, though also a few children, were found. Some lay
in an open grave, others in a ditch, by the roadside or in houses. Most
had been killed by single shots to the head, though the skull of one had
been smashed in. But there were no lurid descriptions of crucifixions. A
German doctor from a regiment in the district had inspected the corpses.
Himmler's own personal doctor, Professor Gebhardt, had, remarkably,
also found his way to Nemmersdorf within a day of the Soviet troops
leaving, though, presumably, someone of his rank was not needed
simply to establish the cause of death. Already, it seems, leading Nazi
authorities had earmarked Nemmersdorf for special notoriety. Propagandists were swiftly on the scene following the recapture of the area,
keen to exploit Soviet ill-deeds to bolster the German determination to
fight, and not slow to exaggerate where it served their purposes.[60]

Naturally, German propaganda made the most of the exposé of
Soviet atrocities. The most grisly scenes may have been a fabrication.
On the other hand, the atrocities were not simply a propaganda invention or later concoction. General Werner Kreipe, Luftwaffe Chief of
Staff, visiting the Panzerkorps 'Hermann Göring' near Gumbinnen and
in the Nemmersdorf area within hours of the Red Army pulling out,
claimed in his diary entry that bodies of women and children were
nailed to barn doors, and ordered the outrages to be photographed as
proof.[61] If the photographs were taken, they have long since disappeared.

A machine-gunner among the German troops who entered Nemmersdorf on 22 October recorded in the diary jottings he kept secreted in his uniform the discovery of 'terrible incidents involving mangled bodies', some mutilated, one old man pierced with a pitchfork and left hanging on a barn door, sights 'so terrible that some of our recruits run out in panic and vomit'.[62] The numbers killed in Nemmersdorf may have been smaller than alleged, though some of the more inflated figures probably included those also killed by Red Army soldiers in other nearby localities.[63] Conceivably, too, there were fewer rapes than claimed, though some certainly took place and the later behaviour of the Red Army on its passage through eastern Germany offers no grounds to presume the best of its soldiers. Colonel-General Reinhardt visited the district on 25 October. He wrote to his wife the following day that 'the Bolsheviks had ravaged like wild beasts, including murder of children, not to mention acts of violence against women and girls, whom they had also murdered'. He was deeply shaken by what he had seen.[64] Whatever doubts are raised about the actual scale of the murders and rapes, and necessary though it is to remember the nature and purpose of propaganda exploitation, the atrocities were no mere figment of propaganda. Terrible things did happen in and around Nemmersdorf.

Moreover, whatever the truth about the precise details of the atrocities, propaganda acquired a reality of its own. In terms of the impact of Nemmersdorf, its likely effect was to underpin the determination of soldiers to fight on at all costs in the east, to struggle to the utmost to avoid being overrun by the Red Army and to encourage civilians to take flight at the earliest opportunity. The image of Nemmersdorf turned out to be more important than precise factual accuracy about its horrific reality.

IV

The propaganda machinery was soon in action. Goebbels instantly recognized the gift that had come his way. 'These atrocities are indeed dreadful,' he noted in his diary, after Göring had telephoned him with the details, 'I'll make use of them for a big press campaign.' This would ensure that the last doubters were 'convinced of what the German people can expect if Bolshevism really gets hold of the Reich'.[65] Head of the Reich Press Office Otto Dietrich gave out instructions for the presentation of the story by the *Deutsches Nachrichtenbüro* (DNB; German News Agency), responsible for circulating news items within and outside Germany. 'It is specially desirable', the directive ran, 'that the DNB report brings out the horrific Bolshevik crimes in East Prussia in a big and effective way and comments on them with extreme harshness. The monstrous Soviet bloodlust must be denounced in the layout and headlines.' It was not a matter of attacks on big landowners and industrialists, it had to be stressed, but on ordinary people, targeted for annihilation by Bolshevism.[66]

The headlines duly followed. 'The Raving of the Soviet Beasts' bellowed the Nazi main newspaper, the *Völkischer Beobachter*, on 27 October.[67] 'Bolshevik Bloodlust Rages in East Prussian Border Area', and 'Bestial Murderous Terror in East Prussia' proclaimed regional newspapers in eastern Germany.[68] Other organs of the coordinated press followed suit.[69] Maximum shock was the intention in the stories of plunder, destruction, rape and murder. Commissions of doctors, it was said, had confirmed the murder of sixty-one men, women and children and the rape of most of the women. There was reference to a crucifixion. Photographed lines of corpses conveyed graphic images of the horror.[70] A front-page photograph of murdered children in the *Völkischer Beobachter* had an accompanying warning of what would happen if Germans did not sustain their defences and fighting spirit.[71]

The mood in eastern parts of Germany made a propaganda campaign on the revelations from Nemmersdorf timely. Reports from propaganda offices had acknowledged, before news of Nemmersdorf had broken, that 'the gains of territory by the Bolsheviks in East Prussia had produced deepest consternation', all the more so since Gauleiter Koch had declared in a speech only days earlier that no more land would be given up to the enemy. Bitter reproaches were also made against Koch by East Prussian refugees, arriving in Danzig in a pitiable state and saying that they had first been told by retreating soldiers that 'the Bolsheviks were on their heels'.[72] It was in this climate of wavering morale that Goebbels saw the propaganda value of the Red Army atrocities.

The sensationalized propaganda barrage was, however, less successful than Goebbels had expected. The first reactions indicated that there was some scepticism about reportage seen as a propaganda manufacture.[73] In this Goebbels was hoist with his own petard. Earlier in the month he had given directions to his propaganda specialists to portray 'the conditions in the areas occupied by the Anglo-Americans exactly as dramatically and drastically as in those occupied by the Soviets'. This had been a response to accounts 'that our people, should it come to it, would prefer to fall to Anglo-American rather than Soviet occupation'. Such a possibility could not be left open to the ordinary citizen – 'the little man' – because it would reduce the determination to fight. 'On the contrary, he must know . . . that if the Reich is lost, to whichever enemy partner, there is no possibility of existence for him.'[74]

In reality, the Nazi authorities were well aware that the people of those parts of the west that had already fallen to the Americans had been on the whole well enough treated and had often, indeed, welcomed the enemy and attuned rapidly to occupation.[75] Goebbels himself recognized that reports of atrocities committed by British and American troops were not believed, and that it was easy for people – apart from Party functionaries – to give themselves up to the British or Americans since they would be treated leniently. People thought the Americans especially were not as bad as they had been portrayed in the German press.[76] Propaganda reports were now telling Goebbels that evacuees from the west were spreading the feeling that 'peace at any price' would be preferable to the continuation of the war.[77] And, certainly in parts of the Reich far away from the travails of the east German population, people were inclined to see the accounts of refugees as exaggerated.[78]

Propaganda backfired, too, in another way. One report commented 'that the highlighting of Bolshevik atrocities in the East Prussian border areas' was rejected 'since the propaganda about Nemmersdorf signified in a certain sense a self-incrimination of the Reich because the population had not been evacuated on time'.[79] The allegations were countered only with weak (and false) arguments which claimed that the area directly behind the fighting zone had long been evacuated, that the surprise Soviet assault had overrun refugee treks but that the local population of Nemmersdorf had already left, that the numbers evacuated by the Party had been entirely satisfactory and proof of its energetic and successful work, and – with some contradiction – that people had had to work behind the lines as long as possible to bring in the harvest that was much needed for provisioning the rest of the Reich with food.[80] All in all, Goebbels himself was eventually forced to concede that 'the atrocities reports are not bought from us any longer. In particular, the reports from Nemmersdorf have only convinced a part of the population.'[81]

Elsewhere, far away from the eastern borders of the Reich, another – extremely telling – reason was given for being unimpressed by the horror propaganda about Nemmersdorf. The SD office in Stuttgart reported in early November that people were calling the press stories 'shameless' and asking what the intention of the leadership might be in publishing pictures of the atrocities. Surely the Reich's leaders must realize, the report went on,

> that every thinking person, seeing these gory victims, will immediately contemplate the atrocities that we have perpetrated on enemy soil, and even in Germany. Have we not slaughtered Jews in their thousands? Don't soldiers tell over and again that Jews in Poland had to dig their own graves? And what did we do with the Jews who were in the concentration camp [Natzweiler] in Alsace? The Jews are also human beings. By acting in this way, we have shown the enemy what they might do to us in the event of their victory. . . . We can't accuse the Russians of behaving just as gruesomely towards other peoples as our own people have done against their own Germans.

There was no need to get too worked up 'because they have killed a few people in East Prussia. After all, what does human life amount to here in Germany.'[82]

The Reich was a large country. And Stuttgart was almost as far from Nemmersdorf as it was possible to be. Revealing as these reported remarks are about knowledge of German crimes against humanity, especially of genocidal actions towards Jews, the people of Stuttgart could feel that there was much distance between themselves and whatever Soviet atrocities had taken place on the Reich's easternmost borders. The population of the eastern areas of Germany had every reason to be more alarmed at the proximity of the Red Army. For ordinary civilians, helplessly squeezed between the refusal of the Party authorities to evacuate them westwards and the oncoming assault from demonized enemy forces, the horror propaganda from Nemmersdorf almost certainly helped to induce a sense of intense fear. Certainly, there was profound relief when the Wehrmacht beat off the incursion and some stability returned to the area.[83] In trumpeting the successes in repelling the enemy, propaganda did not hesitate to emphasize the value of all the work that had gone into building the fortifications in the east, which, it was claimed, had held up the Red Army. The *Volkssturm* engagement was also glorified.[84] But Goebbels was keen not to overplay the 'miracle of East Prussia'. It was important, he remarked, 'not to praise the day before evening'.[85] This was a sensible sentiment. When the Red Army returned to East Prussia, this time to stay, in January 1945, blind panic, not determination to fight to the last, characterized the behaviour of the vast majority of the civilian population of the region.

It would be as well, however, not to presume that scepticism or cynicism about the propaganda reports about Nemmersdorf meant that Goebbels' efforts had been fruitless. Contrary to indications that the atrocity stories had failed in their impact, the summary report from propaganda offices in mid-November claimed that those who had initially doubted the written accounts had altered their views in the light of the published photographs. People were 'filled with hatred', ready to fight to the extreme.[86] However varied the response of the civilian population had been, it seems certain that for two groups in particular – groups that bore power – Nemmersdorf carried a message less of panic than of the need to hold out at any cost.

For representatives, high and low, of the Nazi Party and its affiliates, the violence and cruelty of the invaders in East Prussia had offered a foretaste of what seemed certain to await them should they fall into Soviet hands. Hitler himself reacted characteristically to the news and pictures from Nemmersdorf. 'He swore revenge and fanned the flames of hatred,' his most junior secretary, Traudl Junge, later wrote. '"They're not human beings any more, they're animals from the steppes of Asia, and the war I am waging against them is a war for the dignity of European mankind," he fumed. "We have to be hard and fight with all the means at our disposal."'[87] Hitler, least of all, was under no illusions about his fate should the Soviets capture him. On no account could that be allowed to happen. The route he would eventually take out of catastrophic defeat was already prefigured. He had informed the Gauleiter of Vienna and former Hitler Youth leader, Baldur von Schirach, as early as mid-1943 that the only way he could end the war was by shooting himself in the head.[88]

He extended the implications of his own fate to that of the German people. He had told his assembled Gauleiter as long ago as October 1943 that the German people had burnt their bridges; the only way was forward. Their very existence was at stake.[89] He was not alone in the sentiment that there was nothing to lose. Goebbels was glad that bridges had been burnt; it bound people to the cause. In informing Party leaders of the mass killing of the Jews the previous autumn, Himmler had also been deliberately spreading the complicity, so that those present knew that there was no escape from the conspiracy of the implicated.[90] At lower levels of the Party, too, the behaviour of many functionaries on the approach of the enemy – attempts to conceal membership of Nazi organizations, burning insignia, hiding uniforms and, most commonly, flight – betrayed their anxieties about what awaited them if they fell into enemy hands. But where the petty apparatchiks might hope for safety in obscurity, the Nazi bigwigs were left with no obvious choice other than to hold out. Desperation bred determination.

The other crucial sector in which the impact of Nemmersdorf and all that it signified was unmistakable was within the army, especially among those soldiers who came from eastern parts of Germany. In the west, the collapse following the Allied breakthrough in France had brought disarray and damaged morale. The recovery there could not conceal the fervent desire among many soldiers for a swift end to the purgatory of continued fighting. It was possible to see falling into enemy hands in the west as a release. The likely death sentence appeared to be to fight on rather than end up a captive. In the east, the feelings were very different. Colonel-General Reinhardt reflected undoubted widespread sentiments when he saw what the Soviet troops had done in East Prussia almost immediately following their expulsion from the area. He wrote to his wife of the 'rage, the hatred, which fills us since we have seen how the Bolsheviks have wrought havoc in the area that we have retaken, south of Gumbinnen'. 'There can be no other aim for us', he added, 'than to hold out and to protect our homeland.' For soldiers from East Prussia and neighbouring regions, it was no longer a matter of abstract patriotic defence of the homeland, however, let alone fighting for the cause of the Führer. The lives and well-being of their loved ones were at stake. The fury and thirst for revenge at what had been done was palpable. 'I was there yesterday [25 October 1944] in this area to visit my troops after their successful attack,' Reinhardt went on, and 'experienced the blind fury with which they have slain entire regiments'.[91]

A glimpse, if at a later date, of the impact of events in East Prussia on the mentalities of ordinary soldiers far from the areas in possession of the Red Army is provided by the diary of a member of the Wehrmacht Commander-in-Chief's staff in Norway. The reports of 'murder, torture, rapes, abduction to bordellos, deportations' had a devasting effect on the troops, he recalled. It encouraged the 'mystical belief' that salvation would come at the last. Those with a clearer view of the likely future kept quiet since maintaining the discipline that, below the surface, had weakened was the imperative, and this seemed feasible only 'with the aid of false hopes'. Concern for relatives was, however, growing by the hour.[92]

Of course, soldiers, even those from the directly affected eastern border areas of the Reich, did not all think alike. But sufficient numbers fighting on the eastern front, and also many of those transferred to the west, appear to have been convinced that they were indeed engaged, as Hitler, Goebbels and others kept reminding them, in a struggle for their very existence, and that of their comrades and loved ones back home. The Soviet incursion served as a graphically horrible reinforcement of existing stereotypes about the 'Bolsheviks'.[93] It was not in the first instance a matter of firm ideological belief in Nazi doctrine or the redemptive powers of the Führer.[94] It was simply a belief that, in the east at least, it was a life-or-death struggle against barbaric enemies. And for those less than wholly convinced, there was the intensified apparatus of repression, control and severe punishment within the Wehrmacht itself. A rising trend in death sentences for desertion, unwillingness to fight, undermining morale and other offences mirrored the decline in Germany's military fortunes.[95]

The 'war of annihilation' on the eastern front had always been qualitatively different from the nature of the conflict in the west. The ideological confrontation in the east, the savagery of the fighting on both sides, the 'barbarisation of warfare'[96] that openly targeted the wholesale destruction of civilian life, and, not least, the genocidal dimension present from the launch of 'Operation Barbarossa' in June 1941, had no real equivalents in the west, even though their impact was felt throughout the German-occupied parts of the European continent. This is not to underplay the severity of the bitter fighting in the west, such as in Normandy following the Allied landings, where German troops, certainly down to the collapse in mid-August, had fought tenaciously and with losses that for a time matched the rate of attrition in the east.[97] Nor is it to forget the harshness of civilian life under German occupation beyond eastern Europe, let alone the tentacles of genocidal policy that reached out into all corners of the Nazi empire. The subjugated peoples of the Balkans, Greece, Italy (in the last phase of the war) and other countries suffered grievously from mounting atrocities and merciless reprisals for any form of resistance as occupying German forces became more desperate. The Germans perpetrated atrocities in the west, too, most horrifically the massacre by the Waffen-SS of hundreds of villagers at Oradour-sur-Glane in France in June 1944. But what was rare in the west was the norm in the east. Awareness of the fundamentally different character of the war in east and west had been recognized throughout German society since the invasion of the Soviet Union in 1941. The incursion of the Red Army onto German soil, and the terrible experiences for the civilian population that ensued, now sharpened the perceptions of that division between eastern and western fronts, both for soldiers and civilians.

For the latter, experiences of the war in the west were now almost entirely dominated by the wanton destruction and terror from the skies. Goebbels' postbag was almost exclusively taken up with letters – which he thought 'to some extent alarming' – about the effects of the air raids and the despair that there was no defence against them. What was the use of morale, the letter-writers were asking, if the bombing was wrecking the means to carry on the fight? The letters, Goebbels remarked, reflected a worrying level of apathy in continuing the struggle.[98] For most people in the western regions so badly afflicted by the bombing, the end of the war could not come soon enough. It would mean liberation from the misery. True, few preferred the prospect of life under an occupying force. But life would nevertheless go on. Propaganda claims that conquest by the western Allies would destroy German existence were widely disbelieved. There was little fear of the Americans or British. The fear here was of the bombers. 'Fear, fear, fear, nothing else is known to me,' wrote one mother in September 1944, worried sick about her daughter at school as bombers crossed the skies in broad daylight, and anxious too about her husband at the front. At least he was in the west, she wrote. 'To fall into the hands of the Soviets would mean the end.'[99]

In the eastern regions, fear of the Soviets was all-encompassing, and borne out by Nemmersdorf and what that signified. It encouraged the readiness among civilians to dig ditches, undergo any necessary privations and do all that was humanly possible to fend off the worst. It also produced mass panic when occupation was imminent. Naturally, people in these regions, too, desperately wanted the war to end. But for most of them, still largely unaffected by the bombing that was a daily scourge for the western population, the end of the war in any acceptable way had to entail release from the dreadful fear of a Soviet takeover and saving their families, possessions and homeland from occupation by a hated and feared enemy. So desire for a rapid end to the terrible conflict was mixed with the desire for the war to continue until those ends were attained. This meant that hopes had to be invested in the capacity of the Wehrmacht to continue the fight and to stave off the worst.

For soldiers, the divide between east and west was little different. Certainly, troops on the western front fought doggedly and resolutely. According to later reflections of a high-ranking officer under Model's command, they had no great ideals any longer, though there was often still some flickering belief in Hitler and hopes in the promised miracle weapons. Most of all, they had nothing more to lose.[100] Their fighting qualities were often grudgingly admired by the western Allies. But outright fanaticism was mainly to be found among units of the Waffen-SS. And, for most soldiers, the prospect of capture was not the end of the world. On the eastern front, fanaticism, though not omnipresent, was far more commonplace. The mere thought of falling into Soviet hands meant that holding out was an imperative. No quarter could be expected from the enemy. Nemmersdorf showed, it seemed, that fears of Soviet occupation were more than justified, that propaganda imagery of 'Bolshevik bestiality' was correct. The war in the east could not be given up. There could be no contemplation of surrender when what was in store was so unimaginably terrible.

V

Increasingly dreadful though the predicament was of the German population, bombed incessantly in the west and living in terror of Soviet invasion in the east, the fate of Nazism's prime ideological target, the Jews, was infinitely worse.

Hitler had sought in the spring to harden fighting morale and commitment to Nazi principles of all-out racial struggle when he addressed a large gathering of generals and other officers about to head for the front. He told them how essential it had been to deal so ruthlessly with the Jews, whose victory in the war would bring the destruction of the German people. The entire bestiality of Bolshevism, he ranted, had been a product of the Jews. He pointed to the danger to Germany posed by Hungary, a state he depicted as completely under Jewish domination, but added that he had now intervened – through the occupation of the country that had taken place in March – and that the 'problem' would soon be solved there, too. The military commanders interrupted the speech on several occasions with rapturous applause.[101] They were being made complicit through their knowledge of what had happened to the Jews in much of Europe and was now happening in Hungary.

In the summer of 1944, as the Red Army was smashing through Army Group Centre in Belorussia, trainloads of Jews were still being ferried from Hungary to their deaths in the massive extermination unit in Auschwitz-Birkenau, in Upper Silesia. By the time the deportations were stopped in early July by a Hungarian leadership responding to the mounting pressure from abroad, the Nazi assault on the largest remaining Jewish community in Europe had accounted for over 430,000 Jews.[102] The crematoria in Auschwitz struggled to keep up with the numbers being gassed to death – more than 10,000 a day that summer.[103] At the end of July, the Red Army, advancing through Poland, had liberated Majdanek near Lublin, and encountered for the first time the monstrosity of the death camps, publicizing the findings in the world's press (though few in Germany had access to this).[104] Auschwitz-Birkenau was, however, still carrying out its grisly work. With the closure of Bełżec, Sobibor and Treblinka in 1943, and a final burst of exterminatory work at Chełmno in the summer of 1944, Auschwitz-Birkenau, the largest death camp, was the last in operation. Jews from the Łódź ghetto in Poland were gassed there in August; transports from Slovakia and the camp at Theresienstadt on what had once been Czech territory arrived in September and October. In November, satisfied that the 'Jewish Question' had, to all intents and purposes, been solved through the killing of millions and anxious at the growing proximity of the Red Army, Himmler ordered the gassing installations to be demolished.[105]

It is striking how little thought of what might be happening to Jews appears to have impinged upon the consciousness of Germans, wholly and not unnaturally preoccupied with their own suffering and anxieties. Propaganda continued to pour out its anti-Jewish vitriol, blaming Jews for the war, and linking them with Germany's destruction.[106] But these were by now weary platitudinous abstractions. Most ordinary citizens appear to have given no consideration to the actual fate of the Jews or to have pondered much about what might have happened to them. Relatively few people within Germany had first-hand, detailed knowledge of the murderous events that continued to unfold to the east; the 'Final Solution' was, of course, officially still preserved as a closely guarded state secret. But, in any case, overwhelmed by their own anxieties, few Germans were interested in what was happening, far away, to an unloved, where not thoroughly hated, minority.

For most, it was a case of 'out of sight, out of mind', apart from the nagging worry that the ill-deeds perpetrated by German overlords might well come back to haunt them in defeat and occupation. This concern was present in two ways, both more subliminal than overt. As the reported comments from Stuttgart, referred to earlier, indicate, there was a gathering sense that Germany was now reaping what it had sown, that the misery its population was undergoing amounted to retribution for what had been done to the Jews and others. And another sentiment not infrequently encountered in this period was that the Jews would return with the occupying forces to take their revenge. The sentiment, commonplace enough, was directly expressed in one letter home from the front in August 1944. 'You know that the Jew will exact his bloody revenge, mainly on Party people. Unfortunately, I was one of those who wore the Party uniform. I've already regretted it. I urge you to get rid of the uniform, it doesn't matter where, even if you have to burn the lot.'[107] Not a few, especially no doubt among hardened Nazi believers, felt that the bombing and destruction of German towns and cities itself amounted to that revenge. Incessant Nazi propaganda about the power of world Jewry had made a lasting mark.[108]

For the few Jews remaining within the Reich, living as pariahs, keen to keep a low profile, with almost no contact with non-Jews, it was a shadowy world, a completely uncertain, highly precarious, anxiety-ridden existence – though in ways that contrasted with the anxieties and uncertainties of the mass of the population. The academic Victor Klemperer, an intelligent observer living in Dresden whose marriage to a non-Jew had enabled him to avoid deportation, was full of apprehension simply at the late return of his wife from a rare and brief absence from their home. She was carrying parts of the secret diary he was keeping to be hidden by a friend in Pirna, not far away. If it should fall into the hands of the authorities it would spell death not just for himself, but for his wife and for friends he had mentioned by name.[109] He and his wife did share with the mass of the population the fear of bombing. However, here too there were major differences. Bombing for Nazism's victims was a sign of Germany's impending defeat and personal liberation from a terroristic regime.[110] But Klemperer's existential fear was that he would survive a raid, be evacuated, separated from his wife and sent somewhere to be gassed.[111] There was anxiety, too, shared with friends, about surviving another winter of war with provisions of food and fuel scarcely sufficient to keep a person alive. 'Another winter is a horrible prospect,' he wrote.[112] Another acquaintance looked grimly into the future, foreseeing malnutrition, shortage of medicines, spread of epidemic diseases, no end to the war and eventually death for all remaining bearers of the yellow star. Klemperer was aware, if without detail, of the fate of the Jews of eastern Europe. In these very days he was given another report by a soldier on leave of 'gruesome murders of Jews in the east'.[113]

His reaction to the events in East Prussia also contrasted with that of the non-Jewish population. While they had their fears of Bolshevism confirmed, his own worry was what the implications were for Jews. He remarked on the new agitation against Jews unleashed by Martin Mutschmann, the Gauleiter of Saxony, then added: 'and the Bolshevik atrocities in East Prussia, about which the people probably believed, could be turned against us'.[114]

For the countless other victims of the regime – Jews, hundreds of thousands in concentration camps, more than 7 million foreign workers and prisoners of war,[115] and further millions of former political opponents of the Nazis – the end of the war was a moment they yearned for. In autumn 1944, however, that end was still not in sight. Their misery was set to go on.

VI

Intense war-weariness was by now widespread throughout much of German society, within the civilian population and also among ordinary soldiers. One keen foreign observer in Berlin recalled, long after the events, his sense that autumn that Germans felt themselves to be in an avalanche gathering pace as it headed for the abyss. What made them carry on was a question repeatedly in his mind and that of his associates. Beyond terror he thought 'inertia and habit' – apathy and the need for some normality, a search for routine even in the midst of extreme abnormality, which he saw as 'not a specific German, but a universal characteristic' – provided some explanation.[116] To such speculation could be added the sheer debilitating lethargy that arose from constant intense anxiety about the fate of loved ones, ever-present fear of bombing, the daily dislocations of sheltering from (or clearing up after) air raids, overwork and exhaustion, the queuing for greatly reduced rations, malnutrition, and the constant sense of helpless exposure to events beyond anyone's control. Since there was no option, no obvious course of action open to individuals that would not result in self-destruction and would in any case change nothing, people simply got on with their lives as best they could.

Politically, the war-weariness meant extensive and growing aversion to the Nazi regime, though with no potential to turn sentiment into action. Not just the Nazi Party, but Hitler himself was drawn into the front line of criticism for bringing war to Germany and causing such misery.[117] An outward sign was that the 'Heil Hitler' greeting was disappearing.[118] 'Providence has determined the destruction of the German people, and Hitler is the executor of this will,' was said by one SD station at the beginning of November to be a common view.[119] Except in such negative ways, as a cause of the horror and obstruction to ending it, Hitler, once almost deified by millions, had come by now to play little overt part in people's consciousness.

A dwindling proportion of Germans were, it is true, still unbending in their support for the regime, retaining a fanatical determination to fight to the last. Most, however, increasingly saw themselves as victims of Hitler and his regime, often now overlooking how they had in better times idolized their leader and cheered his successes, and how their own treatment of others was rebounding in misery for themselves. The war had come home to Germany, a battered, broken country, its industrial and transport framework collapsing, besieged by economically and militarily superior forces to the east and west. Whatever hopes had been invested in 'wonder weapons' had largely evaporated. Only further devastation lay in store. Most people simply wanted the war to end –

and hoped that Anglo-American occupation would keep the Bolsheviks from their throats.[120]

Such feelings, if not universal, were widely held – though to no avail. They were not shared by those in power – by the regime's leadership, the High Command of the Wehrmacht, military commanders, and those directing the Party, whether at the centre or in the provinces. Moreover, though the system had taken a terrible pounding through military defeats and relentless bombing, it still continued – more or less – to function. Astonishing resilience and even more remarkable improvisation enabled state, Party and military bureaucracies to operate, if not normally, then still with some effectiveness. Above all, the mechanisms of control and repression were in place. No organizational capacity to challenge them existed.

And at the very pinnacle of the regime, there was, as always, not the slightest inclination to contemplate either negotiation or surrender. Hitler made this plain, yet again, in his proclamation of 12 November.[121] He left no one in any doubt: as long as he lived, the war would go on. He had, in fact, been planning for weeks what, given the resources available, would almost certainly be a final, desperate attempt to turn the tide. Remaining on the defensive could prolong the conflict, he reckoned, but would never wrest the initiative from the enemy. A decisive strike was imperative. If such a venture were to be attempted, the imperilled eastern front appeared to be the obvious choice. After all, the prospect of a Bolshevik breakthrough and ultimate victory was too ghastly for anyone to contemplate. The Army Chief of Staff, Guderian, responsible for the eastern front, put the case strongly. But against Guderian's advice, Hitler was adamant that an offensive would have the greatest chance of success, not somewhere along the extensive eastern front, but at a specific vulnerable point of the Allied lines in the west, with the intention of driving on to Antwerp.[122] Inflicting an incisive defeat on the western Allies would not simply be crucial for the war in the west; it would also revive morale and then allow forces to be transferred to the east to bolster the chances of repelling the expected winter offensive of the Red Army. If it failed, however, not only would the western Allies be able to continue their march on the borders of the Reich against a greatly weakened Wehrmacht, but the eastern front would be left enfeebled and exposed.

It was, as all in the know could see, a highly risky strategy. A betting man would not have put much of a wager on its chances of success. But, from Hitler's perspective, it was almost all that was left. 'If it doesn't succeed, I see no other possibility of bringing the war to a favourable conclusion,' he told Speer.[123] On 16 December, the new offensive was unleashed on the Americans with unexpected ferocity. Germany's last serious military hope of affecting the outcome of the war now lay in the balance.

4

Hopes Raised – and Dashed

Victory was never as close as it is now. The decision will soon be reached. We will throw them into the ocean, the arrogant, big-mouthed apes from the New World. They will not get into our Germany. We will protect our wives and children from all enemy domination.

I shall march once more through Belgium and France, but I don't have the smallest desire to do so ... If [only] this idiotic war would end. Why should I fight? It only goes for the existence of the Nazis. The superiority of our enemy is so great that it is senseless to fight against it.

Contrasting views of German soldiers during
the Ardennes offensive, December 1944

I

All the hopes of the German leadership now rested on the great offensive in the west. If successful, it could, they thought, prove a decisive turning point in the war. If it failed, the war would be effectively lost. But remaining on the defensive would simply mean eventually being crushed between the advancing western and eastern powers, who would be able to exploit their superior resources and seemingly limitless reserves of manpower. General Jodl, responsible for strategic planning, summarized the thinking at the beginning of November. 'The risk of the great aim, seeming to stand technically in disproportion to our available forces, is unalterable. But in our current situation we can't shrink from staking everything on one card.'[1]

The card to be played was a swift and decisive military strike aimed at inflicting such a mighty blow on the western Allies that they would lose the appetite for continuing the fight. This would lead to the breakup of what was perceived as an unnatural coalition of forces facing Germany. Hitler's own characteristic thinking was plainly outlined in his address to his division commanders four days before the beginning of the offensive. 'Wars are finally decided', he asserted, 'by the recognition on one side or the other that the war can't be won any more. Thus, the most important task is to bring the enemy to this realization.' Even when forced back on the defensive, 'ruthless strikes' had the effect of showing the enemy that he had not won, and that the war would continue, 'that no matter what he might do, he can never count on a capitulation – never, ever'. Under the impact of severe setbacks and recognition that success was unattainable, the enemy's 'nerve will break in the end'. And Germany's enemy was a coalition of 'the greatest extremes that can be imagined in this world: ultra-capitalist states on one side and ultra-Marxist states on the other; on one side a dying world empire, Britain, and on the other side a colony seeking an inheritance, the USA'. It was ripe for collapse if a blow of sufficient power could be landed. 'If a few heavy strikes were to succeed here, this artificially maintained united front could collapse at any moment with a huge clap of thunder.'[2]

The first deliberations for an offensive in the west had taken place at precisely the time of German crisis on that front – during the collapse in Normandy in mid-August. By mid-September the decision for the offensive, given the code-name 'Watch on the Rhine' (later changed to 'Autumn Mist'), was taken. Utmost secrecy was of the essence. Only a few in the High Command of the Wehrmacht and among the regime's leaders were in the know. Even Field-Marshal von Rundstedt, restored as Commander-in-Chief West on 5 September, was told only in late October of the aims of the operation.[3] Jodl's plans for the attack went through a number of variations before Hitler's order to go ahead was given on 10 November. Then the intended launch of the offensive in late November had to be postponed several times because of equipment shortages and unseasonal good weather – the attack was depending on poor weather to ground enemy aircraft – before the final date was set at 16 December. The military goal was to strike, as in 1940, through the wooded Ardennes in the gap between the American and British forces, advancing rapidly to take Antwerp and, in tandem with German divisions attacking towards the south from Holland, cutting the enemy lines of communication with the rear, encircling and destroying the British 21st Army Group and the 9th and 1st US Armies in a 'new Dunkirk'. It would, according to Hitler's directive for the operation, bring 'the decisive turn in the western campaign and therefore perhaps of the entire war'.[4]

The situation, on the eastern as well as the western front, had deteriorated drastically since the idea for the offensive had initially been conceived. On the eastern front, the Soviet incursion into East Prussia had, it is true, been repelled but the most acutely threatened area had meanwhile become Hungary, a crucial source of oil and other raw materials. German troops were engaged there in bitter attritional fighting throughout the autumn in fending off the Red Army's attempt to take Budapest, ordered by Stalin at the end of October.[5] In the west, meanwhile, American troops stood on German soil in the Aachen area. After taking the city in late October, their advance during the following weeks in the densely wooded hills beyond the *Westwall*, the Hürtgenwald, between Aachen and Eupen and Düren to the east had encountered ferocious defence and proved extremely costly to the Americans.[6] By the time the Ardennes offensive began, the American advance had reached only the river Roer, near Jülich and Düren.[7] Further to the south, the Americans had greater success, though again at a cost and only after tough resistance by the Wehrmacht. In Lorraine, General Patton's 3rd US Army eventually forced the surrender of the heavily fortified town of Metz on 22 November, though, battle-weary and combating driving rain, sleet and mud as well as the enemy, it was unable to continue the advance to Saarbrücken. In Alsace, the 6th US Army Group of General Jacob Devers, encountering weaker German defences, drove through the Vosges Mountains to take Strasbourg on 23 November and reach the Rhine near Kehl.[8] Even so, the German leadership – attributing, typically, the fall of Strasbourg to treachery within Alsace – was encouraged by the stiffened resistance during the autumn that had held the western Allies at bay.[9]

In the eyes of Hitler and his chief military advisers, Keitel and Jodl, the enemy inroads since the summer strengthened rather than weakened the case for the planned western offensive. The pressure, military and economic, on Germany was relentlessly intensifying. The tightening vice, they felt, could be loosened only through a bold strike. German losses of men and equipment had mounted sharply over the autumn, predominantly on the eastern front but also in the west. But so had those of the enemy. The American casualties in fierce autumn fighting for relatively minor territorial gains totalled almost a quarter of a million men, dead, wounded or captured.[10] Hitler impressed upon his commanders that the time to strike against an enemy that had suffered high losses and was 'worn out' was ripe.[11] Beyond that, the eastern front – the heavy fighting in Hungary notwithstanding – was for the time being seen to be relatively stabilized, though no one was in doubt that a big new offensive would soon be launched. This was seen as all the more reason to press home the advantage of a German offensive in the west without delay.

Heavy priority was accorded to the demands of the western offensive in allocation of men and armaments. Three armies of Army Group B were to take part. The 6th SS-Panzer Army, led by SS Colonel-General Sepp Dietrich, one of Hitler's toughest and most trusted military veterans, and the 5th Panzer Army under its brilliant commander and specialist in tank warfare, General Hasso von Manteuffel, were to spearhead the attack in the north and centre of the front.[12] The 7th Army, under General Erich Brandenberger, was assigned the task of protecting the southern flank. Some 200,000 men in five panzer and thirteen People's Grenadier divisions were assigned to the first wave, supported by around 600 tanks and 1,600 heavy guns. However, many of the men were young and inexperienced. Some divisions came, already battle-weary, from the fighting on the Saar. Fuel shortages were a major concern, even with some supplies taken from the hard-pressed eastern front. And an even bigger worry was the weakness of the Luftwaffe. All available planes – including two-thirds of the entire fighter force – were assembled for the attack. Hopes had to be placed in bad weather limiting the massive supremacy in the air of the Allies. Even so, the Wehrmacht began with a substantial numerical advantage in ground-troops and heavy armaments in the 170-kilometre-wide attack zone.[13] The element of surprise would be vital to make this momentary superiority tell. But even surprise would not be enough if the offensive could not be sustained.

There were grounds enough for scepticism about the chances of success. Both Rundstedt and Field-Marshal Model, Commander-in-Chief of Army Group B, thought the aim of Antwerp, around 200 kilometres away, far too ambitious, given the strength of available forces. They favoured a more limited aim of beating back and destroying the Allied forces along the Meuse, between Aachen and Liège. But Hitler wanted no 'little solution', no 'ordinary' victory. He would not be moved from the aim he had stipulated for the offensive. In the end, Rundstedt and Model declared themselves to be 'fully in agreement' with Hitler's ambitious plan. Privately, both remained extremely dubious. Model thought it had 'no chance'. Dietrich and Manteuffel also bowed, their own doubts still unassuaged, to the imperative.[14] Like most military commanders, they saw it as their duty to raise objections to the operational plan but then, when these were rejected, to fulfil to the best of their ability the orders of the political leadership, however futile they deemed these to be. Hitler still had the capacity, however, to make the impossible seem possible. Manteuffel himself accepted that Hitler's addresses to the divisional commanders on 11 and 12 December had made a positive impact. 'The commanders', he later wrote, 'took away from this conference a picture of the enemy's overall situation. They had been given an appreciation of the situation from the one source in a position to see the full military picture and it seemed to give an assurance of favourable conditions.'[15]

In the top echelons of the High Command of the Wehrmacht, there was no readiness to back the well-founded misgivings of those who would lead the offensive. Keitel and Jodl were daily in Hitler's immediate proximity and remained heavily under his domineering influence. Both remained believers in his unique qualities as Führer, adepts of his form of charismatic authority.[16] If they harboured doubts, they kept them to themselves. Jodl refrained from any criticism of Hitler's decision even when interrogated by his Allied captors in May 1945.[17]

On 15 December Rundstedt put out his 'order of the day', exhorting his troops on the eve of battle. 'Soldiers of the western front!' he proclaimed. 'Your great hour has struck. Strong attacking armies are marching today against the Anglo-Americans. I don't need to say any more. You all feel it: it's all or nothing!' Model's own ringing exhortation followed: 'We will not disappoint the trust of the Führer placed in us, nor that of the homeland, which has forged the sword of retaliation. Advance in the spirit of Leuthen' (the legendary victory of Frederich the Great in the Seven Years War, almost two centuries earlier).[18] At 5.30 a.m. on 16 December, an hour-long artillery barrage began. About 7 a.m., before sunrise on a frosty morning, with thick cloud offering protection from enemy aircraft, the German infantry marched out of the dawn mist and began their assault. Germany's last major offensive was under way. The stakes could scarcely have been higher. They were indeed, as Jodl had put it, all placed on one card.

II

Nor had the civilian leadership of the Reich given up hope that depressing autumn. Whatever illusions Nazi leaders harboured, however ready they were to delude themselves and listen to their own propaganda, they were intelligent enough to see how rapidly the situation was deteriorating. Yet they still somehow hoped against hope that Hitler would find a way out, that the Allied coalition would collapse under the weight of its own contradictions, or that the deployment of new 'wonder weapons' could bring a dramatic change of fortunes.

Few Nazi leaders were apprised of the plan for the Ardennes offensive. One who was, however, was Albert Speer, among the most resigned about Germany's inevitable fate (to go from his later account) but possibly the most crucial of Hitler's immediate lieutenants in enabling the war to continue. Without Speer's efforts, drive and organizational skill in the autumn of 1944 in making the armaments available, the Ardennes offensive would not have been feasible however much Hitler and his top military aides wanted it.

It is striking, in fact, how late the almost complete collapse of the economy took place and how great the efforts were, even then, to overcome the increasingly insuperable difficulties. In their post-war interrogations, Speer and the leading figures in his ministry were adamant that the damage to Germany's economic infrastructure only became insurmountable during the autumn of 1944, largely as a consequence of the systematic destruction of the transport and communications network through a relentless Allied bombing campaign that had begun in October. Whatever their private thoughts about Germany's chances of avoiding defeat, the actions of Speer's able and energetic subordinates showed they were far from resigned to inevitable disaster. They performed organizational near miracles (if in part by grossly inhumane exploitation of foreign workers) to enable the economy to continue functioning at all, prolonging the war in its most destructive phase.

Some indeed, most notably Karl Otto Saur, the ruthless head of the Technical Department, retained an astonishingly optimistic view of Germany's chances almost down to the end of 1944.

By the autumn of 1944 it was impossible to manufacture enough to compensate for the losses.[19] Heavy air raids caused a sharp drop in the availability of steel for manufacture of ammunition.[20] Coal production was cushioned until late autumn by reduced deliveries for winter stocking, but catastrophic from November onwards, while serious shortages of most indispensable basic products mounted in the second half of 1944. Speer reckoned that there was a drop in armaments production of 30–40 per cent across 1944, worsening sharply as the year went on. By late autumn there were critical shortages of fuel and gas. The emergency needs of the Luftwaffe could be met only until around October. Aviation fuel levels could not be sustained following the attacks earlier in the year on the synthetic oil plants, though minimum production of motor spirit and diesel oil continued to the end of the war. By autumn, anti-aircraft defence was being accorded priority over fighter production. Speer estimated that some 30 per cent of the total output of guns in 1944 and 20 per cent of heavy calibre ammunition together with up to 55 per cent of armaments production of the electro-technical industry and 33 per cent of the optical industry went on anti-aircraft defences, meaning diminished armaments provision for the front and a weakening in the fighting power of the Wehrmacht. Emergency transport arrangements meant that armaments production could be more or less sustained until late autumn. By then, increasingly damaging attacks on the transport network, including crucial attacks on canals in late autumn, were causing massive disruption to both civilian and military supplies, to the growing concern of the OKW. The severe lack of fuel and other supplies so evident at the outset of the Ardennes offensive, which worried Model and Dietrich, arose in good part from the transport difficulties as the number of railway wagons available for armaments fell by more than a half. Speer went so far as to claim that transport problems, meaning that adequate fuel supplies could not be provided to the frontline troops on time, were decisive in causing the swift breakdown of the Ardennes offensive.[21]

Speer's departmental heads broadly agreed with his assessment that late autumn was the time when the economic crisis became overwhelming. According to Hans Kehrl, head of the Raw Materials and Planning departments, the concentrated Allied attacks on the Reich's transport system had an increasingly drastic effect on production from October onwards and became a decisive factor after December. He estimated that the drop in output owing to lack of transport facilities was around 25 per cent from June to October, but 60 per cent between November and January 1945.[22] The effects on the distribution of raw materials were particularly severe. Werner Bosch, in Kehrl's department, highlighted the critical shortage of cement, needed for building works (including the extensive underground factories run largely on slave labour), as supplies halved from November onwards. He allocated the dwindling supplies through rigorous rationing on a system of priorities. He claimed after the war that he had realized by spring 1944 that the war could not be won and thought (as, he imagined, did Speer himself) that Germany's leadership should have sought peace terms as soon as possible. 'As it was, however,' he remarked, 'people in his position could do nothing except get on with their own work.'[23] Whatever his post-war claims and his private reflections at the time, Bosch, in 'getting on with his own work' so effectively in the interests of the war effort, had helped to keep things going even in such desperate straits.

The impact of the transport crisis on iron and steel production in the escalating crisis of the autumn was extremely grave. Supplies from Belgium and France had dried up during the summer, but German production remained almost at full capacity until September before entering upon a steep decline from October onwards, and was down by half in December from 2 to 1 million tons in the month.[24] Hermann Röchling, head of the Reich Iron Federation and a member of the Technical Department in Speer's ministry, pointed out the huge drop, about 350,000 metric tons a month, in raw steel when Lorraine and Luxemburg fell out of production, then the big fall of around 50 per cent in production from the Saar and the Ruhr district, partly on account of disruption of the railways through bombing.[25] In the Ruhr, Germany's biggest industrial heartland, steel production had been sustained at relatively stable levels, despite increased difficulties, during the first nine months of 1944, according to Dr Walther Rohland, head of the main committee for the iron-producing industry in the Speer Ministry and Deputy Chief of the Reich Iron Federation. Reserves were, however, almost used up by September. Then, from October, a drastic deterioration set in as the transport crisis deepened.[26]

According to Günther Schulze-Fielitz, head of the Energy Department, the total capacity of Germany's power stations had expanded during each year of the war. Electricity supplies held up well until November but then declined sharply as coal deliveries became seriously impaired. By November, coal stocks at power stations were down by 30 per cent compared with the previous year. Many had sufficient coal for only a week.[27] As most of the reports acknowledged, the impact of the incessant air raids on transport installations was uppermost in the production problems by late 1944. By the end of the autumn the difficulties were becoming impossible to surmount.

Without the constant improvisation in all production areas by Speer's capable subordinates, the decline would undoubtedly have set in earlier and been more steep. Richard Fiebig, head of the main committee for railway vehicles, pointed out, for instance, that through efficiencies his department 'not only succeeded in balancing the losses of workshops through bombing and loss of territory, but we actually increased the output'. From September, 1,100 to 1,200 locomotives per month were being lost to enemy raids, but 6,800 were being repaired each month during the autumn, in spite of decreasing repair capacity.[28] Extraordinarily rapid, though inevitably piecemeal, repairs were also made in towns and cities, in factories and workshops, after bombing raids, thanks in no small part to the surplus of manpower through inactive production that the raids themselves had made available. From autumn onwards, between 1 and 1.5 million people were at any one time engaged on work resulting from air-raid damage.[29]

Perhaps most remarkably, according to Saur, owing to long gestation periods in production the total output of weapons increased continuously throughout 1944, reaching its absolute peak for practically all weapon types in December 1944.[30] Saur was prone to excessive optimism (and invariably ready to convey this to Hitler). He went so far as to claim, as 'one of the best informed men in Germany as to the war situation', that, on a purely statistical basis, Germany's situation on the eve of the Ardennes offensive 'looked good'. He pointed out that Germany's total number of soldiers under arms was greater than ever before, as was production of guns, tanks and U-boats in that month and the quantity of weapons and ammunition in the hands of the fighting troops. Of course, as he acknowledged, when it came to the *quality* of the troops, which had certainly fallen as increasingly the young, ill-trained or battle-weary were conscripted, it was a different matter. Saur's final point, emphasizing the great numerical strength of the *Volkssturm*, whose fighting capabilities were widely derided within both the Wehrmacht and in the civilian population, is sufficient indication of the spurious grounds for his apparently optimistic outlook. Nevertheless, it is striking that, far from being resigned to inevitable defeat, Saur still felt that at the outset of the Ardennes offensive 'Germany held many good cards'.[31]

Speer certainly did all he could during the deepening transport and production crisis that autumn to sustain the faltering German war economy. His efforts included a visit to the Ruhr and three to the western front to inspect the extent of the crisis and assess what improvised measures could be taken to improve the dire situation. Each time he reported directly to Hitler, enabling him to put specific proposals in his briefings in the full expectation of gaining Hitler's approval.[32]

On 11 November he informed Hitler of the increasingly serious situation in the Ruhr district, subjected to systematic intense bombing that autumn.[33] Transport was the overriding concern. Speer appointed a plenipotentiary, the head of the Reichsbahn administration, Dr Karl Lammerz, with powers to coordinate transport throughout the region without waiting for directions from Berlin, and also organized emergency measures to keep supplies moving (including food for the civilian population) and set industry to work again. These involved deploying 50,000 foreign workers supplied by Bormann by removing them from digging fortifications, another 30,000 taken from the armaments industry – a sign of the desperation – and 4,500 skilled electricians, pipe-layers and welders brought in from other parts of the Reich. The Gauleiter were ordered by Bormann to draft the local population of their areas, if necessary, to help in the removal of damage. Some 10 per cent of mine-workers were envisaged for this work, even at the cost of temporarily reducing output from the pits – another extraordinary reflection of how bad the situation was. Other emergency measures were put in place to clear the waterways. The local population was to be mobilized, as in times of flood emergencies, to help in repairing the damage. Despite all this, Speer pointed out, it was not possible in the short term to prevent a drastic drop in production. The severity of the damage meant that stockpiles of coal sufficed for no more than ten days and would be exhausted by the end of November if no great improvement could be

made. Rail transport, gas and electricity supplies were seriously threatened. He was, therefore, instigating an emergency programme (including
strict allocation of railway wagons and priority for coal transportation)
that would guarantee at least partial armaments production and sustain
current levels of arms deliveries in the short term.[34]

Between 15 and 23 November Speer visited several units of Army
Group B, the Krupp works at Essen and several other major concerns in
the Ruhr. He made a number of recommendations to overcome the
damage to waterways, shipping and bridges, and improve anti-aircraft
defences. He urged the accelerated expansion of aerodromes to take the
Messerschmitt 262 jet-fighter and other modern planes, and more efficient use of the labour force. He was critical about the sluggishness in
providing the necessary labour from other parts of the Reich, especially
when 128,000 men from the Ruhr, among them skilled workers, had
been conscripted for fortification work outside the area when they were
so badly needed to restore the damaged Ruhr industrial heartland.
He wanted alterations in steel allocation, with priority to be removed
from U-boats and shifted to restoration of transport and reconstruction
of Ruhr industrial works. Otherwise, he could propose only minor
improvements. Lack of transport meant people were having to walk
long distances to work each day over damaged roads. There was a
shortage of shoes, which Speer requested be provided from elsewhere in
the Reich. Because of damage to power stations and electricity cables,
many people were without lighting. He recommended a 'special action'
to provide candles and other means of lighting, including pit-lamps.
Factories could not contact each other since the telephone system was
not fully working, and the Reich postal service did not have the manpower to restore the system. He advocated a communications regiment
from the army to be sent to restore and maintain a communications system for industry. Overall, the tenor of his report was that, despite the
huge damage, there were still unused capacities of labour and resources
if systematically deployed to overcome the worst.[35]

Hitler accepted Speer's recommendations at their meeting at the end
of November. He agreed, for example, that the Reich should provide a
labour force of between 100,000 and 150,000 to assist the Ruhr, and
that all workers from the area conscripted for digging elsewhere should
be returned. He also ordered an improvement in shoe provision for the
Ruhr.[36]

In the build-up to the Ardennes offensive, Speer paid another, shorter, visit to the western front between 7 and 10 December, visiting mainly units of Army Groups B and G to hear their experiences and suggestions on the armaments situation. Major improvements were no longer possible. The armaments industry was by now scraping the barrel. (This had not prevented Speer, however, just before leaving for the western front, impressing a selected audience with an array of improved weapons in preparation.[37]) He was reduced to recommending incentives – additional army stores goods or leave – for troop units with especially low losses of weaponry. He also encouraged intensified propaganda efforts by the NSFOs to explain how well the armaments industry was performing despite all difficulties, and to combat rumours on shortages of tanks and fuel that were damaging troop morale. He pointed out to Hitler that Saar coal and gas were keeping the whole of south-west German industry going. The severe consequences if the Saar fell to the enemy were obvious.[38]

Speer's third trip to the western front took place in the second half of December, during the Ardennes offensive, when he took soundings from a number of units of Army Group B. There was little concrete return from his visit. The most significant part of the report emphasized again the crisis on the railways. The Reichsbahn network in the region had, he reported, been 'almost completely smashed' beyond repair. (Sepp Dietrich complained that his troops were getting no munitions because the communications routes had been destroyed by air raids.)[39] Other methods had to be deployed to ensure that materials were delivered and that inefficiencies, such as leaving loaded wagons at the mercy of air attacks, were reduced. Speer recommended the deployment of Party Local Leaders who, together with stationmasters, could organize alternative transport, get railway wagons unloaded and convey important communications by car or motorbike to the army commanders. However, minor improvisations to try to keep things moving could not gloss over, even for Hitler, the fact that the end was approaching.[40]

With the end of the war and the onset of a post-Hitler era plainly in view, Speer's considerable energies were not least directed, in collaboration with industrial leaders and the army, at preserving what could be saved of German industry.[41] Industrialists were under no illusions about the outcome of the war. Their main concern was avoiding the total destruction of their industries in a futile struggle so that they could be swiftly restored and continue in operation when Hitler was gone. Albert Vögler, head of the Federated Steelworks and among the Ruhr's foremost industrial magnates, a long-standing Hitler supporter, asked the Minister directly, in full recognition of the desolate state of the economy, when Hitler would end the conflict. 'We're losing too much substance,' he said. 'How shall we be able to reconstruct if the destruction of industry goes on like this only a few months longer?'[42]

Neither Speer's later actions to fend off Hitler's 'scorched earth' order, nor that order itself, came out of thin air. Under the ever more obvious fiction that immobilizing rather than totally destroying German industrial installations would enable them to be restored to working conditions as soon as the areas lost to military action were retaken, Speer had been issuing corresponding directives both on the eastern and western fronts since July.[43] In early December he had to contend with instructions from Keitel, indicating Hitler's wish that, where industrial installations could be quickly reconstructed to serve the enemy, they should be completely destroyed, not just paralysed. Keitel emphasized in particular that the Saar coal mines should on no account be allowed to fall undestroyed into enemy hands.[44] Speer evidently intervened directly with Hitler to have the order amended. The same day he wired Saarbrücken: 'all directives stating that coal mines are not to be crippled but destroyed are invalid. The Führer has again stipulated today that he only wants the coal mines to be crippled in the way we have established.' Four days later Keitel transmitted Hitler's decision that industrial installations endangered by the enemy in the area of Army Group G were merely to be crippled, not destroyed, and that all contrary orders were cancelled.[45] Speer's exertions to head off the destruction of Germany's industry were not, however, over yet. The big conflict with Hitler on this front still awaited him.

Speer was clear-sighted enough to see the scale of the mounting disaster. But his strenuous efforts to keep the collapsing war economy functioning never wavered. Whatever motives he had, his efforts helped to maintain his position of power and influence at a time when they were under threat.[46] To one so power-conscious, this mattered. Of course, Speer and his able subordinates in the Armaments Ministry, realists as most of them were (apart, perhaps, from the incorrigible super-optimist Saur), knew full well that they could not prevent the inexorable disintegration of the war economy. Without their extraordinary endeavours and capacity for improvisation, however, it is difficult to see how the German war effort could have staggered on until May 1945.

III

The other members of the power quadrumvirate – Goebbels, Himmler and Bormann – also strived to the utmost during the fraught autumn weeks to ensure there was no slackening of the war effort. They gave no hint whatsoever that the war was unwinnable, maintaining a complete grip on the population through propaganda, organization and unrelenting coercion.

One task was to provide the Gauleiter, crucial figures in the power apparatus in the regions, with the backing they felt they needed. Towards the end of October, Bormann had passed on to Himmler a copy of a communication from Gauleiter Friedrich Karl Florian, the provincial boss of the Düsseldorf area and spokesman of the western Gauleiter, about the 'extremely serious and difficult situation' caused by air raids on cities and the transport network. Florian stated that this could not be mastered, and could become threatening, unless accelerated aid from the Reich were forthcoming. Meetings with individual ministers or their officials had so far been without powers of decision. The western Gauleiter now sought 'new ways' to persuade Hitler to order a meeting of ministers, to be chaired by Bormann, to coordinate measures on food, transport, armaments, labour and other urgent issues without delay. Bormann agreed to the meeting but at Hitler's request handed responsibility for it to Himmler.[47]

The meeting took place on 3 November, attended by representatives of the Party, the Wehrmacht, business, and State Secretaries from relevant ministries in the insignificant location of Klein-Berkel in Lower Saxony, not far from Hameln in the Hanover area, well secluded from the threat of air raids. One of Himmler's bright ideas was that towns away from the beleaguered western and eastern areas could sponsor a lorry carrying an electricity generator. The town's name would be proudly displayed on the vehicle, which would come with a driver. 'In this way', Himmler suggested, 'something could be done in good spirit and with humour.' Just as unpromising was his suggestion of creating mobile flak units on trains and lorries to shoot down low-flying bombers. This initiative was to be accompanied by a competition for sharpshooters, organized by the Party, with the winners rewarded with the Iron Cross Second Class. Another suggestion unlikely to be overwhelmed by a rush of volunteers was the setting up of short training sessions on defusing bombs so that ordinary citizens, not just specialists, could help save lives − although often at the expense of their own. Lessons could be learnt from the Russians, who, if no motorized vehicles were available, used ponies and traps, sledges and even prams to carry munitions to the front. 'We have a lot to learn in improvisation,' remarked Himmler.

Manpower had to be pumped into the Gaue of Essen, Düsseldorf and Cologne-Aachen for fortification work to free up labour from these areas to repair the railways. Keeping coal moving and the arteries to the front open was vital. Men were to be housed in barracks and fed in canteens. He would have Bormann dispatch 100,000 men from the Gaue in central Germany to help build the entrenchments. Himmler undertook to provide additional labour from Polish, Slovakian and Russian prisoners of war for railway work. He would also supply around 500–600 prisoners currently held in four goods trains belonging to the SS Railway Construction Brigade, and find another ten trains stuffed with prisoners to complement them. Another 40,000 workers were to be drawn from the mammoth construction body, the *Organisation Todt*, and 500 vehicles commandeered from Italy to move them around. He exhorted the Gauleiter to coordinate emergency food distribution following air raids to ensure that one area was not privileged over another.

He emphasized the value of the *Volkssturm* (to be provided, he declared, with 350,000 rifles before the end of the year). The Warsaw rising had shown − to Germany's cost, he implied − that there was no better defensive position than a ruined city. The *Volkssturm* existed to mobilize the endless resources within the German people for patriotic defence. Fighting to the last bullet in the ruins to defend every German city had to be in deed, not just words. It is hard to imagine that his own words were greatly reassuring for his audience. He ended with a rhetorical flourish, perhaps heard with differing levels of conviction, evoking patriotic defence, a vision of the future and loyalty to Hitler. 'We will defend our land, and are at the start of a great world empire. As the curve sometimes goes down, so one day it will go up again.' He believed all present agreed that the difficulties, however great, could be mastered.

'There are no difficulties that cannot be mastered by us all with dogged tenacity, optimism and humour. I believe all our concerns are small compared with those of one man in Germany, our Führer.' All that was to be done was no more than duty towards 'the man whom we have to thank for the resurrection of Germany, the essence of our existence, Adolf Hitler'.[48]

Himmler had naturally been unable to offer any panacea and was in no position to meet the Gauleiter's demands, given the scale of the transport crisis. The Gauleiter were far from satisfied. All they gained was the hope that sufficient aid would come from the Reich to tide over the worst of the crisis. For the rest, they had to resort to 'self-help' and passing on to the District Leaders responsibility for repairs to the railway in their own areas. The meeting, Goebbels concluded, had come to nothing.[49]

If the Gauleiter were left to cope as best they could, Himmler's address had nevertheless ruled out any alternative to retaining a positive and constructive approach to the worst difficulties. As high representatives of the regime, they were expected not to bow to problems – a sign of weakness and lack of resolve – but to show initiative in finding improvised solutions. Not least, Himmler appealed to their loyalty to Hitler, whose 'charismatic authority' rested ultimately on the personal bonds built into the Nazi system. And as arch-loyalists for many years, who owed their power entirely to Hitler, and who had nothing to lose, the Gauleiter were far from ready to contemplate deserting him. Their bonds to Hitler might have weakened. But they had not broken. The public face of the regime was still not flinching.

The notion of the power of will to overcome difficulties, central to the operation of 'charismatic authority' throughout the system, ran in its essence completely counter to impersonal bureaucratic administration – the basis of all modern states. The Party had always distinguished between the positive, desirable qualities of 'leadership of people' (Menschenführung) and the negative, arid attributes of mere 'administration'. Leaders, at whatever level, 'made things happen'. Bureaucrats simply administered rules and regulations which invariably, unless overridden by 'will', blocked initiative and sapped dynamism. Yet the Party, despite its unbureaucratic ethos, in seeking to implement the wishes and long-term goals of the Führer had, of course, in reality always been intensely bureaucratic as an organization. The tension in trying bureaucratically to work towards unbureaucratic ends had been there from the start, had increased greatly after the takeover of power and had intensified dramatically in conditions of total war.[50]

In late 1944, when less and less could be achieved, the Party bureaucracy went into overdrive.[51] Time and energy were expended by a bloated Party officialdom on the most trivial matters. The Party Chancellery squandered countless hours, for instance, drawing up regulations on the minutiae of *Volkssturm* service – stipulating duties, regulating training periods, laying down rules about clothing and equipment, dealing with exemptions and, among the most notable absurdities, designating letterheads and service seals and providing detailed descriptions of the insignia to be used by different ranks.[52] Goebbels described the bureaucracy involved as 'laughable'.[53] But it was unrelenting. When Bormann moved to Hitler's new field headquarters at Ziegenberg, near Bad Nauheim in Hessen, prior to the start of the Ardennes offensive, he found 'teleprinters were unsuitably installed, no teleprinter cables connected, neither typewriter desks nor shelves set up in the tiny room where my typists have to work'.[54] Even so, the bureaucratic output from his Party Chancellery continued unabated.

The regime's unfolding of bureaucratic, controlling energy at all levels was little short of astonishing. Orders poured out. Every official, however minor, groaned under the suffocating load of paperwork on the desk (despite efforts to save paper).[55] The Reich Post Minister wrote to all the offices of state, at both Reich and regional levels, complaining bitterly that the postal system was greatly overburdened through the increase in bureaucracy. 'A swelling mass of communications like an avalanche' was how he described it, at precisely a time when the damage to the rail network and postal installations, together with loss of personnel to the Wehrmacht, had gravely affected the efficiency of the service.[56] His urgent entreaties to reduce the level of post fell on deaf ears.

More and more was controlled, orchestrated, regulated, ordained, militarized, directed and organized, yet less and less resulted from all the effort – except, crucially, the stifling of all remaining limited levels of personal free space in the system. If 'total society' has a meaning in the sense that little or nothing not subjected to regime control existed any longer, and that opinion deviating from the official stance could be openly expressed only at great personal risk, then Germany towards the end of 1944 was approaching such a state.

As living conditions worsened drastically under the pounding from Allied bombs, the pressure on the population intensified. The total-war effort, for instance, far from subsiding after the extreme exertions of the late summer, redoubled its attempt in the autumn to dredge up all possible remaining reserves of manpower for the Wehrmacht. Goebbels pointed out at the beginning of November that by this time 900,000 extra men had been provided for the Wehrmacht. But he admitted it was not enough. The losses in the previous three months had numbered 1.2 million. He wanted Hitler's support for pressing a reluctant Speer to surrender more men from the armaments sector. Speer eventually agreed to give up 30,000 men, though only temporarily until they could be redeployed once the transport situation had improved. Goebbels could not accept the condition, so the matter was left to be resolved by Hitler. As so often, no decision was forthcoming.[57]

More important for Goebbels, however, was for him to have authority from Hitler to 'comb out' the Wehrmacht for additional personnel to be sent to the front, as he had done earlier in the civilian sector. He finally managed to gain Hitler's signature to a decree to this effect on 10 December. Goebbels felt revitalized, bursting with new energy, and determined to overcome all opposition within the army itself to raise new forces for Hitler. He expected – once more working through a small directing staff and the Gauleiter at the regional level – to attain very positive results in the New Year. He was convinced that only his total-war drive had made the coming western offensive at all possible. He now hoped, he said, to be able to give the Führer the basis of an offensive army in the east, as the 'combing out' of the civilian sector had provided one for the west.[58]

It was, of course, wishful thinking. But in these weeks Goebbels veered between an evident sense of realism about Germany's plight, brought home to him most forcefully through the destruction of one German city after another through Allied bombing (which, unlike Hitler, he saw at first hand in visits to bombed-out localities), and continued hope that willpower, shored up by propaganda, would sustain the fight, whatever the odds, until the shaky enemy coalition cracked. 'The political crisis in the enemy camp grows daily' was only one of repeated assertions that the internal divisions, and the losses they were suffering, would split the coalition before long.[59] Numerous diary entries hint at scepticism about Germany's position. And when he viewed the impressive new, highly modern U-boats being built in Bremen at the end of November, he sighed despairingly that it was all too late.[60] Yet he had far from given up hope. Following a long talk with Hitler – lasting deep into the night – a few days later, when the embattled Führer exuded confidence, expounded excitedly on the forthcoming offensive and envisioned a grandiose rebuilding of German cities and revitalization of culture after the war, Goebbels was so excited that he could not sleep.[61] He was still, as he always had been, in thrall to Hitler.

Propaganda, in his view, had the vital task of reinforcing the will to resist, 'in strengthening the backbone of the nation again and restoring its diminished self-confidence'.[62] Ceremonies held throughout Germany where the newly created *Volkssturm* swore their oaths of allegiance – around 100,000 men in ten separate ceremonies in Berlin alone on Sunday, 12 November – were part of this task. In seasonal mist and with the ruins of the Wilhelmplatz as a macabre backdrop, Goebbels addressed the arrayed *Volkssturm* men from the balcony of the Propaganda Ministry. 'Some are already armed,' he recorded in his diary – unwittingly acknowledging the impoverished levels of support for the new organization. In fact, rifles, bazookas and some machine guns had been handed out just before the ceremony. Few of the men knew how to use them, but in any case they had to give them up again once the ceremony was over. Silence fell across the square as, lacking uniforms, they doffed their caps and hats in an oath to the Führer before marching past 'in sacred earnestness'. Everything was filmed to make a big impression in the newsreels. The optical effect was excellent, remarked Goebbels' aide Wilfred von Oven. But what the cameras did not show were young boys and soldiers on leave standing on the footpaths and doing their best not to laugh at the march-past. The *Volkssturm* was not worth 'a shot of powder' in von Oven's view.[63]

As a further attempt to maintain fighting spirit, Goebbels had in 1943 commissioned the colour film *Kolberg* – a grand spectacular aimed at turning the defence of the Pomeranian coastal town of that name during the Napoleonic Wars into a heroic epic to inspire the present-day defenders of the Reich.[64] By the end of 1944 the film – with an enormous cast of extras, apparently including 187,000 soldiers temporarily removed from active service at a time when new recruits for the front were being so desperately sought – was almost ready. Goebbels was hugely impressed, on seeing a rough-cut at the beginning of December, by what he called a 'masterpiece' that 'answered all the questions now bothering the German people'. He had great expectations of the film, which he thought worth 'a victorious battle' in its likely impact on the mood of the public.[65] But he feared 'scenes of destruction and despair' would have the effect that in the current situation many Germans would decide against viewing it.[66] As the comment betrays, Goebbels was fully aware of the uphill task he faced in overcoming the deep pall of gloom in Germany as the disastrous year of 1944 neared its close.

IV

The reports reaching Goebbels from the regional propaganda offices left no doubt of the worrying state of morale. News of the success in repelling the Red Army in East Prussia made scarcely a dent in the depressed mood in early November. Feelings ranged from extreme anxiety about the future and anger at being left defenceless as bombs rained down on German cities to wearied resignation (also among Party members, especially in the west) and fatalism. Large parts of the population just wanted 'peace at any price'.[67] In western regions, where the population was most exposed to the nightly horror of devastation from the skies, now being inflicted upon most of Germany's big industrial cities, the mood was at rock bottom. Amid the jangled nerves and constant worry, Goebbels noted, 'outright anger towards the Party, held responsible for the war and its consequences', could be heard.[68]

It was scarcely surprising. Cologne, for instance, was subjected to another huge attack on the night of 30 October in what one witness described as the city's 'death blow'. The quarter of a million people still living there – until the heavy raids started there had been around 800,000 – had no gas or electricity. The little water available was only to be had at hydrants in the street. The NSV distributed meagre food rations to people standing in queues. Almost all remaining habitable parts of the city were now destroyed. There was a stampede to leave as masses of refugees gathered with their few possessions at the Rhine bridges. But an immediate organized evacuation was impossible because of lack of transport. The rail crisis meant trains could not be laid on. Any military vehicle going east was stopped and loaded to capacity with those fleeing the city. There was much bitterness directed at the regime and a sense of the futility of the conflict. The exodus lasted for more than a week. Cologne was now 'virtually a ghost city'. As Goebbels put it, 'this lovely Rhine metropolis has at least for the time being to be written off'.[69]

Among the remnants of the population, housed in improvised barracks or surviving in cellars in the ruined shell of the city, groups of dissident youths, foreign workers, deserted soldiers and former Communist Party members took to despairing kinds of partisan-like active resistance, which reached its climax in December. With hand grenades and machine guns that they had managed to steal from Wehrmacht depots, they waged their own war against the Cologne police, killing the head of the Gestapo in the city and, in one incident, engaging in a twelve-hour armed battle with police before being overwhelmed. Only with difficulty did the Gestapo attain the upper hand before taking savage vengeance on the 200 or so members of the resistance groups whom they arrested.[70]

No similar action materialized in the other cities of the Rhine–Ruhr industrial belt. But hundreds of thousands experienced similar misery to that of the population of Cologne following the devastating raids on Bochum, Duisburg, Oberhausen and other major cities of the region over the autumn. The mood in the Ruhr was bad.[71] The air war was creating 'a downright despairing mood', Goebbels noted from the reports reaching him.[72] There was only a single topic of conversation: 'the war-weariness of all people'.[73]

Still, there was no collapse of discipline either in the workplace or in the army. People carried out to the best of their ability what they took to be their duty.[74] There were no signs of sabotage, strikes or – beyond the events in Cologne – other prominent forms of resistance.[75] Dr Walther Rohland thought shortly after the end of the war that the reason for what he saw as the extraordinary effort made by workers who had little enthusiasm for the war (or the regime) was that 'each single person felt clearly that on the one hand there was no opportunity for the individual to take action against the war'. 'However, if the war was lost, then, in contrast to 1914–18, Germany also, and with her the possibilities of existence for the individual, would be lost'.[76] Such fears were given sustenance by the propaganda gift of the 'Morgenthau Plan' – as the programme prepared by the US Secretary to the Treasury, Henry

Morgenthau, to split up post-war Germany into a powerless, dismembered country with a pre-industrial economy swiftly became known to the German public.[77]

On 12 December Goebbels went to the Ruhr district to assess the situation for himself, and while he was there witnessed a heavy air raid on Witten, turning much of the town into a raging inferno. He also saw the misery of the 100,000-strong population of Bochum, deprived of all amenities, existing in primitive conditions in cellars and little more than holes in the ground. His speech in the Krupp factory in Essen failed to rouse the grim-faced workers who had been dragooned into hearing him, collars turned up against the bitter cold, hands deep in their pockets. The applause was meagre and had scarcely died down when the sirens began to wail. The Propaganda Minister and his entourage had swiftly to take cover in the vaulted cellars deep underground, where they encountered 'grey, disconsolate faces'. Little was said, but the glances on the men's faces were 'not friendly'.[78] Goebbels was made fully aware of the strength of feeling among the Party and industrial leaders of the Rhine and Ruhr about the failings of Göring (blamed for the inability to protect German cities against the 'gangsters of the air'), and also Ribbentrop (held generally in contempt, and seen as inept in his conduct of foreign policy), but came away convinced of their continued 'blind, unshakeable faith' in Hitler.[79] In early December, Goebbels was still persuading himself that 'faith in the Führer is largely unshaken and many' – after seeing the troop build-up near the western front and sensing a coming offensive – 'are again beginning to believe in a German victory'.[80]

It was in the main a delusion. It is true that among the Party elite, those wielding power in the regions as well as at the centre of the regime, there were no signs that loyalty towards Hitler was starting to flake.[81] And in enabling the regime to continue to function, this is what mattered. Among the civilian population, however, beyond Party diehards and sections of youth, it was in the main a different matter. By the end of November, propaganda reports were indicating 'the danger of a crisis in confidence in the leadership' which 'can no longer be ignored'. The concern was seen as important and urgent.[82] For the first time, Hitler had failed to speak in person – Himmler read out his proclamation – at the annual gathering in Munich of the Party 'Old Guard' for the Putsch commemoration on 8 November. Immediately, rumours flared up (mostly arising from foreign speculation) that he was dead, or seriously ill, had suffered a nervous breakdown, or had fled and that Himmler or Goebbels had taken over.[83] Still, popular belief in Hitler had not altogether vanished. And indeed, even at this late hour there were those who clung as a drowning man clings to a piece of wood to their long-held faith in the Führer, and in his ability to save Germany. But such people were in a dwindling minority. Hitler's charisma, in the sense of its popular appeal, was by now fast fading.

On the eve of the Ardennes offensive, Goebbels recorded in his diary a somewhat sobering assessment of popular feeling on the basis of the reports – themselves inevitably tending to emphasize the positive wherever they could – sent in by the regional propaganda offices. 'The scepticism in the German public continues,' he noted. 'There's no proper faith in German powers of resistance ... There have been too many military disappointments recently for the people to be easily able to build up hopes.'[84]

Generalizations about attitudes among soldiers are hazardous. Rank, temperament and earlier approaches towards Nazism affected their mindset. There were reports, for instance, of poor morale among the new recruits of the People's Grenadier divisions.[85] Among battle-hardened veterans, however, it was often a different story. Confidence instilled by generals such as Model was a further factor affecting morale. The situation on the different fronts – and parts of the fronts – produced widely varying experiences and perspectives.

In the late autumn of 1944, away from the continuing bitter fighting in Hungary, the eastern front was relatively quiet. A naval officer who had been based in Memel, then Gotenhafen (now Gdynia), on the Baltic near Danzig, was shocked in the autumn when he travelled through southern Germany. He felt as if he had been until now living on an isolated island as he encountered repeated bombing attacks from low-flying aircraft and constant controls by the military police in the overcrowded compartments of slow-moving, greatly delayed trains. The experience made him and his fellow officers 'deeply pessimistic, in part even despairing'. During the return journey, when almost all in the train were en route to fight the Soviets, he was struck by the unequivocal criticism of the Party and its functionaries. These were blamed for the unstoppable partisan warfare in the east, seen to have been caused by their brutal treatment of the population.[86]

Another officer, based in south-west Germany, was also deeply affected by what he saw while on leave in late November. Though he did not have far to travel, even short rail journeys were difficult. His heavily delayed train was packed with refugees and evacuees, many of them women and children. He was struck, as they journeyed through villages near the front, by the crowded roads, full of people carrying their few possessions and hoping to find refuge somewhere in the Reich. He eventually reached home in Emmendingen only to be told of the bombing on 27 November of nearby Freiburg, a town with a medieval core of picture-book attractiveness not far from the Swiss border to the south, without strategic or industrial significance, and with a population of more than 100,000. When he travelled to Freiburg a couple of days later, he could scarcely believe his eyes. Practically the entire old town had been obliterated. Only the glorious Gothic minster, its tall spire the very symbol of the town, was left standing, if badly damaged, much as Cologne's cathedral had withstood everything the Allies had thrown at the city. Almost 3,000 bodies lay beneath the rubble. It was a terrible picture of devastation. The helpless rage of the survivors, amid the all-embracing misery, was directed only in part at the Allied bombing crews; it was aimed more at the Nazi Party and its leaders who had provoked such outrages. When his leave was over, the officer travelled northwards through Mannheim and Koblenz, again deeply saddened and troubled by the destruction of once lovely towns. Amid the ruined buildings of Koblenz, at the confluence of the Rhine and the Mosel, he was reminded of how the 'prophecy' that Robert Ley, the Labour Front leader, had made in 1933 had in an unintended sense come true: 'in ten years' time you won't recognize your town.'[87]

This sardonic comment reflected a weary resignation at the scale of the destruction. Such sentiments were commonplace. But other attitudes among soldiers were less pessimistic, and still supportive of the regime and what they took to be Germany's aims in continuing the struggle. One sergeant, writing home in early December, spoke wistfully of the coming 'feast of peace' at Christmas. However, the bombs were still raining down and the bells not ringing out for the peace 'which is so yearned for by all peace-loving peoples'. 'Our enemies', he continued, 'have no understanding for this wish', and so 'we, the entire German people, still stand during this feast in a fierce struggle against these degenerate peoples, led by Jewish parasites who know no fatherland nor have one'.[88]

Within the SS, unsurprisingly, outrightly Nazified views were still prevalent. An SS corporal, sympathizing with his family's living conditions after an air raid on Munich but relieved that they were well, blamed the 'air terror' on the Jews 'because the damned Jews are worried about their sack of money and see that the entire world slowly understands that they are guilty of wars and are making money out of blood and tears'. He believed, however, 'that we will be victorious, though it will still cost much sacrifice and suffering'.[89] Along with many other soldiers, he had great hopes of the V2 rockets launched at Antwerp and London, after published reports of the destruction they had caused in the British capital. 'The V2 are all the talk with us,' he wrote in mid-November. 'Perhaps they can be fired on America. . . . I believe for certain that the final victory will be ours.'[90] A corporal, writing home the same day, hoped that the V2 would 'bring a decision with England' in 1945. Then it would be Russia's turn in 1946. 'I can't help it. I have the feeling that all will be well,' he commented.[91] A gunner writing to his family from Schneidemühl in Pomerania rejoiced at the news of the V2 attacks on England. 'Great, isn't it?' he remarked. The arrogance of the Allies, he felt, was being paid back in kind. His confidence had also been bolstered by the way, seemingly against the odds, German troops had managed to stabilize the fronts. 'The German soldier has again proved that he is not yet beaten after five years of war,' he proudly stated.[92]

An Army High Command censorship report in early November, which came into Allied hands, indicated that such attitudes were not isolated. Of course, it was sensible to avoid negative comments in letters that passed under the censor's eyes and could have dire repercussions, but there was no requirement to express outrightly pro-Nazi or glowingly positive comments on the war. Yet the German censor's report stated: 'In spite of the fact that there are now more letters showing a rather weak belief in the final victory, the whole of the mail still proves a strong confidence. They still trust the Führer as much as ever, and some even think that the destiny of the German people depends on him alone.' The main qualification was the increased doubts about new weapons and the view that 'all our efforts are useless if the new weapons are not committed very soon'.[93]

Among higher officers, though attitudes towards the Nazi leadership varied, there was no hint of disloyalty to Hitler. For the sustenance of the regime, this was crucial. Even those far from enthusiastic about Nazism and writing privately could still find much to applaud in Hitler. In diary comments he made in late December, Colonel Curt Pollex, in charge of officer training at Döberitz, the troop-training grounds west of Berlin, was critical of the Party and the 'bigwigs' running it but complimentary about Hitler. He remarked positively on the need for National Socialism and the justification for the war (blame for which he attributed to Roosevelt and Stalin). Germany had to break the Versailles Treaty, he claimed, and the timing of the war had been correct. Some of Hitler's underlings were rogues and idiots who had deceived him and the people. But, despite evident crass errors in military matters, 'big-mouth propaganda' and other nonsense, Colonel Pollex still thought the direction of the state leadership was right. If Hitler was ill and could no longer cope, then he should resign; but no decent person of judgement should underrate what he had achieved.[94]

Beyond continued loyalty to Hitler, there was in the officer corps still an independent 'code of honour'. This had not hindered complicity in atrocities in the eastern campaigns, but it did offer its own block on action that might undermine the war effort. Major-General Johannes Bruhn, commander of a People's Grenadier division before being captured on the western front in November 1944, and regarded by his captors as 'anti-Nazi' in attitude, spoke of suggestions emanating from Switzerland that German generals should lay down their arms. 'That couldn't be reconciled with their honour. It couldn't possibly be done: it's absolutely out of the question,' he remarked to fellow officers, unaware that his comments were being bugged by his British captors. 'The officer corps loves its country, and believes implicitly in its own respectability and ideas of honour and lives accordingly; and like a trusting child considers it quite impossible that it is being wrongly led, and that the command is other than it says it is, and that they have stained their hands with blood etc. in the most revolting way.'[95]

Such fragments of a mosaic never build into a complete picture. As far as it is possible to generalize, it seems that morale within the Wehrmacht was somewhat better than within the civilian population. Attitudes varied widely and as in the civilian population scepticism, apathy and resignation were evident among soldiers, alongside anxiety about loved ones suffering and dying in the bombing raids, and worry about the future. A rise in the number of desertions, though punishable by death, tells its own story.[96] About 350 members of the Wehrmacht each month in the second half of 1944 were sentenced to death for desertion.[97] Precise motives for desertion are not easy to establish. Probably, fear and desperation played a big part. Most soldiers were by now, like the civilian population, war-weary, just longing for the fighting to stop and to be able to get out of the daily misery and back home. However, there was also commitment, determination, a sense of patriotic duty and, among a minority, still a belief in Hitler. The vast majority of soldiers – probably without much reflection – did what they were told to do by their officers. The unquestioning obedience that was the axiom of military life, not just in Germany, continued to prevail. 'If the troops don't want [to fight], it's all hopeless,' remarked Colonel Pollex.[98] Despite everything, the troops *did* want to fight – or at least were prepared to do so. Whatever they thought of the war, Hitler's leadership, Germany's plight, their own hopes of survival, for the overwhelming number of ordinary soldiers there was no sense of any alternative but to continue fighting. Unlike the last months of the First World War, there was no danger of mutiny in the ranks feeding into internal collapse.

V

There was, indeed, optimism among the German troops who advanced into the Ardennes on the early morning of 16 December. Many, according to General von Manteuffel, still believed in Hitler's ability to turn the tide through new 'wonder weapons' and U-boats, and saw it as their task to win him time.[99] The early stages of the offensive were so successful that the optimism and belief seemed justified. The cloak of secrecy over the operation had worked superbly. The Allies were caught completely unawares. And the bad weather, significantly hindering Allied air strikes, was exactly what the Germans wanted. Enemy forward positions were swiftly overrun. On the northern flank, Dietrich's 6th SS-Panzer Army, hampered by bad roads and transport difficulties as well as stiff resistance, made relatively slow progress, though its most advanced troops included the SS-Panzer Regiment 1, commanded by the brutal SS-Obersturmbannführer Joachim Peiper, which left a trail of atrocities in its wake, murdering more than eighty American prisoners of war near Malmédy as it went on its way. Further south, Manteuffel's 5th Panzer Army made initial spectacular progress, breaking the American lines, taking some 8,000–9,000 prisoners, and opening up a gap of more than 30 kilometres in the front. His troops poured through the opening, and had pressed forward by 18 December – though, held up by barely passable roads and detonated bridges, still more slowly than the operational plan required – almost to the Meuse, a distance of some 100 kilometres, where they encountered heavy American resistance at the vital communications point of Bastogne. The town had to be taken and the Meuse crossed if the planned advance on Antwerp was to have the remotest chance of success. But the offensive was slowing. And on 19 December, Eisenhower halted Allied offensive action along the rest of the front in order to rush reinforcements to the Meuse. Hitler's offensive was on the verge of stalling.[100]

To the troops this was far from clear. One lieutenant was impressed that day, he recorded in his diary, as the 'endless columns of prisoners pass; at first, about a hundred, half of them negroes, later another thousand'. When his vehicle stuck, he found none other than Field-Marshal Model – 'a little, undistinguished looking man with a monocle' – directing traffic. The roads, the junior officer noted, were 'littered with destroyed American vehicles, cars and tanks. Another column of prisoners passes. I count over a thousand men.'[101] Another lieutenant, with explicitly Nazi views, was elated at the offensive and delighted in the brutality as he thought the tables were now being turned on the Americans. 'You cannot imagine what glorious hours and days we are experiencing now,' he told his wife in his letter home.

It looks as if the Americans cannot withstand our important push. Today we overtook a fleeing column and finished it . . . It was a glorious bloodbath, vengeance for our destroyed homeland. Our soldiers still have the same old zip. Always advancing and smashing everything. The snow must turn red with American blood. Victory was never as close as it is now. The decision will soon be reached. We will throw them into the ocean, the arrogant, big-mouthed apes from the New World. They will not get into our Germany. We will protect our wives and children from all enemy domination. If we are to preserve all tender and beautiful aspects of our lives, we cannot be too brutal in the deciding moments of this struggle.[102]

Such extreme attitudes (encouraged by propaganda concoctions on the terror of American 'negro soldiers', including the base calumny that 'drunken niggers murder German children'[103]) were almost certainly no rarity, but conceivably less representative than the contrasting views entered in the diary of a soldier, killed in January, whose unwillingness to fight was coloured by the destruction of his home in Hamburg and the blame he attached for this personal tragedy and the wider calamity of the war to Hitler and the Nazis. 'On the 16th December, about 05.30 in the morning, we attacked,' he wrote. 'I shall march once more through Belgium and France, but I don't have the smallest desire to do so ... If [only] this idiotic war would end. Why should I fight? It only goes for the existence of the Nazis. The superiority of our enemy is so great that it is senseless to fight against it.'[104]

How most soldiers felt as they advanced into the Ardennes is impossible to assess. Their main consideration was probably survival – living to tell the tale – coupled with daring to hope that this offensive might indeed prove a turning point on the way to a peace. Letters and diary jottings from soldiers serving in the Ardennes and on other fronts suggest that such hopes were widespread. 'I think the war in the west is again turning,' wrote a corporal from the 3rd Panzer Grenadier Division on 17 December. 'The main thing is that the war will soon be decided and I'll be coming home again to my dear wife and we can again build a new home. The radio is now playing bells from the homeland.'[105] Another corporal learnt of the attack when Field-Marshal Model's proclamation to his soldiers was read out in the barracks. 'Hopefully, the change will now come for Germany to a successful final struggle and peace in the foreseeable future,' he jotted in his diary.[106] An NCO based in the Courland echoed the sentiment. 'The news from yesterday's OKW report, that the offensive in the west has begun, will certainly have filled you with great joy,' he wrote. 'We were all thrilled here. No one had reckoned with that before Christmas. Let's hope that it will bring the decision and with it the end of the war in the west.'[107]

At home, the mood was also suddenly lifted at the news of the offensive. The first the public heard was through the brief OKW report on 18 December. Goebbels was personally elated and more than ready to take the credit for making the offensive possible by raising troops to take part through his ruthless total-war drive. It showed, he thought, what could be done through toughness, resilience and refusal to capitulate in

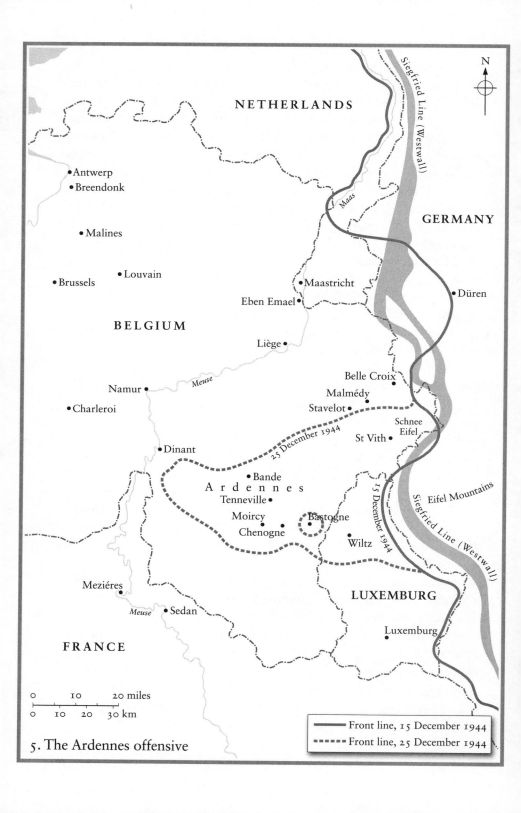

5. The Ardennes offensive

| | Front line, 15 December 1944 |
| | Front line, 25 December 1944 |

the face of difficulties or be discouraged through 'minor setbacks'. He nevertheless advocated caution in the reportage in order not to arouse exaggerated expectations.[108] Newspapers publicized the offensive for the first time on 19 December, and, following Goebbels' instructions, without trumpet-blowing.[109] The response to the German attack was, even so, immediate and hugely enthusiastic. 'Great surprise' and a 'deep inner joy' were recorded by propaganda offices as early reactions to the OKW news. There was a sense of being 'freed from a nightmare'. 'What a lovely Christmas present' was a sentiment frequently heard. That such an offensive could be launched had in itself significantly raised confidence in the leadership and the strength of the Reich, even if it was abundantly plain 'that the whole of France and Belgium would not be reconquered immediately'.[110] A day later, Goebbels was convinced that the impact on morale within the Reich was unquestionably successful. 'The few sentences in the OKW report on Monday [18 December] have prompted a mood in the country which recalls the great times of our offensives,' he recorded. 'In Berlin that evening the entire Christmas schnapps rations were consumed. The people are deeply joyous that we have again gained the initiative, especially since no one in the public, other than the few in the know, had expected that. The surprise is all the greater as a result.'[111]

The Wehrmacht's own propaganda agents, secretly taking soundings in Berlin, acknowledged the 'very good mood', despite trying to dampen the excessive optimism of the 'hurrah-patriots'. Some thought the French and Belgians would this time welcome German troops with open arms after they had had the chance to experience 'Anglo-American occupation'.[112] A positive impression was also gleaned by those outside the German propaganda apparatus. A Swedish correspondent in Berlin reported great enthusiasm at the news of the offensive, exhilaration and confidence among soldiers and a lifting of the gloom that had earlier prevailed.[113] But the euphoria could not last. Already by Christmas it was fading.

The news from the front remained positive for some days. Hitler himself was in high spirits, like a man rejuvenated.[114] The small town of Saint-Vith on the north of the front was taken on the 21st, but, further south, the more important Bastogne, heavily besieged (and tying down three German divisions in the process), still held out. Manteuffel's troops, from the 5th Panzer Army, bogged down in mud as well as facing fierce resistance, could make only slow progress. On 23 December they reached Buissonville and Celles, about 7 kilometres from the Meuse, east of Dinant. But that was as far as they got. The high point of the offensive had already passed.

Rundstedt had expressed doubts on 20 December about the chances of crossing the Meuse (though Model was at this time still more optimistic).[115] Karl Otto Saur, close to supplanting Speer as Hitler's blue-eyed boy in the Armaments Ministry, said after the war that he had realized the offensive had failed as early as 19 December (implying that this was the date at which he knew the war was lost).[116] Model told Speer on 23 December that the offensive had failed.[117] It was plain to any perceptive soldier by 24 December, General Guderian later commented, that the offensive had finally broken down.[118] By Christmas, the American and British reinforcements rushed to the area had shored up Allied defences. On 26 December, armoured units from Patton's 3rd US Army, which had hastened northwards, finally broke through to the encircled American troops in Bastogne and ended the siege.[119] Model still vainly hoped for a regrouping of forces to regain the initiative near Bastogne, and at least cement more limited goals than Antwerp, which he acknowledged was now out of reach. But Manteuffel's advance was at an end. It had been spectacular while it lasted, but could go no further.

Meanwhile, the weather had cleared and Allied aircraft were now fully able to exert their superiority as their ceaseless attacks – the Allies flew six times more sorties during the offensive than Göring's crippled Luftwaffe – pounded German supply lines. Reinforcements of men and *matériel* were, as Rundstedt admitted on 27 December, impossible under these circumstances.[120] Allied losses of 76,890 men killed, wounded or captured actually outnumbered the 67,461 on the German side. But the German losses could not be made good, nor could the 600 tanks which the Allies had destroyed. Whatever gloss was put upon it, the last great German offensive had failed.

The failure only gradually became apparent to the German public. Goebbels soon began to hint at setbacks in the offensive and accepted by 29 December that the advance could go no further, that the Germans would be happy to hold on to their territorial gains. But there was a time lag in popular recognition. As the end of the year approached, with the offensive stalled, many people, noted Goebbels, still had high hopes, nourished by soldiers returning from the west and talking of getting to

Paris before New Year. It was 'naturally absolute rubbish', he remarked, but added: 'Large parts of the German people are convinced that the war in the west could be ended in the forseeable future.'[121] Yet only two days later, on the very last day of 1944, he offered a contradictory assessment, on the basis of reports from the regional propaganda offices. 'The German people attaches no exaggerated illusions to the western offensive,' he now stated, and had in mind only 'smaller aims, though naturally everyone earnestly wishes that we will come to a decisive blow in the west'.[122] The bubble had burst. It was a sobering return to realities. One officer, based in the west, drew his own conclusion from Field-Marshal Model's New Year proclamation to his soldiers, in which he had declared: 'You have withstood the tests of the year 1944. You have held watch on the Rhine.' This meant, the officer concluded, that after being forced to give up 'fortress Europe', holding on to 'fortress Germany' would indeed prove a success.[123]

VI

After the failure of the Ardennes offensive, it was as good as impossible – apart from the incorrigible optimists who insisted on the coming 'wonder weapons' or a split among the Allies – to hold out any further realistic hope of a positive end to the war for Germany. The regime, almost all Germans could see, was utterly doomed. No one beneath Hitler, who as always ruled out any alternative to fighting on, was, however, either able or willing to do anything about it. So nothing changed internally.

The sixth war Christmas was a muted affair, with much talk of striving further for the yearned-for peace and even more of holding out against mighty enemies. At the most miserable New Year celebrations in memory, Hitler's exhortations offered few hopes of major change in 1945. Amid the routinely effusive outpourings of the propaganda offices about the revitalizing effect of the 'Führer speech', it was impossible to conceal the widespread disappointment that Hitler had no reassurance to offer on the deployment of new weapons, the status of the offensive in the west (which he did not even mention), and, most crucially, the breaking of the terror from the air. Many people, it was said (without a trace of irony) were left with tears in their eyes at the end of the speech. Some, in fact, were unable to hear it because they were without electricity.[124] For all its bombast and the usual bile poured out on the 'Jewish-international world conspiracy' that was bent on destroying Germany, Hitler's speech could promise no more than further hardship, suffering and bloodshed without an end in sight.[125] Whatever the miserable prospects, for ordinary people at the base of society, civilian and military, there was little to be done other than struggle on with their daily existence.

The Nazi regime remained an immensely strong dictatorship, holding together in the mounting adversity and prepared to use increasingly brutal force in controlling and regimenting German society at more or less every point. It left little room for opposition – recognizably as suicidal as it was futile. With varying degrees of enthusiasm, ranging from the hundred-percenter hold-out-to-the-last contingent down to the majority simply going through the motions, officialdom – high and low – continued to do its duty. Here, too, most civil servants could not see any alternative. So the bureaucratic wheels kept turning, and with them the attritional grind of controls was sustained. No matter, however trivial, was beneath their attention. Amid the myriad concerns of local civil servants, as they tried to cope with huge social dislocation after air raids, refugee problems, housing shortages, food rationing and many other issues, they never lost sight of the need to complete forms and have them officially stamped for approval. Officials in the Munich police department spent time and energy (as well as using reams of precious paper) in December 1944 making sure that five cleaning-buckets were ordered to replace those lost in the recent air raid, deciding how to obtain copies of official periodicals that regulations said had to come from post offices (even though these were now destroyed), or obtaining permission for a usable iron heater to be taken to police headquarters, left without heating after the last bombing.[126] At the top of the bureaucratic tree, the head of the Reich Chancellery, Lammers, his powers meanwhile largely usurped by Bormann, had little more to do than remind Reich authorities of the Führer's wish that the sending of Christmas and New Year greetings should be greatly restricted to minimize the burden on transport and postal services.[127]

The overlapping, often competing, bureaucracy of the Party was equally cumbersome and even more oppressive for ordinary citizens. Practically every aspect of civil defence was now orchestrated by the

Party. The frequent whine of the sirens produced frenetic attempts to usher people into air-raid shelters, organize the clearance of damage after the devastation, try to provide welfare and accommodation for those without homes (with the help of the hopelessly overstretched NSV) and arrange emergency food distribution (still holding up remarkably well, in contrast to the near famine towards the end of the First World War), among an array of other tasks. In a different society, such efforts might have met with gratitude and approval. By now, however, few beyond the ranks of the diehards could find much else than feelings of anger and bitterness towards the Party functionaries who, even at this stage, combined their attempts at welfare with ceaseless hectoring and haranguing through pointless propaganda and with the surveillance and monitoring that could have dire consequences for any who stepped out of line.

At a higher level of the Party, the Gauleiter, whatever their mounting inner despair at the ever deteriorating situation following the short-lived raising of hopes, had little option but to stick with Hitler. In their own provinces, they were still figures of real power, capable of ferocious repression against any lesser mortals who appeared to pose a threat. Beyond their own domain, however, they were a divided group, and incapable of any unified positive action to avoid the gathering maelstrom of self-destruction, certain only that their own destinies were bound up with the inevitable demise of the regime.

Survival strategies varied, though they usually involved some refusal to accept reality. Göring was probably among the more realistic in recognizing the irredeemable destruction of the Luftwaffe, though he still paid frequent visits to airfields to spur on his demoralized air crews. He retreated as much as he could to the luxury of his palatial country residence at Carinhall, in the Schorfheide 65 kilometres north of Berlin, well away from Hitler's proximity and the malign influence of Bormann. There he could surround himself with fawning friends and relatives, dress in outlandish garb, pop his codeine pills and bemoan the failings of Luftwaffe generals.[128] He had long been a spent force. Ribbentrop was still insisting, a week into January, that the Ardennes offensive had been a success and telling the Japanese ambassador, Oshima Hiroshi, that 'Germany now holds the initiative everywhere'. He was adamant that the Allied coalition was bound to split if Germany and Japan could hold out until the end of 1945 and harboured illusions that peace could even at this late hour be negotiated.[129] Robert Ley, when he was sober, fell into reveries about a coming social revolution, remaining at the same time one of Hitler's most fanatical lieutenants in advocating an all or nothing showdown with the enemy.[130]

Bormann was another with flights of fancy, as, evidently, was his wife, Gerda. Writing to her on 26 December, as the Ardennes offensive was petering out and with it Germany's last military hope of success, he referred to her 'ideas about things to come' as 'by no means extravagant', and outlined his own future scenario.

> There is no doubt that in the future we shall be compelled to build important factories and the like deep beneath the earth's surface. Wherever towns and villages are built on a slope it will be necessary at once to dig deep shafts into the hill or mountainside, with special cellars – storerooms – for all inhabitants. In the new manor farms which we are going to build in the north, the buildings will have to be constructed with three or four basements, and collective shelters must be built at various points for the whole village community from the start.

Gerda found the plans for post-war construction intriguing, but was 'boundlessly furious at the thought that we, with our innate longing for light and sunshine, should be compelled by the Jews to make our abodes as if we were beings of the underworld'.[131]

Himmler, who in mid-December, when he was temporarily based in the Black Forest as Commander-in-Chief of the newly formed Army Group Upper Rhine, was rumoured to have fallen into disgrace at Führer Headquarters, cherished the belief that Britain would come to see that its interests lay in joining forces with Germany to combat advancing Soviet power on the Continent. He thought of himself as an essential element of that continued fight.[132] Goebbels remained among the more clear-sighted Nazi leaders, cautious from the outset about the chances of a major triumph in the Ardennes. He too, however, ended the year in good spirits, convinced that the offensive had widened the conflict between the Allies, that the Germans had won back the initiative in the west and reduced the pressure on the western front.[133] The enigmatic Speer was the least given to fanciful illusions among Nazi leaders. He knew the full extent of Germany's economic plight. And he had seen at first hand the realities of the Ardennes offensive, the hopelessness, despite the initial successes, of the attempt to break the stranglehold of mightily superior enemy forces. For Speer, so he later claimed, 'with the Ardennes offensive the war was at an end', apart from the drawn-out process of enemy occupation of Germany.[134] But Speer's desire for power and influence, as well as ambitions, even now, to play some part in a world after Hitler, kept him going. However resigned he was to Germany's impending defeat, he saw no way out – and no course of action other than doing all he could to sustain the German war effort.

Among the generals – beyond the leadership of the OKW where, in Hitler's direct proximity, illusions still held sway – there was widespread recognition that defences were now desperately overstretched, resources as good as at an end, the chances of staving off powerful enemies minimal. General of the Waffen-SS Karl Wolff, formerly chief of Himmler's personal staff and now 'Plenipotentiary General of the German Wehrmacht' in Italy, became finally convinced that the war was irretrievably lost through conversations with young SS officers who had been part of the spearhead of the Ardennes offensive.[135] Guderian probably spoke for most generals in his frustration with Hitler's leadership and the crass inflexibility which had worsened Germany's position. He acknowledged the size of the odds stacked against the Wehrmacht, given the immense disproportion in military might of the enemy. He felt, nevertheless, that it was necessary to continue to strain every sinew in the struggle to fend off the assault on the Reich, and to gain time – perhaps for the Allied coalition to crack, perhaps for some negotiated end to the nightmare, perhaps . . . who knew for what?

Aware of what was coming on the eastern front, Guderian pleaded in vain with Jodl for the transfer of troops from the west. Jodl refused, insisting that they were needed to retain the initiative in the west.[136] The subsidiary offensive in Alsace, code-named 'North Wind', for which the troops, desperately needed in the east, were allegedly so vital, had been intended to bolster the southern flank of the major offensive in the Ardennes. Ordered by Hitler on 21 December, and started on New Year's Eve, it made little headway and ground to a halt as early as 3 January.[137] The consequence of this predictable failure, on top of losses from the Ardennes offensive, was to leave the overall military situation substantially worse than it had been in mid-December. In the west, the Luftwaffe was effectively now finished. Some 80,000 much-needed soldiers – a number raised under such extreme difficulties – had been lost, huge quantities of armaments had been destroyed and fuel supplies were rapidly running out. In the east, the expected offensive could only be faced with maximum apprehension – made worse by the losses in the west. Even so, the generals had no alternative in mind other than to follow Hitler's orders, however insane they thought them to be. Neither the will nor the organizational capacity was there to challenge his authority as a group, let alone face him individually with any ultimatum to avoid the looming catastrophe. A glimpse into the prevailing mentality can be gleaned from a comment made by Göring at the beginning of November to General Werner Kreipe, just dismissed from his post as Chief of the General Staff of the Luftwaffe. Kreipe had pressed Göring – still exuding optimism that the enemy would be defeated, and that their coalition would split – to confront Hitler and urge him to find a political way out. The Reich Marshal refused point-blank, saying that to do so would take away the Führer's self-belief.[138]

At the very pinnacle of the regime, Hitler could still muster his tried and tested act of supreme confidence and optimism, however bleak the reality. Even at this stage he was able to fire up those around him. More importantly, given the fragmentation in the subordinate leadership and their inability to pose any collective criticism of his leadership, let alone think of a united and frontal challenge to his authority, he could continue to demand the impossible and expect his orders to be obeyed. He still hoped and vainly expected that the Allied coalition would crack. His own hold on reality was waning, but had far from vanished. Beneath the veneer of indomitability that his role of Führer demanded, he was eminently capable of realizing the consequences of the unfolding disaster. His Luftwaffe adjutant, Nicolaus von Below, found him one evening after the failure of the Ardennes offensive, depressed and admitting that the war was lost – characteristically attributing it to betrayal and the failings of others. For him now the struggle was about his place in history – a heroic end, not a cowardly capitulation for the country as in 1918. 'We'll not capitulate,' Below recalled him saying. 'Never. We can go down. But we'll take a world with us.'[139]

Following the failure in the Ardennes, defences in the west were severely weakened. They would nevertheless hold reasonably firm for a few weeks yet, until the major Allied onslaught in March. But in the east, catastrophe was imminent.

5

Calamity in the East

The machine of duty, the will and the unquestioned 'must' application of the last ounce of strength work automatically within us. Only seldom do you think about the big 'what now'.
Colonel-General Georg-Hans Reinhardt, Commander-in-Chief of Army Group Centre, 20 January 1945

The conviction that a victory of the Soviets would mean the extinction of life of the German people and of every individual is the general feeling of all people.
Propaganda report on the popular mood, 24 January 1945

I

The storm broke on 12 January 1945 and raged with savage ferocity for the next three weeks. By the end of the month, vital eastern regions of the Reich – East Prussia to the north, East Brandenburg (between the Oder and what had once been the Polish border), Silesia with its crucial heavy industry to the south – and all of what remained of occupied Poland had been lost. The Wehrmacht had suffered huge, irreparable losses in intensely fierce and bitter fighting. The German civilian population had faced unspeakable horror as it fled in panic. The Red Army now stood on the banks of the Oder, the last natural barrier before Berlin. The roof had fallen in on the Third Reich.

The great Soviet offensive had been expected. The German General Staff even calculated exactly when it would start.[1] But when it came, the Wehrmacht was still ill-prepared for it.

In the main, this simply reflected the crass imbalance of forces. Across the entire eastern front of around 2,400 kilometres the estimated enemy superiority was immense: eleven times more infantry, seven times more tanks, twenty times more guns, twenty times stronger in air-power.[2] The discrepancy was smallest in the north of the front, in East Prussia, though massive even there. Further south, the central part of the front, it was overwhelming. German losses in the last six months of 1944 had been almost as high as in the whole of the previous three years, since the attack on the Soviet Union, and practically all possible reserves – often of ill-trained and unsuitable men – had by now been scraped together.[3] In the path of the Red Army along the Vistula, defending a sector of around 725 kilometres, stood the 9th Army, the 4th Panzer Army and the 17th Army, all part of Army Group A, commanded by Colonel-General Josef Harpe and significantly weakened over previous months. The Army Group's southern flank in the Carpathians was protected by Colonel-General Gotthard Heinrici's 1st Panzer Army. In the north of the front, guarding East Prussia, the route of the Russian invasion of the Reich in 1914, was the rebuilt Army Group Centre, under Colonel-General Georg-Hans Reinhardt, whose 3rd Panzer Army, 2nd and 4th Armies, together with 120 battalions of about 80,000 badly equipped *Volkssturm* men, had to cover around 650 kilometres of extensively fortified terrain. In all, Harpe commanded around 400,000 men, Reinhardt about 580,000. Between them they had some 2,000 tanks at their disposal.[4]

Facing them were the daunting Soviet forces that had been assembled for the big push towards the Reich's borders. In the centre of the front, on the middle reaches of the Vistula, and prepared for the major thrust, was the 1st Belorussian Front of Marshal Georgi Zhukov. Marshal Ivan Konev's 1st Ukrainian Front was poised further south on the Vistula. Between them, Zhukov and Konev commanded an awesome force of almost 2.25 million men, some 6,500 tanks, 32,000 heavy guns and more than 4,500 aircraft. Their objective was to drive some 500 kilometres to the Oder, towards Posen and Breslau, capture the Silesian industrial region, and take position for the final advance on Berlin. In the north, the subsidiary part of the offensive, the 3rd Belorussian Front under General Ivan Chernyakhovsky in cooperation with Marshal Ivan Bagramyan's 1st Baltic Front was set to begin the assault westwards through East Prussia, directed towards the heavily fortified bastion of

Königsberg, while the 2nd Belorussian Front commanded by Marshal Konstantin Rokossovsky, aimed to drive north-westwards from the Narev river in Poland towards the East Prussian coast. The combined strength amounted to almost 1.7 million men backed by 3,300 tanks, 28,000 heavy guns and 3,000 aircraft.[5] The attack from east and south, much as in 1914, towards the heavily fortified area of the Masurian Lakes, aimed to seize Königsberg, cut off East Prussia from the rest of Germany and destroy the major German forces defending the province.

Crushing though the defensive burden facing the German army was, their plight was made worse by the unwieldy and divisive command structure of the Wehrmacht, which had the effect of leaving Hitler, at its head, unchallengeable. All power of decision rested in his hands, in the military as well as the political sphere. No mechanism existed to take it from him, even as he determined on actions that lacked all rationality and were hugely costly in continuing to prosecute a war that was patently lost, and when moves to end it ought to have been urgently demanded of him or of anyone stepping into his place.

At a time of utmost military crisis the long-standing crucial division in the Wehrmacht command structure, dating back to the organizational changes that followed Hitler's assumption of command of the army in December 1941, was glaringly magnified, and highly damaging.[6] The essential lack of coordination was rooted in the split between the responsibilities of the High Command of the Wehrmacht (OKW) and those of the High Command of the Army (OKH). The OKW was responsible for strategic planning on all fronts except the eastern front. This front, where the Luftwaffe and navy played only minor roles, was the province of the OKH. The problem was compounded since Hitler's chief subordinates at the OKW, Field-Marshal Keitel and General Jodl, were guaranteed to back him at every call. Though they could not block any influence that the commanders-in-chief of the navy and Luftwaffe (Dönitz and Göring) might bring to bear on Hitler, as regards the war on land they formed an insuperable barrier to any propositions that they did not favour or that Hitler opposed. Beyond this, even, there was the added great difficulty that Hitler, since December 1941, had been the Commander-in-Chief of the Army, interfering regularly in tactical dispositions. Increasingly distrustful of his generals in such a decisive theatre, he had resolutely and persistently refused to contemplate appointing a commander-in-chief for the eastern front to parallel the position of Field-Marshal von Rundstedt in the west or that of Field-Marshal Albert Kesselring in Italy. A coordinated military command in the east, beneath Hitler, was therefore impossible. And any strategic planning of General Guderian, Chief of the Army General Staff, was made doubly difficult: first, because he had to surmount Hitler's objections in the army command itself; and secondly, because he had to confront Hitler's allocation of priorities to other theatres.

Guderian encountered such difficulties on three separate visits he made to Hitler's western headquarters between 24 December 1944 and 9 January 1945. His entreaties for the recognized weakness on the eastern front to be bolstered by the transfer of divisions from the west were turned down flat by Hitler. The eastern front would have 'to make do with what it's got', Hitler declared. He dismissed the careful figures put together by Colonel Reinhard Gehlen of the Foreign Armies East department of the General Staff as gross exaggerations, part of a Soviet 'enormous bluff' – a view echoed by Himmler. Jodl also backed Hitler's refusal to move troops eastwards, continuing to attribute decisive importance to the western front. The most Guderian eventually squeezed out of Hitler, on his second visit, was the transfer of four divisions. However, Hitler insisted that these be sent not to the broad part of the eastern front threatened by the coming offensive, but to Hungary, where the attritional battles around Budapest had raged for weeks and would continue until mid-February.

Only with the Soviet offensive under way and the attempted breakthrough in the Ardennes and Alsace definitively over was Hitler finally prepared to move forces to the east. But Guderian was infuriated to learn that these forces, too, the redoubtable 6th SS-Panzer Army of Sepp Dietrich, back from the Ardennes, were to be sent to Hungary. Protecting the Hungarian oilfields, so crucial to the German war effort, was the chief consideration.[7] Hitler, following pressure from Armaments Minister Albert Speer, deemed the few oilfields there still available to Germany indispensable to the war effort and to be held at all cost, even if it meant weakening the defences of Army Groups A and Centre.[8] In fact, the Danube, for all the intense fighting there, was rapidly turning into a sideshow to the main event about to unfold on the eastern front. But when Guderian, on 9 January, showed him the detailed assessment of troop figures in the Soviet build-up that he had obtained from Gehlen Hitler responded in fury that the man who had devised them was 'completely idiotic' and should be sent to a lunatic asylum. He also predictably refused to allow Harpe and Reinhardt to withdraw to the more defensible positions they had advocated, spouting his usual condemnation of generals who thought only of retreat. And during the Soviet onslaught he overrode Guderian's objections and insisted on the transfer of a formidable armoured corps, the *Großdeutschland*, from Reinhardt's hard-pressed army in East Prussia to help shore up defences in Poland – only to find that Kielce, which they had been meant to defend, had already fallen. Before then, Guderian had told Hitler that the eastern front was 'like a house of cards': one push and it would collapse.[9] It was an all too reasonable prophecy.

In their post-war memoirs, German generals often tended to lay the blame for the military catastrophe almost wholly at Hitler's door. His own domineering, interfering and increasingly erratic military leadership without doubt notably worsened the extent of the disaster and thereby the scale of the human losses. But such personalized blame overlooks the support the generals had given in better times to Hitler's unfettered command and the structures that had given him such total dominance in the military sphere. Even as battlefield fortunes had turned remorselessly against Germany after 1942, the generals made no concerted attempt to alter the command structures. In March 1944 all the field-marshals had presented Hitler with a sworn declaration of their unwavering loyalty.[10] And following the failure of Stauffenberg's plot in July 1944, they had simply acknowledged that nothing could be done, however absurd the orders appeared to be. Moreover, Hitler was far from bereft of support among the generals for his decisions, however irrational they subsequently seemed, as the records of his military conferences demonstrate. His refusal to accede to Guderian's request to move large numbers of troops from the west to shore up the eastern front, for example, was, however bluntly put, little more than a reflection of realities. Any major transfer from the west would have laid bare defences on that front and might at best have delayed, but almost certainly could not have prevented, the Red Army's breakthrough. In the stretched and splintered Wehrmacht of early 1945, few had anything approaching an overall view of the situation and most generals were above all anxious to hold on to what they could of their own men and resources. Guderian's main support came from the commanders of the Army Groups directly in the Soviet path. Even here, however, his reluctance, with few exceptions, to recommend sensible retreat to more defensible lines (since he knew Hitler would reject such a suggestion) meant an ultimate readiness to accept orders in the full knowledge that they would have disastrous results.[11] Even with a different supreme head of the Wehrmacht, the calamity about to beset Germany in the east could not have been prevented. Only immediate capitulation could have achieved that. But the full extent of the disaster could have been significantly lessened. A more rational defensive strategy, together with orchestrated evacuation of the threatened civilian population, could have held off the Red Army for longer and in so doing possibly saved countless lives.

II

At 4 a.m. on the icily cold morning of 12 January, the 1st Ukrainian Front began a huge artillery bombardment against the positions of the German 4th Panzer Army across the Vistula, some 200 kilometres south of Warsaw. Even the immediate impact seemed to indicate what was to follow. By midday, the barrage alone had destroyed the 4th Panzer Army's headquarters, disabled two-thirds of its artillery, and left a quarter of its men dead or wounded. By the end of the day, Soviet infantry had broken through to a depth of more than 20 kilometres across a 40-kilometre front while tank spearheads had pushed forward more than 32 kilometres, crushing German resistance in their path. Kraków was taken on 19 January, the beautiful city still unscathed since the Germans had had no time to destroy it. Just over a week later, on 27 January, Red Army soldiers came across the horrific site of the huge concentration camp complex at Auschwitz, where more than a million Jews and other victims of Nazi terror had been exterminated. They liberated around 7,000 emaciated and ill prisoners left cowering in the remains of the camp as the Germans had retreated. By 28 January, nearby Katowice had fallen. German forces managed to escape destruction as they evacuated the area. But by next day, nearly all of Upper Silesia, Germany's last intact, vital industrial belt, was in Soviet hands. Before the end of the month, Breslau, capital of Silesia, had been encircled. The city, a designated 'fortress' whose fanatical leadership had determined on holding out to the end, would not fall until May. It was a futile act of defiance, at enormous human cost, which scarcely inconvenienced the Soviet steamroller. Already on 22 January advance troops had crossed the upper reaches of the Oder, near Brieg, between Oppeln and Breslau, and established a bridgehead – rapidly reinforced – on the western banks. By the end of the month five of Konev's armies had taken up positions on or over the Oder, though large-scale crossings of men and equipment had been difficult as the thick carpet of ice over the river started to break up.

A massive barrage in the thick fog of early morning on 13 January announced the beginning of a mighty assault on East Prussia by Chernyakhovsky's 3rd Belorussian Front, followed next day by the northward thrust of Rokossovsky 2nd Belorussian Front. Ferocious German resistance, together with the heavy snow that initially hampered Soviet air support for the offensive, meant the advance was less speedy than further south. After the first few days, however, defences started to crumble. Tilsit fell on 20 January. Chernyakhovsky's forces poured through the so-called Insterburg Gap towards Königsberg, though the massively fortified city itself was to hold out, despite an intense battering, until April. Goldap, Gumbinnen and the area around Nemmersdorf in the east of the province, scene of the notorious incursion of the Red Army in October, were retaken. Advancing from the south, Rokossovsky's troops found that the great Nazi monument commemorating the battle of Tannenberg and victory over the Russians in 1914 had been blown up by the Germans, who had hastily exhumed the remains of Field-Marshal Hindenburg, hero of Tannenberg, and his wife, and shipped them on a cruiser westwards out of Pillau.[12] Hitler's former headquarters, the Wolf's Lair, near Rastenburg, was overrun, Red Army soldiers wandering in amazement around the concrete ruins of the arch-enemy's command centre. Once the Soviet forces had overcome the battery of fortifications in the Allenstein area by 23 January, the way was clear to strike for the sea. The main railway line from Königsberg to Berlin was severed. By 26 January the main forces of the 5th Guards Tank Army reached the Frisches Haff – the huge, shallow lagoon stretching for more than 80 kilometres from near Elbing to Königsberg – at Tolkemit, east of Elbing. With that, East Prussia was cut off from the rest of the Reich.

The trapped 4th German Army, to Hitler's fury, abandoned the heavily fortified defences of Lötzen amid the Masurian Lakes and tried to break out to the west, aiming to reach the river Nogat and the Vistula beyond, and advancing about 32 kilometres before being forced back on Heiligenbeil. A last attempt to break out was blocked on 30 January. Most of the remaining German forces – the bulk of them comprising twenty-three divisions of the 4th Army – were now compressed between the Red Army and the sea in a sizeable enclave, about 60 kilometres long and 20 kilometres wide along the Frisches Haff south-west of Königsberg, centred on Heiligenbeil. Remnants of the 3rd Panzer Army, some nine badly mauled divisions, still held the Samland peninsula, to the north-west of Königsberg, and with it, crucially, the harbour at Pillau. The rest were left to defend the encircled fortress of Königsberg itself. In all, around half a million soldiers were cut off.[13] By the end of January, after a little over two weeks of ferocious fighting, almost the whole of East Prussia lay in Soviet hands.

On 14 January, Zhukov launched his 1st Belorussian Front from bridgeheads on the Vistula, driving on remorselessly through heavy fighting to encircle Warsaw with the help of attached Polish divisions, and racing westwards through central Poland towards Łódź and Posen – the gateway to Berlin. The speed and savagery of the assault swept away German defences. When Polish and Soviet troops entered Warsaw on 17 January, scarcely a building was still intact. The German destruction of the city during and after the uprising, carried out under Himmler's express instructions, following Hitler's order, had been savage in the extreme. The occupiers had engaged in a last orgy of wanton destruction before they left, fleeing westwards, German troops offering only scant resistance from the rearguard. The big textile city of Łódź was seized by General Vasily Chuikov's 8th Guards Army on 19 January, with little resistance and no demolition, so fast had been the Soviet advance. Two days later, Soviet tanks reached the outskirts of Posen, government and communications centre of what the Nazis had called the 'Wartheland'. They were, however, for the time being unable to overcome heavy fortifications to crush the resistance of the 25,000 or so German troops trapped in what had been deemed a 'fortress', whose remnants were eventually stormed only in mid-February. Other Soviet divisions were meanwhile driving north-west towards the Baltic coast of western Pomerania, at the same time protecting the flank of Zhukov's main forces headed due west towards the middle stretches of the Oder. One unit reached the frozen river on 30 January and managed to cross

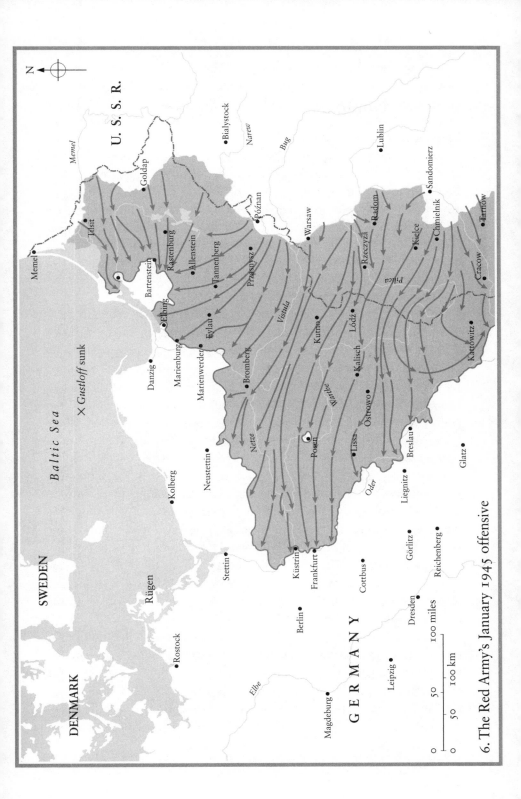

6. The Red Army's January 1945 offensive

it next morning to establish a small but significant bridgehead north of Küstrin. Berlin was now in sight, no more than about 80 kilometres away. Zhukov, and to the south Konev, swayed by the speed and scale of their successes, had their eyes set for a short time on a rapid triumphal drive to the Reich capital, each already envisaging a hero's return to Moscow. But the Red Army's advance had slowed as German resistance had intensified. And heavy losses of men and equipment had been suffered. Zhukov's men, like Konev's, were in need of a respite before the big push for the German capital. Momentary hopes of a dash to Berlin to bring a swift end to the war had to be abandoned. It was more important to consolidate strength for the final phase.[14]

III

The unfolding military disaster for the Wehrmacht conveys little or nothing of the unimaginable agony of the civilian population caught up in the offensive. As they advanced so quickly through formerly occupied parts of Poland, the troops of the Red Army could envisage themselves as liberators of the Polish people – though the subjugated Poles often simply felt one brutal conqueror was being replaced by another. When they reached Reich territory, however, Soviet soldiers saw themselves as avengers. The Germans had shown no mercy as they had laid waste Soviet towns and villages, burning homes and farmsteads, slaughtering innocent civilians. Red Army soldiers, and their commanders, saw no need for restraint now they were the conquerors, advancing through the land of those who had brought them such misery, raping, plundering, murdering as they went. Soviet propaganda encouraged revenge through maximum brutality. The brief incursion in October, for which the name 'Nemmersdorf' had become the symbol, now paled into insignificance in comparison with the scarcely imaginable horror experienced during the onslaught in January 1945.

Just as they had the previous October, Nazi officials, clinging to their own propaganda that the Soviet attack would be repulsed, contributed to the unfolding disaster by their stubborn refusal to give the orders for evacuation in time. In East Prussia, Gauleiter Erich Koch set the tone.[15] He continued, in empty sloganeering, to preach entirely unjustified optimism and to exhort the population to defend their province to the last.

This did not stop him on 21 January encouraging his own secretary to leave with her fellow villagers while she could.[16] His wife had already taken a special train to Bavaria the previous day.[17] Koch himself left Königsberg with his entourage on 28 January and moved his headquarters to the security of a bunker on a naval air base in Neutief on the Frische Nehrung near Pillau.[18] Koch also insisted that no subordinate officials should permit evacuation without his authorization. Not surprisingly, there was intense anger and bitterness directed at the Party's representatives, though even now faith in Hitler had not completely vanished.[19] Last-minute attempts to organize evacuation were often made by local Party leaders and the NSV. Most families however, as the panic at the thought of falling into Soviet hands spread like a contagion, did not wait for orders but resorted to self-help. For many it was too late.[20]

Even by East Prussian standards, where the winter was invariably hard, this was an intensely cold January, with temperatures falling as low as minus 20 degrees Celsius. The prospect – days and nights out in the open without warm clothing, making painfully slow headway on icy roads in biting winds or on tracks blocked by drifting snow, trying to avoid becoming caught up in the fighting – was frightening in the extreme. Some, too infirm or weak to take the risk, decided not to go, and to await in trepidation the arrival of the Soviet occupiers. Some could not face the future and took their own lives. Cyanide was easily available, at least in Königsberg, and there was much talk of using it.[21] But, for most, clinging to life and fear of the Russians were greater than worries about the cold or anxiety about the future. There was no time to wait. 'Panic grips the people as the cry goes up: "the Russians are close",' recalled one woman. 'Then a man comes by on horseback, shouting in a loud voice: "Save yourselves, you who can. The Russians will be here in half an hour." We're overcome by a paralysing fear.'[22] In such scenes of chaos, people hurriedly gathered what few belongings they could, threw them onto handcarts, sledges or horse-drawn wagons, left their homesteads, abandoned practically all their possessions and their livestock, and fled into the unknown. Retreating German soldiers grabbed anything they could find and loaded it onto lorries, slaughtering cattle left roaming the fields as they went.[23]

In the first days after the start of the invasion, trains to the west, into Pomerania, were the means of escape for tens of thousands. Chaotic scenes unfolded at railway stations as people desperately tried to clamber into the departing trains. The big square in front of Königsberg's main station was jammed with rows of refugee wagons. Armed guards held people back in the station, though Party members and others with 'connections' were found places. The Wehrmacht had priority use of the insufficient number of trains available. Soldiers forced their way onto the only trains departing.[24] Refugees had to wait – often in vain. Conditions were appalling, with no toilet facilities or food and drink for the crowds milling round the platforms.[25] Thousands were stranded as the last trains pulled out. By 23 January trains that had headed west were returning, the lines blocked by the Soviets.[26] A few were lucky enough to find transport in military vehicles travelling westwards, even in open-top lorries where they were exposed for long hours to the extreme cold. The majority, however, had to resort to treks, in columns of covered wagons. Those from the western parts of the province were the most fortunate. In the east, the treks were often unable to make progress on roads blocked by snow or army vehicles before being overtaken by Soviet tanks, or otherwise falling into the hands of the dreaded enemy after finding themselves embroiled in fighting zones. Once the rail connection to the Reich was severed, only two means of flight – both extremely perilous – were left.

One way was to escape by ship from Pillau, the harbour opening from the Frisches Haff onto the Baltic. But the first ship to lift off refugees only arrived a fortnight after the launch of the Soviet offensive.[27] Soon, the harbour-town was besieged by tens of thousands who had trekked mainly from the north-eastern parts of the province. Every house was full. People slept where they could, in barns and cow-byres, even exposed to the bitter cold in the open on the dunes. Big communal kitchens were hurriedly set up to provide basic meals.[28] When they finally arrived, the ships, filled to the gunnels with refugees, including sick patients evacuated from hospital, suffered long delays before leaving. Those on board had the constant worry of attacks from the air.[29] One woman, a teacher who had already endured, after a long wait, more than twenty-four hours on the open deck of a small ship with her elderly mother, travelling round the coast before even reaching Pillau, had then to 'stand around all day with thousands in the filth of the harbour and wait.... Everywhere broken glass, dirt and excrement. It's impossible to get a ship. Only families with several children are let through.' It was twelve miserable, uncertain and dangerous days before she and her mother eventually reached Rügen.[30]

By the end of January, around 200,000 refugees were crammed onto the Samland, still in German hands. Around 150,000 had also flooded at first into Königsberg, thinking the fortified city was a sanctuary. Once it became impossible to leave by train, many of these, too, headed for Pillau in the hope of escaping by sea. Nursing staff of military hospitals in Königsberg rejected the chance to join them, and decided to stay to look after the wounded.[31] By the end of January, when Königsberg was cut off, about 100,000 were still stranded there, though more were able to leave when the connection to the Samland was opened up again for a brief time in mid-February. Many lost their lives in the crossings when their small boats went down. The German navy sent help in the rescue effort. Over the next months, 679,541 refugees were ferried from Baltic harbours to the west (450,000 from Pillau), along with 345,000 wounded and a further 182,000 soldiers, though many more could have been shipped to safety if the navy had not given priority to military demands.[32]

The alternative was to cross the frozen Haff to the narrow spit of land, the Frische Nehrung, little over a kilometre wide at its broadest point and running for about 70 kilometres along its northern shore, and to head westwards for Danzig (or in some cases eastwards to try their luck in Pillau). By the latter part of January, hundreds of thousands of desperate refugees from all over East Prussia had defied the bitter cold, raging hunger, thirst, frostbite and attacks from the air by Soviet planes to reach the ever smaller cusp of land still in German hands at the southern end of the Haff and, amid mounting chaos, attempt the crossing over the ice to the frozen dunes of the Nehrung. Day and night for weeks thousands of trekkers, haggard and anxious families leading their heavily laden horse-drawn wagons or pushing prams or home-made wooden trucks and sledges carrying all their belongings, an easy target for low-flying Soviet planes, trudged fearfully over the carpet of ice on routes marked out by the military towards what they hoped was safety. Even this escape route was blocked for a time when the German navy used an ice-breaker to force a channel through the frozen Haff to allow three new torpedo boats through from Elbing to Pillau and prevent their falling into Soviet hands. Thousands were trapped on the ice until rapidly improvised pontoon bridges allowed a way across again.[33]

Once on the Nehrung, the misery was far from over. On the narrow, unpaved track, chewed up by military vehicles as well as the refugees' wagons, progress was painfully slow and the columns were exposed to repeated terror from the air. For many, the hazardous journey ended in tragedy. The extreme cold took its toll, especially of infants and the elderly. Others died of sheer exhaustion, or were caught in air raids. In some cases, despairing efforts to get away had ended with wagons and the families on board tipping through breaks in the ice into the dark waters of the Haff. One farmer's wife, after struggling for eight days to reach the Haff, watched in horror as rows of wagons fell into the holes just left by a bombing raid.[34] Nor, amid such traumas, did Nazi controls ease up. SS men and military police regularly searched the treks for men aged between sixteen and sixty to serve in the *Volkssturm*.[35] In all, perhaps as many as 30,000 perished on the treks.[36] But by the time it started to melt in late February nearly half a million had escaped across the ice.

In one way or another, defying all the perils, most of East Prussia's population of about 2 million at the beginning of the year, managed to flee. In so doing, they avoided the unspeakable fate of the half a million from the province who fell into Soviet hands. Though there were plenty of honourable exceptions, many of the Red Army soldiers did their best to impersonate the caricatures of Nazi propaganda in their bestial behaviour, with the toleration if not outright encouragement of their superior officers. 'A blind feeling of hatred' was how a Red Army veteran described the attitude of the Soviet troops as they entered Reich territory. 'The German mother should curse the day that she bore a son! German women have now to see the horrors of war! They have now to experience what they wanted for other peoples!' wrote one soldier in a letter home. 'Now our soldiers can see how German homes burn, how their families wander round dragging their viper's brood with them. . . . They hope to stay alive. But for them there is no mercy,' wrote another.[37] Alcohol played its part. Looting and plundering were endemic among frequently drunken soldiers from desperately poor parts of the Soviet Union who thought they were entering a land of plenty on encountering the war-torn eastern regions of Germany. They commented in wonder in letters home at the stores of food and drink they found. 'Everybody eats what he has appetite for and drinks as much spirits as he wants,' wrote one. 'I'm wearing riding-boots, have more than one watch . . . in a word, I'm swimming in riches,' another proudly proclaimed.[38] For them, anything they could steal counted only as a token form of recompense for what they and their families and their fellow countrymen had suffered at the hands of the German enemy.

The thirst for revenge was seemingly unquenchable. Houses were ransacked and destroyed, buildings set alight, sometimes entire parts of towns and villages burnt down. German men were often callously and arbitrarily shot, many severely beaten or otherwise mishandled. Anyone recognized as a Nazi functionary was summarily executed. Those in possession of a uniform, even a railway worker or fireman who had no role in the Nazi Party, were likely to be similarly dispatched. It is thought that as many as 100,000 people in the eastern parts of Germany were killed in such fashion.[39] The rape of women, young and old, often many times over – a mass phenomenon and act of revenge through inflicting maximum humiliation on the defeated male population by the degradation of their wives and families – was a terrible hallmark of the first encounter with the Soviet conquerors, mentioned in innumerable eyewitness accounts.[40] 'Can you hear?' one farmer despairingly asked as cries came from his house. 'They've got my thirteen-year-old daughter for the fifth time already this morning.'[41] Such horror was commonplace. Some estimates reckon that 1.4 million women – close to a fifth of the female population – were raped in the eastern provinces conquered by the Red Army in these weeks.[42] Fortunate indeed were women who managed to hide or otherwise avoid the bestiality. Those Germans who survived such horrors were, however, condemned to endless further misery: to the harshness of further maltreatment and forced labour under Soviet occupation, or – the fate of about a quarter of a million Germans – to transport in the most dire conditions, accompanied by huge death rates, to labour camps mainly in the industrial regions of the USSR, where brutal working conditions extracted a further heavy toll.[43]

What happened in East Prussia also occurred, with variants, throughout the German east. Whereas the flight of the East Prussian and Silesian population took place over the best part of four months, the German minority living in the parts of Poland that had not fallen to the Soviets had only about two weeks to make their escape as Zhukov's and Konev's armies raced towards the Oder. Only around a half of them, mainly from the western regions closest to the Reich, could avoid being overtaken by the rapidly advancing Red Army. East Brandenburg, with an almost entirely German population of over 600,000, had been taking in refugees from the Wartheland in western Poland for days before huge panic at the imminent arrival of the Russians led to a stampede to reach safety across the Oder. The Nazi authorities of the region had until almost the end of January refused to give orders to evacuate the province in the optimistic belief that the lines of fortifications would provide a formidable barrier to the Red Army. Consequently many Germans fell into enemy hands as the area was swiftly overrun.[44]

The largest German population east of the Oder–Neiße line was in Silesia, home of more than 4.5 million at the beginning of 1945. In Silesia, not far from the Reich border and from routes into the Sudetenland and Bohemia, not all the territory fell immediately to the Red Army, and, unlike in more easterly regions, there was also some warning of the Soviet advance. Conditions for flight were, therefore, more favourable than in East Prussia and other eastern regions. More than 3 million were able to flee by one means or another into parts of former Czechoslovakia or westwards into the Reich towards Saxony and Thuringia. In the Upper Silesian industrial district to the south, however, which was in Soviet hands by the end of January, only women and children had been permitted to leave. The local Gau leadership, following Speer's demands, ordered the men to remain behind to keep production going as long as possible. Many nevertheless fled on overcrowded trains and buses, on lorries or on foot. Important industrial installations were sometimes reportedly left intact in the panic. There was no time to detonate them.[45] Even so, hundreds of thousands were overrun by the Red Army.

To the north, in Lower Silesia, the evacuation order, pressed for by the military authorities (who had, however, elsewhere at times also played their part in delaying evacuation to prevent blocking supply routes[46]), had in most instances been given out earlier, and most inhabitants were able to get away – often trekking in wagons or on foot in icy weather since the means of transport by rail and road rapidly proved inadequate. In Breslau, the capital and by far the biggest city in Silesia, the thunder of artillery on 20–21 January brought urgent orders – backed by heavy pressure from the Party – for women, children, the old and the sick to leave the city. There were, however, not enough trains or motor vehicles to cope with the mass evacuation. There were reports of children being trampled to death in the stampede to board the few trains available and station waiting-rooms being turned into morgues.[47] Without transport, around 100,000 people, mainly women, were forced to head off into the winter night and brave the extreme cold on foot, hauling prams, sledges and carts along the icy roads, battling through snowdrifts, carrying just a few belongings. Bodies of infants who had perished in the bitter weather had to be left in the roadside ditches. Many women, unable to go on, returned and were among the 200,000 or so civilians in Breslau when the vice closed on the city in mid-February.[48]

Further north, an enclave of the West Prussian coast, centred on Danzig and Gotenhafen (Gdynia), was also engulfed in the refugee crisis. From mid-January onwards the area became the temporary destination of countless thousands fleeing northwards from the path of Rokossovsky's armies and pouring westwards from East Prussia as the province was cut off, across the last opening of the Frische Nehrung or arriving by boat from Pillau. By the end of the month, the area was teeming with close to a million refugees to add to its 3 million population. The NSV and German Red Cross were overwhelmed by the numbers. It was impossible to offer anything like sufficient care for the many who were ill, weak or injured from the terrible treks. Barracks and temporary camps had to be used to accommodate the mass influx. Many tried to travel further as soon as they could, but could find no place on the hugely overcrowded trains and ships. Among the vessels carrying away refugees, many of them sick and wounded, was the big former 'Strength through Joy' cruise vessel, the *Wilhelm Gustloff*, that eventually set sail from Gotenhafen, after long delays, on 30 January, crammed with perhaps as many as 8,000 persons on board – four times its peacetime complement. That evening the ship was torpedoed by a Soviet submarine and sank into the icy waters after little more than an hour. Possibly around 7,000 drowned in the worst maritime catastrophe in history, with nearly five times as many lost as in the sinking of the *Titanic*.[49] It was one of many disasters at sea over the following weeks. Nevertheless, between late January and the end of April, some 900,000 escaped over the Baltic and a further quarter of a million by land through Pomerania, before this region, too, was swallowed up by the Soviet advance.[50] A final horror still awaited the 200,000 or so, many of them refugees who had earlier managed under the greatest difficulties to flee from East Prussia, as Danzig and the surrounding area were taken in a maelstrom of violence by the Red Army in the last days of March.[51]

Even when the refugees escaped the worst, they still faced immense difficulties – and were far from assured of a warm welcome at their destination. By the end of January, 40,000 to 50,000 were arriving each day in Berlin, by train for the most part. The overwhelmed authorities, unable to cope with the mass influx and fearful of importing infectious diseases, did their best to move them on or have trains rerouted around the Reich capital.[52]

In this unending catalogue of misery and suffering, it is hard to conceive of anything worse than the fate of those in the eastern regions of Germany fleeing from the Red Army in the appalling conditions of that dreadful January. Yet the fate of the regime's racial victims was indeed worse: their horror was far from at an end. Even at this time the murder machinery of the SS showed no respite.

For around 6,500–7,000 Jews, rounded up from subsidiary camps in East Prussia of Stutthof concentration camp (itself located in West Prussia), hastily closed down on 20–21 January as the Red Army approached, scarcely conceivable days of terror began as they were marched off, not in a westwards direction like other inmates, but *eastwards*. The initial aim seems to have been to march them to a small satellite camp at Königsberg prior to transporting them by sea to the west, presumably from the port of Pillau, in order to retain them in German hands and prevent their liberation by the Red Army. But they never arrived in Pillau.

The prisoners, sent in recent months to Stutthof from the Baltic regions, Poland and elsewhere, were guarded on their forced march by over twenty SS men and up to 150 members of the *Organisation Todt* (including Ukrainians, Latvians, Lithuanians, Estonians, Belgians and Frenchmen). After the lengthy trek, in horrific conditions, to reach Königsberg, they were marched onwards to the small and once attractive Baltic town of Palmnicken, on the picturesque Samland coast. Many Jews were shot even on the way to Königsberg. Still more were killed, their bodies left on the streets of the East Prussian capital, as the death march to Palmnicken began. The remainder were herded off, clothed in little more than rags and wooden clogs. Though hardly able to walk on the snow and ice, any Jews lagging behind or falling down were shot. The guards killed more than 2,000 on the 50-kilometre march from Königsberg to Palmnicken, leaving the bodies by the roadside. Some 200–300 corpses were found on the last stretch of little over a kilometre as the remaining 3,000 or so prisoners straggled into Palmnicken on the night of 26/7 January.

When it became plain that there was no prospect of ferrying the prisoners to the west, the question of what to do with them took an even more lethal turn. Ideas now surfaced about getting rid of them altogether. The head of the state-run amber works in Königsberg and the East Prussian Gau leadership eventually agreed that the guards would drive the Jews into a disused mineshaft and seal up the entrance. The frozen, exhausted and bedraggled Jews nevertheless met a rare expression of sympathy as the estate manager ordered food for the prisoners and said that as long as he lived nobody there would be killed. His mine-director bravely refused to open up the shafts that they were to be driven into.

On 30 January, however, the courageous estate manager was found dead. He had received threats from the SS and was thought to have taken his own life; either that, or, as some thought, he had been murdered. The idea of entombing the Jews in the mine was, nevertheless, abandoned. That same evening, the local mayor, a long-standing and fanatical member of the Nazi Party, summoned a group of armed Hitler Youth members, plied them with alcohol and sent them, along with three SS men, who were to explain the task ahead, down to the disused mine. The boys were left to guard around forty to fifty Jewish women and girls who had earlier tried to escape, until they were taken out, in the dim light of a mine-lamp, to be shot by a group of SS men, two by two. The Soviets were thought by this time to be very close. The SS men were anxious to 'get rid of the Jews no matter how'. They decided to solve their problem by shooting the rest of their captives.

The following evening, 31 January, the improvised massacre took full shape. Shielded from the village by a small wood, the SS men, their flares lighting up the night sky, drove the Jews onto the ice and into the frozen water using the butts of their rifles and mowed them down on the seashore with machine guns. Corpses were washed up along the Samland coast for days to come. One woman was so shaken at what she saw, she later recalled, 'that I covered my eyes with my hands. . . . We then quickly went on walking because we could not stand the sight.' The SS had not been altogether efficient in their massacre; some Jews survived and managed to clamber back up the beach. The survivors met varied reactions. One German refused to help three of them, saying 'that he did not intend to feed Jewish women'. Another, however, hid them, gave them food, and protected them till the arrival of the Red Army. Doctors and nurses in the local hospital treated some wounded survivors. Two Polish labourers also gave them help. About 200 out of the original 7,000 survived.[53]

IV

People in other parts of Germany were not prepared for the dreadful news from the east that soon started to spread like wildfire, or for the tales of horror from those who had managed to escape the mayhem. The success of the Wehrmacht in repelling the Soviet incursion into East Prussia the previous October and reassurances about German defences in the east meant that there was no psychological readiness for the scale of the disaster that gradually became clear in the second half of January.

The first brief mention of the start of the Soviet offensive in the *Völkischer Beobachter*, reproducing the Wehrmacht report, suggested that the attack had been expected and that German defences had been successful.[54] Within a few days, however, newspapers started to adopt a more anxious tone.[55] The public swiftly caught the note of alarm that crept in about the speed of the Soviet advance, all the more when reports of the evacuation of the civilian population could not conceal the scale of the danger, and were more than amplified by the tales of their experiences carried by the stricken refugees as they poured west. Propaganda offices throughout Germany reported that 'the improved mood of the past weeks caused by our western offensive and the Führer's speech has disappeared in the wake of the Soviet major offensive. People are now looking to the east with the utmost concern and paying little attention to all other fronts and to political events.' 'The slump in mood', the summary report continued, 'was intensified by the disappointment that no one in any Gau, not even in the east, had reckoned with such speedy and big successes of the Soviets.' Widespread expectation of the offensive had been accompanied by much apprehension, but also a belief that the German leadership was well prepared and would regain the upper hand in the east. There was astonishment, then, that the Red Army had gained so much territory so quickly, and that German defences, presumed to be solid, has been so easily overrun.

The shock waves rippled through Germany. A severely depressed mood was accompanied by deep worry about the future. Discussion was dominated by the events on the eastern front and there was much criticism of the media, which had given the impression that all preparations had been made to counter the awaited attack. The German leadership were reproached for underestimating Soviet strength and morale, criticism underscored by the massive advances that the Red Army continued to make despite the reported destruction of huge numbers of Soviet tanks. Notable shock was caused by the advance into the Upper Silesian industrial belt, raising fears about sustaining German armaments potential. Worries about the fate of the civilian population in the threatened regions were only mentioned in last place.

Modifying such a downbeat set of reports came the inevitable emphasis on the resilience of the population – a reflection, without doubt, of opinion mainly registered in the more Nazified sectors of the population. Despite the slump in mood, the propaganda offices declared that there was no apathy or slackening of work effort. Instead, it was claimed, there was a determination to do everything possible to fight 'unconditionally' in the 'hour of decision' and to comb out 'anyone who can bear weapons' to send to the front in the hope of repelling 'the danger of Bolshevism'. Comments that such efforts were too late and pointless were rare. The holding – by and large – of the Reich borders in the west gave grounds for hope that a transformation could at some point be brought about in the east. The purpose of the German western offensive – to prevent a double attack by the enemy, east and west – had, it was said, become clearer. No one was prepared to accept that all the sacrifice, suffering and misery had been in vain. There was complete understanding, therefore, for whatever restrictions were needed in the interest of the war effort and for the 'toughest resistance' and defence at any price.[56]

Though hardly mirroring accurately a cross-section of attitudes, such reported views do indicate the unyielding stance of a still sizeable proportion – how large is impossible to say, though if it was a minority, it was a powerful one – unprepared to admit defeat and ready to do anything to combat the threat from the east. Even as the sense that the war was irredeemably lost became increasingly commonplace, anxiety about what defeat would bring intensified a desperate refusal to give in. 'The conviction that a victory of the Soviets would mean the extinction of life of the German people and of every individual is the general feeling of all people' was said to have bolstered the readiness to fight on and radicalized intolerance towards those seen to be shirking their duty.[57]

The lengthy summary report from the propaganda offices contained no mention of atrocities perpetrated by Red Army soldiers, or the horrors of the treks. But accounts of the refugees flooding westwards soon seeped through to the rest of the population. Immediately after the beginning of the Soviet offensive, propagandists had been warned to counter views that the Bolsheviks were not as bad as they had been painted (arising from known instances of humane treatment of German prisoners of war) by emphasizing atrocities – including reports from Memel refugees of Soviet soldiers on the hunt for German women and of mothers raped in front of their own children.[58] Goebbels, though aware of the 'indescribable' misery of those enduring the treks, was nevertheless initially hesitant about publishing reports on Bolshevik atrocities because of the panic they would cause.[59] There was quite justified panic, nevertheless, and the horror stories of the refugees were told wherever they went. 'The refugees arriving here from the eastern Gaue', ran one report from distant regions of Bavaria, 'are bringing for the most part quite shattering news of the misery of the fleeing population which, partly in panic, has sought refuge from the Bolsheviks within the Reich.'[60] Instead of keeping silent on the atrocities, German propaganda turned, therefore, to using them as a weapon to sustain the fight. 'How the Soviets Rampage in East Germany. Eyewitnesses Report on the Gruesome Extermination Methods of the Bolsheviks', proclaimed the headline in the *Völkischer Beobachter* on 9 February and, in variants, repeatedly in subsequent weeks.[61]

Letters still trickling west from the afflicted areas in the early phase of the Soviet offensive also painted a graphic picture of the appalling conditions in the east and the great anxiety about the future. One letter, from Josef E. from the Glogau district on the Oder, describing the state of refugees fleeing from the Warthegau and the dread of having to leave all that was precious behind, remarked that everything had turned out so different from the hopes of the future once fostered. How long would it be, he asked, before 'the whole of East Prussia – Posen – Silesia is deluged with the eastern hordes'? Then it was only a short way to Berlin. 'If the tempo of the Russians can't be stopped, and that doesn't look likely, then anyone can work out how long the war can last. I'm hoping for an end with horror rather than horror without end,' he concluded, repeating a phrase commonly heard at this time.[62]

People beyond the afflicted zones had their own pressing anxieties, however, and, despite widespread dismay at the Soviet breakthrough, the loss of the eastern territories and the prospect of a lost war, could often spare little concern for the plight of the refugees. Those with fathers, sons, husbands and friends caught up in the bitter fighting during the Soviet onslaught were understandably beset with worry about the fate of their loved ones at the front. 'Dear boy, I've just heard the Wehrmacht report and learnt that you are again engaged in fighting,' wrote one mother to her son, cut off in Courland. She had heard nothing from him in over a month and feared the worst. 'I was upset about what you have to cope with and hope you can still get away. . . . Dear God has to bring an end to it soon, but who knows how. We just hover between worry and expectation. "Without you, where would be my strength and courage?",' she ended, quoting a religious text.[63] With many so anxious about their own relations, the suffering of others played a secondary role.

In Upper Bavaria, where in the absence of the promised new weapons people were said to have little hope of the Soviets being repelled from Reich territory, the mood was apparently more dominated by concern about transport and postal difficulties, and the likely food shortages that would result from the loss of territory in the east.[64] In Franconia, events in the east were overshadowed by the complete destruction of the lovely old centre of Nuremberg through a severe bombing raid on 2 January, which had killed 1,800 people and demolished 29,500 buildings, leaving much of the city's population without homes.[65] Ursula von Kardorff, a Berlin journalist, admitted that her senses were so deadened that she could scarcely imagine the horrifying scenes reported to her at first hand of what happened at the railway station in Breslau after the order had been given to leave the city – of refugees trampling on each other in their desperation, corpses being thrown out of unheated goodswagons, trekkers stuck on the roads, delirious mothers unable or unwilling to see that the babies they were carrying in their arms were dead. A few days later, she remarked on the gruesome atrocity reports that reached her desk day after day. 'Goebbels' propaganda brain is evidently again working feverishly,' she commented, before asking: 'Or is it all true? I don't believe anything any longer before I have seen it myself.'[66]

By this time, there was a chance to do so. The first trains bursting with refugees were already arriving in Berlin from Silesia. An open lorry reached the city packed with children, many of them dead after ninety-six hours exposed to the extreme cold.[67] 'Columns of lorries crowded with refugees and luggage in bags and sacks roll through the Berlin streets,' wrote the Berlin correspondent of a Swedish newspaper on 24 January in a dispatch that came into Allied hands. 'The invasion of Berlin by the refugees is now so striking that the population of the Reich capital has fully realised how the eastern danger is tempestuously approaching the frontiers and Berlin itself.'[68]

In a city preoccupied with its own problems – a transport system near collapse, food and coal shortages, electricity cuts, constant worries about air raids – the refugees were not universally welcomed. Few wanted to share their often already overcrowded apartments or meagre food rations.[69] Porters at the main stations were apparently reluctant to help those leaving the trains; some people complained, probably unfairly, that National Socialist 'sisters' preferred their warm rooms to helping the new arrivals (though their aid and that of other Party organizations was often acknowledged by the refugees); there were worries about the lack of food, especially milk for infants, and complaints that 'we have so little, and now there are all these refugees'. By the end of the month, the city was teeming with the incomers, who poured out their anger and bitterness regardless of the consequences. There was enormous resentment at Party functionaries who had saved themselves first, shown little interest in others, not given warnings in time, and managed to find places in trains leaving for the Reich.[70] 'Those who have lost everything also lose their fear,' an observer remarked. The police temporarily refrained from intervening.[71]

The stories of the refugees had, unsurprisingly, a depressing effect on Berliners. There was a widespread fear that once the Red Army seized the Upper Silesian industrial region the war was as good as lost. People asked repeatedly where the long-awaited 'wonder weapons' meant to turn the tide of war were, and why they were not being used against the Russians after they had been so much talked and written about. There was frank disbelief that they existed; they were seen as no more than a figment of propaganda. Even if the Red Army could be halted, there was scepticism that Germany would be in a position to go on the offensive again. And people regarded as mere propaganda the claim that the Soviets had expended their last forces and were incapable of a new offensive of their own.[72] When, on the morning of 3 February, some 1,500 American planes dropped over 2,000 tons of bombs on Berlin in the heaviest raid of the war on the Reich capital, leaving 5,000 dead, injured or missing, the fate of the stricken population in the east took a back seat as panic temporarily gripped the city. However, reports of the continued Soviet advance in the east prompted great anxiety and talk about an evacuation of Berlin – worries sharpened by the erection of roadblocks. Sarcastic wits asked with black humour how long it would take the Red Army to pass through the roadblocks. The answer to the joke was an hour and five minutes: an hour to laugh at the barricades and five minutes to demolish them.[73]

The population was said to be under no illusions about the consequences of a lost war 'and what those can expect who fall into the hands of the Russians. People basically agree, therefore, that it's better to fight on to the last drop of blood and accept all deprivations rather than lose the war or surrender prematurely.'[74] The sense of fighting to the last was certainly not shared by all. For many, perhaps most, a fatalistic mood prevailed. 'Don't think too much, do your duty and have faith. The German will master this Huns' storm,' wrote one woman to a friend based with the Luftwaffe in East Prussia.[75] According to the recollections of a foreign journalist who experienced life in the German capital at the time, intensified restrictions and controls, transport difficulties and worsening food supplies, constant fear of the bombs and worries about the future, prompted many to look to escapism, often in drink.[76] But the reported determination to hold out did signify an important strain of opinion which had been underpinned by the reports of the atrocities in the east. Unlike the situation in the west, where there was no great fear of British or American occupation, the justified dread of what defeat at the hands of the Soviets would bring was a significant component in support for continuing the fight in the east, especially among those most directly threatened.

By this time, belief in Hitler had waned so strongly that it had little to do with any continued readiness to fight on among the civilian population. A eulogistic article on New Year's Eve by Goebbels in *Das Reich*, the prominent Berlin weekly, lauding Hitler's 'genius', had been strongly criticized, according to the SD in Stuttgart. In the light of what had happened, people were saying, 'the Führer is either not that genius depicted by Goebbels, or he had intentionally unleashed this world conflagration.' Some were looking back at what Hitler had written in *Mein*

Kampf, where 'twenty years ago he had pointed out his aims. There are people who are prepared to claim that there lies the origin of the war'. The conclusion was drawn by many that 'the Führer had worked for war from the very beginning'.[77]

A spark of lingering faith in his powers had, nevertheless, not been totally extinguished. Some refugees in Berlin apparently said 'that the Führer would soon lead them back again into their homeland', and it was claimed, in standard propaganda fashion, that 'faith in the Führer is so great that even a small success quickly improves the mood of very many again'.[78] A German Red Cross sister, writing home from the relative quiet of a naval hospital in La Rochelle in dismay 'that the Bolsheviks are now in our beautiful Germany', evidently wanted to trust Hitler's promise of final victory in his New Year address, but added: 'it's damned hard to believe it.'[79] Another woman brushed away such doubts. Despite her horror at events in the east and bombs raining down on German cities, and her anxiety about the future, she still felt confidence in a leadership 'that only wants the best and greatness for the people', regretted that Party members 'did not uphold the Führer's idea better', and was certain that the war 'must simply end in victory for us' since a Jewish 'diabolical state leadership' could not hold out in the long run.[80]

A genuine, naive belief in Hitler – perhaps most commonly still encountered among younger Germans, though here, too, by now very much a minority taste – was registered in an otherwise pessimistic diary entry of a teenager from Siegen in southern Westphalia, whose mother was ridden with anxiety about relatives who had not managed to escape from the encirclement of Königsberg. Without radio since the last air raid, the girl was unsure precisely where German troops stood, but saw only too clearly how bad the situation was. Germany needed troops in the east; but then the British and Americans would attack in the west. And now, at the evacuation of Breslau, people were having to flee in the east as well as the west. 'Our poor, poor Führer,' was her immediate thought. 'He will probably no longer be able to sleep at night and had only the best in mind for Germany.' She was unsure of her own future, but clung on to two hopes: that God would recognize that the German people had been punished enough (for what she did not say); or 'that the Führer still has a secret weapon to use'. Perhaps the weapon was so destructive, she mused, that the government hesitated to deploy it. Whatever the case, there was nothing any ordinary person could do, she added, fatalistically. Things would take their course. She ended by regretting that her school would reopen at the beginning of February: 'Still having to learn at such a time? Horrible!' she remarked.[81]

Germany was a shrinking country, its eastern parts severed, its western borders threatened, its population subjected to mounting threats of invasion as well as constant bombardment. City dwellers had to face severe privations as gas and electricity supplies were restricted, water often available only at street standpipes and food rations tightened. People frequently had to walk or cycle to work, since public transport systems functioned only partially at best. In country areas not as yet scarred by the war, conditions were generally better. There was food to be had – often hoarded, despite the penalties for doing so. Nor, except for areas on the edge of urban conglomerates, was there the nightly terror of air raids, although anyone at work in the fields might be exposed to the ever more frequent attacks from 'low-flyers'. It was, however, no rural idyll. Huge and increasing numbers of refugees from bombed-out cities and then from the ravaged regions of the east had to be put up – not always graciously – in already cramped and crowded accommodation, and fed from falling ration allowances. In areas close to the front, soldiers too had to be found billets. Incomers were often far from grateful for what was on offer, complaining about primitive conditions and showing reluctance to help out in farm work.[82]

Whether in town or countryside, those with a 'brown' background in the Nazi Party or one of its subsidiary organizations could not fail to recognize how widely they were by now despised by much of the population. But they were still the holders of power. Despite gathering criticism, people were rightly wary of being too outspoken and paying the consequences. Anyone with a history of anti-Nazi views had to be especially careful. The numbers of those sure the war was lost was growing daily. Few could be other than fearful of the future. But there was still a dwindling minority prepared to believe – perhaps more from desperation than conviction – that Hitler had something up his sleeve, even at this late hour. Many who had lost faith in the Führer nevertheless saw no alternative to fighting on if the land was not to fall to the feared Bolsheviks. Then there were the desperadoes who had allied themselves so closely with the Nazi regime for so long that they had a vested interest in continuing the struggle since they had no future once it was over. The Soviet breakthrough in the east triggered the start of their final fling. With nothing to lose, the radicalism of the Party fanatics threatened any who stood in their way.

Whatever the varied attitudes, ranging from outright anti-Nazis to still fervent loyalists, the mass of divided, dislocated and disillusioned Germans could do little or nothing to shape what the future held for them. Beyond the refusal of the Nazi leadership, most obviously and crucially Hitler himself, to contemplate capitulation, the continuation of an evidently lost war rested heavily upon the capacity of the regime to raise troops and provide them with armaments, and on the willingness and determination of the Wehrmacht to fight on even when the only outcome seemed certain to be disastrous defeat.

V

Letters home from the front inevitably indicate a range of attitudes among ordinary soldiers. Most, in fact, avoided any political comment and confined themselves to private matters. Of those who expressed opinions about the war, some were defeatist (despite the dangers of such views being picked up by the censors, with dire consequences for the writer) and others simply resigned to what they had to face; but most still exuded optimism and resilience – often perhaps to assuage the anxieties of relatives. A corporal based in Courland did not hold back in his criticism of Party functionaries who, he said (in sentiments commonplace within Germany), would ruthlessly sacrifice everything rather than serve at the front. 'If only common sense could triumph among tyrants,' he wrote, adding, perceptively, 'but they know that they themselves are in any case doomed. So they will first ruthlessly sacrifice the entire people.'[83] In another letter home, a soldier, recounting stories he had heard from an eyewitness of the 'indescribable rage' of refugees as they fled from the Red Army, thought they would soon have Communism 'if the Americans don't save us from it'.[84] A sergeant writing from Breslau was fearful, but fatalistic: 'The Russians are getting ever closer, and there's the danger that we'll be encircled. But our life is in God's hand and I still hope that we'll see each other again.'[85]

A quite different tone was more usual. 'The very serious situation at present shouldn't take away our confidence!' wrote one soldier. 'It'll be different, believe me! We must, must have patience and mustn't, mustn't lose faith.'[86] Another, asking for necessary material sacrifice at home, thought it would be possible with courage to hold the front and force back the 'great steamroller from the east'.[87] An NCO based in East Prussia expressed his sadness at the 'refugee misery', but also the anger that it provoked, a feeling shared unquestionably by many soldiers and a further motivation to uncompromising efforts to fend off the Soviet threat.[88] A corporal, upset that the Tannenberg monument in East Prussia had had to be blown up and worried about the possible loss of Silesian industry, still strongly believed, he wrote, that Germany would eventually master the enemy.[89] An injured grenadier, in a field hospital in Germany after being transported by sea from Pillau out of the East Prussian cauldron, was confident, despite the worrying situation. 'We must have faith,' he declared. 'I believe for certain that a change will soon come. On no account will we capitulate! That so much blood has already been spilt in this freedom fight cannot be in vain. The war can and will end in German victory!'[90]

How representative such attitudes were is impossible to tell, though, as in these letters, hopes and fears were surely especially prominent in the minds of most soldiers overwhelmed by the crisis in the east. Political opinion is barely mentioned. It was, of course, dangerous to voice criticism of the regime. But expressly pro-Nazi feeling was also seldom registered. Contempt for Party functionaries was by now widespread in the Wehrmacht, as among the civilian population, though it surfaces only rarely in the letters home, for obvious reasons. On the other hand, attitudes supportive of Nazism were not always clearly definable. The regime's extreme nationalism fed into the feeling that the homeland must be protected, come what may. And years of strident anti-Bolshevik propaganda and racist stereotyping matched, for many soldiers, their own experience of the brutal practices of the Red Army and shored up their determination to resist the onslaught of those whom, influenced by Nazi indoctrination, they frequently saw as 'Asiatic hordes' or 'Bolshevik beasts'. Propaganda slogans such as 'Victory or Siberia' or 'We are Fighting for the Lives of our Wives and Children' were probably not without effect, even if it cannot be judged how well they were received.[91] One junior officer, serving in the west but closely following the reports of events in the east with deepening sadness and pessimism, probably echoed the views of many when he jotted in his diary: 'Enough of slogans. They no longer cut any ice.'[92] On the western front at this time,

Allied army psychiatrists investigating the mentality of captured Germans reckoned that about 35 per cent of them were Nazis, though only about 10 per cent 'hard core'. The remaining 65 per cent showed, they estimated, no clear signs of what they saw as a Nazi personality type.[93] Whether such assessments on the eastern front would have reached similar conclusions cannot be known.

Whatever their private views, the rank-and-file could not influence events. Overwhelmingly, they simply obeyed orders. The number of desertions was rising, even on the eastern front, but they represented, nevertheless, a tiny proportion of those serving. There were signs of sagging morale, certainly, but, countered by severe punishment, this never threatened to turn into outright mutiny. Crucial to the continued readiness to fight was in any case less the behaviour of the ordinary soldiers than the stance of their commanders.

The inner tensions of the military leader trying, in desperate days, to stem the flow of the Red Army's inexorable march through East Prussia can be seen in the daily diary entries and letters home to his wife of Colonel-General Reinhardt, in the eye of the storm as Commander-in-Chief of the beleaguered Army Group Centre. Reinhardt, a firm regime loyalist, wrestled with problems of conscience more widely felt in the military leadership as he struggled to reconcile responsibility to those under his command with obedience to Hitler, even when the orders he received diametrically contradicted his own judgement on what he knew to be necessary. After the war he still saw no alternative to his actions. Resignation, unless Hitler demanded it, had not been possible. Even the thought of feigning illness to lay down his command had caused him 'the most serious psychological struggles'. Under the illusion that he could personally influence events, and that 'it was pointless to sacrifice himself' since a willing successor would easily be found, he saw no alternative to remaining in post.[94]

Mid-evening on 14 January, with the offensive in its earliest stages, Hitler telephoned to hear Reinhardt's view of the situation of his Army Group, but abruptly ended the conversation before the commander had a chance to express his concern at the shortage of reserves. Hours later, during a restless night, Reinhardt received Hitler's order to transfer two vital panzer divisions to Harpe's hard-pressed Army Group A, struggling to hold the Soviet advance on the Vistula. This would further weaken his limited reserves. But he was told there was no point in protesting; the Führer's decision was final. Reinhardt noted that the consequences in East Prussia could only be 'catastrophic'. Removing the last reserves would inevitably bring an enemy breakthrough very soon. 'Monstrous blow for us! But has to be borne, as our position is also dependent on Harpe,' he stoically jotted in his diary.[95]

Reinhardt was having to contend with Guderian as well as Hitler. On 15 January Guderian initially refused to allow him to shorten the north-eastern corner of the front. Reinhardt, desperate for reserves, appealed to Hitler, who this time supported him as Guderian backed down. On 17 January Hitler, supported by Guderian, rejected Reinhardt's fervent plea to pull back the 4th Army to save much needed reserves to help support the struggling 2nd Army further to the west. Reinhardt's hour-long telephone call to Hitler to put the case was difficult. Hitler said at the outset that, because of his hearing problems as a result of the attack on his life the previous July, General Wilhelm Burgdorf, his Wehrmacht adjutant, would conduct the discussion. Reinhardt and his Chief of Staff, Lieutenant-General Otto Heidkämper, also a firm regime loyalist, suspected that their case was not fully or clearly represented by Burg-dorf. In any case, it was to no avail. Hitler was convinced, he said, that withdrawals did not save forces, because the enemy simply advanced to more favourable positions. This type of retreat, he claimed, had led to catastrophe at every point of the eastern front. He then rejected Rein-hardt's request to allow the 4th Army to retreat to the Masurian Lakes and was dismissive about the value of the fortifications in Lötzen. The most that Reinhardt achieved was to retain two divisions that Guderian had wanted to transfer to the OKH.[96]

Reinhardt's nerves were jangling as he struggled to cope with the crisis. They were not improved when on 19 January he witnessed terrible scenes of devastation after fleeing civilians had been hit by a bombing raid that left a trail of corpses, wrecked vehicles and horses torn in pieces by the roadside.[97] He asked himself in a letter to his wife how it was possible to carry on under such a heavy and painful burden. He gave his own answer: 'the machine of duty, the will and the un-questioned "must" application of the last ounce of strength work automatically within us. Only seldom do you think about the big "what now".'[98]

Another entreaty from Reinhardt on the evening of 20 January to withdraw the increasingly imperilled 4th Army to safer lines in the

Masurian Lakes was bluntly rebuffed by Hitler – a decision found incomprehensible by the leadership of Army Group Centre since the situation was becoming critical and encirclement almost certain. Guderian promised to try to persuade Hitler to change his mind, but held out little hope. Reinhardt spent another sleepless night. 'Still no permission to retreat,' he noted in his diary on 21 January. 'I'm now in the most severe anguish over whether I should disobey.' That morning he again begged Guderian and the head of the OKH command staff, General Walther Wenck, to get him an immediate decision, 'otherwise trust in the leadership will collapse altogether'. 'Unbelievably tense hours' went by. Reinhardt smoked one cigarette after another until he had none left. Guderian rang mid-morning to say that Hitler had again rejected a withdrawal of the 4th Army.

Reinhardt decided once more to speak directly with Hitler in an attempt to 'save what can be saved'. He had another long struggle to try to surmount Hitler's stubborn rejection of retreat to the Masurian Lakes district as the only hope of holding the front. He found the conversation distressing, he wrote to his wife, 'because I fought so much with my entire feelings and sense of duty and conflicts of conscience between wanting and having to obey and feeling of responsibility for my task'. The turning point in the discussion came when Reinhardt vehemently claimed that, if the withdrawal did not happen, East Prussia and the Army Group would collapse. He had, Reinhardt continued, been bombarded with requests for support from his subordinate commanders and had to say that the question of confidence from below was now a serious factor. He knew of no solution other than the one he had proposed. If this were again to be rejected, he feared he would lose control. After almost two hours Hitler conceded. He gave permission for the retreat to the lakes. 'Thank God!' Reinhardt noted. 'I was near despair. Is suicide desertion? Now probably yes! Thank God,' he repeated, 'that the crisis of confidence has been overcome. I wouldn't have been able to face my commanders. They doubted me, justifiably. Now God must help us see that it is not all too late.'[99]

It *was* too late. No sooner had Hitler finally agreed to allow the 4th Army to pull back to the fortified zone centred on Lötzen than further Soviet advances endangered the area. Already that same evening, 21 January, Reinhardt acknowledged that the Lötzen position was no longer safe, and a move westwards to the 'Heilsberg triangle' was imperative. As he travelled to Königsberg next day in a heavy snowstorm, Reinhardt was dismayed at the sight of the refugees in the appalling weather. It upset him, he told his wife, that 'they were driven off and roughly handled by us if they were blocking our roads with their vehicles and holding up vital troop movements'. The threat to the 4th Army was, meanwhile, becoming graver. Impassable roads meant Reinhardt could not reach the 4th Army's commander, General Hoßbach, on 23 January to assess the overall situation. By that evening, as further depressing news of Soviet advances came in, Reinhardt, blaming the belated permission to retreat, recorded in his diary: 'We are, then, encircled.'

His view by now was that a 'breakthrough to the west', which Hoßbach had urged as the only hope, had to be undertaken. He informed the OKH of the decision that evening – though he omitted to mention his conviction that his forces were too weak both to attempt this and at the same time to hold Königsberg and the Samland. Nor – since it was plain that Hitler would reject the move out of hand – did he report the intention to give up the Lötzen area and retreat entirely to a new defensible position near Heilsberg. The OKH agreed, unaware of the full extent of the crisis, and promised to send forces eastwards from the Elbing area to meet up with the 4th Army pushing westwards. When he and Hoßbach met next morning, Reinhardt, no doubt put under pressure to act by Hoßbach, whose confidence in his Commander-in-Chief had been waning over recent days, gave the order to accelerate the breakout. Reinhardt worried that it was being attempted too late and continued to fret about whether he ought to have disobeyed Hitler's earlier persistent refusal to allow a retreat. 'I cannot survive this catastrophe,' he lamented. 'I'll be blamed, even though my conscience is clear, except that I was perhaps, from a sense of duty, too obedient.'

Next day, 25 January, Reinhardt faced a further inner conflict. He had suffered a severe head injury that morning when he was badly cut by flying glass following a grenade explosion at a field headquarters he was visiting. Bloodied and haggard, he pleaded in vain with Guderian to withdraw the front further. Guderian, backing Hitler's stance, insisted on holding the position on the lakes near Lötzen. Reinhardt, from his sickbed, struggled again the following afternoon to gain a favourable decision from the OKH as the threat to the 4th Army worsened. He was promised a decision by 5 p.m., which he had said was the last possible moment. At 5.30 p.m. Hitler's order eventually came through, but permitted only a limited withdrawal to positions which, in fact, had already been overrun by the Red Army. Hitler continued to insist on holding the position around Lötzen. Reinhardt told Hoßbach, repeatedly pressing for a decision, that if he had received none by 7.15 p.m. he would order the withdrawal himself. Amid rising tension, both Guderian and Wenck at the OKH, remarkably, were unavailable to speak to Reinhardt on the telephone. Hoßbach rang at 7 p.m. to say he needed immediate permission to break out; he could wait no longer. Reinhardt gave the order. He had no choice, he noted; the advantage of the position on the lakes had in any case been lost. He had no forces strong enough to retain it. 'My conscience is clear in favour of the attack . . . on which everything depends,' he added. 'I firmly believe that the success and sustaining of our attack is more important to the Führer than the lake position.' He was wrong. Hitler, feeling he had been deceived, exploded in blind fury at the news that the 4th Army had given up Lötzen, accusing Reinhardt and Hoßbach of treason. He later calmed down. But a scapegoat was needed. That night the loyalist, if conscience-stricken, Reinhardt, along with his Chief of Staff, Heidkämper, was dismissed.

VI

Striking throughout the drama was not only Hitler's absurd obtuseness in refusing to concede sensible withdrawals, but also Reinhardt's unhappiness at having to entertain the idea of disobedience even in such extremes. Significant, too, is that Reinhardt and the leadership of Army Group Centre felt they could rely upon no support from the OKH or from the military entourage around Hitler. The distrust of Burgdorf, Hitler's Wehrmacht adjutant, was plain. But so too was the feeling that Guderian, as Chief of the General Staff, would side with Hitler. When, therefore, the complete withdrawal of the 4th Army to the Heilberg area was recognized as the only remaining option, even if it meant the loss of Königsberg and the Samland, this had to be kept not only from Hitler, but also from the OKH. Gauleiter Koch, still trumpeting the need to hold onto 'Fortress East Prussia' down to the last man, had also to be kept in the dark, since he would immediately tell Hitler. The lines of military as well as political command that kept Hitler's leadership position untouchable and ensured that his orders were carried out, however nonsensical, remained, then, intact throughout the crisis. Hoßbach embellished his own reputation by claiming after the war that he had disobeyed Hitler in unilaterally ordering the attack to the west to break out of the encirclement. In reality, however, down to Reinhardt's dismissal on 26 January he was acting with the full support of his Commander-in-Chief. The decision, reluctantly to act against Hitler's wishes because he felt he had no choice, appears to have been in the first instance Reinhardt's, rather than Hoßbach's.

The aim of Army Group Centre's leadership in retreating to Heilsberg was to move to a more defensible position. Once there, further consideration could be given to whether there was anything left of East Prussia to try to save. Hoßbach's view, so he wrote shortly after the war, was more radical still. He knew East Prussia was lost, he stated. He saw the only option as trying to save the German forces trapped there so that they could fight again.[100]

This became an end in itself. Desperation produced its own dynamic. Hoßbach, like other military leaders, later claimed that the reason he had fought on was to protect and save the civilian population. The truth was different: saving the army came first. Of course, commanders, as Reinhardt's diary notes and letters as well as other contemporary accounts make plain, were frequently shaken and saddened by the plight of the refugees in the depths of the East Prussian winter. Retreating soldiers often did what they could to carry refugees with them or help where they could, though this amounted to little. The misery they witnessed had a depressing effect on troop morale.[101] Unquestionably, the Wehrmacht wanted where possible to prevent the population falling into the hands of the Soviets. But the streams of refugees on the frozen roads threatened to hamper the breakthrough to the west. Reinhardt's orders on 22 January showed where the priorities lay. 'Treks that disturb troop movements on the main roads', ordered Reinhardt, 'are to be removed from these roads . . . It's painful, certainly. But the situation demands it.'[102] 'The civilian population has to keep back,' Hoßbach in turn told his subordinate commanders of the 4th Army two days later. 'It sounds horrible, but can't unfortunately be altered, since, tough though it is, it's a matter now after the loss of East Prussia of getting the military forces there back to the homeland with some fighting power.'

'Treks have to get down off the roads,' he put it bluntly to Reinhardt later the same evening.[103] Repeatedly, the retreating army put the order into practice, manhandling refugees and their carts off the roads as they forced their way westwards.

Military logic can, of course, at times determine that the civilian population has to suffer in the short term to allow the armed forces to reorganize in order to benefit that population in the longer term. But there was little sign of clear strategic thinking in the mayhem of East Prussia in January 1945. Rescuing the troops so that they could fight again, Hoßbach's avowed aim, did not attempt to explain the purpose of fighting on. Precise motivation is not easy to discern, for leaders or for troops. Gaining time until the enemy coalition split was becoming a fainter hope by the day. 'Now it's a question of holding in the west and developing German partisan war in the east,' one colonel stated – the only hope in 'a fight to the death'. This still left the ultimate purpose unsaid, and was in any case an aim rapidly being overtaken by events.[104] 'Defence of the Fatherland' was an abstraction. And where would it be defended? At the Oder (and the Rhine)? Within the Reich itself? In the Reich capital until all was destroyed? The savagery of the Soviet attack, and the dread of falling into enemy hands, a sense of self-preservation, loyalty to immediate comrades facing the same fate, and anxieties about loved ones back home provided sufficient motivation for most ordinary soldiers – when they reflected at all on why they were continuing the fight. For those leading them, there was perhaps another element. Reinhardt's diary remark that an almost automated sense of duty drove on his actions, with little or no thought to further consequences, probably applied to most military leaders, and not just on the eastern front.

This meant that the military leadership, devoid of any alternative strategy for ending the war, was objectively continuing to work towards the regime's only remaining goal – of fighting to the last, whatever the cost in material destruction and human lives. Hitler's decisions during the January crisis in the east furthered that goal alone. As always, generals found wanting were discarded as easily as used shell-cartridges, even if, like Reinhardt, their task had been hopeless. Hitler replaced Reinhardt with Colonel-General Lothar Rendulić, a trusted Austrian, tough, shrewd and capable – though no more capable than Reinhardt had been of mastering the impossible task in East Prussia. In Hoßbach's view, he arrived without any understanding of the overall situation, had no relationship with the troops now placed under his command, 'probably acted on binding orders of Hitler' and greatly overestimated the strength of the forces at his disposal. He clashed immediately with Hoßbach over the intended breakthrough to the west at the cost of abandoning Königsberg and the Samland to their fate, saying he would not support a move he described as 'worthy of death'.[105] Only now did Hoßbach act independently, against the wishes of the Army Group leadership. The breakout went ahead, but, lacking in sufficient strength, was already floundering by 30 January when Hoßbach, too, was sacked and replaced by General Friedrich-Wilhelm Müller, competent though without experience of high command, who broke off the attempt to reach the Vistula.[106]

Further south, an enraged Hitler had already dismissed the chief of Army Group A, Colonel-General Harpe, blamed for the abandonment of Warsaw despite the order to hold the city at all costs.[107] His replacement, the commander who most epitomizes Nazi values, the brutal Colonel-General Ferdinand Schörner, lost no time in imposing his own ruthless discipline on retreating troops, mercilessly rounding up deserters and carrying out exemplary executions.[108] He demanded of his subordinate officers that they put down immediately any sign of desertion or indiscipline without concern for the fine points of a legal trial. Justice was subordinate to the general interest. 'After all, war is also not "fair",' he reasoned.[109] Much later, when he returned from imprisonment in Russia and was facing trial in West Germany, Schörner claimed that on taking up his command he found demoralization of troops, millions of refugees on the roads preventing ordered troop movements and disintegration of fighting units. He had been able to restore the situation and through tough measures had eventually stabilized the front. His aim, he stated, had nothing now to do with 'final victory' or the regime, but was solely the prevention of the Red Army advancing into Germany and saving hundreds of thousands of refugees from the Bolsheviks.[110] This conveniently overlooked his determination, even at this desperate stage, to do all he possibly could to implement Hitler's 'fight to the last' policy in the most fanatical fashion.

On 25 January Hitler took the opportunity of the personnel changes to redesignate the Army Groups, bringing them more in line with reality. Army Group A, taken over by Schörner, became Army Group Centre; Army Group Centre, placed under Rendulić, was renamed Army Group

North; and Army Group North, stranded in Courland despite Guderian's entreaties to evacuate the 200,000 or so much-needed troops trapped there for better deployment on the heavily stretched fronts elsewhere, was turned into Army Group Courland under the command of Colonel-General Heinrich von Vietinghoff, who was moved to the frozen north from sunnier climes on the Italian front. The changes reflected the need felt by the leadership to combat signs of wavering morale and the potential collapse of the front from within through the imposition of ruthless discipline. 'Triumph of the will' through blind obedience was set to replace totally the imperatives of military professionalism. To reinforce this, the head of the OKW, Field-Marshal Keitel, demanded unconditional obedience in carrying out orders and ordered the imposition of the death penalty by military courts for anyone failing in this.[111] In the most remarkable move, Hitler created a new force, Army Group Vistula, to shore up the tottering defences of north-eastern Germany and block the assault on the line of the Oder north of Glogau and Soviet penetration of West Prussia and Pomerania. Astonishingly, and in a move that smacked of desperation, he gave the command to Heinrich Himmler – skilled at the merciless treatment of helpless political and racial victims, certainly, but whose only experience of high-level front-line military leadership had been his brief and unsuccessful command of the hastily assembled Army Group Upper Rhine in the preceding weeks. His role was to restore order to the wavering front and, through harsh discipline, ensure an unrelenting fight to the end.[112] His troops consisted at first largely of what was left of the forces of the 9th and 2nd Armies, though by mid-February he commanded some forty divisions.[113]

One of Hitler's firmest backers in the unconditional fight to the end was Grand-Admiral Dönitz, whose actions belie the post-war image he cultivated of the unpolitical, purely professional military man. Dönitz was a real hardliner, totally committed to the fight against Communism. He never wavered in his complete support for Hitler, whom, he said in post-war interrogations, he saw as a man of 'extreme chivalry and kindness'. He insisted that his relations with Hitler had been purely those 'of a soldier, who was in his activities entirely limited to his province; that is to his soldier's interests',[114] and presented himself as primarily concerned only with the fate of the stricken civilian population of the east. He declared that, after the opening of the Soviet offensive on the eastern front in January, saving the inhabitants of the eastern provinces was the most important task for the German soldier, and he proudly recounted the navy's role in ferrying more than 2 million Germans to the west in the remaining months of the war.[115] Yet he reached agreement with Hitler on 22 January that dwindling coal reserves 'must be reserved for military tasks and could not be used to take away refugees'. Transport of refugees by sea could only be undertaken as long as there was no hindrance to the fighting troops. Dönitz's main priority was shipping provisions to the troops trapped in East Prussia and the Courland. Refugees desperately hoping for ships to take them from Pillau and other Baltic harbours had to wait.[116]

As the head of the Luftwaffe, Hermann Göring, though effectively in disgrace for the failings of air defence and present at Führer Headquarters only when he had to be, remained loyal, however resigned he was to Germany's impending fate.[117] Colonel-General Robert Ritter von Greim, Commander-in-Chief of the 6th Air Fleet on the eastern front, already in mind as a possible replacement for Göring, was another convinced National Socialist, a participant in the putsch attempt of 1923, and utterly committed to Hitler to the very end. Other senior Luftwaffe officers were also fanatical about continuing the fight, however hopeless it seemed. Whether or not leaders of the Luftwaffe felt this way, hopes that something could be saved for the future made most of them ultra-cautious about doing anything that would prompt disfavour.[118]

Guderian, as Chief of the Army General Staff, was as a consequence of his disagreements with military dispositions becoming increasingly frustrated and estranged from Hitler, though, as we have noted, he had usually come down on his side when Reinhardt had desperately been trying to get decisions to retreat in East Prussia. However much he disagreed with Hitler's decisions, Guderian accepted them and tried to implement them as well as he could. Soon after the attempt on Hitler's life in July 1944 he had wanted every General Staff officer to be an NSFO.[119] He had also served on the 'Court of Honour' that had thrown fifty-five army officers out of the Wehrmacht in disgrace.[120] He remained a loyalist, if by now a disillusioned one. And at the top of the Wehrmacht, lapdog loyalty was assured in Keitel and Jodl. The military establishment, contrary to its later claims, remained, therefore, committed to Hitler, and to a strategy which, ruling out any form of capitulation, could logically only lead to further immense bloodshed and ultimate self-destruction.

What above all enabled the military struggle to continue, though at inevitable cost on other fronts, was the belated acceptance that massive reinforcements for the east had to be found. Losses on the eastern front in January and February were more than 450,000.[121] But the front had to be strengthened beyond these losses. The navy and the Luftwaffe made available tens of thousands of sailors and airmen for the land war.[122] The Replacement Army scraped together many more, often from those in reserved occupations previously exempted from call-up. The *Volkssturm* mobilized in total over half a million men, grossly lacking in weapons, to serve on the eastern front, suffering horrendous losses as they did so.[123] But since genuine reserves were as good as exhausted, and new recruits were often scarcely trained boys of sixteen or seventeen, many of the reinforcements could only come from the west or the south. On 19 January, six days into the Soviet offensive, Lieutenant-General August Winter, deputy head of the Wehrmacht Operations Staff, presented a memorandum whose basic premiss was that the war would be decided over the coming weeks in the east. Winter stated the necessity, forced by the emergency in the east, 'at the cost of other theatres of war and with conscious acknowledgement of the serious risk involved for the western theatre of concentrating maximum forces in the eastern theatre for the great decisive battle'.[124] The order resulted in a further forty divisions being dispatched to the east. Aircraft, anti-aircraft batteries, tanks and heavy artillery were now overwhelmingly also sent east, to the neglect of other fronts. By 12 February, thirty-three divisions had been sent to the eastern front, with another twelve to follow by early March. But eighteen of these divisions could be provided only by weakening the fight against the British and Americans in the west and in northern Italy.[125] The eventual final phase of the Allied advance in the west was, therefore, directly presaged by the collapse of the Wehrmacht in the east.

In the meantime, increasing desperation on the part of the regime's leaders and their representatives at lower levels, coupled with the evident signs that morale was crumbling at home as well as on the fronts, intensified the resort to measures of extreme repression. These were now directed not just at helpless, persecuted minority groups, but at the German population itself. The terror that had been exported eastwards for so long was coming home to the Reich.

6

Terror Comes Home

The Führer expects that the Gauleiter will implement the task placed before them with the necessary severity and consistency and ruthlessly suppress every sign of disintegration, cowardice and defeatism with the death sentences of the summary courts martial. Anyone not prepared to fight for his people but who stabs it in the back in its gravest hour does not deserve to live and must fall to the executioner.

Bormann's directive on the establishment
of summary courts martial, 15 February 1945

I

For the mass of the German population, the consequences of the inability to repel the enemy in the west through the Ardennes offensive had still not sunk in before the onslaught from the east in the second half of January 1945. The traumatic impact of this calamity now brought home to almost everyone that the end of the war was approaching; that Germany faced total defeat and enemy occupation in the near future. The days were plainly numbered for a regime that in ever more people's eyes had brought such misery upon the country. With this recognition, the signs of disintegration within the civilian population and among ordinary soldiers started to mount. The regime responded in characteristic fashion: by hugely stepping up the repression at home.

Of course, repression had been an intrinsic part of the Nazi regime from the outset. The legal profession had fully collaborated in the escalating persecution and responded at every stage to the extra-legal violence of the police and the Party's organizations by intensifying its own repression. But the repression of the pre-war years, omnipresent though it was, had concentrated on 'outsider' groups. The regime's social and political control rested ultimately on the general acknowledgement by Germans that it would act ruthlessly against those who stood in its way or were deemed in some way or another to be its enemies. As long as the repression was aimed at 'outsiders' and 'undesirables', however, it was accepted, even welcomed, by the majority of the population.[1] And as long as individuals who did not belong to a politically or racially targeted group conformed, or did not have the misfortune to be deemed an 'inferior' in some way, to be excluded from the 'people's community', they were not likely to fall into the clutches of the Gestapo.

Once the war started, the violence built into the system gained new and powerful momentum. In the main, it was exported. The brunt of it was borne by the peoples of the countries conquered in the early, triumphant phase of the war. But repression at home against any signs of political non-conformity also intensifed. Jews, as always the top-ranking racial enemy and blamed incessantly in relentless propaganda for the war, were subjected to ever worsening, horrific persecution, especially when deportations to the east began in 1941.[2] And terroristic repression was arbitrarily directed at the increasing numbers of foreign workers from the conquered countries, especially when the fortunes of war turned against Germany – a point symbolically marked by the catastrophe at Stalingrad in the winter of 1942/3. By this time, the legal system had effectively capitulated to the untrammelled might of the SS-police security apparatus. As the losses at the front mounted alarmingly and the pressures on the civilian population within Germany grew commensurately during the course of 1944, the regime became ever more sensitive to signs of dissent. Even so, criticism of the regime widened, as the authorities' own monitoring services plainly indicated. Hitler's own popularity – the focal point of 'positive' propaganda – had by now visibly waned. The Party was suffering a severe drop in its standing. Morale at the front, especially after the collapse in France, was wavering.

Dissolving support for the regime, which propaganda struggled vainly to combat, meant inexorably a greater recourse to terroristic repression. Following the attempt on Hitler's life on 20 July 1944, and with Germany facing mounting adversity in the last months of the year, the population, as we have seen in earlier chapters, was increasingly forced into line in the total-war drive. Incautious remarks or any signs of what were deemed defeatism or subversion were ruthlessly punished. It was becoming an ever more dangerous regime for its own citizens.

Even so, from February 1945 onwards the terror within Germany moved to a new plane. The regime's leaders, Hitler at the forefront, could now plainly see that, short of a miracle, defeat was staring them in the face. Propaganda parroted slogans aimed at boosting the readiness to hold out and fight on. But for most people now this was obviously whistling in the wind. As propaganda failed, violence intensified. The regime's reflex to outright violence marked a combination of fear, desperation, defiance and revenge. Fear of another 1918; increasing wariness of the explosive potential of the millions of foreign workers in the country; desperation at the impending total defeat and the collapse of the regime; defiance of all forces – internal as well as external – seen to be dragging Germany to perdition; and revenge against all those who had stood against Nazism and would rejoice at its downfall: the combination created a new level of violence arbitrarily directed against anyone seen to block or oppose the fight to the finish.

The worst of the retribution was, as ever, reserved for the regime's designated enemies. The last months would prove murderous for Jews, foreign workers, prisoners of war and concentration camp internees as the vestiges of control over increasingly untrammelled violence dissolved. But the majority German population was now also subjected in increasing measure to wild reprisals for perceived defeatism. The slightest ill-judged remark or perceived minor opposition to the self-destructive course of the regime could prove disastrous for any individual. As the military fronts closed in on the Reich, the terror, once exported, was rebounding in the death-throes of the regime on the population of Germany itself. It was a mark of increasing desperation. Just as with the vain efforts of propaganda, terror could do nothing to halt the continued slide of morale. But it was more than sufficient to prevent any prospect of the misery, suffering and, by now, detestation of the Nazi regime in wide swathes of the population being converted into the type of revolutionary mood that had characterized the last stages of the First World War in 1917–18.

II

By the end of January, the regime was becoming seriously concerned at the signs of collapsing morale, both at home and – even more worryingly – at the front. Even from within the SS – however difficult it was, there above all, to admit it – there were voices prepared to acknowledge a deepening crisis.

On 26 January SS-Hauptsturmführer Rolf d'Alquen, staff officer in the propaganda department of Army Group Upper Rhine, wired a panicky message to his brother in Berlin, Standartenführer Gunter d'Alquen, editor of the SS newspaper *Das Schwarze Korps*. 'The mood among the fighting troops has become more nervous and serious by the day on account of the events on the eastern front,' he stated. Many who came from the eastern regions had their personal anxieties. 'If the situation gets worse in the next days,' he continued, 'it can be reckoned that the fighting spirit of the troops will be paralysed by worries that can no longer be borne.' The mood among the civilian population of the area was similar, he indicated. He wanted 'a redeeming word from Führer Headquarters' and asked, cautiously but pointedly, if it was possible to ascertain whether Hitler had told his entourage what he had in mind to master the crisis. Both among the troops and in the civilian population, it was clear that the front could only be held for a short time with existing weapons, he remarked. What hopes remained were invested in a weapon 'that could nullify all that has been endured and all setbacks, and produce the decisive change on the fronts'.

He requested that the state of morale at the front should be brought to the Führer's attention. This, almost certainly, did not happen. But his account did reach Himmler. D'Alquen's message was relayed to Rudolf Brandt, Himmler's personal adjutant, with a covering note that it was 'typical for the psychological situation of the troops, but also for those there responsible for propaganda'. Himmler lost no time in replying. Though the troops had suffered setbacks, he declared, it was d'Alquen himself who was most depressed. His suggestion was 'absolutely impossible'. The troops must be told to do their duty, however hard it was. When the west was protected, the Wehrmacht in the east would be ready to absorb the assault before 'becoming active again'. 'From you yourself', Himmler closed, 'I expect the inner bearing of an SS man.'[3]

A few days later, Himmler's own newly created Army Group Vistula was reporting that the officers 'no longer had the troops firmly in hand' and 'signs of dissolution of the worst kind' were occurring as soldiers – and not just in occasional instances – 'pulled off their uniforms and tried in every way to obtain civilian clothing in order to get away'.[4] The western Allies did not, however, for their part, based on their interrogations of captured soldiers, expect large-scale desertions. 'The strongest deterrent against desertion continues to be fear of retaliation against one's family,' was their assessment. The feeling that the end of the war was close was a further reason not to take the high risk of deserting. Around 65 per cent of those interrogated in mid-February thought the war would be over in weeks. They fought on, it was adjudged, through desire for self-preservation, apathy (about all but their own immediate military situation) and an automatic sense of obedience.[5] In the mayhem of the evacuations from the east, soldiers were said to be mingling with the evacuees, 'marking time' and trying to avoid further fighting, 'in expectation of the coming end', since the military police had either disappeared themselves or were helpless to control the massively overcrowded trains.[6]

Martin Bormann, in the Party Chancellery, was in no doubt, from reports he was receiving, of soldiers affecting civilian morale through their defeatist attitude. 'What? You're still listening to Hitler?' one soldier who had returned to the Magdeburg area was heard to remark. He was off home, he said, and by the time the authorities had found him the war would be over anyway. Luckily for him, no one took his details and he got away with it. In the Sudetenland, soldiers pouring back in flight from the east were said to present a depressing sight. Often, they would enter shops to demand goods even though they had no ration coupons. When challenged, they retorted that the war was over anyway and there would be no need for ration cards. Their view was that the consequences of defeat would not be as bad as they were painted.[7] From the Cologne-Aachen area in early February, Bormann heard of a 'gathering inner uncertainty' and belief in 'a certain leadership crisis' in the Wehrmacht, though the Waffen-SS was seen to stand out in distinction.[8]

These impressions of low morale among soldiers within Germany were reinforced by a report of an NSFO – couched, naturally, in Nazi language – of his impressions gathered during a journey through several parts of the country. He registered 'symptoms of threatening developments for the future'. Deserters often found support among the civilian population, he claimed, also for their allegations that sabotage by officers – echoes of the Stauffenberg plot still reverberated here – had caused Germany's defeat. Discipline was undermined and officers themselves apathetic, the report noted. People in central Germany, naturally worried by events in the east, were telling soldiers on the western front that they should let in the Americans so that the Bolsheviks would not get to them, a view he regarded as an obvious danger to morale. Stories that armaments factories had been closed down because of coal and transport difficulties were also affecting morale. Soldiers hearing that the armaments industry was no longer working saw the war then as unquestionably lost. Predictably, the report concluded that drastic measures needed to be taken to counter such worrying signs, advocating 'flying courts martial', 'merciless' implementation of orders and 'radical measures carried out with all force' as a necessary response.[9]

Reports from the eastern regions of Germany in mid-February could only have made depressing reading for Himmler. He heard that recognition of German military impotence was 'the root of almost all signs of demoralization among the troops', who generally accepted that the war was lost. Looting of property by the Wehrmacht in places where the civilian population had fled, also seen as a sign of collapsing morale, was commonplace. Many soldiers, officers and *Volkssturm* men were to be found detached from their units and wandering in the woods on the eastern banks of the Oder, trying to cross into Germany. Their morale was suitably poor. In despairing mood, they often blamed National Socialism for all their suffering, viewed the war as lost and wanted peace at any price. Himmler and the SS, it was acknowledged, were also openly criticized. And leaders among the groups of stragglers were telling them not to resort to arms if they encountered Soviet troops, but to surrender without a fight.[10]

Among the civilian population, morale had dipped to an equally low ebb. Propaganda reports in mid-February indicated 'a profound lethargy' as an attitude said to be prevalent among the middle class and peasantry. Their resigned view – 'a creeping poison' – was that all was lost anyway, and the war would be over within a few months.[11] Soldiers travelling through Berlin reported that the mood in the west was 'catastrophic', as everyone was just waiting for the end of the war, which could not be long delayed. In the Reich capital itself, pessimism had caught hold among the population. There was widespread criticism of failed promises of new weapons, though fear of the consequences of falling into the hands of the Soviets was said to underpin a readiness to fight on.[12] Fatalism and dulled indifference were commonplace. 'We'll take it as it comes. We can't alter things,' people felt. 'Everything that looks like propaganda or is spoken as such is flatly rejected,' it was reported.[13] Similar disbelief in propaganda claims was registered in southern Germany, where the mood was 'very depressed' and there was little hope in a favourable end to the war for Germany, especially since the promised new weapons had never materialized.[14] People in Vienna thought they had been led up the garden path about the new weapons. There was a general feeling that the situation was hopeless. Alongside widespread apathy, individuals were fearful. Many were said to be contemplating suicide. 'I've already taken all steps to do away with my family,' was one comment. 'I've enough poison.'[15] The war was 'the same swindle' as in 1914–18, the rural population in the Alpine district of Berchtesgaden were saying. 'If people had imagined in 1933 what was to come, they would never have voted for Hitler,' was the view in an area where once huge crowds of 'pilgrims' had gathered to try to catch a glimpse of the Führer at his nearby residence on the Obersalzberg.[16]

The resignation, apathy, dislocation and sheer fatigue at the attritional suffering – quite apart from the suffocating repression of the regime – meant, however, that the collapsing morale could not be converted into a revolutionary fervour. Reports by observers from neutral countries smuggled out to the western Allies provided graphic descriptions of the depressed mood in Berlin as preparations were made for the defence of the city, the chaotic situation on the railways, panic buying of food in central Germany and the appalling living conditions throughout the country. But such reports were adamant that there was no possibility of an internal revolution.[17]

Even so, the Nazi authorities were taking no chances. For them, the alarm bells were now ringing loudly, despite repeated routine protestations about the 'solid inner bearing' of the people. A worrying indicator was the crumpling of the Party's authority and collapse in its standing. This had largely disintegrated in the west the previous autumn. Now it was the same in the east – and increasingly everywhere. Refugees flooding in from the east were from late January onwards pouring out their bile on the failings of Party officials in the botched evacuations – prominent among them as a target the East Prussian Gauleiter, Erich Koch.[18] Relations between the army and the Party were tense. Given the current mood on the eastern front, Himmler was told (in response to a suggestion that Party leaders should be sent to serve effectively as political commissars with the troops) that individuals in Party uniform would be killed.[19] The Party uniform, it was claimed, acted like a red rag to soldiers.[20] It was little different among the civilian population. Party functionaries, well aware of their unpopularity, had to be reminded by the Munich Gauleiter, Paul Giesler, of their obligation to wear their uniform on duty – and ordinary Party members their badge at all times – under penalty of exclusion from the Party.[21] The intense hatred and contempt for the representatives of a Party by now widely seen as responsible for Germany's ruination was meanwhile as good as ubiquitous. Cases of what were understandably seen as gross dereliction of duty by Party leaders scandalized the population and pushed their public standing still further into the mire.[22]

Hans Frank, Hitler's viceroy in the General Government of Poland, was hugely corrupt even by Nazi standards. In his domain almost 2 million Jews had been gassed to death in the camps at Bełżec, Sobibor and Treblinka and a reign of terror imposed on the subjugated Polish population. Frank fled on 17 January from the Wawel Castle in Kraków, where he had lived since 1939 in untold luxury and despotic splendour. He and his large entourage headed first to a castle at Seichau in Silesia. When they moved again on 23 January, they left behind rooms littered with the remnants of large stores of food and wine, much of it squandered in a lavish farewell party, to the fury of a local population that had been forced to acclimatize to the privations of war. Lorry-loads of valuables and looted art treasures were sent on to Frank's eventual residence amid the Bavarian lakes.[23]

However, it was the flight by Gauleiter Arthur Greiser from his headquarters in Posen in mid-January that gained particular notoriety. Greiser, who was to be executed in 1946 by the Poles upon whom he had inflicted years of torment and suffering in the 'Warthegau', had been one of the most ruthless of the Nazi provincial rulers. He was proud of having the ear of Hitler and Himmler, and had played a significant part in establishing the Chełmno death camp in his region, where more than 150,000 Jews were gassed between the end of 1941 and 1944. With the Red Army rapidly advancing and by 17 January almost at the borders of his Gau, Greiser still kept up appearances about the strength of German defences. Inwardly, he was close to panic. Unwilling to see his Gau as the first to be evacuated, he refused to give the necessary orders. A partial and belated order for the easternmost parts of the Gau was eventually given on the night of 17/18 January, after Greiser had witnessed thousands of troops running away. But most of the population were unaware of their peril. He still professed to his staff that Posen would be defended. In reality, he knew that there was no possibility of stemming the Soviet onslaught. On 20 January, Greiser called Führer Headquarters and gained Hitler's approval, passed on to him by Bormann, to evacuate the Party offices in Posen and move his entourage to more secure surrounds in Frankfurt an der Oder. Greiser told his staff that he was being recalled to Berlin by order of the Führer to undertake a special task for Himmler. That evening, accompanied by an aide, he fled from Posen. Whatever lorries could be found were sequestrated for the transfer of the property and files of the Gau offices; the initial objections of the military authorities were overcome on the grounds that the evacuation was an order of the Führer. Greiser's flight left the Gau in chaos and a frantic stampede of the population trying to escape by whatever means they could. Most were overtaken by Soviet troops. Around 50,000 died fleeing from the Warthegau.[24]

The Hitler order was a complication when criticism of Greiser arose within the Party itself. It transpired, however, that Greiser had engineered the permission to leave at a time when evacuation was being refused to ordinary citizens – Posen had been designated a fortress town, to be held at whatever cost – and had misled Hitler into believing that the fall of the city was imminent. (In fact, the Red Army was then still about 130 kilometres away, and Posen did not finally capitulate until late February.) Goebbels, long an admirer of Greiser but aware of the damage he had now caused the Party, regarded the Gauleiter's action as shameful, cowardly and deceitful. He thought Greiser should be put before the People's Court (where a death sentence would have been the certain outcome), but could not persuade Hitler – presumably embarrassed by his own authorization – to impose the severe punishment he felt was merited.[25] As it was, the 'Greiser case', propaganda agencies reported, was still 'doing the rounds' weeks later, amplifying the accounts from refugees about 'the failure of the NSDAP in the evacuation of entire Gaue'.[26] Bormann was forced to issue a circular to the

Party, attempting to counter the negative rumours about the behaviour of the political leaders in the Warthegau. He defended Greiser, stating that he was prepared to serve with the military command in Posen but left the city on the express orders of the Führer. He threatened harsh punishment for any functionaries leaving the population in the lurch.[27]

Greiser was, in fact, far from the last of the Party 'bigwigs' to leave his charges stranded after demanding of them that they should hold out to the last. But he was, for Goebbels, 'the first serious disappointment', an indicator that 'everything was breaking up' and the end was not far off.[28]

III

The signs that the determination to hold on was starting to wobble even within the Party itself now prompted moves to shore up the faltering morale by strenuous and repeated exhortation – backed at every point by merciless punishment for those seen to fail in their duty.

On 23 January, Wilhelm Stuckart, as acting Reich Plenipotentiary for Administration (deputizing for Himmler in the latter's capacity as Reich Minister of the Interior), demanded that administrative officials of state authorities in the eastern Gaue (including Mark Brandenburg and Berlin) carry out their duties to the last possible minute in areas threatened by the enemy before then attaching themselves to the fighting troops. Rigorous measures were to be taken against those seen to fail. When Stuckart circulated his missive to the highest state authorities on 1 February, he included a copy of Himmler's order, issued two days earlier, stipulating that anyone leaving his position in any military or civilian office without being ordered to do so should be punished by death. An added list of 'punishments' specified that those guilty of cowardice and dereliction of duty were to be shot immediately. To reinforce the message, Himmler drew attention to the examples from the town of Bromberg, where Party and state officials had behaved less than heroically on the approach of the Red Army. The police chief had apparently deserted his post. A local army commander had gone against orders in retreating from a defensive position. The Government President (head of the regional administration) and the mayor of Bromberg were subsequently degraded and sent to serve in punishment battalions faced with especially dangerous tasks, as was the Party's District Leader, having first been expelled from the Party. All had been forced to attend the execution of the Police President, SS-Standartenführer Carl von Salisch, shot by firing squad for cowardice. The army commander was also shot.[29] On 11 February, Himmler put out a proclamation to the officers of Army Group Vistula, whose command he had just taken over, expecting of them 'a model of bravery and steadfastness' in the decisive phase of the struggle against the 'Jewish-Bolshevik danger', and a 'fanatical will to victory and burning hatred against these Bolshevik sub-animals', but reminding them that the police chief in Bromberg had been shot for not fulfilling the demands of his office.[30]

Bormann was by now, on Hitler's behalf, repeatedly instructing Party leaders on the need for exemplary behaviour (also from their wives, some of whom had left threatened areas before evacuation orders had been issued), again with the threat of severe reprisals for those found lacking.[31] He felt it necessary to pass on Hitler's reminder that all orders were binding, to be implemented 'if necessary by draconian measures' and to be carried out by subordinates 'without contradiction' and swiftly. The German people had to understand more than ever at this time 'that it was led by a strong and determined hand', that 'signs of disintegration and arbitrary actions would be ruthlessly nipped in the bud' and that neglect by subordinate organs of the Party would 'on no account be tolerated'.[32] Any Party leader failing in his duties, abandoning his people to find safety for himself and his family or gain some other advantage, distancing himself from the NSDAP, or 'fleeing as a coward instead of fighting to the last' was to be evicted from the Party, brought before the courts for judgement and subject to 'the most severe punishment'.[33] In his circular – stated to be not for publication – on 24 February 1945, the twenty-fifth anniversary of the promulgation of the Party Programme, Bormann reminded all Party members in unequivocal terms that anyone thinking of himself, of quitting and making off, would be a 'traitor to the people and murderer of our women and children'. Only steadfastness down to death without concern for one's own life served as a defence against 'the elemental storm from the steppes, the methods of the inner-Asiatic hordes'. The Führer demanded, and the people expected, of every Party leader 'that he holds out to the end and is never concerned for his own salvation'. For the Party rank-and-file, too, the call of the hour meant to follow unconditionally the sense of higher duty. 'Anyone seeking to save his life is with certainty, also through the verdict of the people, condemned to death. There is only one possibility of staying alive,' he declared (with some contradiction); 'the readiness to die fighting and thereby to attain victory.'[34] For now, the Party still – just about – held together.

As discipline slackened worryingly in the Wehrmacht, too, there was a similar resort to threats of drastic sanctions. Hitler let it be known through Keitel, at the time that the eastern front was collapsing and his own orders were being challenged by his generals in East Prussia, that if military leaders failed to carry out commands unconditionally or transmit absolutely reliable dispatches he would demand 'the most ruthless punishment of those guilty' and would expect the courts to be severe enough to pass the death sentence.[35]

One plain indicator of the collapsing front was the enormously swollen number of 'stragglers' heading back to Germany. Though many had genuinely become separated from their units, others were feigning detachment from their units in the hope of avoiding further front service. The distinction between those who had deserted and those who, genuinely or not, had 'lost' their units was increasingly blurred. Intensified efforts were now made to pick up 'stragglers' and return them to the front, sometimes using special military police detachments.[36] Even on the wildly overcrowded station in Breslau in late January, as desperate evacuees fought to get on the last trains west, military police were searching for anyone in uniform to send them back to fight the Russians.[37] At the end of the month, Himmler appealed to the German people to adopt a hard line towards 'shirkers', 'cowards' and 'weaklings' who were failing in their duty. He urged women, especially, to show no sympathy for 'shirkers' who tagged onto evacuation treks travelling westwards. 'Men who take themselves from the front are not deserving of bread from the homeland,' he declared. They had instead to be reminded of their honour and duty, be treated with contempt and be sent back to the front.[38] The Wehrmacht laid down detailed regulations for seizing 'stragglers' and returning them to frontline duty, ominously adding 'in so far as in individual cases judgement by a military court is not necessary'.[39]

The commandant of Schneidemühl, a designated fortress, was commended by Himmler in late January for shooting down retreating soldiers with a pistol then hanging a notice round their necks saying 'this is what happens to all cowards'.[40] The 'bitter experiences in the east', Bormann noted, showed that in the face of enemy inroads 'there is no longer an absolute reliance on the steadfastness of the front troops'. Consequently, in early February, in preparation for the expected enemy offensive in the west, he asked Himmler to provide an increased number of 'interception squads' of the kind that had been successful in the collapse in France the previous summer to pick up retreating soldiers 'through rigorous intervention' and return them to 'joyful fulfilment of their duty'. The squads were to be backed up, he told the western Gauleiter, by all the force at the disposal of the police and *Volkssturm*.[41] From the local level upwards, regular reports were to be sent to the Gauleiter in the eastern regions, and from there to military commanders, on the 'stragglers' caught. Western Gauleiter were also to pay particular attention to the problem on account of expected hostilities in the region.[42]

A few days later, Himmler transmitted an order to the Higher SS and Police Leaders in the western regions advocating use of maximum severity, in tandem with the military authorities, in rounding up 'stragglers' and 'shooting looters and deserters on the spot', in order to remove any obstacles from the western front in the forthcoming 'heavy attacks'. Bormann had the order passed on in 130 copies to all Party leaders at central and regional level.[43] 'Should anyone intervene too harshly', Himmler stated, in 'combing out towns and barracks for so-called stragglers or soldiers journeying about with pretended march and travel orders', it was better than not intervening at all.[44] He had by then, on 12 February, announced the implementation in Army Group Vistula of an order, which he found 'so excellent', put out for Army Group Centre by the inimitable Colonel-General Schörner. Among the exhortations, in classical Nazi diction, to fanatical hatred against the enemy and the need for iron resolve with 'our homeland at stake', was the threat that 'stragglers who don't immediately register for redeployment or follow orders' would be placed before a court martial and charged with cowardice.[45] The result in such an event was invariably a foregone conclusion. Schörner's way of dealing with 'trained stragglers', as he dubbed them, was even in Goebbels' eyes 'fairly brutal'. 'He lets them be hanged from the next tree with a notice attached saying: "I'm a deserter and have refused to protect German women and children." That, naturally, has a good deterrent effect on other deserters or those who think of deserting,' the Propaganda Minister observed.[46]

At the end of February, Bormann reckoned there were up to 600,000 soldiers in the Reich avoiding front service. A priority throughout the Reich was to track them down and round them up. The public had to be made aware of the problem and a tough approach adopted, in contrast to 1917–18. Drastic measures were necessary if ducking out of duty was not to spread. 'Every shirker has to be aware that he will with great probability be caught in the homeland and then without doubt will lose his life.' At the front, there was the mere possibility that he would die. At home, avoiding his duty, he would certainly do so, and in dishonour. Only when this message sank in 'shall we master this cowardice disease', he concluded.[47]

Some estimates put the number of deserters down to the end of 1944 at more than a quarter of a million. This can be no more than informed guesswork, and may well include honest 'stragglers' as well as those who, for whatever reason, could take no more and took enormous risks to lay down their arms. The figure relates, however, to the period before the collapse of the eastern front in January sent the numbers of 'stragglers' (and those actually deserting) spiralling – perhaps doubling – in the last four months of the war.[48] If the overall scale of the phenomenon must remain no more than an approximation, at least the figures for those punished for desertion by military courts – though not arbitrarily shot or otherwise 'executed' in arbitrary action – are known. Compared with 18 cases in the German army in the First World War, those in the Wehrmacht sentenced for desertion during the Second World War numbered, in a sharply rising trend, some 35,000. Around 15,000 of these received the death penalty.[49]

Apart from desertion, any perceived undermining of the war effort brought rapid and harsh retribution. The contrast in severity, both with the sentencing in the German army in the First World War and with that of the Allies in the Second, is striking. For a variety of perceived serious offences, a total of 150 German soldiers had been sentenced to death in the First World War, 48 of whom were actually executed. German military courts passed, in all, some 30,000 death sentences against German soldiers during the Second World War, with 20,000 carried out. During the Second World War the British executed 40, the French 103, the Americans 146.[50]

The higher the rank, the less likely it was that perceived military failings would incur severe sanction. Generals might be dismissed, as

Harpe, Reinhardt and Hoßbach had been on the eastern front in January. But they were not disgraced, let alone sentenced to death or subjected to other forms of severe punishment (though not a few voices in the public could be heard still talking darkly, in tones reminiscent of the aftermath of the July plot in 1944, of 'traitors and saboteurs' in high places[51]). Still, as the military situation worsened and the regime became increasingly ready in its mounting desperation to resort to violence within, even high officers needed to tread warily. Colonel Thilo von Trotha, in the Army General Staff, would have recognized the warning shot across the bows from a personal acquaintance, none other than Colonel-General Schörner, in late February. 'Among ourselves, a frank word,' wrote Schörner. 'I received a hint yesterday, *most confidentially*, of course, that your attitude to the Party and its representatives is occasionally somewhat reserved. One could have the impression that you don't place sufficient value in certain things such as the National Socialist leadership of the army. . . .' 'Dear Trotha,' he continued, 'I trust you have understood me. Either we succeed in having fanatical supporters and unconditional loyalists of the Führer at the top, or things will go wrong again.'[52]

A few days later, in a lengthy and secret missive to the commanders-in-chief and generals in command, Schörner amplified this message in a broad attack on the failure of leadership in the staffs of some parts of the army. He praised the soldiers who had learnt to be brutal and fanatical in 'almost four years of an Asiatic war', and had recently in fighting on the river Neiße taken no prisoners. In contrast, he scourged the indifference, bourgeois lifestyles, lack of 'soldier personalities' and 'defeatist tiredness of spirit' of officers who were unable to stir the troops through fanaticism. 'I am in agreement with the commanders-in-chief and generals in command and with every front soldier,' he wrote, 'that in the Asiatic war we need revolutionary and dynamic officers.' Stalin, he added, would have got nowhere if he had waged war with bourgeois methods. Schörner demanded 'clear and unambigous fanaticism, nothing else'.[53]

The scarcely veiled threat in Schörner's letter to Trotha and his exhortation to leading generals is a further pointer to the lack of unity in the higher ranks of the army. Though many high-ranking officers had long since inwardly turned against the Nazi regime, the spectrum of attitudes reached at the opposite extreme as far as fanatics like Schörner. In such a climate of division, distrust and fear, any prospect of a common front against Hitler could be completely ruled out.

The divisions ran throughout society. Far from the united 'community of fate' trumpeted by Nazi propaganda, this was a riven society where individuals looked more and more to their own narrow interests – acquisition of the necessities of life and, above all else, survival. 'Never have the German people lived in such inner division,' was the verdict of one colonel in February 1945.[54]

Despite the flood of reports telling them they were fighting a losing battle, Goebbels' propaganda chiefs intensified rather than lessened their efforts as Germany's plight worsened. Newspapers were distributed in Ruhr cities even after the worst bombing raids (though a suggestion that they be dropped by aeroplane was rejected as absurdly impractical).[55] But even Goebbels himself was sick of the empty pathos of repeated exhortations to 'Believe and Fight', or to stay 'With the Führer to Final Victory'.[56] In the absence of reliable information and in often frank disbelief of official reports, rumour inevitably spread like wildfire and was difficult to control, most of all when it related to evacuation of the population in areas close to the front.[57] One suggestion (later adopted) was to dispatch special units of, in all, around 1,500 Political Leaders of the Party to key points on the eastern and western fronts to stiffen morale, notably in the west, given the expected hostilities there, to prevent 'signs of crisis' arising as had been the case in the east as areas had been evacuated and then fallen to the Red Army. The special propaganda units would not come under Wehrmacht command, but be directed by Bormann and Himmler, with the task of 'organizing and mobilizing the entire strength of the people of the areas in question for total deployment and the war effort'.[58]

Directives for verbal propaganda issued in mid-February tried to do the near impossible in emphasizing the positives for Germany in the current war situation. The Soviet advance into German eastern territories had been at such a cost of men and *matériel* that the Bolshevik fighting strength was decisively weakened, it was claimed, opening 'an extraordinary chance' for German counter-attacks. The German leadership knew that attack was the best form of defence, and would act accordingly. In the west, the length of Allied supply lines was a weakness, whereas German lines were short, units more easily manoeuvrable and, through the addition of the People's Grenadier divisions, the Wehrmacht was stronger than the previous summer in Normandy. Not least, the deep-echelon fortifications system, it was claimed, allowed reserves to be directed at the right moment to positions under pressure and at the same time force the enemy into a damaging war of attrition.[59]

Little of this sounded convincing. And rallying-cries such as Himmler's to his divisional commanders in Army Group Vistula, passed on for wider circulation, that 'strong hearts triumph over mass and *matériel*', accompanied by examples of heroic action at the front, must have sounded empty to most people.[60] Other than in reinforcing defiance among the already committed regime loyalists, propaganda was for the most part by now visibly failing in its objectives.

There was, however, one notable exception. Fear, all the more so after the traumatic events in January, was the prime motivator to hold out and fight on in the east. It formed a bond – even in a negative way forging a kind of integration as all else was falling apart. And in embellishing the already existing – and well-justified – anxieties of the consequences of Soviet conquest, propaganda still had a significant role to play, both among civilians and in the Wehrmacht. Troops were drilled with the need to combat the 'Asiatic storm from the east', and reminded through examples from distant history – such as the defeat of the Hungarians near Augsburg in 955 and of Ottoman forces besieging Vienna in 1683 – that such attacks had always been repelled by fanatical defence when the enemy reached German soil.[61] Even for some leading Nazis, playing on the fears of a population whose nerves were so stretched through the emphasis on Soviet atrocities went too far.[62] But there could be no question of playing down one of the last effective propaganda weapons to hand. Already in mid-February propaganda preparations were being laid for the defence of Berlin. Leaflets were drafted, addressed to 'The Defenders of Berlin', urging 'fanatical hatred' in the fight to repel the Bolsheviks. 'It's about countless German women and children who place their trust in you,' the draft proclamation ran. 'Every house a fortress, every street passage a mass grave for the Red hordes.' 'Hatred against hatred! Fight to the last! Bloody revenge and thousandfold retaliation for the Bolshevik atrocities in our homeland!'[63]

Fear of Bolshevism was undoubtedly an important factor in sustaining the readiness to fight on, particularly in those parts of Germany most obviously exposed to advances by the Red Army. The further the population was removed from the immediate threat of Soviet occupation, and the more probable it was that the area would fall to the western Allies, the less direct resonance, however, the shrill anti-Bolshevik hate-propaganda was likely to have. And in the western parts of the Reich, there was little outright fear of Anglo-American occupation, other than among diehard Nazis and funtionaries of the regime. Reports filtering back from areas already occupied even led to claims that the behaviour of the Americans was better 'than our German troops'.[64] The reality was that, however much the propaganda machine went into overdrive, only a dwindling minority of Germans remained fully committed to the regime. These did, however, include among their number those who still had power of life and death in their hands. A word out of place could bring a denunciation and the direst of consequences. As the hold of the regime slipped and propaganda was widely disbelieved, repression was increasingly all that was left.

A major reflection of the enhanced emphasis on repression and terror within was the decree issued on Hitler's orders on 15 February by the Reich Justice Minister, Otto Georg Thierack (and impatiently awaited by Gauleiter in threatened areas[65]), introducing the establishment of summary courts martial (*Standgerichte*) in areas threatened by the enemy. Each court was to be chaired by a judge and to comprise in addition a Political Leader of the NSDAP or one of its affiliates and an officer of the Wehrmacht, the Waffen-SS or police. The members of the court were to be nominated by the Gauleiter, as Reich Defence Commissar for the region. The court was to deal with all offences that could endanger fighting morale and could issue only three verdicts: death penalty, exoneration or transfer to a regular court. The Reich Defence Commissar was to confirm the verdict and determine place, time and manner of an execution. 'The Führer expects', Bormann added in his covering ordinance to the Gauleiter, 'that the Gauleiter will implement the task placed before them with the necessary severity and consistency and ruthlessly suppress every sign of disintegration, cowardice and defeatism with the death sentences of the summary courts martial. Anyone not prepared to fight for his people but who stabs it in the back in its gravest hour does not deserve to live and must fall to the executioner.'[66] Some days earlier, Bormann had informed the Gauleiter that this now gave them 'the weapon to destroy all those pests of the people' and declared his expectation 'that this instrument will be used as the Führer would wish, ruthlessly and without respect to the standing or position of the person concerned'.[67]

Bormann's guidelines, indicating Hitler's wishes, give clear enough indication that the new courts had little to do with conventional justice. They were, in fact, no more than a façade for increasingly arbitrary and wild terror, 'instruments of destruction in legal drapery'.[68] Death sentences were scarcely more than a formality, all the more so since the judges were themselves under pressure to show their loyalty.[69] Around 6,000–7,000 death sentences are known to have been handed out by the summary courts martial, though in countless other cases the executioners did not even wait for the farce of a quasi-judicial sentence.[70] The summary justice became even more arbitrary and unconstrained after 9 March, when their reach was extended by Hitler's decree creating the 'flying court martial' (fliegendes Standgericht).[71] The courts travelled around Germany dealing with those accused of undermining the war effort in whatever way, and wasting no time before reaching their verdict – usually sentence of death, meted out by the senior officer presiding over the court, and without any appeal.[72] By then, all semblance of centralized control over judicial action was visibly disintegrating, and authorized lawlessness and criminality in the name of upholding the struggle of the German people were becoming rampant as the last phase of the regime was entered.

IV

In lashing out wildly at anyone seen to impair in the slightest the imperative of fighting to the last in an obviously lost war, the regime was like a wounded animal in its death-throes. Any action that smacked of nonconformity could spell disaster for ordinary German citizens. For the designated internal enemies of the regime, the terror by now knew no bounds. Armies of foreign workers (many of them from the Soviet Union and other parts of eastern Europe) and vast numbers of prisoners in jails and concentration camps were now exposed, within Germany itself, to the untrammelled brutality of the regime's desperate henchmen. The terror, greatly escalating since the autumn, was hugely magnified by the impact of the collapse of the eastern front.

The closer Germany's enemies approached the borders of the Reich, and the more imminent defeat became, the more the representatives of the regime saw cause to worry about the security threat from the millions of foreign workers labouring under conditions of near slavery to keep the armaments industry going and to keep the country fed (since almost half of those employed in agriculture were foreigners). The precise number of foreign workers by February 1945 is unknown. The previous summer, there had been not far short of 6 million, all forced labourers, and almost 2 million prisoners of war registered within Germany – in all comprising over a quarter of the total workforce. Of these, some 4.5 million – probably, in fact, an underestimate – were from the east, predominantly Poland and the Soviet Union, and were regarded both as racial inferiors and as a particular danger.[73] The threat of internal unrest, not in terms of a revolution by the German population but as a possible rising by internal enemies, not least foreign workers, was taken seriously by the regime. Instructions were laid down, for example, at the beginning of February for the defence of the government district in Berlin in the event of internal unrest.[74]

The feeling that foreign workers could pose a serious problem as military defeat loomed was not confined to Nazi paranoiacs. Even the previous August, one general in British captivity had mused that 10 million foreign workers would rise up at the approach of enemy armies.[75] Women – their husbands and sons away at the front, or dead – left to run farms with the aid of foreign workers, were worried about their personal safety (though as it turned out they seldom had actual cause to fear).[76] In the big cities, the anxieties were palpable. In Berlin the previous autumn Friedrichstraße station had housed, according to Ursula von Kardorff, a young journalist, an 'underworld' almost excusively inhabited by foreigners, including 'Poles with glances of hatred', and a 'mix of peoples such as was probably never to be seen in a German city'. Any outsider was looked at with suspicion, she wrote. The foreign workers were reputedly 'excellently organized', with their own agents, weapons and radio equipment. 'There are 12 million foreign workers in Germany,' she said in a telling exaggeration perhaps reflecting her own inner concern, 'an army in itself. Some are calling it the Trojan Horse of the current war.'[77]

Numerous reports pointed out that foreign workers were becoming increasingly assertive as they sensed the end of their torment approaching.

They were also a very visible presence in big cities. The perception that they were an internal danger mirrored in good measure the appalling living and working conditions to which they had been reduced. Bombing had left hundred of thousands of them homeless, with no alternative but to frequent air-raid shelters, station waiting-rooms, or other public places, or find the floor of a ruined office or apartment block to lay their heads down. Food shortages meant they were often forced to steal or loot bombed-out buildings to survive. As any semblance of an ordered society broke down – the fabled 'peace and quiet' beloved of the German middle classes was long a thing of the past – the foreign workers offered an obvious scapegoat for the upsurge in criminality and lawlessness. Their image had come to resemble the caricature portrayed by the increasingly worried authorities, who reacted with characteristic harshness. Minor offences were dealt with savagely. Foreign workers were regarded not just as brigands, but also as saboteurs, though in fact there was little action that amounted to political resistance; for the most part it was simply a daily struggle for survival.[78]

Already in November 1944 Himmler had issued a decree empowering regional offices of the Gestapo to implement 'measures of atonement' as 'reprisal for grave acts of terror and sabotage'. The measures were to be directed 'usually against persons from foreign peoples who don't come into question as perpetrators but belong to the entourage of the perpetrator'.[79] The terror was plainly aimed to serve as a deterrent, opening up thereby a freeway to arbitrary killings, decided at the local level. Gestapo execution squads were recruited in numerous cities and equipped with a general remit to shoot 'looters, deserters and other rabble'.[80] The decentralization of any control over executions effectively became complete by February 1945 when the head of the Security Police, Ernst Kaltenbrunner, authorized local police chiefs to use their own discretion on when they saw fit to execute foreign workers, especially Russians.[81] The heads of the Gestapo stations in Düsseldorf, Münster, Dortmund and Cologne had been warned on 24 January that 'elements among the foreign workers and also former German Communists' would take advantage of the current situation to engage in 'subversive' action. In all reported cases, the response should be 'immediate and brutal'. Those involved were to 'be destroyed, without requesting special treatment beforehand from Reich Security Head Office'.[82]

Arbitrary executions of foreign workers now became commonplace. At least 14 Russians were executed by a shot in the back of the head, then tumbled into a ready-made pit, in a labour camp near Dortmund on 4 February; 24 members of a presumed subversive group, the 'Kowalenko Gang', were hanged or shot in Duisburg between 7 and 10 February; 74 persons were murdered in Cologne[83] (where, as we noted in an earlier chapter, something approaching a local war between dissidents and the police had been going on since the autumn) on 27 February and another 50 hanged in Gestapo headquarters on the day before the Americans occupied the city at the beginning of March. In the north of Germany, the Kiel Gestapo regularly carried out mass executions from January onwards, totalling around 200 prisoners by the end of April. One such was the shooting of 20–25 persons in late January or early February, and 17 Russian prisoners on 1 March. In the east of the country, in the penitentiary of Sonnenburg, near Frankfurt an der Oder, as many as 753 Gestapo prisoners, among them around 200 foreigners, were massacred on 30–31 January.[84] Even this was only the beginning of an orgy of killings of foreign workers in big cities across Germany in the final weeks of the war.

For the legions languishing in Germany's prisons and concentration camps, the situation was even worse. The concentration camp population at the beginning of 1945 numbered around 700,000 prisoners from all over Europe, just under a third of them women, an estimated 200,000–250,000 of them Jews, the rest mainly political internees, watched over by 40,000 SS guards. A further 190,000 or so prisoners, many of them interned for 'political' offences, were held in German penal institutions at this time.[85] This entire population of the dispossessed, beyond the reach of any conventional judicial constraints, however harsh, and utterly exposed to the whim of their captors, was now in the greatest peril. Hitler had made no bones about the need to eradicate any internal threat on enemy approach. Probably in February 1945 he issued verbal orders to blow up the concentration camps on the approach of the Allies. According to Himmler's masseur, Felix Kersten, the Reichsführer-SS told him at the beginning of March that 'if National Socialist Germany is going to be destroyed, then her enemies and the criminals in concentration camps shall not have the satisfaction of emerging from our ruin as triumphant conquerors. They shall share in the downfall. Those are the Führer's direct orders and I must see to it that they are carried out down to the last detail.'[86]

Himmler himself had already, in June 1944, passed executive powers to the Higher SS and Police Leaders to take necessary action in the event of a rising of prisoners on enemy approach.[87] Camps were to be evacuated and those interned there moved back into other camps. Should this not be possible, they were to be liquidated.[88] In January Himmler ordered the evacuation of the camps in the east, telling their commanders that Hitler held them responsible for ensuring that no prisoner should fall alive into enemy hands.[89] Precise responsibilities were, however, as so often in the Third Reich, left unclear. When the camps came to be evacuated, it was amid much confusion and panic rather than through precise implementation of clear orders from above.[90]

Two imperatives, at least partially contradictory, played their part in the confusion. One was that prisoners should not fall living into the hands of the enemy, presumably to prevent their giving testimony about the barbarity of their treatment, and also because they might be used as hostages in any possible deal with the Allies. The other – offering the most slender of lifelines for the prisoners – was the need, still bizarrely felt even at this juncture, to retain them for their economic value as slave-labourers for the war effort. Extermination versus economic exploitation had long been a contest of Nazi racial policy. The contest continued to the last.

Himmler was by now playing a double game, demonstrating his unquestioned loyalty by maximum ruthlessness and brutality, exactly along the lines that Hitler would wish, while seeing his concentration camp empire as a pawn in possible feelers towards the western Allies with an eye on retaining a place in the post-Hitlerian order. Resorting to a long-held view in leading Nazi circles, he continued to entertain the vague notion that Jews could be used as hostages or a bargaining tool with the enemy. An attempt had already been made, in spring 1944, to barter the lives of Hungarian Jews for lorries to be used on the eastern front, in a fairly transparent tactic to try to split the enemy coalition. And in October 1944, Himmler met the former Swiss Federal President, Jean-Marie Musy, the go-between in an attempted deal to arrange the release of Jews in German hands against a payment of 20 million Swiss francs from Jewish sources in the United States. Himmler and Musy met again in the Black Forest on 12 January, when the Reichsführer agreed to transport 1,200 Jews to Switzerland every fortnight in exchange for $1,000 for each Jew to be paid into a Swiss account in Musy's name.

On 6 February the first train-load of Jews from the camp at Theresien-stadt in north-west Bohemia did actually reach Switzerland, and 5 million Swiss francs were deposited in Musy's account. But Ernst Kaltenbrun-ner, involved in his own soundings (which eventually came to nothing) to ransom Jews, sabotaged the deal. Kaltenbrunner brought to Hitler's attention press reports of the arrival of the first transport of Jews in Switzerland, together with an intercepted piece of intelligence suggest-ing, wrongly, that Himmler had negotiated with Musy about asylum for 250 Nazi leaders in Switzerland. An enraged Hitler promptly ordered that any German who helped a Jew to escape would be executed on the spot. Himmler immediately halted the transports, though he was soon to attempt another route to try to use the Jews as a bargaining pawn with the Allies, this time through Sweden. For now, Hitler and Himmler still needed each other. But Hitler's suspicions of his 'loyal Heinrich' can only have been sharpened by what he had learnt.[91]

It would be asking too much to look for coherence in Nazi policy in these weeks, even in the area of killing the defenceless, in which the regime excelled. In any case, the speed of the Soviet advance in the east, where some of the largest camps were situated, meant that decisions were usually taken 'on the ground', in maximum haste and often cha-otically, by the local SS leadership, and frequently lacked any clarity of goal other than to evacuate the camp forthwith and prevent the enemy taking the prisoners alive.[92] Mass killing of huge numbers of prisoners at the last minute, as guards were taken by surprise by the rapidity of the Soviet advance, was impractical. Leaving them alive for the enemy to find was explicitly ruled out (though in practice this sometimes hap-pened with those too weak to transport away). That left forcing them, weakened and emaciated by their capitivity, ill-clothed and with scarcely any food, to be moved westwards, often on foot since insufficient trans-port was available, through the ice, snow and glacial winds of midwinter. The result was predictably murderous, but the horror was more usually a matter of improvisation within the remit of general guidelines rather than following clearly prescribed orders from above. For the guards, in any case, the haste of the marches, and the shooting or clubbing to death of stragglers and others who could not keep up the pace, was less dictated by the worry that the prisoners would fall into enemy hands than the fear of being taken captive themselves.[93]

The chaos of the actual evacuations of camps and prisons did not

The 'quadrumvirate' of Nazi grandees: (*above*) Martin Bormann (*left*), Heinrich Himmler (*right*); (*below*) Joseph Goebbels (*left*), Albert Speer (*right*).

Captured German prisoners near Falaise in early September 1944.

German civilians leaving Aachen on 19 October 1944, two days before the city fell to the Americans.

Military leaders: (*above*) Wilhelm Keitel (*left*), Alfred Jodl (*right*); (*below*) Heinz Guderian (*left*), Karl Dönitz (*right*).

The rural population digging a defensive trench near Tilsit in September 1944.

Erich Koch, Gauleiter of East Prussia, inspects food provisions in his province, August 194.

German soldiers viewing corpses in Nemmersdorf (East Prussia) following Soviet atrocities during the Red Army's incursion in October 1944.

After initial successes, the Germans are forced to retreat during the Ardennes offensive in December 1944.

Front commanders: (*above*) Walter Model (*left*), Georg-Hans Reinhardt (*right*); (*below*) Ferdinand Schörner (*left*), Gotthard Heinrici (*right*).

Ill-equipped *Volkssturm* men on the eastern front in October 1944.

Volkssturm men march past Goebbels in Berlin on 12 November 1944.

Four prominent Gauleiter: (*above left*) Arthur Greiser (Wartheland), (*right*) Josef Grohé (Cologne-Aachen); (*below left*) Karl Hanke (Lower Silesia), (*right*) Karl Holz (Franconia).

Death and devastation through Allied bombing: (*above*) Dresden, (*below*) Nuremberg.

Young Germans near Frankfurt an der Oder, armed with the 'Panzerfaust' and cycling off the front, February 1945.

Passers-by in Berlin glance at the propaganda placard: 'Our walls break, but not our hearts'.

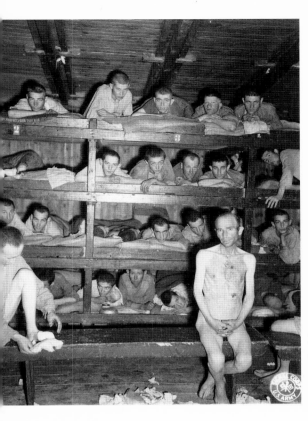

Prisoners in Buchenwald concentration camp immediately after its liberation by American troops in April 1945.

Prisoners on a death march from Dachau in late April 1945.

Germans in Königsberg surrender to the Red Army on 9 April 1945 at the fall of the beleaguered East Prussian city.

White flags fly from houses in Worms as the Americans take the Palatinate town in late March 1945.

General Heinrich von Vietinghoff (*left*) and General of the Waffen-SS Karl Wolff (*right*) ere instrumental in the German surrender in Italy on 29 April 1945 – the only surrender to precede Hitler's death.

Field-Marshal Wilhelm Keitel signs the complete German capitulation at Karlshorst, near Berlin, on 8 May 1945.

The End: an angel high on the spire of the minster in Freiburg surveys the legacy of destruction left by the war.

mean that no plans had been laid for the removal of the incarcerated when the enemy arrived. The judicial authorities in Berlin had, in fact, already in late 1944 devised guidelines for evacuating the inmates of penal institutions, which were passed on in early 1945 to areas close to the front lines. Prisoners were divided according to the severity of the offence and racial criteria. Remaining Jews and 'half-Jews', Sinti and Roma, Poles, and the most serious categories of habitual criminals, psychopaths and 'asocial subversive prisoners' were on no account to be freed or allowed to fall into enemy hands. If they could not be transferred to the police and removed, they had to 'be neutralized by shooting them dead' and the evidence 'carefully cleared up'.[94] The Soviet advance was so fast, however, that the 35,000 or so prisoners in seventy-five jails and penitentiaries in the path of the Red Army could not be transported back to central Germany in any orderly fashion.

Forced marches of prisoners who were in no physical condition to endure the treks of more than 30 kilometres a day on icy roads and tracks with hardly any food and without warm clothing or adequate footwear were chaotically undertaken. Many simply dropped by the wayside, exhausted, frozen and starving. Others were shot by trigger-happy guards, themselves desperate to flee from the oncoming Soviets. In one march of women prisoners, forced to cover 36 kilometres in a day in a temperature of minus 12 degrees Celsius, only 40 out of 565 arrived at their destination. But on some marches, a third of the prisoners managed to escape. Their guards were often too few in number and more concerned to save their own skins than to bother about the prisoners. Some guards just left their charges and fled into the unknown. Even so, the death rate during the prison evacuations was high, while several thousand prisoners were simply shot dead in their penitentiaries in the last months of the war to add to those who died on the forced marches.[95]

For the inmates of the concentration camps, the death toll on the forced marches was far higher still. By 27 January, when the Red Army reached Auschwitz, by far the biggest concentration camp (which, with its nearby satellites, had combined a huge slave-labour complex with an immense extermination capacity), only about 7,000 of the weakest prisoners – barely more than living skeletons – remained of a camp population that had once comprised as many as 140,000 terrorized individuals, the bulk of them Jews. Gassing operations had been halted in November 1944. About 1.1 million victims, around a million of them Jews, had perished there.[96] Killing installations had been dismantled, and attempts made to erase the traces of the camp's murderous activities.[97] The unexpected swiftness of the Soviet advance had caused panic among the Auschwitz guards, though reasonably clear guidelines had been laid down for the clearance of the camp. These included orders from the camp commandant, SS-Sturmbannführer Richard Baer, to shoot stragglers on the march or any prisoner trying to flee.[98]

Beginning already on 17 January some 56,000 prisoners, resembling 'columns of corpses',[99] had marched off, in great fear and abject misery, scantily clad and without food, trudging through heavy snow in piercing cold. Some were forced to push wheelbarrows carrying the guards' belongings. Another 2,200 were transported by train six days later in open coal wagons with no protection from the glacial conditions. The guards scarcely knew where they were going, apart from the targeted destination of the camp of Groß-Rosen, some 250 kilometres to the west. Minimal food supplies were requisitioned in the villages the prisoner columns passed through. What rest the prisoners were allowed had often to be spent in the open; even barns or schoolrooms could sometimes not be used for overnight stays since they were already full of refugees. 'Any of the prisoners who could not go further was shot,' recalled just over a year later one member of a column of about 3,000, mainly Jews, who left Auschwitz-Birkenau on foot in freezing conditions on 18 January. 'It was a complete shooting-festival.'[100]

'Every hundred metres there's an SS milestone' – the SS's own term for another corpse they had left in the gutter by the roadside with a bullet in the head – recalled another survivor, who endured sixteen days of the barely imaginable horror before arriving at Groß-Rosen. On the first awful night of the march, he had been forced to stand with the other prisoners for eight hours overnight in the freezing cold of a factory yard belonging to one of Auschwitz's subsidiary camps, without food or drink, not even permitted to move to relieve himself. By the time they moved on next morning, seventy prisoners were dead. The column tramped on as if in a trance, prisoners eating snow to quench a raging thirst. Whenever there was a fragment of food to be had, prisoners in near delirium fought each other for it, to the amusement of their guards.[101] On one day, 23 January, after marching for nine hours through the fierce cold, the prisoners caught a glimpse of a signpost telling them that they were 2 kilometres farther from Gleiwitz than when they had started that morning. Little wonder that some thought the torture had no point, other than marching on until they were all dead. Some yearned for death to end their misery, and the SS were glad to oblige. For others, survival was all that counted.[102] For many, there was no survival. Up to 15,000 Auschwitz prisoners, most of them Jews, died on the marches.[103]

For those who reached Groß-Rosen, the agony of the marches was far from over. Initially a small camp, Groß-Rosen, at an important rail junction in Silesia 60 kilometres south-west of Breslau, had swollen to become a huge complex comprising numerous subsidiary camps, and held 80,000 prisoners. As camps and prisons in the General Government of Poland had been closed down over previous months and new prisoners had arrived on almost a daily basis – many of them swiftly to be pushed out again – Groß-Rosen's overcrowding reached monstrous proportions, with some of the barrack-huts forced to house up to nine times their normal complement. Hygiene and sanitation were as good as non-existent, illness and infestation rampant. Rations consisted of bread and a spoonful of jam, with half a litre of salty soup distributed three times a week. 'We are a thousand men lying in a room with space for maximum two hundred,' jotted one prisoner in his diary notes. 'We can't wash, we get half a litre of swede-broth and 200 grams of bread. Up to today there are 250 dead in our barracks alone.'[104] And as conditions deteriorated, the terror inflicted by the guards became even more arbitrary.

Many of the tens of thousands teeming into Groß-Rosen from Auschwitz were there only a couple of days before being transported onwards in open railway wagons on journeys that could last up to a fortnight before arrival at one of the equally overcrowded and grotesquely brutal hellholes in the Reich, such as Bergen-Belsen, Buchenwald, Flossenbürg, Dora-Mittelbau or Mauthausen (in Austria). On 8–9 February, the main camp at Groß-Rosen was itself evacuated in chaotic haste, though some of the outlying auxiliary camps fell into Soviet hands before the prisoners could be removed. The prisoners received a piece of bread each for the journey before being crammed like cattle into open goods-wagons, so tightly and without protection against the bitter elements that many did not survive the journey. Others were shot even on the way to the station and some while trying to escape. Many others – 500 in one transport of

3,500 – were murdered at the station. Bodies lay strewn along the railway lines.[105] Around 44,000 prisoners from Groß-Rosen reached other camps within the Reich. The number who died en route is not known, but was evidently very large.[106]

For a third huge concentration camp complex in the east, at Stutthof near Danzig at the Vistula estuary, detailed evacuation plans had been worked out the previous summer. The idea was to ship a section of the prisoners westwards from Danzig and Gotenhafen (Gdynia), while the remainder would head over land to a temporary stationing at Lauenburg in Pomerania, before being moved on to camps in the Reich itself. A number of subsidiary camps were closed down at the approach of the Red Army in January and the 22,000 prisoners, the majority of them women, held there were moved out. The massacre at Palmnicken in East Prussia, mentioned in the previous chapter, was the result of one such evacuation, but was far from the sole slaughter of prisoners removed from the subsidiary camps, particularly those not capable of undertaking the forced march, whom the SS did not know what to do with. The threat from the Red Army's advance to the vicinity of Elbing and Marienburg on 23–4 January, leaving them only about 50 kilometres from Stutthof, led also to the hastily reached decision to evacuate the main camp. On 25 January, each taking 500 grams of bread and 120 grams of margarine for the trek, around 11,000 prisoners were forced out into the wintry wastes for a seven-day march to Lauenburg. German and the small number of Scandinavian prisoners were better treated than the Jews, Poles and Soviets. Clear orders were given that the prisoners were to march in rows of five and that any trying to flee or showing any signs of rebellion were to be ruthlessly shot down. By the time they reached Lauenburg, between 1 and 4 February, two-thirds of the prisoners were dead. Most were unfit to travel further into the Reich. An estimated 85 per cent – 9,500 out of 11,000 who started the terrible march to Lauenburg, mostly Jews – did not survive.[107]

Some 113,000 concentration camp prisoners, in all, set out on the death marches in January and February.[108] A cautious estimate is that at least a third did not survive. Those on the marches could expect little help from the villagers of the places they passed through. The guards did what they could to keep the prisoners segregated and, where there was some contact, prevented attempts by anyone prepared to show sympathy by throwing them a piece of bread or another morsel. In other instances, people were hostile to the prisoner columns. Whether from fear of the guards, of the prisoners or of both, or approval of the treatment of the Reich's 'enemies', most bystanders kept their distance. Often, too, the marches were passing through already evacuated districts or diverted to avoid contact with refugee treks.[109] Of those who did manage to survive the terrible ordeal, the barely describable suffering was far from at an end. Having reached grossly overcrowded concentration camps within Germany, where conditions of existence – it could scarcely be called living – were deteriorating drastically by the day, in the last, wild weeks of the Third Reich they were forced to endure still further death marches even more chaotic than those they had already barely survived.

V

In another way, too, terror came 'home into the Reich' on a new scale. This was the terror from the skies, given its lasting symbol by the Allied raids on 13–14 February 1945 which ruthlessly obliterated the historic and beautiful centre of Dresden, a city labelled, on account of its cultural glory, 'Florence on the Elbe'.

By this time, hardly any German city or town of any size had wholly escaped the horrors of the Allied bombing campaign and many had experienced death and destruction at the hands of the bombers on numerous occasions. Arthur 'Bomber' Harris had presided over the campaign to destroy German cities since 1942.[110] Northern and western cities, most easily reachable from British bases, had been the first to be targeted. By 1943, British night-time 'area bombing' was linked to daytime American so-called 'precision raids' (often, in fact, considerably less than precise) as the severity of the attacks grew in the proclaimed strategy of 'round-the-clock bombing'. In a specially terrible and devastating attack on Hamburg in July 1943, around 40,000 citizens perished in horrific firestorms. The cities of the Rhine–Ruhr industrial belt were relentlessly and repeatedly attacked as the bombing intensified over 1943 and 1944. Cologne, Essen (home of Krupp), Dortmund, the Ruhr 'coal-pot' Bochum, and other major parts of the industrial conurbation were reduced to heaps of rubble. As Allied control of the skies grew and air bases could be situated closer to Germany, cities in the middle and south of the country became more frequent targets. Kassel and Darm-stadt, Heilbronn, Stuttgart, Nuremberg and Munich were among those to suffer fearful attacks. The great metropolis Berlin, its sheer size as well as distance from enemy bases an obstacle to the level of destruction caused in some other cities, was attacked 363 times in all during the course of the war. The heavy raid on 3 February inflicted the worst destruction in the capital to date, laying waste the government district and the historic buildings of the city centre (though, luckily for Berliners, causing only a fraction of the death toll the Allies had intended).[111]

There was a sharp escalation of the bombing as Allied strength grew and the Luftwaffe was increasingly rendered ineffective. In 1942, a total of 41,440 tons of bombs were dropped on Germany. In 1943 the figure rose to 206,000 tons, and in 1944 expanded more than fivefold to 1,202,000 tons. And 471,000 tons, or more than twice the amount dropped in the whole year of 1943, were dropped between January and the end of April 1945.[112] The 67,000 tons dropped by the RAF in March 1945 amounted, in fact, to almost as much as the entire tonnage unloaded onto Germany during the first three years of the war.[113] Some of the most devastating attacks were made on near defenceless popula-tions in the very last weeks of the war with the near obliteration of Pforzheim, 'Gateway to the Black Forest', on 23–4 February, killing 17,600 people (a quarter of the population), and the savage bombing – militarily quite pointless – of Würzburg, on 16 March, leaving 4,000 dead out of 107,000 inhabitants as incendiaries destroyed 90 per cent of the beautiful baroque centre, a cultural gem, within seventeen minutes.[114]

Germany was paying a dreadful price, reaping the whirlwind for what it had begun, even before the war, with the merciless bombing of Guernica in 1937, then, once the war had started, in the ruthless attacks on Warsaw, Rotterdam, Coventry and densely populated parts of Lon-don. In all, it is adjudged that Allied bombing of Germany killed close to half a million people. A third of the population suffered in some way. More than a quarter of the homes in Germany were damaged by attacks from the air.[115]

In this terrible catalogue of death and destruction through enemy bombing, the ferocious attack on Dresden on 13–14 February holds a special place. There were perfect conditions for complete aerial annihilation: good weather for bombing, the almost total absence of air defences, the lack of provision by the Nazi leadership of even semi-adequate air-raid shelters (apart from the bunker built for the use of Gauleiter Martin Mutschmann), and a city overcrowded by the accommodation of thousands of refugees to add to the population of 640,000. All this was the target of a double British incendiary and explosive attack of enormous severity that ensured the complete fire-storm which turned the old town into a raging inferno. This was followed by a further heavy raid next lunchtime, now by the Americans.

People taking cover in makeshift shelters were suffocated. Those on the streets were sucked into the devouring firestorm. When survivors emerged onto the streets after the first attack, they were caught up in the second, which magnified greatly the ferocity of the firestorm and wid-ened the area of devastation. Those diving into the large reservoir in the middle of the city to escape the flames, among them people who were injured or non-swimmers, found that, unlike swimming-pools, there was no easy way of getting out, since the walls were of smooth cement, and many drowned. On the burning streets, charred corpses lay everywhere. Basements and cellars were full of bodies. In the main station, which had been crammed with refugees, there were 'corpses and parts of bodies wherever one looked, in the tunnel passages and waiting-rooms in hor-rific numbers. Nobody got out of here alive.'[116] In the pandemonium, the difference between death and survival was a hair's breadth – often a mat-ter of pure luck. The best hope was to reach the Elbe, and the safety of the river. When the firestorm finally blew itself out and the bombers of next day's raid had dispatched their lethal loads and left for home, Dresden was a city of the dead.[117] But for a few, remarkably, the night of horror brought salvation. The remaining Jews of the city had been awaiting their imminent deportation, and were aware what that meant. In the chaos, they were able to rip off their yellow star, join the homeless 'aryan' masses, and avoid deportation to their deaths.[118]

Even at this late stage of the war, and amid all the mayhem of the ruined city, the regime showed a remarkable capacity for organizing an improvised emergency response. Aid teams were dispatched to Dresden the morning after the attack. Two thousand soldiers and a thousand prisoners of war, together with repair teams from other cities in the region, were rushed in. A command post and communications system were erected to coordinate work. Within three days, 600,000 hot meals a day were being distributed. Martial law was declared and looters arrested and, in numerous cases, executed forthwith. The gruesome task of collecting charcoaled bodies started, some of it undertaken by prisoners of war. With bureaucratic precision, the city's authorities collected and counted the corpses. More than 10,000 were buried in mass graves on the edge of the city. Thousands more were cremated between 21 February and 5 March in huge pyres on the Altmarkt, in the centre of town. The official report on the victims of the bombing, compiled in March, spoke of 18,375 dead, 2,212 seriously injured, 13,718 slightly injured, and 350,000 homeless. Taking account of others still presumed to be lying beneath the masses of rubble in the inner city, the report estimated the death toll at 25,000 – still accepted as the most reliable figure.[119]

This figure is lower than the grim toll of mortalities in Hamburg in July 1943, though as a proportion of the population higher (if considerably smaller than in Pforzheim, which, measured in this macabre way, suffered the worst raid of the entire war).[120] The shock of Dresden was all the greater since it had long presumed that, as such a cultural jewel, it would be spared the fate of other big cities in the Reich. Of course, Munich's reputation as a city of priceless art and architecture had offered no protection against as many as seventy-three air raids.[121] And the centre of Würzburg, a testament to the rococo genius of Balthasar Neumann, was almost totally wiped out in March.[122] But Munich, apart from its art treasures, was the 'capital of the [Nazi] movement' (as it had been labelled since 1933). And the flattening of Würzburg (where despite the level of destruction the death toll was perhaps a fifth of Dresden's) might have been a bigger shock had it preceded, not followed, the bombing of the Saxon capital. Dresden had been a huge attack, and, with the end of the war in sight, had caused immense loss of life and had destroyed a city of singular beauty. Perhaps all this was sufficient of itself to turn Dresden, of all the cities mercilessly pounded from the air, into the very symbol of the bombing war.

There was, however, something else. Dresden gave Goebbels a propaganda gift. He seized upon an Associated Press report, which, remarkably, passed the British censor, and spoke not inaccurately of a policy of 'deliberate terror bombing of great German population centres'.[123] Within days he was castigating a deliberate policy to wipe out the German people by terror-attacks aimed, not at industrial installations, but at the population of a peaceful centre of culture and the masses of refugees, many of them women and children, who had fled from the horrors of war. The numbers of refugees in the city and killed in the attack were inflated in the reportage (though many had, indeed, fallen victim to the bombing, and the Allies were well aware that refugees had poured into the city in recent weeks in the wake of the Red Army's advance). Also deliberately misleading was the image of a city without war industries, devoid of military significance. Its position as an important railway junction gave it some importance, and most of its industry was involved in war production. The attempt to disrupt the passage of German troops through Dresden to reinforce the eastern front, and thereby to assist the Soviet offensive, was, in fact, the rationale behind the bombing of Dresden along with other eastern cities (including Berlin).[124] It was, nevertheless, the case that the main target in Dresden had been the heavily populated area of the old town, not the more outlying industrial installations. Not least, Goebbels magnified the number of victims, by the simple device of adding a 'o' onto the official figure. Instead of 25,000 dead – itself a vast number – Goebbels created a death toll of 250,000.[125] From horrific reality, he created even more horrific – and long-lasting – myth.

He and other Nazi leaders also used the bombing of Dresden to emphasize the need to fight on – the only response possible, his weekly newspaper *Das Reich* claimed, to the threat to Germany's existence posed by the western Allies as much as by the Soviets.[126] It seems unlikely that most ordinary Germans drew this conclusion from the devastating attack. True, there were voices to be heard – echoing Goebbels – that Germany would not be forced by terror to capitulation.[127] But they were probably the exception. Letters to and from the front speak of the horror at the news of what had taken place, but not of strengthened morale or determination to hold out.[128] Doubtless, the prevalent hatred of 'air gangsters' gained some new sustenance. For the most part, however, the destruction of Dresden probably signified for most people not the need to resist to the last, but the helplessness against such wanton devastation and the futility of fighting on while Germany's cities were being obliterated. And Dresden, the most glaring manifestation of the Nazi regime's inability to protect its own population from the bombers, brought no deflection of the mounting antagonism of the German people towards their own leaders. 'Trust in the leadership shrinks ever more,' ran a summary of letters monitored by the Propaganda Ministry in early March. 'Criticism of the upper leadership ranks of the Party and of the military leadership is especially bitter.'[129]

VI

The horror inflicted on Dresden did little or nothing to hasten the end of the war. But it was a reminder to many that the end was not far off. The regime's leaders, too, were well aware – not that they would openly acknowledge it – that the game was up, that it would be a matter of weeks, not months, before Germany was totally crushed. They could intensify the terror and repression directed now also at their own population and throttle any possibility of a repeat of 1918. But they were powerless to stop the flood tide of impending defeat.

The outward façade of invincibility had to be maintained. Robert Ley, the Labour Front Leader, whose public utterances – and reputation for drunkenness – were an embarrassment to Goebbels and other leading Nazis,[130] even managed to draw positives from the Dresden inferno, declaring that as a consequence the struggle for victory would no longer be distracted by concerns for the monuments of German culture.[131] Yet privately Ley could see as well as anyone how desperate the situation was on the fronts.[132] Even within leading SS circles, Himmler held to the myth that the war would turn out well for Germany. Rituals were to continue as usual. Himmler wrote to Obersturmführer Freiherr von Berlepsch to congratulate him on the birth of his eighth child and let him know that the 'light of life' (*Lebensleuchter*) – part of the pseudo-religious cultism within the SS – for little Dietmar could be sent only after the war.[133] The Reichsführer-SS let it be known among his leading aides that he wanted every year in May to establish which book he would give to higher SS leaders at the 'Julfest' – the order's pagan version of Christmas. A list was to be provided by 30 April 1945 on which the titles of the books in question were to be presented.[134] And replying to the father of one of his godchildren, who had written to thank him for all the presents to his family, mentioning that a Christmas plate (*Jul-teller*) had arrived broken, Himmler had Rudolf Brandt, his aide, provide assurance that, should a small contingent be available after the war, 'I will gladly again send you a Christmas plate'.[135] Speaking privately to Albert Speer, Himmler kept up pretences. 'When things go downhill, there's always a valley-bottom, and only when that's reached, Herr Speer, do they go up again.'[136] This maintenance of illusions came from a man, wavering between his own growing sense of delusion and hard-headed awareness of realities, who was already making tacit overtures to the enemy with an eye to his post-war future.

A curious mixture of unreality and 'business as usual' prevailed, too, in the highest ranks of the state bureaucracy. Lutz Graf Schwerin von Krosigk, the long-serving Finance Minister who had held office since 1932, before Hitler's accession to power, dispatched numerous letters in early 1945 to Nazi leaders and government ministers offering advice on the conduct of the war. Little notice was taken of them. His main preoccupation, however, was the desolate state of Reich finances. In January he compiled a lengthy dossier, sent to leading figures in the regime, which began by stating: 'The current finance and currency situation is characterized by rising costs of war, falling state income, increased money supply and smaller purchasing power of money.' It was urgently necessary, he concluded, drastically to restrict money supply by reducing Reich expenditure and by increases in postage, rail and local transport prices, and by raising taxation on tobacco and alcohol, visits to the cinema, hotel accommodation, radio licence fees and newspapers, as well as increasing the war supplement on gas, water and electricity prices. With remarkable logic – justifying the post-war impression of him as an individual of singular ineptitude, an utter 'ninny'[137] – he reasoned that 'it cannot be objected that essential provisions for the population are thereby being made more expensive' since 'a large part of the population has already been entirely without regular access, or with only restricted access, to water, gas and electricity for months'.[138] He presented his proposals for a fourfold rise in property tax to a meeting of ministers on 23 February, lamenting Bormann's absence from the meeting and his unwillingness to discuss the dangers of a collapse of the currency. All he could get out of the Party Chancellery was a suggestion that a programme should be devised by state officials after which Bormann would be able to judge whether it could be 'politically implemented'.[139] In any normal political system, the imminent collapse of the state currency would have been a matter of the utmost priority. To the Nazi leadership, in the conditions of February 1945, it was of no consequence. Undeterred, Krosigk continued to work on his plans for tax reform, which were criticized in late March by Goebbels – as if they were about to be implemented – for placing the burden upon consumer tax rather than income tax. By that time, it was at best an arcane issue: most of the country was under enemy occupation.[140]

Constantly in Hitler's close proximity, Martin Bormann was more aware than most of the true scale of the disaster closing in on Germany. His frequent letters to his wife, Gerda, show his anxious recognition of the plain realities of the military situation, brought home to him at first hand by the bombing of the Reich Chancellery on 3 February. The day following this heavy raid, he feared (he wrote) that 'the worst phase of our fortunes is still to come' and told Gerda frankly 'how very unpleasant – indeed, if I am completely honest, how desperate the situation really is'. But pretence had to be maintained, and he added: 'I know that you, like myself, will never lose your faith in ultimate victory.'[141] Next day he wrote again, first with scarcely veiled pessimism about the outlook on the western front, but then reverting to a form of fatalistic hope in the future:

> Anyone who still grants that we have a chance must be a great optimist! And that is just what we are! I just cannot believe that Destiny could have led our people and our Führer so far along this wonderful road, only to abandon us now and see us disappear for ever. A victory for Bolshevism and Americanism would mean not only the extermination of our race, but also the destruction of everything that its culture and civilisation has created. Instead of the 'Meistersinger' we should see jazz triumphant . . .[142]

Gerda replied: 'One day, the Reich of our dreams will emerge. Shall we, I wonder, or our children, live to see it?' Martin interpolated some words in his wife's letter at this point: 'I have every hope that we shall!'[143] In another letter to her, a little later, he added: 'As I have often emphasized, I have no premonitions of death; on the contrary, my burning desire is to live – and by that I mean to be with you and our children. I would like to muddle on through life, together with you, as many years as possible, and in peace.'[144]

Goebbels was, for many Germans, the outward face of the regime in the last months, appearing in public more frequently than any other Nazi leader, visiting troops at the front as well as urging on bombed-out civilians – a constant driving force, in his radio broadcasts and newspaper articles, to ever greater efforts to hold out and fight on. He still worked feverishly to drum up new recruits for the Wehrmacht and, now, to plan the defence of Berlin (for which he saw Bolshevik methods in Leningrad and Moscow as a possible model).[145] He remained among the most utterly fanatical Nazis, widely regarded alongside Himmler as one of 'the strong men' of the regime.[146] He urged rapid sentencing by drumhead courts martial and execution to address the 'miserable mood' among the 35,000 'stragglers' and deserters recently rounded up, looking to Stalinist methods to restore order and combat sunken morale.[147] His fanaticism led him to advocate the execution of tens of thousands of Allied prisoners of war in response to the bombing of Dresden.[148] He was still a figure of remarkable dynamism, able not just to put on a show for the masses, but also to fire up those in his entourage and continue to represent the face of optimism and defiance. Yet he was among the most clear-sighted of the Nazi leaders. When, in early February, his wife Magda lamented the loss of so many territories that Germany had once conquered and the weakness now unable to prevent the threat to Berlin itself, Goebbels replied: 'Yes, sweetheart. We've had it, bled white, finished. There's nothing to be done.'[149]

Despite such sentiments, he had not conceded defeat. He still saw in late February, so his aide Wilfred von Oven recorded, a slim chance of avoiding complete disaster if Germany were to gain some time, then – a delusion he shared with other leading Nazis – negotiate to let in the western Allies to join in a fight against Bolshevism. But he readily admitted that Hitler did not share this view and still insisted that 1945 would bring the decisive change for the better in Germany's fortunes.[150] He was sceptical about Hitler's extraordinary adherence to undiluted optimism.[151] But a visit to the Führer bunker was nevertheless invariably an antidote to any fleeting moments of depression. The atmosphere there, increasingly given to flights from reality, usually dissipated his doubts and pandered to his willingness to believe in some near miraculous change in war fortunes.[152] After one visit, in mid-February, he came away enthused by discussions with the architect Hermann Giesler, who had just shown a fascinated Hitler his model of Linz as it was to be after the war. Giesler told Goebbels, as he had indicated to Hitler, that he thought most German towns could be rebuilt within three to five years. Goebbels found himself, as in 1933 at the end of the struggle for power, longing to take part in the work of reconstruction.[153] He still pressed, as he had long done, for a radicalization of the home front, the dismissal of Göring and Ribbentrop (both of whom he regarded as utter failures and an obstacle to any new initiatives), and a search even at this late stage for a political solution to end the war. But he remained, as always, a faithful acolyte of Hitler, unwilling and unable to take an independent step. He saw Hitler as a stoical disciple of Frederick the Great, fulfilling his duty to the end, 'a model and an example to us all'.[154] For Goebbels, too, reality and illusion were by this time closely interwoven.

More realistic than other Nazi leaders in his appraisal of the situation was Albert Speer. On 30 January, as it happened the twelfth anniversary of the 'takeover of power', he submitted a lengthy memorandum to Hitler outlining the armaments situation for February and March. He pointed out the dire consequences from the loss of Upper Silesia, hitherto Germany's last intact coal-producing area. He provided figures demonstrating the dramatic fall over the previous year of weapons and munitions production. At the current levels of coal and raw steel capacity, it was, he wrote, impossible to sustain the German economy for long. Collapse could only be delayed for a few months. After the loss of Upper Silesia, the armaments industry was no longer remotely in a position to cover the demand for weaponry to replace losses at the front. Speer concluded his memorandum in underlined bold type: 'The material superiority of the enemy can accordingly no longer be countered by the bravery of our soldiers.'[155]

Goebbels drew the logical conclusion from the memorandum – which he recognized as showing 'things as they really are' – that Speer was indicating the need to try to find a political way out of the war. But he saw no prospect of that.[156] He was right to be pessimistic. Hitler forbade Speer to give his memorandum to anyone else – somewhat belatedly, since Goebbels and others had already seen it – and, referring specifically to its conclusions, told him coldly that he alone was entitled to draw conclusions from the armaments situation.[157] That was an end to the matter, as Speer acknowledged.

Hitler's authority was still intact.[158] In sustaining his unchallengeable leadership position, he could thank, now as before, in no small part his provincial chieftains, the Gauleiter. Although he had to insist in early February that the Gauleiter blindly follow orders from Berlin and stop the tendency 'to govern in their own way' – actually a tendency that grew, rather than diminished, in the last weeks of the war – he was soon afterwards lavishing praise on them for their utter dependency in controlling matters of civil defence.[159] Most of them, like Gauleiter Albert Forster of Danzig-West Prussia, had probably given up hope of a positive outcome to the war for Germany.[160] But whatever their private feelings and the secret hopes some of them cherished of escaping the tightening vice, they remained a group of outright loyalists.

Summoned to what turned out to be their last meeting with Hitler, in the Reich Chancellery on 24 February 1945, the twenty-fifth anniversary of the promulgation of the Party Programme, the Gauleiter – minus Koch and Hanke, unable to leave East Prussia and Breslau respectively – initially shared criticisms and complaints with each other, not least about Bormann. But they were 'all still full of belief in victory', at least on the surface. In truth, they were anxious about betraying any defeatist sentiment. Karl Wahl, Gauleiter of Swabia, had the feeling, so he wrote later, that 'they all lived on the moon'.[161] When Hitler finally arrived, they were shocked at his appearance – that of an old, ill, physical wreck of a man, whose left arm shook the whole time. Tears came into Wahl's eyes at the sight of such a decrepit individual; for him, it was 'the end of the world'.[162]

Hitler had begun the meeting by shaking hands with each individual Gauleiter for what seemed an age, looking them in the eye as he did so. But his speech, an hour and a half long, was a disappointment. He spoke at great length, as he had done so often, about the past – the First World War, his entry into politics, the growth of the Party, the triumph of 1933, the reshaping of Germany thereafter – but hardly touched upon what they had come to hear: how Germany stood in the war. What he had to say about the impact of new U-boats and jet-planes was less than convincing. The much-vaunted 'miracle weapons' were not even mentioned. It seemed a far cry from the old Hitler. But after the formal proceedings, he relaxed visibly in their company over a simple meal until, their own conversations petering out, they all found themselves listening, as ever, to a monologue. Hitler spoke now with a verve earlier lacking about the certainty that 'the alliance of madness' ranged against Germany would break up into two irreconcilable fronts, and of the dangers for the west in a pyrrhic victory that would raise Bolshevism to a dominant position in Europe. 'Our depressed mood evaporates,' recalled one Gauleiter, Rudolf Jordan, Party boss of Magdeburg-Anhalt. 'The disappointment of the last hours has vanished. We experience the old Hitler.' They were left in no doubt: he would fight on to the bitter end.[163]

That much was clear, as it always had been. There could be no talk of defeat, no talk of surrender. It was good to have burnt one's bridges.[164] On the evening of 12 February the communiqué from the Yalta Conference, where Stalin, Roosevelt and Churchill had met for a week in crucial deliberation to determine the post-war shape of Europe, was read in Berlin. The communiqué stipulated that Germany would be divided and demilitarized, the Nazi Party abolished, and war criminals put on trial. There could now be no lingering doubt for Nazi leaders that Germany's fate was sealed; there would be no negotiated end to the war; 'unconditional surrender' meant just that.[165] For Hitler, it simply confirmed what he already knew. 'I've always said: "there can be no question of a capitulation!"' was his response to Yalta. 'History does not repeat itself!'[166]

7

Crumbling Foundations

Is there nobody there who will restrain the madman and call a halt? Are they still generals? No, they are shitbags, cowardly poltroons. They are cowards! Not the ordinary soldier.
Diary entry of an officer in the west, 7 April 1945[1]

I

By March 1945, Allies were closing in east and west for the kill as the Reich's military weakness was fully exposed.[2] The eastern front was reinforced at the expense of the west, but the troops were invariably already battle-weary and, increasingly, ill-trained young recruits. The huge losses could simply no longer be made good. The fighting strength of divisions had fallen drastically. The greatly weakened, though still tenaciously fighting, German forces faced an impossible task in trying to halt the Red Army, once it had regrouped and consolidated its supply lines after the big advance of January. In the west, the Ardennes offensive had inflicted a temporary shock rather than a major reversal on the western Allies. They soon regathered and prepared for the assault on the western frontiers of the Reich, against a Wehrmacht whose impoverished resources were incapable, despite its tough rearguard action, of repelling immensely superior might. The task was rendered completely hopeless through the near total impotence of the Luftwaffe, whose limited capability in the west had been cut back in order to supply – wholly ineffectively – the eastern front.

After the disasters of January, the Army High Command did all it could to reinforce the front in Pomerania and along the Oder. Army

N

DENMARK

North Sea

Hamburg • Aumühle
• Neuengamm

Elbe

Lüneburg
Bremen •
• Bergen-Belsen

NETHERLANDS

Weser

• Hannover

Amsterdam •
Hildesheim •
Magdeburg •

The Hague •

Rhine

• Bocholt
• Lippstadt

BELGIUM
• Bochum
Osterode •

• Düsseldorf
Mittelbau-Dora •

Brussels •
Cologne
Kassel •
GERMANY

Aachen
Erfurt

Maas
• Bonn
Buchenwald •

Remagen • • Linz

Sinzig
Hirzenhain •
Neustadt an der Orla •

Koblenz
Frankfurt

Mosel
Main

Luxemburg •
• Trier

Reims •

• Saarbrücken
Nürnberg •

Rhine
Heilbronn •
• Schwäbisch Hall

Schwäbisch Gmünd •

Strassburg •
Stuttgart •

Danube

FRANCE
Augsburg •
Dachau •
Munich •

Mülhouse •

Rhine

Innsbruck •

| 0 | 50 | 100 miles |

| 0 | 50 | 100 km |

• Berne

SWITZERLAND

7. The Collapse of the Third Reich, March 1945

Copenhagen

SWEDEN

Baltic Sea

Gotenhafen

Stolp • • Danzig

Zetthun • • Bütow • Stutthof • Heilsberg

Peenemünde

Anklam • • Swinemünde

Stettin •

Vistula

• Ravensbrück

Sachsenhausen • Küstrin

Nauen • • **BERLIN** Posen •

Potsdam *Warthe*

Oder

• Calau • Glogau

• Torgau • Baranow

• Leipzig • Strehla Haynau • • Breslau

• Moritzburg *Oder* Klosterbrück

Dresden Groß-Rosen • Oppeln

• Hindenburg

• Auschwitz

Gleiwitz

Prague •

• Flossenbürg

PROTECTORATE OF
BOHEMIA AND MORAVIA **SLOVAKIA**

Mauthausen Pressburg

Linz • • Vienna

Salzburg *Danube*

• Obersalzberg • Budapest

——— Front lines, March 1945
- - - - - Front lines, April 1945

Group Vistula, commanded by Himmler and comprising twenty-five infantry and eight panzer divisions, defended an extensive sector running from Elbing in the east to the Oder, little more than 80 kilometres north-east of Berlin. The whole of its southern flank, however, faced the Red Army, impatient to press northwards towards the Baltic coast. Once a weak German counter-offensive in mid-February had fairly easily been parried, the loss of Pomerania – allowing the Soviets to secure their northern flank for the coming assault on Berlin – swiftly became unstoppable. On 4 March, the Red Army reached the Baltic coast between Köslin and Kolberg. The coastal town of Kolberg was a vital strategic stronghold. The spectacular colour film *Kolberg* (referred to in an earlier chapter), which Goebbels had commissioned, depicted the town's heroic defence against Napoleon's forces.[3] This time there was, however, to be no heroic defence. Kolberg was besieged on 7 March and declared by Hitler a 'fortress' to be held at all costs. The town commandant held out only until the civilians – including around 60,000 refugees, many of them wounded – could be shipped away by the navy,[4] then left himself over the sea on 18 March, along with the town's remaining defence force.[5]

Other Pomeranian strongholds were lost soon afterwards. By 20 March, after days of bitter fighting, Stettin's harbour and wharves had been wrecked and could no longer be used by the German navy, though German troops held onto a bridgehead and the city itself, now largely deserted, fell to the Soviets only towards the end of April. Gotenhafen (Gdynia) held out until 28 March and the key city of Danzig till 30 March, enabling the navy to ferry many desperate refugees and wounded civilians and soldiers to safety. By this time, German forces in Pomerania had been broken, then crushed. What remained of them, around 100,000 men, retreated to the long thin Hela peninsula, facing Gdynia in the Bay of Danzig, and the Vistula delta, where they remained down to the capitulation. Overall, between the beginning of February and middle of April Army Group Vistula suffered losses of around 143,000 officers and men killed, wounded or missing.

In East Prussia, the battered forces of Army Group North still comprised thirty-two divisions in early February, twenty-three of them, belonging to the 4th Army, in the heavily fortified Heilsberg pocket, about 180 kilometres long and 50 deep. A second grouping was besieged in Königsberg, a third, the 3rd Panzer Army, contained on the Samland peninsula. For a brief time in mid-February, intense fighting opened up a corridor from the encircled Königsberg to Pillau, the last remaining port in German hands in the province. This enabled some civilians in Königsberg to escape and provisions to be brought in for the garrison. Once the corridor was closed off again, the fate of the remaining inhabitants of Königsberg was sealed, though capitulation did not follow until 9 April. Meanwhile, the position of the troops in the Heilsberg pocket had worsened sharply. The replacement of Rendulić by Colonel-General Walter Weiß as Commander-in-Chief Army Group North on 12 March could bring no improvement. By 19 March, the German pocket was reduced to an area of no more than about 30 kilometres long and 10 deep, exposed on all sides to intense Soviet firepower. By the time the last remnants of the 4th Army were transported across the Frisches Haff from Balga, then to safety from Pillau on 29 March, only 58,000 men and around another 70,000 wounded could be rescued out of an original complement of half a million. The eight divisions left on Samland continued to fight on for some weeks until Pillau was eventually taken on 25 April, when the broken and demoralized remainder retreated to the Frische Nehrung. There they stayed – though with further losses through repeated heavy Soviet bombardment – until the end of the war.

On the Oder, the German 9th Army, under General Theodor Busse, sought, with weakened forces, to hold the defences of the heavily fortified town of Küstrin and the designated fortress of Frankfurt an der Oder. Reinforcements were rushed to the area, but could not compensate for the blood-letting in the fierce fighting – the Panzer Division Kurmark alone lost between 200 and 350 men a day – and the Soviets were able gradually to extend their bridgehead. By early March, Küstrin could be supplied only through a narrow corridor, 3 kilometres wide, which was closed off on 22 March. Much of Küstrin fell on 13 March after bitter street-fighting over previous days, but what remained of the fifteen battalions defending the town under the leadership of SS-Brigadeführer Heinz Reinefarth – the former police chief in the Wartheland who had also been prominent in the savage brutality used to put down the rising in Warsaw – retreated within the old fortress walls. When an attempted counter-offensive to relieve the siege failed, amid high German casualties, Guderian was made the scapegoat. He became the last Chief of the General Staff to be dismissed by Hitler, on 28 March, when he was replaced by General Hans Krebs. A second attempt to reach Küstrin that same day had to be abandoned after a few hours. Reinefarth ignored Hitler's order to fight to the last and the garrison of almost a thousand officers and men managed to break out of the encirclement on 30 March, just before Küstrin fell. For this disobedience he was court-martialled and was fortunate to escape with his life.

Further south on the Oder, in Lower Silesia, the Red Army made rela-tively slow progress. Schörner's Army Group Centre, comprising some twenty infantry and eight panzer divisions, battled ferociously, though in the end vainly. The Germans fought hard to keep open a corridor to Breslau, though once this was closed by 16 February some 40,000 troops (along with 80,000 civilians) were sealed off in the Silesian capital. Another 9,000 were encircled to the north in Glogau. Tough German resistance was unable to prevent the Soviets reaching the right bank of the Neiße near its confluence with the Oder by 24 February. In mid-March, a big drive by the Red Army in the Oppeln area overcame fierce fighting to surround and destroy five German divisions. Around 30,000 Germans were killed, another 15,000 captured. When Ratibor fell on 31 March, the last large industrial city in Silesia was lost to the Germans. What was left of Army Group Centre was forced back onto the western reaches of the Neiße and south-west into the Sudetenland.

On the southern flank of the eastern front, where nineteen infantry and nine panzer divisions were located, the intense fighting around Budapest which had lasted for weeks was finally reaching its dénoue-ment. Ferocious street-fighting – ultimately in the sewers – came to an end on 13 February. Between them, the Germans and Hungarians had lost 50,000 men killed and 138,000 captured in the battle for Buda-pest. Soviet losses were even higher. Heavy fighting continued to the west of Budapest. Hitler insisted, against Guderian's advice, on a counter-offensive centred on Lake Balaton. A successful outcome, so ran the strategic thinking, would free nine divisions to be sent to the Oder for an eventual counter-offensive there in May. It would also block the Soviet approaches to Vienna. Most crucially, it was vital to the continuation of Germany's war effort to retain control of the remaining oil wells in the region. Sepp Dietrich's 6th SS-Panzer Army, refreshed since the fail-ure in the Ardennes, was sent down to spearhead the attack, which began on 6 March. The German forces battled their way forwards around 20–30 kilometres over a 50-kilometre stretch, but after ten days, amid heavy losses and exhaustion, the attempt ran out of steam. General Otto Wöhler, Commander-in-Chief Army Group South, gave out orders to fight to the last. But even the elite troops of the 6th SS-Panzer Army preferred retreat to pointless self-sacrifice. The orders were disobeyed as Dietrich's men fought their way back westwards into Austria in some disarray, narrowly avoiding complete destruction, but abandoning much heavy equipment as they went. In blind fury, Hitler ordered that Sepp Dietrich's units, including his own bodyguard, the 'Leibstandarte-SS Adolf Hitler', should be stripped of their armbands in disgrace. Even General Hermann Balck, the tough panzer commander in Hungary, who himself had telephoned Guderian to request action be taken against intact units of the Leibstandarte retreating with all their weapons, thought the degradation too harsh a punishment.[6] Worse than the prestige issue of the armbands, from a German perspective, was that by the end of March the oilfields were lost, along with the whole of Hungary. The Austrian border now lay directly in the path of the Red Army.

By the end of March, the Red Army had made significant headway on all parts of the eastern front. Berlin was now under imminent threat. In the west, too, February and March saw German defences put up stiff opposition, but ultimately crumble as the western Allies were able to cross the Rhine, the last big natural barrier protecting the Reich, and advance deep into Germany itself.

By February 1945, Germany's western front was defended by 462,000 soldiers in fifty-nine divisions (about a third as many as on the eastern front). These were hopelessly outnumbered by the forces of the western Allies, who by this time had more than 3.5 million men on the European continent. The German divisions were smaller than earlier in the war, on average just under 8,000 men, and the actual fighting strength of each of them only about half that number – many of them young recruits, already worn down by constant fighting. Tanks, artillery and aircraft, like manpower, had had to be sacrificed for the eastern front. It was made clear to the commanders of the western army groups – Army Group H in the north under Colonel-General Johannes Blaskowitz (who had replaced Colonel-General Kurt Student on 28 January), Army Group B in the centre of the front under Field-Marshal Walter Model, and Army Group G in the south led by Colonel-General of the Waffen-SS Paul Hausser – that, given the situation in the east, they could reckon with reinforcements of neither men nor *matériel*. The imbalance with the armaments of the western Allies was massive – and most pronounced in the air, where Allied supremacy was as good as total.

Before the Allies could tackle the crossing of the Rhine, they faced tenacious defences west of the great river from north to south. In Alsace, French and American troops had already forced the Germans back across the Rhine near Colmar in early February. The main Allied attack began, however, further north, on 8 February. Despite initial slow progress against fierce resistance, abetted by bad weather and the opening of dams to hamper tank and troop movements, Canadian and British forces pushing south-eastwards from the Nijmegen area and Americans pressing north-eastwards from around Düren took Krefeld on 2 March and by 10 March had encircled nine German divisions near Wesel, capturing 53,000 prisoners, though many German troops were nonetheless able to retreat over the Rhine, destroying the bridges as they went. By this time, once the Americans had reached the Rhine south of Düsseldorf on 2 March, a long stretch of Germany's most important river was in Allied hands, and with that a vital artery for delivery of Ruhr coal and steel blocked. On 5 March, American troops broke through weak defences (many manned by the *Volkssturm*) to reach Cologne. The following morning the retreating Germans blew up the Hohenzollern bridge in the city centre, the last remaining crossing in the Rhine metropolis. The problem for the Allies of gaining a bridgehead on the eastern bank of the Rhine was, however, soon solved by a slice of good luck. German troops retreating at Remagen, farther south, between Bonn and Koblenz, had failed to detonate the explosives laid and the Americans, to their great surprise finding the bridge intact on 7 March, crossed and swiftly formed a small bridgehead on the eastern bank. Desperate German attempts to clear it meant that precious reserves were sucked into Remagen, to no avail.

Farther south, Trier fell on 1 March. General Patton's 3rd US Army, after struggling since mid-February to overcome strong resistance, was able to force the defenders back across the Rhine and Mosel by 10 March – the day after Field-Marshal von Rundstedt had been relieved of his command for the last time and replaced as Commander-in-Chief West by the tough Field-Marshal Albert Kesselring, adjudged to have acquitted himself well in the rearguard action in northern Italy. Three days later the Americans were crossing the Mosel and preparing to attack the Saarland, still producing about a tenth of German iron and steel. Kesselring refused to evacuate such a vital industrial area. Intense fighting followed, but there could be only one outcome. The German forces eventually retreated into the eastern Saarland, then the Palatinate, and finally across the Rhine, suffering severe losses (also inflicting them on the enemy). By 25 March the Saar was lost to Germany. By that time the Americans had also occupied Kaiserslautern, Worms and Mainz. Meanwhile, Koblenz had fallen on 17 March.

Six days later the entire stretch of the Rhine from Koblenz to Ludwigshafen was in American hands, and a second bridgehead over the river had been established at Oppenheim, south of Mainz, where troops had crossed in assault boats in a daring manoeuvre on the night of 22/3 March. That day, the British commander, Field-Marshal Montgomery, led his forces over the Lower Rhine at Wesel and by the end of March had consolidated an extensive bridgehead on the eastern bank of the river. The basis for the assault on the Reich's biggest industrial region, the Ruhr, was thereby laid. Farther south, now the Americans were over the Rhine, fierce German resistance was unable to halt their progress deep into the western parts of the Reich. Mannheim, Ludwigshafen and Frankfurt am Main were in American hands by 29 March, Heidelberg two days later. From here on, the advance into central Germany and, to the south into Bavaria, would rapidly unfold.

In the defence of Rhine positions, the Germans had suffered appalling losses, with more than 60,000 men killed or wounded and 293,000 taken prisoner. The loss of tanks, artillery and other heavy weaponry as the troops had been hastily forced back over the Rhine and Mosel was huge. German fighting-power, weak enough at the onset of the Allied offensive, was now drastically diminished. Even the paper strength of the divisions, itself much reduced during the fighting of February and March, belied the reality that only a minority – many of them raw recruits – were by now capable of frontline service. Defences otherwise were dependent upon the poorly equipped *Volkssturm* and hastily assembled units transferred from the Luftwaffe and navy.

If Allied superiority on all fronts in manpower and armaments was ultimately simply overpowering, the characteristic refusal by Hitler and the High Command of the Wehrmacht to countenance tactical retreats until it was too late exacerbated the losses. Coupled with this was the rejection of all entreaties by Guderian and others to withdraw German forces still located outside the Reich's borders. These included, most prominently, 200,000 battle-hardened troops stranded in Courland, together with forces occupying the Low Countries, Scandinavia and still fighting in northern Italy. The main reason for the catastrophe nevertheless lay in the consistent refusal by the Reich's leadership to surrender and determination to fight on when any realistic hope had long been extinguished.[7]

By the end of March, then, Germany's enemies were across the Oder in the east and across the Rhine in the west. That even now there was a readiness to fight on when little if anything could be gained, though continued destruction and heavy loss of life were thereby guaranteed, is little less than astonishing. The readiness should not, however, be mistaken for widespread popular commitment to the German war effort. In the east, it is true, fear of the Soviets was a strong deterrent to defeatism and willingness to surrender. For most people, however, whether in the army or among the civilian population, there was simply no alternative but to struggle on under the terroristic grip of the regime in the dwindling parts of the Reich that were still not occupied.

II

All the indications point to a slump in morale within the Wehrmacht, especially in the west, as the defences gave way and the enemy pressed into the Reich. It was matched by the state of civilian morale. The regime reacted to try to combat the signs of disintegration, as always, through ramping up still further its propaganda efforts and through ferocious repression to serve as a deterrent.

The Party went to great lengths in March 1945 to intensify propaganda efforts to sustain and improve the fighting spirit within the Wehrmacht and among the civilian population. At the start of the month, Bormann sought support from the Gauleiter for a new propaganda drive that aimed to avoid any empty slogans but to reinforce a fanatical will to resist. A 'Special Action of the Party Chancellery' was set up to organize intensive propaganda activity through deputations of Party functionaries (in Wehrmacht uniform) and army officers.[8] Propaganda, it was accepted, had to be improved.[9] Based on recommendations from

Goebbels, it had also to be far more realistic than hitherto – an oblique recognition of some of the failings of hopelessly optimistic prognoses. Soldiers had to be given answers to the central questions preoccupying them: whether there was still a point in fighting; and whether the war could be won. A number of themes had to be highlighted: that Germany still had enough supplies of armaments and food and sufficient reserves of manpower and *matériel* (none of which was true, belying the emphasis on realism); the development of new 'miracle' weapons (on which there was by now all too justified widespread disbelief);[10] the effectiveness of the 'Panzerfaust' (the German type of bazooka, widely associated with the *Volkssturm*'s despairing defensive efforts); and the fact that the Americans had to deploy their forces over a huge area (which, of course, had not stopped them making massive inroads through German defences).[11]

None of this was much of a recipe to restore the rapidly waning confidence and slumping morale. Party speakers serving with the Wehrmacht were selected to address the troops – all the more necessary since transport difficulties were preventing written material from reaching them. In the Gau of Hessen-Nassau, arrangements were made to bus Party speakers chosen by the Reich propaganda leadership to frontline troop units. The leaflets such speakers were to distribute included reminders to 'think of the mass murder of Dresden' to encourage them in the belief that the British and Americans, as their destruction of the homeland through terror-bombing showed, were no better than the Bolsheviks. The only lesson was to stand and fight to the last.[12]

Another approach was to try to deflect attention from complaints and grievances by turning the spotlight on the enemy. This included disparaging the Americans as inferior to the Germans in every respect other than the sheer might of their weaponry, and the claim that Britain was at the limits of its tolerable losses. More remarkably, criticism of German mishandling of occupied territories was to be met with assertions that German measures had, in fact, been superior to those of the Allies, that 'we could in any case have a really good conscience in the question of treatment of most of the peoples hostile to us'. Understanding for the tasks of the Party and its achievements in the war effort could be improved through comparing these with the running of the First World War.[13]

The 'speaker action' included advice on how to deal with commonplace criticisms. Defeatist talk, for instance, had to be met with insistence that only determination and the will to resist could master the crisis. Blame attached to the Party for the war was to be countered by emphasizing that war had been declared on Germany, not the other way round, and that the enemy aimed to destroy not just the leadership but the very existence of Germany; that it would be far worse than after 1918. A rejoinder to the widespread view that the 'air terror' was the most unbearable burden of all and accompanying expressions about unfulfilled promises was that hardships had temporarily to be endured to allow time to produce better weapons. Pessimistic remarks that Germany had been unable to do this with its industry intact and could therefore hardly hope to do so with so much of it destroyed were to be turned round by saying that the loss of territories meant a smaller industrial output sufficed. Finally, dejection at enemy inroads in east and west had to be faced down by instilling confidence that counter-measures had been taken and would become stronger, that the fight was continuing at the front and at home, and that it was necessary to hold out to allow time for military and political decisions to ripen. The tenor of all speeches had to be an insistence that Germany would not lose the war, but would still win it. The people had to be given the conviction that there was a united fighting community which would on no account give in, but would be determined to endure the war with all means in order to gain victory.[14]

Little of this could sound convincing to any but the wilfully blind and obtuse. People in Berlin likened propaganda to a band playing on a sinking ship.[15] Most soldiers as well as civilians could see the hopelessness of the situation and form their own judgements on the feeble attempts of propaganda to contradict the glaringly obvious. The diary entries of a junior officer on the western front, who kept a careful eye on propaganda statements, comparing them with reality as he saw it, give one impression of feelings as the Americans advanced through the Rhineland. 'Wherever you go, only one comment: an end to the insanity,' he observed on 7 March, the day after Cologne had fallen. He did admit, however, that the occasional optimist, such as one of his comrades, a former Hitler Youth leader and 'a great show-off', still existed – though such figures could provide no grounds for their optimism. He could barely believe the reports of street-fighting in the ruins of Bonn. 'Ruins!' he remarked. 'That is the legacy for people after the war. How differently Ludendorff acted [at the end of the First World War] when he recognized that all was lost. To some extent still conscious of his respon-sibility.' The unspoken criticism of Hitler was obvious. Commenting on what proved to be the last 'Heroes' Memorial Day' on 11 March, the diarist noted: 'How the dead are being misused, their memory and their sacrifice. . . . There should and must now be an end.'[16]

Reports reaching the Propaganda Ministry in early March told of many soldiers looking bleakly towards a bitter end to the war.[17] Goebbels himself acknowledged in early March in exhorting Party prop-agandists to ever greater exertions that troop morale was a problem in parts of the army.[18] On 11 March he noted that 'the morale of our troops and our population in the west has suffered exceptionally. . . . Something can only now be achieved in the west through brutal measures, other-wise we'll no longer be master of the developing situation.'[19] Hitler briefly contemplated scrapping the Geneva Convention, which stipu-lated good treatment for prisoners of war, to encourage his soldiers to fight as hard on the western as on the eastern front.[20] But there were problems in the east, too. Guderian felt forced to provide a vehement denial of a scathing report about defeatist attitudes even among the general staff of Schörner's Army Group Centre. Though the report was inevitably coloured by the usual Party antagonism towards General Staff officers, the officers' recorded criticism of the poor quality and wavering resolve among the infantry is unlikely to have been fabricated.[21]

In Danzig, there was talk of 'a second Stalingrad', since the army gave the impression of being paralysed and lacking in initiative. Hun-dreds of soldiers were said to have deserted their posts at Küstrin (described as no more than 'one single heap of rubble' at the end of the siege), where there were plain signs of demoralization. They had fled westwards along with *Volkssturm* men only to be picked up by the Security Police and forced back into their units. Given the reported scale of looting by German troops in Küstrin, people muttered grimly that the Russians could be no worse.[22] Looting of houses and other property by retreating soldiers was by now, however, almost everywhere a com-monplace occurrence, despite the threat of severe sanctions for those involved.[23] There were other indications of army indiscipline. A Party District Leader in the Halle-Merseburg region reported a minor mutiny of 200 soldiers from a panzer division, and complained about the inabil-ity of police checks at stations to pick up deserters. At the fall of Trier, most of the *Volkssturm* defenders were said to have gone over to the enemy. Others did all they could to avoid military duty.[24] German troops on the Mosel, surprised by American tanks, had simply fled in whatever vehicles were to hand, leaving their arms and equipment behind.[25]

Of course, there were plenty of exceptions to the widespread longing of so many ordinary soldiers for the end of the war. One long letter home from a battalion sergeant-major based in Wiesbaden, just after the Americans had crossed the Rhine at Remagen, reveals an undiluted Nazi mentality and sense of unbroken defiance – though his own comments make plain that he was a rarity among his comrades, and he admitted that 'we can no longer rely 100 per cent on our soldiers'. He scorned American hopes, as he saw them, that Germans would lay down their weapons, or would fight with them against the Russians, as 'Jewish tricks'. Though he admitted the situation was extremely grim, he refused, he said, to lose his belief

> that we'll nevertheless win the war. I know that I'm laughed at by many people or thought mad. I know that there are only a few apart from me who have the courage to claim this, but I say it over and again: the Führer is no scoundrel, and not so bad as to lie to an entire people and drive it to death. Up to now the Führer has always given us his love and promised us freedom and carried out all his plans. And if the Führer prays to God that He may pardon him the last six weeks of this war of the nations then we know that there must and will be an awful and terrible end for our enemies.

It was, therefore, imperative to stay 'brave and strong. What use are all our material advantages if we end up later somewhere in Siberia?' he added. He was confident that Germany would strike back within the next few weeks with new weapons that would 'end this desolate situation' and decisively turn the war in Germany's favour. 'We must firmly believe in Germany's future – believe and ever more believe. A people that has so courageously lost so much blood for its greatness cannot perish. . . . Only our faith makes us strong, and I rely on the words of the Führer that at the end of all the fighting there will be German victory.'[26]

As the Allies crossed the Rhine and pushed into Germany, such naivety was distinctly a minority taste. By the end of March, only 21 per cent of a sample of soldiers captured by the western Allies still professed faith in the Führer (a drop from 62 per cent at the beginning of January), while 72 per cent had none. A mere 7 per cent still believed in

German victory; 89 per cent had no such belief.[27] A detailed report to the Propaganda Ministry from Hessen-Nassau in late March, as the Americans were advancing into the Main valley, painted a dismal picture of disintegration, antipathy between the military and Party leadership in the area, organizational disorder, and civilians refusing orders to evacuate, on the grounds that they had nowhere to go and, in any case, 'it's all over'. Many people, propaganda offices reported in March, had given up hope and there was a widespread view that the war was lost for Germany – though there remained a readiness, it was claimed, to continue doing their duty since it was recognized that capitulation would mean the 'complete destruction of the German people'.[28]

The defeatism was furthered, and much bitterness caused, by troops fleeing eastwards as fast as they could go, leaving badly trained and poorly equipped *Volkssturm* units behind and displaying a complete lack of 'comradely' behaviour towards the wounded and civilian evacuees as they brusquely commandeered vehicles for their retreat.[29] The long-serving Gauleiter of the area, Jakob Sprenger (who had already requested permission to set up summary courts martial in his Gau), added that the morale of the troops was influenced by the defeatism of the civilian population. The sense that defeat, at least at the hands of the western Allies, would mean the end of German existence was scarcely apparent. White flags had been shown in various places on the approach of enemy troops and the erection of tank barriers blocked.[30]

The population of numerous places on the Mosel acted in similar fashion, exhorting the troops to cease fighting to avoid further destruction.[31] A despairing SD agent wrote to Bormann of his bitter disappointment, shared with the many now serving on the western front who had come from the east and had, like himself, lost everything at the hands of the Bolsheviks, when they saw the defeatist attitude of the civilian population in Gau Moselland as Allied troops approached. People showed friendliness towards the Americans, he reported, but hostility towards their own troops. Propaganda attempts to inculcate hatred of the enemy were a complete failure. The Hitler greeting had disappeared from use; no rooms any longer had pictures of the Führer adorning them; white flags had replaced the swastika banner. Weapons were concealed or thrown away. There was, of course, no willingness to serve in the *Volkssturm*. And the attitude towards the Party was one of total 'annihilatory' rejection.[32]

In the Rhineland, civilians were said to have hurled insults at soldiers, accusing them of prolonging the war and causing additional misery by blowing up bridges and digging tank traps. They cut wires and engaged in minor acts of sabotage, prepared white flags of surrender, burnt Party emblems and uniforms and encouraged soldiers to put on civilian clothes and desert.[33] Such acts of localized opposition were, even so, not typical of the majority of the population. The longing for an end to the war was certainly near universal, but doing anything to shorten it was highly risky. Most people were not prepared to risk their lives at the last moment. This, together with an ingrained acceptance of authority, meant that resigned compliance rather than resistance was the norm.[34] And however extensive outward expressions of rejection of the continued war effort were on the western front, they were rare if not non-existent in the east, where the civilian population was wholly dependent on the fighting troops to keep the feared enemy from their throats.

Army discipline still held by and large, and not just in the east. Even so, desertion by troops was by now a serious concern for the military and Party leadership. Goebbels noted in early March that 'the desertion plague has worryingly increased. Tens of thousands of soldiers, allegedly stragglers but in reality wanting to avoid frontline service, are said to be in the big cities of the Reich.'[35] Discussions in the Party Chancellery to tackle the problem included the suggestion – found to be impracticable in the circumstances of mounting disorganization – of a nationwide 'general raid' on a specific day to round up all detached soldiers. Another was to leave executed deserters hanging for a few days in prominent places, a tactic said to have been effectively deployed in the east as a deterrent. (One woman, describing her flight from Silesia as a young girl, recalled her horror at seeing four corpses left to swing from lamp-posts with notices pinned to their bodies, telling passers-by: 'I Didn't Believe in the Führer', or 'I am a Coward'.[36]) Such fearsome reprisals, which probably had much support from those who felt they were doing their utmost for the war effort,[37] were to be accompanied by emphasizing the motto of Gauleiter Hanke, holed up in besieged Breslau, that 'he who fears death in honour will suffer it in dishonour'.[38] On 12 March, Field-Marshal Kesselring, the new Commander-in-Chief West, announced as one of his first orders the establishment of a motorized special command unit of military police to round up 'stragglers', who, he declared, were threatening to endanger the entire prosecution of the war in the west. Three days earlier, a 'flying court martial' (mentioned in the previous chapter) had been set up under the fervent loyalist Lieutenant-General Rudolf Hübner – a dentist in civilian life and cheerful executioner who allegedly said it gave him great satisfaction to shoot a general who had neglected his duty – to counter desertion and defeatism.[39] The first victims were five officers found guilty of failing to detonate the bridge at Remagen and peremptorily condemned to death.[40] Four were shot that very day. The fifth, luckily for him, had been captured by the Americans.[41] Model and Kesselring proclaimed the verdict to all their troops as a deterrent example, adding that the 'greatest severity' was expected of the courts martial.[42]

As the desperation increased, other frontline commanders also threatened, and deployed, harsh enforcement of discipline, even if Colonel-General Schörner stood out, as we have seen, for the scale of his brutality. Rendulić ordered unwounded 'stragglers' who had left their units to be summarily shot. Himmler, as Commander-in-Chief of Army Group Vistula, published orders that after 25 March any 'straggler' would be sentenced by drumhead court and shot on the spot.[43] Demands for fanatical defence of the Reich accompanied such severity. Unambiguous politicized fanaticism, as Stalin's troops had displayed, was required by Schörner in the east.[44]

In the west it was scarcely less savage. Paul Hausser, a Waffen-SS general commanding Army Group G in the south of the front, recommended the imprisonment of family members as a deterrent and ordered his soldiers under pain of punishment immediately to open fire on any soldier seen crossing the lines.[45] The Commander-in-Chief of Army Group H, based in the Netherlands, Colonel-General Blaskowitz, was certainly no SS extremist. In fact, he had been castigated by Hitler in 1939 for 'Salvation Army methods' for courageously criticizing the barbarity of the SS in Poland. But in the harshness of the treatment of his own troops in the last war months, Blaskowitz was no different to other generals, threatening deserting soldiers on 5 March with being 'summarily condemned and shot'.[46] 'The enemy must have to fight for every step in German land through the highest possible bloody losses,' Rundstedt had ordered at the beginning of March.[47] His successor in the western command, Kesselring, sought the assistance of the Party's Gauleiter to impress upon the public the need to fight for German towns and villages, now within the war zone, with absolute fanaticism. 'This struggle for the existence or non-existence of the German people does not exclude in its cruelty cultural monuments or other objects of cultural value,' he proclaimed.[48] Jodl appealed to commanders in the west to ensure that the enemy encountered a 'fanatical will to fight' among troops defending the Reich. Regard for the population, he added, could currently be no consideration.[49]

Generals were no mere tools of Hitler, much as they claimed to have been such in their post-war apologetics. They acted from conviction, doing all in their power to inspire, and compel, their troops to ever greater efforts. Though they subsequently liked to portray themselves as professional soldiers doing no more than their patriotic duty, they were in fact the most indispensable component of the dying regime. Though few shared Schörner's undiluted belief in the doctrine of National Socialism, they all accepted some of its articles of faith. The combination of extreme nationalism (meaning belief in German superiority and the unique glory of the Reich) and anti-Communism, together with a passionate resolve to prevent the occupation and – as they mostly believed – the destruction of Germany, sufficed to sustain their undiminished exertions in a lost cause. A distorted sense of duty was a strong additive. Without their extraordinary commitment to continuing the struggle when rational assessment demanded an end to the destruction, the regime would have collapsed.[50]

Among the military leaders displaying greatest fanaticism in the final weeks of the Reich, counter to the post-war image he cultivated, was Grand-Admiral Karl Dönitz, Commander-in-Chief of the Navy. His series of short situation reports were seen as so valuable by Bormann for their defiant fighting spirit that he had them sent out to Gauleiter and other leading Party functionaries. The first of Dönitz's reports, on 4 March, began:

> There is no need to explain to you that in our situation capitulation is suicide and means certain death; that capitulation will bring the death, the quick or slower destruction, of millions of Germans, and that, in comparison with this, the blood toll even of the harshest fighting is small. Only if we stand and fight have we any chance at all of turning round our fate. If we voluntarily surrender, every possibility of this is at an end. Above all, our honour demands that we fight to the last. Our pride rebels against crawling before a people like the Russians or the sanctimony, arrogance and lack of culture of the Anglo-Saxons.

He appealed for a sense of 'duty, honour and pride' to fight to the last.[51]

In the navy, more than in the Luftwaffe (where morale had suffered from its heavy losses and from the drastic decline in public standing as Allied bombers dominated the skies) or the army, such appeals were not without effect. In 1918, the revolution had begun with the mutiny of sailors in Kiel. Sailors schooled in the Third Reich were well aware of this 'stain' on the navy's history. Not that there was any likelihood of a repeat in 1945. As in the other branches of the Wehrmacht, attitudes and forms of behaviour varied widely. War-weariness was evident. But desertion, mutiny and indiscipline in the navy were rare. For the most part, morale remained high and readiness to fight on was present to the end – when, indeed, thousands of sailors were transferred to help in the battle of Berlin. Since taking over as Commander-in-Chief at the end of January 1943, Dönitz had done all he could to instil in the navy the 'most brutal will to victory' that derived from National Socialist ideology. Bolstering the readiness to utmost resistance in the 'fight with the western powers, Bolshevism and Jewry' was the message passed on by one of his subordinate officers, the head of a destroyer flotilla based at Brest.[52] How much this sort of rhetoric shaped the unbroken fighting spirit of ordinary sailors is nevertheless hard to judge. Other factors may well have been more significant.

Dönitz had ensured that naval crews had good welfare provision – material and psychological. And the war at sea, for all its perils, was somewhat detached from the daily brutalities of the land war in the east. For some, indeed, the part they played in helping to rescue tens of thousands of stranded refugees gave the continued war some purpose and sense of idealism. Others perhaps found purpose in the claims of the naval leadership that the continued war at sea was tying down enemy forces, and that the navy would be an important bargaining counter in any negotiated settlement. Most important of all, however, was almost certainly the feeling of comradeship, enhanced by the close confines of a ship or submarine, where class divisions were less apparent than on land as officers and men lived cheek by jowl sharing exactly the same dangers.[53]

Finally, as in the remainder of the Wehrmacht and among the civilian population, there was another factor at work, impossible to quantify, but doubtless widespread: passive acceptance of the situation since there was no obvious alternative. If this did not amount to positive motivation, it certainly did not pose any barrier to the military system continuing to function – and, with that, to the war continuing.

III

High-ranking military officers had possibilities of a wider perspective on the war than might be expected among the rank-and-file. What did the generals see as the purpose of still fighting on at this stage? Was there any sense of rationality, or was nothing left beyond a fatalistic dynamic that could not be halted short of total defeat? Was there any clear-sightedness at all?

Colonel-General Heinrich von Vietinghoff-Scheel, in the last phase of the war Commander-in-Chief of the German forces in Italy, pointed out a few years later that, following the great increase of size of the army in the course of the conflict, the number of generals by 1945 had risen to around 1,250, though he estimated that only about fifty had any insight into the overall strategic position. Addressing the question of potential political power of the generals to block the disastrous course of the war, he took the view, naturally involving more than a tinge of apologetics, that 'even among the field-marshals, the slightest attempt to bring together a majority to unified action against Hitler would have been condemned to failure, and become known to Hitler, apart from the fact that the troops would have refused to go along with such a move'. He rejected the notion that generals serving at the front could have resigned in protest. This would simply have meant abandoning their troops, and would have flown in the face of all sense of comradeship and honour. It would have been cowardice. Finally, voluntary capitulation would have been feasible only if the troops had been prepared to follow the order, which they would not have done, he claimed.[54]

The war, Vietinghoff wrote on release from captivity, was unquestionably lost once the Rhine front had collapsed in March 1945. Ending it at that point would have spared countless victims and massive destruction. It was the duty of the Reich leadership to draw the consequences and negotiate with the enemy. Since Hitler refused to entertain such a proposition, this duty fell to everyone in a position of responsibility able to do something to achieve that end. 'In this situation, the duty of obedience reached its limits. Loyalty to the people and to the soldiers entrusted to him was a higher duty' for the commander. However, in taking such action he had to be sure that the troops would follow him. This Vietinghoff still felt, at the beginning of April, with German troops holding a line south of Bologna, unable to guarantee. The majority of the troops, he claimed – an exaggerated claim at this stage, in all probability – still had faith in Hitler. And the regime would swiftly have blamed the commander for treachery, exhorting the troops not to obey him. Solidarity among the fighting troops would have collapsed, as some would have wanted to carry on the fight, others to surrender.[55] It would be some weeks yet before Vietinghoff finally agreed to a capitulation in Italy. Even then, he was unsure until late in the day, so he later implied, about the readiness of the troops to surrender.

Post-war memoirs by former military leaders frequently, like Vietinghoff's, have a self-serving flavour. They can nonetheless still illustrate ways of thinking that shaped behaviour. Vietinghoff shared the sense of obedience, honour and duty that had long been bred into the officer corps and posed a psychological barrier to anything that smacked of treason. He at least did eventually act, though by then the Red Army was almost literally at the portals of the Reich Chancellery. His uncertainty about the readiness of the troops to follow orders to surrender also sounds plausible. And whether he would have sought a partial capitulation even at such a late stage had he been serving on the eastern or western front might reasonably be doubted. For all its apologetics, Vietinghoff's account gives an indication of why German generals could not contemplate breaking with the regime.

Though numerous generals confided their opinions to paper after the end of the war, contemporary expressions of their private views are relatively rare. Few generals in those hectic weeks had time to compile diary entries or other current reactions to events. They had in any case, like everyone else, to be wary of expressing any critical, let alone defeatist, comments that might fall into the wrong hands. Penetrating their public stance is, therefore, difficult.

Some insight into the mentality of German generals in the last phase of the war can be gleaned from the private conversations – which they did not know were being bugged – of those in British captivity. These were, of course, by now viewing events from afar and without any internal insights into developments. On the other hand, they could express their views freely without fear that they would be denounced as traitors or defeatists and suffer for their criticism of the regime. Strikingly, despite recognition that the war was undoubtely lost, these high-ranking officers drew quite varied conclusions – depending, in part, on their susceptibility to Nazi thinking and propaganda. Some of the more Nazified officers believed that 'if Bolshevism triumphs today, then it will be a question of the biological annihilation of our people'. Speculation after the failure of the Ardennes offensive that Rundstedt might surrender in the west in order to fight on in the east was dismissed as impracticable. The western Allies would not accept a partial surrender; Rundstedt could in any case do nothing because SS panzer divisions among his Army Group would not allow it; and there was the fear that anyone attempting such unilateral action would be killed immediately.[56] Non-Nazi, relatively critical, officers were still in February and March 1945 evoking 'elementary military honour' in demanding that 'nobody in the front line, not even the commander-in-chief, can even consider whether or not he should carry on fighting'. Honour was a crucial consideration. 'Whatever defeats they may yet suffer,' ran another comment, 'this nation can only go down with honour.'[57]

A lower-ranking officer, captured at Alzey (between Worms and Mainz) in mid-March 1945, gave his Allied interrogators his own views, based on what he had gleaned at Army General Staff headquarters at Zossen, on why the Germans kept on fighting. The 'realists' in the General Staff, he said, 'expected the Rhine and Elbe lines to collapse and meant to go down fighting. Whilst Hitler was in power it was not considered possible for the German forces to lay down their arms.' Any attempt to overthrow him was presumed out of the question after the failure of the Stauffenberg plot the previous July. The intentions were to hold the line of the Oder as long as possible and when this was no longer tenable to make a fighting withdrawal to the Elbe. In the west, the priority was to wipe out the Remagen bridgehead. It was not anticipated that the Allies would be able to cross the Rhine anywhere else. In the north, troops would be withdrawn from western Holland to hold the line on the Lower Rhine. 'It was believed', he added, 'that the line of the Elbe in the east and of the Rhine in the west could be held for as long as proved necessary. It was envisaged that sooner or later a split would occur between the US and UK on the one hand and the USSR on the other, which would enable Germany to restore her position.' The re-emergence of the Luftwaffe, with production of jet-fighters as a first priority, was seen as a prerequisite for the strategy, so oil refineries and other vital installations were provided with especially heavy anti-aircraft defences.[58]

One contemporary glimpse of the thinking of a high-ranking officer based inside the Reich, away from the front lines, is afforded by letters (cautiously couched to avoid anything smacking of defeatism) of Colonel Curt Pollex, from 9 January 1945 Chief of Staff to the head of Wehrmacht Armaments. Pollex was a cultured individual and no Nazi. But he was fatalistic and passive, accepting that he could do nothing other than continue with his duties – which, of course, helped the regime in his own sphere still function – and brace himself for the hurricane soon to come. He had a realistic sense of impending disaster, but felt in his way as helpless as the millions of soldiers and civilians in lowly positions to do anything to prevent it, or see any alternative.

'Everything is carrying on at present as if it would be all right at the end,' he wrote on 5 March. He mentioned hopes in the U-boats, but was evidently sceptical. He did not know how anyone could still believe Goebbels, still proclaiming the impact of V-weapons. He was equally dubious about talk of 'an aeroplane that they call Germany's bird of fate', something to change the course of the war. If a change was to come, it had to be very soon, he remarked drily. He just carried on with his duties. 'My people understand me,' he added. He immersed himself in his work, 'acting as if everything were as it is written in the news-paper'. But he refrained from criticizing Goebbels' speech at the end of February, leaving open the outcome of future developments and whether the Führer and Goebbels might prove right in the end. Perhaps there would after all be a change in fortune. 'The Führer claims it will be so. I'm just a poor fool with no sixth sense who unfortunately sees noth-ing,' he remarked, with scarcely veiled sarcasm. He had not imagined the Americans crossing the Rhine so quickly. 'But it's not fully out of the question that we could still master this situation,' he added, again seem-ing to doubt his own words. There were still those, he acknowledged, who shared Hitler's confidence in final victory; plainly, he was not among their number. It was obvious to him that Hitler would not capitulate. He thought it would end with a battle on the Obersalzberg. There were 'wonderful things in preparation', but they would come too late. Even now, however, there were signs that he had not altogether given up hope. Conflict between the Russians and the Americans would still give Germany a chance, just as a motor-race could be decided by a puncture 100 metres from the finishing line. Away from such reveries, work seemed pointless. He was just going through the motions. Orders by now had in any case little effect. An 'ostrich-policy' operated as people buried their heads in the sand.[59]

Pollex could entertain his quasi-philosophical reflections, well away from the front. Colonel-General Gotthard Heinrici, brought in on 20 March by Hitler to replace Himmler – whose command of Army Group Vistula had laid bare his evident incapacity for military leadership – and use his recognized abilities as a defensive strategist to try to hold the front in Pomerania, made his assessments much closer to the action. An archetypal Prussian career officer who had served in the First World War and had long experience of command in the Second, Heinrici was a strong patriot but had always kept his distance from the Party. Soon after the war, in British captivity, he provided his own explanation for the continued fight down to the end, however despairing the situation. He praised the fighting spirit, determination and resolute defence of German troops on the Oder against greatly superior enemy might. He was well aware of the deficiencies in armaments, the lack of fighting experience of around half his troops, and the fact that some of the more experienced soldiers, having narrowly survived so many battles, had lost the will to fight to the last as the end approached. None of this overshadowed, however, the overall strategic picture, which, he said, was clear both to the leadership and to the ordinary soldier. As long as German forces could hold the Rhine, the defence of the Oder did not seem hopeless, and was certainly worth fighting for. Once the enemy was over the Rhine and pressing on towards the Elbe, however, ordinary soldiers inevitably asked themselves whether there was any point to carrying on. What made them do so he attributed primarily to their sense of 'patriotic duty to halt the advance of the Russians'. It was clear to every soldier what could be expected from the Russians. And it was seen as imperative to protect the civilian population as far as possible from the sort of horror that had occurred east of the Oder. Beyond that, he said, the military leadership believed that it could not undermine any possible bargaining position in negotiations through premature collapse. When hopes that the Oder could be held proved

vain and German defences were smashed, disintegration swiftly followed. 'If the soldier decided to fight on, then this was no longer to halt
the enemy but to save his own life or not to fall into Soviet captivity.'
Terror, he stated, was no longer sufficient to compel soldiers to fight.
Survival alone was now the driving force.[60]

After the war, Dönitz argued – attributing much responsibility to the
Allied insistence on unconditional surrender – that 'no one in authority
could have signed an instrument of capitulation without knowing full
well that its terms would be broken' by soldiers in the east refusing to
accept orders to stay and enter Soviet captivity and instead, like the civilian population, choosing to flee westwards.[61] Whatever his self-justificatory
motivation in such remarks (which clash with his contemporary demands
for a fanatical fight to the last), Dönitz did have a point in the implication
that the millions still serving on the eastern front would have felt betrayed
and might well have taken matters into their own hands in trying to get
to the west. Whether this would have been worse for them than what did
actually happen is a moot point.

In the east especially, a passionate desire for an end to the war, detestation of the Party, criticism of the regime, and even loss of faith in
Hitler were perfectly compatible with soldiers' continued determination
to repel the Russian invaders on Reich soil who posed such a threat to
families and homes. And ultimately, as Heinrici points out, when all
idealism had vanished and pure desperation took hold, soldiers fought
on for self-survival.

In the west, the situation was different. Certainly, on the western
front, despite the attempts of propaganda, equivalent anxieties about
falling into the hands of the Americans or the British rarely existed
beyond the ranks of Party functionaries. Once the enemy had reached
German soil and then crossed the Rhine, there was, even so, still much
determination to repel the invader. Unable to see beyond the immediate
battlegrounds, many soldiers were compelled to believe, beyond what
their senses were telling them, that they were still fighting to gain time –
for the leadership to fend off the Soviets, seek a worthwhile peace
settlement, see the breakup of the enemy coalition. Who knew exactly?
Moreover, units on the western front also included many soldiers whose
homes and families were in eastern or central regions of Germany and
who saw fighting on as necessary as long as the British, Americans and
French remained in alliance with the Soviets. Some unquestionably

thought the western Allies would eventually see sense and realize that the real war was against Russia. 'Germany is saving Europe and England and America from being gobbled up by Bolshevik Russia,' claimed officers captured in the west. 'The British and Americans will one day . . . awaken to the real situation and will join the Germans in holding off Russia.'[62] Beyond such motives were more immediate, unpolitical feelings: the unwillingness, as in most armies, to leave close friends and comrades in the lurch. The sense of comradeship often provided its own motivation for fighting on when idealism was lacking.

And ultimately there was the sense that there was nothing to be done about it. There was no potential for mutiny or rising to overthrow the regime. The scale of harsh repression was simply too great. Stepping out of line was little less than suicidal. And when it happened, desertion was usually an individual act, not mass mutiny. It reflected a desperate attempt at personal survival, not a collapse of the military order.[63] Apart from the savagery of reprisals and fears for one's family, the capacity to organize any mutiny was as good as absent, in part because the sheer intensity of the fighting and scale of losses at the front left no chance to organize political action, partly too because constant losses left little continuity in the manpower of troop units. There was nothing for it, therefore, but to struggle on.

The situation in 1945 contrasted sharply with the revolutionary conditions of 1918.[64] 'In 1918 we experienced more open revolutionary tendencies,' commented one cavalry general in British captivity in March 1945. 'As the end drew near, the men were already behaving in a very insolent fashion. They don't do that now.'[65] In the last months of the First World War, there had been a gathering collapse of authority in the military command. Perhaps as many as a million soldiers in the final weeks, encouraged by the stirring revolutionary mood at home, among workers and soldiers in home-based garrisons, and aware of peace demands in the Reichstag, voted with their feet against continuing to fight. In 1918 military discipline had been much in line with that of the other belligerent powers, losses were smaller, German cities had not been reduced to rubble, civil society was largely intact, pluralist politics continued to exist; most crucially, there had been no brutal Russian occupation of eastern Germany and threat to the Reich capital itself, and there had been no western invasion of the Reich. German troops could return home seemingly undefeated in the field.

There had also been the Workers' Councils in factories, bodies to give voice to the simmering unrest and to organize mass strikes and protest meetings. There had been no equivalent of the Nazi Party ensuring through its ruthless hold over the population that 'organizational space' to engender a popular uprising was totally unavailable. Not least, there was no equivalent to the terroristic police apparatus of 1945. In 1918, rejection of the Kaiser and Germany's ruling class, extensive within the army and within the population, could be openly expressed and ultimately transformed into revolutionary action. In 1945, detestation of Hitler and the regime or heated criticism of policies that had produced the misery of a lost war were sentiments best swallowed. The faintest whiff of insurrectionary sentiment could spell instant brutal retaliation.

Paradoxically, therefore, increasing defeatism among ordinary soldiers not only failed to prompt them to lay down their arms or rise in mutiny against their superior officers but was compatible with continued readiness to fight on. Exhausted, demoralized troops provided no basis for insurrection. If one sentiment could sum up the myriad views of soldiers, it was probably fatalism – hoping for the best because that was all anyone could do. They saw no alternative but to carry on. Change could only come from above, but there were no indications that it ever would.

IV

For the civilian population, the sense of helplessness as the maelstrom gathered force was almost totally embracing. In bomb-ravaged big cities, conditions by March 1945 were intolerable, though the countryside, for all its privations, fared better. The misery was near universal as people simply awaited the end of the war, unable to do anything to hasten it, left to their fate to face the continued bombing and the inroads of the enemy, with all the uncertainty, anxiety and – in the east – downright fear that entailed. The only hope was that the war would soon end and that the British and Americans would arrive before the Russians.[66] A graphic display of feeling in one Alpine village, said to mirror 'the true attitude of the people', was the refusal of the soldiers, *Volkssturm* men and civilians assembled for Heroes' Memorial Day on 11 March to return the 'Sieg Heil' to the Führer at the end of the Wehrmacht commander's speech.[67] The SD summed up attitudes at the end of March: no one wanted to lose the war, but no one believed Germany could now win it; the leadership was to blame (confidence in it had collapsed 'like an avalanche' in recent days), there was much criticism of the Party, 'certain leaders' and propaganda; the Führer was still 'the last hope' of millions – a necessary ritualistic concession in such reports – but was more vehemently 'by the day included in the question of confidence and the criticism'; finally, the feeling that fighting on was pointless was by now eating at the readiness to continue, at self-belief and at belief in other people.[68]

Shortage of food was becoming a big issue in the cities. Owing to lack of transport, acute shortages – exacerbated by hoarding, especially by military personnel – had existed in Rhineland cities before the Allies arrived.[69] 'Hunger, terror from the air and the military situation' determined the popular mood, according to a report from Stuttgart in late March. 'A large section of the population is already completely at an end as regards bread, fats and foodstuffs.'[70] There were serious worries about food supplies in Berlin, too, as rations were reduced again.[71] Many claimed they already had nothing to eat – though 'painted and powdered ladies wearing expensive furs and afternoon dresses' were said still to frequent the few remaining restaurants.[72] Anxieties were said to be mounting over likely future acute shortages. The Allies, it is true, had reported adequate supplies of food hidden away – some of it allegedly looted from the homes of neighbours who had evacuated – when they marched through the Rhineland.[73] But even in the country, where farmers especially always seemed to have sufficient in store, the diminished rations were making themselves felt. 'Just enough if you can sleep the whole day,' bemoaned one worker in south Germany, where there was much 'bad blood' over shortages of potatoes and other foodstuffs.[74] Many individuals tried to pretend that they had lost their ration cards as applications for substitute cards soared after the drop in rations was announced.[75] Directives from Bormann – perhaps emanating from Hitler himself – instructing the Gauleiter to coordinate measures to make more use of wild vegetables, fruits, berries, mushrooms and herbs to mitigate food-ration reductions, and wild medicinal herbs to compensate for shortage of medicines, were unlikely to have been warmly welcomed.[76]

Cuts in electricity and gas supplies and severe coal shortages were commonplace in big cities. Drains were often blocked by bomb damage. Water could in some places be had only from standpipes in the street. People in some rural areas had to resort to cooking on stoves fired with peat.[77] Schools and universities had mainly closed by now. Some schools were requisitioned as field hospitals for the wounded.[78] Floods of refugees placed a massive additional burden on housing and other public services. Welfare work was made more difficult by the lack of unified control, resulting – typical for the Third Reich – in conflicting demands from different agencies.[79] Hospitals could not cope with the high numbers of casualties from air raids. In early March, Bormann ordered the incorporation of the personnel of hospitals and clinics into the *Volkssturm*.[80] There was huge disruption of the railways. If a journey had to be undertaken and even if a place on a train could be found, delays of many hours were to be expected. People coped as best they could under the extremely difficult circumstances. But the cuts in public services had complicating side effects. Electricity cuts meant, for instance, that shops were shutting early, when it became too dark for business, leaving no possibility for those in work to buy food in the early evening hours. And once the electricity was restored, in mid-evening, there was often an air-raid alarm so that people had no time to eat.[81]

A source of particular concern to the millions of families desperate for news of sons, brothers, fathers or other close relatives at the front was that postal services were in a state of near collapse. By late March, post offices had often been put out of action by bombing. Telephone, telegraph and rail communications had largely broken down for ordinary citizens, and often, too, for public authorities and businesses.[82] The Reich Post Minister, Wilhelm Ohnesorge, laid down stipulations for ensuring a minimum postal service. If trains were unavailable, motor vehicles had to be used to shuttle post to the nearest functioning railway station. If no vehicles were available, local transport had to be requisitioned. In the last resort, the most urgent post was to be carried by bicycle or on foot in rucksacks.[83]

There was, it is true, still a veneer of what passed for 'normality' in the diminishing parts of Germany not under occupation or sucked into the fighting zones, though anything resembling civic society had long since vanished. One of the few places bomb-threatened people of big cities found any semblance of communal activity in these weeks was in the air-raid shelter.[84] Work itself, however hard, tedious and long, must have been for many a distraction from the heavy worries and burdens of daily life. And wages and salaries continued to be paid as Germany collapsed. Newspapers still appeared – though by March there were only 814 of them (compared with 2,075 daily papers in 1937), and they were only two to four pages in length. Periodicals had been cut back still further because of the shortage of paper and other difficulties; only 458 out of 4,789 in pre-war times were still in circulation.[85] Radio remained the most important means of communication (though power cuts meant big interruptions to programmes), not just for propaganda but also for entertainment programmes. The main transmitters in big cities continued to function to the end. Not least, the radio was crucial for giving warnings of approaching bombers, while receivers in air-raid shelters passed on Party directives following raids.[86] Despite stiff penalties, many continued surreptitiously to listen to enemy broadcasts, especially the BBC. People could still find escapism in the cinema. Entertainment films provided a temporary release from the horrors and misery of reality. They were more attractive than the 'fight-on' propaganda conveyed through films like *Kolberg* (which can only have reminded people of what was actually happening in the town at the time) or newsreels that could only show Germany's desperate plight. However, bombing of cinema buildings, blackouts and air-raid alarms had taken their toll on attendance. And for those who did go to the cinema, leaving the building was to re-enter a reality beyond the imagination of any film producer.

Outside the most war-ravaged zones and the worst bombed areas of the big cities, a still functioning, if hugely creaking, bureaucracy and the far-reaching tentacles of Party control ensured that skeletal and emergency administration, accompanied by much hand-to-mouth improvisation, continued in some measure to operate.

Routine administration carried on – even with much reduced personnel through recruitment to the Wehrmacht. Forms, more of them than ever, had to be completed, reports filed, the myriad tasks of minor bureaucracy (which civil servants down the ranks had always done) still undertaken. The usual local health and social welfare, finance and economic issues, even building planning, continued amid the mayhem, however unreal it often seemed.[87] And local police stations were still sending in their reports on maintenance of 'order' down to the end. Much of the work of local and regional authorities was, however, inevitably preoccupied with finding housing for those bombed out of their homes, trying to cope with the influx of refugees, organizing food rations and distribution of increasingly stretched provisions, regulating air-raid measures[88] and the deployment of the hard-pressed fire service (many of whom were volunteers, taken out of their normal work for fire-brigade duties).[89] Few of the lower-ranking civil servants were by now, if they ever had been, inspired by gung-ho Nazi propaganda and sloganeering about fighting to the last ditch. But hardly any would have contemplated doing anything other than what they saw as their duty to ensure that they carried out their work as conscientiously and efficiently as possible. They were merely small cogs in a big machine. But they did their best, even at this late stage, to ensure that the machine continued to function as well as possible.

In any case, much of their work had been usurped by Party functionaries.[90] Here the level of political commitment was still far greater, and where it was flagging a sense of self-protection against possibly costly reproaches from higher Party offices could produce its own activism.[91] Local and District Leaders, down to Block Leaders based in tenement blocks, would do all they could to carry out the directions of the Gauleiter in all matters of civil defence, organizing anti-aircraft batteries, the running of air-raid bunkers, clearing up after air raids and, through the NSV, providing whatever social welfare was possible.[92] But all this frenetic activism was coupled with still unceasing attempts to mobilize the population and instil in them the need to fight on. However ineffective the actions of the local Party functionaries were in practice, and whatever antipathies they now encountered as the end approached, they still served as a crucial control mechanism on the population. Even the NSV, the huge Party welfare organization (which had employed more than 60,000 people full-time, mainly women, in mid-1944[93]), was in essence still a vehicle for political control, whatever work it did – in addition to (and often in competition with) state-run welfare – to help the victims of bombing raids, provide for wounded soldiers, organize evacuations or take care of refugees. The Party's organizational structures, still incorporating (if affiliates are included) huge numbers of citizens, mobilizing young Germans as 'flak helpers' in anti-aircraft defence, and half a million women for service as 'Wehrmacht assistants' (then some of these even for fighting),[94] ensured that the overwhelming majority of citizens remained compliant even as the regime crumbled. Few were prepared to risk stepping out of line. Political dissidence could prove lethal for any individual, and was regarded by most people as not just foolhardy but unnecessary as the end loomed.

At higher levels of state administration, the erosion had intensified. Following the heavy bombing of the government district of Berlin in early February, especially, the work of major state ministries was heavily impaired. New addresses were circulated almost weekly as improvised accommodation had to be found for the ministerial staff. The Finance Minister, Schwerin von Krosigk, for example, had to move his office to his home in the suburb of Dahlem.[95] Parts of ministries were now increasingly evacuated from the Reich capital. It was seen by many as 'rats leaving the sinking ship'.[96] Coordination of work was ever more difficult. Written communication between ministerial officials could often only be achieved now through a courier service. And much of the work was merely trying to reconstitute files destroyed in bombing raids. Central government administration increasingly resembled rearranging the deckchairs on the *Titanic*.[97]

Practically all matters of substance outside the military sphere had anyway been taken over by the Party. The Gauleiter remained the key figures in the provinces still not occupied – bulwarks of loyalty to Hitler and diehards without a future, who in varying degrees according to ability, temperament and attitude represented the radical drive of the Party to mobilize all forces for the 'last stand', even when any semblance of rationality told them that all was lost. Gauleiter Wilhelm Murr of Württemberg, for instance, Party boss in the region since 1928, was determined, in the face of the evident longing of the people of the area for peace, that there would be no surrender in his domain. He threatened instant execution for anyone showing a white flag or obstructing German defences.[98] Karl Wahl, the Gauleiter of Swabia, centred on the city of Augsburg in the west of Bavaria, had also run his province without interruption since 1928. He counted as one of the less extreme of the Gauleiter (an image he was keen to burnish after the war), and as a result did not stand high in the esteem of Hitler and Bormann.[99] In mid-March, however, after the debacle of Remagen, Wahl recommended to Bormann the use of suicide pilots to fly their planes loaded with bombs into the Americans' temporary supply bridges over the Rhine. A new heroism, not known in history, was needed, he claimed. 'There are surely sufficient loyal followers of the Führer who would be prepared to sacrifice themselves if they could save the people through their deed. . . . Is it not better that a few dozen choose to die than that, by not undertaking this essential emergency measure, tens of thousands must lose their lives . . .'[100] Nothing came of the idea. Perhaps Wahl proposed it cynically, reckoning with its rejection but believing it would uphold his credentials as a fanatical backer of the Führer's cause. Even so, the proposal illustrates the stance that Germany's ruling cohorts felt they had to display in the last weeks of the war. It was rapidly coming to be the rule of the desperadoes.

By the end of March Wahl was promoting in his Gau the creation by Goebbels and Labour Front leader Robert Ley of partisan organizations to engage in terroristic guerrilla activity to hinder the enemy advance (and at the same time to combat and deter defeatism), the so-called 'Werwolf' and 'Freikorps "Adolf Hitler"'.[101] The idea of a partisan-style movement had been first mooted in 1943, and it took preliminary organizational shape under the aegis of the SS in the autumn of the following year, when the name 'Werwolf' – resonating in German tradition with connotations of ferocious defiance as well as shadowy lupine terror – was attached to it.[102] Some guerrilla activity was carried out on the eastern front and to a lesser extent in the west in the winter months of 1944–5, though it could inflict no more than pinpricks on the advancing enemy. Its most notable activities were terroristic in nature. A number of American-appointed mayors in the newly occupied parts of western Germany were assassinated, for instance, most notably the Mayor of Aachen, Franz Oppenhoff, in March 1945. Once the western front had crumbled and the Allies were pressing deep into Germany, underground resistance movements began to gain more importance in Nazi thinking, particularly when the Party leadership started to show interest in them. Martin Bormann saw their potential for tackling defeatism and possible insurgency within the Reich. But 'Werwolf' took shape, however dimly, in public consciousness only when Goebbels turned it into a propaganda enterprise, muscling in on the territory both of the Party Chancellery and of the SS, though with Hitler's backing.

On 1 April, Werwolf Radio began broadcasting its tirades against the Allies, exultant news of real or imaginary acts of sabotage, and dark threats against 'defeatists' and 'traitors' in the homeland.[103] Just before this, Ley, one of the zanier zealots in the last phase, had approached Hitler with the notion of creating an organization similar to that of the

Werwolf, aimed at mobilizing young fanatical activists, equipped with little more than bicycles and bazookas, to shoot down approaching enemy tanks. Hitler agreed to the establishment of a Freikorps bearing his own name. Goebbels' only objection was that it was under the leadership of a man he regarded as little more than a clown. He himself expected much of the partisan activity, chiefly 'to hunt down every German traitor on the side of the western enemy', though he prided himself that the Werwolf had caused horror in the enemy camp and aroused fears of a 'partisan Germany' that would cause unrest in Europe for years.[104] This was an overestimation of Allied fears – though the Allies certainly took seriously the prospect of having to combat guerrilla warfare as they fought their way through Germany, and of the likelihood of a 'national redoubt' in the Alps where the Nazis would continue to hold out.[105] It also grossly overrated the appetite for partisan activity among the exhausted German people.

Overall, the Werwolf and Freikorps 'Adolf Hitler' added up to little. Their victims – an estimated 3,000–5,000 killed (including continued post-war activity) were not insignificant in number.[106] But for the Allies, they were – beyond the worries they initially aroused – no more than a minor irritant. And among the German population they had little support – though there was undoubtedly some appeal to fanaticized Hitler Youth members.[107] Their main capacity was to terrorize, and this they did to the very last days of the war, when they were still engaged in sporadic and horrific murders of those wanting to avoid rather than promote pointless destruction as the Allies marched in. Ultimately, the partisan organizations of these weeks represented the regime's lasting and massive capability for destructiveness. But just as great in these weeks was its capacity for self-destructiveness.

V

The deepening fissures in the foundations were now starting to show, too, among the regime leadership. One sign was the increasing desperation with which, even at this late hour, efforts were made to prompt a search for a political solution to the end of the war. As war fortunes had plummeted, leading Nazis – among them Goebbels, Ribbentrop, Göring and even Himmler – had pondered seeking a negotiated exit route from the path leading inexorably towards Germany's doom. But whenever tentative suggestions had been made for exploring an opening, whether with the western powers or even with the arch-enemy, Bolshevik Russia, Hitler had been dismissive. He persisted with his dogmatic stance that negotiations were carried out from a position of strength, so could only follow a major German military success. The Ardennes offensive had been a last attempt to acquire such a bargaining position. Since then, the calamitous cave-in on the eastern front followed by the disastrous collapse in the west as the Allies pushed over the Rhine and Mosel meant that hopes of acquiring any sort of worthwhile negotiating position became more illusory by the day. Even at the beginning of March, Hitler purported to believe – or at least held to the fiction – that the Rhine could be held, the Soviets pushed back, and some sort of deal then done with Stalin.[108] He was shrewd enough to know how unrealistic this was, even before the Rhine was crossed. Any negotiated end would, in any case, have inevitably meant Hitler's own end, as he well knew. Negotiations would now more than ever have amounted to capitulation. This would have upturned everything that had driven his political 'career': that there would be no repeat of the 'shameful' capitulation of 1918.

Hitler retained at the core an extraordinary inner consistency – a dogmatic inflexibility that had terrible consequences for his country. Refusal to contemplate negotiations was for him both logically consistent and easy since his own life was forfeit anyway whether Germany capitulated or fought on. It was not that he worked out a 'choreography' of downfall.[109] It was quite simply that there was no way out. With the war lost (as even he, inwardly, by now recognized) there could be no possible alternative in his mind to fighting on to the last. Going down in glory was for him, wedded to the heroic myths of the Germanic past, inconceivably greater than the 'coward's' way out of surrender – and negotiations from weakness amounted to the same thing. The 'heroism' would set an example for later generations, as he emphasized to Goebbels.[110] To his soldiers, he underlined once again on Heroes' Memorial Day in mid-March: 'The year 1918 will . . . not repeat itself.'[111]

Of the top-ranking Nazi leadership below Hitler, only Goebbels, still the worshipping acolyte, was prepared to follow the same line to its logical conclusion. He had at numerous points wanted to negotiate. But after the Allies crossed the Rhine, he was clear-sighted enough to see that Germany's last hope of a political settlement had collapsed.[112] His decision, as he told Hitler in early March, that he, his wife Magda and their six children would stay in Berlin come what may was consistent with his view that fighting on with honour was all that was left.[113]

He was scornful when he heard, early in March, that Ribbentrop – whom he utterly despised (a sentiment that unified the otherwise scarcely harmonious Nazi leadership) – was making overtures to the western powers. He was then irritated when these led to exaggerated stories in the western press, but full of derision when the 'abortive escapade' predictably came to nothing. At least it was plain, he remarked, 'that hopes of an internal revolution in Germany against National Socialism or the person of the Führer are illusory'.[114]

Even now, however, Ribbentrop had not wholly given up. In mid-March, immediately following this failed attempt, he summoned Dr Werner Dankwort, deputy ambassador in Stockholm, to fly back to Berlin. He told an incredulous Dankwort that it was now a matter of gaining time to unleash the new weapons, long in preparation but now almost ready, which would restore the initiative to Germany, turn around the fortunes of war and fend off the threat to the country's existence. 'Germany has won the war if it does not lose it,' he said, with his own brand of reasoning. The western Allies had rejected every attempt he had made to help prevent the westwards advance of Bolshevism. Other ways had to be tried. Dankwort was left to ponder these thoughts over the following days, when he was summoned twice more to Ribbentrop's presence. On his third visit, Ribbentrop, in some excitement, informed him that the redoubtable Soviet emissary in Stockholm, Mme Alexandra Michailowna Kollontay, was leaving for Moscow and not expected to return. He wanted Dankwort to find a suitable intermediary to propose a message for her to take to Moscow: that the western Allies would, once the war was over, use their military superiority to remove from the Soviet Union territory it had conquered during the war, and that Germany alone would be in a position to guarantee a large portion of the lands would stay in Soviet hands.

It was an unlikely proposition. In any case, as Ribbentrop told Dankwort, he had first to obtain the Führer's approval. The Foreign Minister promptly rang Hitler's bunker, to be told that the Führer was in a briefing which would last until midnight. An air-raid alarm disturbed the wait, allowing Dankwort to experience the dismal mood – 'below zero' – as the Foreign Minister's staff descended into the cellars. Ribbentrop himself disappeared into his private air-raid shelter. It was after midnight when the all-clear sounded and, back in Ribbentrop's office, the call from Hitler finally came through. It was a short conversation. Dankwort heard Ribbentrop say in a resigned tone: 'Thank you. Good night.' The Foreign Minister turned to Dankwort. 'The Führer let me know that he regards every attempt as pointless. We must fight to the last moment.' Dankwort could scarcely believe the pointlessness of his arduous journey to the Reich capital. He took the first plane he could back to Stockholm, heartily relieved to escape from the Berlin madhouse.[115]

Himmler had by now for some time been secretly looking to a possible future after Hitler, while continuing to show himself to be the most loyal of the Führer's paladins. SS-Brigadeführer Walter Schellenberg, head of the Foreign Intelligence Service in the Reich Security Head Office, had persuaded Himmler in mid-February to meet Count Folke Bernadotte, a member of the Swedish royal family and vice-president of the Swedish Red Cross. Bernadotte was in Berlin to explore possibilities of negotiating the release of prisoners, especially those from Scandinavia, from concentration camps. From Himmler's point of view, it was a chance to show himself in a good light – conciliatory, an honest broker – and to look to a possible opening to the west. The Swedish connection was taken further in March through the intermediacy of Himmler's masseur, Felix Kersten, who had moved to Sweden, though he retained property in Germany. The fact that the end of the war was evidently approaching, that Hitler as adamantly as ever excluded all possible exit routes other than going down in flames, and that Himmler had no intention of joining him in the self-immolation made the Reichsführer open to the potential that Bernadotte and his foreign connections might offer. When Goebbels visited him in hospital in Hohenlychen at the beginning of March, where the Reichsführer was suffering from an angina attack, Himmler accepted that the morale of the troops had slumped and that the war could not be militarily won, but he thought from instinct that 'a political possibility' would open up sooner or later.[116]

By the middle of March, he was all the more ready to contemplate alternatives after enduring an almighty dressing-down from Hitler over his failings as Commander-in-Chief of Army Group Vistula. (Hitler had apparently already in February rebuked Himmler as a 'defeatist'. In his command of the defence of Pomerania, Himmler had actually been too weak to countermand tactical interference from Hitler which he knew to be catastrophic, as well as demonstrating that he had no knowledge of how to handle an army.[117]) Hitler, in his characteristic search for scapegoats, held Himmler personally responsible for the inability to hold the Red Army in Pomerania, reproaching him with 'secret sabotage' and direct disobedience. The Reichsführer was relieved of his command on 20 March. The retreat, against orders, of Sepp Dietrich's 6th SS-Panzer Army in Hungary, resulting in Hitler's furious demand that Himmler remove the insignia of the 'Leibstandarte Adolf Hitler', was a further humiliation for the Reichsführer. Guderian claimed to have tried on 21 March, just prior to his own dismissal, to persuade Himmler to use his foreign connections to try to secure an armistice.[118] Himmler refused point-blank. He could still not risk an open breach with Hitler.

Himmler had the reputation of being the most feared man in Germany. But he himself knew that was not true. He was fully aware that he remained completely dependent on a higher power. He feared Hitler even at this stage – and with justification. But a serious estrangement had now clouded their relations. Himmler was practically in disgrace. His resentment must have encouraged him to take further his soundings with Bernadotte. Against Hitler's wishes, he agreed to allow concentration camps to be handed over to the enemy (a promise he did not keep), and permitted small numbers of Jews and thousands of Scandinavian prisoners to be released. There was still no direct suggestion from Himmler that he might be involved in negotiations with the west. But by the beginning of April, Schellenberg – doubtless at Himmler's prompting – was sounding out Bernadotte about the possibility of arranging a capitulation on the western front. Bernadotte refused, saying that the initiative had to come from Himmler. At this juncture it was still not forthcoming. But Bernadotte recalled Schellenberg telling him that Himmler had talked of a capitulation in the west and 'but for Hitler' would not have hesitated to ask him to approach the Allied Supreme Commander, General Eisenhower. It would not be long before Himmler made his move.[119]

In the meantime, one of Himmler's former closest associates, SS-Obergruppenführer Karl Wolff, head of his personal staff until being transferred in September 1943 to Italy as Supreme SS and Police Leader there, then from July 1944 as Plenipotentiary General of the German Wehrmacht (effectively German military governor in the occupied parts of the country), had already edged towards capitulation south of the Alps. Through intermediaries, Wolff had in February secured a link to the American secret service, the OSS, and arranged a clandestine meeting in Zurich on 8 March with its head of European operations, Allen W. Dulles. Another meeting followed on 19 March, when Wolff undertook to arrange for the unconditional surrender of German forces in Italy. Various interests pushed in the same direction. Wolff plainly had an eye on saving his skin through gaining immunity from prosecution for war crimes. The Wehrmacht leadership in Italy, certainly once Kesselring (who would not commit himself to Wolff's move) had been replaced on 10 March by the more sympathetic if still highly cautious Vietinghoff, was favourably disposed to steps towards ending a conflict that could now be continued only at huge and senseless cost.

The Allies saw obvious gain in liquidating the front south of the Alps, where the two armies of Army Group C, around 200,000 men,[120] were still fighting a tenacious rearguard battle, and eliminating the danger of continued resistance centred on the feared Alpine redoubt. Even Hitler, who seems to have had a vague indication of Wolff's intentions (though not his detailed plans, which amounted to treason), was prepared to let him proceed – at least for the time being. He had been non-committal – taken by Wolff to be a tacit sign of approval – when the latter had, in early February in Ribbentrop's presence, carefully hinted at negotiations through his own contacts to win time for Germany to develop its secret weapons and to drive a wedge through the Allied coalition. The use of Italy as a possible bargaining pawn in any dealings with the western powers meant that there was no attempt made from Berlin to halt Wolff's manoeuvring.

Nor was Wolff, in fact, the only leading Nazi trying to secure a deal with the Allies in Italy. None other than the feared head of the Security Police, Ernst Kaltenbrunner, was at the same time taking his own secret soundings about a separate settlement with the western Allies. Nothing conclusive had materialized from either Wolff's or Kaltenbrunner's feelers by the end of March. Still, it was the case by now that the head of the SS, the head of the Security Police, and the SS leader in Italy were all, independent of each other, pursuing ways to avoid the Armageddon that Hitler was inviting. Mutual distrust and fear of Hitler ruled out any collaboration in either bypassing or confronting him. Nevertheless, the leadership of the Third Reich was starting to crumble.[121]

The most enigmatic member of Hitler's court was also beginning to distance himself from Hitler. Over the previous months, Albert Speer had consistently tried to prevent the complete destruction of German industrial plant as the Wehrmacht retreated. This had an obvious rationale for the war economy: it meant production could continue as long as possible, and possibly be restored if lost territory were to be recaptured. But by the spring of 1945 other motives were taking over. Speer's close connections with industrialists inevitably led him to look to a world beyond Hitler, where it would be necessary to rebuild their factories. He recognized that even after a lost war the country would require an economic infrastructure; the German people would survive their Dictator and need a functioning economy to support them. Not least (and increasingly), considerations of his own future after likely defeat – perhaps hoping to inherit what was left of power in the Reich – made him insist on temporary immobilization of industry, not its wanton destruction.[122]

Hitler's thinking ran, as it always had done, along diametrically opposed lines. In his characteristic fashion of posing only stark alternatives he had early in his 'career' declared that Germany would be victorious or it would cease to exist. The more any semblance of victory had evaporated, the more his thoughts had turned to the opposite pole: defeat would be total, the German people would have deserved to go under through proving too weak, and there was, therefore, no need to make provision for their future. Destruction wherever and whatever the cost, to bar the enemy advance and its inroads into Germany, was what he wanted. Speer had often had to struggle to water down the orders for destruction of industrial plant, which the High Command of the Wehrmacht had been ready to pass on, to turn them merely into immobilization. Usually, as we have seen in earlier chapters, he had succeeded, pandering to Hitler's lingering hopes, in persuading the Dictator to accede to his wishes by arguing that the Reich would need the industries again when it reconquered the lost territory. It was an argument, however contrived, to which Hitler was susceptible. But with the enemy now on Reich territory and the fiction of reconquest harder to uphold, the issue of destruction or immobilization was bound to arise again – and in radical fashion.

At the beginning of March, the deliberate destruction of the transport infrastructure by the military was causing great concern to Ruhr industrialists.[123] Speer, who had meanwhile secured control over transport to add to his other extensive powers,[124] travelled west to reassure them that temporary paralysis, not permanent destruction, of industry and transport infrastructure remained the policy. Any opposition to the orders to this effect had to be 'broken'. He repeated his key argument. 'We can only continue the war if the Silesian industrial belt, for example, or also parts of the Ruhr district are again in our hands. . . . Either these areas are brought back . . . or we have definitively lost the war.' A unified approach was essential. It was pointless to paralyse industry only to find that the military were destroying all means of transport. He would speak to the commanders-in-chief of the Army Groups and try to obtain a directive from Hitler. He went on to underline the duty to ensure the repair of water supplies and provide food for the civilian population. After food, coal was the most urgent area of production. Alongside troop transports, food supplies would have priority, even over armaments, a point he said he had cleared with Hitler. These measures were not put forward on humanitarian grounds, but to retain the 'strength of resistance of the population'. The war, Speer's remarks made plain, was far from over. He spoke further of concentrating steel production on munitions. And he repeated the priorities for transport which Hitler had decided – on his suggestion – for areas being evacuated: troop transports first, then foodstuffs, and finally, where possible, refugees.[125]

Hitler was still insisting on the evacuation of the population from the threatened western areas back into the Reich so that men capable of fighting should not be lost to the enemy. The Gauleiter of such areas knew how impracticable this demand was. Goebbels saw it as another 'heavy loss of prestige' for Hitler's authority.[126] Even Goebbels accepted that evacuation was not possible, influenced by a report Speer had given him in the middle of the month. Speer, he commented, had expressed irritation at the evacuation orders. He had taken the view 'that it is not the task of our war policy to lead a people to a heroic downfall'. The Armaments Minister told Goebbels that the war was in economic terms lost. The economy could hold out for only another four weeks – implying until about mid-April – and would then gradually collapse.

Speer, noted Goebbels, 'strongly opposes the position of destroyed earth. He explains that if the artery of life through food and in the economy should be cut off to the German people, that must be the enemy's job, not ours.' If Berlin's bridges and viaducts were to be detonated as planned, the Reich capital would face imminent starvation.[127]

A conflict was plainly brewing. Speer had learnt that Hitler intended the destruction of factories, railways, bridges, electricity and water installations rather than allow them to fall into enemy hands. He approached Guderian, seeking his help to prevent the madness of measures which would destroy the crucial economic infrastructure and ensure lasting misery and poverty for the civilian population. He and Guderian agreed that the detonation of bridges, tunnels and railway installations required special permission. A furious Hitler refused to implement the draft decree.[128] On 15 March, Speer gave an unvarnished picture of realities. The collapse of the economy was no more than four to eight weeks away, after which the war could not be continued militarily. A firm order was needed to prevent the destruction of vital installations in Germany. 'Their destruction means the elimination of every further possibility of existence for the German people.' Speer concluded: 'We have the duty to leave the people all possibilities that could secure them reconstruction in the more distant future.'[129]

Speer passed the memorandum to Nicolaus von Below, Hitler's Luftwaffe adjutant, and asked him to deliver it at a suitable moment. Below eventually did so on 18 March, though the Dictator already knew what was coming. In an attempt to lessen the anticipated hefty reaction and demonstrate his continued loyalty, Speer asked for a signed photograph of Hitler for his fortieth birthday next day.

He also gave Hitler another memorandum – one which he never mentioned after the war.[130] It was a shorter document, and couched in a wholly different tone. It began by stating that, since economic collapse was unavoidable, drastic measures were needed to defend the Reich at the Oder and the Rhine. Defence beyond these borders was no longer possible. So for the coming eight weeks, it was crucial to take every ruthless measure needed to mobilize all possible resources, including the *Volkssturm*, for the defences along these two rivers. Forces currently in Norway and Italy should be transferred to serve in this defence. Only such measures had a chance of securing the front. He concluded: 'Holding out tenaciously on the current front for a few weeks can gain respect from the enemy and perhaps thus favourably determine the end of the war.'[131]

Speer's motive in producing this second memorandum is unclear. Possibly he hoped it would soften the blow of the first, though he never subsequently claimed this. His silence about the second memorandum is telling, since its wording ill fitted his cultivated post-war image of being the one Nazi leader to have tried to act humanely and broken with Hitler before the end. Perhaps more likely, it was written to try to head off any charges – dangerous in the climate – by Hitler or those in his entourage that he was a defeatist and practically a traitor to the cause.[132] Maybe, since the 'current front' on the Rhine was on the verge of being lost, it was an obliquely clever way of encouraging Hitler to draw the conclusion that now was the time to end the war.[133] If so, it is odd that Speer never made this point in any of his post-war statements. The final possibility is that Speer actually believed what he was saying – that a last-ditch effort could still wring some sort of deal from, presumably, the western Allies. He later sought to portray himself as one whose early recognition of Germany's inevitable defeat made him selflessly work for the preservation of the economic basis needed for the people's survival. But the memorandum of 18 March shows how late he was in accepting that the war was irredeemably lost.[134] His efforts to restrict the destruction of the economic infrastructure and acceptance that, economically, Germany was close to the end were still compatible with an assumption that the war could not be won but was not yet totally lost. Up to this point, Speer told Hitler only a few days later, he had still believed in a good end to the war.[135] It was not rhetoric. As the memorandum shows, until then Speer had remained a 'believer' of sorts. The continued destruction that fighting on would inevitably entail might have been reconciled by Speer with his attempts otherwise to restrict demolition of the economic infrastructure on the grounds that this was 'collateral' damage rather than wilful self-destruction. At the very least, with this memorandum Speer was showing Hitler that he still stood by him.[136] The conflict with Hitler over destruction of the means of production was a serious one. But it did not amount to a fundamental rejection of the leader to whom he had been so closely bound for more than a decade.

Hitler wasted no time in providing his answer to Speer. Already on 18 March he overrode all objections in ordering the compulsory evacuation of the entire civilian population of threatened western areas.

If transport was not available, people should leave on foot. 'We can no longer take regard of the population,' he commented.[137] Next day came Hitler's notorious 'scorched earth' decree, his 'Nero Order', completely upturning Speer's recommendations to spare destruction wherever possible. 'All military transport, communications, industrial and supplies installations as well as material assets within Reich territory, which the enemy can render usable immediately or within the foreseeable future, are to be destroyed.' Responsibility for the implementation of the destruction was placed in the hands of the military command as regards transport and communications and the Gauleiter as Defence Commissars in the case of industry and other economic installations.[138]

Down to 18 March, Speer, for all his criticism of measures guaranteed to destroy any basis of post-war reconstruction, had, as his memorandum of that day shows, still believed that there was something to be gained from continuing the war. But on that day, then confirmed by the 'scorched earth' decree, his attitude dramatically changed. The breaking-point came when Hitler told him point-blank: 'If the war is lost, then the people too is lost. This fate is irreversible.' It was not necessary, therefore, to provide even for their most primitive future existence. On the contrary, it was better to destroy even this basis, because 'the people had shown itself to be the weaker, and the future belongs exclusively to the stronger people of the east. What will remain after this struggle will be in any case only the inferior ones, since the good ones have fallen.' At these words, Speer told Hitler in a handwritten letter he delivered to the Dictator some days later, he was 'deeply shocked'. He saw the first steps to fulfilling these intentions in the destruction order of the following day.[139]

During the days that followed, backed by Walther Rohland and his colleagues in the Ruhr Staff of his Ministry, Speer travelled through western Germany trying (partly by using Nazi arguments that the installations were necessary to sustain production for winning the war) to overcome the initial readiness of the Gauleiter to implement Hitler's order. How easy it would have been in practice for them to carry out the destruction might actually be doubted. It seems likely that industrialists and factory bosses would have cooperated with local Party functionaries to block many attempts at senseless destruction.[140] Speer also persuaded them that Hitler's evacuation orders were impracticable.[141] Model, too, after some hesitation came round to accepting Speer's arguments and agreed to keep destruction of industrial plant in the Ruhr to a minimum, though the military, as implementation orders show, would have been prepared to carry out the destruction.[142] In Würzburg, Gauleiter Otto Hellmuth, generally seen as one of the more moderate Party bosses, was all set to go ahead with implementing the 'Nero Order'. It would, indeed, be pointless though, he admitted, if there were no chance of a change in the situation at the last minute. He asked Speer when the decisive 'miracle weapons' were going to be deployed. Only when Speer told him bluntly: 'They're not coming', did he agree not to destroy the Schweinfurt ballbearing factories.[143]

Hitler had, however, meanwhile learnt of Speer's efforts to sabotage his order. When the Armaments Minister, on his return to Berlin, was summoned to meet him, he met a frosty reception. Hitler demanded that he accept that the war could still be won. When Speer demurred, Hitler allowed him twenty-four hours to consider his answer. On his return – after composing a lengthy, handwritten justification of his position, which, in the event, he did not hand over – Speer said merely: 'My Führer, I am unconditionally behind you.'[144] That sufficed. Hitler felt his authority intact; there had been no loss of face; Speer had backed down.[145] A brief glimpse of the old warmth between the two returned. Speer exploited the situation to obtain from Hitler the crucial concession and vital qualification of his earlier order, that the implementation of any destruction lay in the hands of his Armaments Minister.[146] With that, Speer was able to prevent the 'scorched earth' that Hitler had ordered (though the Wehrmacht nevertheless blew up numerous bridges within Germany as it retreated).[147] It was an important victory, even if it might cynically be interpreted as aimed as much at securing Speer's own future existence as that of the German people.[148] And on top of Hitler's inability to insist that his evacuation orders were carried out, it was a further sign, as Goebbels recognized, that Hitler's authority was waning.[149]

This was, nevertheless, not the point of collapse. The foundations were shaking. But they still – just about – held together. Decisive in that, as ever, was the leadership position of Hitler himself. Though the leaders of the Third Reich plainly saw Hitler's days as numbered, they still knew that they openly crossed him at their peril. Ribbentrop dared not take his peace feelers further without Hitler's imprimatur. Himmler and Kaltenbrunner were extremely careful to hide their own soundings.

Wolff, too, knew what dangerous ground he was treading, though at least he had some geographical distance between him and Berlin. And Speer had ultimately retreated from complete confrontation. He had avoided the possibility of the severe sanctions that might then have arisen, even if he now saw Hitler's favour in armaments matters turn from him to his long-standing rival, Karl Otto Saur. In no case had any of the paladins looking to their own positions in a post-Hitler future openly challenged the Dictator. Apart from fear of the consequences, since Hitler could still call upon powerful military and police forces to back him, each of them still acknowledged that his own powers still rested on the higher authority of the Führer. Divided among themselves, fearful of the consequences, and still beholden to Hitler, they posed no threat of a fronde.[150] Hitler's power was set to go on to the end.

8

Implosion

*We're issuing orders in Berlin that practically don't even arrive,
let alone can be carried out. I see in this the danger of an extraordinary diminution of authority.*

Joseph Goebbels, diary entry, 28 March 1945

I

Berlin in April 1945 was a city bracing itself for the storm about to
blow. All possible preparations were being hastily made to try to counter the coming onslaught from the east. Everyone knew that it could not
be long before the city was engulfed in the fighting. The mood had
reached rock bottom. Only the occasional expression of gallows humour
punctuated the fatalistic acceptance that there was no way out.[1] But as
the seemingly interminable dark days of those truly terrible winter
months of 1944–5 gradually gave way to a sunny and warm spring,
some Berliners tried their best to shut out the war for a few fleeting
moments.

For anyone passing through the Tiergarten, the beautiful park in the
centre of the city (if now horribly damaged, occupied by heavy artillery
and serving as a source of much needed firewood), beneath trees coming
into bloom and accompanied by the chirping of the birds, or looking
out from the balconies of spacious villas in the Grunewald, on the western outskirts of Berlin, the war could seem far away (though the ruins
of some villas could provide a swift reminder). But fleetingly pleasant
activities, unremarkable strands of peacetime everyday life, were in
early April 1945 no more than an attempt to 'seize the day', to grasp

what might be one of the last chances of enjoyment before grim reality overtook them.

Others sought to 'seize the night' as women and soldiers in districts of central Berlin frantically engaged in 'a hectic search for pleasure' in shelters, basements of buildings reduced to rubble and dark pathways through the ruins. Looting and thieving were commonplace. Despite the harsh penalties, a black market flourished in food and almost any material goods to be found. Resort to any form of alcohol – including stolen medical supplies – served for many to blot out fears of what was in store.[2]

Whatever illusions people still briefly entertained swiftly passed. And in any case only a few were in a position to share them. Most were too worn down by cares and worries, trying to cope with the severe privations of daily existence. For the city, like every other big city in the country, was in physical appearance and the psychological disposition of its inhabitants deeply scarred by the war. The main feature of Berlin's outward appearance was, in fact, not just the devastated city centre, the desolate façades, the bomb craters, the ruined buildings that were no more than empty shells, but its emptiness – the lack of traffic and people on the streets, the shops bereft of goods, the houses without furniture.[3] At night, 'a ghost town of cave-dwellers was all that was left of this world metropolis', noted one observer.[4] Practically every evening, as people ate their meals by flickering candlelight – since electricity usage was heavily rationed – sirens would announce the latest air raid and lead to the nightly descent into the nearest shelter. It was a sharp tug out of any reveries – a reminder that the end was fast approaching, and that the Red Army was only a short distance away, poised to launch its attack on the Reich capital.

Hitler's own dreamworld during nocturnal visits to the cellars of the New Reich Chancellery as he sat by the model, constructed by his architect Hermann Giesler, of his home town of Linz as it would appear at the end of a victorious war provided him, too, with a momentary distraction from the clammy pressure of the war. Beyond that, his fantasies fitted the mask that he wore even now, refusing to concede to himself or anyone else that his world had collapsed into ruins. He had, at the latest since the failure of the Ardennes offensive, known that defeat was certain. But he could not openly admit it. This was part of the continuing act of the indomitable Führer which he had unceasingly upheld throughout the mounting adversity – the constant pretence, to himself as well as his entourage, that all would eventually turn out well. His dreams and illusions were a defiance of the reality gripping him most of the time – of a lost war, and of an imminent end that had to follow his own death. Since he could never contemplate surrender, as long as he lived the immense suffering and destruction of the war would continue. And since he would not allow himself to be captured, suicide was the only way out. His monstrous ego had led him long since to conclude that the German people had proved themselves unworthy of him. Their defeat had shown them to be weak. They did not deserve to survive. He could weep no tears for them. But he had yet to decide when and where to end his own life.

For those in his entourage, who saw him on a daily basis, his authority remained utterly unquestioned. Beyond the bunker, deep below the garden of the Reich Chancellery in the centre of Berlin, that he had made his last home since returning from the western front in mid-January, it was a different matter. The Reich itself had drastically shrunk. Goebbels pointed out on 9 April that German possessions were by now reduced to little more than a narrow band running southwards from Norway to the Adriatic coast of northern Italy.[5] Much of what had been the Reich was by now under enemy occupation and beyond Hitler's reach. And for most ordinary people in areas still under German rule, Hitler had long been a shadowy presence, someone encountered only through the occasional proclamation or newsreel pictures – though they were aware that as long as he lived there would be no end to their misery. For the Gauleiter, the regional rulers of the Reich, his writ was ceasing to run. It was not that they thought of openly challenging his authority. They had been his loyal viceroys for years, the pivot of his power in the provinces. And even now the consequences of any rebellious acts were to be feared. But huge communications problems and the advances of the western Allies meant that control from Berlin was scarely possible any longer. They had to tackle the situation confronting them directly, not await often unrealistic and impracticable orders from Berlin. In any case, it was obvious that Germany could hold out at best for only a week or two longer. Most of Hitler's henchmen thought of little beyond saving their skins. Few of them contemplated leaping into the funeral pyre with their Leader.

As Nazi rule disintegrated ever more rapidly and fragmentation took the place of any semblance of centralized governance, the regime increasingly 'ran amok'.[6] Police, SS, and regional and local Party officials took matters into their own hands in the ferocious repression of anything hinting at rebellion or attempts to prevent senseless last-minute destruction. 'Internal enemies' were at extreme risk as Nazi desperadoes turned on them in the last agony of the regime, determined to exact revenge for their hostility, and to ensure that they would not be able to exult in triumph at the downfall of Nazism. And the fate that had befallen the prisoners of the concentration camps in the east was inflicted upon those in the remainder of the Reich, forced out of the horrendous hellholes and, in one final spurt of intense terror, dragooned onto seemingly aimless death marches. Now, as before, as the regime visibly fell apart its leaders in the Party and in the military lacked both the unity of spirit and will and the organizational capacity – which the Italian Fascist leaders had exercised in toppling Mussolini in July 1943 – to confront Hitler and try, even at the final hour, to halt Germany's descent into the abyss. The last act in the drama remained, therefore, to be played out.

II

With the loss of the Rhine front in March, any lingering logic to continuing the war in the west had evaporated. Nevertheless, the generals fought on. Keitel and Jodl in the High Command of the Wehrmacht and the Commander-in-Chief West, Field-Marshal Kesselring, had believed, so they later claimed, to the end of March that they could prevent the total collapse of the front on the Rhine and stabilize for a while the position in the west.[7] The only faint rationality was presumably the old one of buying time for the western Allies to recognize that their true enemy lay in the east, bringing the collapse of the 'unholy' coalition with the Soviet Union and allowing the remnants of the Wehrmacht to find new purpose by joining with the western powers against the Red Army. If that did represent the thinking at the time, it was by now even more obviously the mere pipe dream it had always been. With victory so close, the last thing on the minds of Roosevelt and Churchill was breaking with the Soviet allies who continued to bear the brunt of the human losses in the fight to crush Hitler's regime.

The total collapse in the west was unstoppable. The swift American advance, once US troops had consolidated positions over the Rhine, had driven wedges between Model's Army Group B in the Ruhr and the Army Groups H to its north and G to the south. By 2 April, Model's forces, still numerically strong but with weak heavy weaponry, were cut off in the Ruhr and could be supplied only from the air. Two days later, the American 9th Army began its attack to destroy the surrounded German forces. They had to surmount initial fierce resistance, but the outcome was never in doubt. Mayors of some major cities, encouraged by leading industrialists and backed by Social Democrats, Communists and other anti-Nazi groups, emerging from years of suppression, surrendered without a fight. Duisburg, Essen, Solingen, Bochum and Mülheim fell without inflicting further unnecessary suffering on populations deprived of the most basic amenities and forced to dwell in cellars, bunkers and bombed-out buildings. In contrast, fighting continued for four days before Hamm was taken and Dortmund eventually fell only after being encircled then stormed by powerful American forces on 13 April.[8] By this time, Model had reported that about two-thirds of his army lacked weapons. Troops were now deserting in droves, simply disappearing into the woods or the ruined cities, and a number of commanders surrendered their units.

American forces had in the meantime advanced deep into central Germany. By the middle of April they had pushed into Thuringia, taking Erfurt, Weimar and Jena, from where they pressed south towards Coburg and Bayreuth, as well as advancing into Saxony to the outskirts of Halle, Chemnitz and Leipzig and to the north-west, capturing Hanover and Braunschweig. By 11 April they had reached the Elbe. There was no longer a German front to speak of. Continued fighting was, nevertheless, sporadically fierce and the Americans still encountered pockets of tenacious resistance. As in the Ruhr, the civic officials of numerous towns and cities preferred surrender to senseless destruction. Gotha, Göttingen and Weimar were among those that capitulated without a fight. In Magdeburg, by contrast, the refusal of the city's military commandant to surrender on 17 April prompted a devastating attack by 350 planes the same afternoon before the last resistance faded the following day.

To the north, the British and Canadians made slower progress against the still relatively strong forces of Blaskowitz's Army Group H. But by

N

NORWAY

*Oslo

Channel Islands
Alderney
Guernsey
Sark
Jersey
FRANCE

Courland
Baltic Sea
U.S.S.R.

SWEDEN

North Sea

Baltic Sea

DENMARK

*Copenhagen

Hela Peninsula

Flensburg*

Rügen

Greifswald*

Danzig*

Hamburg*
Aumühle*

Stettin*

Vistula

*Bremen

NETHERLANDS
*Amsterdam
*The Hague

Weser

Elbe

Oder

*Berlin

Hannover*
Magdeburg*

Warthe

Rhine

GERMANY

BELGIUM
*Brussels
Maas
*Cologne

Kassel*

Leipzig*
Erfurt*

*Dresden

Breslau*

Landeshut*

Oder

Frankfurt*
Main

Neuern*
Elbe

Prague*

LUXEMBURG
*Luxemburg
Mosel

*Saarbrücken

Nürnberg*

Murrhardt*
*Stuttgart   *Danube*

Strassburg*

FRANCE

Rhine

Munich*

Linz*

Vienna*   *Pressburg

Danube

Salzburg*

AUSTRIA

SWITZERLAND
*Berne

Innsbruck*   *Inn*
*Mayrhofen

Drave

☐ Territory held by Germany

0   50   100 miles
0 50 100 km

8. Dönitz's Reich, 1 May 1945

10 April the British had reached Celle, north-east of Hanover, and, further north, reached the Weser, south of Bremen, while the Canadians had forced their way northwards through the Netherlands almost to the coast. The major North Sea ports and links to Denmark and Norway remained, however, in German hands and the Wehrmacht in the north-west constituted one of the last relatively intact bases of power for the Nazi regime.

In southern Germany, the situation was more ominous. Hitler dismissed Colonel-General of the Waffen-SS Paul Hausser, Commander-in-Chief of Army Group G, on 2 April, after he had wanted to retreat to the south and south-east. His replacement, General Friedrich Schulz, tried to implement Hitler's orders to hold out for two to three weeks to gain vital time, so it was claimed, to introduce jet-planes which would transform the military situation, and pressed all available forces into a display of fanatical resistance in the area of Aschaffenburg, on the Main. Until the middle of the month, he succeeded in blocking the American advance until he was outflanked by the 3rd US Army heading south from Thuringia, at which the retreat of Army Group G turned into flight. American and French troops had meanwhile advanced towards Stuttgart. Heilbronn, an important railway junction on the eastern bank of the river Neckar, was taken only after intense fighting. The town was defended by a relatively heavy concentration of Wehrmacht troops supported by *Volkssturm* contingents. Its citizens, terrorized by a fanatical Nazi leadership, had been unable, as in many other places, to instigate moves to capitulate without a struggle. The result was that Heilbronn suffered a week's bitter but futile fighting before the inevitable surrender. That was the exception. Most places were able to engineer a surrender and avoid being blown to smithereens in a senseless attempt to hold out.

The French had easily taken Karlsruhe and other towns in Baden without a struggle, though for reasons still unclear they almost completely destroyed Freudenstadt in the Black Forest. By the middle of the month they were set to attack Freiburg, which fell to them with little fighting on 21 April. Stuttgart, the capital city of Württemberg, was surrendered the next day without a struggle, despite the insistence of the Gauleiter on a fight to the last, after the Nazi leaders had fled. Prominent anti-Nazis had managed to persuade the mayor, a long-standing Nazi himself, to spare the city pointless destruction. The French swiftly took control of Stuttgart and the surrounding areas. For local inhabitants, fear of the Nazis – who in most cases skedaddled – turned into anxiety about the French conquerors. Unlike the Americans, whose occupying forces were largely disciplined, the French troops, especially it seems a minority of the feared colonial troops from North Africa, looted extensively and perpetrated numerous rapes on entering German villages and townships, as reports by the local clergy and others made plain. In Freudenstadt, the worst instance, the raping, looting and pillaging went on for three days.[9]

In the meantime, driving south through Franconia, American troops encountered resistance, sometimes heavy, but took town after town – most surrendered without a fight – before on 16 April reaching Nuremberg, the very shrine of Nazism. Hitler ordered the 'city of the Reich Party Rallies' to be defended to the last. The fanatical Party leadership, with nothing to lose and *Götterdämmerung* mentality intact, refused to capitulate. It simply delayed the inevitable. After four days of fierce fighting and further unnecessary bloodshed and destruction the former Party stronghold and symbol of Nazi power eventually fell. It was 20 April, Hitler's birthday.[10]

On 15 April the western Allies had laid down their immediate future objectives: in the north, press on to Lübeck, consolidate positions on the Elbe in central Germany, and in the south, advance to the Danube and into Austria. That same day Hitler stipulated that, should the Reich be split into two by enemy advance through central Germany, Grand-Admiral Dönitz in the north and Field-Marshal Kesselring in the south should take command of the defence as his delegates in whichever part of the country he himself was not situated.[11]

The Wehrmacht in the west was by now in a truly desolate situation. And in the east, the awaited big Soviet offensive, directed at Berlin, was set to begin before dawn of the very next day, 16 April.

In East Prussia the Soviets had finally broken the siege of the once beautiful, now devastated city of Königsberg. On 9 April, with his forces on the verge of complete destruction and the city an inferno, its commandant, General Otto Lasch, finally surrendered – though only when Red Army soldiers stood outside his bunker. The defence of Königsberg had cost the lives of 42,000 German soldiers and 25,000 civilians. Some 27,000 soldiers left in the garrison at the end entered Soviet captivity.[12] In a towering rage, Hitler had Lasch sentenced in his absence to death by hanging – a sentence impossible to have been carried out – and his family imprisoned.[13] He also dismissed General Friedrich-Wilhelm Müller, last commander of the 4th Army, which, apart from remnants still holding out in the Samland, was by now effectively defunct. By the time the harbour at Pillau eventually fell, on 25 April, only 3,100 of an army once comprising half a million soldiers were left, barricaded on the Frische Nehrung until the end of the war.[14]

To the south-east, there had been a further great disaster: after a siege lasting nearly two weeks the Austrian capital, Vienna, fell, a ruined shell, to the Red Army on 13 April, after days of intense street-fighting that continued into the heart of the city with heavy losses on both sides. The Soviets could now push further westwards into Austria on both sides of the Danube. Few German soldiers forced to retreat further into a shrinking Reich could have placed much faith in Hitler's empty words two days later: 'Berlin stays German, Vienna will be German again, and Europe will never be Russian.'[15]

By then Zhukov's troops, massed on the Oder only some 70 kilometres from Berlin, awaited the signal to launch the attack which, they were confident, would destroy Hitler's regime and bring them victory. A mighty army had been assembled for the battle of Berlin. Zhukov's 1st Belorussian Front and, further north, preparing to attack westwards from Pomerania, the 2nd Belorussian Front under Rokossovsky together comprised 1.4 million men, with more than 4,000 tanks and 23,000 pieces of heavy artillery. To the south, Konev's 1st Ukrainian Front, ready to be launched from bases on the Neiße, had a further 1.1 million men and 2,150 tanks. Each of the fronts was backed by massive air support, amounting in all to 7,500 planes. Facing them were Heinrici's Army Group Vistula (an outdated name, since they were now preparing to fight west of the Oder), consisting of the 3rd Panzer Army under Manteuffel to the north and the 9th Army under General Theodor Busse, directly guarding the approaches to Berlin, together with, defending the attack from the Neiße and protecting the southern outreaches of the city, part of Schörner's Army Group Centre (the 4th Panzer Army under General Fritz-Hubert Gräser). The German forces amounted in total to a million men, 1,500 tanks and armoured vehicles, and 10,400 artillery pieces, backed by 3,300 fighter planes. The imbalance in forces was compounded by the fact that many of the Germans were young, ill-trained recruits, while the air-strength was purely nominal since so many planes were grounded through lack of fuel. Only the three concentric rings of deep-echeloned fortifications barring the path to the capital gave an advantage to the defenders.

Zhukov's offensive began at 3.30 a.m. on 16 April with an immense artillery barrage amid a battery of searchlights aimed at blinding the enemy and illuminating the path of attack. But German defences held for two days before, after ferocious fighting and huge losses on both sides, the heavily fortified Seelow Heights, a steep outcrop of hills ranging 90 metres above the Oder valley between Seelow and Wriezen and the last formidable natural defensive barrier outside Berlin, fell to Zhukov's troops. With this, Busse's 9th Army was split into three parts and forced into retreat in the north, centre and south of the front. Konev's offensive from the Neiße, meanwhile, had broken through more easily, driving the defenders back towards Dresden but, even more menacingly, rapidly advancing northwards towards Berlin and the rear of Busse's army. By 20 April, the 1st Belorussian Front had forced its way through the outer defensive ring around Berlin and its right flank was preparing to press the advance to the north of the city. Berlin was on the verge of being encircled. South of Berlin, Konev's tanks had reached Jüterbog, the German army's major ammunition depot, and were about to overrun Zossen, its communications centre. Zhukov's forces had taken Bernau, north of the capital, early in the morning. A few hours later, his guns opened fire directly on Berlin.[16]

III

In the last desperate weeks, in which the gains from fighting on were hard to rationalize, Hitler's front commanders remained paralysed from taking any action other than continuing the struggle, whatever the cost in lives and destruction. Since they had attempted nothing to halt the gathering self-destructive (as well as massively devastating) momentum over previous months, there was no likelihood of their doing anything when the end was so close. On the contrary, through an almost Darwinistic selection achieved by the dismissal of so many generals, only hardline loyalists, committed to continuing the fight whatever the cost, were left in key posts.

Field-Marshal Kesselring, Commander-in-Chief West (though by now with little of a western front to command), had for a time in the

1930s been Chief of Staff in the Luftwaffe, commanded an air fleet in the early years of the war, then sealed his reputation as a tough commander-in-chief in Italy, a military leader of high professional competence who took care to keep out of politics.[17] He was an arch-loyalist, always exuding real or contrived optimism, however grim the military situation, and invariably impressed by Hitler's will to hold out. It was little surprise that Speer had no success in trying to persuade him not to implement Hitler's 'Nero Order' to destroy Germany's economic infrastructure on retreat.[18] Speer was again disappointed in the field-marshal when Kesselring arrived in the Führer Bunker in early April to inform Hitler of the hopelessness of the situation. After only a few sentences, Hitler interrupted with a lengthy disquisition on how he was going to turn the tables on the Americans. Whether he was genuinely convinced, or, more likely, taking the easy way out, Kesselring was soon agreeing with Hitler's fantasies.[19]

After the war, in his self-serving memoirs, Kesselring gave a glimpse of his mindset in mid-April, with the Ruhr lost and the battle for central Germany unfolding. He saw meaning in sustaining the fight in the Harz Mountains in order to hold up the enemy's advance 'until a stronger, organised striking force came to the rescue'. He had in mind the 12th Army, scraped together at the end of March and stationed east of the Elbe and in the region stretching from Dessau to Bitterfeld and Wittenberg. 'Only with its help could there be a certain assurance that the course of events on the Russian front would not be influenced from the west and the splitting of Germany into two halves be prevented.' His views, he stated, coincided with those of the High Command of the Wehrmacht. 'At that moment I did not examine the question of the effect of these operations on the outcome of the war, which was no longer a matter for profitable thought. All I was trying to do was to prolong the battle by all available means in front of the Harz to give time for our operations on the Russian front to mature.' Even if the Russians and the western Allies were to meet on the Elbe or in Berlin there would still be a justification for continuing the war: 'the imperative necessity to gain time for the German divisions engaged in the east to fight their way back into the British and American zones'.[20]

The Commander-in-Chief of Army Group B, encircled in the Ruhr, Field-Marshal Model, had long been numbered among Hitler's most trusted generals, and was described by the Dictator towards the end of

April 1945 as having been his 'best field-marshal'.[21] Like Kesselring, Model had disingenuously insisted, while serving Hitler to the best of his ability, that he was 'unpolitical'. Like almost all of his fellow generals, in fact, he shared at the least partial identities with Nazism – including detestation of Bolshevism, and belief in both the superiority of German culture and Germany's rightful supremacy in Europe. As the war had turned irredeemably against Germany, his own fanatical will to stave off defeat and prevent the victory of the Reich's enemies was reflected in his unwaveringly confident proclamations to his soldiers and orders for ruthless punishment of 'inferior elements in the civilian population' who displayed a defeatist or hostile attitude.[22] He echoed demands of the regime to 'hold out' at all costs, and even the vocabulary of Nazi propaganda. At the end of March, his proclamation to his sub-commanders had described the duty of officers as setting an example to their men, if need be through their own deaths, and convincing them of the need to continue the struggle 'even more than before . . . down to self-sacrifice'. He demanded immediate action against those sections of the civilian population who had been 'infected by Jewish and democratic poison of materialist ideas' and put the protection of their own belongings above 'unconditional support for the fighting troops'.[23]

Model remained conscious of his loyalty and obedience to Hitler even as German hopes crumbled. This was still the case after his strategic recommendations on the Ardennes offensive had been ignored, and even after a confrontation with Kesselring about a possible breakout from the Ruhr had led to his vehement denunciation of Keitel and Jodl at Wehrmacht High Command.[24] Increasingly in conflict with this, as the end approached, was his sense of soldierly duty. Unlike Kesselring, he was amenable to Speer's entreaties not to destroy vital economic infrastructure. But he refused all attempts to persuade him to surrender his encircled army. (Feelers towards a possible capitulation had initially been made by Walther Rohland, Speer's tank expert, with Colonel-General Josef Harpe, now commanding the 5th Panzer Army in the west. Harpe, who had been dismissed from his command during the retreat in the east in January, refused to act since going against the will of Model and the five western Gauleiter would have meant certain condemnation to death.)[25] Hitler's order, following the fall of Königsberg, to have families arrested in the event of capitulation or refusal to accept orders, apparently weighed heavily with Model.

By 17 April the fighting in the Ruhr was over. When all hope had gone for his troops, Model dissolved his Army Group rather than formally capitulate to the enemy. Some 317,000 German soldiers and 30 generals entered captivity. Model had long seen suicide as the only honourable way out for a field-marshal, and had hinted for some weeks at his own death in defeat. He shot himself in the woods near Duisburg on 21 April.[26]

Field-Marshal Schörner – Hitler's favourite commander and the last one to whom he gave the field-marshal's baton, on 5 April – was, as we have had cause to note in earlier chapters, notorious for his brutality even among his peer group of tough generals, all of them strict displinarians. Anything other than driving his troops on to continue the fight against what he saw as an 'Asiatic' enemy was here inconceivable. While Schörner did not have an equivalent anywhere else in the army, he had no monopoly of ruthlessness towards his own troops. The successor to SS Colonel-General Hausser as Commander-in-Chief of Army Group G in southern Germany, General Schulz, issued orders for 'the most severe measures' to be taken to prevent the possibility of soldiers taking to flight at the appearance of enemy tanks. Every soldier leaving his position in battle without a command had to be made aware of what awaited him. Acknowledging the shortage of weaponry, he demanded that soldiers compensate with small arms and the Panzerfaust.[27]

Fighting on had become an end in itself. As Kesselring's reflection, quoted above, indicated, it was not thought worthwhile to contemplate how actions might affect the outcome of the war. Most generals were perfectly capable of rational assessment of the situation. They chose instead to overlook their own dire assessments of the lack of weaponry, shortage of men and minimal prospects against overwhelming force to stress the need to do everything 'not to disappoint the onward-driving will of the Führer'.[28]

This fitted par excellence the stance of those in Hitler's own direct military entourage. Here, independence of judgement had never existed. Though General Jodl had on earlier occasions not refrained from speaking frankly to Hitler, he remained an ultra-loyalist, still in thrall to the 'genius' of the Führer. Field-Marshal Keitel had never throughout his career shown a flicker of willingness to stand up to Hitler, and was not going to start now. And with Guderian's dismissal as Chief of the General Staff at the end of March, the last semblance of feisty determination to counter what he saw as calamitous operational decisions was gone. His replacement, General Hans Krebs, was a capable staff officer, but had scarcely been selected for his readiness to challenge higher authority. Personally far more emollient than Guderian, he was quickly assimilated into the bunker community and amounted to little more than a cipher. The division of responsibilities between the High Commands of the Wehrmacht and of the Army had long been a structural weakness in the running of the war. Now, with the war almost over, the division ceased to be significant. But the new unity, in kowtowing to Hitler at every turn, was even more disastrous than the former split had been. And, certainly, nothing to deflect Hitler from his decisions was to be expected of the commanders-in-chief of the Luftwaffe and navy, Göring and Dönitz. Göring had long been out of favour. But when he attended military briefings his lasting humiliation made him, if anything, even more determined to show his mettle and back Hitler. Dönitz, for his part, proved himself in these last weeks to be among the most fanatical of Hitler's military leaders in insisting on the fight to the last.

On 7 April, Dönitz, echoing Hitler's own sentiments, declared: 'We soldiers of the navy know how we have to act. Our military duty, which we unerringly fulfil, whatever happens around us, leaves us standing as a rock of resistance, bold, hard and loyal. Anyone not acting in this way is a scumbag and must be hanged with a notice round his neck saying "Here hangs a traitor who from the most base cowardice has helped German women and children to die instead of protecting them like a man".' On 19 April he commended the example of a prisoner of war in Australia who had 'quietly bumped off' Communists in the camp and said he would be promoted to a leadership position on his return. 'There are more such men in the navy', he added, who show their 'mastery of difficult positions' and prove their 'inner value'. Just over a week earlier, Dönitz expounded his own views on the presence of the enemy deep inside German territory. Capitulation, he stated, meant the destruction of Germany through Bolshevism. He defended National Socialism, and Hitler's policies, as necessary to prevent the Russians overrunning Germany. Grumbling, moaning and complaining was fruitless, and born of weakness, he declared. 'Cowardice and weakness make people stupid and blind.' The leadership was aware of all possibilities. The Führer alone, years ago, had clearly seen the threat of Bolshevism. 'At the latest in a year, perhaps within this year, the whole of Europe will recognise

Adolf Hitler as the only statesman of standing.' Europe's blindness would one day be removed and result in political possibilities for Germany. Dönitz urged a commitment to duty, honour, obedience, hardness and loyalty. He demanded of his commanders ruthless action against any officers failing in their soldierly duty. A crew would always go down with their ship in honour rather than surrender it. The same principle applied to the fight on land. Every naval base would be defended to the last, in accordance with the Führer's orders. It was victory or death. The navy would fight to the end. This would earn it respect in coming times. It had to represent the will to existence of the people. There was no situation that could not be improved by heroism. Every alternative led to 'chaos and inextinguishable disgrace'.[29]

Dönitz's unconditional obedience to Hitler's will and conviction in the need to continue the fight was equally plainly expressed in a meeting with a number of Gauleiter and other leading Party figures in northern Germany on 25 April. Interestingly, the question was raised at the meeting – by whom is not stated – whether it might be better to end the fighting 'in the interest of maintaining the substance of the German people'. Dönitz replied that the assessment of this question was 'exclusively a matter of the state leadership embodied by the Führer and nobody had the right to deviate from the line laid down by him. The action of the Führer was exclusively determined by concern for the German people' – though, as we know, Hitler had actually stated on more than one occasion that they did not deserve to survive. 'Since the capitulation must in any case mean the destruction of the substance of the German people, it is from this standpoint too correct to fight on,' Dönitz added. He stated his determination 'to put into action what was ordered by the Führer'.[30]

Among the very few frontline generals to show any independence of mind and try to assert himself against Hitler in the last weeks was Colonel-General Gotthard Heinrici, presented with the unenviable task of defending against massively superior forces the coming attack on Berlin from the Oder. Other than Model, there was no general better equipped to conduct a defensive struggle. But Heinrici was well aware that his forces were weak in armour and heavy artillery, and had large numbers of young, ill-trained soldiers. He was therefore appalled to learn at the beginning of April that Hitler was depriving him of several reserve divisions (including two panzer divisions) and relocating them to Army Group Centre, now forced back into defending what was left of the Protectorate of Bohemia and Moravia. Heinrici had been summoned to Berlin on 6 April to outline his defensive preparations for the forthcoming offensive.

At the meeting in the Führer Bunker, the general, accompanied only by his operations chief, Colonel Hans-Georg Eismann, had to face not just Hitler but his entire supporting military entourage, including Keitel, Jodl, Dönitz, Göring, Krebs and Himmler. He coolly summarized the situation of his Army Group. A particular weakness was the front near Frankfurt an der Oder, where defences depended heavily upon the *Volkssturm*. Heinrici asked for 'fortress' status for Frankfurt to be given up, and the eighteen battalions holding the city to be redeployed in his own defensive forces. Hitler, seeming at first to accept the proposal, suddenly erupted into a thunderous outburst of fury at generals and advisers who failed to understand him. The rage soon subsided, but Heinrici was granted only six out of the eighteen battalions he had wanted. The general emphasized the weakness of his infantry reserves and requested reinforcements of at least three divisions. For an imminent battle of such significance, the situation was unacceptable, he stated. For a moment there was silence. Then Göring volunteered 100,000 men from the Luftwaffe, followed by Dönitz and Himmler, who said they would provide between them 30,000–40,000 men from the navy and SS. Heinrici's objection that these were young recruits not trained and inexperienced in hard infantry defensive warfare was ignored. Weapons for them could only be provided by taking them from units of foreign troops serving with the Germans.

When Heinrici pointed out the weakness not just of his infantry, but also of his armoured formations, after losing important units to Schörner, Hitler told him that the Red Army would launch its offensive not at first towards Berlin but towards Dresden, then Prague. Heinrici looked in astonishment at General Krebs, but the Chief of the General Staff backed Hitler, saying the possibility could not be ruled out. Throughout, Hitler, supported by his entourage, had swept over the serious problems which Heinrici had raised and provided the most optimistic gloss possible. At the end of the audience, Heinrici questioned whether the fighting quality of the troops could withstand the opening barrage of the attack, and asked again where, since the outcome of the battle depended on it, he could find replacements for the inevitable losses. Hitler reminded him of the reinforcements promised by the Luft-waffe, navy and SS. On the first question, he told Heinrici that he bore the responsibility for conveying 'faith and confidence' to the troops. If all possessed this faith, 'this battle will be the bloodiest defeat of the war for the enemy and the greatest defensive success', he concluded. Leaving the Reich Chancellery some while later, after a prolonged wait in the bunker because of an air raid, Heinrici and Eismann sat in silence in their car until the general said simply: 'It's come to this for us.'[31]

Heinrici was to undergo worse conflict with Hitler's military advisers in the High Command of the Wehrmacht later in the month as the battle of Berlin reached its denouement. But his audience with the Dictator on 6 April already highlighted the ambivalence of his continuing stance. He thought Hitler was mistaken and wrong-headed in his decisions. Never-theless, he felt obliged to implement these decisions to the best of his ability. As he saw it (making every allowance for the fact that his post-war memoirs were intended to vindicate his own actions), his duty was a patriotic one – to defend Germany, not serve Hitler and National Socialism. But carrying out what his conscience and upbringing told him was his duty could only be done by helping to sustain the regime. He was, it is true, unlike Kesselring open to Speer's request not to imple-ment Hitler's 'scorched earth' decree. But that was about as far as his defiance went, as an incident in mid-April demonstrates. Speer, visiting Heinrici in his headquarters near Prenzlau, broached the question of assassinating Hitler and asked whether the general was prepared to act. (The question was purely rhetorical since Speer's talk of killing Hitler was no more than hypothetical, and backed by no preparation. He possibly raised the matter with thoughts already in mind of his defence when faced with charges of participation in the regime's crimes.) The answer was prompt and straightforward. In a personal sense, Heinrici said he had no bonds to Hitler or his entourage. But as a soldier he had sworn an oath of allegiance and as a Christian he had learnt 'thou shalt not kill' (killing in war was plainly a different matter). He could imagine that in extreme circumstances he could reject the obedience bound up in the oath. 'But as a soldier, to murder the supreme commander, to whom I swore an oath of loyalty, in the face of enemy attack, that I cannot do!' He was, moreover, sure that it would prompt later belief in a 'stab in the back'. Speer agreed. They were, he acknowledged, trapped. They could only go on.[32]

Whatever their varying attitudes towards Hitler and National Socialism, ranging from fanatical commitment to little more than contempt, no general – and the same applied to the vast majority of the soldiers in their commands – wanted to see Germany defeated, least of all to be subjugated by the Bolsheviks. The consequence of doing all in their power to prevent this happening was the prolongation of the war, and of the lifespan of the Nazi regime, with all the suffering this entailed. Hopes that, even now, something could be salvaged from the war and Germany 'saved' outweighed the desire for an end to Nazism. For some, indeed, there was no estrangement from Nazism and the lingering dream that a miracle could still happen. In his retirement near Würzburg after his dismissal for 'failure' in East Prussia, Colonel-General Reinhardt, for example, could plaintively ask 'when and how the salvation that we still believe in will come'. A week later, just like Hitler and Goebbels, he saw in President Roosevelt's death on 12 April 'a glimmer of hope'.[33]

Meanwhile, the deadly machinery of war ground on. Reserves of manpower were exhausted.[34] Orders were still going out involving the Party in cooperating with the Wehrmacht to round up 'stragglers' and send them back to the front.[35] But whatever the brutal methods used, the numbers amounted to a mere drop in the ocean. At the end of February, Hitler had approved using 6,000 boys born in 1929, some of them therefore not yet sixteen years old, to strengthen rear defensive lines, as well as the training of a 'Women's Battalion'.[36] But by April boys were being sent out to fight not in the rear, but in the front lines. The Reich Youth Leader, Artur Axmann, agreed at the end of March to establish 'panzer close-combat units' of the Hitler Youth. At the start of April the first battalion of 700 Hitler Youth was ferried out on lorries to fight as close-combat troops to shoot down tanks near Gotha.[37] When the Soviet offensive began, fifteen- and sixteen-year-olds were to find themselves facing up to the onslaught from Russian tanks. The Waffen-SS were still press-ganging young Germans to join up a month later even as the Soviets were battling their way into the centre of Berlin.[38] It was far from the case, however, that all young Germans had to be coerced into almost suicidal combat. Whether through indoctrination in the Hitler Youth, idealism, or a sense of adventure, many went willingly to the front, some ready even at this desperate stage of the war to offer the last sacrifice for their country.[39] Few could have been prepared for what lay in store. Most of the Hitler Youth recruits were in any case far from being fanatics ready to die for their country, and were just frightened, disorientated boys, forced into action and often wantonly slaughtered in a hopeless cause.[40]

Improvisation was by now the order of the day. In the south of Germany, the *Volkssturm* were used to carry out road repairs after bombing raids to enable troop movements to continue. Most road-workers were by this time in any case serving with the *Volkssturm*, it was pointed out. Orders were still being dispatched for the hasty erection of tank barriers by means of the 'ruthless and comprehensive deployment of the entire population'. The dearth of equipment for the fighting troops was partly to be made good by distribution from Wehrmacht stores in the path of enemy advance. In Württemberg, Army Group G was grateful to come across 100,000 pairs of boots to replace the down-at-heel footwear of the troops, along with large amounts of leather clothing.[41]

Astonishingly, Hitler himself had to order, in the last week of his life, that all stocks of weapons and equipment left lingering for more than a week on wagons at railway stations should be unloaded and supplied to the troops.[42] None of this was any more than papering over the cracks. But it contributed towards enabling some sort of a fighting force to continue operations in the increasingly desperate circumstances. And pretences had to be maintained. Remarkably, amid the extraordinary shortages of men and *matériel* in a lost war, preparations were still made in mid-April for an exhibition of the latest armaments models to be displayed in the courtyard of the Reich Chancellery for Hitler's usual birthday inspection on 20 April.[43]

Generalizations about mentalities among the rank-and-file of the armed forces are obviously hazardous. And however varied the political attitudes of individual soldiers, sailors and airmen, the overwhelming number probably simply accepted that they had no choice but to do what they were ordered to do: fight on. The character of the fronts certainly affected attitudes. There was almost certainly greater tenacity, determination to fight, and even belief in Hitler among those directly facing the Red Army in the east, where the ideological conflict was most pronounced, than among the troops on the collapsing western front. How representative was a letter home at the beginning of April from an NCO serving with the 12th Panzer Division cut off in Courland cannot be known, but it indicates that Nazified ideas were still present in his unit: 'Some will regard the war in these critical days as lost,' he wrote.

> But the war is only lost if we surrender. Even should Germany capitulate, would the war be over for us? No, the horror would be only just really beginning and we would not even have weapons to defend ourselves. As long as we have weapons and the firm belief in our good cause, nothing is lost. I believe firmly in a decisive shift in fortunes. Providence, which sent us the Führer, will not allow all the terrible sacrifices to have been in vain and will never abandon the world to the annihilatory terror of Bolshevism.[44]

There were, however, contrasting attitudes, even among soldiers in the east. Reflective diary entries in mid-April from an NCO based in Prague, with obvious anti-Nazi feelings, display critical distance from the regime, a realistic view of the hopelessness of the position, and a sense that the fate now embracing the Reich had been earned by the crimes in the east that Germans had committed. He estimated that about 10 per cent of the soldiers, with reference to statements by Hitler and Goebbels, still believed in 'a technical miracle'. Remarkably, there was speculation about the splitting of the atom, and that Germany possessed a weapon of such force that it would make England disappear from the face of the earth. Even worse than such talk, the diarist thought, was that a great sector of the German population, while not believing in the existence of such a weapon, regretted that Germany did not have one which it could use to destroy all its enemies in one strike: then 'we would be the victors'. In such notions he saw the extent of the brutalization and moral decay which Nazi education had produced. 'This people will have nothing to complain of in its own fate,' he commented. He had heard in the last days several times from older soldiers who had experienced the first two years of the Russian campaign the saying that all guilt is avenged on earth. They saw reports, he thought partly exaggerated, of Bolshevik atrocities in the occupied eastern parts of Germany as proof of this. 'Many think consciously of the things that they themselves saw or had to carry out and which have to be set against what is allegedly taking place now. "We are guilty ourselves, we've earned it" – that's the bitter recognition that many struggle through to.'[45]

Two days later the same soldier commented on the fighting in central Germany and the surrender of Königsberg, with the attendant condemnation to death *in absentia* of the German commandant and arrest of his family. He saw the demands of the Nazi leadership to defend every town and village to the last as leaving no lingering doubt about 'the fanatical will and the method to try to counter the imminent threat of collapse. Everyone not involved in the defence or acting against the decreed measures will be threatened with death.' However, he thought there was growing acceptance of unconditional surrender, and that mass desertion and internal unrest would spread in the following days. The signs of rising anger were evident. People were saying more openly what they had earlier secretly thought, and 'the insight into the true situation and the intentions of our leadership is growing'. 'In these days the last arguments are being knocked out of even the most hard-nosed optimist,' he wrote. 'Soon nobody and nothing will be able to justify further resistance. The slogan of heroic downfall will then in its naked madness be plain to the entire people.'[46]

However divided they were in their political stance, for soldiers awaiting the Red Army's Oder offensive, east of Berlin, a prominent motive for continuing to fight was unquestionably defence of the homeland against a hated enemy. More telling in the heat of battle was the group cameraderie of the fighting unit. And most important of all in the last resort was the desire for self-preservation. German soldiers were well aware that they could expect no quarter from the Red Army if they were captured. They often knew, sometimes at first hand, of earlier German atrocities in the east. What awaited them on capture, they were sure, was death or at best indefinite slave labour far away in the Soviet Union.

Propaganda vilifying the enemy and depicting the horrors awaiting them should the Bolsheviks prevail, rammed home to the troops in pep-talks from NSFOs, naturally, then, fell on its most fertile ground in the east. For troops being pushed relentlessly back in north-western, central and southern Germany there was a less clear focus. Fear of the enemy was far less pronounced. At the same time, revulsion at the notion that foreign enemies were occupying German soil doubtless spurred on many. A group of fourteen- and fifteen-year-old boys, evacuated from the Ruhr, who volunteered for service in the SS in Lower Franconia in early April 1945, had themselves mixed motives. Some were ardent Nazis, others sought cameraderie and adventure. But all of them wanted to 'save the Fatherland'.[47] There were still, if in a minority, plenty of ardent Nazis present in the armed forces, especially among younger soldiers. In one letter that came into British hands in April, a lieutenant serving in Lower Saxony told his parents in Westphalia: 'I simply cannot believe that the Führer will sacrifice us senselessly. Nobody will be able to rob me of my faith in "Him". He is my All. . . . Who knows what experiences I shall have before we meet again, but I am an officer and will gladly do all I can for my Fatherland, more – much more, even – than duty requires.'[48] Volunteers were not lacking for service as suicide-pilots, with the aim of ramming their fighters into Allied bombers. More than 2,000 men immediately came forward, motivated by the loss of their homeland in the east, the death of their families through Allied bombing, or Nazi fanaticism. The kamikaze-style tactic proved unsuccessful and the self-sacrifice pointless: only eight bombers were brought down through ramming, at a cost of 133 German planes and the lives of seventy-seven pilots.[49] Waffen-SS units still showed astonishing levels of morale, fighting-power and commitment to the regime, as well as utter ruthlessness in blowing up houses where white flags were flying and taking reprisals against individuals raising them. In varying degrees, differing from person to person, ideological commitment, fanatical loyalty, a sense of comradely duty, fear of the consequences of non-compliance and sheer lack of alternative drove on the German will to resist.[50]

Perhaps, other than a vague notion that their actions were helping somehow to 'save' Germany, many soldiers in the west had no clear rationale for why they were still fighting. For in the west, too, self-preservation was the most prominent motive, according to a survey of 12,000 soldiers' letters during March. In almost all, the wish was expressed to survive the last phase of the war and rejoin their families.[51]

An impression of a disintegrating army can be glimpsed from the diary account, cited on occasion in earlier chapters, of Lieutenant Julius Dufner. By April 1945, Dufner was based in the Bergisches Land south of Remscheid, near Wermelskirchen, then in nearby Solingen as Model's orders came through for the dissolution of Army Group B. On 13 April he heard rumours that soldiers had thrown away their weapons and that the war in the west was over. As troops retreated, men and women were exhorting them to lay down their arms, offering accommodation and civilian clothing. Two days later there were further rumours, that Hitler, Göring and Goebbels had been shot or committed suicide. Inhabitants were pulling down tank barriers in Solingen. Wehrmacht goods were being distributed to the local population. Children were running round in steel helmets discarded by soldiers. Hatred against the Party was now able to find voice. 'Everything smelling of the Party was seen as fair game,' he noted. By 16 April nearly all the soldiers were wearing civilian clothes and acting as if they had been dismissed from army service, though an actual order to that effect had still not come through. Their senior officer, a major, was dressed in an ill-fitting suit and sports cap, giving up any pretence at command. The last munition dump was detonated. The following day, 17 April, in the ruined city centre of Solingen, as German prisoners were loaded onto lorries to be taken into captivity, and American GIs, smoking Camel cigarettes and chewing gum, took over the town, he set out for home in Baden (where he arrived nearly a fortnight later) in civilian clothing, and on the bicycle that he had obtained by offering his motorbike and 100 Reich Marks in exchange. For him, the war was over.[52] Other soldiers, particularly those tensely awaiting the battle on the Oder, were less lucky.

IV

The regime's control in western areas was by now in an advanced stage of dissolution. Propaganda reports gave Goebbels an 'alarming' picture of demoralization. There was no longer reluctance to voice sharp criticism of Hitler himself, and no fear of the Americans. White flags were put out as they approached, and they were greeted with enthusiasm, regarded as protectors against the Soviets. The population were often directly opposed to their own troops who wanted to continue the fight, with a predictably depressing effect on the soldiers. There was a good deal of looting. Alongside the defeatism and widespread fatalism, many people were now talking of suicide as the best way out. Characteristically Nazified demands were voiced for drastic action against those seen as responsible for Germany's plight. People pointed to the peremptory punishment of those who had failed to detonate the Remagen bridge and thereby allowed the Americans to cross the Rhine; they wanted similar treatment for those responsible for the 'catastrophe in the air war', even demanding the death penalty for Göring. Some believed – as did Hitler himself – that treason was behind the collapse on the western front.[53]

So negative were the reports reaching Bormann that he felt it necessary to write a lengthy complaint to Ernst Kaltenbrunner, Chief of the
Security Police, at the tone of the 'typical SD report', which generalized
broadly from a small number of individual cases to paint a bleak picture. Bormann accepted that some segments of the population – but not
the population – had welcomed the Americans, though he attributed
this to an inability to counter the propaganda effect of enemy radio and
to the readiness of people to believe that the war would soon be over,
and with that a release from the constant bombing raids. For his part,
he was convinced that, as after 1918, there would soon be 'a very strong
sobering process'.[54]

According to General Schulz, Commander-in-Chief of Army Group
G, in a telex on 8 April to Karl Wahl, Gauleiter of Swabia, 'the fighting
of the last days has clearly shown that the population in the zone close
to the front uses all means to deter soldiers from any fighting and resistance in order to protect their property from destruction'. As a
counter-measure, he urged the evacuation of the population near the
combat zone. Wahl took the view that this did not yet apply to the
population of his Gau.[55] A few days later, he nevertheless complied with
an order to evacuate a zone either side of the Danube as a preventive
measure in case it was drawn into the fighting area. Women and children were ordered to leave within two hours on foot or bicycle since no
transport was available, and to use side roads to keep the main routes
clear for the troops.[56] In many parts of the west, evacuation, as Goebbels acknowledged, was impracticable. 'We're issuing orders in Berlin
that practically don't even arrive, let alone can be carried out,' he wrote,
seeing in this 'the danger of an extraordinary diminution of authority'.[57]
Removing a largely unwilling population was impossible. No transport
was available. And there were no areas to send them to. Evacuation
orders of the Führer could simply not be implemented and were quietly
forgotten.[58]

In the south, following the collapse in Hungary and Austria, chaos
arose from tens of thousands of refugees fleeing from the Soviets.
Gauleiter August Eigruber of Gau Oberdonau complained bitterly to
the Party Chancellery that Gau Bayreuth and Gau Munich-Upper
Bavaria would not accept fifteen trainloads of refugees, numbering
around 100,000 people, from Vienna, the Lower Danube and Hungary,
nor, despite orders, send urgently needed cereals to Gau Upper Danube,

which had no corn supplies left. The refugees had been left in railway sidings for several days. Munich eventually agreed to take its share. Gau Tirol was also forced into accepting some, though the Gauleiter, Franz Hofer, said that while he would do what he could for Germans, he could do nothing for Hungarians, Croats and Slovenes. No one wanted to take the Hungarians. Gauleiter Fritz Wächtler in Bayreuth stubbornly continued to refuse to cooperate. The Party Chancellery sought in vain to get him to respond to its demands, eventually sending a special courier to obtain a reply. Wächtler had also failed to provide the daily situation reports to which, it was said, the Führer attached great importance.[59] His unwillingness or inability – Bayreuth was suffering severe air raids at the time – to comply with orders from Berlin was a further indication of the gathering dissolution of the regime.

The collapsing communications network also contributed to the undermining of central control. By early April it was almost impossible to sustain contact between Berlin and the Gaue in southern Germany and Austria. A motorbike courier service was proposed to relay urgent messages. The 'communications calamity' had never been so great.[60] Where communications still functioned, they brought an unceasing flood of new decrees and directives from Bormann, 'thoroughly useless stuff' according to Goebbels, and largely ignored by Gauleiter who did not even have time to read them. The Propaganda Minister contemptuously dismissed Bormann's efforts, saying he had turned the Party Chancellery into 'a paper Chancellery'.[61]

A glimpse of the profound lack of realism at lower levels of the Party, existing to the end, can be found in the directive of the Kreisleiter of Freiberg in Saxony, as late as 28 April. 'Now that a certain stabilization of the situation has taken place,' he wrote (two days before Hitler's suicide), 'it is necessary again to turn intensively to Party work.' A whole array of duties followed.[62]

In Vienna, the Party was in a desolate state weeks before the city fell to the Red Army. There were reports of a rebellious mood among the working class (which indeed manifested itself in attempts by underground Communist groups to assist the Soviets when they entered the city), and high levels of antagonism towards the Party. Functionaries were insulted, even spat at, and did not dare walk round after air raids unless armed. There was strong criticism of the Gauleiter (and one-time Hitler Youth leader), Baldur von Schirach, and of Hitler. Women were said to have been especially prominent in the agitation, even inciting troops to mutiny.[63]

Goebbels could still try to claim, not least for Hitler's benefit, that the 'Werwolf' activity marked a return to the revolutionary ethos of the Party's 'time of struggle' before the 'seizure of power' in 1933.[64] He continued to press for radical action. And he acted ruthlessly without hesitation. When 200 men and women stormed bakers' shops in a district of Berlin to get bread he saw it as a symptom of 'inner weakness and budding defeatism', deciding instantly to stamp it out 'with brutal methods'. Two of those singled out as ringleaders, a man and a woman, were summarily sentenced to death by the People's Court that afternoon and beheaded the next night. Posters, radio broadcasts and a meeting held by the Kreisleiter about the incident aimed at discouraging any repetition.[65]

As Goebbels knew, such ruthlessness could not hide the evident fact that the Party was disintegrating. The constant propaganda slogans to 'hold out to the last', and to go down fighting in defence of towns and villages stood in stark contrast to the behaviour of many Party functionaries who disappeared into thin air at the approach of the enemy. The Party Chancellery repeatedly reminded functionaries to set the best example to the population. The Führer expected political leaders to master the situation in their Gaue with lightning speed and maximum severity, Bormann told them in mid-April. They had to educate their District Leaders in the same way. 'Leaders by nature have burnt their bridges and show extreme commitment,' he added. 'The honour of each one is worth only as much as his steadfastness, his commitment and his deeds.'[66] The appeals fell mainly on deaf ears. 'The poor examples presented by the Party have had an extraordinarily repellent impact on the population,' Goebbels remarked at the beginning of April. Its reputation had been badly tarnished.[67] A few days later, he admitted that the behaviour of Gau- and Kreisleiter in the west had led to a huge drop in confidence in the Party. 'The population believed it could expect that our Gauleiter would fight in their Gaue and, if necessary, die there. This has not been the case in any instance. As a result, the Party is fairly played out in the west.'[68]

Some Gauleiter (and beneath them many Kreisleiter and lower functionaries of the Party) had simply left the people in their areas in the lurch and fled.[69] Much to the disgust of Goebbels, Josef Grohé, Gauleiter of Cologne-Aachen, had failed to defend his Gau in March as the Americans entered and left in advance of the civilian population with his staff in a motor boat. He retained a skeletal staff for a short time at Bensberg, then dissolved his Gau administration entirely on 8 April and moved to Field-Marshal Model's headquarters before discarding his uniform a week later and setting out under an assumed name in a vain attempt to locate his family in central Germany.[70] Albert Hoffmann, Gauleiter of Westphalia-South, had tried in previous weeks through 'extreme severity' to combat signs of collapsing morale and defeatism in his Gau. But, despite giving Speer the impression that he backed his attempts to prevent unnecessary destruction, he personally ordered a number of bridges to be blown up and made plans for his departure at the beginning of April. He moved to the headquarters of Model's Army Group B and was seldom seen thereafter in his Gau offices. Without consulting either Hitler or Bormann, at a meeting with his Kreisleiter on 13 April he announced the dissolution of the Nazi Party in Gau Westphalia-South, fled that same evening and vanished before joining his family in the middle of May disguised as a farmhand.[71] Gauleiter Koch, who for years had ruled East Prussia with a rod of iron and had been the target of much hatred for the belated and mismanaged evacuation of the population in January, was still in April producing slogans in the besieged provincial capital such as 'Victory is Ours – Königsberg will be the Grave of the Bolsheviks'.[72] At the same time he was making preparations to take himself, his family and his possessions to safety. He made a final departure from East Prussia by air on 25 April, just before the harbour at Pillau was taken by the Red Army and the fate of around 100,000 refugees still stranded on the Samland was sealed. From the Hela peninsula he transferred to the ice-breaker *Ostpreußen*, apparently with his Mercedes on board, and sailed to Denmark before travelling on to Flensburg, where he vainly demanded a U-boat to take him to South America.[73]

If these were the most blatant cases of the flight of the Party's 'Golden Pheasants', few Gauleiter were prepared to entertain the prospect of the 'heroic' death that the image of the leading Nazi 'fighters' demanded. Only two out of forty-three serving Gauleiter, Karl Gerland of Kurhessen and the notably brutal Karl Holz of Franconia died at their posts in the fighting.[74] Holz's last report from Nuremberg, sent late in the evening on 17 April, painted a depressing picture of the situation in the city (though the most negative sections were crossed out, perhaps in the Party Chancellery's Munich office). The troops were worn down by the enemy superiority in *matériel*. The poor morale of 'stragglers' was evident. One group of thirty or so men had approached the enemy with white flags before being shot down by machine-gun fire from their own side. The population simply awaited its fate, cowering in the cellars and bunkers. He proudly reported that he had sent out some of his staff to organize the Werwolf, and that his Gau had managed to assemble within only a few weeks a regiment of tank-destroying troops from the Hitler Youth, who had fought courageously, though with big losses, so that one battalion was already nearly 'wiped out'. He and the mayor of the city, Willi Liebel, had decided to stay in Nuremberg and fight rather than leave the city.[75] Next day, Nuremberg was under fire.

Holtz's report to Hitler declared that 'in these hours my heart beats more than ever in love and loyalty to you and the wonderful German Reich and people', and 'that the National Socialist idea will be victorious', for which he was rewarded with the Golden Cross of the German Order, the highest honour of Party and state. Just before midnight on 19 April, Holz again wired Hitler – for the last time: 'Our loyalty, our love, our lives belong to you, my Führer. All our good wishes for your birthday' (the next day). He refused to contemplate surrender and threatened even now to have anyone showing a white flag shot. On that day, 20 April, the 'city of the Reich Party Rallies' surrendered. Holz had just dispatched the local SA leader to fight his way through to report to Hitler 'that we have defended Nuremberg to the last man'. His final act was to order the SS men in his company to open fire on some policemen who were trying to cross to the Americans. An absolute fanatic to the end, Holz was among a group that continued the fighting in the ruins of the police headquarters, where he was killed.[76]

Farther east, Gauleiter Karl Hanke was coming to symbolize the genuine Nazi 'hero' in the beleaguered city of Breslau. The situation there was worsening daily. From the beginning of April, with the loss of the aerodrome at Gandau, even provisioning of the city from the air was no longer possible. Houses were bulldozed, inflicting further misery on local inhabitants, in order to construct an emergency air-strip. The living conditions of the population, still numbering more than 200,000, were meanwhile indescribable, and became almost impossible when non-stop bombing raids on Easter Monday, 2 April, obliterated practically the entire city centre.[77] They were paying a terrible price for Hanke's decision in January to defend 'Fortress Breslau' to the last. In Nazi eyes, however, he signified the indomitable spirit that refused to capitulate.

For his personal leadership of the defence of Breslau, and to his great delight, Hitler bestowed upon the Gauleiter the Golden Cross of the German Order.[78] In mid-April, Albert Speer sent Hanke a personal letter effusively thanking him for his personal friendship, 'for all that you have done for me', and praising him for his 'achievements as defender of Breslau', through which he had 'given much to Germany today'. 'Your example,' Speer went on, 'yet to be recognized in its greatness, will later have the inestimable high value for the people of only few heroes of German history.' He did not pity him, Speer concluded. 'You are heading for a fine and honourable end to your life.'[79] The 'hero' had, however, no intention of going down with the city he had condemned to near total destruction. Hours before Breslau's capitulation on 5 May, Hanke would make his escape in a Fieseler Storch, perhaps the only plane ever to leave the improvised air-strip in the city.[80]

V

The brutal message which Bormann dispatched in Hitler's name to members of the Party on 1 April clearly signalled, in its call to utter ruthlessness in demanding a fight to the last, the gathering desperation of the regime's leadership:

After the collapse of 1918 we devoted ourselves with life and limb to the struggle for the right of existence of our people. Now the high point of our test has come: the danger of renewed enslavement facing our people demands our last and supreme effort. From now on the following applies: The fight against the enemy who has forced his way into the Reich is to be uncomprisingly conducted everywhere without pity. Gauleiter and Kreisleiter, other political leaders and heads of affiliates are to fight in their Gau and district, to conquer or to fall. Any scumbag who leaves his Gau when under attack without express order of the Führer, anyone not fighting to the last breath, will be proscribed and treated as a deserter. Raise your hearts and overcome all weaknesses! Now there is only one slogan: conquer or fall! Long live Germany. Long live Adolf Hitler.[81]

It was a callous attempt at the final hour to turn back the tide. It could do nothing to stave off collapse as the inexorable military defeat grew closer by the day. Even so, in these last weeks it set the tone for the gathering wave of unbridled violence against the regime's declared enemies as its control crumbled.

Even the regime's high representatives were not immune from its venom. Gauleiter Fritz Wächtler – a prominent functionary in Thuringia almost since the time he joined the NSDAP in 1926, appointed Thuringian Minister of the Interior in 1933, and since 1935 Gauleiter of the Bayerische Ostmark with honorary status as an SS-Obergruppenführer – had, as we saw, been unresponsive to missives from the Party Chancellery towards the end of the first week of April. This may have contributed to the readiness of Bormann and Hitler to believe the malicious report of his deputy that Wächtler had deserted his Gau. Whether communications difficulties prevented Wächtler from letting Führer Headquarters know his position is unclear. He certainly did face major problems at the time. Bayreuth, the seat of his Gau headquarters, had been heavily bombed three times in early April, and by the middle of the month looked like a ghost-town. Most of the *Volkssturm* men, who had been mobilized to defend the city, fled, followed by the Kreisleiter and his staff, before American tanks reached the outskirts in the night of 13 April. The Party had by then effectively abdicated its power in the city, which was defended by no more than 200 or so soldiers under a 'combat commandant' (*Kampfkommandant*).

Wächtler also secretly left Bayreuth about the same time with his Gau staff to head south and take up residence in a hotel in Herzogau, a district of the small town of Waldmünchen, in the Upper Palatinate, close to the Czech border. It seems probable that Wächtler was transferring his command post rather than deserting. But his deputy and long-standing rival, Ludwig Ruckdeschel, who had himself transferred his base to Regensburg, chose not to see it like that. It appears that Ruckdeschel contacted Führer Headquarters in Berlin, accusing Wächtler of desertion. In the early morning of 19 April, Ruckdeschel and a squad of 35 SS-men arrived at Wächtler's hotel. Ruckdeschel ignored Wächtler's plea that he had removed his staff to organize resistance from Waldmünchen, and without hesitation pronounced the death sentence. Screaming 'dirty treason', Wächtler was taken away, stood up against a nearby tree and immediately shot dead by a firing-squad.

Ruckdeschel proclaimed that Wächtler had been thrown out of the Nazi Party and executed for cowardice in the face of the enemy, threatening any 'scoundrel and traitor' acting similarly with the same fate.[82]

For ordinary citizens, compliance through fear of instant and arbitrary reprisals was a rational form of behaviour. Anyone showing the least sign of opposing the regime's own death wish of senseless 'holding out' against impossible odds faced great peril. Himmler decreed on 3 April that 'in a house in which a white flag appears, all males are to be shot'. He was responding to an initiative from the Party, referred to him by the OKW, which had recommended the burning down of any house showing a white flag.[83] On 12 April, the High Command of the Wehrmacht issued an order, signed by Keitel, Himmler and Bormann, that every town was to be defended to the last. Any offer or promise by the enemy should the town surrender was to be rejected out of hand. The assigned 'combat commandant' was personally responsible for ensuring that the defence of the town was carried out. Anyone acting against this order, or any official seeking to hinder the commandant in fulfilling his duty, would be sentenced to death. Publishing this order in Nuremberg, the Gauleiter and Reich Defence Commissar for Franconia, Karl Holz, added his own rider: 'Every traitor hoisting a white flag will without fail be hanged. Every house where a white flag is hanging will be blown up or burnt down. Villages that raise white flags communally will be burnt down.'[84]

Despite such uncompromising orders, backed by ruthless terror (even if the threat to burn down entire German villages does not appear to have been carried out), there were numerous cases of localized opposition. Few people wanted to end their lives in a futile show of 'heroism' or to see their homes and workplaces blown up senselessly. Whether they were able to avoid the worst of the destruction varied from place to place, depending on local conditions and the actions of those still holding the reins of power in their hands. Representatives of the dying regime in threatened areas – local government officials, Party functionaries, town commandants who were handed military control over a locality – did not behave uniformly. In western regions, localized power-struggles often decided whether a town was surrendered without a fight or went down in a hail of destruction.[85] Many mayors of towns and even local Party leaders behaved responsibly in defying demands to fight on. This could, however, bring savage reprisals if local desperadoes – Party fanatics or SS men, usually – gained the upper hand. In other instances, regime zealots still controlled the local levers of power and condemned inhabitants of towns or villages to unnecessary death and destruction in the final hours before occupation – and before, as a rule, they themselves fled at the last minute. There was no clear pattern.

In many eastern areas, the approach of such a feared enemy brought not thoughts of handing over a town or village without a fight, but panic and attempts to flee – usually after Party representatives, knowing what awaited them if they fell into Soviet hands, had abandoned them. Cottbus in Brandenburg was one of many such examples. Almost all the civilians in the town and surrounding area fled westwards in the days before the Soviet assault on Cottbus began on 21 April. By the early hours of the next morning, all the regular troops, including an SS panzer unit, had pulled out, destroying bridges as they went. Only the *Volkssturm* and a few groups of 'stragglers' remained to defend the town. The last 200 soldiers or *Volkssturm* men fled that day. 'That was the last of the German Wehrmacht that I saw,' recalled one eyewitness. The Party Kreisleiter also vanished. The 'fortress commandant' in Cottbus accepted that without regular troops the town was indefensible. This decision, and the speed of the Red Army's advance, meant that the last act in the fall of the town came quickly and without further fighting or additional pointless destruction (though Soviet soldiers set on fire houses in which they found Nazi symbols).[86]

The fate of a village or town depended heavily upon the stance of the combat commandant and the actions of prominent citizens. The lovely university town of Greifswald, close to the Pomeranian coast, was fortunate in avoiding destruction. The rector of the university, a fifteenth-century foundation, and a small group of professors and prominent citizens were able to gain the backing of the combat commandant for the surrender of the town to the Soviets without a fight, despite the insistence of the Kreisleiter that it be defended even if it held up the Red Army for only an hour. Without the support of the combat commandant (who encouraged citizens to put out white flags from their homes), the Party officials in the town were powerless.[87]

In western Germany, probably more than in eastern areas, the collapsing control of the regime offered possibilities, despite the terror, for groups of citizens, women often prominent among them, sometimes led by local 'worthies' such as priests or doctors, to take the initiative to prevent the destruction of their townships. They could, if they were fortunate, win support from the mayor or other local government officials and win over the combat commandant.[88] Much hinged upon the individuals concerned, their readiness to take action, the stance of the local Party officials, and the presence of the SS or Wehrmacht troops insistent upon terrorizing any seen as 'defeatists'. In Stuttgart, the mayor, Dr Karl Strölin, himself a Nazi, was persuaded by anti-Nazi local notables to ignore the demands of the Gauleiter of Württemberg, Wilhelm Murr, who was fanatically determined to fight on and punish any who stood in his way. Strölin, gaining the support of the new combat commandant's superior and through him the Wehrmacht commander in the area, opened clandestine negotiations with the Allies. On 22 April Stuttgart was surrendered without a struggle.[89]

On occasion, direct action prevented the worst. In the picturesque small town of Bad Windsheim in Lower Franconia, in the most spectacular of a number of demonstrations led by women against the destruction of their towns, 200–300 women, some of them with their children, protested in early April about the decision of the local military commander to hold out against the imminent arrival of strong American forces.[90] After a tense confrontation, Bad Windsheim eventually fell without being subjected to total destruction and heavy loss of life. Such courageous protests were, however, not always effective. In Lahr, in the south of Baden, a large group of women in rebellious mood, hurling insults at Hitler and the Party, persuaded a delegation of the town's officials to seek agreement from the local Wehrmacht commandant to surrender without a fight. Waiting for the return of the delegation, the women hoisted white flags throughout the town, and started the bell tolling to signal surrender. Their hopes were premature. The delegation returned empty-handed. The SS commandant insisted on the defence of Lahr, warning the women that if the white flags were not withdrawn that evening his own men would open fire on the town. Instead of surrender, battle raged throughout the night and into the next day before the town fell to the French, who then looted houses and shops, saying that the SS had behaved worse in France.[91]

Such actions to try to avoid futile destruction when all was obviously lost could provoke a drastic response. Hundreds of German citizens fell victim to uncontrolled violence in the last weeks of the Nazi regime. Examples could be multiplied without difficulty.[92] Following the women's demonstration in Bad Windsheim, for instance, one woman, wrongly selected (probably because of her reputation as a critic of the NSDAP) as the ringleader by a hit-squad sent down by the Gestapo in Nuremberg, was cold-bloodedly shot in front of her husband and daughter and a notice pinned to her body announcing that 'a traitor has been executed'.[93] In Schwäbisch Gmünd, a small town in Württemberg not far from Stuttgart, the Kreisleiter and combat commandant had two men executed just before midnight on 19 April, hours before the Americans entered the town without a fight. One of the men was known to have been an opponent of the Nazis since 1933, when he had been arrested for distributing anti-Nazi pamphlets and returned from his stay in a concentration camp a changed person, psychiatrically disturbed. The other was a former soldier, no longer fit to fight after a serious injury. In a heated argument about handing over the city or fighting on, with the certainty of the destruction of the lovely town with its beautiful medieval minster, they had been heard to shout, probably under the influence of alcohol, 'Drop dead Hitler. Long live Stauffenberg. Long live freedom.' The two were removed from their police cells late at night, taken to a wood at the edge of the town and shot dead. The local Nazi representatives were ensuring, with their last act of power, that long-standing opponents would not live to enjoy their downfall. Even as the executions were taking place, the Kreisleiter and his entourage were preparing to flee from the town.[94]

An extreme case was the arbitrary shooting dead of four civilians, among them a pastor, in a suburb of Heilbronn on 6 April when the local Kreisleiter, Richard Drauz, and a group of fanatics (three of them in the *Volkssturm*) fleeing by car together with him as the Americans approached came across a street in which white flags hung from several houses. In a rage, he stopped the car, ordering his men 'out, shoot, shoot everybody'. Drauz's accomplices arbitrarily shot down their victims, men and women, within a frenzied few minutes, narrowly missing several others, before driving off.[95]

Others fell victim not to random shootings or the actions of hit-squads, but to the brutal summary 'justice' of the 'flying court martial'. One such mobile court travelled through parts of southern Germany in a grey Mercedes under the leadership of Major Erwin Helm, 'a special kind of berserker', proud of an earlier head-wound that had left part of his brain protruding through his skull. Passing close to the village of

Zellingen in Lower Franconia at the end of March, Helm's attention was drawn by the commander of the local *Volkssturm* battalion, a doctor, to a sixty-year-old farmer, Karl Weiglein, who had allegedly made a sarcastic comment during a pep-talk for the battalion, then later remarked that those responsible for blowing up the nearby bridge over the Main should be hanged. Helm's instant reaction, before hearing any details of the incidents, was that Weiglein should be executed. When the hurriedly constituted court martial – there was no defender – took too long over its deliberations, Helm threatened to proclaim the sentence himself and prepared the place of execution while the 'court' was meeting. As soon as the inevitable death sentence was pronounced, he hung a notice round Weiglein's neck: 'Sentenced to Death for Sabotage of the Wehrmacht and Mutiny'. In a particularly sadistic move, Weiglein was hanged from a branch of the pear-tree just beneath the window of his farmhouse while insults were hurled at his horror-struck wife.[96]

Walter Fernau, an NSFO and member of Helm's squad who had prosecuted Weiglein and demanded the death sentence, still justified it many years later. 'I really cannot say to you', he told his interviewer decades after the event, 'that at the time I thought that was too harsh.' He took the view that Weiglein was guilty even though the case against him was not proven. The situation necessitated harsh measures, he argued. There was also the deterrent effect. Helm said, Fernau claimed to recall, 'that he has to be hanged and kept on display so that the Zellingen *Volkssturm* people see, well, if we step out of line we'll get the same as him'. The court rightly, in his view, did not have powers to give prison sentences. A few months in prison while others were dying would have been unjust. From the first to the last day of belonging to Helm's battalion, said Fernau, 'I never had the sense that I had made myself guilty.'[97]

Though anyone seen to stand in the regime's way now ran the serious risk of summary execution, the main targets of the 'crimes of the last phase' were nevertheless not random, but real or imagined opponents of the regime, defeatists, 'subversives', supposed 'shirkers', presumed deserters or 'cowards', or anyone welcoming the end of Nazism or the arrival of the enemy. In this sense, the violence differed from the style of savagely arbitrary collective reprisals that had frequently been inflicted earlier in the war on the peoples of Nazi-occupied Europe. When directed by Germans against their fellow countrymen in the last weeks, the horror had a different pattern. Old scores were settled. Personal animosities, little to do with ideology, played their part. So did feelings of sheer revenge. Long-standing opponents were arbitrarily dispatched to prevent their enjoying their moment of triumph.

Ideological indoctrination was, however, far from insignificant. Now as before, the worst of the murderous violence was directed at the per-ceived racial or political enemies of the regime, foreign workers and, above all, concentration camp prisoners. Out of 288 'crimes of the last phase' bringing convictions in post-war trials in West Germany, 114 (39.6 per cent, the highest single proportion) related to the shooting of prisoners and foreign workers. Apart from members of the Gestapo and other police units, *Volkssturm* men and prison personnel were most prominent among the convicted killers.[98]

Prominent individuals who had been involved in the resistance to Hitler could not be allowed to witness his downfall. Among those who had formerly belonged to the opposition within the *Abwehr* (German military counter-intelligence) Hans von Dohnanyi, who had worked for Hitler's downfall since 1938, was hanged in Sachsenhausen concentra-tion camp on 9 April after a farcical 'trial' before an SS court martial. A similar fate in Flossenbürg the same day befell Admiral Wilhelm Canaris, former head of the *Abwehr*, Colonel Hans Oster, who had been part of a plot against Hitler in 1938 and had leaked German invasion plans to the Dutch in 1940, and the evangelical theologian Dietrich Bonhoeffer, whose courageous attempts to persuade the western Allies to support the resistance in Germany had come to nothing. In Dachau, Georg Elser, the Swabian joiner who had tried to blow up Hitler in 1939 was also murdered (without even the semblance of a trial).[99] But such killings were merely the tip of the iceberg. With the regime lurching almost visibly out of control, prisoners, whether in concentration camps or in state penitentiaries, lived or died at the whim of their guards or jailers. Violence towards prisoners, already escalating wildly, now became ubi-quitous.[100] It was even prompted in some cases by the military leadership. When his forces were cut off in the Ruhr, Field-Marshal Model ordered on 7 April that prisoners in penitentiaries, including those under remand for political offences, should be handed to the police for 'examination'. The execution of more than 200 prisoners followed. There were numer-ous other killings in the final hours before penal institutions were evacuated, or before the Allies arrived. Where an official executioner could not get to a penitentiary on time, prison officials – rewarded with money and cigarettes – carried out the killings. In one subsidiary of Emsland camp, a young apprentice chimney-sweep, wearing an army captain's uniform, turned up and ordered the execution of dozens of prisoners. Astonishingly, his orders were followed, a sign of the mounting chaos in the collapsing regime. More than a hundred prisoners were executed over the next few days.[101]

VI

Amid the gathering mayhem and murderous frenzy, the violence and killing of the death marches of concentration camp prisoners in the final weeks of the regime mark a separate unholy chapter.

The hurried, often chaotic, evacuations and subsequent terrible death marches of prisoners from Auschwitz, Groß-Rosen, Stutthof and other camps in the east, which we followed in Chapter 6, had at least a semblance of underlying rationale – from the regime's perspective. The prisoners were to be kept out of the hands of the enemy and brought back into the interior of the Reich where – in theory, though scarcely in practice for such emaciated, exhausted, frozen, starved, beaten and otherwise maltreated human beings – they could be available for labour, or, as Himmler saw it, as potential pawns in any deal with the Allies. Those who were not killed en route, or who did not die from exhaustion or exposure to the bitter winter conditions, eventually reached camps within Germany, including Bergen-Belsen.

Following two days of negotiations and, amazingly, Himmler's permission to hand over rather than evacuate the camp – unaware (given the dramatic decline in the already dreadful conditions in the camp over recent weeks) of exactly what horrors he was revealing, and hoping to exploit his 'humanitarian' gesture in his dealings with Bernadotte – British troops entered Bergen-Belsen on 15 April. Most SS guards had by then left. Around 50,000 prisoners, in a state closer to death than life, were liberated. Thousands of decomposing corpses, many of them dead in the typhus epidemic that had raged for weeks lay around. Some 37,000 had died since February, more than 9,000 in the two weeks before the liberation of the camp. Another 14,000 were to die from the effects of their suffering in the camp in the following weeks.[102] That

Bergen-Belsen was handed over, not evacuated, was a unique occurrence. The typhus epidemic ruled out evacuation.[103] In all other camps, an attempt was made to remove the prisoners before the camp could be taken by the enemy.

In March, as part of his attempt to reach some arrangement with the Allies, Himmler had ordered that Jews should be treated like other prisoners, informing camp commandants that they were no longer to be killed, and that the death rate among prisoners should be reduced by all possible means.[104] On the last day of March, the commandant of Buchenwald was expecting the camp to be handed over to the Allies. Within less than a week that had diametrically altered. Himmler now ordered the camp's prisoners, where possible, to be sent to Flossenbürg.[105] In this, as an order sent to the commandant of Flossenbürg in mid-April made clear, he reverted to the policy that there could be no question of surrendering concentration camps and that no prisoner should be allowed to fall alive into enemy hands.[106] Hitler's reaction to reports that newly liberated prisoners from Buchenwald had made their way to nearby Weimar and had looted and raped had probably caused the reversion.[107] Himmler now pressed for the swift evacuation of Mittelbau-Dora and Buchenwald. During the night of 4/5 April removal of the Mittelbau prisoners in the direction of the concentration camps in Sachsenhausen, Ravensbrück and Mauthausen began, and ended within forty-eight hours or so.[108]

On 11 April American soldiers reached the camp complex at Mittelbau-Dora, where they found 700 ill and emaciated prisoners, soon afterwards encountering further horrific scenes as they liberated the subsidiary camps. When the Americans arrived in Buchenwald, the largest camp in Germany, on 13 April, an unimaginably gruesome experience, they found around 21,000 prisoners – many little more than walking skeletons – remaining in the camp out of the complement of 48,000 little more than a week earlier. The rest had set out, by rail or on foot, between 7 and 10 April, heading for the concentration camps many kilometres away to the south of Flossenbürg and Dachau, themselves bursting at the seams with swollen numbers of prisoners.[109] These camps, too, and those still remaining at Mauthausen (not far from Linz in Austria), Sachsenhausen (just outside Berlin), Neuengamme (near Hamburg) and Ravensbrück (a women's camp, about 80 kilometres north of Berlin), would evacuate their prisoners capable of marching, under catastrophic circumstances and with no obvious destination, during the second half of April.[110]

The Buchenwald prisoners were among the numerous long columns of bedraggled, gaunt, shrunken figures from the remaining concentration camps now being driven by their merciless guards hundreds of kilometres criss-cross through parts of Germany in disastrous conditions that defy description or obvious rationale. The prisoners were at this stage of the war plainly not of any use as forced labour (even if capable of working). And given the pace of the Allied advance, they would, even if they reached their destinations, obviously fall in the near future into enemy hands. No consideration appears to have been given to the notion of killing all the prisoners in the camps, which, given the speed of the Allied advance, would in any case scarcely have been practicable. But if those removed were eventually going to be killed anyway, there was little logic to the lengthy treks beforehand. Himmler had not, it is true, given up expectation that the prisoners – or the Jews among them – could be used as pawns in some deal with the Allies. As long as they were alive and within his power, they might still serve a purpose in his illusory scheme.

This dubious rationale apart, the death marches were completely pointless, except as a means of inflicting still further enormous suffering on those designated as the regime's internal enemies. But the commandants and the guards treating the prisoners on the marches with such sadistic brutality did not seek any rationale. Their system still functioned – after a fashion. They remained, even in its dissolution, set in the same mentality that had earlier seen them torture prisoners pointlessly or force them to carry out pointless backbreaking labour.[111] Ultimately, by April 1945 the regime just did not know what to do with the hundreds of thousands of prisoners still in its domain. In the gathering chaos of the last weeks, the death marches reflected the futile flailing of a regime on the verge of its own destruction but retaining its murderous capacity to the very end.

As the regime collapsed, decisions on what to do with the prisoners were left increasingly to those guarding them. Only unclear or confused guidelines, though leaving much scope for initiative, came from Himmler and the now faltering concentration camp central administration. Camp commandants were wary of acting prematurely, so gave evacuation orders at the last minute. Max Pauly, commandant of Neuengamme, near Hamburg, told interrogators after the war that in April 1945 he did not know what to do with his prisoners.[112] When the marches set out, the fate of the prisoners was entirely in the hands of their guards – by this time far from all SS men, and including many drawn from the *Volkssturm*. How many were firm believers in Nazi ideology, or even genuine regime loyalists, cannot be known. But all had been in some way 'schooled' in how to deal with the 'enemies of the people'. There was no control over the guards' actions, no sanction for what they did. Their decisions on who should live or die were arbitrary.

Prisoners were dispatched without a thought on a daily basis by guards to whom they were totally anonymous, lacking all identity. One blond-haired SS guard, only about twenty years old, casually shot a thirteen-year-old boy on a march from Sachsenhausen because he could not keep up with the fast pace, almost running speed. In their anger and despair, the boy's elder brother, a Jesuit priest, and his father tried to jump on the SS man, but he simply 'fired a few volleys from his machine gun at them'. 'The machine guns rattled unceasingly' as many prisoners were mowed down in the first two days. When, after a night in a barn, one prisoner refused to continue the march, the same young SS brute simply shot him dead, then a few minutes later turned his gun on the prisoner's distraught brother-in-law who had lagged behind. By now, the blond SS man simply 'pulled out prisoners who, in his opinion, did not walk fast enough and shot them on the spot'.[113]

The guards thought of little besides themselves and their task of delivering their charges at the destination. As long as prisoners were capable of walking, obeying instructions, and serving the needs of their guards – not least keeping them away from the front – they might survive. But any sense that they had become a burden for the guards meant their instant death.[114] Once on the marches, no obvious distinction seems to have been drawn by the guards about the prisoners. All, Jewish or not, were subject to their arbitrary murderous actions.[115]

In some cases, the killings became full-scale massacres. In Celle, 35 kilometres north-east of Hanover, almost 800 prisoners, men and women, fell victim on the night of 8/9 April. The railway wagons transporting them – Russians, Poles and Ukrainians predominantly, some but far from all Jewish – from two satellite camps of Neuengamme at Salzgitter to nearby Bergen-Belsen were caught during a heavy air raid while standing in the station at Celle. Hundreds of prisoners burnt to death while trapped in the wagons.[116] Those who escaped the inferno were able to take flight into the nearby woods. The manhunt rapidly set up to track them down consisted not only of their SS guards, but *Volkssturm* and SA men, local police and Party functionaries, soldiers stationed nearby, members of the Hitler Youth, and also groups of local citizens who spontaneously joined in. When one thirteen-year-old boy enquired about the identity of the prisoners, as shots rang out in the woods, he was told 'they could well be Jews'. The crowd was easily persuaded that the escapees were dangerous criminals and Communists. The mass shooting of probably around 200 prisoners was thus portrayed, and evidently viewed, as self-protection.[117]

Shortly afterwards, between 9 and 11 April, about 3,000–4,000 prisoners, many of them from Mittelbau-Dora heading for Bergen-Belsen, Sachsenhausen and Neuengamme camps, arrived in the village of Mieste, near Gardelegen, about 40 kilometres north of Magdeburg. When damaged tracks prevented their train from continuing, and the prisoners were force-marched to Gardelegen, the local Kreisleiter, Gerhard Thiele, exploiting stories that escaped prisoners had looted and raped in a village not far away and declaring that he would do everything to prevent such an occurrence in his area, made preparations to have them killed. There was great urgency since the Americans were closing in on the town. The SS were aided in the meantime in guarding the prisoners by detachments from the Wehrmacht, Hitler Youth, the *Volkssturm*, the local fire brigade and other organizations. When objections were raised that the site of the cavalry school he had proposed for the killing was too close to the town centre, Thiele came up with the idea of a large barn in an isolated position in a field on the outskirts. On 13 April, more than 1,000 prisoners, Jews among them though predominantly 'politicals', were herded into the barn. Petrol was poured on the straw, the large doors were sealed, and the barn was set alight. Some prisoners trying desperately to escape were shot by the guards. The remainder died in the flames. Next day, the Americans arrived while the attempt was still being made to bury the charcoaled remains of the prisoners.[118]

Unlike the earlier death marches that had left from the camps in the east, the thousands of prisoners who had been in every conceivable way degraded and dehumanized now trekked through Germany itself, before the eyes of the German public. As in Gardelegen, their guards were often a motley bunch. Most were drawn from the SS and were well armed and often accompanied by dogs which they did not hesitate to turn on the prisoners. But a march from Ravensbrück in mid-April was guarded only by lightly armed 'older men', thought to be auxiliary police. Others had guards composed of SA men or ethnic Germans from different parts of eastern Europe.[119]

Beatings and shootings of prisoners also took place before the eyes of the public, with no attempt to hide them. The hostile stance of the German population dominates the recollections of the victims, thankful though those doubtless were who benefited momentarily from any sign of human kindness. Post-war German accounts, on the other hand, had good reason to emphasize sympathy for the prisoners and condemnation of the crimes of the SS guards.

Acts of solidarity, friendship or support from bystanders seem at any rate to have been relatively rare. Years of demonization of Jews and indoctrination in racial stereotypes, along with the stoked-up fear of the 'people's enemies' – reinforced through lurid radio reports of former Buchenwald prisoners rampaging and marauding through Weimar, and similar stories used to justify the massacre at Gardelegen – had clearly not been without their baleful effect. However much Germans saw themselves, increasingly, as victims of Hitler and the Nazi regime, many of them were not ready to extend their sympathies to concentration camp prisoners, least of all Jews, or to embrace the true victims of Nazism as part of their 'community'. The human wrecks before their eyes looked like the caricatures of 'subhumans' rammed home in incessant propaganda. But in all their evident frailty, they were still, perversely, seen by many as a threat. 'What crimes they must have committed to be treated so cruelly,' was one comment. Another person, justifying the shooting by Wehrmacht soldiers of thirteen escaped prisoners (recaptured with help of the local population), remarked: 'They were political prisoners and mere criminals.'[120] Survivors of the marches recounted, depressingly but unsurprisingly, numerous cases where they had been insulted, jeered at, spat at, had had stones thrown at them, or were refused food and drink by local inhabitants. In some cases, German civilians, as at Celle, aided guards to capture prisoners who had escaped, and apparently participated in the killing.[121]

Alongside the horrific instances of callous support for murderous action, there were, nevertheless, indications that some civilians, even if they were the exceptions, tried to give food or succour to the prisoners passing through their villages. A British report on the massacre at Celle stated that numerous citizens tried, in the face of threats and abuse from the perpetrators, to aid the prisoners by giving them first aid or comforting them.[122] Around 1,250 weak and starving prisoners who arrived in Hütten in Württemberg at the beginning of April were said to have been given food by some local families. The local mayor apparently succeeded in bringing in some supplies for the prisoners and appealed to the Wehrmacht for help. A Wehrmacht officer and veteran of the First World War, called to the scene, then organized a meal for around 200 sick prisoners who remained after the others had been marched off. He also ordered the dead to be properly buried.[123]

In Altendorf, a village in the Upper Palatinate where 650 prisoners stopped on the night of 21/2 April on their trek from Buchenwald to Dachau, thirteen prisoners who hid in a barn were hunted down by their SS guards with dogs and pitchforks. Twelve were caught and immediately shot. The thirteenth, a Pole, was able to escape when the head of the local constabulary chose not to hand him over to the SS and allowed him to be fed before he disappeared. The dead victims were then buried by *Volkssturm* men in a mass grave in the cemetery, in contrast to many instances when local inhabitants elsewhere rapidly dug improvised graves where the prisoners had been killed, or simply pushed the corpses into a roadside ditch and covered them over.[124] The examples could be multiplied of inhabitants recalling feelings of shock and shame at the beatings and shootings that they witnessed, of providing prisoners with food and drink (not just when the guards simply requisitioned it), or, more rarely, of assisting escape or not betraying hiding-places.[125]

Most people, however, it seems reasonable to surmise, simply remained passive – not participating, but also showing no opposition – as the maltreatment and murder occurred beneath their gaze. The bystanders' own fear of the reactions of the guards to support for the prisoners understandably played a part. With the war so close to its end, few were ready to invite retribution, least of all in the cause of prisoners whose guilt was for the most part taken for granted. But some evidently did risk retribution through signs of sympathy for the prisoners. Fear could not, therefore, have been the sole cause of the prevalent passivity. Even so, it was probably less the case that 'broad social support . . . was given to the killing'[126] than that few were prepared to risk their own well-being by acting against guards ruthlessly wielding power in attempting humanitarian gestures which, they felt, would change nothing towards people with whom they could not identify. That was enough to make them accomplices to murder. The passivity allowed the killing to continue until the guards fled on the approach of the enemy and the prisoners were liberated not by Germans themselves, but by their conquerors.

VII

In the Berlin bunker on 20 April the Nazi grandees, having congratulated Hitler on his birthday, avowed their lasting loyalty and said what for most of them would be their final farewells, were chafing at the bit to depart before the roads out of the capital became blocked. Goebbels apart, hardly any were anxious to join their Leader on the funeral pyre. Whatever their long-standing rhetoric about fighting or dying, when it came down to it they thought predominantly about saving their own skins. Göring's copious belongings were packed and on their way to Berchtesgaden. He had sent his wife and family to relative safety there some weeks earlier. His ranch at Carinhall, north of Berlin, was now deserted and waiting to be detonated. A few weeks later he was telling Allied interrogators that until late in the day he had thought Germany might be able to fight to a stalemate.[127] Now he was off – to await an uncertain end, but certainly not self-immolation in the Berlin catacombs.

Speer headed north to Hamburg, though he felt he had not properly said goodbye to the man who had dominated his life for more than a decade, and with whom even now he could not completely break the ties which had bound them together. To remedy this he was to make an arduous (and pointless) fleeting return to the bunker on 23 April. Perhaps he was even now thinking that, once the end had come, all might not be lost for him, and hoped that Hitler would anoint him as his successor.[128] To Speer's dismay, Hitler could scarcely bring himself to offer more than a perfunctory goodbye.[129]

Himmler was also on his way north, and set to continue his clandestine dealings with Count Bernadotte in the hope of extracting something out of the disaster for himself even at the end. In his desperation he was even willing to meet a prominent member of the Jewish World Congress and to agree to the release of female Jews from Ravensbrück concentration camp. He was also ready to make a promise he could not have kept even had he wanted to – that no more Jews would be killed. He had ordered the SS to fight to the last, and never to capitulate.[130] He himself was contemplating doing precisely the opposite of what he had preached.

Bormann, the *éminence grise* of the regime, must have been aware by now that his leadership of the Party Chancellery had become little more than an empty title. Few Gauleiter were even in a position to receive his directives. He could not leave the bunker. That was clear. But once Hitler was dead, which could not be far off, he had every intention of escaping both his own demise and the clutches of the Russians.

Goebbels, the last of the quartet who, beneath Hitler, had dominated internal politics in the last months and ensured that the regime continued to operate until the end, had, whatever his public rhetoric and notwithstanding his private flights of fantasy, clearly seen what was coming for quite some time. He continued to do all he could to help in the fight to fend off the Soviets. Even on Hitler's birthday, he laid on Berlin buses to carry soldiers out to the Oder front.[131] But he knew it would be in vain. By then he had had his personal belongings destroyed. The originals of the diaries he had diligently kept for over twenty years were among them. However, he ensured that this daily record of his role alongside Hitler in Germany's lost but 'heroic' fight – what he saw as his lasting legacy for future generations – would be preserved for posterity by sending out three copies into hiding.[132] He and his wife Magda then made ready to move into the Führer Bunker to join Hitler. They knew that in doing so they were taking the decision to end their lives. They had already decided to kill their six children.[133]

By next morning, 21 April, the government district in the heart of Berlin was being shelled. There was a rumble like distant thunder, but unceasing and growing louder by the hour.[134] The Soviets were now only about 12 kilometres away to the east. As the encirclement of the city advanced, a unit of the Red Army liberated some 3,000 prisoners – mainly sick women and children – left behind in Sachsenhausen concentration camp when most of the prisoners had been marched off on 20 April.[135] By 24 April Busse's 9th Army was caught in a tightening Soviet vice. Colonel-General Heinrici's warnings of this fate had been ignored by Hitler and his military advisers.[136] Heinrici would eventually have the dubious distinction of being the last of Hitler's generals to be dismissed, on the night of 28/9 April, when he finally refused to carry out an utterly impossible order from Keitel and Jodl.[137] By then his army was breaking up in a westward stampede of soldiers desperate to avoid Soviet captivity. The constant interference in his command by unrealistic orders had ultimately proved too much for him. But there was also a personal grievance: he felt deeply insulted at the way Keitel and Jodl had treated him, 'unworthy', he thought, of the manner in which the commander-in-chief of an Army Group should be addressed and 'unbearable' for an officer with forty years of service behind him.[138]

Heinrici's stance even in these last days, and that of Field-Marshal Keitel and General Jodl, said much about Hitler's generals. When Heinrici objected to Keitel and Jodl about the minimal prospects of the slightest success in what his Army Group Vistula was expected to undertake, he was simply told it was his duty to rescue the Führer. Hitler's main advisers, he felt, either could not or would not accept the true situation and realize that the battle of Berlin was lost. But Heinrici did not offer his resignation. Instead, as he stated in a description of the battle he compiled less than a month later, 'the bond of my duty of obedience as a soldier, the impossibility of rejecting orders to save the Supreme Commander of the Wehrmacht' meant that he felt unable to refuse 'without committing treason'. 'After the OKW had placed "the saving of the Führer" at the head of all orders, this took precedence over other military considerations.'

For Keitel, however, even Hitler's death would not prevent the continuation of the struggle. If Berlin could not be saved, he suggested to Heinrici, the Army Group should carry on the fight in northern Germany. Heinrici retorted that this was neither economically nor militarily possible. 'The will to fight on the part of the soldiers was already falling sharply and would collapse altogether with the news of the death of the Führer.' Keitel answered that this news would therefore have to be delayed as long as possible. Further resistance was necessary in order to enter negotiations with the western enemies. Germany still possessed numerous bargaining counters, such as Denmark, Norway and Bohemia, that would serve as a good basis for negotiation. Heinrici thought Keitel was completely detached from reality, though his awareness of the preparations being made by Dönitz in Plön, in line with Hitler's orders, to continue the fight in the northern half of the country as long as possible made him take the proposition seriously.[139]

On 25 April the Reich was cut in two as American and Soviet troops met at Torgau, on the Elbe. By noon that day Berlin was completely encircled. The city centre now came under increasingly heavy artillery bombardment. Berlin had been declared a fortress, to be defended to the last. The forces to do so were weak indeed, compared with the Soviet behemoth. But Dönitz was among the military leaders who took the view that the battle for Berlin was necessary whatever the cost to the civilian population since they would otherwise be deported to Russia without any attempt to prevent their undergoing such a fate.[140] As it was, civilians had to experience the misery, suffering and death that accompanied the relentless destruction of their city. Soviet troops had to fight their way practically block by block. But amid intense and bitter street-fighting they pressed inexorably on towards the epicentre of Nazi rule in the Reich Chancellery.[141] They knew Hitler was there.

A combination of near hysteria and outright fatalism had by then caught hold in the bunker. Hitler had placed illusory hopes, not defused by Keitel and Jodl, who knew better but were still fearful of giving him bad news,[142] in the newly and hastily constituted 12th Army under General Walther Wenck, fighting on the Elbe, and, especially, in a counter-offensive to the north of Berlin led by SS-Obergruppenführer Felix Steiner's panzer corps. When he had learnt, on 22 April, that Steiner's attack had not taken place,[143] the pent-up feelings had exploded in a torrential outburst of elemental fury. Hitler admitted openly for the first time that the war was lost. He told his shocked entourage that he was determined to stay in Berlin and take his life at the last moment. He seemed to be abdicating power and responsibility, saying he had no further orders for the Wehrmacht. He even implied that Göring might have to negotiate with the enemy.[144] But, astonishingly, he had pulled himself together again, refused to concede a grain of his authority, and exuded as always undiluted optimism in his military briefing just moments after speaking privately about his imminent death and the burning of his body.[145] The act, which had slipped for a brief moment, was back in place.

Keitel was sent to Wenck's headquarters with orders – totally unfeasible, but temporarily cheering up Hitler once more – to march on Berlin. The High Command of the Wehrmacht was now split between Krampnitz, near Potsdam (later moving north, until finally based with Dönitz in Plön), and Berchtesgaden. Despite the despairing outburst during his temporary breakdown, Hitler was still in no mood to relinquish control. Göring learnt this when, mistaking the information he had received about Hitler's eruption as denoting incapacity or unwillingness to lead any longer and assuming, therefore, that on the basis of the long-standing succession law he should take over, he was peremptorily dismissed from all his offices and put under house arrest at the Berghof. Bormann, an arch-enemy for years of the Reich Marshal, could savour a last triumph.

Even now the generals in charge of Berlin's defence would not contemplate capitulation. When General Kurt von Tippelskirch arrived on 27 April to take over the 21st Army, hastily put together from whatever units could be found, he had a long conversation with Heinrici, with whom he had served in Russia, about the position of Army Group Vistula. They acknowledged that every day brought further immense destruction to what remained of the Reich. Only capitulation could prevent it. Yet such a decision was still impossible, Tippelskirch argued. It would mean acting against the will of the Führer (and Jodl had recently emphasized that negotiations were impossible as long as Hitler lived).[146] Moreover, an attempt to capitulate would be unsuccessful. The mass of the soldiers would refuse to obey orders to hand themselves over 'and start on the road to Siberia', and would seek to find their own way home. The enemy would then claim the conditions of capitulation had not been met. The war would continue. So would the destruction of the land. The soldiers would be taken prisoner anyway. No good would, therefore, have been served. But 'the Army Group would bear the disgrace of capitulation and desertion of the Führer'. 'The fight must therefore go on, with the aim of bringing the armies gradually so far to the west that ultimately they would fall not into Russian but into Anglo-American captivity.'[147] In this reasoning, plainly, the interests of the army exceeded all other concerns.

Away from the madhouse in the bunker, the remnants of government were in terminal disarray. Most ministerial staffs (with the big exception of the Propaganda Ministry) had been relocated to southern Germany, beginning in March, leaving no more than skeletal arrangements in Berlin. A number of ministers and their staffs had followed in April, welcoming the opportunity to leave. Berlin was now a government capital without government apparatus. The head of the Reich Chancellery, Hans-Heinrich Lammers, had left for Berchtesgaden at the end of March. He went on leave, claiming high blood pressure. In fact, he had suffered a severe nervous breakdown. He had for long served little real purpose. The Reich Chancellery's function had since the previous summer been hardly more than residual, as its powers had drained off to Bormann in the Party Chancellery. In its last days, its acting head was the State Secretary, Friedrich Wilhelm Kritzinger, who was left with the purely theoretical task of coordinating the other ministries and the remainder of the Reich Chancellery civil servants from Berlin. Asked after the end of the war why he had not resigned, Kritzinger seemed scarcely to understand the question. 'As a long-standing civil servant I was duty-bound in loyalty to the state,' he answered, expressing shame at its policies towards Jews and Poles. (Even on the morning of 21 April, as Soviet rockets exploded in the government district of Berlin, civil servants continued to 'work' – doing nothing useful – at their desks.[148]) When asked further why Lammers continued to do all he could for the war effort, Kritzinger replied: 'Well, there had to be some sort of organization. Think just of food for the people. That functioned to the end.' 'Would it have been better had it not functioned to the end?' his interrogator retorted. 'It was war,' shrugged Kritzinger.[149]

On the evening of 20 April Kritzinger gave instructions to the ministerial staffs still in Berlin to leave with all haste for the south by road. That proved impossible. A new order was given to leave next day by air. Not enough planes were available. It was then suggested that they should go to the north instead. Exasperated by now, the Finance Minister, Graf Schwerin von Krosigk, who in previous weeks had pressed Goebbels and Speer to take action that would pave the way for the western Allies to come to terms,[150] demanded a clear order of the Führer, saying he had no intention of being hanged en route by the SS as a deserter. When, after much trying, Kritzinger managed through Bormann to obtain a 'recommendation' from Hitler for the ministers to head north, it was not enough for Krosigk. He now insisted on a written Führer order. Eventually, Kritzinger succeeded in persuading Bormann to get Hitler, for whom this was scarcely the highest priority at the moment, to sign a written order to head for Eutin, far to the north in Schleswig-Holstein. Amid such panicky improvisation, the ministers of a Reich with a long and proud tradition of state service fled the capital and a head of state set on self-destruction.

With Hitler's earlier orders to split the Reich into northern and southern sectors coming into effect, there were by now effectively six centres of government in Germany: Hitler in his Berlin bunker, his authority real and unchallenged – where it could still reach; the High Command of the Wehrmacht, itself now divided between Krampnitz and Berchtesgaden; parts of the Reich cabinet based in the south and the remainder in the north under Dönitz; Göring still presided (until ousted by Hitler on 23 April) over his own remaining Luftwaffe command in Berchtesgaden; while Himmler had what was left of his SS and police power-base in the Lübeck area in the north.[151] There was no semblance any longer of a central government of the Reich.

In the provinces, too, or what was left of them under German control, the regime was also imploding – accompanied, inevitably, by untrammelled violence in its very last days. On 20 April the Gau administration in Augsburg was told that the banks would run out of money within a week. Wages and salaries could then no longer be paid. No banknotes had been received from the Reichsbank for a week. The Bavarian Finance Ministry was printing money, but it would not be ready for eight to ten days, and it was itself awaiting a transport of 300 million Reich Marks from Berlin, after which Swabia would be allocated its share.[152] Whether that happened is unclear, but Swabia had not much longer to limp on before Augsburg was surrendered to the Americans on 28 April.

Near chaos was reported in late April by the Kreisleiter in the small town of Lindau, on the Bodensee at the western tip of Bavaria close to the Swiss border. Drunken German soldiers were rampaging through the streets and looting property. Huge numbers of refugees and deserters had poured into the town. The Kreisleiter sought permission to restore order by having the first hundred seized and shot. Permission, mercifully, does not appear to have been granted. Lindau survived a few more days before surrendering on 2 May.[153]

Violence also preceded the capitulation without a fight of Regensburg, the capital of the Upper Palatinate. The tone was set by Gauleiter Ruckdeschel, who had engineered Gauleiter Wächtler's execution. Ruckdeschel and the Nazi leadership in the city were determined to fight on. In a tense meeting in the city's velodrome on the evening of 22 April, called by the Kreisleiter, Ruckdeschel declared that the city would be 'defended to the last stone'. His speech, broadcast locally, merely succeeded in stirring up fear and dismay. The Americans were only a short distance away, and few people were prepared to go down in flames as the enemy took the town. Next morning some women started going round shops, spreading the word that there was to be another meeting that evening in Moltkeplatz, in the city centre, to demand that Regensburg be handed over to the Allies without a fight. Nearly a thousand people, many of them women with children, turned out. As the crowd started to become restless, it was addressed by a prominent member of the cathedral chapter, Domprediger Dr Johann Maier, who, however, was able to say only a few words before he and several others were arrested.

When Ruckdeschel heard what had happened, he ordered that Maier and the other 'ringleaders' be hanged. A rapidly summoned drumhead court lost no time in pronouncing the death sentence on Maier and a seventy-year-old warehouse worker, Joseph Zirkl. They were hanged in Moltkeplatz in the early hours of 24 April. The terror apparatus had still functioned. But with the Americans on the doorstep, the town's military commandant, its head of regional government, the Kreisleiter and the head of police suddenly vanished into the night. Gauleiter Ruckdeschel had also disappeared. The way was all at once clear for emissaries to hand over the city on 27 April, still largely undamaged by the war.[154]

In other parts of Bavaria, too, representatives of the regime were determined to leave the scene with shows of vengeful last-minute murderous violence, as futile as they were horrific. The Nazis, as they knew, were on the way out. But their capacity for taking violent revenge on their political opponents continued. The murder of more than forty people in different parts of the region, with the Americans in some cases only hours away, was prompted by the proclamation over a captured radio transmitter on the outskirts of Munich on the morning of 28 April of the 'Freedom Action of Bavaria', a courageous but ultimately counterproductive localized rising against the Nazi regime in its final days. The 'Action' was led by three officers in locally stationed Wehrmacht units, Captain Rupprecht Gerngroß, Major Alois Braun and Lieutenant Otto-heinz Leiling. It aimed at impressing the Allies that in Bavaria at least the Nazi regime did not represent the only face of Germany, and sought to achieve the restoration of traditional Bavarian values in the rebuilding of the province. It was unquestionably a brave mistake at this juncture. In encouraging long-standing opponents of the regime in a number of Bavarian towns and villages to open shows of defiance, it was unwittingly signing their death warrant. There was little to be achieved militarily or politically by the rising. Villages, towns and cities were in most cases being handed over through often bold manoeuvring at the appropriate moment by those on the spot. It was inconceivable that an attempted rising, planned and executed in little more than amateurish fashion, could bring an immediate end to the fighting in Bavaria. Instead, it merely served as a provocation for local Nazis still wielding power to take murderous revenge on their opponents, in the process settling some long-standing vendettas.

The Gauleiter of Munich-Upper Bavaria, Paul Giesler, now a cornered fanatic, was behind the worst of the violence. Five men in Munich were taken out on his orders and shot. In Altötting, a Catholic pilgrimage centre, the Kreisleiter led an SS squad which shot five people – local opponents for many years – on a list he had rapidly drawn up. When his hit-squad reported the execution of another three in neighbouring Burghausen, he shouted 'What, only three?' The worst outrage was in the small mining town of Penzberg, somewhat incongruously situated in beautiful Alpine scenery between Munich and Garmisch-Partenkirchen. Local Nazi leaders wanted to blow up the coal mine, heart of the town's economic life, and the waterworks and bridges in the vicinity. To block the destruction, former Social Democrats and Communists participated in an attempt to take over the coal mine and depose the Nazi town leadership. It was not long, however, before the officer of a nearby Wehrmacht unit had the leaders of the revolt, including the former SPD mayor, arrested. With the deposed Nazi mayor, he then drove to Munich, where Gauleiter Giesler peremptorily gave orders that they were to be shot immediately, without trial. On return to Penzberg, about 6 p.m., the sentences for treason were read out and the executions of the seven prisoners were promptly carried out. A Werwolf squad, around 100 strong, given the task by Giesler of dealing with the 'politically unreliable', meanwhile hastened down to Penzberg and that evening hanged a further eight people, among them two women, at different points of the town, placing notices round their necks declaring that they were traitors and in the service of the enemy. The next day, the Americans arrived.[155]

In Berlin, hardly any people were aware of the subterranean drama in the bunker. They had far more pressing things on their minds. They desperately wanted peace – 'an end with horror rather than a horror without end', as the well-worn phrase had it. They had equally desperately wanted the Americans to get to Berlin before the Russians.[156] Even that hope had disappeared. All that was left was fear of what was coming and the desire to survive. The streets were empty, apart from some queues of people outside shops trying to buy the food they needed for a long siege.[157] Most were by now living in cellars 'like woodlice, creeping into the farthest corners',[158] constantly hungry as rations dwindled, without heating because of coal shortages, with little or no gas or electricity, having to stand in long queues to collect water in buckets from street pumps. People had the feeling that they were no longer governed. 'No orders any more, no news, nothing. No swine is bothered about us,' as one woman expressed it.[159] Without electricity, few by now could receive news by radio. As even the last of the two-page broadsheets that passed for newspapers disappeared, they had to rely upon word of mouth to glean fragments of often inaccurate information.[160] At least they were spared the headlines of the *Völkischer Beobachter*, still printed in Munich until 28 April and proclaiming in its headlines that 'Germany Stands Firm and Loyal to the Führer', 'The Führer – Defender of Berlin', or 'The Führer Inflames Berlin's Fighting Spirit'.[161] Anyone expressing such sentiments on the streets of Berlin was thought to be mad. But bodies hanging with notices round their necks proclaiming them to have been 'traitors' were a warning not to speak out recklessly, and still to take extreme care of those still standing behind the fatally wounded regime.[162]

As long as the roads out of Berlin had remained open, thousands – many of them pale, worn-out women and their exhausted children – tried to escape to the west, on foot, in horse-drawn wagons, pushing wheelbarrows and prams containing remnants of their last few possessions.[163] Then the last escape routes were shut off. There was now nothing to do but wait in dread in cellars, wanting the end but fearing what it meant.[164] In the last week of April, the worst fears of many Berliners started to be realized as soldiers of the Red Army arrived.

In the bunker, too, the end was near. The final act in the drama had begun. The regime's ruthlessness in its own death-agonies struck home within the small bunker community itself when Eva Braun's brother-in-law, the dissolute and brutal Hermann Fegelein, an SS leader close to

Himmler, tried to flee and, after being dragged back was summarily sentenced to death and executed. Fegelein was no more than a substitute for the real arch-traitor in Hitler's eyes in the last days of his life: Heinrich Himmler. The Reichsführer-SS had, it seems, like Göring, taken news of Hitler's outburst on 22 April as an effective abdication. He had finally cast off the caution which had dogged him throughout his dealings with Bernadotte and offered to capitulate in the west (though not in the east). This, for Hitler, was the ultimate betrayal. In his last volcanic explosion of rage, he had Himmler, too, thrown out of the Party and ordered his arrest.[165] But his reach no longer stretched far enough to have the Reichsführer-SS, in the north of the country, brought back to Berlin and subjected to a final disgrace and fearsome execution.

With Himmler's betrayal, it seemed as if the fight had gone out of Hitler. In the last act of the drama, he married Eva Braun, his partner of many years, who had decided to end her life alongside him, and drew up his Testament. In its political section it included the names of the ministers in the successor government. Dönitz, his fanatical support throughout recognized – also in sending sailors to fight in Berlin's last battle – was to become Reich President. Goebbels, Bormann, Hanke, Saur, Giesler and Schörner, diehards all of them, were rewarded for their loyalty and zealotry. There was no place for Speer. The task done, and the Soviets almost literally at the gates, all that was left was for Hitler and Eva Braun to make the last preparations to commit suicide. In the mid-afternoon of 30 April, Hitler shot himself and Eva Braun took poison. Dönitz, up in Plön in Schleswig-Holstein, did not learn of Hitler's death until next morning – not long after he had sent a message, presuming him to be still alive, professing his continued unconditional loyalty. The Wehrmacht and the German people – those who were listening – were not informed until the late evening of 1 May that Hitler had fallen 'at the head of the heroic defenders of the Reich capital', a propaganda lie to the last.[166] Joseph and Magda Goebbels had committed suicide that day, after poisoning their six children. The following day, 2 May, the German troops in Berlin were ordered to cease fighting. The Soviet 'hammer and sickle' flag fluttered from the Reichstag.

The war was still not over. Outside Berlin, fighting continued. But with Hitler's death, the insuperable obstacle to capitulation was removed. What had been impossible as long as he was alive became immediately realizable as soon as he was dead. Nothing demonstrates more plainly the extent to which he personally had held together the regime. The bonds with his 'charismatic community' and the fragmented structures of rule that had existed throughout the Third Reich and guaranteed his own unchallengeable power had allowed it, at terrible cost to the German people, to continue to operate until the Russians were at the very portals of the Reich Chancellery.

9

Liquidation

*Since the western enemies continue their support of the Soviets,
the fight against the Anglo-Americans according to the order of
the Grand-Admiral carries on.*

Head of naval operations staff, 4 May 1945

I

Only two or three years earlier, Hitler's death would have stunned the nation. Before the invasion of the Soviet Union plunged Germany into a long, attritional and ultimately unwinnable war, the sense of loss would have been immeasurable in every corner of the country. The reactions to Stauffenberg's assassination attempt in July 1944 show that even then, if Hitler had been killed, the shock waves would have been enormous. By the evening of 1 May 1945, however, when the news of Hitler's death was broadcast, few tears were shed.

There were of course exceptions. The crew of a minesweeper were said to have been close to tears when they heard the announcement, seeing it as the 'final heroic tones' of a long war.[1] An NCO based near Prague recorded the lengthy silence and feelings of dismay that greeted the news in his unit, noting that the death of the Führer was regarded positively as a 'heroic gesture' by the soldiers – 'at least by the majority', he added.[2] Whether the assessment was accurate cannot be known. It is equally impossible to ascertain the common reaction among the soldiers to the proclamation issued on 3 May by the most Nazified of all generals, Field-Marshal Schörner, to his Army Group Centre, largely located now in Bohemia. Schörner described Hitler as 'a martyr to his idea and his belief and as a soldier of the European mission' who had died fighting

348

against Bolshevism 'to his last breath'.[3] Probably, it seems fair to surmise, most soldiers, wherever they were based, were concerned less with the death of the Führer than with their own struggle to escape falling into the clutches of the Red Army.

There were indeed some fanatical supporters of Hitler in every military unit to the end, though usually by now in a minority. One officer recalled how, hearing the news that the Führer had 'fallen', a single young soldier leapt to his feet, raised his arm and shouted 'Heil Hitler', while the others carried on eating their soup as if nothing had happened.[4] There must have been a spectrum of emotions at the news among generals, ranging from relief to sorrow, mingled with a sense of the inevitable. 'Führer fallen! Terrible, and yet expected,' noted one former front commander, Colonel-General Georg-Hans Reinhardt, in his diary.[5] When a small group of senior officers, gathered at the field headquarters of the 3rd Panzer Army in Mecklenburg, heard the announcement, there was no sign that any of them was moved.[6] Even among senior officers in British captivity, divided opinions on Hitler were voiced when they heard of his death. 'A tragic personality, surrounded by an incompetent circle of criminals', 'a historical figure' whose achievements would only be recognized in a future age, summarized the overall view, as they debated whether, having sworn an oath of allegiance to him personally, they were now freed from their military oath.[7]

Among the civilian population, most Germans were too preoccupied with fending off hunger, eking out an existence in the ruins of their homes, avoiding marauding Soviet soldiers, or piecing together broken lives under enemy occupation to pay much attention to the demise of the Führer.[8] A mother in Celle was concerned with a practical issue: whether her children should still greet people with 'Heil Hitler' now that he was dead. 'I told them, they could continue to say "Heil Hitler" because Hitler remained the Führer to the last,' was her judgement. 'But if that seems odd to them, they should say "good day" or "good morning".'[9] In Göttingen, which had been in Allied hands for three weeks, a woman observed that those who had effusively cheered Hitler a few years earlier now scarcely noticed his end. No one mourned him.[10] 'Hitler is dead and we – we act as if it's of no concern to us, as if it's a matter of the most indifferent person in the world,' wrote a woman in Berlin, a long-standing opponent of National Socialism. 'What has changed? Nothing! Except, that we have forgotten Herr Hitler during the inferno of the last days.'[11]

Increasing numbers had come to realize in the last months of the war that Hitler, more than anyone, had been responsible for the misery that had afflicted them. 'A pity that Hitler hasn't been sent to Siberia,' one woman in Hamburg wrote. 'But the swine was so cowardly as to put a bullet through his head instead.'[12] 'Criminals and gamblers have led us, and we have let them lead us like sheep to the slaughter,' was the view of one young woman in Berlin, exposed to the tender mercies of Red Army soldiers and not yet aware of Hitler's death. 'Now hatred is blazing in the wretched mass of the people. "No tree is high enough for him," it was said this morning at the water-pump about Adolf.'[13] The earlier idolization, the personalized attribution to Hitler of praise and adulation for all that had seemed at one time positive and successful in the Third Reich was already being transformed into demonization of the man on whom all blame for what had gone wrong could be focused.

For ordinary people, concerned only with getting through the misery, Hitler's death on the face of it changed nothing. The same was true for soldiers in their billets or still serving on the front, and for naval and Luftwaffe crews, some of whom had been drafted into the increasingly desperate fight on land. Indeed, as Grand-Admiral Dönitz took up the reins of office as President of the German Reich, continuity rather than a break with the immediate past seemed on the surface the order of the day. Nevertheless, a fundamental change had actually taken place. It was as if a bankrupt organization had, with the departure of a managing director who refused point-blank to accept realities, been placed in administration, left with the mere task of winding up orders and the process of liquidation.

With Hitler gone, the chief and unyielding barrier to capitulation was removed. When Bormann's wireless message had informed Dönitz at 6.35 p.m. on 30 April that Hitler had named him as his successor, there was no indication that the Dictator was by then dead. Dönitz had, however, been given immediate full powers to take whatever steps were needed in the current situation.[14] He felt an enormous sense of relief that he could act, immediately summoning Keitel, Jodl and Himmler to discuss the situation.[15] But remaining unsure, Dönitz telegraphed the bunker in the early hours of 1 May – a telegraph left unmentioned in his memoirs – to profess his unconditional loyalty to the Führer he presumed still alive, declaring his intention to do all possible (while knowing it to be a futile aim)[16] to get him out of Berlin and declaring, ambiguously, that he would 'bring this war to an end as the unique heroic struggle of the German people demands'.[17] Only later that morning did Dönitz receive Bormann's message that the Testament was in force. On this clear news of Hitler's death, Dönitz now felt finally that his hands were free.[18]

As long as Hitler had lived, Dönitz had seen himself bound to him as head of state and supreme commander of the Wehrmacht by his oath of military obedience, which the Grand-Admiral saw, like most of his generation who had been schooled as officers, as a sacred commitment. Beyond that, he had totally accepted – as had most leading figures in the military – the 'leadership principle' (*Führerprinzip*) that had been the basis of Hitler's authority in the Party, then in the state and in his military command, throughout the Third Reich.[19] He had consequently, and consistent with his unbending principles, refused all considerations of capitulation and upheld the fanatical continuation of the struggle as long as Hitler was alive. Immediately that he knew Hitler was dead, however, he felt in a position to contemplate a negotiated end to a lost war.[20] There could be no plainer illustration of the absolute centrality to the catastrophic continuation of the war not just of the person of the Führer, but of the structures of rule and mentalities that underpinned Hitler's domination.

Even now there was a process of liquidation of the war, not an immediate end. Dönitz's proclaimed aim, on 1 May, 'to rescue the German people from destruction through Bolshevism', denoted an attempt to give meaning to the continued fight in the east while looking to a negotiated end in the west.[21] All at once, therefore, the question of capitulation – though not in the east – was a real and urgent one. Could general capitulation be avoided, even now? Could the western powers, even at this stage, through partial capitulations, be persuaded to join forces with the Wehrmacht to fight Bolshevism? Could some terms favourable to sustaining the Reich as a political unity be attained? Could a deal be struck that would save the German troops on the eastern front from Soviet captivity? The end was plainly imminent. But whereas Hitler had ruled out capitulation totally and was prepared to take everything into the abyss with him, the new Dönitz administration concerned itself from the beginning with the type of surrender that, it thought, could potentially be negotiated and still stave off the worst – submission to Bolshevism. And whereas Hitler, at least until the visibly crumbling days before his death, had been able to depend upon residual loyalties backed by a high dosage of terror and repression to hold the fading regime together, Dönitz could rely upon neither personal standing nor the backing of a mass Party or huge police apparatus, and was left with little at his disposal beyond the shrinking framework of military leadership, a restricted intelligence network and the residues of ministerial bureaucracy. 'Who is this Herr Dönitz?', General of the Waffen-SS, Obergruppenführer Felix Steiner contemptuously asked on hearing that the Grand-Admiral was to be the new head of state. 'My forces and I are not bound by oath to him. I will negotiate on my own footing with the English at my rear.'[22]

Of the quartet beneath Hitler – and leaving aside military leadership – on whom the governance of the Reich since the previous July had heavily rested, only Speer, though omitted from Hitler's ministerial list in favour of his arch-rival Saur, was retained in the Dönitz administration. As Economics Minister, he was, however, in charge of little but economic ruins. Goebbels, the designated Reich Chancellor in the ministerial list drawn up by Hitler, was alone among the quadrumvirate in acting in accord with the Führer's imperative of going down with the Reich in a 'heroic' end. And even Goebbels had entertained the prospect of a localized capitulation after Hitler's death, committing suicide after trying and failing, together with Bormann, to negotiate an arrangement with Marshal Zhukov in Berlin. Bormann, the nominated Party Minister, was disinclined – like most others in Hitler's entourage – to end his life in a Berlin catacomb and fled from the bunker as soon as he could, supposedly on his way to join Dönitz in Plön. He managed to go only a short distance from the ruins of the Reich Chancellery before swallowing a poison capsule to end his life in the early hours of 2 May to avoid capture by the Soviets. Himmler, in disgrace after being stripped by Hitler of all his powers following his 'treachery', was initially hopeful of finding a position under Dönitz and playing a prominent role in the coming combined struggle against Bolshevism of the western powers in unison with the Reich, but was refused office in the new administration.

Dönitz, as previous chapters have indicated, had proved himself one of the most fanatical Wehrmacht commanders in his backing of Hitler's determination to fight on to the last. 'I know you don't believe me, but I must again tell you my innermost conviction,' he informed a colleague in March. 'The Führer is always right.'[23] His unswerving loyalty to

Hitler had earned him the appellation 'Hitler Youth Quex', named after the 'hero' of the well-known propaganda film.[24] A sign of his undiluted support had been to dispatch more than 10,000 sailors, equipped only with light arms, to Berlin on 25 April to serve in the futile struggle for the Reich capital.[25] By then, Dönitz was already acting as Hitler's delegate, with plenipotentiary powers over Party and state (though not over the Wehrmacht in its entirety) in northern Germany. At Himmler's 'treachery' at the end of April, Dönitz was relied upon by Hitler to act 'with lightning speed and hardness of steel against all traitors in the north German area, without exception'.[26] Hitler, who had long regarded most army generals with little more than contempt, valued Dönitz highly and acknowledged his unwavering support by singling out the navy for praise in its sense of honour, refusal to surrender and fulfilment of duty unto death when composing his Testament.[27] Hitler's nomination of Dönitz to be his successor as head of state – though with the reconstituted title of Reich President, in abeyance since 1934, and not Führer – did not, then, come to those in high positions in the regime as the surprise that it was to those further from the centre of power, or that it might appear to be in distant retrospect.[28]

In any case, Hitler was short of options. Göring, the designated successor for more than a decade and, until his disgrace, Commander-in-Chief of the Luftwaffe, had been dismissed from all his offices following his 'betrayal' on 23 April and was in Berchtesgaden under house arrest. Whether he could have commanded authority over all the armed forces is in any case by this time extremely doubtful. Himmler's only significant experience of military command had been as chief of the Replacement Army since July 1944 and then, in early 1945, a sobering one as a brief and unsuccessful Commander-in-Chief of Army Group Vistula. He had also been peremptorily dismissed from all offices in Hitler's thunderous rage at the end of April. Keitel was no more than the subservient executor of Hitler's orders and held in contempt by many within the Wehrmacht. The only army general in whom Hitler had any confidence at the end was Field-Marshal Schörner. But he was still a front commander, leading the beleaguered Army Group Centre fighting in the former Czechoslovakia. Though much admired by Hitler, Schörner was heartily disliked by many other generals and, even had he been available, would have been unthinkable as head of state. That left Dönitz.

The Grand-Admiral, who made no secret even after the war of the mutual respect between him and Hitler, claimed in an early post-war interrogation that he was chosen as the senior member of the armed forces with the necessary authority 'to put in effect the capitulation'. Since Hitler could not end the war, he asserted, someone else had to do it. 'This war could only be finished by a soldier who had the necessary authority with the armed forces. The point was to insure that the Army would obey, when told to capitulate. . . . The Führer knew that I had the authority.'[29] Years later, Dönitz added a gloss: 'I assumed that Hitler had nominated me because he wished to clear the way to enable an officer of the Armed Forces to put an end to the war. That this assumption was incorrect I did not find out until the winter of 1945–46 in Nuremberg, when for the first time I heard the provisions of Hitler's will, in which he demanded that the struggle be continued.'[30] Whether Dönitz at the time understood that the reason for his appointment was to enable him to bring about a capitulation is highly doubtful. Nothing in Hitler's stance during the last days, or in his dealings with Dönitz, implied that he was handing over power to seek the capitulation which he himself could not undertake.[31] That would have been totally out of character for Hitler, whose entire 'career' had been based on the imperative that there would be no 'cowardly' capitulation as in 1918, and who had on a number of occasions expressed the view that the German people did not deserve to survive him. On the contrary: Hitler saw in Dönitz precisely the military leader whose fanaticism was needed in order to continue the fight to the bitter end.[32]

Dönitz did, in fact, immediately deviate from Hitler's expressed wish that the struggle should on no account be abandoned,[33] and began to explore avenues towards negotiating an end to the war short of complete and unconditional surrender on all fronts. But this was almost certainly not a result of misunderstanding the reason for his appointment as head of state and supreme commander of the Wehrmacht. It was simply the need to bow to military and political reality now that Hitler was dead. The end was near; most of the Reich was under enemy occupation; the population was war-weary in the extreme; loyalties were fragmenting rapidly; and the Wehrmacht was largely destroyed, its remnants on the verge of total defeat.[34] There was little alternative from Dönitz's point of view, now burdened with responsibility not just for the navy but for the entire Reich, to try even at this late stage to negotiate an end which would be less than total disaster.

In a post-war interrogation several months later, Field-Marshal Keitel claimed that 'as soon as Hitler was dead, more or less the principal point was this: if somebody else has the responsibility, then the only thing to do was to seek an immediate armistice and attempt to save whatever can be saved'.[35] This was disingenuous. No immediate armistice was sought. Dönitz, who later asserted that his government programme was clear, that he wanted to end the war as quickly as possible but above all to save as many lives as he could,[36] chose rather to prolong the fight for the time being on both eastern and western fronts in an attempt to buy time to bring back the troops from the east. He had also not altogether given up hopes of splitting the coalition and winning the western powers for a continued war against Bolshevism. In so doing, he did enable hundreds of thousands of soldiers and a far smaller number of civilians to avoid Soviet captivity. But he added a further week of death and suffering to the immense human cost of the war.

I I

For those civilians imminently exposed to the prospect of Soviet conquest, the mortal fear and dread was completely unaltered by Hitler's death. Many, in any case, lacking radio, newspapers and post did not hear the news for days.[37] One macabre way the deep anxiety manifested itself was in an epidemic of suicides in the closing weeks of the Third Reich, which continued into May as complete military defeat and enemy occupation loomed.[38]

Among the Nazi regime's rulers, suicide could be seen and portrayed as heroic self-sacrifice, eminently preferable to the 'cowardice' of capitulation. This was, of course, how Hitler's own death was advertised.[39] For military leaders, too, death at one's own hand was seen as a manly way out rather than yieloding and offering to surrender. In extreme cases, like that of Goebbels, there was the sense that after Germany's defeat there was nothing for him, his wife or his children to live for. His life, stated Goebbels at the end, had 'no further value if it cannot be used in the service of the Führer and by his side'. His wife, Magda, thought along the same lines, giving as justification for taking her own life and those of her children that 'the world to come after the Führer and National Socialism will no longer be worth living in'.[40]

More prosaically, and for many, no doubt, the prime motive, Nazi leaders feared retribution at the hands of the victors, particularly the Russians. 'I do not wish to fall into the hands of enemies who, for the amusement of their whipped-up masses, will need a spectacle arranged by Jews,' was Hitler's own inimitable way of expressing this fear.[41] While most were prepared to take their chance, and disappeared into hiding, or simply stayed where they were and waited to be arrested, a fair number of other leading Nazis and military leaders felt suicide was their only option. Bormann trying to flee from Berlin, and Himmler, Ley and Göring in Allied custody, were among those choosing to end their own lives, along with 8 out of 41 Gauleiter and 7 from 47 of the Higher SS and Police Leaders, 53 out of 554 army generals, 14 of 98 Luftwaffe generals and 11 from 53 admirals.[42]

For ordinary citizens, too, thoughts of suicide were commonplace. This was especially the case in Berlin and eastern parts of Germany, where despair and fear combined to encourage such thoughts. 'Many are getting used to the idea of putting an end to it. The demand for poison, a pistol and other means of ending life is great everywhere,' an SD report had already noted at the end of March.[43] 'All Berliners know that the Russians will soon be in Berlin, and they see no alternative – other than cyanide,' one pastor had remarked around the same time. He blamed the rise in suicidal tendencies on the horror stories in Goebbels' propaganda about the behaviour of the Soviets.[44] This was undoubtedly a major contributory factor. But the propaganda had, as we have seen, some basis in fact, and tales of terrible experiences at the hands of Soviet soldiers, especially the rape of German women, circulated by word of mouth and independently of Goebbels' machinations. Women committed suicide rather than face the likelihood of being raped. Others killed themselves afterwards. More would have done so had they possessed the means.[45]

In Berlin, where suicide statistics, if incomplete, exist, the trend is plain to see. At the peak in April and May, during the battle of Berlin, 3,881 people killed themselves. Overall in 1945 there were 7,057 suicides in the city, 3,996 of them women, compared with 2,108 in 1938 and 1,884 in 1946. In Hamburg, by contrast, there were only 56 suicides in April 1945.[46] In Bremen, flattened by repeated bombing, suicides rose markedly in 1945, but the level remained in fact lower than it had been in 1939.[47] There was a sharp rise in Bavaria in the final phase of the war, though the figure of 42 suicides in April and May 1945 was scarcely on a comparable scale with that of Berlin and accountable at least in part by the disproportionate number of Nazi functionaries there who took their own lives. Some other parts of western Germany also had modestly increased suicide rates in 1945, but nothing remotely comparable with those of Berlin.[48] Plainly, the suicide wave was first and foremost a phenomenon of those parts of Germany where fear of occupation by the Red Army was most acute.

Panic gripped the people in eastern localities as the Red Army approached. Along the front line, in numerous places in Pomerania, Mecklenburg, Silesia and Brandenburg, there were hundreds of suicides. No overall total can be calculated, but it is presumed to have been in the thousands, perhaps tens of thousands.[49] In Demmin, a town in western Pomerania of some 15,000 inhabitants before the war but by this time also housing numerous refugees, more than 900 people, the majority of them women, committed suicide in the three days following the arrival of the Red Army on 1 May.

There was enormous fear in Demmin in the days before the Russians entered. The feeling of terror mounted as the frightening noise of Soviet tanks rolling into the town could be heard. German soldiers fled that morning, blowing up the bridges over the two local rivers as they went. White bedsheets were hung out of windows to offer surrender, though a group of Hitler Youth fired at the Soviets. One man shot his wife and three children before blasting off a Panzerfaust, then hanging himself. Families barricaded themselves into their homes, blocking the doors with furniture. Then they heard loud, foreign voices, banging and kicking at the doors, before Red Army soldiers, many looking very young, broke in, demanding watches and jewellery. The other ominous demand was 'Frau, komm!' Plundering, marauding troops, often under the influence of drink, roamed the streets. The town's representatives were peremptorily shot. The houses of suspected Nazi Party members were set on fire, and the flames spread, engulfing neighbouring properties until much of the town centre was burning.

In the horror, women were paralysed with the all too justified fear of being raped. They tried to hide, or dressed in men's clothes, but were all too often found. Many were raped numerous times. In this scene of Sodom and Gomorrah (as it appeared to one witness), terrified individuals decided on the instant to kill themselves, and sometimes their families, with whatever method was to hand – poison, shooting, hanging, or drowning in the local rivers, the Peene or the Tollense. In one case, the death of thirteen family members is recorded. In another, a mother pushed her two tiny children in a pram while her six-year-old followed on his bike. Under a large oak tree on the edge of town, she poisoned her children, then tried to hang herself but was cut down by Soviet soldiers. She said she had seen propaganda posters claiming that the Russians killed children by putting an axe through their skull. There was something approaching mass hysteria among the townsfolk. Entire families headed for the river, tied themselves together, and plunged into the cold water. Many elderly people were among those who took their lives that way. For weeks afterwards, swollen corpses were found floating in the rivers. In some instances, panic-stricken women took their children by the hand and jumped into the water. One girl, eleven years old at the time, fleeing from her burning home, was dragged back by her grandmother as her mother suddenly grabbed her and made for the riverbank. 'We all thought we were going to burn to death,' she recalled, many years later. 'We had no hope left for life, and I myself, I had the feeling that this was the end of the world, this was the end of my life. And everyone in Demmin felt like that.'[50]

The rampaging of the Red Army and the gross maltreatment of the conquered German population were only gradually brought under control by the Soviet authorities once the war was over. But in the first days of May 1945, the war still continued. And so did the suffering.

III

Dönitz's cabinet, fully formed on 5 May, bore only partial resemblance to the one nominated by Hitler. All that Dönitz had learnt from Bormann, arising from Hitler's Testament, was the names of three intended ministers: Bormann, Goebbels and, to replace Ribbentrop as Foreign Minister, Arthur Seyß-Inquart, the Reich Commissar in the Netherlands.[51] In establishing his administration, set up in the northernmost extremity of the Reich in somewhat primitive accommodation in the Naval Academy at Flensburg-Mürwik after a hasty departure from Plön as British troops approached, Dönitz had to presume that Bormann and Goebbels were dead or captured, while Seyß-Inquart was involved in negotiations with the Allies about a partial capitulation and also therefore unavailable to take up his nominated position. In any case, Dönitz was determined to form his own cabinet, not simply take over one prescribed for him.[52]

Nevertheless, continuity was the hallmark of the new government. What was later claimed to have been an 'unpolitical' cabinet included several high-ranking SS officers and a Party Gauleiter (Paul Wegener of Gau Weser-Ems). The Minister of the Interior, Wilhelm Stuckart, an SS-Obergruppenführer, who had in effect run the ministry as Himmler's State Secretary during the last months of the war, had been a participant in the notorious Wannsee Conference that in January 1942 had determined policy on the 'Final Solution of the Jewish Question'. Herbert Backe, the Minister for Agriculture, had the rank of an SS-Gruppenführer and had helped shape policies imposing starvation on occupied Soviet territories. Otto Ohlendorf, deputy State Secretary in the Reich Economics Ministry, was an SS-Gruppenführer who had formerly headed the SD-Inland in the Reich Security Head Office and had led Einsatzgruppe D in the murder of hundreds of thousands of Jews. As late as 16 May Ohlendorf was in discussion with Dönitz about reconstructing the security service, also for possible use by the occupying powers.[53] (In all, 230 of the 350 or so members of Dönitz's administrative personnel in Flensburg had belonged to the security services.[54])

There was no place for Himmler, viewed as an obvious liability in any prospective dealings with the western Allies. But it was easy to see why he thought he might have a part to play and sought after 2 May to enter the Dönitz government. He offered his services to Dönitz in any capacity, but, enquiring how the Wehrmacht regarded him, perhaps had his eye on taking over as War Minister.[55] Himmler argued that he would be crucial in the struggle against Bolshevism and required only a brief audience with General Eisenhower or Field-Marshal Montgomery to gain recognition of this. He was told in no uncertain terms, however, that 'every Englishman or American who thought for half a second of speaking to him would in the next half a second be swept away by public opinion in England and the USA'.[56] His 'treason' against Hitler in the last days was reportedly also a reason why Dönitz rejected any involvement in his administration by Himmler.[57] Dönitz finally broke off relations with him on 6 May, after which the once mighty and greatly feared police chief, as one prominent member of the Dönitz administration later put it, 'turned himself into a poor petitioner and disappeared without trace'.[58] He fled in disguise before being captured by the British in north Germany, escaping trial and a certain death sentence by swallowing a poison capsule in custody.

Old survivors from pre-Hitler governments who had served throughout the Third Reich were the Labour Minister, Dr Franz Seldte, the Transport Minister and Lutz Graf Schwerin von Krosigk, the former Finance Minister, now elevated to chief minister (*Leitender Minister*) and also placed in charge of foreign affairs. Dr Julius Dorpmüller, Reich Transport Minister since 1937, also continued in office. Speer was brought in to oversee what was optimistically termed 'reconstruction'. Not least, there was continuity in the military leadership. Dönitz's own replacement as head of the navy was Admiral-General Hans-Georg von Friedeburg. But the crucial positions as chief of the High Command of the Wehrmacht and head of the Wehrmacht Operations Staff were held, as before, by Field-Marshal Keitel and Colonel-General Jodl, who had made their way north to join Dönitz shortly after Hitler's death.[59] In the days that followed, Keitel and Jodl, alongside Dönitz and Krosigk, were the key players.[60] The remainder had largely bit-parts.

Forming a cabinet had not been Dönitz's first priority on taking over the government, though he had been keen to appoint a Foreign Minister. He had wanted Hitler's first Foreign Minister, Konstantin von Neurath, but was unable to reach him. Instead, he gave the post to Krosigk, whom he barely knew but had found impressive at a meeting in Plön at the end of April.[61] Krosigk had no obvious qualifications other than the interest he had shown in previous weeks in bombarding Goebbels in particular with wholly unrealistic propositions for seeking a negotiated settlement to the war. He was practically the only choice available to Dönitz and carried no especially harmful baggage from the Hitler years.

It was not just in personnel that there was no clean break with the immediate past. The old forms and structures were maintained. The organization of the High Command of the Wehrmacht – as much of it as had survived – continued to function seamlessly. The Nazi Party was neither banned nor dissolved. Pictures of Hitler still hung in government offices. The 'Heil Hitler' greeting was used even now in the Wehrmacht. And summary courts, with their grisly sentences, were not abolished.[62] Astonishingly, sailors were still being sentenced by court martial and executed even after the signing of total capitulation.[63] Mentalities, too, remained unaltered. Retaining the existence of the Reich by saving what could be saved was a central objective. Ribbentrop, like Himmler, had represented the unacceptable face of the old regime and was excluded by Dönitz from the new administration. But a letter from Ribbentrop to the new head of state composed (though in the event, it seems, not sent) on 2 May, probably in the vain hope that he would be invited to join the new administration, was clearly written with a view to influencing policy direction.

The aim, wrote Ribbentrop, must be to give the Reich government under Dönitz's leadership the chance to rule from a free German territory. Because of the difficulty of the 'unconditional surrender' demand, the attempt should be made to persuade Eisenhower and Montgomery that taking Schleswig-Holstein would be at a high price in Allied lives, and to imply that the British army would someday need the Germans at its side in the fight against the Soviet Union. He suggested an offer to evacuate gradually the German presence in Scandinavia in return for retention of a Reich government in Schleswig-Holstein. This first step would slowly be extended, leaving behind the formula of unconditional surrender and enabling negotiations to take place with the western Allies that would enable them to present an 'alibi' acceptable to the Russians. The programme in foreign policy would be to bring together all Germans in Europe, without subjugation of other peoples and offering freedom of all nations in Europe and cooperation in upholding peace. At home, there would be an 'evolution in ideological questions', where these might threaten peace. He saw only two possibilities for the future. The first would be complete occupation, internment of the Reich government, administration of the country by the Allies and, in the foreseeable future, a return to a limited form of democracy under Allied tutelage including Democrats, Communists and Catholics. National Socialism would be eradicated, the Wehrmacht completely demolished, and the German people condemned to slavery for decades. Alternatively, through the attempt at a policy of cooperation with all nations, at least superficially also with Russia, and recognition of a Reich government and its programme under Dönitz's leadership, Germany would remain as a nation, and with it also the National Socialist system and a smaller Wehrmacht, thus paving the way for recovery for the German people.[64] Ribbentrop, like Himmler, was soon disabused of his hopes of continuing his career.

But variants of the ideas advanced in his unsent letter were certainly not absent from the leaders of the new administration.

Already on 2 May, Dönitz laid down his aims. The only policy was to try to negotiate a series of partial surrenders in the west, while continuing the fight in the east, at least until as many Germans as possible, soldiers and civilians, could be rescued from the clutches of the Soviets. 'The military situation is hopeless,' the minutes of the first meeting of his administration began. 'In the current situation the main aim of the government has to be to save as many German people as possible from destruction through Bolshevism. In so far as the Anglo-Saxons oppose this aim, they must also be combated.' In the east, therefore, 'continuation of the struggle with all available means' was required, while ending the war against the 'Anglo-Saxons' was 'desirable' to avoid further sacrifice. This was blocked, however, Dönitz went on, by the Allied demand for unconditional total surrender, which would mean at a stroke handing over millions of soldiers and civilians to the Russians. The aim was, therefore, capitulation only to the western powers. But since their political conditions made this impossible, it had to be attempted through 'partial actions' at the level of the Army Groups, utilizing existing contacts.[65]

IV

Developments in the Netherlands appeared to hold out some hope. Even in mid-April, the German authorities there had been uncompromising in their determination to stave off the Allies. The biggest danger to the Netherlands was the deliberate inundation of the countryside. The Wehrmacht had flooded 16,000 hectares in coastal areas in July 1944 in an attempt to hinder the Allied advance.[66] The prospect now was that this dire tactic would be extended. At a meeting with leaders of the Dutch Underground Movement, Reich Commissar Seyß-Inquart had threatened destruction of locks and dykes in western Holland, which would have made 'the country uninhabitable during a number of years for several million people', and, had it been carried out, would have inordinately exacerbated the famine of the previous winter. The Allied response had been that, should this happen, Seyß and Colonel-General Johannes Blaskowitz, Commander-in-Chief of the Netherlands, would be treated as war criminals.[67]

With defeat certain and imminent, this reaction evidently concentrated German minds. As soon as Hitler was dead, the stance changed. Seyß, as Dönitz and his colleagues noted, now successfully engaged in talks with Eisenhower's Chief of Staff, General Walter Bedell Smith, to alleviate the food crisis in the Netherlands. Even so, Seyß himself reported on 3 May that a partial capitulation would be difficult to achieve. Smith had offered discussions about possible armistice negotiations, but Seyß, on the instructions of Blaskowitz, had refused, awaiting a directive from Dönitz. Meanwhile, the fight for 'Fortress Holland' was to be continued. However, there was to be 'no flooding of the land'. An 'honourable transition' – surrender by any other name – would, it was thought, bring 'a small credit' to the German administration.[68]

During the morning of 2 May Dönitz had already been confronted with the unexpected news of the surrender of Army Group C in Italy.[69] Moves to engineer a capitulation in Italy dated back to March, to the clandestine meetings in Switzerland, mentioned in Chapter 7, between Himmler's former right-hand man, SS-Obergruppenführer Karl Wolff, and the head of the American intelligence services, the OSS, in central Europe, Allen Dulles. Cautious steps towards a capitulation had quickened throughout April as the military situation in Italy had worsened. The German Commander-in-Chief, Colonel-General Heinrich von Vietinghoff-Scheel, remained anxious that news of the continued dealings between Wolff and Dulles should not leak out. Even at this stage, German generals were fearful of the dire consequences should they be seen to be implicated in treasonable activities. Vietinghoff also argued – justifying his hesitancy, though by the end of April a dubious proposition – that Goebbels would create out of any disclosure of the capitulation soundings a new 'stab-in-the-back' legend, and deflect blame from the Reich leadership on to the 'traitors' in Italy who had prevented a last-minute change in war fortunes.[70]

There were other difficulties. The likelihood, as it seemed, that Hitler would be flown out of Berlin to establish an 'Alpine fortress' in the Berchtesgaden area was a complication, leaving the Gauleiter of the Tyrol, Franz Hofer, torn between his continued loyalty to the Führer and his desire to prevent his province becoming a battleground. Hofer's continued backing for Hitler remained a worry for Vietinghoff and those trying to reach terms with the Allies. His support for the armistice negotiations could not be taken for granted. Field-Marshal Kesselring, based by late April in southern Bavaria and responsible for military direction in the southern part of the Reich (from 28 April for the military command over the entire southern front, covering Italy and the Balkans as well as the south of Germany), was a further problem. As late as 27 April, Kesselring was still hesitant. At a meeting that day in Gauleiter Hofer's house with Vietinghoff, the Gauleiter and the German ambassador in Italy, Dr Rudolf Rahn, Kesselring backed the steps that were being taken and agreed to be associated with them. But he added a cautionary rider. It had to be presumed, he stated, 'that the Führer was basing his proclamation "Berlin will remain German; the fight for Berlin will bring the great turn in war fortune" on a reasoned basis.' As long as he had faith in that, Kesselring added, he could not act on his own accord. He was prepared to let his name be used in the moves towards capitulation, but added 'that an end only came into question for him if the Führer was no longer alive'.[71] The bonds with Hitler were evidently vital for Kesselring even in what were obviously the closing days of his power. Reports on foreign radio stations on the evening of 28 April that Hitler was dead turned out to be untrue. Kesselring still wanted to wait, though the military situation was worsening by the hour. The deterioration was reported by Kaltenbrunner – unaware of the suicide in the bunker – in a message for Hitler sent in the early morning of 1 May, though, because there were no communications with Berlin, relayed to Dönitz. Kaltenbrunner, informed by Gauleiter Hofer, noted the demand for capitulation by 29 April, mentioning, too, the death of Mussolini at the hands of partisans.[72]

Meanwhile, a German delegation had flown to meet Allied representatives in Caserta to be faced with the ultimatum to agree unconditional surrender in Italy or see negotiations broken off. The German position was by then hopeless. The final Allied offensive had begun on 9 April. German forces in Italy, totalling around 600,000 men (including 160,000 Italian troops), were greatly outnumbered by some 1.5 million Allied troops (70,000 of them Italians).[73] By 25 April, the Allies had crossed the Po, sweeping northwards and forcing the Germans into headlong retreat towards the Alps. Surrender was the only sensible option. The capitulation was signed at 2 p.m. on 29 April, to come into effect exactly three days later, on 2 May.[74] It was the only capitulation to be signed before Hitler's death – though by chance it did not come into effect while he was alive. Even now, Kesselring belatedly distanced

N

NORWAY
Bergen ●
Oslo ●

FINLAND
Helsinki ● ● Leningrad

SWEDEN
Stockholm ●

RUSSIA

North Sea

Baltic Sea

DENMARK
Copenhagen ●
Flensburg ●

● Königsberg

IRELAND
● Dublin

GREAT
BRITAIN

● Hamburg

POLAND

London ●

NETHERLANDS
The Hague ●

Weser

● Berlin

Vistula
● Warsaw

Dunkirk ◉

Brussels ●

● Cologne

Oder

● Breslau

BELGIUM
LUX.

● Frankfurt

GERMANY
Elbe

● Prague

SLOVAKIA

Lorient ◉
St Nazaire ◉

Paris ●
Reims ●

Seine

Danube

Bratislava ●

Vienna ●

● Budapest

La Rochelle ◉

FRANCE

Rhine

● Munich

AUSTRIA

RUMANIA

Loire

SWITZ.
Berne ●

Po

● Trieste

Rhône

Ebro

YUGOSLAVIA

● Belgrade

Danube

● Bucharest

BULGARIA

ITALY
● Rome

● Sofia

Istanbul ●

● Tirana

● Caserta

ALBANIA

GREECE

● Athens

ALGERIA
(French protectorate)

TUNISIA
(French protectorate)

Mediterranean Sea

Crete

| | Front line, on 9 May 1945 |

LIBYA
(British and French
occupation)

0   100   200   300 miles

0   200   400 km

9. Europe at the final surrender

himself from what had taken place, and dismissed Vietinghoff and his Chief of Staff, Hans Röttiger, threatening to report the matter to the Führer and demand the necessary consequences for their treasonable actions. His own involvement probably prevented him carrying out this threat, and the Field-Marshal contented himself with the fiction that Vietinghoff and Röttiger were resigning at their own request. Whether the capitulation, though signed, would be effected remained in doubt until the news – authentic this time – of Hitler's death came through and Kesselring finally, at 4 a.m. on 2 May, gave his approval. Kesselring told Dönitz and Keitel that day that the armistice negotiations had taken place without his knowledge or approval, and that he had felt compelled to support the armistice that had been concluded in order to prevent an open revolt.[75] At 2 p.m. that afternoon, the weapons in northern Italy finally fell silent.[76] General Winter, deputy head of the OKW Operations Staff, telexed his chief, Jodl, that day: 'Perfidious behaviour of the Commander-in-Chief there will for all time be inexplicable to me.'[77] As late as this the top military leadership retained its perverse notion of loyalty.

In north-west Germany, East Frisia and Schleswig-Holstein were not yet occupied, and further north Denmark and Norway remained in German hands. On 2 May Jodl sent out instructions to Field-Marshal Ernst Busch, Commander-in-Chief of Army Group North-West, to fight on in order to 'gain time' for negotiations. The orders were, however, swiftly overtaken by events, which were by now moving far too rapidly for Dönitz to have any hope of controlling them. The British advance to Lüneburg and the American push through Schwerin to Wismar meant that overnight the last gateway for Germans to escape westwards from Pomerania and Mecklenburg was sealed off. Army Group Vistula, the 12th Army and the remains of the 9th Army were left to fight their way back to western lines as best they could. With this development, it was acknowledged that there was no longer any point in fighting on against the western forces in northern Germany. It was decided to try to open talks with Montgomery as quickly as possible.[78]

On 3 May, the date on which the city of Hamburg capitulated under threat of renewed British bombing,[79] Admiral-General von Friedeburg was, therefore, dispatched to try to negotiate an armistice in north-west Germany with the British military commander. When Montgomery refused unless German forces in Holland, Denmark, Frisia and Schleswig stopped fighting, offering only to treat Germans fleeing from the east as prisoners of war and not hand them over to the Soviets, increasingly chaotic circumstances in the west forced Dönitz's hand. German troops had flooded back in disorder westwards through Mecklenburg while there was still a chance to escape from the Red Army. And there were signs of disintegration in those troop units already in the west – where the civilian population was said to oppose any continuation of the war with the western Allies – amid fears that they would take matters into their own hands and simply refuse to fight any longer.[80]

After discussing the dilemma with Krosigk, Speer, Keitel, Jodl and Gauleiter Wegener, Dönitz saw no alternative but to comply with Montgomery's demands. On 4 May he approved the signing of the partial capitulation under the terms laid down. At the same time he ordered a halt to the U-boat war. (The order was not, in fact, received by all U-boats. Four further attacks on Allied shipping took place. In the last U-boat attack of the war, on 7 May, shortly before the total capitulation of the Wehrmacht, two freighters were sunk off the Firth of Forth.) On 5 May hostilities officially ceased in the Netherlands, Denmark and north-west Germany. Against earlier intentions to scuttle warships rather than allow them to fall into enemy hands, the Germans agreed to sink no ships. Montgomery left open their continued use for refugee transportation.[81]

Norway, however, where the Commander-in-Chief, Colonel-General Georg Lindemann, was still claiming that his troops (remarkably even now around 400,000 strong[82]) were ready to fight on and requested (in vain) the continued use of the 'Heil Hitler' greeting, remained under German occupation. As late as 3 May Dönitz had continued to regard Denmark and Norway as possible bargaining counters with the western powers. Only now did Dönitz take steps to discard still lingering features of the Hitler regime. Actions of the Werwolf – though only in the west – were now banned and deemed contrary to laws of combat. The 'Heil Hitler' greeting was at last prohibited in the Wehrmacht. Pictures of Hitler were on British orders to be removed from government offices.[83] And only on 6 May did Dönitz finally ban all destruction or temporary dismantling of factories, canals, and rail and communications networks, finally reversing Hitler's 'scorched earth' orders of March.[84]

In the south, too, there were clear signs of disintegration among the troops, and of hostility towards the Wehrmacht by the civilian population in Bavaria and Austria. Kesselring took the view that the end had arrived, and sought permission from Dönitz on 3 May to negotiate with the western Allies.[85] The capitulation to the Americans on 5 May of German forces of Army Group G (Nordalpen), left in a hopeless position in Bavaria and Austria, and that of the 19th Army in the Austrian Alpine region, had been preceded on 3–4 May by the surrender, also to the Americans, of around 200,000 men from General Walther Wenck's 12th Army, once earmarked for extracting Hitler from Berlin, which had battled its way back to the Elbe, and parts of General Theodor Busse's 9th Army.[86] The amenability of the Americans to these partial surrenders gave Dönitz shortlived hope that he could come to an arrangement with Eisenhower that would fall short of total capitulation. He imagined he could still reach a deal to prevent the huge numbers of troops facing the Red Army being taken into Soviet captivity. Announcing the surrender in the west, 'since the fight against the western powers has lost its meaning', Keitel added that 'in the east, nevertheless, the struggle continues in order to rescue as many Germans as possible from Bolshevization and slavery'.[87] Even on 4 May the navy leadership was still declaring: 'Aim of the Grand-Admiral is to remove as many Germans as possible from the clutches of Bolshevism. Since the western enemies continue their support of the Soviets, the fight against the Anglo-Americans according to the order of the Grand-Admiral carries on. The aim of this fight is to gain the state leadership space and time for measures in the political arena.'[88]

Nearly 2 million soldiers of the Wehrmacht remained at risk of falling into Soviet hands.[89] Still fighting against the Red Army were: Army Group Ostmark, renamed from 'South' on 30 April, now pushed back into Lower Austria and comprising around 450,000 men under the command of Colonel-General Lothar Rendulić; Army Group E, with around 180,000 men, fighting a rearguard struggle in Croatia under Colonel-General Alexander Löhr; and Field-Marshal Ferdinand Schörner's Army Group Centre, whose 600,000 or so men were pinned back mainly in the 'Protectorate of Bohemia and Moravia' (large parts of the former Czechoslovakia).[90] In addition, some 150,000 German troops who had been evacuated from East Prussia remained stranded on the Hela peninsula, and 180,000 or so were still cut off and fighting in Courland.[91] The latter were not yet ready to give in. A message to Dönitz on 5 May from the commander of the Courland army informed the

Grand-Admiral that the Latvian people were ready 'in common struggle against Bolshevism to fight shoulder to shoulder with the German Wehrmacht to the last', and asked for instructions about whether the Army Group should fight on as a Freikorps unit if a Latvian state should proclaim independence.[92]

Immediately following his negotiations with Montgomery, and in the hope still of avoiding total capitulation, Admiral von Friedeburg was commissioned on 4 May to contact Eisenhower about a further partial capitulation in the west, while explaining to him 'why a total capitulation on all fronts is impossible for us'.[93] Next day, Kesselring offered the surrender of Army Groups Ostmark, E and Centre to Eisenhower, though the offer was promptly rejected unless all forces also capitulated to the Red Army. Rendulić, unable to make contact with OKW headquarters, promptly sought to arrange a partial surrender of his own forces to General Patton. Even now he had not given up hope of persuading the Americans to join him in repelling the Red Army and went so far as to request permission to allow German troops stationed in the west through their lines to support his eastern front. He eventually capitulated unilaterally on 7 May, after himself fleeing to the Americans and offering the surrender of his forces. The offer was rejected, though the Americans were prepared to allow his troops to cross their lines westwards until 1 a.m. on 9 May and be treated as prisoners of war.[94] On 5 May Dönitz gave Löhr permission – since he argued that it could not be prevented and, in any case, accorded with the political aims of his government – to approach Field-Marshal Sir Harold Alexander, Allied Commander-in-Chief in the Mediterranean, about a surrender with the aim of saving Austria from Bolshevism, accepting its separation from the Reich.[95] Eisenhower refused, however, to accept the capitulation unless it was also made to the Red Army.[96] The main concern remained Schörner's army. Already on 3 May Dönitz accepted that 'the entire situation as such demands capitulation, but it is impossible because Schörner with his army would then fall completely into the hands of the Russians'.[97]

Schörner had reported on 2 May that he could not hold out for long. His Chief of Staff, Lieutenant-General Oldwig von Natzmer, thought two weeks was the maximum, though he continued to insist on an orderly retreat. Preparations for sudden orders to retreat were laid while political options were under consideration.[98] The possibilities of saving

Army Group Centre depended upon the political as well as military situation in Bohemia. Dönitz, together with Keitel, Krosigk, Wegener and Himmler had deliberated on 2 May about holding Bohemia for the time being as a bargaining counter.[99] It was acknowledged that the Protectorate of Bohemia and Moravia, known to be on the verge of revolution, could neither politically nor militarily be sustained in the long run. But with a view to rescuing Germans in the area there were thoughts of having Prague declared an open city and sounding out political options by sending emissaries to Eisenhower. Himmler and the OKW briefly entertained the idea of relocating what was left of German government to Bohemia, but Dönitz ruled out the proposition since the territory was not part of Germany, and the political situation too unstable.[100]

This swiftly proved to be true. Any lingering hopes invested in Bohemia rapidly dissolved with the news that a popular rising had broken out in Prague on 5 May. Immediately, orders were issued to rescue as many soldiers as possible from Soviet hands by retreating westwards.[101] Schörner's men had placed their hopes in the Americans advancing into Bohemia before the Soviets could get there. However, Eisenhower held to his agreement with the Soviets to hold the American advance at a line west of Prague, near Pilsen, and refused General Patton permission to march on the city. Once the uprising broke out, the Red Army's orders to take Prague were brought forward. The Soviet advance on Bohemia began on 6 May, though it was only in the early hours of 9 May – after the general capitulation had been signed – that the Red Army's tanks entered Prague and destroyed the remnants of German resistance in the city. In the intervening four days, several thousand Czech citizens were killed or wounded in brutal German attempts to suppress the rising. There were also bloody acts of vengeance taken against the Germans. Demands of the SS commander in Bohemia and Moravia, SS-Gruppen-führer Carl Graf von Pückler-Burghaus, for Prague to be intensively fire-bombed were vitiated only by the lack of fuel for planes.[102]

The situation for Schörner's troops had meanwhile become critical, not just on account of the uprising in Prague which had prompted the Soviet offensive from the north, blocking possible routes of retreat, but because of events much farther north. On the morning of 6 May Friede-burg let Dönitz know that Eisenhower was insisting on 'immediate, simultaneous and unconditional surrender on all fronts'. Troop units were to stay in their positions. No ships were to be sunk, no aeroplanes to be damaged. Eisenhower threatened a renewal of bombing raids and closure of borders to those fleeing from the east if his demands were not met. 'These conditions are unacceptable,' a meeting of Dönitz, Keitel, Jodl and Gauleiter Wegener concluded, 'because we cannot abandon the armies in the east to the Russians. They are not capable of implementation since no soldier on the eastern front will hold to the command to lay down arms and stay in position. On the other hand, the hopeless military situation, the danger of further losses in the west through bombing raids and combat and the certainty of the inevitable military collapse in the near future compel us to find a solution for the still intact armies.' Since there was no way out of the dilemma, it was decided to send Jodl to explain with all force to Eisenhower 'why a complete capitulation is impossible, but a capitulation only in the west would be immediately accepted'.[103]

In the early hours of next morning, 7 May, Jodl's wire from Eisenhower's headquarters brought the depressing news that the Allied Commander-in-Chief insisted that total capitulation be signed that day, otherwise all negotiations would be broken off. Eisenhower's demand was seen in Dönitz's headquarters as 'absolute blackmail' since if refused it would mean the abandonment of all Germans beyond American lines to the Russians. But with a capitulation to go into effect at midnight on 8/9 May, it would give forty-eight hours to extract at least most of the troops still fighting in the east. With a heavy heart, Dönitz therefore gave Jodl powers to sign the capitulation.[104] At 2.41 a.m. on 7 May Jodl, in the presence of Admiral-General von Friedeburg, signed the Act of Military Surrender together with General Walter Bedell Smith and the Soviet General Ivan Susloparov in Eisenhower's headquarters in Rheims. All military operations were to cease at 23.01 hours Central European Time on 8 May – given the hour's time difference, a minute past midnight on 9 May in London.[105]

The act of capitulation was, however, not yet complete. The text of the surrender document, the Soviets complained, differed from the agreed text, and Susloparov had been given no authorization to sign. This was, however, merely the pretext. Both the issue of prestige – since the Red Army had borne the lion's share of the fighting over four long years – and continued suspicion of the west prompted Stalin's insistence on a further signing, of a lengthier version of the capitulation document, this time by the highest representatives of all sectors of the Wehrmacht as well as leading Allied representatives. This second signing took place in Karlshorst, in the former mess of the military engineering school, now Zhukov's headquarters, on the outskirts of Berlin. The German representatives, flown from Flensburg to Berlin in an American plane, were kept waiting throughout the day on 8 May until the Allied delegation arrived, between 10 and 11 p.m. At last, Keitel, accompanied by Colonel-General Hans-Jürgen Stumpff (representing the Luftwaffe) and Admiral-General von Friedeburg (on behalf of the navy), came slowly through the doorway for the surrender ceremony. Keitel raised his field-marshal's baton in salute. The Allied representatives (Marshal Georgi Zhukov, the British Air-Marshal Arthur W. Tedder (on behalf of Eisenhower), the French General Jean de Lattre de Tassigny, and the US General Carl Spaatz) did not respond.

The German delegation were then invited by Zhukov to sign the instrument of unconditional surrender. Keitel, his face blotched red, replacing his monocle, which had dropped and dangled on a cord, his hand shaking slightly, signed five copies of the capitulation document before putting his right glove back on. It was almost a quarter to one in the early morning of 9 May, so the capitulation was backdated to the previous day to comply with the terms of the Rheims agreement. Once Keitel and the German delegation withdrew, bowing stiffly as they went, their heads sunken, it was time for the Soviet officers to sing and dance the night away.[106] However little appetite the German delegation had, they were given a good meal with caviar and champagne. Somewhat surprisingly, at such a catastrophic moment for their country, Keitel and his fellow officers sipped the celebratory drink.[107] Keitel was asked whether Hitler was really dead, since, it was said, his body had not been found. The Soviets inferred that he might still be ruling behind the scenes.[108]

Once Dönitz had agreed to the capitulation in Rheims, a rapidly accelerated desperate attempt was made to transport westwards troops still on the eastern front before the surrender took effect. Hurriedly, he instructed the Army Groups South-East, Ostmark and Centre to fight their way back to Eisenhower's domain with the aim of being taken prisoner by the Americans.[109] A flotilla of German ships ferried backwards and forwards across the Baltic to try to carry soldiers and – with lower priority – refugees to the west. Overland, soldiers and civilians alike fled in their droves beyond the Elbe and from Bohemia towards Bavaria. Many of the soldiers were from Army Group Ostmark, left leaderless at Rendulić's surrender, and now flooding back pell-mell towards the American lines, up to 150 kilometres away in the west.[110] Wild rumours circulated among soldiers in the east that the Americans would set free their German prisoners and rearm them 'to throw the Bolsheviks out of Germany'. Even though most soldiers were hoping for an end to the war, they would, one recorded in his diary, all have been prepared to fight on if they could attack the Russians alongside the Americans 'for the homeland must sometime be liberated again'.[111]

Schörner endeavoured as ever through ferocious discipline and vehement exhortation to keep his army together. On 5 May he issued a final proclamation to the soldiers of Army Group Centre. 'Only the eastern front of the southern army groups remains unbroken,' he told them. According to the order given him by the head of state and Commander-in-Chief of the Wehrmacht, nominated by the Führer, Grand-Admiral Dönitz, it was the task of his soldiers to carry on fighting 'until the most valuable German people are saved'. It was his intention, he declared, to lead his troops in formation, heads held high 'in proud bearing' back into the homeland. No picture of disintegration was to be conveyed in this final phase. Any attempt to break ranks and seek an independent way back to the homeland 'is dishonourable treason towards comrades and people and must be dealt with accordingly. Our discipline and our weapons in the hand are the guarantee for us to leave this war in decency and bravery.'[112]

The plight of Army Group Centre, once Dönitz had been forced to agree to the capitulation in Rheims, was unenviable in the extreme. Bringing back Schörner's troops was seen as imperative on 6 May, but the capitulation made this impossible.[113] The order to retreat had come too late. The Soviet attack from the north, from Saxony towards Prague, blocked the path.[114] On 7 May a British plane flew a German General Staff officer, Colonel Wilhelm Meyer-Detring, south from Flensburg to meet Schörner to explain the unavoidability of the capitulation in Rheims and press the urgent case for his men to fight their way to the west. From Pilsen, Meyer-Detring was escorted by forty American soldiers to Schörner's field headquarters, where they met next day.[115] He described the background to the unavoidable total capitulation. An orderly retreat, the colonel told Schörner, had been ruled out by the speedy conclusion of the capitulation. He gave Schörner the order to leave all heavy equipment behind and to move his divisions to the south-west as rapidly as possible. Schörner issued the command to comply with the stipulations of the surrender, though was doubtful that troops would obey if it meant abandoning their fellow soldiers fighting to escape Soviet captivity or meaning that they themselves would fall into Russian hands. The Czech uprising had led to a breakdown in commu-nications. 'Leadership possibilities', he added, scarcely existed any longer 'and he saw no possibility everywhere of preventing complete disorganization and non-compliance with the terms'. There was the danger that individual troop sectors or lower-ranking commanders would take matters into their own hands, ignoring orders and simply trying to fight their way to the west.[116]

In his proclamation of 5 May, Schörner had promised his soldiers: 'You can have trust in me, that I will lead you out of this crisis.'[117] But after his return from years of Soviet captivity, Schörner, facing trial in West Germany on account of his brutal treatment of his soldiers under his command,[118] was forced to defend himself vehemently against accu-sations levelled by his own former Chief of Staff, Lieutenant-General Natzmer, that he, the most fervent follower throughout of Hitler and the most ferocious adherent of fighting to the last, had left his troops in the lurch at the end. It was said that on 8 May he had fled in civilian clothing by plane to the Austrian Alps, hiding for some days in a hut before handing himself over to the Americans, who a few weeks later delivered him to the Russians.[119] According to Schörner's own later account, he left Army Group Centre only on the morning of 9 May, when his command had been removed following the capitulation. He had, he claimed, been led to believe from Flensburg that the capitula-tion could be postponed until around 12 May, and he had until then to bring his troops home. Taken completely by surprise by the sudden news of the Rheims surrender, which, through communications difficul-ties, reached him only after a costly delay of several hours, he had been unable to fulfil his promise of 5 May to lead his troops back in forma-tion and instead, on 7 May, had given the orders for an organized flight.[120] To the end of his life he asserted that his flight to Austria had been with the intention of carrying out Hitler's orders to establish an Alpine front to continue the fight.[121] But although Schörner left his troops as he claimed on 9 May when his command had formally ceased following the capitulation, it remains the case that the men whose discipline he had enforced with a rod of iron were now suddenly abandoned to their fate.[122] And the justification he gave for his flight to Austria shows, true or not, that even now he was prepared to argue that he was following an order from Hitler.

Army Group Centre had been the last largely intact Wehrmacht force in the field. The vast majority of its troops were taken into Soviet captivity, along with most other German soldiers still left on the eastern front at the total capitulation. It has been estimated that 220,000 soldiers were taken prisoner by the Red Army between 1 and 8 May, and as many as 1.6 million after the capitulation.[123] Around 450,000 of those earlier fighting in the east had been able – though not all in the last week of the war – to reach the relative security of western lines.[124] Eisenhower's refusal to the end to contemplate any breach of the coalition with the Soviet Union, his insistence at his meeting with Jodl on 6 May upon unconditional surrender on all fronts, and the speed of the final moves to sign the capitulation had ruined Dönitz's intention of bringing the troops in the east back to the west and keeping them out of the hands of the Red Army. At a cost of continuing the war for more than a week after Hitler's death, Dönitz did partially succeed. In the overall balance, no more than around 30 per cent of the 10 million German troops entered Soviet captivity, though far more soldiers had fought in the east than in the west.[125] Despite the flight to the west in the first week in May, the great majority of those on the eastern front when Dönitz took office were still there at Germany's surrender. They were marched off to the east and forced to endure years of Soviet captivity. A great many did not return. On the best estimates, about a third of those captured during the entire war in the east, around a million German prisoners of war, died in Soviet hands.[126]

Dönitz, as we have seen, had endeavoured to postpone the inevitable defeat as long as possible, through a series of partial surrenders calculated to find time to bring back the troops – and, as a much lower priority, civilians – from the east, and also in the hope, if rapidly fading, that even now the wartime coalition of the western powers and the Soviet Union might crack. The strategy was largely, if not totally, a failure, and at a high cost. Did Dönitz have an alternative? Only once

Eisenhower's 'blackmail' (as Dönitz saw it) of complete capitulation within hours could not be avoided were the troops still engaged in the east instructed to fight their way to the west. The order, as the fate of Army Group Centre shows, came too late for most of them. Instead of gambling on the potential of a series of partial surrenders in the west, following the model which had worked in Italy, Dönitz's best option was arguably to have opened the western front completely – ordering the troops in all areas facing the Allies simply to stop fighting and lay down their arms. This would have allowed the western powers to advance their lines immediately and rapidly to the east, shortening the lines to those still trapped there. Simultaneous orders to the three Army Groups still in the east to fight their way back straight away towards the western powers might well, then, have saved far more of them than turned out to be the case, even if the flight from the east had been chaotic rather than the planned and orderly retreat that German military leaders dreamed of.[127] The speculation is, of course, pointless. The mentality in the high ranks of the German leadership ran counter to such notions. Even officers in British captivity had as late as spring 1945 rejected the idea of German officers simply allowing the western Allies to break through as incompatible with military honour.[128] For Dönitz, whose acute sense of military honour had married so easily with his fervent belief in the ideology of National Socialism, orders to troops in the west unilaterally to stop fighting without formal capitulation would have been impossible to contemplate. So the war, even with Hitler dead, could not be immediately ended, but was forced to drag on until, with the civilian population demoralized and resigned to their fate, Germany's armies had either been destroyed or were on the verge of destruction. This time there could be no claim, as in 1918, that the army had been defeated not on the battlefield but through subversion at home.

On 9 May the Wehrmacht issued its final report. 'From midnight the weapons are silent on all fronts. On command of the Grand-Admiral the Wehrmacht has ended the fight that had become hopeless,' it ran. 'The struggle lasting almost six years is thereby over.' The 'unique achievement of front and homeland' would, it stated, 'find its final appreciation in a later, just verdict of history'.[129] The war, caused primarily by Germany's expansionist aims and ultimately spreading to most parts of the globe, had left over 40 million people dead in the European conflict alone (leaving aside those killed in the Far East) – more than four times the mortalities of the First World War, once seen as the war to end all wars.

V

Oddly, the capitulation was not quite the end for the Third Reich. The Dönitz administration, an ever more pointless curiosity, was allowed to continue for a further fifteen days in office, its sovereignty confined to a tiny enclave in Flensburg. SS-uniforms were swiftly discarded and civilian dress adopted. A couple of ministers, Backe and Dorpmüller, were ordered to fly to Eisenhower's headquarters to provide advice on the first steps of reconstruction.[130] Keitel, still Chief of the OKW, was arrested on 13 May and Jodl, who three days after he had signed the capitulation in Rheims was belatedly and by now somewhat pointlessly awarded the Oak Leaves to go with his Knight's Cross, took over the running of a largely redundant OKW. Government business went on – if in a surreal way. It was little more than the pretence of government. Dönitz and his remaining colleagues discussed the issue of the national flag, because the swastika was banned by the enemy powers. Another emblem of Hitler's Reich was at stake. Since pictures of the Führer had been removed or defaced by members of the Allied forces the question arose as to whether as a preventive measure they should all be taken down. Dönitz was opposed since, until now, the incidents had all been localized. Three days later he relented in part, conceding their removal in rooms where there were meetings with members of the occupying forces.[131]

Deprived of all effectiveness, the cabinet still felt it had 'a responsibility to help the German people where it could'.[132] This was hardly at all. A cabinet meeting took place every morning at 10 a.m. in an old schoolroom. It seemed to Speer as if Krosigk, the acting head of government, was making up for all the years under Hitler in which there had not been a single cabinet meeting. Members of the government had to bring their own glasses and cups from their rooms. They discussed, among other things, how to re-form the cabinet and whether to include a Church minister. Dönitz, still addressed as 'Grand-Admiral', was driven backwards and forwards from his apartment 500 metres away in one of Hitler's big Mercedes that had somehow found its way to Flensburg.[133]

This was not the only element of continuity with Hitler's regime that the Grand-Admiral held to. At a meeting with Admiral-General von Friedeburg on 15 May, Dönitz stipulated that 'defamatory orders' to remove medals were to be refused, that the soldier should be proud of his service for the Wehrmacht and people during the war, and that 'the true people's community created by National Socialism must be maintained'. The 'madness of the parties as before 1933 must never again arise'.[134]

On 15 May Speer wrote to Krosigk asking to be released from his duties as Acting Minister of Economics and Production, stating that a new Reich government was needed, untainted by any connection with the Hitler regime. He still cherished hopes that he might be seen as useful to the Americans.[135] He received no reply, and two days later, described as 'Minister Speer', was still involved in the administration.[136] The entire cabinet considered resigning, but did not do so. The prime consideration was the 'Reich idea' and the question of sovereignty. State Secretary Stuckart, now heading the Ministry of the Interior, produced a memorandum stipulating that unconditional surrender did not affect the further existence of the Reich as a state under international law. Germany had not ceased to exist as a state. Moreover, Dönitz had been legally appointed by the Führer as head of state and therefore Commander-in-Chief of the Wehrmacht, whose oath to Hitler had passed to him automatically. Dönitz could only resign by appointing a successor. As regards legal theory, the Reich continued in existence.[137]

The pantomime of the rump Dönitz regime did not last long. On 23 May, Dönitz, Friedeburg and Jodl were suddenly summoned to the temporary headquarters of the Allied Control Commission, located on the steamship *Patria*, a former German passenger ship of the Hamburg-Amerika line, now moored in Flensburg harbour. Three Wehrmacht limousines ferried them the short journey. Dönitz was wearing full dress uniform and carrying his gold-tipped baton. On arrival, they were ushered up the gangplank and into a lounge to await Allied representatives, who entered the room some minutes later. US Major-General Lowell W. Rooks, heading the Allied mission, then read a prepared text: 'I am under instructions . . . to tell you that the Supreme Commander, General Eisenhower, has decided, in concert with the Soviet High Command, that today the acting German Government and the German High Command shall be taken into custody with the several members as prisoners-of-war. Thereby the acting German Government is dissolved.'[138]

The Third Reich was over. The bankrupt concern was liquidated. The long process of reckoning was about to begin. But the debts for crimes against humanity of such magnitude would not, and could not, ever be repaid.

VI

For Germany itself – leaving aside the untold misery and suffering and vast numbers of war casualties suffered by the citizens of other countries – a colossal price was paid for continuing the war to the bitter end. In the ten months between July 1944 and May 1945 far more German civilians died than in the previous years of the war, mostly through air raids and in the calamitous conditions in the eastern regions after January 1945. In all, more than 400,000 were killed and 800,000 injured by Allied bombing, which had destroyed more than 1.8 million homes and forced the evacuation of almost 5 million people, the vast majority of the devastation being inflicted in the last months of the war.[139] The Soviet invasion then occupation of the eastern regions of Germany after January 1945 resulted in the deaths – apart from the immeasurable suffering caused and the deportation of many German citizens to an uncertain fate in the Soviet Union – of around half a million civilians.[140]

German military losses in the last phase of the war were immense, as high in the last ten months of the war as in the four years to July 1944. Had the attack on Hitler's life in July succeeded and the war then been promptly brought to an end, the lives of around 50 per cent of the German soldiers who died would have been saved. A total of 5.3 million servicemen out of the 18.2 million who served in the army, Luftwaffe, navy and Waffen-SS lost their lives during the entire course of the conflict. Of these, 2.7 million died down to the end of July 1944. As many as 49 per cent of deaths, or 2.6 million (more than 1.5 million of them on the eastern front), were killed in the last ten months. Towards the very end 300,000–400,000 were dying each month.[141]

In the ruins of their country, people could look only dimly and with great foreboding into an uncertain future. Enormous relief that the war was finally over mingled with dismay at the catastrophe that had engulfed Germany and anxiety about life under enemy control. For the vast majority, the victory of the Allies was not seen as liberation. And for those in central and eastern Germany, Soviet rule was a fearful prospect. Passivity and compliance marked the behaviour of the subdued German population as the victors took over. After the ferocious pounding the country and its people had taken over previous months, there was no appetite for the sort of insurrectionist guerrilla activity that so often meets an occupying force.[142] Probably, too, a conditioned readiness to comply with authority played its part. Most importantly, the existential demands of daily life did not alter with the capitulation. The drain on energies through doing no more than surviving in the ruins, getting by in chaotic circumstances, finding lost loved ones, mourning personal losses and trying to pick up the pieces of broken families and homes, was enormous.

As the heavy hand of occupation started to be felt, deep recriminations began to be voiced and the arrests of tens of thousands of Nazi functionaries and others implicated in the Hitler regime gathered pace.[143] Germans in high places and low were meanwhile already laying the foundations of their apologia, attempting to establish distance between themselves and the crimes of Nazism. Claims for the exoneration of the Wehrmacht were under way in Flensburg. Keitel, just prior to his arrest, had asserted that the Wehrmacht had had nothing to do with the SS (apart from the Waffen-SS) or SD, and bore no responsibility for them. And as news and what was described as 'mounting enemy propaganda about conditions in German concentration camps' spread, Dönitz and Jodl were among those who saw the need of a public statement 'that neither the German Wehrmacht nor the German people had knowledge of these things'.[144] The myth of the 'good' Wehrmacht, which had such currency for decades in post-war Germany, was being forged.

At the grass roots, a not dissimilar, if differently accentuated, process of dissociation from Nazism was under way. Everywhere, the symbols of Nazism, where they still survived, were rapidly destroyed. No one willingly admitted to having been an enthusiastic follower of the regime. Initially, there were numerous denunciations of those functionaries who, only a year or two earlier, had strutted arrogantly in their Nazi uniforms and acted like 'little Hitlers' in their localities.[145] But as the 'big-shots' were gradually rounded up, the 'major war criminals' put on trial and the attention of the Allies shifted to the process of denazification at lower levels, the impression was increasingly given that hardly anyone had really backed the regime, but had at best under duress gone along with policies dictated by the tyranny of Hitler and his henchmen.

'Everybody pulls away from Adolf, nobody took part. Everybody was persecuted, and nobody denounced anybody,' was the cynical assessment of a young Berlin woman in May 1945, listening to voices in the queues for vegetables and water.[146] A report written in June 1946 by the Lutheran pastor in Berchtesgaden, a predominantly Catholic district nestling below the Obersalzberg, Nazi Germany's 'holy mountain' where Hitler had built his Alpine palace, expressed sentiments that were far from uncommon in the months after the demise of the Third Reich. The pastor spoke of 'all the disappointments under the National Socialist regime and the collapse of the hopes harboured by many idealists'. He also referred to the 'revelation of all the atrocities of this regime'. Then came the dissociation from Nazism. He regretted that 'our people as a whole is nevertheless still held responsible for the misdeeds of National Socialism although the vast majority throughout all those years had only the single wish, to be liberated from this violent regime because it saw its most sacred possessions of family, church and personal freedom destroyed or threatened'. His neighbour, the priest of the Catholic parish of St Andreas in Berchtesgaden, emphasized that 'our truly believing population, good middle-class and farming families, fundamentally rejected Nazism', that 80 per cent of the local Catholic population was opposed to the Party, horrified by the stories of the 'brutal manner' of Party leaders on the Obersalzberg, which had been 'hermetically sealed' off from the village below.[147]

In a prisoner-of-war camp in the winter of 1945–6, Major-General Erich Dethleffsen, former head of operations in Army High Command, began his memoirs of the last weeks of the war with his own reflections – thoughtful, if emphasizing lack of knowledge of barbarity, and guiltless exploitation by a ruthless regime – on how Germans were facing the trauma that still held them in its grip:

> It is still only a few months since the collapse. We haven't yet gained the distance in time, or in mind, to be able to judge, to some extent objectively, what was error, guilt and crime, or inexorable fate. We Germans are still too taken up by prejudice. Only slowly, in shock, and with reluctance are we awakening from the agony of the last years and recognizing ourselves and our situation. We search for exoneration to escape responsibility for

all that which led to the recent war, its terrible sacrifices and dreadful consequences. We believe ourselves to have been fooled, led astray, misused. We plead that we acted according to the best of our knowledge and conscience and knew little or nothing of all the terrible crimes. And millions did know nothing of them; especially those who fought at the front for homeland, house and home, and family and believed they were only doing their duty. But we are also ashamed that we let ourselves be led astray and misused and that we knew nothing. Shame mainly finds expression at first in defiance and undignified self-denigration; only gradually and slowly in regret. That is how it is among the nations. We are experiencing that now in our people . . .[148]

Such words, and many other accounts in similar vein in the early months after Germany's total defeat, convey – even if they can only faintly express – some sense of the trauma felt by people who had undergone the desperate last phase of the war and were now being fully confronted with the magnitude of the crimes committed by their fellow citizens. For the generation that endured the apocalyptic collapse of the Third Reich, it was a trauma that would never fully pass. It is unsurprising, then, that in German memory of the Third Reich, the final Armageddon of 1944–5 came to overshadow all else. The rise of Hitler amid the almost complete rejection of liberal democracy as Germany's economy crumbled, the first triumphant years of the regime when so many had rejoiced at national resurgence and economic recovery, and the early phase of the war with German military power laying the base for the conquest and ruthless exploitation of almost the whole of the European continent: these were more distant, less sharp memories. What had accompanied the 'good times' – the persecution of unloved minorities, first and foremost Jews, and the violent repression of political opponents, the terroristic framework on which the 'people's community' had been built – had been tolerated if not welcomed outright then, and could later be viewed as mere 'excesses' of the regime. 'If only National Socialism hadn't become so depraved! In itself it was the right thing for the German people,' the view expressed by a German officer in British captivity just after the capitulation, was not an uncommon one.[149] According to Allied opinion surveys in the immediate post-war years, about 50 per cent of Germans still thought National Socialism had been in essence a good idea that had been badly carried out.[150]

What really lasted in memory was the experience, devastating for so many Germans, of those last terrible months. It was perhaps not surprising, then, that the Germans thought of *themselves* as the helpless victims of a war they had not wanted, foisted on them by a tyrannical regime that had brought only misery to the land and produced catastrophe.[151] One man from a town in the east, whose mother had killed herself out of fear of the Russians, complained many years later: 'There were memorials for everybody: concentration camp prisoners, Jewish victims, Russians who had fallen. But nobody bothered about the other side.'[152] In the generation that experienced it, this sense of being the victims – exploited, misled, misused – of the uncontrollable tyranny of Hitler and his henchmen that in their name perpetrated terrible crimes (though, it was often averred, less heinous than those of Stalin) has remained, scarcely diluted.

Of course, it was not wholly incorrect. Germans themselves *were* in this final phase of the war indisputably also victims of events far beyond their control. The bombed-out homeless were evidently victims – of a ruthless bombing campaign, but also of the expansionist policies of their government that had prompted the horror. The women, children and elderly people forced to flee their homes and farmsteads in eastern Germany and join the millions trekking through ice and snow were also victims – of the Red Army juggernaut and of the self-serving Nazi leaders in their areas, but also of the war of aggression waged by their government against the Soviet Union that had invited such terrible reprisals. The soldiers dying in their thousands at the fronts in those horrific last months were themselves in a sense victims – of a military leadership using draconian methods to coerce compliance in the ranks, but also of an inculcated sense of duty that they were fighting in a good cause, and of a political leadership prepared for its own selfish ends to take the country into oblivion rather than surrender when all was evidently lost.

Yet, considering themselves victims, few stopped to consider *why* they had allowed themselves to be misled and exploited. Few of those bombed in the Ruhr had given much thought to the arsenal of weapons they were producing for the regime and enabling it to attack other countries and bomb the citizens of Warsaw, Rotterdam, Coventry, London, Belgrade and many other cities, inviting the obliteration of their own cities in return. As long as the bombs were falling elsewhere, on others, they had no complaints. Few of those expelled from East Prussia in such horrific circumstances in early 1945 were willing to recall that the province had been the most Nazified in Germany, that its support for Hitler had been far above average before 1933, or that they had cheered to the rafters during the 1930s as their area benefited from Nazi policies. Most people throughout Germany were unwilling to recollect their earlier enthusiasm for Hitler, their jubilation at his 'successes' and the hopes they invested in a brave new world for themselves and their children to be constructed on German conquest and despoliation of Europe. None wanted to dwell on what horror their own fathers, sons or brothers had inflicted on the peoples of eastern Europe, let alone ponder the reports (or rumours bordering on hard fact) they had heard of the slaughter of the Jews. The gross inhumanity for which Germany had been responsible was suppressed, forced out of mind. What remained, seared in memory, was how the Third Reich had gone so tragically wrong.

And even in those terrible last months of the war, few, it seems, preoccupied as they were by their own pressing existential needs, were prepared to give much thought to the real victims of what was taking place – the armies of foreigners who had been taken to Germany and forced to work against their will, the hundreds of thousands of inmates of concentration camps and prisons, more dead than alive, and the bedraggled and grossly maltreated prisoners, most of them Jews, on the death marches of the final weeks. The racial prejudice that Nazism could so easily exploit was something that few later wanted to admit to. But the old ideas died hard. According to American opinion surveys in October 1945, 20 per cent of those questioned 'went along with Hitler on his treatment of the Jews' and a further 19 per cent remained generally in favour but thought he had gone too far.[153]

A lasting partial affinity with Nazi ideas was not all. As the Third Reich disintegrated, an inevitable ambiguity lingered in most people's minds.[154] The overwhelming desire to see the war end was almost universal in these last months. It went along with the fervent wish to see the back of the Nazi regime that had inflicted such horror and suffering on the people. But one of Nazism's great strengths in earlier years had been its ability to usurp and exploit all feelings of patriotism and pride in the nation and turn them into such a dangerous and aggressive form of hypernationalism that could so easily become racial imperialism. The collapsing regime in 1944–5 did not erase, among all those who had come to detest Nazism, the determination still to fight for their country, to defend their homeland against foreign invasion, and especially – years of anti-Bolshevik propaganda, but also the bitter experience of conquest in the eastern regions, had done their job – to protect against what was viewed as an alien, repugnant and inhumane enemy to the east. So people wanted to see an end to Nazism, but not an end to the Reich. Since, however, the fight to preserve Germany was still directed by the very people whose policies had wrecked the country, the Nazi regime could still, if in a negative way, bank on support from both soldiers and civilians to the end. In western parts of Germany, the relatively lenient treatment by the American and British conquerors (if not by the French) inevitably prompted a more rapid erosion of the regime and swifter process of disintegration in civilian society and within the army than was the case in the east. There, despite the by now almost universal feelings of revulsion towards the Nazi Party and its representatives, people had little choice but to place their trust in the Wehrmacht and hope that it could stave off the Red Army.

The ambiguity in attitudes of ordinary Germans, civilians and soldiers, in the last dreadful months of the war was even more prevalent in the upper echelons of the Wehrmacht's officer corps. We have seen ample evidence, leaving aside fanatics like Dönitz or Schörner who associated closely and directly with Hitler, of the belief-systems and mentalities of generals who felt obliged to carry out orders that they thought were senseless, who were contemptuous of the Nazi leadership, but nevertheless saw it as their unswerving duty to do all they could to fend off enemy conquest, above all in the east. Defence of the homeland, not ideological commitment to Nazism, was what counted for the majority of high-ranking officers. But their nationalist and patriotic feelings sufficed to keep them completely bound up in the service of the regime which they had been so ready to serve in better times. After the failure of the bomb plot of July 1944, scarcely a thought to 'regime change' was given among the generals, who could see more plainly than anyone that Germany was heading for complete catastrophe. This was ultimately crucial. It meant that Hitler would remain in power, the war would go on, and there would be no putsch from within. Only once Hitler was dead did it seem feasible to move towards surrender. And only then, in conditions of complete collapse and impotence, were the links that bound the military leadership to Hitler and his regime reluctantly broken.

Conclusion:
Anatomy of Self-Destruction

This book began by pointing out the extreme rarity of a country being able and prepared to fight on in war to the point of total destruction. It is equally rare that the powerful elites of a country, most obviously the military, are unable or unwilling to remove a leader seen to be taking them down with him to complete disaster. Yet, recognized by all to be taking place and, increasingly, to be inevitable, this drive to all-enveloping national catastrophe – comprehensive military defeat, physical ruination, enemy occupation and, even beyond this, moral bankruptcy – was precisely what happened in Germany in 1945. The preceding chapters have tried to explain how this was possible. They have shown the long process of inexorable collapse of Europe's most powerful state under external military pressure. They have also tried to bring out the self-destructive dynamic – by no means confined to Hitler – built into the Nazi state. Most of all, they have sought to demonstrate that the reasons why Germany chose to fight to the very end, and was capable of doing so, are complex, not reducible to a single easy generalization.

The Allied demand for 'unconditional surrender', often seen as ruling out any alternative to fighting on to the end, provides no adequate explanation. German propaganda of course exploited the demand in its ceaseless efforts to bolster the will to hold out, claiming that the enemy, west and east, intended to destroy Germany's very existence as a nation. But ever fewer people in the last months, as we have seen, believed such messages, at least as regards the western powers.

More significant were the implications of the policy for the regime's elite. Certainly, 'unconditional surrender' was grist to Hitler's mill, insistent as he was that there could be no consideration of capitulation. And 'unconditional surrender' did make it impossible to end the war in the west – which most German leaders, though not Hitler, would have been prepared to negotiate – without also ending it in the east. Even the Dönitz administration following Hitler's death rejected this option – since it meant condemning nearly 2 million German soldiers to Soviet captivity – until Eisenhower gave it no choice in the matter, thus ensuring that the war went on for a further eight days of bloodshed and suffering. On the other hand, the demand for 'unconditional surrender' did not lead to any reconsideration by the Wehrmacht High Command of German strategy from early 1943 onwards – in so far as any overall strategy existed beyond an ideologically framed self-destructive drive to hold out to the point of total perdition.[1] It provided useful justification for fighting on to the end. But it was not the cause of the determination to do so.

The claim that it undermined the possibility of the resistance movement gaining wider support and a greater possibility of toppling Hitler also remains a doubtful proposition.[2] In any case, 'unconditional surrender' did not, of course, prevent an attempted *coup d'état*. Stauffenberg and his co-conspirators in the bomb plot of July 1944 acted in full awareness of the Allied demand, and, had they succeeded, would immediately have tried to sue for peace terms. And most of Hitler's paladins, and numerous generals, would have been willing, as we have noted, at one point or another to parley their way to a settlement, if Hitler had agreed, undeterred by the uncompromising Allied position.

So although 'unconditional surrender' was undoubtedly a factor in the equation, it cannot be regarded as the decisive or dominant issue in compelling the Germans to fight on.[3] Churchill himself later rejected the claim that 'unconditional surrender' had been a mistake which had prolonged the war. In fact, he went so far as to state that an alternative statement on peace terms, which the Allies had several times attempted to draft, would have been more harmful to any German attempts to seek peace since the conditions 'looked so terrible when set forth on paper, and so far exceeded what was in fact done, that their publication would only have stimulated German resistance'.[4]

Nor can Allied mistakes in strategy and tactics, weakening their own efforts to bring the war to an early end and contributing to the protracted end to the great conflict also by temporarily boosting the confidence of the German defenders, be seen as the key factor. Important errors were certainly made, and contributed to the inability of the Allies, after the Normandy landings in the west and the Red Army's surge through

Poland in the east, to finish off Germany by Christmas, as they had in their early optimism initially thought possible.

As we saw in earlier chapters, in the west, the divergence in strategic aims between Eisenhower and Montgomery, underpinned by their personal differences (owing mainly to the latter's overbearing personality and some ingrained anti-American prejudice in the British military elite), prevented full exploitation of the breakthrough in France in August 1944, which had left the German western front in great disarray. As a result, compounded by the British failure to secure the port in Antwerp and by the disaster at Arnhem, the Wehrmacht was able to reinforce western defences and bring the Allied attack almost to a standstill for several precious weeks. The Allies never fully regained their momentum – and suffered a further temporary setback in the Ardennes offensive – until March 1945. On the eastern front, the Red Army's mistakes in operational planning also meant that the massive assault of the summer of 1944, devastating though it was for the Wehrmacht, did not bring an early end to the war. A bold thrust to the Pomeranian coast, which German defence planners had feared, would have cleared the way for a much earlier attack on Berlin than in fact took place and could possibly have brought total collapse long before May 1945.

What might have occurred had the British and Americans in the west and the Soviets in the east taken different strategic decisions can of course only be a matter of speculation. Perhaps the war would have been over much earlier. But just as possibly, other errors or hesitations – war inevitably producing its own frequent surprises and seldom going according to plans laid down on paper – might have played their part and prevented a more rapid conclusion.

In a similar realm of ultimately futile speculation is the question of what the outcome might have been to a successful assassination of Hitler and takeover of the state by the conspirators behind the July plot of 1944. Had they succeeded, Stauffenberg and the successful plotters would unquestionably have sought peace with the west, though almost certainly not in the east. Most likely, the west would have refused consideration of anything other than 'unconditional surrender' on all fronts, since to do otherwise would have split the coalition with the Soviet Union, which rested fundamentally on the complete destruction of German militarism as well as Nazism. With Hitler dead, the leaders of the successful coup would have been faced with the choice of either accepting the terms of complete capitulation or fighting on. Probably, they would have felt compelled to agree to total surrender. The war might, therefore, have been over in July 1944, with the saving of the immense bloodshed that occurred in subsequent months. But would the military leadership, especially in the east, have agreed? And would Nazi diehards, most notably in the SS, have gone along with it? Shored up by a new 'stab-in-the-back' legend focused on the image of the dead, heroic Führer, portrayed as killed by his own officers when leading Germany's fight for existence, powerful internal forces might have resisted and even toppled the new government. Civil war might have ensued.

In the nature of things, the endless fascination of such 'what-if?' speculation can provide no answers. This book has attempted, therefore, to assess not what might have been, but what did in fact happen, and to evaluate on that basis the reasons for Germany fighting on to the end. On the basis of the evidence presented in earlier chapters, it is time to draw the threads of an answer together.

First of all, it was plainly not the case, as has sometimes been claimed, that the population backed Hitler and the Nazi regime to the end. 'The people have no confidence any longer in the leadership,' ran an internal report, one of the many cited above, in March 1945. 'The Führer is drawn more strongly by the day into the question of confidence and into the criticism.'[5] The bonds with Hitler, at the top and bottom of society, had, it is true, at least in the short term been strengthened in July 1944 by the failure of Stauffenberg's bomb plot. As we saw, there was a surge in Hitler's lagging popularity among the civilian population and among frontline soldiers, to go from their letters home. And most of the generals, even those who were far from regime enthusiasts, were utterly dismayed by the attempt on Hitler's life, as their private diary entries and remarks not meant for public consumption demonstrate. But apart from this brief resurgence, Hitler's popularity had been on the wane since winter 1941 and by 1944–5 was in free fall. Significant reserves of his popularity did remain among a dwindling minority of the population – though, to be sure, a minority that still held power. By early 1945, however, support for Hitler was very low.

And by now the Nazi Party was widely hated. As Goebbels admitted, the Party was largely 'played out' well before the end, the target of bitter resentment as its functionaries disappeared into the ether, abandoning the population. Despite the intensified efforts of propaganda, the reports reaching Goebbels spoke with a clear voice. Propaganda could do little or nothing to counter what people were seeing with their own eyes. Its gung-ho messages were increasingly scorned by a population yearning for an end to the war and inexorably turning against the regime which had brought such misery upon Germany. There is little to be said for the view that the 'people's community' retained its cohesion and integrative force behind the war effort. The much-vaunted 'people's community' had in fact long since dissolved as it become a question of 'save yourself, if you can'.

Yet there were important partial affinities that went beyond support for the regime but still objectively underpinned it. Crucially, the regime's existence was intertwined with defence of country and homeland – a cause upheld by most Germans, even when they despised Hitler and the Nazis. The overwhelming proportion of the population, as numerous internal reports acknowledged, yearned for the end of the war. But there was an obvious ambivalence. Few wanted foreign occupation, least of all by the feared Russians. But as long as they fought to their utmost to avoid being overrun by the enemy, Germans were, whatever their motives and desires, helping the regime to continue functioning. And however demoralized, for the vast majority of Germans there was in any case simply no alternative to carrying on.

The role played by terror in this can scarcely be overstated. Without it there may well have been a popular uprising. But the regime was a grave danger to its own citizens, increasingly so after the sharp intensification of terror in February 1945. Very justifiably, people felt greatly intimidated. In the death-throes of the regime the terror, earlier exported, rebounded back onto the population of Germany itself, and not just its persecuted minorities. Among ordinary soldiers, the numbers of deserters, intermingled with 'stragglers', soared. Military courts, as we noted, reacted with harsh exemplary punishment. The summary courts martial introduced in mid-February were no more than kangaroo courts meting out little other than death sentences, and in early March, when such courts were made itinerant, the 'flying court martial' could turn up in any frontline area, and within minutes have sentenced to death those denounced as shirkers, defeatists or subversives, carrying out the sentence instantly. Remarkably, military courts were still passing death sentences even after the capitulation. Among civilians, too, anyone stepping out of line, even in desperation, could to the very end meet brutal retribution. Largely owing to the intimidatory effect of such terror, the popular mood was resigned, war-weary and pessimistic, but not rebellious. Those who dared raise their voices, let alone take any action, against the regime were viciously struck down. Most, sensibly, took the view that they could do nothing – except wait for the end and hope that the Americans and British got there before the Russians.

Yet terror does not explain all. It works as an explanation mainly at the grass-roots level. Tens of thousands of soldiers deserted, and many faced summary execution as a consequence. But even here, and bearing in mind the wider intimidatory effect of the drastic punishment awaiting those refusing to fight, the vast majority did not desert – or even contemplate deserting. They fought on, often fatalistically, even reluctantly, but frequently even in the last desperate weeks with high commitment, even enthusiasm. That cannot be accounted for by terror.[6] And at the higher level of the Wehrmacht, among those senior officers with power of decision and command, terror played little role. Apart from those involved in the bomb plot, generals were not terrorized. Some were dismissed. But they were not executed.

For the German people, and even more for the racial and political victims of Nazism, the intensified terror alongside the terrible suffering could not end until the regime itself was destroyed by military might. This was in no small part because many of those wielding power, in particular those in high places, but also functionaries and representatives of the Party and its affiliates at regional and local level, realized that they had burnt their boats and had no future. Party and SS leaders had been involved in the worst atrocities against Jews and others. Goebbels saw this as a positive factor in ensuring their continued fanaticism and backing for the regime (often underpinned by belief in some ferocious 'Jewish revenge'). Hitler thought exactly the same way. As Nazi rule fragmented, the regime increasingly ran amok as police, SS, regional and local Party officials took matters in the provinces into their own hands. Hundreds of citizens fell victim to uncontrolled violence by Nazi fanatics in the last weeks of the regime, often in the attempt to prevent the senseless destruction of their towns or villages in continued fighting as the enemy approached. Prisoners and foreign workers were now more exposed than ever to the wild and unconstrained violence. And with the enemy on the doorstep, pointless forced marches of thousands of concentration camp prisoners, many of them Jews, left countless numbers dead, the rest terrorized and traumatized.

The 'desperado-actions' of many Party activists in the last weeks reflected the readiness of those who were well aware that they had no future to take enemies down with them, to exact revenge against long-standing opponents, to settle personal scores, and to ensure that those who had rejected the regime should not be around to triumph at its downfall. Though these fanatics were a small minority, they were a minority still wielding power over life and death. Their self-destructive urges paralleled those of Hitler and the regime leadership, helping through their own brutality to guarantee that Nazi power continued and that any manifestations of resistance from below were swiftly extinguished.

The Party and its affiliates increasingly occupied all the organizational space beyond the military sphere after July 1944 and gained hugely extended powers over citizens and over civil administration. Martin Bormann used his proximity to Hitler and his command of the Party's central administration to reinvigorate the Party and push the state administration out of any importance in policy-making. The 'time of struggle' before the Party gained power in 1933 was repeatedly evoked as activists were urged to take radical steps to complete the 'Nazi revolution'.

Below Bormann, a pivotal role was played by the Gauleiter. As Reich Defence Commissars, responsible for civil defence in their areas, they had enormous scope for interference in practically all spheres of daily life (and for imposing summary retribution for non-compliance). They and their subordinates at district and local level controlled, among other things, distribution of welfare, compulsory evacuation of citizens from threatened areas, access to air-raid shelters, clearance of bomb damage, and compulsory recruitment to forced labour on defence installations. And they were key agents for Goebbels' total-war drive to comb out last reserves of manpower from offices and workplaces to raise men for the Wehrmacht. The increase in the Party's dominance did nothing to create a streamlined administration. But it did massively strengthen its grip over government and society. In the last months of the war, Germany was as close to a totally mobilized and militarized society as it is possible to get. The mass of Germans were oppressed, browbeaten and marshalled as never before. There was by now scarcely any avenue of life remaining free from the intrusions of the Party and its affiliates.

A big step towards the complete militarization of society was the introduction of the *Volkssturm* in the autumn of 1944. It was militarily as good as useless. It was lampooned as the awaited 'miracle weapon' and generally derided. And it was a sign, recognized by all, of how desperate things had become. Sensible individuals did all they could to avoid having to serve in it, with justification given its high loss rate, especially on the eastern front. But as a control structure for the regime, it was far from devoid of significance. And its leadership was often in the hands of fervent Nazis, increasingly involved in many policing 'actions', including atrocities against other Germans viewed as cowards or defeatists.

Despite the drain of actual power away from the state bureaucracy – reduced largely to an instrument of administrative implementation – and increasingly into the hands of the Party at all levels, the regime was also sustained to the end by a sophisticated and experienced bureaucratic machine. This surmounted any number of huge difficulties to keep on functioning, if with sharply decreasing effectiveness, especially in the last months, till there was little or nothing left to administer. Without the organizational capacity that came from educated, well-trained civil servants at different levels, the administration would surely have collapsed much earlier. The judicial system, too, still meting out draconian sentences, continued to function to the end, sustaining the radicalized terror against German citizens and against persecuted minorities. Throughout the civil service, there was an almost unthinking loyalty, not specifically to Hitler but to the abstraction of 'the state', and commitment to what was seen as 'duty'. Even for civil servants scornful of Hitler and disdainful of Nazi bosses, it was enough to provide support for a system in terminal collapse. We saw the near incomprehension of Kritzinger, the State Secretary in the Reich Chancellery, when asked by his post-war interrogators why he had continued to work so hard when all was so obviously lost, replying: 'As a long-standing civil servant I was duty-bound in loyalty to the state.' The mentality was replicated at top and bottom of the large civil service.

The savagery of the war in the east provided its own motivation for carrying on fighting and rejecting all thoughts of surrender. This was a war quite unlike the conflict in the west. Military leaders and rank-and-file soldiers alike were well aware that they had been responsible for or implicated in countless atrocities in the east – torched villages, mass executions of partisans, shootings of tens of thousands of Jews. The barbarity of warfare on the eastern front meant, as they well knew, that they could expect no mercy if they fell into Soviet hands.

The propaganda image of Nemmersdorf, scene of Soviet atrocities in October 1944, was worse than the reality – but that had certainly been bad enough. Nemmersdorf encapsulated the fear of Bolshevism, something hammered home over the years in incessant propaganda but now no longer an abstraction. For soldiers fighting in the east, or those elsewhere with families in the threatened eastern regions, there was not simply an ideological reason for fighting on. The ideological fight against 'Asiatic hordes' and 'Bolshevik beasts', and even the patriotic defence of the nation, merged subliminally into a desperate attempt to stave off the very obvious threat to families and homes or to avenge the atrocities of the Red Army. Beyond these motives, soldiers fought out of group solidarity for their immediate comrades and, in the last resort, for their own survival.

Vital to the regime's ability to fight on was, not least, the role of the officer corps of the armed forces. The war brought soaring numbers – to nearly 200,000, including reserve officers, in early 1944 – and a very rapid turnover. The army lost 269,000 officers during the war, 87,000 of them killed. In September 1944 an average of 317 officers a day – mostly low-ranking – were killed, wounded or taken captive. The junior and middle-ranking officers were crucial cogs in the military machine. Many had swallowed tenets of Nazi doctrine in the Hitler Youth and in subsequent training courses, and had been hardened by battle and involvement in murderous 'pacification' and genocidal actions in the east.[7] As we noted, Nazi penetration of the armed forces was sharply intensified after the failed bomb plot with the introduction of the 'Heil Hitler' greeting instead of the traditional military salute and extended use of NSFOs to instil fanaticism and loyalty in the troops. The brutal reprisals against those involved in the Stauffenberg plot and the repeated tirades of vilification of army officers by Nazi leaders, from Hitler downwards, also produced their own pressure not just to conform but to display enthusiastic commitment.

At the top, the generals held the key. Most were too old to have been schooled in Nazism like the more junior officers. But their older nationalist mentalities had blended easily with Nazi ideals and they had wide experience of – and support for – the ideological 'war of annihilation' on the eastern front. Only loyalists were left after the purge that followed the failed bomb plot. That did not prevent serious disputes over tactics developing between individual generals and Hitler. Numerous generals were made scapegoats for defeats or for their inability to fulfil absurd orders. But they were not temperamentally or organizationally capable of challenging Hitler or staging another attempted military coup. Most generals took their oath of allegiance to Hitler extremely seriously and were tortured by the thought that they might be compelled to disobey orders. Even where the oath served as little more than a pretext for compliance and a retreat from any political responsibility on the grounds that they were purely soldiers carrying out their duty, the traditional military imperatives of order and obedience were distorted in the Third Reich to an extreme readiness to yield to the commands of the Führer, however irrational.[8] Ultimately, a deeply inculcated but utterly warped sense of duty provided both motivation and alibi for the Third Reich's military leaders.[9]

The generals were divided among themselves. The bugged conversations of those in British captivity, referred to on several occasions in preceding chapters, reveal sharp divergence in views.[10] It was no different among those generals still holding positions of high command in Germany and on its borders. As fervent nationalists, they saw it as axiomatic to be ready to do their utmost for the defence of the Reich, even where they had inwardly broken with Hitler or despised the Party and its representatives. But some, in fact, remained fanatical backers of Hitler, like the brutal Field-Marshal Ferdinand Schörner, whose ruthlessness in enforcing discipline made him notorious even in the top ranks of the army, or Grand-Admiral Karl Dönitz, who demanded in April 1945 that every ship and naval base be defended to the last in accordance with the Führer's orders, offering his men the choice of victory or death. Most high-ranking officers, like Dönitz, held to the fiction that they were 'unpolitical', and that political decisions were solely and rightly the concern of the state leadership. But without their support, whatever their motives, it is plain that the state leadership could not have continued, and nor could the war.

Even where they disagreed fundamentally with Hitler's tactics, the generals did not dispute his right to issue them, and fought on loyally. Faced with increasingly insane orders for the defence of Berlin,

Colonel-General Heinrici nonetheless felt that to refuse them was to commit treason. The example of Field-Marshal Kesselring, refusing even at the end of April 1945 to condone surrender in Italy as long as the Führer was alive, is a further graphic case.

Crucial in enabling the regime to fight on was also the radicalization of the structure of power beneath Hitler in the last months. In the wake of Stauffenberg's assassination attempt, the regime was swiftly buttressed. Changes were made that shored it up in the last months and ruled out any internal collapse, with power below Hitler largely divided between the four Nazi grandees. Bormann, as we saw, greatly expanded the mobilizing and controlling role of the Party, extending its hold over almost all facets of daily life. Goebbels now combined the key areas of propaganda and mobilization for the total-war effort. Without the million extra men that he raised by the end of 1944, the Wehrmacht would simply not have been able to replace the extraordinary losses it was suffering. Himmler, with his takeover of the command of the Replacement Army (from whose headquarters Stauffenberg had orchestrated the plot to kill Hitler), extended his terror apparatus into the Wehrmacht itself. Only the Replacement Army had been capable of planning the attempted *coup d'état* in 1944. In Himmler's hands, that potential was removed. And Speer achieved miracles of management and organization in producing sufficient armaments, despite the growing crisis of production and transport through Allied bombing and territorial losses, to ensure that the troops still had weapons to fight with. If Speer, who was very late in accepting that the war was irredeemably lost, had worked half as hard, Germany could not have held out for remotely so long.

The quadrumvirate of Bormann, Goebbels, Himmler and Speer – three of them among the most brutal and radical fanatics, the fourth an ambitious, power-hungry organizational genius – was instrumental to the continuation of the war. But the four were divided among themselves and suspicious of each other – a characteristic of the Nazi state. And each of them knew that his power depended on a higher authority – that of Hitler.

Finally, but far from least, we come to Hitler himself. He never deviated from what had been the leitmotiv of his political existence, that there would never, ever, be a 'cowardly' capitulation and internal revolution as there had been in 1918. He consequently and consistently refused all entreaties from his paladins to consider a negotiated settlement. For him, that could only follow a victory, not a defeat. There was never a chance of that, once the vice closed on the Third Reich after the major enemy successes, east and west, from June 1944 onwards. The Allied demand for 'unconditional surrender' simply played to his mentality and convictions. 'Heroic' total destruction was for him infinitely preferable to what he saw as the coward's way out of capitulation. The plight of the German people did not concern him. They had proved weak in the war, and deserved to go under. After the failure of the Ardennes offensive, he was clear-sighted enough to see that his last card had been played. But he clutched at one straw after another in desperation and impotence to turn the tide that was about to engulf him. Suicide was the obvious and likely way out. In fact, it became the only way out. It was simply a matter of time, and of timing, so that he could not be captured by the Russians. It was also the easy way out for him, since he knew that whatever happened he had no future after the war. But as long as he lived, his power – if over a rapidly diminishing Reich – could not be challenged, as Göring and Himmler learnt even in the very last days of his life.

Hitler's personality was self-evidently scarcely insignificant to Germany's continued fight. Generals and political leaders alike found him absolutely intransigent if they proposed any alternative course of action. Even in the last weeks some went in to see him demoralized and disconsolate and came away with new enthusiasm and determination. Under a different head of state, say Göring (until his ousting on 23 April 1945 Hitler's designated successor), it seems highly likely that Germany would have sued for peace at some point earlier than May 1945. It is indeed questionable whether in the event of Hitler's earlier demise Göring (or Himmler, the only other feasible candidate to have succeeded) would have had the internal authority with the generals to continue the prosecution of the war. Such a counter-factual scenario only emphasizes once more how much Hitler's insistence on the continuation of the war provided the major obstacle to halting it. This cannot, however, be regarded solely as a matter of Hitler's domineering personality – his intransigence, his detachment from reality, his readiness to take the country and German people down with him to total perdition – however important this was. Beyond this is the question of why the power elite was prepared to allow him to dictate in such disastrous fashion to the end.

Albert Speer ruminated in pseudo self-reproach in his memoirs about why, when it was obvious that Germany was as good as finished economically and militarily, Hitler was not faced with any joint action from those military leaders in regular contact with him to demand an explanation of how he was going to end the war (with the implication that they might have forced him to do so). Speer thought of such a move coming from Göring, Keitel, Jodl, Dönitz, Guderian and himself.[11] The proposition, as he well knew, was absurd.[12] Structurally as well as individually, the group he mentioned was divided and (his own and Guderian's growing estrangement aside) in any case arch-loyalists, three of whom fervently backed Hitler's 'hold-out' orders.

Confronting Hitler in any organized body, political or military, was completely impossible. The dissolution, from early in the Third Reich and ever more pronounced during the war, of all structures of collective government ensured that. Mussolini's deposition in July 1943 had come from within his own organization, the Fascist Grand Council. And above Mussolini, at least nominally, stood an alternative source of loyalty: the King of Italy. No similar structures existed in Nazi Germany. Hitler was head of state, commander-in-chief of the armed forces, head of government and head of the Party. He had consistently resisted suggestions to reinstate a form of collective government in the Reich cabinet and the creation of a senate of the Nazi Party to determine, among other things, the succession. The Gauleiter were summoned to assemble periodically, but only to hear pep-talks from Hitler. Even in the armed forces, there was a damaging division between the High Command of the Wehrmacht (responsible for operations outside the eastern front) and the High Command of the Army (responsible for only the eastern front).

The problem was compounded by the fact that Hitler was not just supreme commander of the Wehrmacht as a whole, but also Commander-in-Chief of the Army. Even compared with other authoritarian regimes, the personalization of rule in Hitler's regime was extreme. Structures of power, each imbued in varied measure with Nazi ideological values, were all bound to Hitler, gaining legitimacy from his 'charismatic leadership'. The fragmentation of governance reflected the character of Hitler's absolute power, even when this started to wane in the very last weeks. Though Hitler's mass appeal as a charismatic leader had been in steep decline since the middle of the war, the fragmentation of rule beneath him that had been a hallmark of his charismatic rule from the beginning lasted to the end. It was a fundamental reason why an earlier collapse, or a resort to a negotiated settlement – any alternative to the inexorable course to self-destruction – did not take place.

The mindset of the ruling elite had attuned to the character of charismatic domination and underpinned the structural determinants preventing any challenge to Hitler. Among Nazi leaders, the personal bonds forged with him at an earlier time proved almost impossible to break even when the nimbus of infallibility built into the personality cult faded. So did the utter dependence on Hitler for positions of power. Speer admittedly distanced himself, though very belatedly, and even he felt an inward urge to make a perilous and futile last trip back into the Führer Bunker in the very last days to say his personal farewell to the leader he had once idolized. Göring, despite bearing the brunt of Hitler's fury at the failure of the Luftwaffe, never broke with him. His deposition from all his offices on 23 April followed a misunderstanding wilfully exploited by Bormann, one of the Reich Marshal's arch-enemies. Bormann himself was the loyal right hand of his master, turning Hitler's tirades and outbursts into bureaucratic regulations and orders. Himmler was the strong arm of repression who, despite surreptitiously going his own way in the last months in an attempt to retain a position of power in a post-Hitler world, continued to recognize his dependency. The breach with Hitler came at the very last, and, as with Göring, seems to have followed a misunderstanding, when Himmler presumed reports of the Dictator's breakdown on 22 April had meant his effective abdication. The most committed of all the top Nazi leaders, and among the most clear-sighted of Hitler's acolytes, Joseph Goebbels, was one of the very few prepared to stay with him to the end and cast himself on the great funeral pyre of the Third Reich.

Beneath the top echelon of Party bosses, the Gauleiter still presented a phalanx of outright loyalists, whatever their private feelings, who had long since bound themselves irredeemably to Hitler, even though in the last weeks they started of necessity to take independent action as communications with Berlin broke down. Their last collective meeting with Hitler, on 24 February 1945, showed that Hitler's authority was still intact among this important group.

Among military leaders, the stance of Grand-Admiral Karl Dönitz, head of the navy and at Hitler's death his nominated successor as head of state, is illustrative of the lasting bonds with Hitler. In contrast to his post-war reputation of a military professional who had simply done his duty, Dönitz had been one of the foremost fanatics in his support for Hitler's orders to fight to the last, an outright Nazi in his attitude. But with Hitler gone, the chief and unyielding barrier to capitulation was removed. Given overall responsibility and feeling freed from his oath of loyalty to Hitler, Dönitz saw the need to bow to military and political reality and looked immediately to find a negotiated end to a lost war. This sudden reversal of his stance by Dönitz underlines as clearly as anything how much the fight to the end, down to complete defeat and destruction, was owing not just to Hitler in person, but to the character of his rule and the mentalities that had upheld his charismatic domination.

Of the reasons why Germany was able and willing to fight on to the end, these structures of rule and underlying mentalities behind them are the most fundamental. All the other factors – lingering popular backing for Hitler, the ferocious terror apparatus, the increased dominance of the Party, the prominent roles of the Bormann–Goebbels–Himmler–Speer quadrumvirate, the negative integration produced by the fear of Bolshevik occupation, and the continued readiness of high-ranking civil servants and military leaders to continue doing their duty when all was obviously lost – were ultimately subordinate to the way the charismatic Führer regime was structured, and how it functioned, in its dying phase. Paradoxically, it was by this time charismatic rule without charisma. Hitler's mass charismatic appeal had long since dissolved, but the structures and mentalities of his charismatic rule lasted until his death in the bunker. The dominant elites, divided as they were, possessed neither the collective will nor the mechanisms of power to prevent Hitler taking Germany to total destruction.

That was decisive.

Notes

ABBREVIATIONS

BAB	Bundesarchiv Berlin/Lichterfelde
BA/MA	Bundesarchiv/Militärarchiv, Freiburg
BDC	Berlin Document Center
BfZ	Bibliothek für Zeitgeschichte, Württembergische Landesbibliothek, Stuttgart
BHStA	Bayerisches Hauptstaatsarchiv, Munich
DNB	Deutsches Nachrichtenbüro (German News Agency)
DRZW	*Das Deutsche Reich und der Zweite Weltkrieg*
DZW	*Deutschland im Zweiten Weltkrieg*
HSSPF	Höherer SS- und Polizeiführer (Higher SS and Police Leader(s))
IfZ	Institut für Zeitgeschichte, Munich
IMT	International Military Tribunal
ITS	International Tracing Service, Bad Arolsen
IWM	Imperial War Museum, Duxford
KTB/OKW	*Kriegstagebuch des Oberkommando der Wehrmacht*
KTB/SKL	*Kriegstagebuch der Seekriegsleitung*
LHC	Liddell Hart Centre for Military Archives, King's College, London
MadR	*Meldungen aus dem Reich*
NAL	National Archives London (formerly Public Record Office)
Nbg.-Dok.	Nürnberg-Dokument (unpublished trial document(s))
NCO	non-commissioned officer
NL	Nachlaß (personal papers)
NSDAP	Nationalsozialistische Deutsche Arbeiterpartei (Nazi Party)
NSFO	Nationalsozialistischer Führungsoffizier (National Socialist Leadership Officer)
NSV	Nationalsozialistiche Volkswohlfahrt (National Socialist People's Welfare Organization)
OKH	Oberkommando des Heeres (High Command of the Army)
OKW	Oberkommando der Wehrmacht (High Command of the Armed Forces)

OT	*Organisation Todt*
PWE	Political Warfare Executive
RPÄ	Reichspropagandaämter
RPvNB/OP	Regierungspräsident von Niederbayern und der Oberpfalz (Government President (Head of the Regional Administration) of Lower Bavaria and the Upper Palatinate)
RPvOB	Regierungspräsident von Oberbayern (Government President of Upper Bavaria)
RPvOF/MF	Regierungspräsident von Oberfranken und Mittelfranken (Government President of Upper Franconia and Central Franconia)
RVK	Reichsverteidigungskommissar(e) (Reich Defence Commissar(s))
SD	Sicherheitsdienst (Security Service)
SHAEF	Supreme Headquarters Allied Expeditionary Force
StAA	Staatsarchiv Augsburg
StAM	Staatsarchiv München
TBJG	*Die Tagebücher von Joseph Goebbels*
VB	*Völkischer Beobachter*
VfZ	*Vierteljahrshefte für Zeitgeschichte*
YVS	*Yad Vashem Studies*

For the full book titles, see List of Works Cited, pp. 511–32; for details of archives, see List of Archival Sources Cited, pp. 509–10. Contributions in *DRZW* are cited by author only in the Notes; titles are given in List of Works Cited.

PREFACE

1. See, for example, Ralf Meindl, *Ostpreußens Gauleiter: Erich Koch – eine politische Biographie*, Osnabrück, 2007.
2. A good, critical study of Dönitz, long overdue, appeared only after this work had been completed: Dieter Hartwig, *Großadmiral Karl Dönitz: Legende und Wirklichkeit*, Paderborn, 2010.
3. Exemplary, in different ways, are Herfried Münkler, *Machtzerfall: Die letzten Tage des Dritten Reiches dargestellt am Beispiel der hessischen Kreisstadt Friedberg*, Berlin, 1985, and Stephen G. Fritz, *Endkampf: Soldiers, Civilians, and the Death of the Third Reich*, Lexington, Ky., 2004.
4. None better than Antony Beevor's brilliant narrative depiction of the Red Army's assault on the Reich capital, *Berlin: The Downfall 1945*, pb. edn., London, 2007.
5. *Deutschland im Zweiten Weltkrieg*, vol. 6: *Die Zerschlagung des Hitlerfaschismus und die Befreiung des deutschen Volkes (Juni 1944 bis zum 8. Mai 1945)*, written by an Authors' Collective under direction of Wolfgang

Schumann and Olaf Groehler, with assistance from Wolfgang Bleyer, Berlin, 1985.

6. *Das Deutsche Reich und der Zweite Weltkrieg*, edited by various authors for the Militärgeschichtliches Forschungsamt, vols. 7–10, Munich, 2004–8.

7. Two recent works among many might be singled out: Andreas Kunz, *Wehrmacht und Niederlage: Die bewaffnete Macht in der Endphase der nationalsozialistischen Herrschaft 1944 bis 1945*, Munich, 2007; and John Zimmermann, *Pflicht zum Untergang: Die deutsche Kriegführung im Westen des Reiches 1944/45*, Paderborn, 2009.

8. This applies to the excellent works by Dieter Rebentisch, *Führerstaat und Verwaltung im Zweiten Weltkrieg*, Stuttgart, 1989, and Eleanor Hancock, *National Socialist Leadership and Total War 1941–45*, New York, 1991. Martin Broszat's classic *Der Staat Hitlers*, Munich, 1969, dealt in the main with the beginning, rather than the end, of the Third Reich.

9. The extensive study by Dietrich Orlow, *The History of the Nazi Party*, vol. 2: *1933–1945*, Newton Abbot, 1973, for example, devotes little more than 20 of its 538 pages to the period after the Stauffenberg assassination attempt and no more than 8 pages or so to the months January–May 1945, while Kurt Pätzold and Manfred Weißbecker, *Geschichte der NSDAP 1920–1945*, Cologne, 1981, written by two GDR historians, devotes less than a dozen out of 429 pages to the period under consideration in this book.

10. Marlis Steinert's splendid *Hitlers Krieg und die Deutschen*, Düsseldorf and Vienna, 1970, has not yet been bettered as a social history of Germany during the war. It is, however, largely restricted to usage of – highly informative – internal reports on morale, and deals in the main with civilian society, but not with the military. A new and highly promising study of German society during the war is being prepared by Nicholas Stargardt, Magdalen College, Oxford.

11. The outstanding study of American strategy and the military advance into Germany is that of Klaus-Dietmar Henke, *Die amerikanische Besetzung Deutschlands*, Munich, 1995. A graphic description of Allied, as well as German, military experiences at the fronts as Germany was crushed is provided by Max Hastings, *Armageddon: The Battle for Germany 1944–45*, London, 2004.

12. On this issue, see the excellent study of how German experiences in the final war months helped the beginnings of recovery after capitulation by Richard Bessel, *Germany 1945: From War to Peace*, London, 2009.

INTRODUCTION: GOING DOWN IN FLAMES

1. *Justiz und NS-Verbrechen: Sammlung deutscher Strafurteile wegen nationalsozialistischer Tötungsverbrechen 1945–1966*, vol. 1, ed. Adelheid L.

Rüter-Ehlermann and C. F. Rüter, Amsterdam, 1968, Nos. 010, 029, pp. 115–29, 645–59; Elke Fröhlich, 'Ein junger Märtyrer', in Martin Broszat and Elke Fröhlich (eds.), *Bayern in der NS-Zeit*, vol. 6, Munich and Vienna, 1983, pp. 228–57; Stephen G. Fritz, *Endkampf: Soldiers, Civilians, and the Death of the Third Reich*, Lexington, Ky., 2004, pp. 153–8; Hans Woller, *Gesellschaft und Politik in der amerikanischen Besatzungszone: Die Region Ansbach und Fürth*, Munich, 1986, pp. 48–55. Dr Meyer, the town's former military commandant, was sentenced in December 1946 by the Ansbach district court to ten years in a penitentiary.

2. See the valuable collection of essays on the terror of the last phase in Cord Arendes, Edgar Wolfrum and Jörg Zedler (eds.), *Terror nach Innen: Verbrechen am Ende des Zweiten Weltkrieges*, Göttingen, 2006.

3. Members of the Munich police constabulary, for instance, were paid continually through to May 1945. Backpay for a cleaner in the department who had not been paid in April was claimed at the end of June. – BHStA, Munich, Minn 72417, Nr. 2415f27, Gehaltszahlung, 28.6.45, 2415f28, Zahlung von Arbeitslöhnen, 28.6.45. At the other end of the spectrum, Himmler's former chief of his personal staff and in the last phase of the war Wehrmacht plenipotentiary in Italy, General der Waffen-SS Obergruppenführer Karl Wolff, still drew a salary of 2,226.80 Reich Marks (1,551.90 Reich Marks net) in April 1945, at a time when he was in fact secretly plotting the unilateral surrender of German troops in his region. – BAB, BDC, SSO-Karl Wolff, Gehaltsabrechnung, April 1945, 31.3.45. I am grateful to Horst Möller and Michael Buddrus for this information, and to Jonathan Steinberg for the suggestion to look for it.

4. Information kindly provided by Wolfgang Holl, Alexander von Humboldt-Stiftung, Bad-Godesberg, and by Holger Impekoven, currently working on a history of the Stiftung between 1925 and 1945, to whom I am indebted for an exposé of his project.

5. Albert Speer, *Erinnerungen*, Frankfurt am Main and Berlin, 1969, p. 467; BA/MA, N648/1, NL Dethleffsen, Erinnerungen, fo. 7 (1945–6).

6. Andreas Förschler, *Stuttgart 1945: Kriegsende und Neubeginn*, Gudensberg-Gleichen, 2004, p. 10.

7. Christian Hartmann and Johannes Hürter, *Die letzten 100 Tage des Zweiten Weltkriegs*, Munich, 2005, Day 78, 21 Feb. 1945 (and for the following). The football hardly measured up to modern Premiership standards. The teams had to be improvised from what players – often soldiers on leave – were available. The last final for the German championship took place on 16 June 1944 in front of 70,000 spectators in Berlin, when Dresden beat Hamburg 4–0. After that, because of limited transport capacity and the ever worsening war fortunes, matches were restricted to regional 'Sportgaue'.

8. For an interesting comparison of the potential for a *coup d'état* in Italy and in Germany, see Jerzy W. Borejsza, 'Der 25. Juli 1943 in Italien und der 20.

Juli 1944 in Deutschland: Zur Technik des Staatsstreichs im totalitären System', in Jürgen Schmädeke and Peter Steinbach (eds.), *Der Widerstand gegen den Nationalsozialismus*, Munich and Zurich, 1986, pp. 1079–85.

9. Michael Geyer, '*Endkampf* 1918 and 1945: German Nationalism, Annihilation, and Self-Destruction', in Alf Lüdtke and Bernd Weisbrod (eds.), *No Man's Land of Violence: Extreme Wars in the 20th Century*, Göttingen, 2006, p. 40. An almost identical question was posed by Doris L. Bergen, 'Death Throes and Killing Frenzies: A Response to Hans Mommsen's "The Dissolution of the Third Reich: Crisis Management and Collapse, 1943–1945"', *German Historical Institute, Washington DC, Bulletin*, 27 (2000), pp. 26–7: 'We need to ask what made people not only tolerate [Hitler's regime] but fight and kill for it until the bitter end.'

10. Alfred Vagts, 'Unconditional Surrender – vor und nach 1943', *VfZ*, 7 (1959), p. 300. The demand for 'unconditional surrender' had arisen from the perception, especially strong in the USA, that it had been a costly mistake to concede an armistice instead of insisting on German surrender in 1918, thereby opening the way for the 'stab-in-the-back' legend propagated on the German Right that Germany had not been militarily defeated at all in the First World War. This time, the Americans and the British were agreed, there would be no repeat of the mistake and no scope for misunderstanding or misrepresentation. Germany's unconditional surrender was regarded as the very basis for lasting future peace. – See Gerhard L. Weinberg, *A World at Arms: A Global History of World War II*, Cambridge, 1994, pp. 438–9.

11. A number of leading German generals were adamant after the war that the Allied demand had been a mistake and had lengthened the conflict. – Anne Armstrong, *Unconditional Surrender: The Impact of the Casablanca Policy upon World War Two*, New Brunswick, NJ, 1961, pp. 137–47. General Westphal remarked in his memoirs that the demand for unconditional surrender 'had welded us to a certain extent on to the Nazi regime', and that it was impossible to have laid down weapons and opened up the western front to the Allies without being given some sort of security for Germany. He claimed that news of the Morgenthau Plan to break up Germany and turn it into a pre-industrial country, then the result of the Yalta Conference, 'left every initiative by us completely without prospect' and that there was, therefore, no other way than to fight on. – Siegfried Westphal, *Erinnerungen*, Mainz, 1975, pp. 326, 341. Grand-Admiral Dönitz's adjutant, Walter Lüdde-Neurath, also claimed that it had been decisive for the readiness to fight on at any price. – Walter Lüdde-Neurath, *Regierung Dönitz: Die letzten Tage des Dritten Reiches*, 5th edn., Leoni am Starnberger See, 1981, p. 22.

12. Reiner Pommerin, 'The Wehrmacht: Eastern Front', in David Wingeate Pike (ed.), *The Closing of the Second World War: Twilight of a Totalitarianism*, New York, 2001, p. 46. See also the comment of Klaus-Jürgen

Müller, 'The Wehrmacht: Western Front', in the same volume, p. 56, that 'unconditional surrender' added to the fear of senior military leaders of being accused of perpetrating another 'stab in the back'.

13. Bodo Scheurig, *Alfred Jodl: Gehorsam und Verhängnis*, Berlin and Frankfurt am Main, 1991, p. 286, remarks that for General Jodl (and unquestionably for other military leaders) the demand for unconditional surrender provided a 'flimsy excuse' (*'fadenscheiniger Vorwand'*).

14. Walter Warlimont, *Inside Hitler's Headquarters 1939–45*, pb. edn., Novato, Calif., n.d. (original Eng. language edn., London, 1964), p. 316.

15. The classics were Hannah Arendt, *The Origins of Totalitarianism*, New York, 1951, and Carl Joachim Friedrich and Zbigniew Brzezinski, *Totalitarian Dictatorship and Autocracy*, Cambridge, Mass., 1956.

16. See Eckhard Jesse (ed.), *Totalitarismus im 20. Jahrhundert*, Bonn, 1999, for a collection of later evaluations and applications of the concept.

17. See, as representative of the new research trend, Frank Bajohr and Michael Wildt (eds.), *Volksgemeinschaft: Neue Forschungen zur Gesellschaft des Nationalsozialismus*, Frankfurt am Main, 2009.

18. Heinrich Jaenecke, 'Mythos Hitler: Ein Nachruf', in *Kriegsende in Deutschland*, Hamburg, 2005, p. 223.

19. This notion underpinned the path-breaking 'Bavaria Project' in the 1970s. The volumes of essays arising from the project and published in the series *Bayern in der NS-Zeit*, ed. Martin Broszat, Elke Fröhlich *et al.*, Munich, 1977–83, carried the subtitle 'Herrschaft und Gesellschaft im Konflikt' ('system of rule and society in conflict').

20. Robert Edwin Herzstein, *The War that Hitler Won*, London, 1979.

21. See especially, Michael Wildt, *Volksgemeinschaft als Selbstermächtigung*, Hamburg, 2007 (though the work deals only with the pre-war period) and Peter Fritsche, *Life and Death in the Third Reich*, Cambridge, Mass., and London, 2008.

22. *DRZW*, 9/2 (Herf), p. 202.

23. Götz Aly, *Hitlers Volksstaat: Raub, Rassenkrieg und nationaler Sozialismus*, Frankfurt am Main, 2005.

24. See Fritsche, pp. 266–96.

25. Quotations from Fritsche, pp. 269–71.

26. Robert Gellately, *Backing Hitler: Consent and Coercion in Nazi Germany*, Oxford, 2001, pp. 1, 3, 226.

27. For a thoughtful analysis of the importance of the legacy of 1918, not just for Hitler but for the entire Nazi regime, see Timothy W. Mason, *Sozialpolitik im Dritten Reich: Arbeiterklasse und Volksgemeinschaft*, Opladen, 1977, ch. 1.

28. The most forthright statement of this is in Hans-Ulrich Wehler, *Der Nationalsozialismus: Bewegung, Führerherrschaft, Verbrechen*, Munich, 2009, esp. chs. 2, 7, 11, 14, extracts assembled from his monumental *Deutsche*

Gesellschaftsgeschichte, vol. 4: *1914–1949*, 3rd edn., Munich, 2008. The concept of 'charismatic rule' is, of course, drawn from Max Weber. See his *Wirtschaft und Gesellschaft: Grundriß der verstehenden Soziologie*, 5th rev. edn., Tübingen, 1980, pp. 140–47, 654–87. Although Ludolf Herbst, *Hitlers Charisma: Die Erfindung eines deutschen Messias*, Frankfurt am Main, 2010, criticizes notions that Hitler began his 'career' with innate personal charismatic qualities – something few serious historians have claimed – and emphasizes the propagandistic manufacture of his charisma in the 1920s (in an argument that comes close to portraying the Germans as victims of techniques of sophisticated mass seduction), he appears nevertheless to accept that the Nazi regime was based upon 'charismatic rule'.

CHAPTER 1. SHOCK TO THE SYSTEM

1. Rudolf Semmler, *Goebbels – the Man Next to Hitler*, London, 1947, p. 147 (23.7.44). Semmler (real name Semler) was a press officer in the Reich Propaganda Ministry. The original German text of his diary entries appears to have been lost.

2. Max Hastings, *Armageddon: The Battle for Germany 1944–45*, London, 2004, pp. xi, 15, 17.

3. *MadR*, 17, pp. 6645–58, reports for 14 and 22.7.44.

4. This sketch is based upon: Jochen von Lang, *Der Sekretär: Martin Bormann. Der Mann, der Hitler beherrschte*, Frankfurt am Main, 1980; Joachim C. Fest, *The Face of the Third Reich*, Harmondsworth, 1972, pp. 191–206; and *The Bormann Letters*, ed. H. R. Trevor-Roper, London, 1954, pp. vi–xxiii.

5. For a full study of this obnoxious individual, see Ralf Meindl, *Ostpreußens Gauleiter: Erich Koch – eine politische Biographie*, Osnabrück, 2007. See also Ralf Meindl, 'Erich Koch – Gauleiter von Ostpreußen', in Christian Pletzing (ed.), *Vorposten des Reichs? Ostpreußen 1933–1945*, Munich, 2006, pp. 29–39.

6. BAB, R43II/684, fo. 61, Kritzinger to Lammers, 13.7.44. And see Alastair Noble, *Nazi Rule and the Soviet Offensive in Eastern Germany, 1944–1945: The Darkest Hour*, Brighton and Portland, Ore., 2009, pp. 82–3.

7. BAB, R43II/393a, fo. 47, Vermerk for Lammers, 11.6.44.

8. *'Führer-Erlasse' 1939–1945*, ed. Martin Moll, Stuttgart, 1997, pp. 432–3.

9. Bernhard R. Kroener, *'Der starke Mann im Heimatkriegsgebiet': Generaloberst Friedrich Fromm. Eine Biographie*, Paderborn, 2005, pp. 670–73; Peter Longerich, *Heinrich Himmler: Biographie*, Munich, 2008, p. 720 (and now in general the most authoritative account of Himmler's personality and career).

10. Eleanor Hancock, *National Socialist Leadership and Total War 1941–45*, New York, 1991, p. 127.

11. *TBJG*, II/12, p. 522 (22.6.44).

12. *DRZW*, 5/2 (Müller), p. 754.

13. e.g. *MadR*, 17, pp. 6657–8 (22.7.44).

14. BAB, R3/1522, fos. 4–16, Memorandum on 'Total War', 12.7.44. And see Wolfgang Bleyer, 'Pläne der faschistischen Führung zum totalen Krieg im Sommer 1944', *Zeitschrift für Geschichtswissenschaft*, 17 (1969), pp. 1312–29; also Gregor Janssen, *Das Ministerium Speer: Deutschlands Rüstung im Krieg*, Berlin, Frankfurt am Main and Vienna, 1968, pp. 271–2.

15. Peter Longerich, *Hitlers Stellvertreter: Führung der Partei und Kontrolle des Staatsapparates durch den Stab Heß und die Partei-Kanzlei Bormann*, Munich, 1992, p. 195. In his Nuremberg testimony, Speer suggested, presumably with his success in instigating the planned meeting in mind, that his letter had prompted Hitler to appoint Goebbels as Plenipotentiary for Total War (IWM, FO645/161, p. 10, 9.10.45).

16. Dieter Rebentisch, *Führerstaat und Verwaltung im Zweiten Weltkrieg*, Stuttgart, 1989, p. 514.

17. Peter Longerich, 'Joseph Goebbels und der totale Krieg: Eine unbekannte Denkschrift des Propagandaministers vom 18. Juli 1944', *VfZ*, 35 (1987), pp. 289–314 (text pp. 305–14). And see Hancock, pp. 133–6.

18. BAB, R3/1522, fos.23–45, Memorandum on 'Total War', 20.7.44. And see Hancock, pp. 129–33; and Janssen, pp. 272–3.

19. Kroener, p. 705.

20. Speer did not pass the memorandum to Hitler, via the latter's Luftwaffe adjutant, Nicolaus von Below, until 29 July, the day after he sent a copy to Himmler. – BAB, R3/1522, fo. 48, Speer to Himmler, 28.7.44.

21. BA/MA, N24/39, NL Hoßbach, typescript, 'Erinnerungen', May 1945.

22. *Lagebesprechungen im Führerhauptquartier: Protokollfragmente aus Hitlers militärischen Konferenzen 1942–1945*, ed. Helmut Heiber, Berlin, Darmstadt and Vienna, 1963, p. 219 (20.12.43) (Eng. edn., *Hitler and his Generals: Military Conferences 1942–1945*, ed. Helmut Heiber and David M. Glantz, London, 2002, p. 314).

23. Quoted in Andreas Kunz, *Wehrmacht und Niederlage: Die bewaffnete Macht in der Endphase der nationalsozialistischen Herrschaft 1944 bis 1945*, Munich, 2007, p. 61.

24. Heinz Guderian, *Panzer Leader*, Da Capo edn., New York, 1996, p. 336.

25. Friedrich-Christian Stahl, 'Generaloberst Kurt Zeitzler', in Gerd R. Ueberschär (ed.), *Hitlers militärische Elite*, vol. 2: *Vom Kriegsbeginn bis zum Weltkriegsende*, Darmstadt, 1998, p. 278.

26. General Heusinger had evidently changed tack since spring 1944, when he had followed Hitler's line of not yielding a metre in the east and intending a later offensive to win back the Ukraine, providing the expected Allied landing in the west could be repulsed. – Jürgen Förster, *Die Wehrmacht im*

NS-Staat: Eine strukturgeschichtliche Analyse, Munich, 2007, p. 189. After the war Heusinger was a strong critic of Hitler's military leadership.

27. IWM, EDS, F.5, AL1671, 1.8.44; printed in '*Spiegelbild einer Verschwörung*': *Die Opposition gegen Hitler und der Staatsstreich vom 20. Juli 1944 in der SD-Berichterstattung*, ed. Hans-Adolf Jacobsen, 2 vols., Stuttgart, 1984, vol. 2, pp. 654–8 (and see also vol. 1, pp. 125–6, 515).

28. A point made by Förster, pp. 131ff., and in his contribution to *DRZW*, 9/1, p. 621 as well as by Heinemann in the same volume, p. 883. See also Kunz, pp. 105ff.

29. Ardsley Microfilms, Irving Collection, D1/Göring/1.

30. BA/MA, N24/39, NL Hoßbach, typescript, 19.5.45.

31. Hans Mommsen, 'Social Views and Constitutional Plans of the Resistance', in Hermann Graml *et al.*, *The German Resistance to Hitler*, London, 1970, p. 59.

32. Joachim Kramarz, *Stauffenberg: The Life and Death of an Officer, November 15th 1907–July 20th 1944*, London, 1967, p. 185.

33. Marlis Steinert, *Hitlers Krieg und die Deutschen*, Düsseldorf and Vienna, 1970, pp. 476ff.

34. *Spiegelbild einer Verschwörung: Die Kaltenbrunner-Berichte an Bormann und Hitler über das Attentat vom 20. Juli 1944. Geheime Dokumente aus dem ehemaligen Reichssicherheitshauptamt*, ed. Archiv Peter, Stuttgart, 1961, pp. 1–11 (reports from 21, 22 and 24.7.44).

35. BAB, R55/601, fos. 54–63, Tätigkeitsbericht, weekly report of the head of the Propaganda Staff, 24.7.44.

36. BAB, R55/601, fos. 69–70, Tätigkeitsbericht, weekly report of the head of the Propaganda Staff, 7.8.44. Guderian, speaking to General Balck, blamed Field-Marshal Kluge's involvement with the conspiracy for the collapse in the west. – BA/MA, N647/12, NL Balck, Kriegstagebuch, Bd. 11, fo. 89, entry for 10.9.44.

37. The plot immediately gave Hitler his explanation of the disaster on the eastern front. See the comments he made to Jodl at the end of July. – *Lagebesprechungen im Führerhauptquartier*, pp. 246–8 (31.7.44); *Hitler and his Generals*, pp. 446–7. Those close to Hitler passed on the interpretation. Writing to Gauleiter Eggeling in Halle, Bormann claimed that the collapse of Army Group Centre had been connected with the conspiracy, and pointed to the role of Major-General Henning von Tresckow. – BAB, NS6/153, fos. 3–5, Bormann to Eggeling, 8.9.44. Bormann eventually felt compelled to rein in the generalized attacks on the officer corps, particularly some higher officers, in connection with the bomb plot and the collapse of Army Group Centre that had been made in Party meetings. – BAB, NS6/167, fos. 69–71, Party Chancellery, Bekanntgabe 254/44, Stellungnahme zu den Vorgängen im Mittelabschnitt der Ostfront und zu den Ereignissen des 20.7.1944, 20.9.44; also in BAB, NS19/2606, fos. 25–7.

38. BAB, R55/603, fo. 508, Party Chancellery, Abt. II B4, Vertrauliche Informationen, 13.9.44.
39. BAB, R55/603, fo. 380, Hauptreferat Pro.Pol, Dr Schäffer to Abteilung Rfk. Dr Scharping, 18.8.44.
40. BfZ, Sammlung Sterz, Gefr. Günter H., 2.8.44.
41. Heinrich Breloer (ed.), *Mein Tagebuch: Geschichten vom Überleben 1939–1947*, Cologne, 1984, p. 334.
42. Steinert, p. 479.
43. Ortwin Buchbender and Reinhold Sterz (eds.), *Das andere Gesicht des Krieges: Deutsche Feldpostbriefe 1939–1945*, Munich, 1982, pp. 21–2.
44. LHC, Dempsey Papers, no. 72, appendix B, letter (in English translation) to Hfw. Ludwig E., 21.7.44.
45. BA/MA, MSg2/5284, fo. 603, diary of Major Max Rohwerder, entries for 20–21.7.44.
46. BA/MA, MSg2/2697, diary of Lieutenant Julius Dufner, vol. 2, fo. 20, entries for 20–21.7.44. Biographical details about Dr Julius Dufner, born on 25 January 1902, whose diary entries will find reference in the following chapters, are sparse. The first entry in 'Mein Kriegstagebuch', MSg2/2696, fo. 1, for 12.11.40, says he was called up to 3.Inf.Ers.Batl.14 in Konstanz. Later in the war, on 11.3.44, he is mentioned (fo. 190) as a participant in a meeting on that date as Lieutenant 'O.Zahlm.d.R. [Oberzahlungsmeister (head of payments section) in the Reserve] Dr. Dufner, 1.Fest.Pi.Stab. 15, Stabsgruppe [pioneer corps]'. I am grateful to Jürgen Förster for his help in tracing Dufner in the Kartei of the BA/MA in Freiburg. His diary entries (MSg2/2697, fo. 182) were typed up in 1971, 'according to his continuously kept diary'.
47. Manfred Messerschmidt, 'Die Wehrmacht: Vom Realitätsverlust zum Selbstbetrug', in Hans-Erich Volkmann (ed.), *Ende des Dritten Reiches – Ende des Zweiten Weltkrieges: Ein perspektivische Rüchschau*, Munich and Zurich, 1995, pp. 240–41.
48. Förster, p. 136.
49. *DRZW*, vol. 8 (Frieser), pp. 539 ff. for the disaster of the 3rd Panzer Army at Vitebsk in late June.
50. BA/MA, N245/3, NL Reinhardt, Persönliches Kriegstagebuch, fo. 75, 20–21.7.44.
51. BA/MA, N245/2, NL Reinhardt, Auszugsweise Abschriften von Briefen an seine Frau, letter to his wife, fo. 39, 17.8.44.
52. BA/MA, N647/12, NL Balck, Kriegstagebuch, Bd. 11, fos. 77–8, 83–4, entries for 21.7.44, 5.8.44. Balck later described Hitler as 'the cement that bound people and Wehrmacht insolubly together'. – Quoted in John Zimmermann, *Pflicht zum Untergang: Die deutsche Kriegführung im Westen des Reiches 1944/45*, Paderborn, 2009, p. 2.
53. BA/MA, N24/39, NL Hoßbach, typescript, 19.5.45 (four-page interpolation following p. 5).

54. *'Führer-Erlasse'*, p. 433.

55. Kroener, pp. 710–11, 730.

56. Förster, p. 134, and pp. 138–45 for the significance of Himmler's new powers within the army; also Longerich, *Himmler*, pp. 717, 719–21. There was, understandably, little initial enthusiasm among the higher ranks of the Wehrmacht for Himmler's takeover (though they were said to have been won over by a speech he made to generals and other officers at a training course in Sonthofen). – BAB, NS19/3271, fo. 31, Auszug aus der Meldung des SD-Leitabschnittes Danzig, SD report from Danzig, 14.9.44.

57. Kroener, p. 714; Longerich, *Himmler*, p. 722. There was, in fact, a dispute within the high ranks of the SS over responsibilities in recruitment for the Replacement Army. The head of the SS Central Office (responsible for recruitment to the Waffen-SS), Gottlob Berger, successfully extended his own powers in this area not only towards the army, but also towards Jüttner, who in practice was more conciliatory towards the interests of the Replacement Army than his rival within the SS leadership. – Kroener, pp. 714–15. Berger's ambitions to take over all matters concerning recruitment and training for the Replacement Army are evident in his letter to Himmler of 1.8.44 in BAB, NS19/2409, fo. 6.

58. BAB, NS19/4015, fos. 13–32, Himmler speech to officers of Chief of Army Armaments, 21.7.44.

59. BAB, NS19/4015, fos. 42–7, Himmler speech at Grafenwöhr, 25.7.44; IWM, EDS, F.2, AL2708, Himmler speech at Bitsch, 26.7.44 (printed in *Heinrich Himmler: Geheimreden 1933 bis 1945 und andere Aussprachen*, ed. Bradley F. Smith and Agnes F. Peterson, Frankfurt am Main, 1974, pp. 215–37). Himmler did not conceal his contempt when, this time addressing Party leaders in early August, he castigated the air of defeatism which the officers of the General Staff had spread in the army since the beginning of the war in the east. – Theodor Eschenburg, 'Die Rede Himmlers vor den Gauleitern am 3. August 1944', *VfZ*, 1 (1953), pp. 362–78.

60. BAB, NS19/3910, fo. 89, Himmler to Fegelein, 26.7.44.

61. *'Führer-Erlasse'*, p. 438.

62. BAB, R3/1522, fos. 48–9, Speer to Himmler, 28.7.44.

63. Hancock, p. 139.

64. Rebentisch, p. 515.

65. BAB, R43II/664a, 'Totaler Kriegseinsatz', fos. 81–91, fos. 117, 154 for the exemption for the Reich Chancellery, agreed by Hitler. Goebbels' summary of the meeting is in *TBJG*, II/13, pp. 134–7 (23.7.44). And see Rebentisch, pp. 515–16; Hancock, pp. 137–8; and Elke Fröhlich, 'Hitler und Goebbels im Krisenjahr 1944: Aus den Tagebüchern des Reichspropagandaministers', *VfZ*, 39 (1990), pp. 205–7.

66. *TBJG*, II/13, pp. 136–7 (23.7.44).

67. *TBJG*, II/13, pp. 153–5 (24.7.44).

68. BAB, R43II/664a, fos. 119–21 (and fos. 92–118 for drafts and preparatory material).

69. Wilfred von Oven, *Mit Goebbels bis zum Ende*, vol. 2, Buenos Aires, 1950, p. 94 (25.7.44).

70. *TBJG*, II/13, pp. 135, 137 (23.7.44).

71. BAB, R43II/664a, fos. 153–4; Rebentisch, pp. 516ff.; Longerich, *Hitlers Stellvertreter*, pp. 195ff.

72. Von Oven, *Mit Goebbels*, pp. 120–21 (16.8.44).

73. Longerich, *Hitlers Stellvertreter*, p. 197.

74. Hancock, pp. 157, 287 n. 27.

75. Hans Mommsen, 'The Indian Summer and the Collapse of the Third Reich: The Last Act', in Hans Mommsen (ed.), *The Third Reich between Vision and Reality*, Oxford and New York, 2001, p. 114.

76. BAB, NS6/167, fo. 95–95ᵛ, Bormann to the Gauleiter on the 'new combing out action', 19.7.44; *TBJG*, II/13, pp. 134 (23.7.44); Longerich, *Hitlers Stellvertreter*, p. 196.

77. '*Führer-Erlasse*', pp. 428–9. The role of the RVKs would be widened with the second decree (pp. 455–6) on 'Collaboration of Party and Wehrmacht in an Operational Area within the Reich' of 19 September. Bormann passed on to the Gauleiter Keitel's guidelines for cooperation of 27 July (BAB, NS6/792, fo. 1–1ᵛ, Rundschreiben 163/44 gRs., Zusammenarbeit zwischen militärischen und zivilen Dienststellen, 1.8.44, also in NS19/3911, fos. 30–32). See also Förster, p. 133 and n. 9; Kroener, p. 668.

78. Longerich, *Hitlers Stellvertreter*, p. 196. One, among many, examples of the extended power of the Party was in the takeover of control by the Party Chancellery (delegated by Bormann to the Reich Defence Commissars) of air-raid protection and the necessary instruction of the population. See BAB, R43II/1648, fo. 54 Lammers to the Highest Authorities of the Reich, 27.7.44, passing on the Führer decree of two days earlier.

79. See Karl Teppe, 'Der Reichsverteidigungskommissar: Organisation und Praxis in Westfalen', in Dieter Rebentisch and Karl Teppe (eds.), *Verwaltung contra Menschenführung im Staat Hitlers*, Göttingen, 1986, p. 299 for the extended power the RVKs gained after Goebbels' appointment as Total War Plenipotentiary.

80. The somewhat clumsy term was the invention of Dietrich Orlow, *The History of the Nazi Party*, vol. 2: *1933–1945*, Newton Abbot, 1973, p. 474.

81. For Bormann's centralization of Party control, see Orlow, pp. 465–8.

82. IfZ, ZS 988, Interrogation of Wilhelm Kritzinger, State Secretary in the Reich Chancellery, 5.3.47.

83. See Hans Mommsen, 'The Dissolution of the Third Reich', in Frank Biess, Mark Roseman and Hanna Schissler (eds.), *Conflict, Catastrophe and Continuity: Essays on Modern German History*, Oxford and New York, 2007, pp. 110–13 (a reprint of 'The Dissolution of the Third Reich: Crisis

Management and Collapse, 1943–1945', *Bulletin of the German Historical Institute, Washington DC*, 27 (2000), pp. 9–23).

84. Speer, *Erinnerungen*, Frankfurt am Main and Berlin, pp. 401–2; Joachim Fest, *Speer: Eine Biographie*, Berlin, 1999, pp. 306–7.

85. Speer, *Erinnerungen*, pp. 405–7; and for the contradictions in the 'total war' effort, see Janssen, pp. 274–82.

86. *TBJG*, II/13, p. 526 (20.9.44).

87. Adam Tooze, *The Wages of Destruction: The Making and Breaking of the Nazi Economy*, London, 2006, p. 637.

88. BAB, R3/1538, fo. 7, Speer handwritten letter to Hitler, 29.3.45.

89. See *DRZW*, 5/2 (Müller), p. 755.

90. *TBJG*, II/13, p. 147 (23.7.44).

91. Guderian, p. 351.

92. BA/MA, RW4/57, fos. 27–31, Ansprache des Chefs WFSt Gen. Oberst Jodl, 24.7.44. For Jodl's stance after the assassination attempt, see also Bodo Scheurig, *Alfred Jodl: Gehorsam und Verhängnis*, Berlin and Frankfurt am Main, 1991, pp. 282–6.

93. BBC Archives, *The Nazis: A Warning from History* (1997), written and produced for BBC2 by Laurence Rees, Beta Tape 59, pp. 102–3: Karl Boehm-Tettelbach, Luftwaffe Operations Chief on OKW-Führungsstab, interview with Laurence Rees, c. 1995–6.

94. Orlow, p. 465; Kunz, p. 115; *DRZW*, 9/1 (Förster), p. 623. Keitel and Bormann agreed that uniformed members of the Party and the Wehrmacht had the duty to greet each other with the 'Heil Hitler' salute to demonstrate the unity of political will and the common unbreakable loyalty to the Führer. Lammers extended this to civil servants. – BAB, R43II/1194b, fos. 90–94, text of Anordnung from Keitel and Bormann, fo. 93, 26.8.44.

95. *TBJG*, II/13, p. 146 (23.7.44).

96. Manfred Messerschmidt, *Die Wehrmacht im NS-Staat: Zeit der Indoktrination*, Hamburg, 1969, pp. 433–7 (text of the order on p. 435); *DRZW*, 9/1 (Förster), p. 625, (Heinemann), p. 884. Guderian's own account of his appointment as Chief of the General Staff is in his *Panzer Leader*, pp. 339–44, though he does not mention this order. A brief, critical sketch of Guderian is provided by Hans-Heinrich Wilhelm, 'Heinz Guderian – "Panzerpapst" und Generalstabschef', in Ronald Smelser and Enrico Syring (eds.), *Die Militärelite des Dritten Reiches*, Berlin, 1995, pp. 187–208. In the same volume, Peter Steinbach, 'Hans Günther von Kluge – ein Zauderer im Zwielicht', p. 308, describes Guderian as 'the willingly deferential instrument of the undignified "self-cleansing" of the Wehrmacht from "traitors" until a few weeks from the end of the war'.

97. Messerschmidt, *Die Wehrmacht im NS-Staat*, p. 441. On the history (and pre-history) of the NSFOs generally, see Waldemar Besson, 'Zur Geschichte des nationalsozialistischen Führungsoffiziers (NSFO)', *VfZ*, 9 (1961),

pp. 76–116; Gerhard L. Weinberg, 'Adolf Hitler und der NS-Führungs-offizier (NSFO)', *VfZ*, 12 (1964), pp. 443–56; Volker R. Berghahn, 'NSDAP und "geistige Führung" der Wehrmacht 1939–1943', *VfZ*, 17 (1969), pp. 17–71; Messerschmidt, *Die Wehrmacht im NS-Staat*, pp. 441–80; and the comprehensive treatment in *DRZW*, 9/1 (Förster), pp. 590–620.

98. See *DRZW*, 9/1 (Förster), pp. 620ff.

99. Kunz, p. 114.

100. Besson, p. 113; *DRZW*, 9/1 (Heinemann), p. 884.

101. Wolfram Wette, *Die Wehrmacht: Feindbilder, Vernichtungskrieg, Legenden*, Frankfurt am Main, 2002, p. 190. On p. 189, Wette gives the number of full-time (*hauptamtliche*) NSFOs as 623 at the end of 1944. It is unclear why there is a discrepancy with the figure of 1,074 given in *DRZW*, 9/1 (Förster). The training of the NSFOs was carried out by a staff based in the Party Chancellery. By the end of 1944 it had held thirteen training courses, attended by 2,435 participants. Some 1,300 lectures a week were given to members of the Wehrmacht on ideological matters. – Kurt Pätzold and Manfred Weißbecker, *Geschichte der NSDAP 1920–1945*, Cologne, 1981, p. 371.

102. BA/MA, RH19/IV/250, fos. 41–2, Richtlinien für die NS-Führung, Nr. 6/44, Kommandeur der 242. Infanterie-Division, 22.7.44.

103. On a rough estimate – precision is impossible – some 700 officers were arrested and 110 executed for their participation in the attempted coup. – *DRZW*, 9/1 (Heinemann), pp. 882–3.

104. Walter Görlitz, *Model: Strategie der Defensive*, Wiesbaden, 1975, p. 188. More critical towards Model than Görlitz's biography are the biographical sketches in Smelser and Syring, pp. 368–87 (Joachim Ludewig), in Ueberschär, pp. 153–60 (Samuel W. Mitcham Jr. and Gene Mueller), and in Correlli Barnett (ed.), *Hitler's Generals*, London, 1990, pp. 319–33 (Carlo d'Este).

105. Model's 'Tagesbefehl' of 31.7.44, quoted in Manfred Messerschmidt, 'Die Wehrmacht in der Endphase: Realität und Perzeption', *Aus Parlament und Zeitgeschichte*, 32–3 (1989), pp. 38–9 (4.8.89).

106. See Smelser and Syring, pp. 497–509 (Klaus Schönherr) and Ueberschär, pp. 236–44 (Peter Steinkamp). A largely sympathetic portrait of Schörner is provided in Roland Kaltenegger, *Schörner: Feldmarschall der letzten Stunde*, Munich and Berlin, 1994.

107. *DRZW*, 9/1 (Förster), pp. 596–600; Smelser and Syring (Schönherr), p. 504.

108. BA/MA, RH19/III/727, fos. 2–3, Tagesbefehle der Heeresgruppe Nord, 25, 28.7.44.

109. BA/MA, RH19/III/667, fo. 7, post-war recollections of Hans Lederer (1955): 'Kurland: Gedanken und Betrachtungen zum Schicksal einer Armee'.

110. Walter Warlimont, *Inside Hitler's Headquarters 1939–45*, pb. edn., Novato, Calif., n.d. (original Eng. language edn., London, 1964), p. 464.

111. Warlimont, p. 462.

112. Ronald Smelser, *Robert Ley: Hitler's Labor Front Leader*, Oxford, New York and Hamburg, 1988, p. 291, for Ley's speech. The impact on the military was said to have been 'simply catastrophic'. – Wilfred von Oven, *Finale Furioso: Mit Goebbels bis zum Ende*, Tübingen, 1974, p. 505 (29.10.44).
113. Orlow, pp. 462–5.
114. See Förster, pp. 132–3.
115. *TBJG*, II/13, p. 134 (23.7.44).
116. Förster, pp. 131, 134, 139.
117. NAL, WO208/5622, fo. 120A, not contained in the printed edition of these bugged conversations by Sönke Neitzel, *Abgehört: Deutsche Generäle in britischer Kriegsgefangenschaft 1942–1945*, Berlin, 2005 (Eng. edn., *Tapping Hitler's Generals: Transcripts of Secret Conversations, 1942–45*, Barnsley, 2007).

CHAPTER 2. COLLAPSE IN THE WEST

1. The High Command of the Wehrmacht had expected to cut off the Americans by a counter-attack and was taken by surprise at the breakthrough to Avranches. – NAL, WO219/1651, fo. 144, SHAEF: interrogation of General Jodl, 23.5.45.
2. This was the tenor of his discussions with Jodl late on the evening of 31 July 1944. – BA/MA, 4/881, fos. 1–46; printed in *Lagebesprechungen im Führerhauptquartier: Protokollfragmente aus Hitlers militärischen Konferenzen 1942–1945*, ed. Helmut Heiber, Berlin, Darmstadt and Vienna, 1963, pp. 242–71 (Eng. edn., *Hitler and his Generals: Military Conferences 1942–1945*, ed. Helmut Heiber and David M. Glantz, London, 2002, pp. 444–63). See Nicolaus von Below, *Als Hitlers Adjutant 1937–45*, Mainz, 1980, p. 386, for Hitler's thinking about a new offensive in the west; and *DRZW*, 7 (Vogel), pp. 576–7, for the implications for a negotiated end.
3. *DZW*, 6, p. 105.
4. *DZW*, 6, p. 112.
5. Joseph Balkoski, 'Patton's Third Army: The Lorraine Campaign, 19 September–1 December 1944', in Albert A. Nofi (ed.), *The War against Hitler: Military Strategy in the West*, Conshohocken, Pa., 1995, pp. 178–91. BA/MA, N647/12, NL Balck, Kriegstagebuch, Bd. 11, fo. 90, diary entry for 21.9.44, shows Balck's impressions on receiving the command of a 'fresh and confident' Hitler, and of the troops he was taking over as 'mere shadows'. *TBJG*, II/13, p. 528 (20.9.44) gives Goebbels' assessment of Balck as a 'first-class general from the eastern front'.
6. Klaus-Dietmar Henke, *Die amerikanische Besetzung Deutschlands*, Munich, 1995, p. 98. Lieutenant-General Siegfried Westphal, appointed at the beginning of September 1944 as Chief of Staff to Rundstedt in

Oberkommando West, and struck on taking up the post by the poor morale of the retreating troops and the bloated numbers of the rear-lines staff, reckoned that a more determined advance by Eisenhower's forces would have made it impossible to have built up a new front on the western borders of the Reich, and would have allowed an assault on the Reich itself that would have ended the war in the west. – Siegfried Westphal, *Erinnerungen*, Mainz, 1975, pp. 273, 279, 289.

7. The course of military events is based upon: *DRZW*, 7 (Vogel), pp. 550–80, 606–14; *DZW*, 6, pp. 105–19; Gerhard L. Weinberg, *A World at Arms: A Global History of World War II*, Cambridge, 1994, pp. 688–702; Lothar Gruchmann, *Der Zweite Weltkrieg*, pb. edn., Munich, 1975, pp. 295–306; R. A. C. Parker, *Struggle for Survival: The History of the Second World War*, Oxford, 1990, pp. 200–208; Max Hastings, *Armageddon: The Battle for Germany 1944–45*, London, 2004, pp. 1–83; John Man, *The Penguin Atlas of D-Day and the Normandy Campaign*, London, 1994, chs. 6–7; *The Oxford Companion to the Second World War*, ed. I. C. B. Dear and M. R. D. Foot, Oxford, 1995, pp. 809–12; Antony Beevor, *D-Day: The Battle for Normandy*, London, 2009, chs. 19, 21–2, 24, 27.

8. The Luftwaffe, and its Commander-in-Chief, Hermann Göring, were widely blamed by the Nazi leadership, as well as much of the population, for Germany's plight. A letter to Himmler from Gauleiter Joachim Albrecht Eggeling of Halle-Merseburg on 1 September pointed out the image of total impotence in air defences left by the repeated attacks on the hydrogenation plants in his Gau, and the popular view that the collapse of the front in France was solely attributable to the failure of the Luftwaffe. – BAB, NS19/3911, fos. 71–2, 1.9.44. Hitler himself attributed the crisis of the Luftwaffe to Göring's 'own absolute failure'. – *TBJG*, II/12, p. 520 (22.6.44). Speer and Himmler corresponded in September 1944 about the 'lack of leadership in the Luftwaffe and air industry'. Himmler criticized poor planning, production mistakes, long delays in availability of new aircraft and weapons, and the attempt to deploy the prototype jet-fighter, the Me262, as a bomber (an absurd decision, however one that Hitler himself had insisted upon, against Speer's advice). – BAB, NS19/3652, fos. 1–8, 26–8, Himmler to Speer, 5.9.44, and Speer's reply, 8.10.44.

9. Even without access to secret reports, the regular monitoring of the German press and that of correspondents from neutral countries, such as Sweden, based in Germany, gave the British a clear enough indication of the demoralized condition of the retreating Wehrmacht and the chaotic disorganization of the evacuation of western regions. – NAL, FO898/187, fos. 489–90, 522–3, 540–42, 559–61, 577 (reports from 11.9–22.10.44).

10. BAB, R55/601, fos. 73–4, Tätigkeitsbericht, weekly report of propaganda offices, 14.8.44.

11. *MadR*, 17, pp. 6705–8, 'Reports on Developments in Public Opinion',

17.8.44. This was the last report of its kind. Martin Bormann stopped the regular digest of SD reports on account of their defeatist tone.

12. BAB, R55/601, fos. 102–6, Tätigkeitsbericht, weekly propaganda report 4.9.44. Goebbels noted the 'rather dark picture' of morale that emanated from the propaganda reports in his diary entry for 15.9.44 (*TBJG*, II/13, pp. 484–5).

13. BAB, R55/603, fos. 411, 413, Stimmung durch Ereignisse im Westen, 5.9.44.

14. BAB, R19/751, fo. 4, Gebhardt to Himmler, 5.9.44; copy in IfZ, Fa-93.

15. This follows the excellent, detailed account in Christoph Rass, René Rohrkamp and Peter M. Quadflieg, *General Graf von Schwerin und das Kriegsende in Aachen: Ereignis, Mythos, Analyse*, Aachen, 2007, pp. 29–64. This solid research supplants the earlier versions of the dramatic events that emphasize Schwerin's role in defying the evacuation orders in Bernhard Poll (ed.), *Das Schicksal Aachens im Herbst 1944: Authentische Berichte*, Aachen, 1955, pp. 213–56; Bernhard Poll (ed.), *Das Schicksal Aachens im Herbst 1944: Authentische Berichte II*, Aachen, 1962, pp. 65–77, 80–97; Walter Görlitz, *Model: Strategie der Defensive*, Wiesbaden, 1975, pp. 211–12; *DZW*, 6, p. 113.

16. *TBJG*, II/13, pp. 462–3 (12.9.44).

17. *TBJG*, II/13, pp. 491–2 (16.9.44).

18. *TBJG*, II/13, p. 498 (17.9.44). See also Wilfred von Oven, *Mit Goebbels bis zum Ende*, vol. 2, Buenos Aires, 1950, p. 137 (18.9.44); and Olaf Groehler, 'Die Schlacht um Aachen (September/Oktober 1944)', *Militärgeschichte* (1979), p. 326.

19. *TBJG*, II/13, pp. 500–501 (17.9.44).

20. BAB, R3/1539, fos. 12–14, summary report, dated 14.9.44, of Speer's visit to the west, 10–14.9.44.

21. BAB, R3/1539, fos. 17–31, report of 16.9.44 for Hitler on his visit to the western area, 10–14.9.44.

22. BAB, R3/1539, fos. 7–9, draft report by Dorsch on his ministerial trip to the western front, 13.9.44.

23. IWM, EDS, F.2, AL2837A, unfoliated, Kaltenbrunner to Himmler, 16.9.44, sending reports from 12–16.9.44. Few Party functionaries evidently had any intention of following Bormann's instructions that, in areas falling to the enemy, they were to report voluntarily to the Wehrmacht and serve with the fighting troops. – BAB, NS6/167, fo. 100–100ᵛ, Bormann to the Gauleiter, 16.9.44. A letter home from an officer stationed in the west spoke of the 'purest panic' after Gauleiter Josef Bürckel had ordered Germans to leave Lorraine on 1 September. No trains were available, and officials were at the forefront of the flight. – BfZ, Sammlung Sterz, Lt. Otto F., Berghaupten, 13.9.44.

24. BAB, NS19/3809, fo. 16, wire to Standartenführer D'Alquen for immedi-

ate presentation to Himmler, signed Damrau, SS-Standarte 'Kurt Eggers', September, ?13.9.44. Gauleiter Simon, the head of the civilian administration in Luxemburg, moved his office to Koblenz, where he complained at the end of October that he had not received copies of edicts and ordinances, asking for these to be sent to him, including those for the period since the end of August. – BAB, R43II/583a, fo. 151, Der Chef der Zivilverwaltung in Luxemburg an den Reichminister der Finanzen, 31.10.44.

25. BA/MA, MSg2/2697, fos. 39–46, diary of Lieutenant Julius Dufner, entries for 1–18.9.44.

26. For the revival of criticism of the *Etappe* – which had not featured in the early, successful, years of the war – in the wake of the collapse in France, see Bernhard R. Kroener, '"Frontochsen" und "Etappenbullen": Zur Ideologisierung militärischer Organisationsstrukturen im Zweiten Weltkrieg', in Rolf-Dieter Müller and Hans-Erich Volkmann (eds.), *Die Wehrmacht: Mythos und Realität*, Munich, 1999, pp. 380–84.

27. *TBJG*, II/13, pp. 394–5 (3.9.44).

28. *DZW*, 6, p. 106.

29. BAB, NS19/3911, fo. 5, Himmler to HSSPF in west, 23.8.44.

30. BAB, NS19/1864, fos. 7–13, Bormann to Himmler, 29.8.44, Holz to Bormann, 28.8.44, Himmler to Bormann, 1.9.44.

31. BAB, R55/620, fos. 101–3, report by Generalleutnant Dittmar, 26.9.44.

32. BA/MA, RH19/IV/14, Tätigkeitsbericht der Geh. Feldpolizei für September 1944 (27.10.44).

33. BAB, NS19/1858, fos. 1–7, Chef des NS-Führungsstabes des Heeres, Kurze Aktennotiz über Frontbesuch im Westen in der Zeit vom 22.9–3.10.1944, 5.10.44.

34. On 1 September, the OKW passed on an order from Hitler that troops retreating from the west and not needed for relocation to other theatres were to give up weaponry and equipment as they crossed the frontier into Germany, which could then be redeployed for the western front. – BAB, NS6/792, fo. 15–15ᵛ, Oberbefehlsleiter Hellmuth Friedrichs, head of Abteilung II (Parteiangelegenheiten) in the Party Chancellery, to western Gauleiter, 1.9.44.

35. *DZW*, 6, p. 108; BA/MA, RW4/494, fo. 94, Chef des OKW, Maßnahmen gegen Auflösungserscheinungen in der Truppe, 23.9.44.

36. BA/MA, RW4/494, fo. 108, Jodl to Ob.West, etc., 16.9.44; *DZW*, 6, pp. 106–9, partial facsimile of Hitler's order of 16.9.44, p. 109; Heinrich Schwendemann, '"Verbrannte Erde"? Hitlers "Nero-Befehl" vom 19. März 1945', in *Kriegsende in Deutschland*, Hamburg, 2005, p. 158.

37. *DZW*, 6, pp. 119–20; Groehler, pp. 331–2.

38. NAL, WO208/4364, pp. 2–6 (quotation, in English, p. 6) (26–8.10.44).

39. *DZW*, 6, p. 111. For examples of the fanaticism and belief in Hitler among wounded SS men in France, see Beevor, p. 324.

40. Kurt Pätzold and Manfred Weißbecker, *Geschichte der NSDAP 1920–1945*, Cologne, 1981, pp. 369–70.

41. Bernd Wegner, *Hitlers politische Soldaten*, Paderborn, 1982, p. 306.

42. Examples from August and September 1944 in Ortwin Buchbender and Reinhold Sterz (eds.), *Das andere Gesicht des Krieges: Deutsche Feldpostbriefe 1939–1945*, Munich, 1982, pp. 154–61. A number of large samples of soldiers' correspondence in August and September 1944 tested by the censors showed mixed results. Some indicated a slight rise in positive attitudes towards the regime and the war effort. Others pointed in the opposite direction, with a small increase in negative attitudes and trend towards war-weariness. Unsurprisingly, however, political views were expressed (or hinted at) in only a fraction of the correspondence. Most of the letters confined themselves to personal matters. – *DRZW*, 9/1 (Förster), pp. 631–3. The limited indoctrination with the ideals of National Socialism is a general hallmark of letters to and from the front, dominated above all by private concerns. See *DRZW*, 9/2 (Kilian), pp. 287–8. For an assessment of the value of the letters as a reflection of ordinary soldiers' mentalities, see Klaus Latzel, 'Wehrmachtsoldaten zwischen "Normalität" und NS-Ideologie, oder: Was sucht die Forschung in der Feldpost?', in Müller and Volkmann, pp. 573–88.

43. *DRZW*, 9/1 (Rass), pp. 686–90; Christoph Rass, *'Menschenmaterial': Deutsche Soldaten an der Ostfront. Innenansichten einer Infanteriedivision 1939–1945*, Paderborn, 2003, pp. 121–34, esp. pp. 122–3; also Andreas Kunz, *Wehrmacht und Niederlage: Die bewaffnete Macht in der Endphase der nationalsozialistischen Herrschaft 1944 bis 1945*, Munich, 2007, p. 114. Omer Bartov, *The Eastern Front, 1941–45: German Troops and the Barbarisation of Warfare*, New York, 1986, p. 49, estimates that around 30 per cent of officers had been members of the Nazi Party.

44. NAL, WO219/4713, fos. 907–8, SHAEF report, 4.9.44.

45. NAL, WO219/4713, fos. 906–7, SHAEF report, 11.9.44.

46. BAB, R55/601, fo. 104, Tätigkeitsbericht, weekly propaganda report, 4.9.44.

47. *'Wollt Ihr den totalen Krieg?' Die geheimen Goebbels-Konferenzen 1939–1943*, ed. Willi A. Boelcke, Munich, 1969, p. 452; Marlis Steinert, *Hitlers Krieg und die Deutschen*, Düsseldorf and Vienna, 1970, p. 43.

48. BAB, R55/601, fo. 113, Tätigkeitsbericht, weekly propaganda report, 11.9.44.

49. *TBJG*, II/13, p. 388 (2.9.44).

50. *MadR*, vol. 17, p. 6708 (17.8.44); BHStA, MA 106695, report of RPvOB, 6.9.44. The first V2 rocket attack on London on 8 September, causing only a few casualties, was not publicized in the German press. When eventually, two months later, news of the V2 attacks was broadcast, there was a mixed reaction. Satisfaction, revived hopes and an upturn in mood were reported,

though Berliners were said to have been 'not specially impressed'. – Steinert, pp. 511–12; *Das letzte halbe Jahr: Stimmungsberichte der Wehrmachtpropaganda 1944/45*, ed. Wolfram Wette, Ricarda Bremer and Detlef Vogel, Essen, 2001, p. 147 (7–12.11.44).

51. BAB, R55/601, fos. 78–9, Tätigkeitsbericht, weekly propaganda report, 14.8.44.
52. Robert Gellately, *Backing Hitler: Consent and Coercion in Nazi Germany*, Oxford, 2001, pp. 226–30.
53. BAB, R55/623, fos. 56–9, Wochenübersicht über Zuschriften zum totalen Kriegseinsatz, 28.8.44.
54. *MadR*, 17, pp. 6697–8 (10.8.44).
55. Michael Kater, *The Nazi Party: A Social Profile of Members and Leaders, 1919–1945*, Oxford, 1983, p. 263 (figure 1).
56. Figures from Pätzold and Weißbecker, pp. 354, 375, 419 n. 17.
57. *TBJG*, II/13, p. 389 (2.9.44); Eleanor Hancock, *National Socialist Leadership and Total War 1941–45*, New York, 1991, p. 164.
58. On 31 August Bormann ordered schools and universities to continue until their pupils, students or teachers were conscripted for work in armaments, in accordance with the restrictions laid down by Goebbels. – BHStA, Reichsstatthalter Epp 644/2, unfoliated, Party Chancellery circular 209/44, 31.8.44.
59. *DZW*, 6, pp. 230–31; Hancock, p. 148.
60. Dieter Rebentisch, *Führerstaat und Verwaltung im Zweiten Weltkrieg*, Stuttgart, 1989, pp. 520–21.
61. Goebbels decided, however, having gained Hitler's agreement, not to proceed with this further increase of the age limit for women's labour duty. – *TBJG*, II/14, p. 218 (16.11.44).
62. *TBJG*, II/13, pp. 307–9 (24.8.44).
63. BAB, R43II/680a, fos. 135–7, Spende des Führers (*Eierkognak*) an die NSV, costs of supplying the liqueur, 12–18.8.44.
64. BHStA, Reichsstatthalter Epp 681/6, unfoliated, Stuckart to RVKs, 3.9.44; BAB, R43II/1648, Lammers to RVK, 4.9.44.
65. Rebentisch, p. 522.
66. Hancock, pp. 155, 158.
67. Hancock, pp. 151, 156. Goebbels was well aware that 70 per cent of the exempted occupations were in the armaments industry. – *TBJG*, II/13, p. 239 (10.8.44).
68. *DRZW*, 5/2 (Müller), pp. 750, 752, 762, 767; *DZW*, 6, p. 229.
69. *TBJG*, II/13, p. 397 (3.9.44).
70. *TBJG*, II/13, pp. 196–7 (2.8.44).
71. *DZW*, 6, p. 231; *TBJG*, II/13, p. 239 (10.8.44); BAB, R3/1740, fos. 38–9, Speer-Chronik.
72. *DRZW*, 5/2 (Müller), p. 761.

73. Von Oven, p. 124 (1.9.44).
74. Hancock, pp. 162-4; Dietrich Orlow, *The History of the Nazi Party*, vol. 2: *1933-1945*, Newton Abbot, 1973, pp. 470-72; BAB, R3/1740, fos. 43, 81, Speer-Chronik.
75. BAB, R3/1740, fos. 103-4, Speer-Chronik; *TBJG*, II/13, pp. 370 (31.8.44), 378 (1.9.44), 388-9 (2.9.44), 452 (10.9.44), 490 (16.9.44), 525-7 (20.9.44), 568 (26.9.44); von Oven, pp. 127-9 (3.9.44), 134 (10.9.44).
76. *DRZW*, 5/2 (Müller), pp. 764-6. For Bormann's antagonism, see Louis Eugene Schmier, 'Martin Bormann and the Nazi Party 1941-1945', Ph.D. thesis, University of North Carolina at Chapel Hill, 1969 (University Microfilms Inc., Ann Arbor), pp. 304-8, 312-13.
77. *TBJG*, II/13, p. 388 (2.9.44).
78. BAB, R3/1526, fos. 3-19, Speer to Hitler, 20.9.44. See also Hancock, p. 167.
79. Albert Speer, *Erinnerungen*, Frankfurt am Main and Berlin, 1969, p. 407.
80. See *DZW*, 6, p. 228, Speer's Posen speech, 3.8.44; BAB, R3/1527, fo. 13, Speer to Hitler, 3.10.44.
81. BAB, R3/1527, fos. 8-9, Stellungnahme zur Führerinformation v. Dr. Goebbels, 26.9.44; fo. 10-10ᵛ, Speer to Bormann, 2.10.44; fos. 12-15, Speer to Hitler, 3.10.44 (quotation, fo. 12).
82. *TBJG*, II/14, pp. 329-30 (2.12.44).
83. See *TBJG*, II/14, p. 383 (9.12.44).
84. *DRZW*, 5/2 (Müller), p. 754.
85. *DRZW*, 5/2 (Müller), pp. 755-61; *DZW*, 6, pp. 364-5.
86. BAB, R3/1740, fo. 111, Speer-Chronik, mentions some of these aims.
87. Speer's suggestion in his *Erinnerungen*, p. 411, that this emphasis was a tactical device, in case Hitler should hear that installations close to the front had not been destroyed sounds like a later rationalization of something that at the time he genuinely advocated.
88. Speer, p. 410. See also Gregor Janssen, *Das Ministerium Speer: Deutschlands Rüstung im Krieg*, Berlin, Frankfurt am Main and Vienna, 1968, pp. 304-7; Matthias Schmidt, *Albert Speer: Das Ende eines Mythos*, Berne and Munich, 1982, pp. 146-7; and Hans Kehrl, *Krisenmanager im Dritten Reich*, Düsseldorf, 1973, pp. 412-13. Hitler had agreed in August, during the retreat from France, that industrial plant in danger of falling into enemy hands should be temporarily immobilized, not destroyed. – BAB, R3/1512, fo. 57, notes from armaments conferences 18-20.8.44; printed in *Deutschlands Rüstung im Zweiten Weltkrieg: Hitlers Konferenzen mit Albert Speer 1942-1945*, ed. Willi A. Boelcke, Frankfurt am Main, 1969, p. 402. Speer (pp. 411-12) had, however, then been alarmed at signs in early September that Hitler intended a 'scorched earth' policy in Germany. This was from a leading article in the *Völkischer Beobachter* on 7 September, written by Helmut Sündermann, deputy Reich Press Chief, on Hitler's direct instruc-

tions, Speer said (p. 577 n. 13). Goebbels was displeased with the article, written without his agreement, which had been badly received by the public. – *TBJG*, II/13, p. 493 (16.9.44). See also von Oven, p. 137 (18.9.44), who described the article as 'idiotic'.

89. BAB, R3/1539, fos. 7–14, 17–31, reports on visit to the west, 14.9.44, 16.9.44 (quotation, fo. 28); R3/1740, fos. 106–7, Speer-Chronik; BAB, R3/1623, fos. 22, 24–7, 50–52, 66–8, 77–77ᵛ, directives on disabling industry in the west.

90. BAB, R3/1540, fos. 6–23, report on the visit to the western areas, 26.9.– 1.10.44 (5.10.44); description of the visit in R3/1740, fos. 112–25, Speer-Chronik. See also Speer, p. 408.

91. BAB, R3/1583, fos. 110–11, Speer to Himmler, Bewachungs-Mannschaften für KZ-Häftlinge, 29.10.44.

92. Speer, p. 409; Gitta Sereny, *Albert Speer: His Battle with Truth*, London, 1995, p. 460. And see the critical assessment of Speer's claim to have accepted at an early stage that the war was lost, by Alfred C. Mierzejewski, 'When Did Albert Speer Give up?', *Historical Journal*, 31 (1988), pp. 391–7.

93. A point he makes in *Erinnerungen*, p. 411. For the industrialists' preparations for peace, see Ludolf Herbst, *Der Totale Krieg und die Ordnung der Wirtschaft*, Stuttgart, 1982, pp. 345–7 and part V generally.

94. *DRZW*, 5/2 (Müller), p. 302.

95. IWM, Box 367/27, Speer Interrogations, Karl Saur, 11–13.6.45; Box 368/77, Kurt Weissenborn, December 1945–March 1946. And see, for Saur's brutal mode of operation, Adam Tooze, *The Wages of Destruction: The Making and Breaking of the Nazi Economy*, London, 2006, pp. 628–9.

96. *DZW*, 6, p. 266.

97. Around 2.5 million additional foreign workers and prisoners of war were put to work in Germany between the beginning of 1943 and autumn 1944, two-thirds of these from the east. Nearly a third of the labour force in the mining, metal, chemical and building industries in August 1944 consisted of foreign workers. – Ulrich Herbert, *Fremdarbeiter: Politik und Praxis des 'Ausländer-Einsatzes' in der Kriegswirtschaft des Dritten Reiches*, Bonn, 1985, pp. 258, 270.

98. *DZW*, 6, pp. 261–3. See Herbert, pp. 327–31, for increasingly arbitrary and violent persecution of foreign workers as fears of a breakdown of order grew in the last months of the war.

99. *DZW*, 6, pp. 257–9; Peter Hoffmann, *Widerstand, Staatsstreich, Attentat: Der Kampf der Opposition gegen Hitler*, 4th edn., Munich, 1985, p. 635.

100. BAB, NS19/3911, fos. 66–7, Der Höhere SS- und Polizeiführer Spree an den Gauen Berlin, Mark Brandenburg und im Wehrkreis III to Reichsführer-SS Persönlicher Stab and others, conveying Himmler's decree of 20.8.44. Himmler later reinforced the full backing he had given to his

HSSPFs as solely responsible for combating internal unrest, when commanders of Defence Districts sought to exert their own authority in this realm. – BAB, NS19/3912, fos. 17–26, correspondence relating to the competence dispute, 14.9.44 to 5.10.44.

101. *DZW*, 6, p. 233.
102. *TBJG*, II/13, pp. 389–90, 398, 408 (2, 3, 4.9.44).
103. BAB, NS19/751, fo. 3, Party Chancellery Rundschreiben 224/44, Erfassung von zurückführenden und versprengten einzelnen Wehrmachtsangehörigen, 4.9.44; NS6/792, fo. 16–16ᵛ, Himmler to the western Gauleiter, 4.9.44. A repeated order to pick up individuals or units returning over the Reich border following the events in the west was issued on 22 September (NS19/751, fos. 10–12, Party Chancellery circular 258/44). Increased fears of enemy agents, saboteurs and spies led to the police being given the sole right to check papers of members of the Wehrmacht as well as the Waffen-SS and, where necessary, to make arrests. – BAB, R43II/692, fos. 1–2, directive by Keitel and Himmler, 20.9.44.
104. Peter Longerich, *Heinrich Himmler: Biographie*, Munich, 2008, p. 732.
105. *DZW*, 6, p. 108.
106. BAB, NS19/3912, fo. 96, Einsatz von Alarmeinheiten im Kampf um Ortschaften, Guderian's directive, 27.8.44.
107. *TBJG*, II/13, p. 438 (8.9.44); David K. Yelton, *Hitler's Volkssturm: The Nazi Militia and the Fall of Germany, 1944–1945*, Lawrence, Kan., 2002, pp. 39–40.
108. *TBJG*, II/13, p. 464 (12.9.44).
109. Yelton, pp. 7–18; Klaus Mammach, *Der Volkssturm: Bestandteil des totalen Kriegseinsatzes der deutschen Bevölkerung 1944/45*, Berlin, 1981, pp. 31–3; Hans Kissel, *Der Deutsche Volkssturm 1944/45*, Frankfurt am Main, 1962, pp. 15–23; Franz W. Seidler, *'Deutscher Volkssturm': Das letzte Aufgebot 1944/45*, Munich and Berlin, 1989; BAB, R43II/692a, fos. 2–7, 14–20.9.44; *DRZW*, 9/1 (Nolzen), pp. 183–5; *DZW*, 6, pp. 237–8. Goebbels still spoke of the new organization by this name in his diary entry for 21 September 1944. – *TBJG*, II/13, pp. 534–5.
110. Mammach, p. 33. Two days earlier, Himmler had received a list of suggestions sent to him by SS-Obergruppenführer and General der Polizei Richard Hildebrandt, Chief of the Race and Settlement Head Office, to mobilize and organize the civilian population for 'the people's war', a 'German partisan war', to be carried out as a 'freedom struggle' in the homeland. – BAB, NS19/2864, unfoliated, Hildebrandt to Himmler, 19.9.44.
111. BAB, R43II/692a, fos. 8–21; Mammach, pp. 32–3, 55–6 and 168–73 for facsimiles of Hitler's decree and Bormann's order for implementation.
112. Yelton, chs. 2–3. Longerich's claim (*Himmler*, p. 733) that Himmler and Berger were successful against Bormann seems doubtful. Bormann's personal

success in his demarcation disputes with Himmler is underlined by Jochen von Lang, *Der Sekretär: Martin Bormann. Der Mann, der Hitler beherrschte*, Frankfurt am Main, 1980, pp. 298–9. For the recruitment and organization of the *Volkssturm*, undertaken by the Party local leaders (*Ortsgruppenleiter*), see Carl-Wilhelm Reibel, *Das Fundament der Diktatur: Die NSDAP-Ortsgruppen 1932–1945*, Paderborn, 2002, pp. 377–81.

113. Kissel, p. 89; Mammach, p. 58; Yelton, pp. xv, 19–35.

114. *TBJG*, II/13, p. 535 (21.9.44).

115. Mammach, pp. 57–8. No figure for its actual size (which anyway fluctuated) at any one point appears to exist. Because of manpower shortage, exemptions, deferrals and bureaucratic inefficiency the target was never remotely reached in practice. Even so, the numbers drafted were large. The first levy of the *Volkssturm* amounted to 1.2 million men, formed into 1,850 battalions. – Alastair Noble, *Nazi Rule and the Soviet Offensive in Eastern Germany, 1944–1945: The Darkest Hour*, Brighton and Portland, Ore., 2009, p. 149.

116. *TBJG*, II/13, p. 103 (13.7.44); Noble, pp. 100–101.

117. *DZW*, 6, pp. 235, 237; BAB, NS6/792, fos. 6–8 (29.8.44), 9–12 (30.8.44); *DRZW*, 9/1 (Nolzen), pp. 180–82.

118. IfZ, ZS 597, fo. 27, Gauleiter Josef Grohé (1950).

119. *TBJG*, II/13, p. 465 (12.9.44).

120. BHStA, Reichsstatthalter Epp 681/1–8, unfoliated, copy of Hitler's Verfügung 12/44 (1.9.44); BAB, R43II/1548, fo. 36, Lammers an die Obersten Reichsbehörden, transmitting Hitler's order (6.9.44); *'Führer-Erlasse' 1939–1945*, ed. Martin Moll, Stuttgart, 1997, pp. 446–50; *DZW*, 6, p. 237.

121. Quoted (in English) in NAL, FO898/187, fo. 598, PWE report for 4–10.9.44.

122. *DZW*, 6, p. 236. By the end of 1944 the number of conscripts for fortification work on all fronts was over 1.5 million. – *DRZW*, 9/1 (Nolzen), p. 182.

123. BAB, NS19/3912, fos. 11–12, Bormann to Gauleiter, Rundschreiben 302/44g.Rs., Stellungsbau, 6.10.44.

124. BAB, NS19/3911, fos. 35–8, Party Chancellery Rundschreiben 263/44 g.Rs., Zweiter Erlaß des Führers über die Befehlsgewalt in einem Operationsgebiet innerhalb des Reiches vom 19.9.1944, etc., 23.9.44, transmitting Hitler's decree of 19.9.44, and providing guidelines for implementation; BAB, NS19/3912, fo. 27, Rundschreiben 312/44g.Rs., Zweiter Erlaß des Führers über die Befehlsgewalt, etc., 11.10.44, amending one clause of the decree to underline Himmler's overall authority; *'Führer-Erlasse'*, pp. 455–7; *Hitlers Weisungen für die Kriegführung 1939–1945: Dokumente des Oberkommandos der Wehrmacht*, ed. Walther Hubatsch, pb. edn., Munich, 1965, pp. 337–41.

125. *The Bormann Letters*, ed. H. R. Trevor-Roper, London, 1954, p. 88 (27.8.44).

126. *The Bormann Letters*, p. 139 (25.10.44).
127. Pätzold and Weißbecker, p. 375.

CHAPTER 3. FORETASTE OF HORROR

1. *DZW*, 6, pp. 78–9; Andreas Kunz, *Wehrmacht und Niederlage: Die bewaffnete Macht in der Endphase der nationalsozialistischen Herrschaft 1944 bis 1945*, Munich, 2007, pp. 152–3. Those killed on the eastern front numbered 589,425 in the months June to August 1944. In the last six months of 1944, the figure was 740,821 dead. The number of deaths on the eastern front in 1944 as a whole, 1,233,000, amounted to 45 per cent of the mortalities in that theatre since the invasion of the Soviet Union on 22 June 1941. – Rüdiger Overmans, *Deutsche militärische Verluste im Zweiten Weltkrieg*, Munich, 1999, pp. 277–9.

2. *DRZW*, 8 (Frieser), p. 594, who gives the losses for Army Group Centre at around 390,000 men, compared with some 330,000 at Verdun and 60,000 dead and 110,000 captured at Stalingrad. On the four fronts of 'Bagration', the Soviets deployed around 2.5 million men, 45,000 artillery pieces, 6,000 tanks and more than 8,000 planes over a front of around 1,100 kilometres with a depth of advance of 550–600 kilometres over a period of 69 days (22 June to 29 August). – *DRZW*, 8 (Frieser), pp. 526–35, 593, for the size of the Soviet offensive and relative weakness of German forces.

3. *DRZW*, 8 (Frieser), p. 556. Soviet losses were more than 440,000. Gerhard L. Weinberg, *A World at Arms: A Global History of World War II*, Cambridge, 1994, provides a good summary of the developments on the eastern front in this period.

4. *DRZW*, 8 (Frieser), p. 612; Brian Taylor, *Barbarossa to Berlin: A Chronology of the Campaigns on the Eastern Front 1941 to 1945*, vol. 2, Stroud, 2008, p. 218.

5. *DZW*, 6, pp. 52–60; *DRZW*, 8 (Schönherr), pp. 678–718.

6. Hitler himself had given the order, passed on by Himmler, for the total destruction of Warsaw. – BA/MA, RH19/II/213, v.d. Bach-Zelewski to 9th Army command, 11.10.44.

7. *DZW*, 6, p. 410. For a vivid narrative of the horrific events, see Norman Davies, *Rising '44: 'The Battle for Warsaw'*, London, 2004.

8. This figure in *DZW*, 6, p. 70, deviates from that provided by Weinberg, p. 714 (380,000 men lost) and *DRZW*, 8 (Schönherr), p. 819 (286,000 men killed or captured in the Romanian theatre). The basis for the discrepancy in figures is not clear.

9. *DZW*, 6, pp. 62–70; *DRZW*, 8 (Schönherr), pp. 746–819.

10. *DRZW*, 8 (Frieser), pp. 626–7, 668–72; *DZW*, 6, p. 72; Weinberg,

pp. 707–720–21; and the fine, thorough study by Howard D. Grier, *Hitler, Dönitz, and the Baltic Sea: The Third Reich's Last Hope, 1944–1945*, Annapolis, Md., 2007.

11. BA/MA, RH19/III/727: for Schörner's tough orders on taking over command of Army Group North and his demand for fanaticism, mentioning also the fear of being cut off (25.7.44, 28.7.44); his threats regarding discipline and appeal to ruthless fanaticism in the total war 'for our threatened national existence' (12.8.44); his demands for ruthless punishment by military courts in accordance with Hitler's orders (1.10.44); his appeal to fanatical determination after the 'heroic' fightback in Riga (5.10.44); further demands for ruthless action and improvised methods, with threats for those found lacking (7.10.44); his exhortation to his generals to educate their men to fight harder than ever, and order for defensive measures to be adopted in line with Hitler's command to hold the area (18.10.44, 21.10.44); his claim that they were not conducting the war 'uncompromisingly, radically and asiatically enough' (2.11.44); his extreme intolerance of perceived absence of fighting spirit (10.11.44). When Schörner was on trial in West Germany after his return in 1955 from Soviet captivity, he received supportive letters from former comrades who praised his leadership of Army Group North and attributed its survival to his leadership. See BA/MA, N60/73, NL Schörner. However, the court found that the level of his brutality could not be justified, even in the conditions of war on the eastern front in 1944.

12. Heinz Guderian, *Panzer Leader*, Da Capo edn., New York, 1996, pp. 376–7.

13. *DZW*, 6, pp. 70–76; *DRZW*, 8 (Frieser), pp. 623–57 (troop numbers, pp. 657–8); Grier, ch. 3.

14. *TBJG*, II/13, pp. 524–5 (20.9.44), 536–42 (21.9.44).

15. *DRZW*, 8 (Frieser), pp. 602–3 and map, p. 573.

16. Alastair Noble, *Nazi Rule and the Soviet Offensive in Eastern Germany, 1944–1945: The Darkest Hour*, Brighton and Portland, Ore., 2009, pp. 20–22.

17. Noble, chs. 1–3, p. 46 for the evacuee figure.

18. See Noble, pp. 85 and 276 n. 81. British intelligence authorities gleaned much about the panic in eastern Germany from reading between the lines of German newspapers and other publications. See NAL, FO898/186, PWE, Summary of and Comments on German Broadcasts to Germany, fos. 18, 35–8 (reports for 24–31.7.44 and 31.7–6.8.44).

19. *MadR*, 17, pp. 6698–9 (10.8.44).

20. *MadR*, 17, pp. 6702 (10.8.44), 6708 (17.8.44).

21. BAB, R55/601, fos. 73–4, 102–6, Tätigkeitsbericht, weekly propaganda reports, 14.8.44, 4.9.44.

22. Heinrich Schwendemann, 'Ein unüberwindlicher Wall gegen den Bolschewismus: Die Vorbereitung der "Reichsverteidigung" im Osten im zweiten

Halbjahr 1944', in *Schlüsseljahr 1944*, ed. Bayerische Landeszentrale für Politische Bildungsarbeit, Munich, 2007, p. 236.

23. Kunz, p. 249.
24. Quoted Kunz, pp. 250–51.
25. Noble, p. 152.
26. Noble, pp. 95, 100, 107–8, 280 n. 28.
27. Noble, pp. 95–9.
28. BAB, NS6/792, fos. 17–22, Guderian to Wehrkreis commands, etc., 28.7.44; Stuckart to eastern Gauleiter, 28.7.44.
29. BAB, R43II/1648, fo. 36, Lammers to Oberste Reichsbehörden, 6.9.44, transmitting Führer order of 1.9.44; also in BHStA, Reichsstatthalter Epp 681/1–8.
30. *DZW*, 6, pp. 234–5; Ralf Meindl, *Ostpreußens Gauleiter: Erich Koch – eine politische Biographie*, Osnabrück, 2007, pp. 417–22.
31. NAL, FO898/187, PWE, Summary of and Comments on German Broadcasts to Germany, fo. 685 (report for 7–13.8.44, in English); Noble, p. 106.
32. Guderian, p. 360; Noble, pp. 102–3, 127.
33. *MadR*, 17, pp. 6720–6, report to the Reich Treasurer of the NSDAP, 28.10.44.
34. Noble, pp. 108–13; *DZW*, 6, p. 236; also Marlis Steinert, *Hitlers Krieg und die Deutschen*, Düsseldorf and Vienna, 1970, pp. 504–5.
35. Noble, p. 114.
36. *TBJG*, II/13, p. 224 (4.8.44); Noble, p. 107.
37. Noble, p. 108.
38. Noble, pp. 126–7.
39. Noble, pp. 107, 127.
40. BAB, NS19/4016, fos. 99–126, draft of speech, 18.10.44 (quotations, fo. 123); *VB*, 19.10.44.
41. BAB, R55/601, fo. 180, Tätigkeitsbericht, weekly propaganda report, 23.10.44.
42. BAB, R55/601, fol. 208, Tätigkeitsbericht, weekly propaganda report, 7.11.44; Christian Tilitzki, *Alltag in Ostpreußen 1940–1945: Die geheimen Lageberichte der Königsberger Justiz 1940–1945*, Leer, 1991, pp. 283–4, 286, reports for 17.10.44, 19.10.44; Edgar Günther Lass, *Die Flucht: Ostpreußen 1944/45*, Bad Nauheim, 1964, pp. 23–31. And see David K. Yelton, *Hitler's Volkssturm: The Nazi Militia and the Fall of Germany, 1944–1945*, Lawrence, Kan., 2002, pp. 89–96; Noble, p. 151; Steinert, pp. 506–8.
43. Yelton, p. 90.
44. Yelton, p. 91; Noble, p. 151.
45. Yelton, pp. 97–102.
46. Klaus Mammach, *Der Volkssturm: Bestandteil des totalen Kriegseinsatzes der deutschen Bevölkerung 1944/45*, Berlin, 1981; Yelton, p. 75.
47. Yelton, p. 120.

48. BA/MA, RH21/3/730, post–war account written in 1955 by the Chief of Staff of the 3rd Panzer Army, Major-General Mueller-Hillebrand, p. 1.

49. *Die Vertreibung der deutschen Bevölkerung aus den Gebieten östlich der Oder-Neiße*, ed. Theodor Schieder *et al.*, pb. edn., vol. 1, Munich, 1984, pp. 1–4; and see Noble, pp. 130–32.

50. Guderian, p. 376.

51. *DRZW*, 8 (Frieser), pp. 612–19; Noble, pp. 132–5.

52. See Noble, pp. 136–8.

53. Noble, p. 130.

54. BA/MA, N245/3, NL Reinhardt, diary entries for 11, 17, 22.10.44 and 1, 3, 4, 5, 7, 10, 14.11.44 refer to his continuing hefty disputes with Koch – though not directly on the evacuation issue – as does his letter to his wife of 23.10.44, in N245/2, fo. 40. See also N245/15 for his protest to Himmler at Koch's misrepresentation of conditions within his Army Group (letters of 26.10.44 and 27.11.44). Part of the conflict related to Koch's allocation of armaments meant for the army to the *Volkssturm* (BA/MA, RH19/II/213, fo. 303, Reinhardt to Guderian, 31.10.44).

55. *Die Vertreibung*, vol. 1, pp. 4–7.

56. Bernhard Fisch, *Nemmersdorf, Oktober 1944: Was in Ostpreußen tatsächlich geschah*, Berlin, 1997, ch. 5. See also Guido Knopp, *Die große Flucht: Das Schicksal der Vertriebenen*, Munich, 2001, pp. 37–49.

57. Quoted *DRZW*, 10/1 (Zeidler), p. 700, and pp. 682ff. for an excellent account of Soviet propaganda aimed at troops about to fight in Germany, including the role of the arch-propagandist Ilya Ehrenburg. See also Guido Pöllmann, 'Rote Armee in Nemmersdorf am 22.10.1944', in Franz W. Seidler and Alfred M. de Zayas (eds.), *Kriegsverbrechen in Europa und im Nahen Osten im 20. Jahrhundert*, Hamburg, 2002, p. 215.

58. Quoted Manfred Nebelin, 'Nazi Germany: Eastern Front', in David Wingeate Pike (ed.), *The Closing of the Second World War: Twilight of a Totalitarianism*, New York, 2001, p. 98.

59. *Die Vertreibung*, vol. 1, pp. 7–8. Further gruesome reports are presented in Lass, pp. 44–50. The International Commission was a creation of the Propaganda Ministry. It met on 31 October 1944 in Berlin with representatives from Spain, France, Norway, Sweden, Denmark, Estonia, Latvia, Italy and Serbia, before an audience of 600 or so, largely drawn from Berlin Party members, and attended by 100 members of German and foreign press and radio. Predictably it concluded that the Soviet Union had been guilty of serious breaches of international law. – BA/MA, RH2/2684, fos. 7–8, report of Major Hinrichs, Abteilung Fremde Heere Ost, 1.11.44.

60. Bernhard Fisch, 'Nemmersdorf 1944 – ein bisher unbekanntes zeitnahes Zeugnis', *Zeitschrift für Ostmitteleuropa-Forschung*, 56 (2007), pp. 105–14. See also Fisch, *Nemmersdorf*, chs. 6–7.

61. 'Persönliches Kriegstagebuch des Generals der Flieger [Werner] Kreipe als

Chef des Generalstabes der Luftwaffe für die Zeit vom 22.7.–2.11.1944',
entry for 23.10.44, in Hermann Jung, *Die Ardennenoffensive 1944/45*,
Göttingen, 1971, p. 227.

62. Günter K. Koschorrek, *Blood Red Snow: The Memoirs of a German Soldier on the Eastern Front*, London, 2002, p. 293 (22.10.44).

63. BA/MA, RH20/4/593, unfoliated, report of Hauptmann Fricke, to
Armeeoberkommando 4, 26.10.44, enumerated 45 corpses, 26 found in
Nemmersdorf and 19 in nearby Tutteln (together with several more
uncounted charcoaled corpses in a burnt-out byre there). Most of the dead
in Nemmersdorf were not inhabitants of the village but had been on treks
overtaken by the Red Army. Two further reports (BA/MA, RH2/2684,
fos. 2, 5) indicated one woman probably raped then murdered by being
beaten with an axe or spade in Schweizerau on 22 October and 11 civilians, including 4 women who had been raped, found in the dairy at Bahn-
felde, near Schulzenwalde. A list of victims later compiled recorded 90 in a
number of places in East Prussia (the largest number, 26, in Nemmersdorf),
with numerous cases of rape and including the murder of 5 childen whose
tongues, it was claimed, had been nailed to tables. – BA/MA, RH2/2685,
fo. 168. Karl-Heinz Frieser in *DRZW*, 8, p. 620 n. 77, gives a probable
figure of 46 civilian victims in Nemmersdorf itself, not counting adjacent
localities, though he provides no basis for the figure, which is probably a
marginal miscounting of those in Nemmersdorf and Tutteln together. As he
points out (n. 76), Fisch's findings were reliant almost entirely upon answers
to the questions he had posed to survivors still alive in the 1990s. In his
attempt to reveal the propaganda as largely mendacious, he appeared to
verge on occasion towards an over-sympathetic image of the Red Army
soldiers. Pöllmann, p. 214, indicates 26 civilian victims in Nemmersdorf
itself and a further 28 in the immediate vicinity.

64. BA/MA, N245/2, fo. 40. NL Reinhardt, letter to his wife, 26.10.44.

65. *TBJG*, II/14, p. 110 (26.10.44). And see Wilfred von Oven, *Mit Goebbels
bis zum Ende*, vol. 2, Buenos Aires, 1950, p. 170 (27.10.44). Hitler himself
had responded to the news of the atrocities by demanding their propaganda exploitation within the Wehrmacht, and expressed impatience at the
slowness to act in distributing photographs and eyewitness accounts. – IfZ,
Nbg.-Dok. PS-1787. See also David Irving, *Hitler's War*, London, 1977,
p. 893, n. to p. 726.

66. Quoted Steinert, pp. 521-2.

67. Fisch, *Nemmersdorf*, pp. 144, 153 n. 8.

68. Schwendemann, p. 240 n. 41.

69. Some, along similar lines, were monitored by British intelligence services:
NAL, FO898/187, PWE, Summary of and Comments on German Broadcasts to Germany, fos. 439, 457-8 (reports for 23–9.10.44 and 30.10–
5.11.44).

70. Fisch, *Nemmersdorf*, pp. 146–7.

71. *VB*, 1.11.44.

72. BAB, R55/601, fo. 181, Tätigkeitsbericht, weekly propaganda report, 23.10.44. See also Meindl, p. 434.

73. Steinert, p. 522.

74. *TBJG*, II/14, p. 69 (10.10.44).

75. See IfZ, Fa-93, Vorlage for Bormann, 12.10.44, in which Werner Naumann, State Secretary in the Propaganda Ministry, informed him that Germans in western occupied areas were not behaving in compliance with 'national honour'; and Himmler to HSSPF West, 18.10.44 (also in BAB, NS19/751, fo. 21), indicating that enemy press reports revealed 'dishonourable' conduct by German citizens under enemy occupation in the west. See also Klaus-Dietmar Henke, *Die amerikanische Besetzung Deutschlands*, Munich, 1995, p. 172.

76. *TBJG*, II/14, pp. 176 (8.11.44), 189 (10.11.44).

77. BAB, R55/601, fo. 204, Tätigkeitsbericht, weekly propaganda report, 7.11.44; *TBJG*, II/14, p. 192 (10.11.44).

78. BHStA, MA 106696, report of RPvOF/MF, 8.11.44.

79. BAB, R55/601, fo. 210, Tätigkeitsbericht, weekly propaganda report, 7.11.44.

80. BAB, R55/608, fo. 29, Mundpropagandaparole Nr. 4, 7.11.44.

81. *TBJG*, II/14, pp. 192–3 (10.11.44).

82. Otto Dov Kulka and Eberhard Jäckel (eds.), *Die Juden in den geheimen NS-Stimmungsberichten 1933–1945*, Düsseldorf, 2004, p. 546, no. 749, report from SD-Leitabschnitt Stuttgart, 6.11.44; also in IWM, 'Aus deutschen Urkunden, 1935–1945', unpublished documentation, n.d. (*c.* 1945–6), pp. 275–6; and quoted by Steinert, pp. 522–3.

83. BAB, R55/601, fo. 215, Tätigkeitsbericht, weekly propaganda report, 14.11.44.

84. BAB, R55/608, fo. 30, Mundpropagandaparole Nr. 5, 8.11.44.

85. *TBJG*, II/14, p. 169 (7.11.44).

86. BAB, R55/601, fo. 223, Tätigkeitsbericht, weekly propaganda report, 14.11.44. Goebbels had concluded earlier in November that 'the publication of the atrocities of Nemmersdorf has already been sufficient to make clear to every soldier what is at stake'. At Führer Headquarters it was thought that there was no need at present to fire up the morale of the troops by publishing details of Bolshevik atrocities against German soldiers. – *TBJG*, II/14, p. 159 (5.11.44).

87. Traudl Junge, *Until the Final Hour: Hitler's Last Secretary*, London, 2002, p. 145.

88. Nicolaus von Below, *Als Hitlers Adjutant 1937–45*, Mainz, 1980, p. 340.

89. *Hitler: Reden und Proklamationen 1932–1945*, ed. Max Domarus, Wiesbaden, 1973, p. 2045.

90. Himmler had the names of those not present noted on a list – an indication

that the purpose was to ensure knowledge of and complicity in what had taken place. – Irving, pp. 575–6.

91. BA/MA, N245/2, NL Reinhardt, fo. 40 (diary entry, 26.10.44).

92. Udo von Alvensleben, *Lauter Abschiede: Tagebuch im Kriege*, Frankfurt am Main, 1971, pp. 439–40 (12.2.45). Also quoted in Kunz, p. 253.

93. See the negative imagery in letters from the front in *DRZW*, 9/2 (Müller), pp. 80–89.

94. See *DRZW*, 9/1 (Förster), pp. 638–9.

95. Almost 10,000 death sentences in the Wehrmacht (most of them in the army) had been carried out by the end of 1944. – *DRZW*, 9/1 (Echternkamp), pp. 48–50.

96. Part of the title of Omer Bartov's book, *The Eastern Front, 1941–45: German Troops and the Barbarisation of Warfare*, New York, 1986.

97. Antony Beevor, *D-Day: The Battle for Normandy*, London, 2009, p. 522.

98. *TBJG*, II/14, p. 199 (11.11.44)

99. LHC, Dempsey Papers, no. 179, pt. II, p. 8, letter from Johanna Ambross, Munich, 20.9.44. Text in English.

100. BA/MA, N6/4, NL Model, report (for US authorities) on Army Group B from mid-October 1944 to mid-April 1945 by Oberst im Generalstab a.D. Günther Reichhelm, compiled in 1946–7, fo. 1.

101. Hans-Heinrich Wilhelm, 'Hitlers Ansprache vor Generalen und Offizieren am 26. Mai 1944', *Militärgeschichtliche Mitteilungen*, 2 (1976), pp. 123–70.

102. Saul Friedländer, *The Years of Extermination: Nazi Germany and the Jews, 1939–1945*, London, 2007, pp. 615–19; Raul Hilberg, *The Destruction of the European Jews*, New Viewpoints edn., New York, 1973, p. 547.

103. Hilberg, p. 629.

104. Friedländer, p. 628.

105. Hilberg, pp. 630–31.

106. See Jeffrey Herf, *The Jewish Enemy: Nazi Propaganda during World War II and the Holocaust*, Cambridge, Mass., 2006, pp. 246–54.

107. Kulka and Jäckel, p. 544, no. 744.

108. Peter Longerich, *'Davon haben wir nichts gewußt!' Die Deutschen und die Judenverfolgung 1933–1945*, Munich, 2006, pp. 304–11, where recorded criticism of such crude assessments of the bombing is also apparent.

109. Victor Klemperer, *Ich will Zeugnis ablegen bis zum letzten*, vol. 2: *Tagebücher 1942–1945*, ed. Walter Nowojski and Hadwig Klemperer, Darmstadt, 1998, pp. 594–6 (27.9.44).

110. He remarked on how depressed an acquaintance was about the defeat of the British at Arnhem. Otherwise 'they would now have the Ruhr District and the war would be over'. – Klemperer, p. 609 (30.10.44).

111. Klemperer, p. 605 (17.10.44).

112. Klemperer, pp. 609–10 (2.11.44, 12.11.44).

113. Klemperer, p. 616 (26.11.44).

114. Klemperer, p. 609 (30.10.44).

115. Ulrich Herbert, *Hitler's Foreign Workers: Enforced Foreign Labor in Germany under the Third Reich*, Cambridge, 1997, p. 298.

116. IWM, Memoirs of P. E. von Stemann (a Danish journalist based in Berlin from 1942 to the end of the war, compiled *c.* 1980), fo. 183.

117. See BAB, R55/601, fo. 124, Tätigkeitsbericht, weekly propaganda report, 18.9.44.

118. BAB, R55/601, fo. 119, Tätigkeitsbericht, weekly propaganda report, 11.9.44.

119. IWM, 'Aus deutschen Urkunden, 1935–1945', unpublished documentation, n.d. (*c.* 1945–6), p. 276.

120. BAB, R55/601, fo. 124, Tätigkeitsbericht, weekly propaganda report, 18.9.44. fos. 123–4.

121. *Hitler: Reden und Proklamationen*, pp. 2160–67.

122. Jung, p. 103 and p. 218 (Kreipe diary, entry for 16.9.44); Guderian, pp. 370–71.

123. Albert Speer, *Erinnerungen*, Frankfurt am Main and Berlin, 1969, p. 423.

CHAPTER 4. HOPES
RAISED – AND DASHED

1. Quoted *DZW*, 6, p. 125; *KTB/OKW*, vol. 4/I, p. 436, Jodl to Chief of the General Staff at OB West, 1.11.44. See also Bodo Scheurig, *Alfred Jodl: Gehorsam und Verhängnis*, Berlin and Frankfurt am Main, 1991, pp. 303–6, for Jodl's doubts about – though justification of – the Ardennes offensive. When he learnt from Speer that Hitler was about to play his last card, the leading industrialist Albert Vögler presumed, naturally enough, that it would be on the eastern front. 'No one could be so mad as to expose the east in order to hold up the enemy in the west,' he reasoned. – Albert Speer, *Erinnerungen*, Frankfurt am Main and Berlin, 1969, p. 423.

2. *Hitler and his Generals: Military Conferences 1942–1945*, ed. Helmut Heiber and David M. Glantz, London, 2002, pp. 539–40 (12.12.44).

3. Walter Warlimont, *Inside Hitler's Headquarters 1939–45*, pb. edn., Novato, Calif., n.d. (original Eng. language edn., London, 1964), pp. 475–8; *DRZW*, 7 (Vogel), pp. 619–20.

4. Hermann Jung, *Die Ardennenoffensive 1944/45*, Göttingen, 1971, p. 218 (Kreipe diary, 16.9.44); *DZW*, 6, pp. 124–5.

5. John Erickson, *The Road to Berlin*, Cassell edn., London, 2003, pp. 394–7; Brian Taylor, *Barbarossa to Berlin: A Chronology of the Campaigns on the Eastern Front 1941 to 1945*, vol. 2, Stroud, 2008, pp. 248–59.

6. Max Hastings, *Armageddon: The Battle for Germany 1944–45*, London, 2004, pp. 202–25.

7. *DRZW*, 7 (Vogel), p. 615.
8. *DZW*, 6, pp. 212–13; *DRZW*, 7 (Vogel), pp. 615–16; Hastings, pp. 218–20; Joseph Balkoski, 'Patton's Third Army: The Lorraine Campaign, 19 September–1 December 1944', in Albert A. Nofi (ed.), *The War against Hitler: Military Strategy in the West*, Conshohocken, Pa., 1995, pp. 178–91.
9. Wilfred von Oven, *Finale Furioso: Mit Goebbels bis zum Ende*, Tübingen, 1974, pp. 517–18 (3.12.44); *TBJG*, II/14, pp. 339–41 (3.12.44); BAB, R55/608, fo. 34, Verbal Propaganda Slogan, No. 11 (18.12.44). The suddenness of the fall of Strasbourg and the chaotic attempts to evacuate the population were emphasized in an eyewitness account, later sent on to Himmler. – BAB, NS19/606, fos. 2–4ᵛ, report on the events in Strasbourg on 22–3 November 1944 (19.12.44). A propaganda report from Baden underlined the 'enormous shock effect' throughout the region that resulted from the fall of the city. Streams of refugees engulfed the right bank of the Rhine. The depressed mood of the people reached a low point. Trust was 'extremely shaken'. – BAB, R55/21504, unfoliated, Gaupropagandaleiter, Reichspropagandaamt Baden, Bericht über die Propagandaführung im Gau Baden, 15.1.45.
10. Hastings, p. 225.
11. *Hitler and his Generals*, p. 541 (12.12.44) and p. 1038 n. 1556.
12. See Franz Kurowski, 'Dietrich and Manteuffel', in Correlli Barnett (ed.), *Hitler's Generals*, London, 1990, pp. 411–37 for pen-pictures.
13. *DZW*, 6, pp. 126–8; *DRZW*, 7 (Vogel), pp. 621–2; Warlimont, p. 485; Heinz Guderian, *Panzer Leader*, Da Capo edn., New York, 1996, p. 380.
14. Warlimont, pp. 481–5; Guderian, p. 380; Scheurig, p. 305; BA/MA, RH21/5/66: Manteuffel: 'Die 5. Panzerarmee in der Ardennenoffensive' (deposition for US Historical Division, 1946), fo. 50; BA/MA, N6/4, Oberst G. Reichhelm (Model's Chief of Staff), 'Zusammendfassender Bericht über die Kampfhandlungen der deutschen Heeresgruppe B von Mitte Oktober 1944 bis Mitte April 1945' (deposition for US Historical Division, 1946–7), fos. 14–15; Guenther Blumentritt, *Von Rundstedt: The Soldier and the Man*, London, 1952, pp. 264–9; *DRZW*, 7 (Vogel), p. 620; *DZW*, 6, p. 125; Siegfried Westphal, *Erinnerungen*, Mainz, 1975, pp. 294–300: Walter Görlitz, *Model: Strategie der Defensive*, Wiesbaden, 1975, pp. 222–5; David Downing, *The Devil's Virtuosos: German Generals at War 1940–5*, London, 1977, pp. 231–3.
15. Quoted Warlimont, pp. 489–90. Jung, pp. 201–2, argues that the only alternative course of action open to them – to resign – would have given the command to less able generals and increased German losses.
16. See Warlimont, pp. 481–2.
17. NAL, WO219/1651, fos. 144–5, SHAEF: interrogation of Jodl, 23.5.45.
18. Quoted *DZW*, 6, pp. 129–30.
19. For an assessment of the catastrophic collapse, largely in the second half

of 1944, see John Zimmermann, *Pflicht zum Untergang: Die deutsche Kriegführung im Westen des Reiches 1944/45*, Paderborn, 2009, pp. 40–65.

20. IWM, FD 3063/49, Box 368/54, deposition of Speer (13.7.45). On the economic impact of bombing in 1944, see Richard Overy, *Why the Allies Won*, London, 1995, pp. 130–31; and Dietrich Eichholtz, 'Deutschland am Ende des Krieges: Eine kriegswirtschaftliche Bilanz', *Bulletin der Berliner Gesellschaft für Faschismus- und Weltkriegsforschung*, 6 (1996), pp. 22–3, 27–30.

21. IWM, FD 3063/49, Box 367/26, deposition of Speer (13.8.45); Box 368/67, deposition by Saur (2–8.10.45). For the armaments situation leading up to the Ardennes offensive, see Jung, ch. 2.

22. IWM, FD 3063/49, Box 367/34, depositions of Saur and Kehrl (13.8.45).

23. IWM, FD 3063/49, Box 367/28, deposition of Bosch (11.6.45).

24. IWM, FD 3063/49, Box 367/34, deposition of Kehrl (26.7.45).

25. IWM, FD 3063/49, Box 367/34, deposition of Röchling (10.8.45).

26. IWM, FD 3063/49, Box 367/35, suppl. I, deposition of Rohland (22.10.45).

27. IWM, FD 3063/49, Box 367/34, and Box 368/93, depositions of Schulze-Fielitz (10.8.45 and undated, summer 1945).

28. IWM, FD 3063/49, Box 368/84, part II, deposition of Fiebig (25.5.46).

29. IWM, FD 3063/49, Box 367/26, deposition of Speer (13.8.45).

30. IWM, FD 3063/49, Box 368/67, depositions of Saur (2–8.10.45, 7.6.45). Hans Kehrl, *Krisenmanager im Dritten Reich*, Düsseldorf, 1973, p. 407, also pointed to the fact that despite all the mounting difficulties, armaments production was higher in 1944 than in each of the years 1940 to 1943, when Germany was in full command of its economic basis. Even in January 1945, the index of armaments production was higher than that of any war year apart from 1944. – Adam Tooze, *The Wages of Destruction: The Making and Breaking of the Nazi Economy*, London, 2006, pp. 687–8, table A6.

31. IWM, Box 367/27, deposition by Saur (11–13.6.45).

32. See, for these decisions in November and December, *Deutschlands Rüstung im Zweiten Weltkrieg: Hitlers Konferenzen mit Albert Speer 1942–1945*, ed. Willi A. Boelcke, Frankfurt am Main, 1969, pp. 444–58; and for Speer's strenuous efforts to sustain production at this time, Alfred C. Mierzejewski, 'When Did Albert Speer Give up?', *Historical Journal*, 31 (1988), p. 394.

33. Heavy raids had repeatedly hit the big industrial cities and attacked the transport network. Over 50 per cent of American bombs at this time were aimed at destroying transport installations. The British, who dropped more bombs in the last three months of 1944 than in the entire year 1943, concentrated more on the cities, with big attacks on Dortmund, Duisburg, Essen, Cologne, Düsseldorf, Bochum and Gelsenkirchen, but also inflicted severe damage on transport, dropping 102,796 tons, mainly on railway marshalling yards, between November and January 1945. See *DZW*, 6, pp. 163, 166–7; Tooze, p. 650; Jörg Friedrich, *Der Brand: Deutschland im*

Bombenkrieg 1940–1945, pb. edn., Berlin, 2004, p. 150. Alfred C. Mierze-jewski, *The Collapse of the German War Economy, 1944–1945: Allied Air Power and the German National Railway*, Chapel Hill, NC, 1988, chs. 6–7, provides a detailed account of the crippling impact of the bombing on transport in autumn 1944. Speer informed the naval leadership in mid-November of the seriousness of the air attacks. The Reichsbahn had been badly hit. Five major railway stations were out of action. There had been huge drops in coal and steel production (with four-fifths of steel mills damaged or destroyed), and gas supplies had been reduced by 40 per cent. – *KTB/SKL*, vol. 63/II, p. 188 (17.11.44).

34. BAB, R3/1528, fos. 1–48, Speer's report on the Ruhrgebiet, 11.11.44.
35. BAB, R3/1542, fos. 1–21, Speer's report on his trip to Rhine and Ruhr, 23.11.44.
36. *Deutschlands Rüstung*, p. 444 (28.11.44).
37. *TBJG*, II/14, pp. 368–9 (7.12.44).
38. BAB, R3/1543, fos. 3–15.
39. Speer, p. 425.
40. BAB, R3/1544, fos. 56–73 (quoted words, fo. 71).
41. *DRZW*, 5/2 (Müller), p. 771, sees this as, in effect, Speer's 'survival programme' for the last phase of the war.
42. Speer, p. 423. After his trip to the Ruhr in November, Speer engineered Vögler's appointment by Hitler as Plenipotentiary for Armaments and War Production in the Ruhr in order to take decisions on the spot in his name in order to sustain Ruhr production. – *Deutschlands Rüstung*, p. 445 (28.11.44).
43. BAB, R3/1623, fos. 3, 4, 8–10, 22 (26.7.44, 2.8.44), on retreat from the east; fos. 24–7, 46, 50–52, 66–8, 77 (10, 13, 16, 18, 19, 22.9.44), on immobilization of industry in western areas.
44. BAB, R3/1623, fo. 123, Keitel to Speer (6.12.44).
45. BAB, R3/1623, fos. 125–6, Speer to head of Armaments Commission XIIb Kelchner, 6.12.44; Keitel Fernschreiben, 10.12.44. Even now, Speer felt it necessary (fo. 127, 12.12.44) to intervene again, this time with Grand-Admiral Dönitz, to prevent the destruction of wharves and their installations which had been scheduled for destruction by an order of Coastal Command East (*Marinekommando Ost*) on 17 November.
46. A point made by Müller in *DRZW*, 5/2, p. 771.
47. BAB, NS19/1862, fos. 1–5, Bormann to Himmler, 23.10.44.
48. BAB, NS19/4017, fos. 43–56, meeting at Klein-Berkel, 3.11.44.
49. *TBJG*, II/14, pp. 157–8 (5.11.44).
50. See Dieter Rebentisch and Karl Teppe (eds.), *Verwaltung contra Menschenführung im Staat Hitlers*, Göttingen, 1986, pp. 7–32; Peter Longerich, *Hitlers Stellvertreter: Führung der Partei und Kontrolle des Staatsapparates durch den Stab Heß und die Partei-Kanzlei Bormann*, Munich, 1992,

pp. 256–64; and Armin Nolzen, 'Charismatic Legitimation and Bureaucratic Rule: The NSDAP in the Third Reich, 1933–1945', *German History*, 23 (2005), pp. 494–518.

51. Kurt Pätzold and Manfred Weißbecker, *Geschichte der NSDAP 1920–1945*, Cologne, 1981, p. 375; Dieter Rebentisch, *Führerstaat und Verwaltung im Zweiten Weltkrieg*, Stuttgart, 1989, pp. 528–9.

52. All contained, many from November–December 1944, in BAB, R43II/692b: Deutscher Volkssturm, Bd. 2, fos. 1–28. An impression of the mass of heterogeneous business dealt with by the Party Chancellery in this period can be gleaned from the collection *Akten der Partei-Kanzlei der NSDAP*, vol. 1, ed. Helmut Heiber, Munich, 1983, Regesten Bd. 1–2, and vol. 2, ed. Peter Longerich, Munich, 1989, Regesten Bd. 4.

53. *TBJG*, II/14, p. 432 (17.12.44).

54. *The Bormann Letters*, ed. H. R. Trevor-Roper, London, 1954, p. 148 (11.12.44).

55. See *TBJG*, II/14, p. 400 (12.12.44) for the paper shortage.

56. BAB, R43II/583a, fo. 64–64ᵛ, Reichspostminister to Highest Reich Authorities, etc. (7.11.44).

57. *TBJG*, II/14, pp. 146–7 (3.11.44), 191 (10.11.44), 224 (17.11.44), 232 (18.11.44), 268 (24.11.44), 308–9 (1.12.44), 444 (19.12.44); BAB, R3/1529, fos. 3–12, Speer's memorandum to Hitler (6.12.44).

58. *TBJG*, II/14, pp. 394 (11.12.44), 398 (12.12.44); von Oven, pp. 519 (5.12.44), 520–23 (11.12.44). Text of the decree in *'Führer-Erlasse' 1939–1944*, ed. Martin Moll, Stuttgart, 1997, pp. 469–70.

59. *TBJG*, II/14, p. 305 (1.12.44).

60. Von Oven, p. 517 (29.11.44); *TBJG*, II/14, p. 276 (25.11.44).

61. *TBJG*, II/14, pp. 317–34 (2.12.44).

62. *TBJG*, II/14, pp. 159–60 (5.11.44).

63. *TBJG*, II/14, pp. 208–9 (13.11.44); von Oven, pp. 511–12 (12.11.44).

64. On the film, see David Welch, *Propaganda and the German Cinema 1933–1945*, Oxford, 1983, pp. 225–35.

65. *TBJG*, II/14, pp. 310–11 (1.12.44), 345 (3.12.44); Welch, p. 234.

66. *TBJG*, II/14, pp. 469–70 (23.12.44). More changes were necessary, but, as he had hoped, the premiere took place on 30 January 1945, the twelfth anniversary of Hitler's takeover of power.

67. BAB, R55/601, fo. 204, Tätigkeitsbericht, weekly propaganda report, 7.11.44; *TBJG*, II/14, p. 192 (10.11.44) .

68. *TBJG*, II/14, p. 147 (3.11.44); also p. 310 (1.12.44). He acknowledged that the failure of the regime to protect its population in the air war was its greatest weakness in the eyes of the public (p. 165 (6.11.44)). Düren, east of Aachen, one of the most heavily bombed towns of the war, provides an example. Only 13 out of 9,322 buildings were left undamaged by the autumn air attacks and over 3,000 people lost their lives (Friedrich, p. 144).

In late December Himmler reported that the population there was 'completely hostile and unfriendly' and that the 'Heil Hitler' greeting was almost unknown, even among local Party functionaries (BAB, NS19/751, fo. 32, Himmler to Bormann, 26.12.44, also in IfZ, Fa-93).

69. *TBJG*, II/14, pp. 133 (1.11.44), 238 (19.11.44); Robert Grosche, *Kölner Tagebuch 1944–46*, Cologne, 1969, pp. 52–6 (30.10.–6.11.44); LHC, Dempsey Papers, no. 178, pt. II, pp. 7–8 (27.11.44), 'Total War Comes to Cologne' (account of a prisoner of war who witnessed the raid).

70. *Widerstand und Verfolgung in Köln*, ed. Historisches Archiv der Stadt Köln, Cologne, 1974, pp. 395–6; Detlef Peukert, *Die Edelweißpiraten: Protestbewegungen jugendlicher Arbeiter im Dritten Reich*, Cologne, 1980, pp. 103–15; *TBJG*, II/14, p. 426 (16.12.44).

71. *TBJG*, II/14, p. 269 (24.11.44).

72. *TBJG*, II/14, p. 192 (10.11.44).

73. Margarete Dörr, '*Wer die Zeit nicht miterlebt hat . . .': Frauenerfahrungen im Zweiten Weltkrieg und in den Jahren danach*, vol. 3, Frankfurt am Main and New York, 1998, p. 437.

74. *TBJG*, II/14, p. 192 (10.11.44).

75. *TBJG*, II/14, p. 269 (24.11.44).

76. IWM, Box 367/35, suppl. I, deposition of Rohland, pp. 3–4 (22.10.45).

77. Von Oven, p. 518 (3.12.44). The 'Morgenthau Plan', put forward by the Americans at the Quebec Conference in September 1944, had been agreed, apparently with little detailed consideration, by the British (who, surprisingly, seem to have shown scant interest in its proposals). Though President Roosevelt favoured a harsh peace, he was eventually persuaded to back away from the 'Morgenthau Plan' by the combined and determined opposition of his Secretary of State, Cordell Hull, and his Secretary for War, Henry Stimson. – Toby Thacker, *The End of the Third Reich: Defeat, Denazification and Nuremberg, January 1944–November 1946*, pb. edn., Stroud, 2008, pp. 58–60.

78. Von Oven, pp. 524–5 (14.12.44); *TBJG*, II/14, pp. 407–13 (13.12.44). Vivid descriptions of the dreadful conditions following the raids in Bochum ('a dead city') and other major conurbations in the Rhine and Ruhr were given in a secret German censorship report on letters to and from the front, which fell into Allied hands. – NAL, FO898/187, summary of German media reports, fos. 292–5 (27–31.12.44).

79. *TBJG*, II/14, pp. 408–9, 412 (13.12.44).

80. *TBJG*, II/14, p. 377 (8.12.44).

81. Robert Ley, the Party's Organization Leader, sent Hitler a somewhat mixed report on the qualities of the western Gauleiter, after a 14-day visit to the west in November, but there was no hint of disloyalty. – BAB, NS6/135, fos. 12–17, Ley's report to Hitler, 30.11.44; accurately summarized in *TBJG*, II/14, pp. 355–7 (5.12.44).

82. BAB, R55/603, fo. 513, Hauptreferat Pro.Pol. an das RPA Neustadt a.d. Weinstr. (28.11.44).

83. *TBJG*, II/14, pp. 309–10, 316, 344, 382 (1–3.12.44, 9.12.44); BAB, R55/601, fos. 221–2, Tätigkeitsbericht, weekly propaganda report, 14.11.44; von Oven, p. 509 (10.11.44); *Das letzte halbe Jahr: Stimmungsberichte der Wehrmachtpropaganda 1944/45*, ed. Wolfram Wette, Ricarda Bremer and Detlef Vogel, Essen, 2001, pp. 153, 160, 167 (21.11.44, 29.11.44, 9.12.44).

84. *TBJG*, II/14, p. 420 (15.12.44).

85. BAB, NS19/751, fos. 23–5, Chief of SS-Hauptamt Gottlieb Berger to Himmler, 17.11.44 (also in IfZ, Fa-93).

86. Cited in Andreas Kunz, *Wehrmacht und Niederlage: Die bewaffnete Macht in der Endphase der nationalsozialistischen Herrschaft 1944 bis 1945*, Munich, 2007, p. 269.

87. BA/MA, MSg2/2697, fos. 64–7, diary entries of Lieutenant Julius Dufner (27.11–5.12.44). For the bombing of Freiburg, see Peter Zolling, 'Was machen wir am Tag nach unserem Sieg?' in Wolfgang Malanowski (ed.), *1945: Deutschland in der Stunde Null*, Reinbek bei Hamburg, 1985, p. 121; and, especially, Friedrich, pp. 306–11.

88. BfZ, Sterz-Sammlung, U'Fw. Hermann S., 6.12.44.

89. BfZ, Sterz-Sammlung, SS-Rttf. Paul S., 5.12.44.

90. BfZ, Sterz-Sammlung, SS-Rttf. Paul S., 11.11.44. Propaganda offices reported an improvement in the mood of the civilian population in mid-November, which it partly attributed to the announcement of the V2 attacks. – BAB, R55/601, fo. 215, Tätigkeitsbericht, weekly propaganda report, 14.11.44.

91. BfZ, Sterz-Sammlung, Gefr. Michael M., 11.11.44.

92. BfZ, Sterz-Sammlung, Kanonier Felix S., 10.11.44.

93. LHC, Dempsey Papers, no. 199, pt. II, p. 5 (20.12.44), in English.

94. BA/MA, N712/15, NL Pollex, Kriegstagebuch, entry for 26.12.44. Pollex, born in 1898, had served briefly as senior quartermaster (*Oberquartiermeister*) with Army Group Centre in 1942 before being transferred to the Army General Staff and later in the year being promoted to the rank of colonel. In December 1944 he was sent to Döberitz to take charge of officer training courses (*Regimentskommandeur-Lehrgang*) then moved on 9 January 1945 to become Chief of Staff to the Chef der deutschen Wehrmachtrüstung.

95. Sönke Neitzel, *Abgehört: Deutsche Generäle in britischer Kriegsgefangenschaft 1942–1945*, Berlin, 2005, pp. 171, 432–3 (1.1.45) (Eng. edn., *Tapping Hitler's Generals: Transcripts of Secret Conversations, 1942–45*, Barnsley, 2007, p. 127).

96. Benjamin Ziemann, 'Fluchten aus dem Konsens zum Durchhalten: Ergebnisse, Probleme und Perspektiven der Erforschung soldatischer Ver-

weigerungsformen in der Wehrmacht 1939–1945', in Ralf-Dieter Müller and Hans-Erich Volkmann (eds.), *Die Wehrmacht: Mythos und Realität*, Munich, 1999, p. 594; Manfred Messerschmidt, 'Die Wehrmacht in der Endphase: Realität und Perzeption', *Aus Parlament und Zeitgeschichte*, 32–3 (1989) (4.8.89), pp. 42–3. General Schörner justified his ferocious military discipline to his own subordinate leading officers in Courland by the need to combat the rapidly growing number of deserters. – BA/MA, RH19/III/727, fo. 49–49ᵛ, Schörner to all his generals, 5.12.44.

97. Kunz, p. 267.
98. BA/MA, N712/15, NL Pollex, diary entry for 8.12.44.
99. Hastings, p. 228. Major Hasso Viebig, commanding officer of the 277th Grenadier-Division, recalled in British captivity four months after the offensive the determination of the troops, exhilarated that they were advancing again. – Neitzel, *Abgehört*, p. 200 and p. 539 n. 158. See also Zimmermann, p. 94 for the initial boost to morale from the offensive.
100. For the course of the offensive, see *DZW*, 6, pp. 128–34, *DRZW*, 7 (Vogel), pp. 625–32; Jung, chs. 4–7; Lothar Gruchmann, *Der Zweite Weltkrieg*, pb. edn., Munich, 1975, pp. 310–12; Gerhard L. Weinberg, *A World at Arms: A Global History of World War II*, Cambridge, 1994, pp. 766–8; Stephen B. Patrick, 'The Ardennes Offensive: An Analysis of the Battle of the Bulge', in Nofi, pp. 206–24; and Hastings, ch. 8. Peiper's panzer regiment was responsible for the deaths of more than 400 American and Belgian prisoners in all. – *DZW*, 6, p. 130. The Malmédy massacre of 84 prisoners is judiciously discussed by Michael Reynolds, *The Devil's Adjutant: Jochen Peiper, Panzer Leader*, Staplehurst, 1995, pp. 88–97.
101. LHC, Dempsey Papers, no. 241, pt. II, p. 3 (30.1.45), diary entry of Lt. Behmen, 18th Volksgrenadier Division, in English.
102. LHC, Dempsey Papers, no. 217, pt. II, p. 5 (6.1.45), in English.
103. BAB, R55/793, fos. 16–18, Material for Propagandists, No. 19 (11.12.44). Such propaganda had nevertheless limited effect. Goebbels noted in mid-December that the population in the west had no fear of the Anglo-Americans and farmers were reluctant, therefore, to be evacuated. – *TBJG*, II/14, p. 402 (12.12.44).
104. LHC, Dempsey Papers, No. 246, pt. II, p. 3 (4.2.45), in English.
105. BfZ, Sterz-Sammlung, Gefr. W.P., 17.12.44.
106. BfZ, Sterz-Sammlung, Gefr. S.F., 17.12.44.
107. BfZ, Sterz-Sammlung, Uffz. Werner F., 19.12.44.
108. *TBJG*, II/14, pp. 429, 433 (17.12.44), 438–9 (18.12.44), 445 (19.12.44); von Oven, pp. 526–9 (17.12.44, 20.12.44).
109. See *VB*, 19.12.44, where the headline simply read, 'German Offensive in the West'.
110. BAB, R55/601, fos. 249–50, Tätigkeitsbericht, weekly propaganda report,

19.12.44. See also Klaus-Dietmar Henke, *Die amerikanische Besetzung Deutschlands*, Munich, 1995, pp. 316–17.

111. *TBJG*, II/14, p. 450 (20.12.44), and, still in the same vein, p. 468 (23.12.44).
112. *Das letzte halbe Jahr*, p. 183, report for 18–24.12.44 (2.1.45).
113. NAL, FO898/187, summary of German media reports, fo. 315 (18–26.12.44).
114. *TBJG*, II/14, p. 452 (20.12.44).
115. *DRZW*, 7 (Vogel), p. 631.
116. IWM, Box 367/27, p. 7, Speer Ministry Interrogation Reports, deposition of Saur, 11–13.6.45. According to Goebbels' aide Rudolf Semmler, the offensive was by 21 December 'already seen to be a definite failure'. – Rudolf Semmler, *Goebbels – the Man Next to Hitler*, London, 1947, p. 171 (21.12.44).
117. Speer, p. 425.
118. Guderian, p. 381.
119. *DRZW*, 7 (Vogel), p. 629; Hastings, p. 261.
120. *DZW*, 6, p. 133, and p. 137 for the figures that follow.
121. *TBJG*, II/14, pp. 436–7 (29.12.44). He had acknowledged a 'somewhat more critical' situation six days earlier (p. 469 (23.12.44)) and a deterioration on 28.12.44 (pp. 480–81). Wehrmacht propaganda agents in Berlin also commented at this time on the confidence of soldiers returning from the front, but hinted that the enthusiasm at home had waned. – *Das letzte halbe Jahr*, p. 193, report for 25–31.12.44 (3.1.45).
122. *TBJG*, II/14, p. 500 (31.12.44).
123. BA/MA, MSg2/2697, diary of Lieutenant Julius Dufner, fo. 78 (1.1.45).
124. BAB, R55/612, Echo zur Führerrede, summary report to Goebbels, fos. 22–3, 2.1.45; fos. 17–102 for replies of propaganda offices to request for information on the reception of Hitler's speech and that of Goebbels himself, 1–2.1.45.
125. *Hitler: Reden und Proklamationen 1932–1945*, ed. Max Domarus, Wiesbaden, 1973, pp. 2179–85 for the text of the speech.
126. BHStA, Minn 72417, unfoliated, 28.11.44–5.1.45.
127. BAB, R43II/1648, fo. 20, Lammers to Highest Reich Authorities, 17.12.44.
128. *TBJG*, II/14, pp. 282 (27.11.44), 328–9 (2.12.44), 370–72 (7.12.44); David Irving, *Göring: A Biography*, London, 1989, pp. 447–8, 476.
129. Michael Bloch, *Ribbentrop*, pb. edn., London, 1994, pp. 418–19.
130. Ronald Smelser, *Robert Ley: Hitler's Labor Front Leader*, Oxford, New York and Hamburg, 1988, p. 291.
131. *The Bormann Letters*, pp. 152 (26.12.44), 158 (1.1.45)
132. Felix Kersten, *The Kersten Memoirs, 1940–1945*, London, 1956, pp. 238–9 (10.12.44); BAB, NS19/3912, fo. 115, Berger to Himmler, for rumours of Himmler's disgrace (21.12.44). Himmler had been appointed in November

to be Commander-in-Chief Upper Rhine. As head of the Replacement Army, and Chief of Police, Himmler was seen to be in a good position to raise a makeshift army as a defence force to help the German 19th Army try to hold back the Allied drive into Alsace. The newly created Army Group Upper Rhine, stationed in an area between the Black Forest and the Swiss frontier, was heavily patched together from stragglers, *Volksgrenadier* and anti-aircraft units, border police, non-German battalions from the east, and *Volkssturm* men. Refusing to leave his Black Forest headquarters, Himmler created a vacuum which fostered intrigue at Führer Headquarters, possibly involving Bormann and some disaffected influential SS leaders. – Heinz Höhne, *The Order of the Death's Head*, London, 1972, pp. 509–11; Peter Padfield, *Himmler: Reichsführer-SS*, London, 1990, pp. 546, 554–6. Berger requested Himmler to cut short his activity as Commander-in-Chief Upper Rhine and return to Führer Headquarters. His request, he said, 'comes not only from the fabrication of rumours promoted by certain sides with all energy – Reichsführer-SS is in disgrace, the Wehrmacht lobby – Keitel – has indeed triumphed – but because I sense that if Reichsführer-SS is not at Headquarters our political work, as the basis of everything, suffers immeasurably'. Himmler replied (fo. 116), via his personal adjutant, SS-Standartenführer Rudolf Brandt, on 29 December, stating that it would only be a short time before he could place the command of Army Group Upper Rhine in other hands, and that he might have the opportunity to speak briefly about the matter to Berger. Letter and telephone, he added, cryptically, were 'not suitable for this topic'. Himmler's short-lived command of Army Group Upper Rhine, as part of the weak and brief German offensive in Alsace in January, ended in failure. But whatever rumours there had been, they had evidently not undermined his standing with Hitler. According to Goebbels, Hitler was 'extraordinarily satisfied' with the work of the Reichsführer. – Peter Longerich, *Heinrich Himmler: Biographie*, Munich, 2008, pp. 736–7.

133. *TBJG*, II/14, pp. 497–8 (31.12.44); von Oven, pp. 529–30 (26.12.44), 534–6 (28.12.44).

134. Speer, pp. 425–7.

135. NAL, WO204/6384, interview with SS-Obergruppenführer Wolff, fo. 2, 15.6.45.

136. Guderian, pp. 382–4. It has been adjudged that 'the fatal role of the Ardennes offensive was indirectly to weaken the eastern front' through binding forces needed for defence against the Red Army. – Heinz Magenheimer, *Hitler's War: German Military Strategy 1940–1945*, London, 1998, p. 264. However, as Jung, p. 201, points out, even had the Ardennes offensive proved more successful, the transfer of exhausted Wehrmacht units to the east would not have sufficed to hold off the Soviet offensive. See also Henke, p. 342.

137. *DZW*, 6, p. 135; Warlimont, pp. 491–4; IfZ, Nbg.-Dok., PS-1787, Jodl's notes on Hitler's briefings, 22.12.44 (not published in the Nuremberg Trial documentation).

138. Jung, p. 229 (Kreipe diary, 2.11.44).

139. Nicolaus von Below, *Als Hitlers Adjutant 1937–45*, Mainz, 1980, p. 398.

CHAPTER 5. CALAMITY IN THE EAST

1. Heinz Guderian, *Panzer Leader*, Da Capo edn., New York, 1996, p. 382.

2. Guderian, p. 382.

3. *DZW*, 6, pp. 498–9.

4. *DZW*, 6, pp. 503, 509; *DRZW*, 10/1 (Lakowski), pp. 498, 502–4, 531; John Erickson, *The Road to Berlin*, Cassell edn., London, 2003, p. 449.

5. Erickson, pp. 447–9.

6. See Walter Warlimont, *Inside Hitler's Headquarters 1939–45*, pb. edn., Novato, Calif., n.d. (original Eng. language edn., London, 1964), pp. 212–19.

7. Jürgen Förster, 'The Final Hour of the Third Reich: The Capitulation of the Wehrmacht', *Bulletin of the International Committee for the History of the Second World War*, Montreal (1995), pp. 76–7.

8. IfZ, Nbg.-Dok., PS-1787, Jodl's 'Notizen zum Kriegstagebuch', 'Lage am 22.1.45' (23.1.45), not printed in the published trial documents. According to Goebbels, Hitler stated that the first priority was possession of oil, then coal, then a functioning armaments industry. – *TBJG*, II/15, p. 218 (25.1.45). Hungary produced some 22 per cent of the petrol and 11 per cent of the diesel demand of the Reich. – Heinrich Schwendemann, 'Strategie der Selbstvernichtung: Die Wehrmachtführung im "Endkampf" um das "Dritte Reich"', in Rolf-Dieter Müller and Hans-Erich Volkmann (eds.), *Die Wehrmacht: Mythos und Realität*, Munich, 1999, p. 226.

9. Guderian, pp. 382–7, 392–3.

10. Erich von Manstein, *Lost Victories*, London, 1982, pp. 531–2; *DRZW*, 9/1 (Förster), p. 605.

11. Schwendemann, 'Strategie', p. 231.

12. The coffins of Hindenburg and his wife were initially transported to Potsdam's garrison church, then shortly afterwards moved secretly to a safer location in a salt mine near Bernterode (a small town in Thuringia). The Americans found the coffins there on 27 April, the names scrawled on them in red crayon, and in May took them west to Marburg, where the former Reich President and his wife were finally reburied, unobtrusively, at night, in August 1946. – Anna von der Goltz, *Hindenburg: Power, Myth, and the Rise of the Nazis*, Oxford, 2009, pp. 193–6.

13. Heinrich Schwendemann, 'Das Kriegsende in Ostpreußen und in Südbaden

im Vergleich', in Bernd Martin (ed.), *Der Zweite Weltkrieg und seine Folgen: Ereignisse – Auswirkungen – Reflexionen*, Freiburg, 2006, p. 96.

14. Where not otherwise indicated, the above description of the military course of events draws upon *DZW*, 6, pp. 498-517; *DRZW*, 10/1 (Lakowski), pp. 491-542, 568ff.; *Die Vertreibung der deutschen Bevölkerung aus den Gebieten östlich der Oder-Neiße*, ed. Theodor Schieder *et al.*, pb. edn., Munich, 1984, vol. 1, pp. 16E-23E; Erickson, ch. 7; Guderian, pp. 389ff.; Brian Taylor, *Barbarossa to Berlin: A Chronology of the Campaigns on the Eastern Front 1941 to 1945*, vol. 2, Stroud, 2008, pp. 267-79; Heinz Magenheimer, *Hitler's War: German Military Strategy 1940-1945*, London, 1998, pp. 264-71; Max Hastings, *Armageddon: The Battle for Germany 1944-45*, London, 2004, chs. 9-10; and Antony Beevor, *Berlin: The Downfall 1945*, pb. edn., London, 2007, chs. 3-4.

15. Ralf Meindl, *Ostpreußens Gauleiter: Erich Koch – eine politische Biographie*, Osnabrück, 2007, pp. 435-8; Kurt Dieckert and Horst Grossmann, *Der Kampf um Ostpreußen: Ein authentischer Dokumentarbericht*, Munich, 1960, pp. 119-20.

16. Hastings, pp. 322-3.

17. Alastair Noble, *Nazi Rule and the Soviet Offensive in Eastern Germany, 1944-1945: The Darkest Hour*, Brighton and Portland, Ore., 2009, p. 320 n. 168; Meindl, pp. 441-2.

18. Meindl, p. 445. According to Noble, p. 210, Koch initially moved to the comfort of a Pillau hotel, but this was bombed a few days later. See also Isabel Denny, *The Fall of Hitler's Fortress City: The Battle for Königsberg, 1945*, London, 2007, pp. 201-2. In early February, Koch moved his staff to Heiligenbeil to help organize the evacuation of refugees over the ice of the Haff. – Meindl, p. 447.

19. Heinrich Schwendemann, 'Endkampf und Zusammenbruch im deutschen Osten', *Freiburger Universitätsblätter*, 130 (1995), p. 19; Hans Graf von Lehndorff, *Ostpreußisches Tagebuch: Aufzeichnungen eines Arztes aus den Jahren 1945-1947*, pb. edn., Munich, 1967, pp. 18 (23.1.45), 40 (7.2.45).

20. Some of many examples in Edgar Günther Lass, *Die Flucht: Ostpreußen 1944/45*, Bad Nauheim, 1964, pp. 85-7.

21. Lehndorff, pp. 24-5 (28.1.45).

22. *Die Vertreibung*, vol. 1, p. 28 (testimony from 1951).

23. Christian Tilitzki, *Alltag in Ostpreußen 1940-1945: Die geheimen Lageberichte der Königsberger Justiz 1940-1945*, Leer, 1991, pp. 300-304 (report of the Generalstaatsanwalt, 18.1.45). See also Heinrich Schwendemann, 'Tod zwischen den Fronten', *Spiegel Special* 2, Hamburg, 2002, p. 46. Gauleiter Koch encouraged the judicial authorities to take a pragmatic view of the looting in the circumstances. Lehndorff, p. 27 (29.1.45), in his field hospital in Königsberg after a bombing raid, recorded his despair at the looting; also pp. 28-9 (30.1.45). Later accounts have at times

minimized the looting of apartments in Königsberg, emphasizing the severe punishment for 'plunderers'. – Hans-Burkhard Sumowski, *'Jetzt war ich ganz allein auf der Welt': Erinnerungen an eine Kindheit in Königsberg 1944–1947*, Munich, 2009, p. 61.

24. Schwendemann, 'Tod zwischen den Fronten', pp. 44–5.
25. Denny, p. 199.
26. Lehndorff, p. 18 (23.1.45).
27. Beevor, p. 49.
28. Dieckert and Grossmann, p. 129; Lehndorff, p. 39 (7.2.45).
29. Lehndorff, pp. 19, 21 (24, 26.1.45).
30. *Die Vertreibung*, vol. 1, pp. 144–6.
31. Lehndorff, p. 23 (27.1.45).
32. *DRZW*, 10/1 (Rahn), p. 272; Schwendemann, 'Endkampf', p. 20.
33. Lass, pp. 246ff.
34. *Die Vertreibung*, vol. 1, p. 79 (testimony from 1952).
35. Schwendemann, 'Endkampf', p. 20.
36. Franz W. Seidler and Alfred M. de Zayas (eds.), *Kriegsverbrechen in Europa und im Nahen Osten im 20. Jahrhundert*, Hamburg, 2002, p. 220. Vivid descriptions of the mass flight from East Prussia and conditions in the province are provided in the account compiled only a few years after the events by Jürgen Thorwald, *Es begann an der Weichsel: Flucht und Vertreibung der Deutschen aus dem Osten*, pb. edn., Munich, 1995 (1st edn., 1949), pp. 123–99; and in Guido Knopp, *Die große Flucht: Das Schicksal der Vertriebenen*, Munich, 2001, pp. 57–85. A good description of the horrific treks is provided by Richard Bessel, *Germany 1945: From War to Peace*, London, 2009, ch. 4.
37. Manfred Zeidler, *Kriegsende im Osten: Die Rote Armee und die Besetzung Deutschlands östlich von Oder und Neiße 1944/1945*, Munich, 1996, pp. 135–8.
38. Zeidler, pp. 140–41.
39. Schwendemann, 'Endkampf', p. 22.
40. A few of many examples in *Die Vertreibung*, vol. 1, pp. 194, 297; vol. 2, pp. 159–64, 224–34; Lass, pp. 87, 121.
41. *Die Vertreibung*, vol. 1, p. 266.
42. Barbara Johr, 'Die Ereignisse in Zahlen', in Helke Sander and Barbara Johr (eds.), *Befreier und Befreite: Krieg, Vergewaltigungen, Kinder*, Munich, 1992, pp. 47–8, 58–9.
43. The above account of the plight of the East Prussian refugees, where not otherwise indicated, is based on *Die Vertreibung*, vol. 1, pp. 33E–41E, 60Eff., 79Eff., and the reports, pp. 21–154. Figures on Germans deported are in *Die Vertreibung*, vol. 1, p. 83E, and Schwendemann, 'Endkampf', p. 24 (estimating up to as many as 400,000). A number of later graphic oral accounts are given by Hastings, pp. 319ff.

44. *Die Vertreibung*, vol. 1, pp. 26E–32E, 345–404. See also Noble, p. 204 for the refusal of the Gauleiter, Emil Stürtz, to allow precautionary evacuation.

45. BfZ, Sammlung Sterz, Pfarrer Heinrich M., 28.1.45, giving the example of the Blechhammer and Heydebreck synthetic fuel plant in Upper Silesia. The enormous industrial complex at Blechhammer, near Cosel, about 75 kilometres from Auschwitz, had in its heyday nearly 30,000 workers, nearly 4,000 of whom were, shortly before the evacuation in January 1945, prisoners in an outlying camp attached to Auschwitz III (Monowitz). On Blechhammer, see Ernest Koenig, 'Auschwitz III – Blechhammer. Erinnerungen', *Dachauer Hefte*, 15 (1999), pp. 134–52; and Andrea Rudorff, 'Blechhammer (Blachownia)', in Wolfgang Benz and Barbara Distel (eds.), *Der Ort des Terrors: Geschichte der nationalsozialistischen Konzentrationslager*, vol. 5, Munich, 2007, pp. 186–91. A week earlier, Speer had reported to Hitler on the importance of the plant's production of aircraft fuel, urging concentration of the entire Luftwaffe 'in this decisive struggle' for its defence, and seeking the Führer's opinion. He had told the works the same day that he and Colonel-General Schörner would decide when the factory should be put out of action, though only in such a way that would render deployment by the Soviets impossible for two to three weeks. – BAB, R3/1545, fos. 3–7, Speer to von Below, for immediate presentation to the Führer; Speer to the Werke Blechhammer und Heydebreck, both 21.1.45.

46. Schwendemann, 'Tod zwischen den Fronten', p. 44.

47. Paul Peikert, '*Festung Breslau' in den Berichten eines Pfarrers 22. Januar bis 6. Mai 1945*, ed. Karol Jonca and Alfred Konieczny, Wrocław, 1993, p. 29; BfZ, Sammlung Sterz, Pfarrer Heinrich M., 28.1.45; Knopp, *Die große Flucht*, p. 158. Those who managed to find a place on a train then faced a long and grim journey through the bitter cold. Some refugees arrived in Dresden with children who had frozen to death on the way and had to ask railway personnel for cardboard boxes to serve as coffins. – Reinhold Maier, *Ende und Wende: Das schwäbische Schicksal 1944–1946. Briefe und Tagebuchaufzeichnungen*, Stuttgart and Tübingen, 1948, p. 172 (5.3.45).

48. *Die Vertreibung*, vol. 1, pp. 51E–59E, 405–77; Friedrich Grieger, *Wie Breslau fiel . . .*, Metzingen, 1948, pp. 7–8; Ernst Hornig, *Breslau 1945: Erlebnisse in der eingeschlossenen Stadt*, Munich, 1975, pp. 18–19; Peikert, pp. 29–31; Knopp, *Die große Flucht*, pp. 158–62; Noble, p. 202; Sebastian Siebel-Achenbach, *Lower Silesia from Nazi Germany to Communist Poland, 1942–49*, London, 1994, pp. 60–61, 72–4 (where the number of those forced to march off in the direction of Kanth, 25 kilometres southwest of Breslau, is given as 60,000, of whom 18,000 were estimated to have perished, and the numbers of civilians in the city when it was cut off at 150,000–180,000).

49. Hastings, pp. 328–32. Unclarity about the numbers actually on board means the death toll is uncertain. Estimates vary widely. Dieckert and

Grossmann, pp. 130–31, have 904 from 5,000 surviving; Seidler and de Zayas, p. 222, indicate a complement of 6,600 on board, of whom 1,200 were saved and 5,400 drowned. Guido Knopp, *Der Untergang der Gustloff*, 2nd edn., pb., Munich, 2008, pp. 9, 156, reckons the losses to have been as high as 9,000, and (p. 12) that as many as 40,000 refugees lost their lives in this and other sinkings in the last months of the war. Michael Schwartz in *DRZW*, 10/2, p. 591, also accepts a figure of 9,000 dead, but halves the number of refugee victims in sea disasters to 20,000. One of the officers responsible for checking the passengers on board the *Gustloff* claimed to have noted the last figure for registrations as 7,956. This was twenty hours before the *Gustloff* set sail, and one estimate suggests that a further 2,000 people were allowed on board before departure, making the total number, including crew, more than 10,000. – Knopp, *Die große Flucht*, p. 104. Denny, pp. 202–3, has 996 from 9,000 saved. Bessel, p. 75, has 1,239 rescued from over 10,000 on board. Beevor, p. 51, places the number of deaths between 6,600 and 9,000. Two of the subsequent worst disasters occurred almost at the end of the war, with the sinking off Lübeck through British air attack of the *Thielbek* (50 survivors from 2,800 on board) and the *Cap d'Arcona* (4,250 dead from 6,400 on board). The victims were almost all prisoners who had been evacuated by their SS guards from Neuengamme concentration camp near Hamburg on the approach of British forces. – David Stafford, *Endgame 1945: Victory, Retribution, Liberation*, London, 2007, pp. 291–301.

50. Under Gauleiter Franz Schwede-Coburg, the Pomeranian Party leadership, as elsewhere, had exacerbated the plight of the population by refusing to give timely orders for evacuation. – Noble, pp. 205–8.

51. For the above, where not otherwise indicated, *Die Vertreibung*, vol. 1, pp. 41E–51E, 155–201.

52. Beevor, pp. 48–9.

53. Andreas Kossert, '"Endlösung on the Amber Shore": The Massacre in January 1945 on the Baltic Seashore – a Repressed Chapter of East Prussian History', *Leo Baeck Year Book*, 40 (2004), pp. 3–21 (quotations, pp. 15–17); and Andreas Kossert, *Damals in Ostpreußen: Der Untergang einer deutschen Provinz*, Munich, 2008, pp. 148–53; Schmuel Krakowski, 'Massacre of Jewish Prisoners on the Samland Peninsula – Documents', *YVS*, 24 (1994), pp. 349–87; Reinhard Henkys, 'Ein Todesmarsch in Ostpreußen', *Dachauer Hefte*, 20 (2004), pp. 3–21; the eyewitness account by a former member of the Hitler Youth who had been involved in the atrocity, Martin Bergau, 'Tod an der Bernsteinküste: Ein NS-Verbrechen in Ostpreußen', in Elke Fröhlich (ed.), *Als die Erde brannte: Deutsche Schicksale in den letzten Kriegstagen*, Munich, 2005, pp. 99–112; the early account, from 1952, of the former Landrat of the Samland District in *Die Vertreibung*, vol. 1, p. 136; Martin Bergau, *Der Junge von der Bernsteinküste:*

Erlebte Zeitgeschichte 1938–1948, Heidelberg, 1994, pp. 108–15, 249–75; and Daniel Blatman, *Les Marches de la mort: La dernière étape du génocide nazi, été 1944–printemps 1945*, Paris, 2009, pp. 132–40. This terrible episode was also described in Nicholas Stargardt, *Witnesses of War: Children's Lives under the Nazis*, London, 2005, pp. 284–6. Though most eyewitness accounts concur that the mass shooting took place during the night of 31 January–1 February, some imply that it was slightly later. – Henkys, p. 16. Bergau, and, based on his accounts, Kossert, reckon the number of survivors to have been as low as 15, but Blatman, p. 139, citing the conclusions reached by the court which in 1967 tried and convicted one of the perpetrators, gives an estimated figure of around 200.

54. *VB*, South German edn., 15.1.45; *Die Wehrmachtberichte 1939–1945*, vol. 3: *1. Januar 1944 bis 9. Mai 1945*, Munich, 1989, p. 402 (15.1.45).

55. This was registered in British monitoring of the German press: NAL, FO 898/187, PWE, fos. 222–4, Summary of and Comments on German Broadcasts to Germany, 14.8.44–7.5.45.

56. BAB, R55/601, fos. 272–6, Tätigkeitsbericht, weekly propaganda report (24.1.45).

57. BStA, MA 106696, report of the RPvNB/OP, 9.2.45.

58. BAB, R55/793, fos. 7–8, 'Material für Propagandisten, Nr. 25: Betr. Bolschewistische Greuel', 16.1.45.

59. *TBJG*, II/15, p. 190 (23.1.45), p. 216 (25.1.45). By early February Goebbels had changed his mind. He now thought it important to emphasize the Bolshevik atrocities and did not think that publicizing them would produce panic. – *TBJG*, II/15, pp. 322–3 (6.2.45).

60. BStA, MA 106696, report of the RPvNB/OP, 10.3.45. Colonel Curt Pollex, based in Berlin, noted that Soviet atrocities, exploited by German propaganda, were causing 'total panic'. – BA/MA, N712/15, NL Pollex, Auszüge aus Briefen, fo. 14, 23.1.45. For the mood of panic spread by refugees and fear of the Russians, see also Victor Klemperer, *Ich will Zeugnis ablegen bis zum letzten*, vol 2: *Tagebücher 1942–1945*, ed. Walter Nowojski and Hadwig Klemperer, Darmstadt, 1998, pp. 645–6, 649–60 (25.1.45, 29.1.45).

61. *VB*, South German edn., 9.2.45.

62. BfZ, Sammlung Sterz, Josef E., 21.1.45.

63. Jörg Echternkamp (ed.), *Kriegsschauplatz Deutschland 1945: Leben in Angst – Hoffnung auf Frieden. Feldpost aus der Heimat und von der Front*, Paderborn, 2006, pp. 138–9 (28.1.45) and p. 268 nn. 282–6. The letter was returned, marked 'Wait for New Address'. Whether the soldier survived is not known.

64. BStA, MA 106695, report of the RPvOB, 9.2.45.

65. BStA, MA 106696, report of the RPvOF/MF, 8.2.45.

66. Ursula von Kardorff, *Berliner Aufzeichnungen 1942–1945*, pb. edn., Munich, 1981, pp. 228 (25.1.45), 229 (30.1.45).
67. Ruth Andreas-Friedrich, *Schauplatz Berlin: Ein deutsches Tagebuch*, Munich, 1962, p. 124 (22.1.45).
68. LHC, Dempsey Papers, no. 249, pt. II, p. 9 (in English).
69. IWM, Memoirs of P. E. von Stemann, p. 193.
70. *Das letzte halbe Jahr: Stimmungsberichte der Wehrmachtpropaganda 1944/45*, ed. Wolfram Wette, Ricarda Bremer and Detlef Vogel, Essen, 2001, pp. 219–20, 229 (23.1.45, 1.2.45).
71. Andreas-Friedrich, p. 126 (31.1.45).
72. *Das letzte halbe Jahr*, p. 219 (23.1.45), pp. 228–9 (1.2.45).
73. IWM, Memoirs of P. E. von Stemann, p. 197.
74. *Das letzte halbe Jahr*, pp. 235–6 (7.2.45).
75. Echternkamp, p. 129 (20.1.45).
76. IWM, Memoirs of P. E. von Stemann, p. 200.
77. IWM, 'Aus deutschen Urkunden 1935–1945', unpub. documentation, n.d. (*c.* 1945–6), pp. 66–7, 276–8.
78. *Das letzte halbe Jahr*, pp. 218 (22.1.45), 236 (7.2.45).
79. BfZ, Sammlung Sterz, Gisela K., 3.2.45.
80. BfZ, Sammlung Sterz, Luise G., 3.2.45.
81. Heinrich Breloer (ed.), *Mein Tagebuch: Geschichten vom Überleben 1939–1947*, Cologne, 1984, p. 228 (27.1.45).
82. For a good description in one region, see Jill Stephenson, *Hitler's Home Front: Württemberg under the Nazis*, London, 2006, pp. 304–12.
83. BfZ, Sammlung Sterz, Gefr. Heinrich R., 23.1.45.
84. BfZ, Sammlung Sterz, Sold. Willy F., 30.1.45.
85. BfZ, Sammlung Sterz, Fw. Hugo B., 2.2.45.
86. BfZ, Sammlung Sterz, Lt. Thomas S., 23.1.45.
87. BfZ, Sammlung Sterz, Hptm. Emerich P., 20.1.45.
88. BfZ, Sammlung Sterz, Uffz. Hans ——, 24.1.45.
89. BfZ, Sammlung Sterz, O'Gefr. Otto L., 24.1.45.
90. BfZ, Sammlung Sterz, Gren. Kurt M., 30.1.45.
91. Quoted Andreas Kunz, *Wehrmacht und Niederlage: Die bewaffnete Macht in der Endphase der nationalsozialistischen Herrschaft 1944 bis 1945*, Munich, 2007, p. 243, and see also, for racial stereotypes, pp. 269–70.
92. BA/MA, MSg2/2697, fo. 88, diary of Lieutenant Julius Dufner, 25.1.45.
93. NAL, WO219/1587, fo. 860, SHAEF, Directorate of Army Psychiatry Research Memorandum 45/03/12, January 1945.
94. Kunz, pp. 299–300.
95. BA/MA, N245/3, NL Reinhardt, 'Kalenderblätter 1945', fo. 81 (14.1.45); N245/2, Briefe, fo. 41 (15.1.45); N245/15, Generalleutnant Otto Heidkämper

(former Chief of Staff of Army Group Centre), 'Die Schlacht um Ostpreußen' (1953), fo. 32; Guderian, pp. 382–3; *DRZW*, 10/1 (Lakowski), pp. 536–7.

96. BA/MA, N245/3, NL Reinhardt, 'Kalenderblätter 1945', fo. 82 (16–17.1.45); N245/15, Heidkämper, fos. 40–43.
97. BA/MA, N245/2, NL Reinhardt, Briefe, fo. 41 (19.1.45).
98. BA/MA, N245/2, NL Reinhardt, Briefe, fo. 41 (20.1.45).
99. BA/MA, N245/2, NL Reinhardt, Briefe, fo. 41ᵛ (21.1.45); N245/3, NL Reinhardt, 'Kalenderblätter 1945', fos. 82–3 (20–21.1.45); N245/15, Heidkämper, fos. 53–7.
100. The above account relies, except where otherwise stated, on BA/MA, N245/3, NL Reinhardt, 'Kalenderblätter 1945', fos. 83–4 (22–7.1.45); N245/2, NL Reinhardt, Briefe, fos. 41–2 (22.1.45, 26.1.45); N245/15, Heidkämper, fos. 68–72, 76–87; N24/39, 'Erinnerungen von General d.I. a.D. Friedrich Hoßbach', typescript (May 1945), pp. 45–6, 68. See also Friedrich Hoßbach, *Die Schlacht um Ostpreußen*, Überlingen, 1951, pp. 51–73; Guderian, pp. 400–401; Dieckert and Grossmann, pp. 94–5, 110-18; *DZW*, 6, p. 511.
101. e.g. BA/MA, RH21/3/730, fos. 3–6, 'Auskünfte Gen.Major Mueller-Hillebrand (Chef des Stabes) über den Einsatz der 3. Pz. Armee in Ostpreußen, Sept. 1944–Feb. 1945' (1955); 'Auszug aus einem Bericht von Oberst i.G. Mendrzyk O.Qu. bei der 3. Panzer-Armee'.
102. Quoted Schwendemann, 'Das Kriegsende in Ostpreußen', p. 98.
103. Schwendemann, 'Tod zwischen den Fronten', p. 43. I am most grateful to Dr Schwendemann for the reference to the source for these comments, BA/MA, RH20/4/617, unfoliated, Notizen über Ferngespräche 14–25.1.45, Gesprächsnotizen vom 24.1.45 (Hoßbach addressing leading officers at 16.00 hours that day, and speaking to Reinhardt that evening at 22.15 hours), and to Dr Jürgen Förster for obtaining for me a copy of the document.
104. BA/MA, N712/15, NL Pollex, Auszüge aus Briefen, fo. 12, 22.1.45.
105. N24/39, NL Hoßbach, 'Erinnerungen', pp. 46–7; Hoßbach, p. 70. That Rendulić had a less than complete comprehension of the situation in East Prussia when he arrived there seems clear. He had as recently as 17 January been appointed by Hitler as Commander-in-Chief of Army Group Courland, and had been in Courland no more than twelve hours when, on 26 January, he was suddenly informed that he had to take over the command of Army Group North, besieged in East Prussia. – Lothar Rendulić, *Gekämpft, Gesiegt, Geschlagen*, Wels, 1952, pp. 331–2, 336.
106. Guderian, pp. 400–401. Rendulić, pp. 337–55, provides a description of his period, a little over six weeks, in command in East Prussia, until 12 March, though it contains only a few inconsequential lines on Hoßbach's dismissal on p. 343.
107. Guderian, p. 394.

108. Hastings, p. 283; Roland Kaltenegger, *Schörner: Feldmarschall der letzten Stunde*, Munich and Berlin, 1994, pp. 265–6; Siebel-Achenbach, pp. 59, 71–2. Hitler had initially intended Field-Marshal Model to take over the command. It was decided, however, that he was urgently needed in the west, so the command was given to Schörner. – *TBJG*, II/15, pp. 135 (16.1.45), 138 (17.1.45).

109. Quoted *DRZW*, 10/2 (Kunz), p. 39.

110. BA/MA, N60/74, NL Schörner, 'Tragödie Schlesien, März 1945', fo. 2 (1958).

111. BAB, NS6/353, fos. 157–8, Bormann, Bekanntgabe 28/45, Ungehorsam und falsche Meldungen, containing Keitel's order in appendix; also IfZ, Fa-91/4, fo. 1069.

112. Himmler's command had, it seems, already been agreed some days earlier, in the main, according to Goebbels, because 'a firm hand' was needed to turn troops 'flooding back' from the path of the Soviets into new fighting units. Goebbels even suggested making Himmler Commander-in-Chief of the Army, to relieve Hitler of this duty, but Hitler was unwilling to go so far and stated that Himmler first had to prove he could master operational command. – *TBJG*, II/15, pp. 165 (20.1.45), 181 (22.1.45), 195 (23.1.45).

113. *DZW*, 6, p. 513.

114. IWM, FO645/155, interrogations of Karl Dönitz, 30.9.45, p. 5; 2.10.45, p. 2 (in English).

115. IfZ, ZS 1810, Bd. II, fo. 54, Dönitz interview with Barry Pree, 18.11.74.

116. Quoted Schwendemann, 'Endkampf', p. 20; also Schwendemann, 'Tod zwischen den Fronten', p. 45.

117. Goebbels thought Göring, when he spoke with him on 27 January, 'almost defeatist' and depressed, hoping even now that Hitler would try to find a political solution. – *TBJG*, 15/II, p. 250 (28.1.45)

118. *DZW*, 6, p. 572.

119. *DRZW*, 9/1 (Heinemann), p. 884.

120. *DRZW*, 9/1 (Heinemann), p. 882.

121. *DRZW*, 10/1 (Lakowski), p. 559.

122. *DZW*, 6, pp. 575, 591.

123. David K. Yelton, *Hitler's Volkssturm: The Nazi Militia and the Fall of Germany, 1944–1945*, Lawrence, Kan., 2002, p. 131.

124. Quoted *DZW*, 6, p. 513.

125. *DZW*, 6, pp. 513–14.

CHAPTER 6. TERROR COMES HOME

1. See in general, for a similar interpretation, Robert Gellately, *Backing Hitler: Consent and Coercion in Nazi Germany*, Oxford, 2001.

2. For the malevolent depiction of Jews, which showed no diminution as Jews were deported from Germany, see Jeffrey Herf, *The Jewish Enemy: Nazi Propaganda during World War II and the Holocaust*, Cambridge, Mass., 2006, and Herf's contribution, '"Der Krieg und die Juden": Nationalsozialistische Propaganda im Zweiten Weltkrieg', in *DRZW*, 9/2, pp. 159ff.

3. BAB, NS19/2454, fos. 1–3ᵛ: SS-Kriegsberichter-Abteilung, SS-Standarte 'Kurt Eggers', 26–30.1.45.

4. *1945: Das Jahr der endgültigen Niederlage der faschistischen Wehrmacht. Dokumente*, ed. Gerhard Förster and Richard Lakowski, Berlin, 1975, p. 144 (5.2.45).

5. NAL, WO219/4713, SHAEF reports, 15.2.45, 20.2.45. The threat of 'family liability' (*Sippenhaft*) against soldiers judged to be failing in their duty had been issued on numerous occasions by Wehrmacht commanders as a deterrent. It was indeed carried out in some cases, though these were exceptions rather than the rule. See Robert Loeffel, 'Soldiers and Terror: Re-evaluating the Complicity of the Wehrmacht in Nazi Germany', *German History*, 27 (2009), pp. 514–30.

6. Account (in English) of a prisoner of war, captured in the west, who had returned from the eastern front: LHC, Dempsey Papers, no. 273, pt. II, p. 7 (3.3.45).

7. BAB, NS6/135, fos. 44, 118–21, Gauleitung Mageburg-Anhalt, report of 16.2.45; report of Landratsamt in Mähr.-Schönberg, 17.2.45.

8. BAB, NS6/135, fo. 11, Auszug aus einem Bericht des Pg. Waldmann, Inspektion-Mitte, 7.3.45 (referring to impressions gathered in early February).

9. BAB, NS19/3705, fos. 6–13, 'Beobachtungen im Heimatkriegsgebiet', 22.2.45 and covering letter of Bormann to Himmler, 1.3.45.

10. BAB, NS19/2068, fos. 6–6ᵛ, 20–20ᵛ, 'Meldungen aus dem Ostraum', Müllrose, 16.2.45, Mark Brandenburg, 21.2.45. Reports of widespread looting in the Oder area as an indication of demoralization also in *DZW*, 6, p. 514. According to Goebbels' aide, Wilfred von Oven, writing in mid-February, 'the morale of the German soldiers on the eastern front is becoming worse by the day'. – Wilfred von Oven, *Finale Furioso: Mit Goebbels bis zum Ende*, Tübingen, 1974, p. 578 (11.2.45).

11. BAB, R55/601, fo. 284, Tätigkeitsbericht der RPÄ, 21.2.45.

12. *Das letzte halbe Jahr: Stimmungsberichte der Wehrmachtpropaganda 1944/45*, ed. Wolfram Wette, Ricarda Bremer and Detlef Vogel, Essen, 2001, pp. 236–7 (7.2.45).

13. *Das letzte halbe Jahr*, p. 251 (23.2.45).

14. BHStA, MA 106695, report of RPvOB, 9.2.45. And see further examples in Klaus-Dietmar Henke, *Die amerikanische Besetzung Deutschlands*, Munich, 1995, pp. 819–20, and Marlis Steinert, *Hitlers Krieg und die Deutschen*, Düsseldorf and Vienna, 1970, pp. 546ff.

15. BAB, R55/620, fos. 129–131ᵛ, SD report to State Secretary Dr Naumann,

Propaganda Ministry, 'Situation in Wien', 1.3.45. The popular mood in Vienna had been especially poor, according to a report the previous September, when it was claimed that there was widespread defeatism, making the population open to Communist agitation. – BAB, NS6/166, fos. 23–7, Kaltenbrunner to Bormann, 14.9.44. And see Ludwig Jedlicka, 'Ein unbekannter Bericht Kaltenbrunners über die Lage in Österreich im September 1944', in Ludwig Jedlicka, *Der 20. Juli 1944*, Vienna, 1985, pp. 82–6; and Timothy Kirk, *Nazism and the Working Class in Austria*, Cambridge, 1996, pp. 130–32.

16. StAM, LRA 29656, fo. 573, SD-Außenstelle Berchtesgaden, 7.3.45.

17. NAL, WO219/1587, SHAEF summary of intelligence reports from informants, 20–25.2.45.

18. Goebbels noted that 'the fiasco of the East Prussian treks is mainly put down to the Party, and the Party leadership in East Prussia is thoroughly lambasted'. – *TBJG*, II/15, p. 374 (13.2.45).

19. BAB, NS19/3833, fo. 1, Gottlob Berger to SS-Standartenführer Rudolf Brandt, 18.2.45.

20. BAB, NS6/135, fo. 44, report from Gauleitung Magdeburg-Anhalt, 16.2.45.

21. StAM, NSDAP 35, unfoliated, Gauorganisationsleiter München-Oberbayern to Kreisleiter, etc., 21.2.45. At the beginning of January, the Gauleiter had sharply criticized the wearing of 'fantasy uniforms' and 'costuming' as Party officials created their own colour or cut of uniform. – StAM, NSDAP 52, unfoliated, Gauorganisationsleiter München-Oberbayern to Gauamtsleiter and Kreisleiter, 3.1.45.

22. See Henke, p. 829.

23. Mark Mazower, *Hitler's Empire: Nazi Rule in Occupied Europe*, London, 2008, pp. 528–9. Frank was eventually arrested by American troops on 4 May, tried at Nuremberg, and hanged for his part in war crimes and crimes against humanity.

24. IfZ, NO-3501, report of SS-Staf. Hübner, 16.3.45; National Archives, Washington, NND 871063, arrest and interrogation reports on Greiser, 17.5.45, 1.6.45; Jürgen Thorwald, *Es begann an der Weichsel: Flucht und Vertreibung der Deutschen aus dem Osten*, pb. edn., Munich, 1995 (1st edn., 1949), pp. 69–79; Catherine Epstein, *Model Nazi: Arthur Greiser and the Occupation of Western Poland*, Oxford, 2010, pp. 298–304.

25. *TBJG*, II/15, pp. 223 (25.1.45), 231–2 (26.1.45), 357 (11.2.45); von Oven, *Finale Furioso*, p. 551 (23.1.45)

26. BAB, R55/622, fos. 181–2, survey of letters sent to the RPÄ. And see BAB, NS6/135, fos. 30–32, report of 20.2.45 from Lieutenant Klein, NS-Führungsstab OKH Potsdam, on negative impressions of Party members, notably an SS-Obersturmführer, during treks from the Wartheland between 19 and 25 January. Remarkably, as late as 20 February, a month after he

had fled, Greiser submitted a final report, from the security of Karlsbad, to Himmler and Bormann on the setting up and deployment of the *Volkssturm* in the Warthegau. – BAB, R43II/692b, fos. 109–24 (20–21.2.45).

27. BAB, NS6/353, fo. 30–30^v, PK Rundschreiben 65/45, 12.2.45. Only a few days later the Party Chancellery received another dismal report of the failings of the authorities in the Warthegau in January. – BAB, NS6/135, fos. 30–32, report by Lieutenant Horst Klein, NS-Führungsstab OKH Potsdam, with an attached recommendation for Pg. Willi Ruder for the Party, in order to restore confidence in it, to take drastic action against all leading Party members seen to have failed in their duties.

28. Von Oven, *Finale Furioso*, p. 572 (7.2.45).

29. IfZ, Fa 91/4, fos. 1075–8, GBV an die Obersten Reichsbehörden, 1.2.45; *1945: Das Jahr der endgültigen Niederlage der faschistischen Wehrmacht*, p. 152.

30. *1945: Das Jahr der endgültigen Niederlage der faschistischen Wehrmacht*, pp. 152–4.

31. e.g. BAB, NS6/353, fo. 15, PK Rundschreiben 43/45, 30.1.45; fo. 49, PK Rundschreiben 86/45, 17.2.45; fo. 106, Anordnung 23/45, 21.1.45.

32. BAB, NS6/354, fo. 134, PK Anordnung 48/45g, 1.2.45.

33. BAB, NS6/353, fos. 121–2, PK Anordnung 98/45, 23.2.45.

34. BAB, NS6/353, fos. 65–66^v, PK Rundschreiben 113/45, '25. Jahrestag der Verkündung des Parteiprogramms', 24.2.45.

35. BAB, NS6/353, fos. 157–8, PK Bekanntgabe 28/45, 26.1.45 and Anlage.

36. One of these, Feldjägerkommando II, based behind the lines of Army Group Centre, reported picking up 136,000 soldiers in February, leading to almost 200 facing trial and 46 death sentences. It regarded the ratio of those arrested to the number of troops fighting as unexceptional, given the military situation. – *DRZW*, 9/1 (Förster), p. 638.

37. Ursula von Kardorff, *Berliner Aufzeichnungen 1942–1945*, pb. edn., Munich, 1981, p. 228 (25.1.45).

38. IfZ, Fa-91/5, fo. 1239, Aufruf Himmlers, 31.1.45; BAB, R55/610, fos. 161ff., RPÄ Danzig to State Secretary Dr Naumann, Propaganda Ministry, 31.1.45, attaching Himmler's proclamation.

39. BAB, NS6/354, fos. 60–61^v, PK Rundschreiben 59/45g, 'Erfassung von versprengten Wehrmachtangehörigen', 6.2.45, and attached Anlage reproducing OKW order of 2.2.45. A month later, on 5 March, Field-Marshal Keitel passed on Hitler's order that all financial support for the families of prisoners entering captivity without being wounded or having demonstrably fought to the last was to be halted. – Printed in Rolf-Dieter Müller and Gerd R. Ueberschär, *Kriegsende 1945: Die Zerstörung des Deutschen Reiches*, Frankfurt am Main, 1994, p. 163.

40. Andreas Kunz, 'Die Wehrmacht in der Agonie der nationalsozialistischen

Herrschaft 1944/45: Eine Gedankenskizze', in Jörg Hillmann and John Zimmermann (eds.), *Kriegsende 1945 in Deutschland*, Munich, 2002, p. 103 n. 26.

41. BAB, NS19/3705, fos. 1–5, Bormann to Himmler, 'Vorbereitungen für die bevorstehende Feindoffensive im Westen', and attached Rundschreiben to the western Gauleiter, 8.2.45.

42. BAB, NS6/354, fos. 135–6, PK Anordnung 67/45g, 13.2.45.

43. BAB, NS6/354, fos. 81–4, PK Rundschreiben 92/45g, Rs., 20.2.45.

44. StAM, NSDAP 35, Gauleitung München-Oberbayern, Rundschreiben Nr. 5, 22.2.45.

45. BAB, NS19/2721, fo. 4–4ᵛ, Oberbefehlshaber der Heeresgruppe Weichsel, 12.2.45.

46. *TBJG*, II/15, p. 459 (9.3.45). Bodies of uniformed German soldiers hanging from a bridge across the Oder near Frankurt in mid-February were said to have led to thousands of 'stragglers' reporting for further frontline service. – Wilfred von Oven, *Mit Goebbels bis zum Ende*, vol. 2, Buenos Aires, 1950, p. 246 (16.2.45).

47. BAB, NS6/756, fos. 2–6, Bormann, 'Verstärkung der kämpfenden Truppe', 28.2.45.

48. Norbert Haase, 'Justizterror in der Wehrmacht', in Cord Arendes, Edgar Wolfrum and Jörg Zedler (eds.), *Terror nach Innen: Verbrechen am Ende des Zweiten Weltkrieges*, Göttingen, 2006, pp. 84–5, reckons that half a million German soldiers might have been sentenced by military courts over the duration of the war, implying, therefore, that the numbers down to the end of 1944 doubled in the last four months. There were eighteen times as many death sentences as in the period from June 1941 to November 1944. Fritz Wüllner, *NS-Militärjustiz und das Elend der Geschichtsschreibung*, Baden-Baden, 1991, p. 461, estimates a figure of around 300,000 deserters down to the end of 1944. For the organization of the terror apparatus within the Wehrmacht, including the extended use of the *Geheime Feldpolizei*, see John Zimmermann, *Pflicht zum Untergang: Die deutsche Kriegführung im Westen des Reiches 1944/45*, Paderborn, 2009, pp. 139–65.

49. Benjamin Ziemann, 'Fluchten aus dem Konsens zum Durchhalten: Ergebnisse, Probleme und Perspektiven der Erforschung soldatischer Verweigerungsformen in der Wehrmacht 1939–1945', in Rolf-Dieter Müller and Hans-Erich Volkmann (eds.), *Die Wehrmacht: Mythos und Realität*, Munich, 1999, pp. 594–6, 599; Otto Hennicke, 'Auszüge aus der Wehrmachtkriminalstatistik', *Zeitschrift für Militärgeschichte*, 5 (1966), pp. 442–50; Manfred Messerschmidt and Fritz Wüllner, *Die Wehrmachtjustiz*, Baden-Baden, 1987, p. 91; Richard Bessel, *Germany 1945: From War to Peace*, London, 2009, p. 63. The figure of 35,000 underestimates the scale of desertion. One estimate places the figure at more than 100,000. – Manfred Messerschmidt, 'Deserteure im Zweiten Weltkrieg', in Wolfram Wette

(ed.), *Deserteure der Wehrmacht*, Essen, 1995, p. 62. A further 35,000 were sentenced for other contraventions of military law (Ziemann, p. 604). On the procedures for carrying out the death penalty in the Wehrmacht, see Manfred Messerschmidt, *Die Wehrmachtjustiz 1933–1945*, Paderborn, 2005, pp. 393–400.

50. Messerschmidt, 'Deserteure im Zweiten Weltkrieg', p. 61; Haase, p. 85 and p. 100 n. 26; *DRZW*, 9/1 (Echternkamp), p. 50. While the western liberal democracies executed few soldiers, Germany was not alone among authoritarian regimes in its draconian punishment. Japan executed 22,253 soldiers; estimates (though detailed research remains to be carried out) suggest that as many as 150,000 may have been executed in the Soviet Union. – Ulrich Baumann and Markus Koch (eds.), *'Was damals Recht war . . .': Soldaten und Zivilisten vor Gerichten der Wehrmacht*, Berlin-Brandenburg, 2008, p. 184.

51. e.g. BAB, R55/620, fo. 132, SD report to State Secretary Dr Naumann, Propaganda Ministry, 'Stimmung und Haltung der Arbeiterschaft' (reported opinion among workers in Mecklenburg), 1.3.45.

52. BA/MA, N60/17, NL Schörner, letter from Schörner to Oberst i.G. Thilo von Trotha, Generalstab des Heeres, Chef Operations-Abt., 22.2.45. Partially quoted also in Andreas Kunz, *Wehrmacht und Niederlage: Die bewaffnete Macht in der Endphase der nationalsozialistischen Herrschaft 1944 bis 1945*, Munich, 2007, p. 113.

53. BAB, NS6/354, fos. 163–165ᵛ, PK Bekanntgabe 149/45g, 19.3.45, attaching a copy of Schörner's four-page message dated 27.2.45.

54. BA/MA, N712/15, NL Pollex, Colonel Curt Pollex, Auszüge aus Briefen, fo. 35, 18.2.45.

55. BAB, R55/610, fos. 156–9, correspondence related to propaganda in the Ruhr, 19.12.44–12.1.45.

56. Von Oven, *Finale Furioso*, p. 584 (22.2.45).

57. See Bormann's attempt to check the spread of rumour, in BAB, NS6/353, fos. 16–17, 'Bekämpfung beunruhigender Gerüchte über die Frontlage', 1.2.45.

58. IfZ, Fa 91/2, fos. 278–81, 'Vorlage: Sondereinsatz Politischer Leiter an Brennpunkten der Ost- und Westfront', 17.2.45.

59. BAB, R55/608, fos. 35–6, Chef des Propagandastabes, Mundpropaganda-anweisung, betr. Kriegslage, 17.2.45.

60. BHStA, Reichsstatthalter Epp 681/1–8, Reich Minister of the Interior to Reich Defence Commissars, etc., 28.2.45.

61. BA/MA, RH19/IV/228, fo. 10, Hinweis für die NS-Führung der Truppe, 4.2.45.

62. *DZW*, 6, p. 627, citing a letter to Bormann of Joachim Albrecht Eggeling, Gauleiter of Halle-Merseburg, 10.2.45.

63. BAB, NS6/137, fos. 40–41, Flugblatt (im Entwurf): 'An die Verteidiger von Berlin', 24.2.45.

64. Quoted in Steinert, p. 559.

65. *TBJG*, II/15, p. 352 (10.2.45).

66. BAB, NS6/354, fos. 137–138ᵛ, PK Anordnung 79/45g, Standgerichte, 15.2.45, and 'Verordnung über die Errichtung von Standgerichten vom 15. February 1945', *Reichsgesetzblatt*, Teil 1, Nr. 6, 20.2.45, p. 30; printed in Müller and Ueberschär, pp. 161–2.

67. BAB, NS19/3705, fo. 4, Vorbereitungen auf Feindoffensive im Westen, Fernschreiben from Bormann to the western Gauleiter, undated appendix to his letter to Himmler, 8.2.45.

68. Henke, p. 845.

69. Henke, p. 846.

70. Haase, p. 86.

71. *'Führer-Erlasse' 1939–1945*, ed. Martin Moll, Stuttgart, 1997, p. 483; also printed in Müller and Ueberschär, pp. 163–4. For the operation of the summary courts martial, see Messerschmidt, *Die Wehrmachtjustiz 1933–1945*, pp. 411–15; and also Jürgen Zarusky, 'Von der Sondergerichtsbarkeit zum Endphasenterror: Loyalitätserzwingung und Rache am Widerstand in Zusammenbruch des NS-Regimes', in Cord Arendes, Edgar Wolfrum and Jörg Zedler (eds.), *Terror nach Innen: Verbrechen am Ende des Zweiten Weltkrieges*, Göttingen, 2006, p. 114. The extension to the 'flying courts martial' is indicated in Bormann's circular to the Gauleiter, NS6/354, fo. 88ᵛ, RS 123/45g, 9.3.45.

72. See Henke, pp. 846ff., for examples of their practice.

73. Ulrich Herbert, *Fremdarbeiter: Politik und Praxis des 'Ausländer-Einsatzes' in der Kriegswirtschaft des Dritten Reiches*, Bonn, 1985, pp. 270–71, p. 430 n. 3.

74. BAB, R43II/650c, fos. 119–25, Kampfkommandant Reichskanzlei, Führererbefehl v. 4.2.45 über 'Verteidigung der Reichskanzlei bei inneren Unruhen', 4–10.2.45.

75. NAL, WO208/5622, fo. 122A, 29.8.44. The general in question, Dietrich von Choltitz, had been the Wehrmacht commander in Paris at the time of the city's liberation in August 1944.

76. Jill Stephenson, *Hitler's Home Front: Württemberg under the Nazis*, London, 2006, p. 285.

77. Von Kardorff, pp. 208–9 (30.11.44).

78. Herbert, pp. 327–35; Andreas Heusler, 'Die Eskalation des Terrors: Gewalt gegen ausländische Zwangsarbeiter in der Endphase des Zweiten Weltkrieges', in Arendes, Wolfrum and Zedler, pp. 172–82.

79. Quoted Gerhard Paul and Alexander Primavesi, 'Die Verfolgung der "Fremdvölkischen": Das Beispiel der Staatspolizeistelle Dortmund', in Gerhard Paul and Klaus-Michael Mallmann (eds.), *Die Gestapo: Mythos und Realität*, Darmstadt, 1995, p. 398.

80. Gerhard Paul, '"Diese Erschießungen haben mich innerlich gar nicht mehr berührt": Die Kriegsendphasenverbrechen der Gestapo 1944/45', in Gerhard Paul and Klaus-Michael Mallmann (eds.), *Die Gestapo im Zweiten Weltkrieg: 'Heimatfront' und besetztes Europa*, Darmstadt, 2000, p. 548.

81. Paul and Primavesi, p. 399; also Paul, p. 549; Bessel, p. 55.

82. Cited Paul, p. 550.

83. For the special circumstances in Cologne, see Bernd-A. Rusinek, '"Wat denkste, wat mir objerümt han": Massenmord und Spurenbeseitigung am Beispiel der Staatspolizeistelle Köln 1944/45', in Paul and Mallmann, *Die Gestapo: Mythos und Realität*, pp. 402-16.

84. Paul, pp. 553-7; Herbert, pp. 336-7; Nikolaus Wachsmann, *Hitler's Prisons: Legal Terror in Nazi Germany*, New Haven and London, 2004, pp. 332-3.

85. IWM, F.2, AL 1753, statistics from SS-Wirtschafts-Verwaltungshauptamt, totalling 511,537 men and 202,674 women, 714,211 in all on 15 January 1945, guarded by 37,674 men and 3,508 women; Martin Broszat, 'Nationalsozialistische Konzentrationslager 1933-1945', in Hans Buchheim *et al.*, *Anatomie des SS-Staates*, Olten and Freiburg im Breisgau, 1965, vol. 2, p. 159; Wachsmann, p. 395; Daniel Blatman, 'Die Todesmärsche – Entscheidungsträger, Mörder und Opfer', in Ulrich Herbert, Karin Orth and Christoph Dieckmann (eds.), *Die nationalsozialistischen Konzentrationslager*, vol. 2, Göttingen, 1998, p. 1067; Gerald Reitlinger, *The Final Solution*, Sphere Books edn., London, 1971, pp. 501, 639 n. 30; Peter Longerich, *Holocaust: The Nazi Persecution and Murder of the Jews*, Oxford, 2010, p. 418.

86. Felix Kersten, *The Kersten Memoirs, 1940-1945*, London, 1956, p. 277 (12.3.45), and also p. 275 (2.3.45); and *DZW*, 6, p. 643 (where Himmler's reference to a Führer order is dated 5.3.45). Himmler saw Kersten at the sanitorium in Hohenlychen every morning from 4 to 13 March (BAB, NS19/1793, Termine des Reichsführer-SS, fos. 5-15). No specific written order from Hitler for the murder of camp prisoners has come to light, though a general – almost certainly verbal – directive that prisoners were not to be left behind on approach of the enemy seems to have been known to high-ranking SS officers, and may well have been used as an implicit order to kill those in their charge if there was a danger of the camp falling into enemy hands. In practice, however, there were only a few cases of the murder of all prisoners before evacuation. The actual decisions over life and death for the prisoners were taken lower down the leadership ladder, at the local level. – Daniel Blatman, 'Rückzug, Evakuierung und Todesmärsche 1944-1945', in Wolfgang Benz and Barbara Distel (eds.), *Der Ort des Terrors: Geschichte der nationalsozialistischen Konzentrationslager*, vol. 1, Munich, 2005, pp. 300-301.

87. Karin Orth, *Das System der nationalsozialistischen Konzentrationslager: Eine politische Organisationsgeschichte*, Hamburg, 1999, pp. 272-3.

88. No explicit written order to this effect has been found (other than for prisons in the General Government of Poland). – Paul, pp. 550-51 and nn. 31-3; Gabriele Hammermann, 'Die Todesmärsche aus den Konzentrationslagern 1944/45', in Arendes, Wolfrum and Zedler, pp. 122-3, 125; Blatman, 'Die Todesmärsche', pp. 1068-70, 1086; Eberhard Kolb, 'Die letzte Kriegsphase: Kommentierende Bemerkungen', in Herbert, Orth and Dieckmann, p. 1131; *DZW*, 6, p. 643.

89. *Kommandant in Auschwitz: Autobiographische Aufzeichnungen des Rudolf Höss*, ed. Martin Broszat, pb. edn., Munich, 1963, p. 145 n. 1; Saul Friedländer, *The Years of Extermination: Nazi Germany and the Jews, 1939-1945*, London, 2007, p. 648; Daniel Blatman, 'The Death Marches, January–May 1945: Who Was Responsible for What?', *YVS*, 28 (2000), pp. 168-71, 198-9.

90. Rudolf Höss gives a vivid impression of the chaos in *Kommandant in Auschwitz*, pp. 145-7.

91. Walter Schellenberg, *Schellenberg*, pb. edn., London, 1965, pp. 167-70; Peter R. Black, *Ernst Kaltenbrunner: Ideological Soldier of the Third Reich*, Princeton, 1984, pp. 228-30; Friedländer, pp. 621-5, 647-8; Peter Longerich, *Heinrich Himmler: Biographie*, Munich, 2008, pp. 728-30; Heinz Höhne, *The Order of the Death's Head*, London, 1972, pp. 524-5; Hammermann, p. 126; Yehuda Bauer, *Jews for Sale? Nazi-Jewish Negotiations, 1933-1945*, New Haven, 1994, pp. 239-51; Simone Erpel, *Zwischen Vernichtung und Befreiung: Das Frauen-Konzentrationslager Ravensbrück in der letzten Kriegsphase*, Berlin, 2005, pp. 97-154 (where the number of camp prisoners saved by such action by the end of the war, most notably through the Swedish initiative, is given as 15,345, of whom 7,795 were Scandinavians – a proportion which, however, as she points out, underrates the number of non-Scandinavians rescued). Intelligence reports to the western Allies claimed that the negotiations about the liberation of a number of Jews had caused a 'sensation' in Berlin, and had been condemned by leading Nazis, including Julius Streicher. – NAL, WO219/1587, fo. 734, SHAEF report, 25.2.45.

92. Blatman, 'Die Todesmärsche', pp. 1069-72; and Daniel Blatman, *Les Marches de la mort: La dernière étape du génocide nazi, été 1944-printemps 1945*, Paris, 2009, pp. 96-100, 127-31.

93. Orth, p. 279.

94. Wachsmann, pp. 324-5.

95. Wachsmann, pp. 325-33.

96. Laurence Rees, *Auschwitz: The Nazis and the 'Final Solution'*, London, 2005, p. 301, based upon figures supplied by the Auschwitz-Birkenau Museum.

97. Sybille Steinbacher, *Auschwitz: A History*, London, 2005, p. 124.
98. Andrzej Strzelecki, 'Der Todesmarsch der Häftlinge aus dem KL Auschwitz', in Herbert, Orth and Dieckmann, p. 1103; Danuta Czech, *Kalendarium der Ereignisse im Konzentrationslager-Auschwitz-Birkenau 1939–1945*, Reinbek bei Hamburg, 1989, pp. 966–7.
99. *Kommandant in Auschwitz*, p. 146 (where Höss also used the term 'columns of misery').
100. ITS, Tote 80, fo. 00030a, Häftlingstransport von Birkenau nach Gablonz, 2.4.46. See also *Kommandant in Auschwitz*, p. 146; and Czech, p. 968.
101. Monika Richarz, *Jüdisches Leben in Deutschland: Selbstzeugnisse zur Sozialgeschichte 1918–1945*, Stuttgart, 1982, pp. 443–6 (account by Paul Heller based on diary jottings kept at the time).
102. Richarz, pp. 448, 450–51.
103. Strzelecki, p. 1102; Blatman, *Les Marches de la mort*, pp. 112, 140.
104. Richarz, p. 452.
105. ITS, Tote 80, fo. 60282a, Marches de la Mort, Groß-Rosen – Leitmeritz, 4.4.46.
106. Isabell Sprenger, 'Das KZ Groß-Rosen in der letzten Kriegsphase', in Herbert, Orth and Dieckmann, pp. 1113–24. On one march alone (p. 1122), 500 out of 3,500 died.
107. Orth, pp. 282–7; Blatman, *Les Marches de la mort*, pp. 126–32; Blatman, 'The Death Marches', pp. 174–9. See also Olga M. Pickholz-Barnitsch, 'The Evacuation of the Stutthof Concentration Camp', *Yad Vashem Bulletin*, 16 (1965), pp. 37–9. According to the SS's figures, the prisoners in Stutthof had numbered 18,436 men and 30,199 women (48,635 persons in all) on 15 January 1945. – IWM, F.2, AL 1753, SS-Wirtschafts-Verwaltungshauptamt List of Concentration Camps with numbers of guards and prisoners 1. & 15.1.45. When the evacuations began, this number had fallen to 46,331 prisoners. – Blatman, 'The Death Marches', p. 175, based (cf. n. 43) on the last roll-call of 24.1.45.
108. Blatman, *Les Marches de la mort*, p. 140.
109. Hammermann, pp. 140–41; Sprenger, pp. 120–21; Katharina Elliger, *Und tief in der Seele das Ferne: Die Geschichte einer Vertreibung aus Schlesien*, Reinbek bei Hamburg, 2006, pp. 71–4 (where she mentions seeing as a girl the column of misery of Auschwitz prisoners passing through her village, near Ratibor in Silesia, and throwing bread down before hastily closing her window as the guard reacted negatively).
110. See Richard Overy, *Why the Allies Won*, London, 1995, pp. 112–33, for an assessment of Harris and Allied bombing strategy, concluding (p. 133) that 'the air offensive was one of the decisive elements in Allied victory'. The policy of 'area bombing' of cities had already been decided – following a change in tactics suggested by Churchill's scientific adviser Lord Cherwell (earlier known as Professor Frederick Lindemann) on account of the failure

of precision bombing – just before Harris took over Bomber Command on 22 February 1942. Harris, who had an excellent rapport with Churchill at this time, was the inspirational driving force behind the implementation of the policy, dedicating himself 'to the vital necessity of striking at Germany in her homeland, where it would really hurt'. – Henry Probert, *Bomber Harris: His Life and Times*, London, 2001, pp. 122, 126–46; Max Hastings, *Finest Years: Churchill as Warlord 1940–45*, London, 2009, pp. 246–9.

111. Frederick Taylor, *Dresden: Tuesday 13 February 1945*, pb. edn., London, 2005, p. 216.

112. Lothar Gruchmann, *Der Zweite Weltkrieg*, pb. edn., Munich, 1975, pp. 197–8, 280–81, 414.

113. Taylor, p. 427.

114. Jörg Friedrich, *Der Brand: Deutschland im Bombenkrieg 1940–1945*, pb. edn., Berlin, 2004, pp. 108–9, 312–16; Taylor, p. 428.

115. Rüdiger Overmans, 'Die Toten des Zweiten Weltkriegs in Deutschland', in Wolfgang Michalka (ed.), *Der Zweite Weltkrieg: Analysen, Grundzüge, Forschungsbilanz*, Munich and Zurich, 1989, p. 860; Friedrich, p. 63; *DRZW*, 10/1 (Boog), p. 868; *United States Strategic Bombing Survey*, New York and London, 1976, vol. 4, pp. 7–10.

116. Müller and Ueberschär, p. 160 (report from 1955 by Theodor Ellgering, who in 1945 was Geschäftsführer des Interministeriellen Luftkriegsausschusses der Reichsregierung in Berlin, on his impressions on entering Dresden immediately after the raid to organize the grim salvage operations).

117. Based on Taylor, chs. 21–4. See also Götz Bergander, *Dresden im Luftkrieg*, Weimar, Cologne and Vienna, 1994, esp. chs. 9–12; Friedrich, pp. 358–63; *DRZW*, 10/1 (Boog), pp. 777–98; Olaf Groehler, *Bombenkrieg gegen Deutschland*, Berlin, 1990, pp. 400–12; Rolf-Dieter Müller, *Der Bombenkrieg 1939–1945*, Berlin, 2004, pp. 212–20; Paul Addison and Jeremy A. Crang (eds.), *Firestorm: The Bombing of Dresden, 1945*, London, 2006, esp. pp. 18–77 (contributions by Sebastian Cox and Sönke Neitzel) and pp. 123–42 (Richard Overy's discussion of the post-war debate); and Max Hastings, *Armageddon: The Battle for Germany 1944–45* (London, 2004), pp. 382–7.

118. Victor Klemperer, *Ich will Zeugnis ablegen bis zum letzten*, vol. 2: *Tagebücher 1942–1945*, ed. Walter Nowojski and Hadwig Klemperer, Darmstadt, 1998, pp. 661, 669, 675–6 (13–14.2.45, 19.2.45). Discrimination against Jews even went so far as to refuse them entry to 'aryan' shelters during air raids. – Klemperer, p. 644 (20.1.45).

119. This paragraph is based on Taylor, pp. 397–402, 508. An eighteen-year-old soldier, shocked to the core by what he saw in Dresden, noted in his diary that there was talk of over 200,000 dead. – Klaus Granzow, *Tagebuch eines Hitlerjungen 1943–1945*, Bremen, 1965, p. 159 (18.2.45).The propaganda claims of up to a quarter of a million victims are judiciously assessed and dismissed by Rolf-Dieter Müller, 'Der Feuersturm und die unbekannten

Toten von Dresden', *Geschichte in Wissenschaft und Unterricht*, 59 (2008), pp. 169–75. An evaluation of all available evidence, and of the wildly differing figures given for the numbers of dead (with some claims of half a million dead), by a specially nominated Historians' Commission which reported in 2010, arrived at the figure of 25,000 – the estimate already made in the official investigations of 1945–6. – www.dresden.de/de/02/035/01/2010/03/pm_060.php, 'Pressemitteilungen. 17.03.2010. Dresdner Historiker-kommission veröffentlicht ihren Abschlussbericht'.

120. Taylor, p. 463.
121. Friedrich, pp. 331–3, 533–6.
122. Friedrich, pp. 312–16.
123. Taylor, pp. 413–14; *DRZW*, 10/1 (Boog), p. 798.
124. Taylor, ch. 15.
125. Taylor, pp. 412–24, 506. Goebbels' aide, Wilfred von Oven, estimated in his diary entry for 15 February a total of 200,000–300,000 victims, and went on to write of a historically unprecedented killing of '300,000 women, children and defenceless civilians within a few hours'. – Von Oven, *Finale Furioso*, pp. 580–82 (15.2.45).
126. *Das Reich*, 4.3.45, p. 3, with the headline: 'The Death of Dresden. A Beacon of Resistance'. The bombing, the article claimed, was an attempt to compel capitulation through mass murder so that the 'death sentence' could be carried out on what was left. 'Against this threat', it concluded, 'there is no other way out than through fighting resistance.' See also Bergander, pp. 184–5; and Taylor, p. 425.
127. Klemperer, p. 676.
128. BfZ, Sterz-Sammlung, letters of DRK-Schwester Ursel C., 16.2.45, 20.2.45; O'Gefr. Rudolf L., 16.2.45, 18.2.45; O'Gefr. Ottmar M., 26.2.45. Only a single letter in Jörg Echternkamp (ed.), *Kriegsschauplatz Deutschland 1945: Leben in Angst – Hoffnung auf Frieden. Feldpost aus der Heimat und von der Front*, Paderborn, 2006, p. 152, mentions the bombing of Dresden, but then only to indicate worry about the population and relatives in the area. One letter that came into the hands of the British army, dated 20 February, though sent from Unna in Westphalia and with no direct reference to the attack on Dresden, did speak of bitterness and sense of impotence at the 'terror-flights' heading for Germany, but determination to fight on and conviction of victory. – LHC, Dempsey Papers, no. 288 Pt. II, p. 8 (18.3.45). The Berlin population seems to have been understandably concerned about the raids on the capital but, to go from reports covering February 1945, no comments about Dresden were registered by the Wehrmacht agents gathering information on popular opinion in the city, though some general feeling was expressed (e.g. p. 252) that the war was almost over and it was pointless to continue. – *Das letzte halbe Jahr*, pp. 248–93. The Government Presidents of Bavarian provinces gave no

indication, in their reports for March 1945, of reactions of the population, preoccupied with its own concerns, to the Dresden bombing.

129. BAB, R55/622, fo. 181, Briefübersicht Nr. 10, 9.3.45.

130. See von Oven, *Finale Furioso*, p. 579 (12.2.45), for Goebbels' fury at Ley's public claim that holding the Red Army at the Oder had been 'The German Miracle', at a time when tens of thousands were fleeing in panic and trying desperately to reach the western banks of the Oder.

131. Cited in Taylor, p. 428; Erich Kästner, *Notabene 1945: Ein Tagebuch*, Berlin, 1961, pp. 55–6 (8.3.45); Jacob Kronika, *Der Untergang Berlins*, Flensburg, 1946, p. 70 (22.3.45). Goebbels, often frustrated by Ley's outspoken statements, noted in his diary the outrage at the latter's comments about Dresden. – *TBJG*, II/15, p. 457 (9.3.45). Ley's article, 'Without Baggage' ('Ohne Gepäck') had appeared on 3 March in *Der Angriff*, 53, p. 2. In a broadcast from the encircled Breslau two days later, Gauleiter Hanke picked up the theme, declaring that what had once been seen as essential cultural property (*unerläßliche Kulturgüter*) could be now viewed on closer inspection as 'the thoroughly dispensable matter of civilization' (*durchaus entbehrliches Zivilisationsgut*). – Kästner, p. 47 (5.3.45).

132. See David Irving, *Goebbels: Mastermind of the Third Reich*, London, 1996, p. 503.

133. BAB, NS19/1022, fo. 5, Brandt to Berlepsch, 3.1.45. The *Lebensleuchter* appears to have taken the form of a large candle in an elaborate Nordicstyled holder. According to a file notice, Himmler agreed a few days later to have all children of teachers at 'NAPOLAs' (Nationalpolitische Erziehungsanstalten) – Party schools (by this time under SS control) – presented with the 'light of life'. SS-Obergruppenführer Heißmeyer, head of the NAPOLAs, was to give a list of the children to Himmler's adjutant, SS-Standartenführer Dr Rudolf Brandt. The number of candleholders available was, however, Brandt warned, currently very small and they were intended only for a third or fourth war child, so that he did not know whether Himmler's promise could be fulfilled. Heißmeyer said he would acquire the requisite details under a pretext and leave it to Brandt to decide to what extent the distribution of the candleholders could be carried out. The file notice on this absurd issue appears to have been consulted on the first day of February, March and April 1945, presumably with little or no action to follow. – BAB, NS19/424, fo. 2, Vermerk, 9.1.45.

134. BAB, NS19/1318, fo. 3, Brandt to Berger, 10.1.45.

135. BAB, NS19/2903, fo. 3, Brandt to Justizwachtmeister Ernst Krapoth, Oberhausen, 1.3.45.

136. Albert Speer, *Erinnerungen*, Frankfurt am Main and Berlin, 1969, p. 435.

137. H. R. Trevor-Roper, *The Last Days of Hitler*, pb. edn., London, 1962, pp. 119–20, 134, 140.

138. IWM, EDS, F.3, M.I. 14/368 (2), unfoliated, Krosigk: Memorandum zur heutigen Finanz- und Währungslage, 10.1.45; IWM, EDS, F.3, M.I.14/368 (1), unfoliated, distributed to Bormann, Goebbels, Göring, Economics Minister Walther Funk, and Price Commissar Hans Fischböck (8.2.45). In post-war interrogations, Krosigk reaffirmed the sharp deterioration in Reich finances after July 1944 on account of the worsening military situation. People were not saving; money had to be printed. There was a huge and growing tax deficit by early 1945. – Ardsley Microfilms, Irving Collection, D1/Göring/1, Krosigk interrogation, 4.6.45; according to Funk (interrogation 4.6.45), holdings in gold had dropped from 900 million Marks in 1940 to 400 million by 1944.

139. IWM, EDS, F.3, M.I. 14/368 (1), Krosigk to Speer, 26.2.45 (also in M.I. 14/285 (no. 26), Personal Papers of Albert Speer); Krosigk to Bormann, 26.2.45, 27.2.45; Krosigk to Funk, 28.2.45; Krosigk to Dr Gerhard Klopfer, head of the legal section of the Party Chancellery and a key right-hand man of Bormann, 27.2.45. See also Speer's letter to Krosigk on the financial situation, BAB, R3/1624, fo. 5, 14.2.45, and Speer, p. 435. Krosigk had sought a meeting with Speer on 13 February. – IWM, EDS, F.3, M.I. 14/369, unfoliated, Krosigk to Speer, 13.2.45.

140. *TBJG*, II/15, p. 613 (28.3.45).

141. *The Bormann Letters*, ed. H. R. Trevor-Roper, London, 1954, p. 170 (4.2.45).

142. *The Bormann Letters*, p. 173 (5.2.45).

143. *The Bormann Letters*, p. 177 (7.2.45).

144. *The Bormann Letters*, p. 186 (19.2.45). When she fled to the Tyrol in late April, accompanied by her nine children, Gerda Bormann took both her own and her husband's letters with her. She died of cancer in March 1946, but her papers, including the letters, were saved by sympathizers. See *The Bormann Letters*, pp. viii, xxii–xxiii.

145. *TBJG*, II/15, pp. 328-9 (7.2.45), 334-5 (8.2.45), 357, 359 (11.2.45). Goebbels admitted that he needed a new directive from Hitler if he were to overcome obstacles to meet the target of 768,000 men needed by the following August and force the armaments industry to give up a monthly quota of 80,000 men, which they were resisting. His frustrations were recorded by von Oven, *Finale Furioso*, pp. 575-7 (8.2.45).

146. Von Oven, *Finale Furioso*, p. 587 (25.2.45).

147. *TBJG*, II/15, p. 364 (12.2.45).

148. Rudolf Semmler, *Goebbels – the Man Next to Hitler*, London, 1947, pp. 183-4 (18-20.2.45); Ralf Georg Reuth, *Goebbels*, Munich and Zurich, 1990, pp. 581-2. The suggestion appealed to Hitler, and was dropped only when it was pointed out by his military advisers that such an appalling breach of the Geneva Convention could backfire drastically, since the Allies

might use their superiority in the air to start using gas and chemical warfare and, anyway, held more prisoners than those in German hands. – *IMT*, vol. 35, pp. 181–6, doc. 606-D. Hitler had already told Goebbels before the attack on Dresden that, should the British go over to gas warfare he would have 250,000 British and American prisoners of war shot. – *TBJG*, II/15, p. 368 (12.2.45).

149. Von Oven, *Finale Furioso*, p. 571 (7.2.45).

150. Von Oven, *Finale Furioso*, pp. 587–8 (25.2.45); and see also p. 577 (9.2.45). Goebbels suggested in mid-February providing an opening to the British, but Hitler thought – as he invariably did – that the right point for this had not been reached. In any case, Goebbels had just told Hitler that it was crucial to hold the west; that was more important than losing territory in the east. – *TBJG*, II/15, pp. 367–8 (12.2.45).

151. *TBJG*, II/15, pp. 337 (8.2.45), 366 (12.2.45).

152. Von Oven, *Finale Furioso*, p. 582 (16.2.45).

153. *TBJG*, II/15, pp. 379–81 (13.2.45).

154. *TBJG*, II/15, p. 383 (28.2.45).

155. BAB, R3/1535, fos. 18–28, Zur Rüstungslage Februar–März 1945, with statistical appendices, fos. 29–31, quotation fo. 28, 30.1.45.

156. *TBJG*, II/15, p. 290 (1.2.45).

157. Speer, p. 432.

158. Speer, p. 428, refers to Hitler's clash with an angry Guderian over withdrawal of troops from the Courland, which the latter had pressed for, as a possible sign of a drop in authority. The fact was, however, that Hitler's word was final. The troops cut off in the Courland remained there.

159. *TBJG*, II/15, pp. 311 (5.2.45), 338 (8.2.45).

160. Von Oven, *Finale Furioso*, p. 588 (25.2.45). Forster claimed to have told Hitler directly to seek negotiations with the western powers. However, Hitler's secretary Christa Schroeder, *Er war mein Chef: Aus dem Nachlaß der Sekretärin von Adolf Hitler*, Munich and Vienna, 1985, p. 74, recalled what was, presumably, a subsequent meeting from which Forster, who had been determined to tell Hitler in most forthright terms of the despairing situation in Danzig, came away revitalized and certain that Hitler could save Danzig.

161. Karl Wahl, '... *es ist das deutsche Herz': Erlebnisse und Erkenntnisse eines ehemaligen Gauleiters*, Augsburg, 1954, p. 385. Almost twenty years later Wahl produced a very similar, but if anything even more apologetic, version of the meeting, in Karl Wahl, *Patrioten oder Verbrecher*, Heusenstamm bei Offenbach am Main, 1973, pp. 155–61.

162. Wahl, '... *es ist das deutsche Herz'*, p. 386.

163. Rudolf Jordan, *Erlebt und erlitten: Weg eines Gauleiters von München bis Moskau*, Leoni am Starnberger See, 1971, pp. 251–8 (quotations, pp. 257–8).

164. *TBJG*, II/15, p. 323 (6.2.45); Speer, p. 431.

165. *TBJG*, II/15, p. 377 for Hitler's recognition that Yalta meant there would be no break in the coalition; and p. 381 for the communiqué, and Goebbels' reaction to it. A British intelligence report on 22 February suggested that 'the very hopelessness of Germany's fate after the war may be one of the reasons for the continuance of a struggle which daily becomes more desperate'. – Hastings, *Armageddon*, p. 417. For the negotiations at Yalta, see *DRZW*, 10/2 (Loth), pp. 289–300. The outcome of the Conference was not immediately made known to the German public, though detailed information – gleaned in the main from illicit listening to foreign broadcasts – soon seeped out. – *Das letzte halbe Jahr*, pp. 251–2 (23.2.45).

166. Speer, p. 433.

CHAPTER 7. CRUMBLING FOUNDATIONS

1. BA/MA, MSg2/2697, diary of Lieutenant Julius Dufner, fo. 151, 7.4.45.

2. On all fronts, the Germans could muster in early 1945 almost 320 weakened divisions, including those tied up in peripheral areas such as Norway and the Courland. East and west, their enemies faced them with around 630 full-strength divisions, nearly 500 of them on the eastern front alone. – http://www.angelfire.com/ct/ww2europe/stats.html.

3. The film was awarded a number of prizes. It appears, however, to have run for only a few days in Berlin, and to have been shown mainly for Party members and for the Wehrmacht. See David Welch, *Propaganda and the German Cinema 1933–1945*, Oxford, 1983, p. 234. Hitler, according to Goebbels, was delighted at the impact of the film, which was said to have made a huge impression on the General Staff. – *TBJG*, II/15, p. 370 (12.2.45).

4. BAB, NS6/134, fo. 14, Kurzlage des Ob.d.M., 17.3.45. Himmler requested, though with little effect, assistance from Karl Kaufmann, Gauleiter of Hamburg and Reich Commissar for Shipping, on 8 March in providing ships to transport refugees from Danzig. – BAB, NS19/2606, fos. 60–61, Himmler's request – passing on one to him from Gauleiter Albert Forster – and reply from Kaufmann, 8.3.45.

5. Goebbels wanted to block mention of the evacuation in the Wehrmacht report. 'On account of the strong psychological effects of the Kolberg film, we can do without that at present,' he noted. – *TBJG*, II/15, p. 542 (20.3.45).

6. BA/MA, N647/13, NL Balck, Kriegstagebuch, Bd. 12, fo. 13.

7. The above course of military events draws upon: *DZW*, 6, pp. 517–61; *DRZW*, 10/1 (Zimmermann), pp. 409–43, (Lakowski), pp. 550–608; *DRZW*,

8 (Ungváry), pp. 919–43; Lothar Gruchmann, *Der Zweite Weltkrieg*, pb. edn., Munich, 1975, pp. 418–35; Heinz Guderian, *Panzer Leader*, Da Capo edn., New York, 1996, pp. 411–29; Brian Taylor, *Barbarossa to Berlin: A Chronology of the Campaigns on the Eastern Front 1941 to 1945*, vol. 2, Stroud, 2008, pp. 280–306; John Erickson, *The Road to Berlin*, Cassell edn., London, 2003, pp. 443–7, 508–26; Klaus-Dietmar Henke, *Die amerikanische Besetzung Deutschlands*, Munich, 1995, pp. 343–64, 377–90; Gerhard L. Weinberg, *A World at Arms: A Global History of World War II*, Cambridge, 1994, pp. 798–802, 810–14; Antony Beevor, *Berlin: The Downfall 1945*, pb. edn., London, 2007, ch. 8; Max Hastings, *Armageddon: The Battle for Germany 1944–45*, London, 2004, ch. 12.

8. Kurt Pätzold and Manfred Weißbecker, *Geschichte der NSDAP 1920–1945*, Cologne, 1981, p. 378.

9. BAB, NS6/137, fo. 6, Vermerk from Willi Ruder, head of the Arbeitsstab für NS-Führungsfragen in the Party Chancellery, 5.3.45; fo. 29, draft circular for distribution to the Gauleiter, 5.3.45.

10. The V1 cruise-missile and V2 rocket had long since failed to live up to expectations. Shortages of fuel and pilots greatly restricted the deployment of the Me262 fighter, jet-propelled and with higher speeds than anything the Allies could match. Only 200 or so were used, with heavy losses, and prototype new rockets and planes were barely in production by the time hostilities ceased. – *DRZW*, 10/1(Boog), pp. 828–9. Only a handful of the fleet of new, technologically advanced U-boats, which Dönitz persuaded Hitler would prove so crucial, were available by the end of the war. – Howard D. Grier, *Hitler, Dönitz and the Baltic Sea: The Third Reich's Last Hope, 1944–1945*, Annapolis, Md., 2007, pp. xviii–xix, 170–79.

11. BAB, NS6/137, fos. 19–21, draft of propaganda directives for the Wehrmacht, 9.3.45.

12. BAB, NS6/136, fos. 1, 16–19, Parteirednereinsatz, 6.3.45, 13.3.45, 24.3.45.

13. BAB, NS6/137, fos. 9–14, Vorlage, probably for Pg. Gerhard Klopfer, from SS-Obersturmbannführer Dr Beyer, of SD office III/V, with attached partial copy of the sketch of a lecture by SS-Obersturmbannführer von Kilpinski and covering letter of 19.3.45 from Ernst Kaltenbrunner, head of the SD, 20.3.45.

14. BAB, R55/610, fos. 182–3, Westfalen-Süd, Merkpunkte zur Versammlungsaktion Februar/März 1945, 12.3.45.

15. *Das letzte halbe Jahr: Stimmungsberichte der Wehrmachtpropaganda 1944/45*, ed. Wolfram Wette, Ricarda Bremer and Detlef Vogel, Essen, 2001, p. 310 (31.3.45).

16. BA/MA, MSg2/2697, diary of Lieutenant Julius Dufner, fos. 123–7 (entries for 5, 7, 9, 12.3.45). Hitler did not lay the wreath in Berlin on the final 'Heroes' Memorial Day'. Göring substituted for him.

17. BAB, R55/622, fo. 181, Briefübersicht Nr. 10, 9.3.45.

18. BAB, NS6/137, Der Reichspropagandaleiter der NSDAP an alle Gau-propagandaleiter, 5.3.45.

19. *TBJG*, II/15, p. 471 (11.3.45).

20. Guderian, p. 427.

21. BAB, NS6/169, fos. 115–21, Guderian to Bormann, 26.2.45; Bericht des Dienstleiters der Partei-Kanzlei, Pg. Mauer, undated. The characteristic demeaning of General Staff officers, part of the standard reportage of Party propagandists, is repeated, for example, in NS6/374, fo. 18, report to Dr Gerhard Klopfer, head of Abteilung III (Staatliche Angelegenheitern) in the Party Chancellery, by Oberleutnant Koller, part of the Sondereinsatz team, 16.3.45, and in NS6/140, fos. 44–5, Vorlage for Bormann, signed by Willi Ruder, 6.3.45, offering critical comments on General Staff officers attending an NSFO course in Egerndorf. Even Goebbels rejected the constant attempt to make Wehrmacht officers the scapegoats for the military defeats of the previous two years as a crass oversimplification, with harmful consequences for the authority of officers. – *TBJG*, II/15, p. 406 (3.3.45). The Party Chancellery itself thought the repeated talk about sabotage and failure of officers (which for long it had promoted) had to be halted if trust between the Party leadership and the Wehrmacht was to be improved. – NS6/137, fo. 27, Vorlage for Bormann, 7.3.45.

22. BAB, NS19/2068, fos. 57, 65, Meldungen aus dem Ostraum, 15.3.45 (includes reports from Danzig, Stettin and Küstrin); in addition, for Küstrin, NS6/135, fos. 190, 192–8, part of a long report for Borman from the Kreis-leiter of Küstrin-Königsberg, 5.4.45.

23. BAB, NS6/354, fos. 100–101ᵛ, Bormann: Rundschreiben 156/45g, Plün-derungen durch deutsche Soldaten in geräumten Gebieten, to Gauleiter and other Party functionaries, 24.3.45, attaching a copy of Keitel's order of 8.3.45 threatening punishment by court martial for any soldier suspected of looting. See also NS6/135, fo. 83, Pg. Noack (of Abt. IIF of the Party Chancellery, Arbeitsstab für NS-Führungsfragen) to NS-Führungsstab der Wehrmacht, reporting complaints about plundering of property by soldiers, 14.3.45; and fo. 199, Vermerk für Pg. Stosch, re plundering, 19.3.45.

24. *DZW*, 6, pp. 549–50; Sönke Neitzel, *Abgehört: Deutsche Generäle in britischer Kriegsgefangenschaft 1942–1945*, Berlin, 2005, p. 190, 9.3.45 (Eng. edn., *Tapping Hitler's Generals: Transcripts of Secret Conversations, 1942–45*, Barnsley, 2007, pp. 141–2).

25. BAB, NS6/135, fos. 79, 97, Erfahrungs- und Stimmungsberichte über die Haltung von Wehrmacht und Bevölkerung, 23.3.45, 29.3.45.

26. BfZ, Sammlung Sterz, O'Wm. Peter B., 9.3.45.

27. Henke, p. 806 and n. 132.

28. BAB, R55/601, fos. 295–7, Tätigkeitsbericht, weekly propaganda reports, 21.3.45.

29. BAB, NS6/169, fos. 4–9, Bericht des Hauptgemeinschaftsleiters Twittenhoff

über den Sondereinsatz der Partei-Kanzlei in Hessen-Nassau, for period 24–30.3.45. The consequence of providing a realistic description was the recommendation that Twittenhoff was not suitable for further work in the 'Special Action' of the Party Chancellery.

30. BAB, NS6/169, fo. 49, Vorlage an Reichsleiter Bormann, 19.3.45; fo. 51, Sprenger to Bormann, 14.3.45.

31. *DZW*, 6, pp. 550–51; *1945: Das Jahr der endgültigen Niederlage der faschistischen Wehrmacht. Dokumente*, ed. Gerhard Förster and Richard Lakowski, Berlin, 1975, pp. 212–14, Staff of Army Group G to Gauleiter Gustav Simon about signs of a hostile attitude towards German troops and flight, in drunken condition, of the *Volkssturm* at the attack of the Americans on Trier. For further examples of a negative stance of the civilian population towards the Wehrmacht – even one case, in Göttingen, when civilians were said to have fired on their own tanks – see John Zimmermann, *Pflicht zum Untergang: Die deutsche Kriegführung im Westen des Reiches 1944/45*, Paderborn, 2009, p. 75.

32. BAB, NS6/51, fos. 1–3, Letter from Hauptmann Heinz Thieme, Pzjäger Abt. 246, SD agent, Abt. Ostland, to Bormann, 15.3.45.

33. Marlis Steinert, *Hitlers Krieg und die Deutschen*, Düsseldorf and Vienna, 1970, p. 559; Neitzel, *Abgehört*, p. 190 (9.3.45) (Eng. edn., *Tapping Hitler's Generals*, p. 141). See also Saul K. Padover, *Psychologist in Germany: The Story of an American Intelligence Officer*, London, 1946, pp. 219, 230, 270, for his experiences of defeatist attitudes and Germans welcoming the arrival of the Americans.

34. See John Zimmermann, 'Die Kämpfe gegen die Westalliierten 1945 – ein Kampf bis zum Ende oder die Kreierung einer Legende?' in Jörg Hillmann and John Zimmermann (eds.), *Kriegsende 1945 in Deutschland*, Munich, 2002, pp. 130–31.

35. *TBJG*, II/15, p. 406 (3.3.45).

36. Katharina Elliger, *Und tief in der Seele das Ferne: Die Geschichte einer Vertreibung aus Schlesien*, Reinbek bei Hamburg, 2006, p. 107.

37. Workers in Berlin were reported in March as saying that no punishment was severe enough for the cowardice of deserters. – *Das letzte halbe Jahr*, p. 277 (3.3.45).

38. IfZ, Fa-91/2, fos. 330–31, Parteikanzlei, Vermerk für Pg. Walkenhorst, 10.3.45. For Hanke's brutal rule in Breslau in the last months of the war, see Guido Knopp, *Der Sturm: Kriegsende im Osten*, pb. edn., Berlin, 2006, pp. 150–62.

39. *DZW*, 6, p. 548, for Rundstedt's order. For Kesselring's advocacy, after taking command in the west, of ruthlessness towards deserters and those seen to be failing in their duty, see Andreas Kunz, *Wehrmacht und Niederlage: Die bewaffnete Macht in der Endphase der nationalsozialistischen*

Herrschaft 1944 bis 1945, Munich, 2007, pp. 276, 279. Hitler's order to establish the 'flying court martial' is printed in Rolf-Dieter Müller and Gerd R. Ueberschär, *Kriegsende 1945: Die Zerstörung des Deutschen Reiches*, Frankfurt am Main, 1994, pp. 163–4; see also Neitzel, *Abgehört*, pp. 202–3, 540 n. 161 (Eng. edn., *Tapping Hitler's Generals*, pp. 150–51). Hübner, a fanatic who had long been involved in attempts to instil Nazi ideology into the troops, was given unrestricted powers to impose the death penalty. – DRZW, 9/1 (Förster), pp. 580–82; Manfred Messerschmidt, *Die Wehrmachtjustiz 1933–1945*, Paderborn, 2005, p. 413. Flying courts martial had been in use by Army Group North since 3 February. – BAB, NS6/354, fo. 88, RS 123/45g, Maßnahmen zur Stärkung der Front durch Erfassung Versprengter (passing on to the Gauleiter an order of the Commander-in-Chief Army Group North, Colonel-General Lothar Rendulić), 9.3.45.

40. *1945: Das Jahr der endgültigen Niederlage der faschistischen Wehrmacht*, pp. 229–30.
41. Henke, p. 348.
42. DZW, 6, p. 548.
43. DZW, 6, p. 522; *Stettin/Szczecin 1945–1946*, Rostock, 1994, pp. 35, 37.
44. BAB, NS6/354, fos. 163–165ᵛ, PK Bekanntgabe 149/45g, 19.3.45, transmission by Bormann of Schörner's secret circular of 27 February.
45. DZW, 6, p. 539.
46. Zimmermann, *Pflicht*, p. 338; Christopher Clark, 'Johannes Blaskowitz – der christliche General', in Ronald Smelser and Enrico Syring (eds.), *Die Militärelite des Dritten Reiches*, Berlin, 1995, pp. 35, 43.
47. DZW, 6, p. 545.
48. Quoted in DRZW, 10/1 (Zimmermann), p. 316; and Zimmermann, *Pflicht*, p. 293.
49. BAB, R3/1623a, fo. 71a, Bormann to the Gauleiter, Reichsleiter, Reich Youth Leader, etc., 30.3.45, passing on Jodl's circular of the previous day to commanders of the Army Groups and the Defence Districts in the west. Jodl still believed that any sacrifice was worthwhile to win time and bring about a split in the unnatural enemy coalition. – Bodo Scheurig, *Alfred Jodl: Gehorsam und Verhängnis*, Berlin and Frankfurt am Main, 1991, pp. 313–14, 319.
50. For the unprompted initiatives of the generals in the last phase to ensure the continued, utmost military effort, see DRZW, 10/1 (Zimmermann), pp. 307–36.
51. BAB, NS6/134, fo. 19, Dönitz, Kurzlagebericht vom 4.3.45.
52. DRZW, 9/1 (Förster), pp. 554, 584–6. See, for Dönitz's fanatical leadership of the navy, Sönke Neitzel, 'Der Bedeutungswandel der Kriegsmarine im Zweiten Weltkrieg', in Rolf-Dieter Müller and Hans-Erich Volkmann (eds.), *Die Wehrmacht: Mythos und Realität*, Munich, 1999, pp. 259–62.

53. Kathrin Orth, 'Kampfmoral und Einsatzbereitschaft in der Kriegsmarine 1945', in Hillmann and Zimmermann, pp. 137–55.

54. BA/MA, N574/22, NL Vietinghoff, 'Die Generale', 25.7.49.

55. BA/MA, N574/19, NL Vietinghoff, 'Kriegsende in Italien', fos. 44–5 (1950). See also DRZW, 10/1 (Zimmermann), p. 321; and Zimmermann, Pflicht, pp. 297–8.

56. Neitzel, Abgehört, pp. 180–81, 185 (quotation, p. 186) (28–31.1.45, 18–20.2.45) (Eng. edn., Tapping Hitler's Generals, p. 138). Also NAL, WO208/4365, reports of monitored conversations of prisoners of war, nos. 251–3, 28–31.1.45. A former corps commander, a lieutenant-general, later told his British captors that Rundstedt had favoured capitulation after the failure of the Ardennes offensive, and reckoned with the support of a majority of the higher ranking members of the officer' corps, but knew that the hold of the Nazi regime meant that there was no chance of undertaking negotiations and that no member of the Wehrmacht would be authorized to contact the Allies for such a purpose. – LHC, Dempsey Papers, no. 317 pt. II, p. 5, (16.4.45).

57. Neitzel, Abgehört, pp. 184–5, 187 (14–15.2.45, 2–3.3.45) (Eng. edn., Tapping Hitler's Generals, pp. 137, 139).

58. NAL, WO208/5543, interrogation reports on German prisoners of war, 16.4.45, 'Enemy Expectations, Intentions and Sources of Information', 16.3.45.

59. BA/MA, N712/15, NL Pollex, fos. 43, 44, 47, 49–51, 54, 57, 59–61, 65, entries for 3.3.45, 5.3.45, 8.3.45, 12.3.45, 21.3.45, 25.3.45, 27.3.45, 31.3.45.

60. BA/MA, N265/118, NL Heinrici, fo. 74a–b (1952).

61. Karl Dönitz, Memoirs: Ten Years and Twenty Days, Da Capo edn., New York, 1997, p. 432.

62. LHC, Dempsey Papers, no. 307, pt. II, app. A (6.4.45).

63. Andreas Kunz, 'Die Wehrmacht in der Agonie der nationalsozialistischen Herrschaft 1944/45: Eine Gedankenskizze', in Hillmann and Zimmermann, p. 131.

64. See Kunz, Wehrmacht und Niederlage, pp. 36–44.

65. Neitzel, Abgehört, p. 189, 9.3.45 (Eng. edn., Tapping Hitler's Generals, p. 141).

66. Steinert, pp. 570–71.

67. StAM, LRA 29656, fo. 576, report of SD-Außenstelle Berchtesgaden, 4.4.45; fo. 592, report of Gendarmerie-Posten Markt Schellenberg, 24.3.45.

68. MadR, 17, pp. 6732–40 (report to the Propaganda Ministry, 28.3.45, undated SD report from the end of March); see also Steinert, pp. 572–6; and Henke, pp. 815–16.

69. BAB, R55/603, fos. 533–8, extracts from weekly Tätigkeitsberichte der Reichspropagandaämter of 20–23 March (4.4.45).

70. Quoted Steinert, p. 570.

71. NAL, FO898/187, Summary of and Comments on German Broadcasts to Germany, fos. 79–80, 140–41, monitoring of German press reports (26.2.45–4.3.45, 26.3.45–1.4.45).

72. *Das letzte halbe Jahr*, pp. 281 (3.3.45), 311 (31.3.45); LHC, Dempsey Papers, no. 291 pt. II, p. 5, (21.3.45), citing a report of 7 March sent by the Berlin correspondent of a Swedish newspaper.

73. NAL, WO219/4713, SHAEF reports on conditions in the newly occupied areas, 14.3.45.

74. StAM, LRA 29656, fos. 574, 580, report of SD-Außenstelle Berchtesgaden, 7.3.45.

75. BHStA, Reichsstatthalter Epp 528, unfoliated, Bayerische Staatsminister für Wirtschaft, Landesernährungsamt Bayern, Abt. B, 22.3.45.

76. BAB, NS6/353, fo. 146, Anordnung 184/45, 26.3.45.

77. LHC, Dempsey Papers, no. 308, pt. II, p. 8 (7.4.45), citing a letter from Vreden, a small town close to the Dutch border, from 19 March as an example typical of the situation just east of the Rhine before the Allied offensive.

78. IWM, EDS, F.3, M.I. 14/369, correspondence of Krosigk and Education Minister Bernhard Rust, etc., 23–6.3.45.

79. BAB, NS6/353, fo. 75, Bormann, Rundschreiben 125/45 (10.3.45).

80. BHStA, Reichsstatthalter Epp 686/1, unfoliated, draft order of Bormann, in cooperation with the Reichsführer-SS and the Reichsgesundheitsführer, Heranziehung der Gefolgschaftsmitglieder der Krankenhäuser, Kliniken usw. zum Dienst im Deutschen Volkssturm, 9.3.45.

81. BAB, R55/603, fo. 529, Reichspropagandaamt Mark Brandenburg, Referat Volkssturm, to Reichsministerium für Volksaufklärung und Propaganda, Berlin, 5.3.45.

82. An example: the owner of two major newspapers, the *Münchener Neueste Nachrichten* and *München-Augsburger Abendzeitung*, desperate to receive reports from the *Deutsches Nachrichtenbüro* but unable to contact Berlin could only do so when the Gauleiter of Munich-Upper Bavaria, Paul Giesler, gave him special permission to telephone from his command post twice a day – StAM, NSDAP 13, fos. 144530–33, exchange of letters from Gauleiter Giesler and Herr Direktor A. Salat, Firma Knorr & Hirth, 2–14.3.45.

83. BAB, R470 altR48/11, Reichspostminister an die Presidenten der Reichspost-Direktion, 26.3.45.

84. See Dietmar Süß, 'Der Kampf um die "Moral" im Bunker: Deutschland, Großbritannien und der Luftkrieg', in Frank Bajohr and Michael Wildt (eds.), *Volksgemeinschaft: Neue Forschungen zur Gesellschaft des Nationalsozialismus*, Frankfurt am Main, 2009, pp. 129–35.

85. *DZW*, 6, p. 628; Oron J. Hale, *The Captive Press in the Third Reich*, Princeton, 1973, pp. 306–7.

86. *DRZW*, 9/1 (Blank), p. 415.

87. For example, instructions were sent out in early March to local authorities in Bavaria to alter arrangements for budgetary plans for 1945, emphasizing that local taxes should be passed on time to the towns and rural districts. – StAM, LRA 31908, unfoliated, Deutscher Gemeindetag, Dienststelle Bayern, Haushaltspläne der Gemeinden und Gemeindeverbände für 1945, 7.3.45. The Landrat in Berchtesgaden was still enquiring on 28 April 1945 when building work on new barracks, commissioned the previous August to extend accommodation for evacuees, would begin. – StAM, LRA 31645, unfoliated, Landrat Berchtesgaden to OT-Sonderbauleitung, 28.4.45.

88. On the policing of air-raid shelters, see *DRZW*, 9/1 (Blank), pp. 385-8.

89. By late March firemen in small communities of Sachsen-Anhalt were complaining that they were being called away from their work, where they were urgently needed, almost daily and often unnecessarily, at the 'pre-alarm' stage by the frequency of air raids. – IWM, EDS, F.3, M.I. 14/369, Krosigk to Goebbels, 26.3.45. Some people registered for voluntary fire service to try to escape recruitment to the *Volkssturm*. – StAM, LRA 31919, Gauleitung München to HSSPF Mühe on training of *Volkssturm* and air protection, including attempted regulation by the Regierungspräsident of Oberbayern of air protection service and service of voluntary firemen in the *Volkssturm* of 30.12.44 and the dispute of firemen serving in the *Volkssturm* of 25 and 31.1.45 and 21.2.45.

90. *DRZW*, 9/1 (Blank), p. 384.

91. Bernhard Gotto, *Nationalsozialistische Kommunalpolitik: Administrative Normalität und Systemstabilisierung durch die Augsburger Stadtverwaltung 1933–1945*, Munich, 2006, p. 373, surmises, most likely correctly, that Party representatives in Augsburg operated more through 'actionism' than idealism in the very last phase of the war.

92. For the organizational and controlling functions of the Party's Block Leaders (who in the mid-1930s had numbered around 200,000), see Detlef Schmiechen-Ackermann, 'Der "Blockwart": Die unteren Parteifunktionäre im nationalsozialistischen Terror- und Überwachungsapparat', *VfZ*, 48 (2000), pp. 594-6.

93. Pätzold and Weißbecker, p. 375. See also Herwart Vorländer, *Die NSV: Darstellung und Dokumentation einer NS-Organisation*, Boppard, 1988, p. 183 for the NSV's mobilizing and control function. Unpaid workers for the NSV and the German Red Cross numbered more than a million. Although the NSV welfare activity was always underpinned by Nazi racial objectives, the work that it carried out in the crisis conditions of the last months of the war made it popular, even among many Germans who were negatively disposed towards the regime. – Vorländer, *Die NSV*, pp. 173-6, 186; Herwart Vorländer, 'NS-Volkswohlfahrt und Winterhilfswerk des

deutschen Volkes', *VfZ*, 34 (1986), pp. 376–80; Armin Nolzen, 'Die NSDAP und die deutsche Gesellschaft im Zweiten Weltkrieg', in *Kriegsende in Deutschland*, Hamburg, 2005, pp. 192–3.

94. See *DRZW*, 9/1 (Nolzen), p. 191; and Armin Nolzen, 'Von der geistigen Assimilation zur institutionellen Kooperation: Das Verhältnis zwischen NSDAP und Wehrmacht, 1943–1945', in Hillmann and Zimmermann, pp. 90–92.

95. IWM, EDS, F.3, M.I. 14/369, Krosigk to Speer, 13.2.45.

96. IWM, EDS, F.3, M.I. 14/369, Krosigk to Goebbels, 22.3.45.

97. This paragraph, when not otherwise referenced, is based on Dieter Rebentisch, *Führerstaat und Verwaltung im Zweiten Weltkrieg*, Stuttgart, 1989, pp. 529–30.

98. Jill Stephenson, *Hitler's Home Front: Württemberg under the Nazis*, London, 2006, p. 324.

99. Gotto, p. 363.

100. StAA, Gauleitung Schwaben, 1/30, fos. 328904–6, Wahl to Bormann, 17.3.45; also Gotto, pp. 374–5.

101. StAA, Kreisleitung Augsburg-Stadt, 1/8, fos. 300554–5, Rundspruch an alle Kreisleiter, 30.3.45. Every Gau was to produce 100 'volunteers', and Wahl laid down – on what criteria it is not clear – the contingents from each district in his region. He criticized the Kreisleiter in mid-April for doing too little to gain recruits. – Gotto, p. 375.

102. Perry Biddiscombe, *Werwolf! The History of the National Socialist Guerrilla Movement 1944–1946*, Toronto and Buffalo, NY, 1998, pp. 12–14 (where the derivation of the name is discussed).

103. Biddiscombe, pp. 38, 128, 134–9.

104. *TBJG*, II/15, pp. 630 (30.3.45), 647 (31.3.45). For Ley's extreme radicalism in advocating a fight to the last, see Ronald Smelser, *Robert Ley: Hitler's Labor Front Leader*, Oxford, New York and Hamburg, 1988, pp. 291–2.

105. Biddiscombe, pp. 266–8; Henke, pp. 837–45.

106. Biddiscombe, p. 276, and ch. 5 for many instances of minor, uncoordinated and sporadic resistance to the Allied occupiers by former Hitler Youth members, former SS men and other Nazi diehards that punctuated the late spring and summer of 1945 and beyond, though they were only tangentially related to the Werwolf groups that had been established in the last weeks of the war.

107. Biddiscombe, p. 282, uses Allied assessments to suggest that 10–15 per cent of Germans supported the partisan movement, though this probably conflates general backing for continued resistance to the Allies and support for the regime with specific support for Werwolf activities. See Henke, pp. 948–9, for a more dismissive appraisal of support.

108. *TBJG*, II/15, pp. 422, 424 (5.3.45). Hitler had also thought the Mosel could be defended. – *TBJG*, II/15, p. 533 (18.3.45).

109. As suggested by Bernd Wegner, 'Hitler, der Zweite Weltkrieg und die Choreographie des Untergangs', *Geschichte und Gesellschaft*, 26 (2000), pp. 493–518; also in *DRZW*, 8, pp. 1192–1209.

110. *TBJG*, II/15, p. 479 (12.3.45).

111. *Hitler: Reden und Proklamationen 1932–1945*, ed. Max Domarus, Wiesbaden, 1973, p. 2212.

112. *TBJG*, II/15, pp. 422–3 (5.3.45).

113. *TBJG*, II/15, p. 425 (5.3.45). For Goebbels' fantasies of heroism as the end approached and his wife's reluctant determination to stay in Berlin and accept not only her own death, but that of her children, see Ralf Georg Reuth, *Goebbels*, Munich and Zurich, 1990, pp. 587–8. Magda had apparently accepted both the certainty of Germany's defeat and that death 'by our own hand, not the enemy's' was the only choice left. – David Irving, *Goebbels: Mastermind of the Third Reich*, London, 1996, p. 506 (though based on recollections, reproduced in an article on Magda in a periodical in 1952 (Irving, p. 564 n. 9), of her sister-in-law Eleanor (Ello) Quandt, whose testimony as Irving acknowledges (p. 564 n. 19) was not always reliable).

114. *TBJG*, II/15, pp. 426–7 (5.3.45), 525 (17.3.45), 532–3 (18.3.45); and see Michael Bloch, *Ribbentrop*, pb. edn., London, 1994, p. 422; Reimer Hansen, 'Ribbentrops Friedensfühler im Frühjahr 1945', *Geschichte in Wissenschaft und Unterricht*, 18 (1967), pp. 716–30; and Hansjakob Stehle, 'Deutsche Friedensfühler bei den Westmächten im Februar/März 1945', *VfZ*, 30 (1982), pp. 538–55; Gerhard L. Weinberg, *A World at Arms: A Global History of World War II*, Cambridge, 1994, pp. 783–4.

115. IfZ, ZS 1953, 'Iden des März. Ein zeitgeschichtliches Fragment über den letzten Kontaktversuch Ribbentrops mit Moskau in der Zeit vom 11.–16. März 1945', fos. 1–13 (no date, probably early 1950s). For a description of Mme Kollontay, 'the grand old lady of Soviet diplomacy', and for Ribbentrop's vain attempts to instigate some form of negotiated peace with the Soviet Union in early 1945, see Ingeborg Fleischhauer, *Die Chance des Sonderfriedens: Deutsch-sowjetische Geheimgespräche 1941–1945*, Berlin, 1986, pp. 58–61, 268–75.

116. *TBJG*, II/15, pp. 450–51 (8.3.45).

117. BA/MA, RH21/3/420, fos. 34, 40, post-war account (1950) by Colonel-General Erhard Raus (former Commander-in-Chief of the 3rd Panzer Army in East Prussia, who had taken command in Pomerania of remaining forces of the 11th SS-Panzer Army) of his meetings with Himmler on 13.2.45 and 7.3.45, and his report to Hitler on 8.3.45.

118. Guderian, p. 426.

119. The above paragraph is based on: Folke Bernadotte, *The Fall of the Curtain*,

London, 1945, pp. 19–47; Walter Schellenberg, *Schellenberg*, pb. edn., London, 1965, pp. 171–5; Felix Kersten, *The Kersten Memoirs 1940–1945*, London, 1956, pp. 271–83; Peter Padfield, *Himmler: Reichsführer-SS*, London, 1990, pp. 565–6, 578–9; and Peter Longerich, *Heinrich Himmler: Biographie*, Munich, 2008, pp. 742–8, 967–8 nn. 131–2. In a post-war interrogation, Schellenberg – who was keen to assert both his own importance and his attempts to influence a negotiated settlement – claimed that in December 1944, in the Reichsführer's presence, he even touched on the possibility of the elimination of Hitler. – IWM, FO645/161, interrogation 13.11.45, p. 15 (1945–6).

120. *DZW*, 6, p. 152.
121. John Toland, *The Last 100 Days*, London, 1965, pp. 73, 238–44, 478–81; Padfield, pp. 573–8; Weinberg, p. 818; Peter R. Black, *Ernst Kaltenbrunner: Ideological Soldier of the Third Reich*, Princeton, 1984, pp. 242–5; BA/MA, N574/19, NL Vietinghoff, 'Kriegsende in Italien', fos. 41–6.
122. For interesting speculation on Speer's power ambitions at this juncture, see *DRZW*, 10/2 (Müller), pp. 74–84; and Müller's remarks in the conclusion to the volume, p. 718.
123. Albert Speer, *Erinnerungen*, Frankfurt am Main and Berlin, 1969, p. 442.
124. He had engineered Hitler's approval to his new responsibilities on 14 February, exploiting the illness of the Transport Minister Julius Heinrich Dorpmüller. – *DRZW*, 10/2 (Müller), p. 82.
125. BAB, R3/1623a, fos. 18–23, Aktennotiz Speer, 7.3.45. That very day, Paul Pleiger, head of the Reich Association of Coal, pointed out to Speer how serious the coal situation was following the loss of Upper Silesia, the transport problems that had effectively ruled out Ruhr coal, and the big drop in production from the Saarland. Unless things improved, he pointed out, it would be impossible to provide coal for armaments or avoid the collapse of transport, electricity and gas. – IWM, F.3, M.I. 14/163, Pleiger to Speer, 7.3.45. On 14 March Hitler ordered that because of severely reduced transport capacity, priorities in areas to be evacuated had to be determined by their value for the prosecution of the war: the Wehrmacht, coal, then food materials. Refugees could be accommodated only where there was available space. In passing on the order next day to relevant authorities, Speer pointed out that it was on his suggestion. – BAB, R3/1623a, fos. 27–8.
126. *TBJG*, II/15, pp. 579 (23.3.45), 603 (27.3.45).
127. *TBJG*, II/15, pp. 500–501 (14.3.45), 511–12 (15.3.45).
128. BAB, R3/1623a, fos. 31–8, OKH, Chef Transportwesens/General der Pioniere und Festungen, draft, no precise date in March given; Speer to Gen. stab des Heeres-General der Pioniere und Festungen, 15.3.45; OKH, Chef Transportwesens/Gend di Pi u Fest, 14.3.45; Speer, p. 442; Guderian, pp. 422–3.

129. BAB, R3/1536, fos. 3–12; *IMT*, vol. 41, pp. 420–25. Drafts (fos. 28–30) were appended of orders limiting destruction and giving Speer the powers to decide on exceptions to immobilization; Speer, pp. 442–3.

130. See Heinrich Schwendemann, '"Drastic Measures to Defend the Reich at the Oder and the Rhine . . .": A Forgotten Memorandum of Albert Speer of 18 March 1945', *Journal of Contemporary History*, 38 (2003), pp. 597–614; also Heinrich Schwendemann, '"Verbrannte Erde"? Hitlers "Nero-Befehl" vom 19. März 1945', in *Kriegsende Deutschland*, p. 163; and, for a different interpretation, *DRZW*, 10/2 (Müller), pp. 86–8. An extract from the memorandum was already published by Gregor Janssen, *Das Ministe-rium Speer: Deutschlands Rüstung im Krieg*, Berlin, Frankfurt am Main and Vienna, 1968, p. 311, though without commentary, beyond pointing (p. 310) to its connection with Keitel's order that morning to evacuate the population from the fighting zone west of the Rhine. Dietrich Eichholtz, *Geschichte der deutschen Kriegswirtschaft 1939–1945*, vol. 3: *1943–1945*, Berlin, 1996, p. 662 n. 212, confines himself to the comment that Speer had 'doubtless tactical aims' with the memorandum. Neither Gitta Sereny, *Albert Speer: His Battle with Truth*, London, 1995, pp. 476–7, nor Joachim Fest, *Speer: Eine Biographie*, Berlin, 1999, pp. 336–8, mentions it.

131. BAB, R3/1537, fos. 3–6 (18.3.45).

132. Hitler spoke to Goebbels in highly negative terms in late March about Speer being 'unreliable' and 'failing' at a critical time and showing a 'defeat-ist' character, tendencies 'incompatible with the National Socialist view of the war'. – *TBJG*, II/15, pp. 619–20 (28.3.45).

133. This is the gist of Müller's interpretation in *DRZW*, 10/2, p. 87.

134. For Speer's late conversion to the need to save the 'means of existence of the . . . people in a lost war', see Henke, pp. 431–2.

135. BAB, R3/1538, fo. 16, handwritten letter by Speer to Hitler, 29.3.45.

136. Schwendemann, '"Drastic Measures"', p. 605, suggests, perhaps going too far, that Speer was seeking 'to show Hitler a way out, by offering the Führer his services as a kind of saviour, thus securing his favour'.

137. Speer, pp. 444–5; BAB, R3/1623a, fos. 39–43, two Fernschreiben of Keitel, 18.3.45; implementation order of Bormann, 19.3.45.

138. BAB, R3/1623a, fos. 46–7, 'Zerstörungsmaßnahmen im Reichsgebiet', Lt.-Gen. August Winter (Deputy Chief of the OKW Operations Staff) to Speer, 20.3.45, passing on Hitler's order of the previous day (printed in *IMT*, vol. 41, pp. 430–31, and *Hitlers Weisungen für die Kriegführung 1939–1945: Dokumente des Oberkommandos dep Wehrmacht*, ed. Walther Hubatsch, pb. edn., Munich, 1965, pp. 348–9).

139. BAB, R3/1538, fos. 14–15, Speer to Hitler, 29.3.45; *IMT*, vol. 41, pp. 425–9; Speer, pp. 445–6.

140. See Henke, pp. 432–5; *DRZW*, 10/2 (Müller), p. 93; and Eichholtz, pp. 663–9. In some factories, crucial component parts were taken out of machines

and hidden so that they could later be reinstated. – Zimmermann, *Pflicht*, p. 60.

141. Speer, pp. 450–59; BAB, R3/1661, fos. 5–8, Reiseprogramm Speer, Schulze-Fielitz, Hupfauer, etc., 22–5.3.45; fos. 20–22, Walter Rohland: Niederschrift über die Ereignisse vom 15.3 bis 15.4.45; R3/1623a, fo. 50, Bormann to the Gauleiter, passing on Hitler's evacuation orders with the stipulation that the evacuation was not a matter for debate, and that the accommodation of the evacuees within Germany simply 'had to be mastered' through improvisation; *IMT*, vol. 41, pp. 491–3 (Rohland's testimony at Nuremberg).

142. Speer, pp. 448, 453–4, for Model's stance. The Wehrmacht's head of transport spoke of creating 'a transport desert' in abandoned areas. – BAB, R3/1623a, fo. 59, Chef des Transportwesens der Wehrmacht, Fernschreiben 29.3.45 (referred to in Speer, p. 459).

143. Speer, pp. 454–5; BAB, R3/1626, fo. 14, unknown eyewitness account, 13.9.45.

144. Speer, pp. 457–61 (quotation p. 460).

145. This is how Hitler saw it, in speaking of the matter to Goebbels soon afterwards. – *TBJG*, II/15, p. 643 (31.3.45). Speer's own depiction of his defiance was almost certainly at least in part contrived. See *DRZW*, 10/2 (Müller), pp. 94–5.

146. Speer registered with a note in his files Hitler's agreement that 'scorched earth' was pointless for a small area like Germany and could only have an effect in a huge country like Russia. He immediately transmitted Hitler's amended order leaving implementation in Speer's hands. – BAB, R3/1623a, fos. 75, 78–80, 85–6 (30.3.45). On 3 April (fos. 106, 108) he replied to the request from Gauleiter Ueberreither (Niederdonau) for clarification on destruction of waterworks and power stations in his region by stating: 'According to the Führer order of 30.3.45 there is no scorched earth', and stipulating only temporary immobilization which 'fulfils the stated aim of the Führer'.

147. The OKW stipulated on 3 April that, despite the Führer order for the destruction of all installations that might be useful to the enemy, it could prove expedient in some cases to limit this to a 'lengthy breach' (*nachhaltige Unterbrechung*) which could be repaired for German use if there was a probability of retaking the bridges. The Wehrmacht was keen to establish its sole responsibility for the destruction of military installations. A few days later, a revised directive emphasized the need to destroy operationally important bridges, as determined by the OKW, with the most severe punishment for failure to carry this out. – *KTB/SKL*, part A, vol. 68, pp. 46 (3.4.45), 75–7 (5.4.45), 128 (8.4.45).

148. Henke, p. 434. A far more positive interpretation of Speer's motives is provided in the early assessment by Reimer Hansen, 'Albert Speers Konflikt mit Hitler', *Geschichte in Wissenschaft und Unterricht*, 17 (1966), pp. 596–621,

based heavily upon the documents and evidence presented to the Nuremberg Trials. Later research – particularly since the publication of Matthias Schmidt, *Albert Speer: Das Ende eines Mythos*, Berne and Munich, 1982 – has tended to be far more critically disposed towards Speer. See, for example, Alfred C. Mierzejewski, 'When Did Albert Speer Give up?' *Historical Journal*, 31 (1988), pp. 391–7, and, more recently, the contribution by Rolf-Dieter Müller to *DRZW*, 10/2.

149. *TBJG*, II/15, p. 613 (28.3.45).
150. See also on this point, *DRZW*, 10/2 (Müller), p. 92.

CHAPTER 8. IMPLOSION

1. *Das letzte halbe Jahr: Stimmungsberichte der Wehrmachtpropaganda 1944/45*, ed. Wolfram Wette, Ricarda Bremer and Detlef Vogel, Essen, 2001, p. 338 (10.4.45).
2. For destruction in the Tiergarten and Grunewald and the nightly activity in the city ('eine hektische Genußsucht'), see the diary entries of the Danish correspondent Jacob Kronika, *Der Untergang Berlins*, Flensburg, 1946, pp. 79, 91, 98–9, 149 (30.3.45, 7.4.45, 10.4.45, 23.4.45). A description – though perhaps drawing in part on distorted memory – of Berlin, shortly before the Soviet attack, can be found in IWM, 'Second World War Memoirs of P. E. v. Stemann', Berlin correspondent between 1942 and 1945 of the Danish newspaper *Berlinske Tidende*, fos. 236–7. Vivid depictions of the city in April 1945 are provided by David Clay Large, *Berlin*, New York, 2000, pp. 358–9, and Roger Moorhouse, *Berlin at War: Life and Death in Hitler's Capital 1939–45*, London, 2010, pp. 365–9.
3. Goebbels remarked in his diary on the emptiness of Berlin's streets at Easter 1945 (*TBJG*, II/15, p. 668, 5.4.45).
4. Quoted in Moorhouse, p. 367.
5. *TBJG*, II/15, p. 692.
6. A fitting term, used by Hans Mommsen, 'The Dissolution of the Third Reich: Crisis Management and Collapse, 1943–1945', *Bulletin of the German Historical Institute, Washington DC*, 27 (2000), p. 20, and Stephen G. Fritz, *Endkampf: Soldiers, Civilians, and the Death of the Third Reich*, Lexington, Ky., 2004, ch. 5.
7. *DZW*, 6, p. 561; and NAL, WO219/1651, fo. 145, SHAEF digests of postwar interrogations of Jodl and Kesselring, 23.5.45.
8. American losses in the battle for the Ruhr totalled around 10,000 men. – *DZW*, 6, p. 564.
9. For the behaviour of French troops, see Heinrich Schwendemann, 'Das Kriegsende in Ostpreußen und in Südbaden im Vergleich', in Bernd Martin (ed.), *Der Zweite Weltkrieg und seine Folgen: Ereignisse – Auswirkungen – Reflexionen*,

Freiburg, 2006, pp. 101, 104; and Richard Bessel, *Germany 1945: From War to Peace*, London, 2009, pp. 116–17, 158–9. Evidently, the very skin colour of the North African soldiers in the French army gave rise to great anxiety among the population which had often never before seen other than white people. This may have led to exaggeration of the numbers of rapes said to have been perpetrated by 'colonial' troops. Numerous parish reports indicating rape and looting – though there were many cases where none were reported – are contained in Josef F. Göhri, *Die Franzosen kommen! Kriegsereignisse im Breisgau und in der Ortenau*, Horb am Neckar, 2005, pp. 17, 24–5, 43, 46, 50, 53, 60, 82, 88, 91, 94, 98, 119, 124–5; and Hermann Riedel, *Halt! Schweizer Grenze!*, Konstanz, 1983, pp. 233, 237–8, 263, 305 (where more than 200 cases were mentioned). See also Bernd Serger, Karin-Anne Böttcher and Gerd R. Ueberschär (eds.), *Südbaden unter Hakenkreuz und Trikolore: Zeitzeugen berichten über das Kriegsende und die französische Besetzung 1945*, Freiburg in Breisgau, Berlin and Vienna, 2006, pp. 253, 257, 269, 311–25; Manfred Bosch, *Der Neubeginn: Aus deutscher Nachkriegszeit. Südbaden 1945–1950*, Konstanz, 1988, p. 34; *Der deutsche Südwesten zur Stunde Null*, ed. Generallandesarchiv Karlsruhe, Karlsruhe, 1975, pp. 102–3; Paul Sauer, *Demokratischer Neubeginn in Not und Elend: Das Land Württemberg-Baden von 1945 bis 1952*, Ulm, 1979, pp. 18–20; *Von der Diktatur zur Besatzung: Das Kriegsende 1945 im Gebiet des heutigen Landkreises Sigmaringen*, ed. Landkreis Sigmaringen, Sigmaringen, 1995, pp. 92–3.

10. The above, where not otherwise indicated, is based on *DZW*, 6, pp. 561–71; *DRZW*, 10/1 (Zimmermann), pp. 443–60; Fritz, chs. 3–6; Lothar Gruchmann, *Der Zweite Weltkrieg*, pb. edn., Munich, 1975, pp. 425–32; *The Oxford Companion to the Second World War*, ed. I. C. B. Dear and M. R. D. Foot, Oxford, 1995, pp. 481–5; Max Hastings, *Armageddon: The Battle for Germany 1944–45*, London, 2004, pp. 481–502.

11. *Hitlers Weisungen für die Kriegführung 1939–1945: Dokumente des Oberkommandos der Wehrmacht*, ed. Walther Hubatsch, pb. edn., Munich, 1965, pp. 355–6. Dönitz and Kesselring were given full powers over the defence of their own zone only in the event that a break in communications prevented the transmission of Hitler's orders and decisions. Otherwise Hitler's own unified operational leadership was to remain unaltered. On 20 April, in line with the expectation that he would leave for the south, Hitler empowered Dönitz, in the north, to issue directives on defence to the civilian authorities in his 'zone'. In the military sphere, Dönitz's remit was confined to the navy, since Hitler finally decided on 25 April to remain in Berlin and to retain his operational direction of the Wehrmacht via the OKW in Rheinsberg. – Herbert Kraus, 'Karl Dönitz und das Ende des "Dritten Reiches"', in Hans-Erich Volkmann (ed.), *Ende des Dritten Reiches – Ende des Zweiten Weltkriegs: Eine perspektivische Rückschau*, Munich and Zurich, 1995, pp. 7–8 and p. 20 n.

17. The split of the Reich became reality with the meeting of Soviet and American troops at Torgau on 25 April.

12. *DZW*, 6, p. 523. A graphic description of the last days in Königsberg before the capitulation (and criticism of Lasch's reluctance to capitulate until the last minute, and to save his own skin) is provided by Michael Wieck, *Zeugnis vom Untergang Königsbergs: Ein 'Geltungsjude' berichtet*, Heidelberg, 1988, pp. 168–222.

13. His wife and daughter were arrested and placed in a military prison. News of their punishment was publicized. – Robert Loeffel, 'Soldiers and Terror: Re-evaluating the Complicity of the Wehrmacht in Nazi Germany', *German History*, 27 (2009), pp. 527–8.

14. Schwendemann, p. 97.

15. In the proclamation, Hitler raised once more the spectre of the extermination of the German people that, he claimed, would follow Bolshevik conquest. 'While old men and children are murdered,' he railed, 'women and children are denigrated to barrack-whores. The rest will march off to Siberia.' Alerting the troops to any sign of treachery from their own officers, Hitler ordered that any officer not well known to the men giving orders for retreat was to be 'dispatched on the spot'. – *Hitler: Reden und Proklamationen 1932–1945*, ed. Max Domarus, Wiesbaden, 1973, pp. 2223–4.

16. Drawing on *DZW*, 6, pp. 686–705; *DRZW*, 10/1 (Lakowski), pp. 631–49; *DRZW*, 8 (Ungváry), pp. 944–55; Gruchmann, pp. 434–6; John Erickson, *The Road to Berlin*, Cassell edn., 2003, pp. 563–77; Brian Taylor, *Barbarossa to Berlin: A Chronology of the Campaigns on the Eastern Front 1941 to 1945*, vol. 2, Stroud, 2008, pp. 307–20; *The Oxford Companion to the Second World War*, pp. 125–7; Antony Beevor, *Berlin: The Downfall 1945*, pb. edn., London, 2007, chs. 15–16; Karl-Heinz Frieser, 'Die Schlacht um die Seelower Höhen im April 1945', in Roland G. Foerster (ed.), *Seelower Höhen 1945*, Hamburg, 1998, pp. 129–43; Manfried Rauchensteiner, *Der Krieg in Österreich 1945*, 2nd edn., Vienna, 1984, ch. 6; Theo Rossiwall, *Die letzten Tage: Die militärische Besetzung Österreichs 1945*, Vienna, 1969, pp. 78–183.

17. For sketches of the man and his career, see: Sam L. Lewis, 'Albert Kesselring – Der Soldat als Manager', in Ronald Smelser and Enrico Syring (eds.), *Die Militärelite des Dritten Reiches*, Berlin, 1995, pp. 270–87; Elmar Krautkrämer, 'Generalfeldmarschall Albert Kesselring', in Gerd. R. Ueberschär (ed.), *Hitlers militärische Elite*, vol. 1: *Von den Anfängen des Regimes bis Kriegsbeginn*, Darmstadt, 1998, pp. 121–9; and Shelford Bidwell, 'Kesselring', in Correlli Barnett (ed.), *Hitler's Generals*, London, 1990, pp. 265–89.

18. BAB, R3/1661, fo. 20, 'Niederschrift über die Ereignisse vom 15.3. bis 15.4.1945', no date, signed by Walther Rohland (entry for 23.4.45); Albert

Speer, *Erinnerungen*, Frankfurt am Main and Berlin, 1969, p. 446. Kesselring passed on Hitler's 'scorched earth' order of 19 March next day to his subordinate commanders. – Krautkrämer, p. 128 n. 10.

19. Speer, pp. 463–4. General Westphal later pointed out that Kesselring, on taking over from Rundstedt as Commander in Chief West, replied sceptically to the attempt to provide him with a realistic briefing of the situation by stating that the Führer had given him a different account. – Siegfried Westphal, *Erinnerungen*, Mainz, 1975, p. 327.

20. *The Memoirs of Field-Marshal Kesselring*, Greenhill Books edn., London, 1997, pp. 266, 269.

21. Joachim Ludewig, 'Walter Model – Hitlers bester Feldmarschall?' in Smelser and Syring, p. 368.

22. *1945: Das Jahr der endgültigen Niederlage der faschistischen Wehrmacht. Dokumente*, ed. Gerhard Förster and Richard Lakowski, Berlin, 1975, p. 230 (18.3.45).

23. Quoted *DRZW*, 10/1 (Zimmermann), p. 332 (29.3.45); see also Manfred Messerschmidt, 'Krieg in der Trümmerlandschaft: "Pflichterfüllung" wofür?' in Ulrich Borsdorf and Mathilde Jamin (eds.), *Über Leben im Krieg: Kriegserfahrungen in einer Industrieregion 1939–1945*, Reinbek bei Hamburg, 1989, pp. 171, 177.

24. Carlo D'Este, 'Model', in Barnett, p. 329; Kesselring, pp. 250–55, attributed much of the blame for the plight of Army Group B to Model's operational decisions.

25. BAB, R3/1626, fos. 15–17, 'Kapitulationsverhandlungen mit Generalfeldmarschall Model und Gauleiter Hoffmann', notes compiled in internment in 'Dustbin', June 1945, by Rohland. And R3/1661, fo. 21, 'Niederschrift über die Ereignisse vom 15.3. bis 15.4.1945', no date, signed by Walther Rohland (entries for 31.3, 2.4, 8.4, 13.4.45); Walter Rohland, *Bewegte Zeiten*, Stuttgart, 1978, pp. 105–7. Model also refused to entertain the plea in a personal letter to him from US Lieutenant-General Matthew Ridgway on 17 April, declaring that his oath to the Führer meant he must fight to the end. – Hastings, p. 482; Messerschmidt, p. 177.

26. Ludewig, pp. 382–4; Rohland, p. 107; Walter Görlitz, *Model: Strategie der Defensive*, Wiesbaden, 1975, pp. 263–8; John Zimmermann, *Pflicht zum Untergang: Die deutsche Kriegführung im Westen des Reiches 1944/45*, Paderborn, 2009, p. 2. The order to make families the guarantors of soldiers fighting to the last was signed by Keitel on Hitler's behalf on 5 March. – *1945: Das Jahr der endgültigen Niederlage der faschistischen Wehrmacht*, p. 207. Strikingly, the initiative for this came from within the Wehrmacht. – Ulrike Hett and Johannes Tuchel, 'Die Reaktionen des NS-Staates auf den Umsturzversuch vom 20. Juli 1944', in Peter Steinbach and Johannes Tuchel (eds.), *Widerstand gegen den Nationalsozialismus*, Bonn, 1994, p. 387.

27. Cited *DRZW*, 10/1 (Zimmermann), p. 327 (7.4.45).
28. *DRZW*, 10/1 (Zimmermann), pp. 331–2.
29. IWM, EDS, F.3, AL2697, 'Doenitz orders Resistance to the last. 3 Orders – 7, 11, and 19 April 1945'.
30. *KTB/SLK*, part A, vol. 68, pp. 331–2A, Kriegstagebuch des Ob. d. M., 25.4.45.
31. BA/MA, N265/112, NL Heinrici, fos. 1–17 (written during captivity, 1945–7 and incorporating memoirs of Colonel Eismann). Though entitled 'Der Vortrag bei Hitler am 4.IV.1945', the meeting appears in fact (see fo. 20) to have taken place not on the 4th but on 6 April. Heinrici had already composed a briefer, though in essentials similar, account of the meeting on 12 May 1945 (BA/MA, N265/108, fos. 3–9, where he dates it to 'about ten days before the beginning of the battle for Berlin').
32. BA/MA, N265/112, NL Heinrici, fos. 23–4. Speer, p. 471, dates the meeting to the 15th, not 14 April (as Heinrici has it), and mentions the discussion only of sparing the destruction of Berlin's installations, not the issue of killing Hitler (which he alludes to, however, elsewhere in his memoirs). In later drafts of parts of his memoirs dating from 1966 or thereabouts, Heinrici again mentions the discussion with Speer about killing Hitler and his rejection of political murder because of his Christian convictions. He adds two points which were not mentioned in his earlier version. An assassination attempt would have been pointless, because of Hitler's security, greatly tightened since July 1944. And, should such an attempt have nevertheless succeeded, the result would have been revolution 100 kilometres behind the front lines against the Russians. The ensuing chaos would have removed from the leadership all possibility of successful negotiations over an armistice. Whether such notions were in his mind in April 1945 or not is unclear. He drew the conclusion, in the later memoirs, that he had no alternative but to carry out his commission to hold the Oder line to the best of his ability. – BA/MA, N265/26, fos. 22–3 (*c.* 1966). On Speer's claims to have considered assassinating Hitler, see Matthias Schmidt, *Albert Speer: Das Ende eines Mythos*, Berne and Munich, 1982, pp. 147–51.
33. BA/MA, N245/3, NL Reinhardt, Kalenderblätter 1945, fo. 87, entries for 5.4.45, 13.4.45.
34. A telex from the Army Personnel Office on 13 April assigned small numbers of officers to the 'Führer-Reserve' of several Army Groups but pointed out that they now had to manage their own manpower resources and could not reckon with further allocations in the foreseeable future. – IWM, EDS, F.3, M.I. 14/163, FS to OB Nordwest, etc., 13.4.45. Seven new divisions were somehow thrown together in early April and given light armaments. But they were made up of seventeen-year-olds. They were meant for the defence of Thuringia, but would not be ready for service for a fortnight. – *TBJG*, II/15, p. 685 (8.4.45). By that time, Thuringia was lost.

35. e.g. StAA, Kreisleitung Günzburg 1/42, Gaustabsamt Gau Schwaben to named Kreisleitungen, 11.4.45.

36. BAB, NS6/756, fos. 2-6, Verstärkung der kämpfenden Truppe, 28.2.45.

37. BAB, NS6/135, fo. 160, Vorlage (for Bormann), re Panzernahbekämpfungstrupp der Hitler-Jugend, 3.3.45.

38. Information from Dr Hermann Graml, Institut für Zeitgeschichte, Munich, on his own experience in the Reich Labour Service in the last days of April 1945. Heavy pressure was put on boys to join. It could be resisted if sufficient determination were shown, for example by emphasizing strong allegiance to the Catholic Church, or, as in Dr Graml's case, by producing call-up papers for the Wehrmacht. A contemporary in Württemberg claimed much later to recall that her then seventeen-year-old brother received a letter in February 1945 telling him that he had volunteered for the Waffen-SS, which had not been the case. He hurriedly volunteered for the Reich Labour Service to avoid it. – *Zeitzeugen berichten ... Schwäbisch Gmünd – Erinnerungen an die Zeit von 1930 bis 1945*, ed. Stadtarchiv Schwäbisch Gmünd, Schwäbisch Gmünd, 1989, p. 312.

39. See the testimony assembled in Nicholas Stargardt, *Witnesses of War: Children's Lives under the Nazis*, London, 2005, pp. 268-9, 294-7, 303, 307.

40. Günter C. Behrmann, '"Jugend, die meinen Namen trägt": Die letzten Kriegseinsätze der Hitlerjugend', in *Kriegsende in Deutschland*, Hamburg, 2005, p. 175.

41. StAA, Kreisleitung Günzburg 1/43, Strassen- und Flußbauamt, Neu-Ulm, 13.4.45; Gauleitung Schwaben, 1/28, fos. 328841-2, 328845, Heeresgruppe G to Gauleitung Schwaben, 13.4.45, Bormann to all Gauleiter, 13.4.45, passing on Keitel's directive of 10.4.45; fos. 328807-8, Bormann's order to ten named Gauleiter in central and southern Germany, 13.4.45; Gauleitung Schwaben, 1/29, fo. 328843, Aktnotiz für den Gauleiter: Versorgungslage der Wehrmacht und ziviler Behörden, 16.4.45; fo. 328835, note for Gauleiter Wahl from the Kreisleiter of Neu-Ulm, who, since the enemy was approaching, saw the need to call on the *Volkssturm* and the people's levy to undertake entrenchment work and increase the number of barriers, 20.4.45.

42. BAB, R3/1622, fo. 102, Speer directive, transmitting Hitler's order, 24.4.45; printed in *'Führer-Erlasse' 1939-1945*, ed. Martin Moll, Stuttgart, 1997, p. 497.

43. BAB, R3/1618, fo. 22, re Führer-Vorführung, 12.4.45.

44. BfZ, Sammlung Sterz, Uffz. Werner F., 1.4.45. Most soldiers' letters, and those they received, were unpolitical in content and dealt in the main with inconsequential family or private matters. A report from one censors' office for March stated on the basis of intercepted and controlled mail that 91.8 per cent of letters checked over the month were 'colourless', 4.7 per cent positively disposed towards the regime and 3.5 per cent negative (the last figure certainly underplaying true sentiments, given the dangers of expressing

criticism). A separate control, under slightly different criteria, for the last eight days of March gave results of 77.08 per cent 'colourless', 8.82 per cent 'positive', 6.64 per cent 'negative' and 7.46 per cent 'neutral'. The report included 113 varied extracts from the letters. – BA/MA, RH20/19/245, fos. 31–43, Feldpostprüfstelle bei AOK.19, Monatsbericht für März 1945, 3.4.45. For the organization of post to and from the front, see Richard Lakowski and Hans-Joachim Büll, *Lebenszeichen 1945: Feldpost aus den letzten Kriegstagen*, Leipzig, 2002, pp. 18–29.

45. BfZ, Sammlung Sterz, Tagebuch Uffz. Heinrich V., 10.4.45.
46. BfZ, Sammlung Sterz, Tagebuch Uffz. Heinrich V., 12.4.45.
47. Fritz, pp. 90–91.
48. LHC, Dempsey Papers, no. 319, pt. II, pp. 8–9 (18.4.45). The fate of the officer is not known.
49. *TBJG*, II/15, pp. 658 (1.4.45), 684, 687 (8.4.45), 692 (9.4.45); *DRZW*, 10/1 (Boog), pp. 830–83; Christian Hartmann and Johannes Hürter, *Die letzten 100 Tage des Zweiten Weltkriegs*, Munich, 2005, entry for Day 33, 7 April 1945. Hartmann and Hürter give the figure of 23 bombers destroyed. This seems close to the actual American figure of 17 bombers and 5 fighters destroyed in the air-battle, though most of these losses were apparently not directly caused by ramming. Some months earlier, a young man, a journalism student whose brother had fallen on the eastern front, and evidently a keen Nazi, expressed his disappointment to the SS newspaper, *Das Schwarze Korps*, at being rejected for suicidal service as a one-man torpedo because there had been too many applicants. Love of Germany, he said, was his motive. – BAB, NS19/2936, handwritten letter, no date (end of 1944 or beginning of 1945).
50. Fritz, pp. 72, 78–9, 88–9, 92.
51. Andreas Kunz, *Wehrmacht und Niederlage: Die bewaffnete Macht in der Endphase der nationalsozialistischen Herrschaft 1944 bis 1945*, Munich, 2007, p. 254.
52. BA/MA, MSg2/2697, diary of Lieutenant Julius Dufner, fos. 154–61, entries for 13–20.4.45. Goebbels referred earlier in the month to the demoralization of the troops in Gau Weser-Ems, similar, he said, to reports that had until then come in from western parts of the Reich, as soldiers went about in loose groups, some throwing away their weapons, and engaging in looting. – *TBJG*, II/15, p. 673 (4.4.45).
53. *TBJG*, II/15, pp. 654–5, 659–60 (1.4.45). According to the diary notes of Goebbels' aide, Rudolf Semmler, reports were emerging in early April from every town or village where American or British troops were approaching 'that large numbers of the population are showing white flags and sheets'. – Rudolf Semmler, *Goebbels – the Man Next to Hitler*, London, 1947, p. 190 (5.4.45). See the diary entries reproduced in Gerhard Hirschfeld and Irina

Renz, 'Vormittags die ersten Amerikaner': Stimmen und Bilder vom Kriegsende 1945, Stuttgart, 2005, pp. 119, 125, 133, for examples of joy or relief
at the arrival of American troops.

54. IWM, EDS, F.2, AL2682, Bormann to Kaltenbrunner, 4.4.45.

55. StAA, Gauleitung Schwaben, 1/28, fo. 328839, Schulz to Gauleitung Schwaben, 8.4.45, with handwritten note by Wahl at foot.

56. StAA, Kreisleitung Günzburg 1/43, fos. 00991, 00999, Kreisleiter to all
Bürgermeister, Ortsgruppenleiter and Ortsamsleiter der NSV, 18.4.45, and
(undated) order of Kreisleiter.

57. TBJG, II/15, pp. 612–13 (28.3.45), a comment also related to Hitler's
orders for the destruction of industry.

58. TBJG, II/15, p. 684 (8.4.45). The difficulties of feeding refugees sent to the
Allgäu in the Alpine region of southern Bavaria led to demands for the
influx to be halted. – StAA, Gauleitung Schwaben, 1/29, fos. 328886–7,
report of Landesbauernführer Pg. Deininger on 'Ernährungslage', 14.4.45.

59. IfZ, Fa-91/5, fo. 1120d, Lagemitteilung Gauleiter Eigruber, 9.4.45; BAB,
NS6/277, fo. 101–101ᵛ, Dienstleiter Hund, Parteikanzlei München, to GL
Wächtler, Bayreuth, 10.4.45; fo. 31, Hund to Pg. Zander, Dienststelle Berlin, 10.4.45; fos. 8–9, Lagebericht of Gauleitung Salzburg, 10.4.45, Fernschreiben, Hund to Bormann, 14.4.45; fo. 11, Aktenvermerk, 17.4.45. Gauleiter
Hugo Jury in Gau Niederdonau also sought advice from Bormann (fo. 92)
about where to send 30,000 refugees from Silesia, currently in the District
Iglau in the Protectorate who had to be brought into the Reich. He said he
would do his utmost to accommodate those who came from his Gau, but
was evidently unwilling to receive those from outside. Gauleiter Eigruber
later recalled the chaotic conditions as tens of thousands of Hungarian refugees, and 15,000 Jews from the Lower Danube and Styria who were dispatched to Mauthausen concentration camp, were sent to his domain,
which had no food for them. – IWM, FO645/156, interrogation of August
Eigruber, 3.11.45.

60. BAB, NS6/277, fo. 130, Funkspruch Walkenhorsts an Reichsleiter Bormann, 5.4.45 (also IfZ, Fa-91/5, fo. 1106). Also: fos. 110–12, Vermerk for
Bormann from Pg. Zander, 5.4.45; fo. 113, Walkenhorst, telefonische Vorlage an den Reichsleiter, 5.4.45; fo. 15, Aktenvermerk referring to the
inability of Gauleiter Siegfried Uiberreither of Styria to reach Berlin with
an urgent message for General Jodl; fo. 4, Pg. Walkenhorst zur telefon-
ischen Durchgabe nach Berlin (on varied communications difficulties and
attempts to overcome them), 12.4.45.

61. TBJG, II/15, p. 677 (4.4.45).

62. 1945: Das Jahr der endgültigen Niederlage der faschistischen Wehrmacht,
pp. 346–8.

63. BAB, NS6/756, fos. 7–9, Vermerk für Chef der Sicherheitspolizei und des

SD, Parteifeindliche Einstellung der Wiener Arbeiterbevölkerung nach den Luftangriffen, 10.3.45. See also fos. 14–15 for a report dated the previous day by Gauleiter Ernst-Wilhelm Bohle, head of the Nazi Party's Auslandsorganisation, on his impressions of Hungarian women and other foreigners behaving as if Vienna were a holiday resort, and fos. 12–13 for an account sent to Walkenhorst on 2 April of the poor situation in the city and lack of leadership of the Wehrmacht and of the Party. See also *TBJG*, II/15, pp. 687, 693 (8–9.4.45). A brief indication of the collapse in Vienna as seen by the regime is provided by Karl Stadler, *Österreich 1938–1945 im Spiegel der NS-Akten*, Vienna, 1966, pp. 401–4. See also, for the rapidly worsening conditions and mounting problems for the Nazi leadership in Vienna in the weeks before the city fell, Rauchensteiner, pp. 154–7, 163–6.

64. *TBJG*, II/15, pp. 666, 680 (2.4.45, 4.4.45).

65. *TBJG*, II/15, pp. 683, 687, 693 (8.4.45, 9.4.45).

66. BAB, NS6/353, fo. 103, RS 211/45, 'Einsatzpflicht der Politischen Leiter', 15.4.45. A month earlier, referring to previous similar directives, Bormann (fo. 80, Rundschreiben 140/45, 'Persönlicher Einsatz der Hoheitsträger', 17.3.45) had exhorted high-standing representatives of the Party to cooperate with troops in assisting the population in the fighting zone and to set an example of fighting morale.

67. *TBJG*, II/15, p. 659 (1.4.45).

68. *TBJG*, II/15, p. 672 (4.4.45).

69. For example, despite their exhortations, accompanied by threats, to hold out, most of the Kreisleiter in Württemberg fled as Allied troops approached. – Christine Arbogast, *Herrschaftsinstanzen der württembergischen NSDAP: Funktion, Sozialprofil und Lebenswege einer regionalen Elite 1920–1960*, Munich, 1998, p. 260. One Kreisleiter from the Black Forest, who turned up in Munich to offer his services to the Party Chancellery, was immediately ordered to return to serve with the *Volkssturm* and warned that his arrival in an official car could be seen as nothing other than flight. – BAB, NS6/277, fo. 24, Aktenvermerk, 20.4.45.

70. IfZ, ZS 597, fo. 113 (1950); *TBJG*, II/15, p. 672 (4.4.45); Karl Höffkes, *Hitlers politische Generale: Die Gauleiter des Dritten Reiches. Ein biographisches Nachschlagewerk*, Tübingen, 1986, pp. 112–13. The Security Police had disbanded their office on 7 March, and, destroying records, fled in civilian clothes with false identity cards. – NAL, KV3/188, interrogation of Ostubf. Karl Hans Paul Hennicke, head of SD-Abschnitt Köln-Aachen, 11.4.45.

71. Ralf Blank, 'Albert Hoffmann als Reichsverteidigungskommissar im Gau Westfalen-Süd, 1943–1945: Eine biografische Skizze', in Wolf Gruner and Armin Nolzen (eds.), *'Bürokratien': Initiative und Effizienz. Beiträge zur Geschichte des Nationalsozialismus*, vol. 17, Berlin, 2001, pp. 201–2.

72. Ralf Meindl, *Ostpreußens Gauleiter: Erich Koch – eine politische Biographie*, Osnabrück, 2007, p. 452.

73. Wilfred von Oven, *Finale Furioso: Mit Goebbels bis zum Ende*, Tübingen, 1974, pp. 635–7 (12.4.45); Meindl, p. 455; Alastair Noble, *Nazi Rule and the Soviet Offensive in Eastern Germany, 1944–1945: The Darkest Hour*, Brighton and Portland, Ore., 2009, p. 240; Isabel Denny, *The Fall of Hitler's Fortress City: The Battle for Königsberg, 1945*, London, 2007, p. 230; Speer, p. 498. Whether, as Oven claimed (p. 636), Koch had influenced Hitler in condemning General Lasch, commander of Königsberg, to death *in absentia* for his 'cowardly' capitulation is doubted by Meindl, p. 454.

74. Höffkes, p. 24.

75. BAB, NS6/277, fos. 76–8 (17.4.45). Printed in Karl Kunze, *Kriegsende in Franken und der Kampf um Nürnberg im April 1945*, Nuremberg, 1995, pp. 217–19.

76. Kunze, pp. 243–4, 265, 283–5; Höffkes, p. 156. The local attempts of courageous individuals and groups of citizens in Central Franconia to prevent the mania of Nazi fanatics from bringing about the destruction of their towns can be seen in Hans Woller, *Gesellschaft und Politik in der amerikanischen Besatzungszone: Die Region Ansbach und Fürth*, Munich, 1986, pp. 46–57.

77. Ernst Hornig, *Breslau 1945: Erlebnisse in der eingeschlossenen Stadt*, Munich, 1975, pp. 129–31; Hans von Ahlfen and Hermann Niehoff, *So kämpfte Breslau: Verteidigung und Untergang von Schlesiens Hauptstadt*, Munich, 1959, p. 83; Friedrich Grieger, *Wie Breslau fiel . . .*, Metzingen, 1948, pp. 23–4; Joachim Konrad, 'Das Ende von Breslau', *VfZ*, 4 (1956), p. 388.

78. *TBJG*, II/15, pp. 692–3 (9.4.45). Höffkes, p. 122, dates the award to 12 April, though Goebbels refers to the granting of the honour already on 9 April.

79. BAB, R3/1625, fo. 2, Speer to Hanke, 14.4.45.

80. After his flight from Breslau, Hanke was captured on 6 May by Czech partisans, though not recognized, and was killed early the following month while trying to escape. – Höffkes, pp. 122–3; Michael D. Miller and Andreas Schulz (eds.), *Gauleiter: The Regional Leaders of the Nazi Party and their Deputies*, CD-ROM, n.d. (*c.* 2004), vol. 1.

81. BAB, NS6/353, fo. 151, Anordnung of Bormann to all Reichsleiter, Gauleiter and Verbändeführer, 1.4.45; also in IfZ, Fa-91/4, fo. 1099.

82. Ferdinand Stadlbauer, 'Die letzten Tage des Gauleiters Wächtler', *Waldmünchner Heimatbote*, 12 (1985), pp. 3–10; Höffkes, pp. 360–61; Joachim Lilla, *Die Stellvertretenden Gauleiter und die Vertretung der Gauleiter der NSDAP im 'Dritten Reich'*, Koblenz, 2003, pp. 100–101.

83. Text in *Justiz und NS-Verbrechen: Sammlung deutscher Strafurteile wegen*

nationalsozialistischer Tötungsverbrechen 1945–1966, Register, ed. C. F. Rüter and D. W. De Mildt, Amsterdam and Munich, 1998, p. 199; Klaus-Dietmar Henke, *Die amerikanische Besetzung Deutschlands*, Munich, 1995, p. 787. Himmler's draft of 29.3.45, and the OKW telex and draft sent to him, are in BA/MA, RH/20/19/196, fos. 103–5.

84. Reproduced in Fritz Nadler, *Eine Stadt im Schatten Streichers*, Nuremberg, 1969, p. 41; *Justiz und NS-Verbrechen, Register*, p. 199. Himmler's decree of the same day, ordering that 'every village and town will be defended and held with all possible means' is printed in *Justiz und NS-Verbrechen, Register*, p. 200 and in Rolf-Dieter Müller and Gerd R. Ueberschär, *Kriegsende 1945: Die Zerstörung des Deutschen Reiches*, Frankfurt am Main, 1994, p. 171.

85. See, for example, the good local study by Herfried Münkler, *Machtzerfall: Die letzten Tage des Dritten Reiches dargestellt am Beispiel der hessischen Kreisstadt Friedberg*, Berlin, 1985.

86. Heinz Petzold, 'Cottbus zwischen Januar und Mai 1945', in Werner Stang and Kurt Arlt (eds.), *Brandenburg im Jahr 1945*, Potsdam, 1995, pp. 121–4.

87. Norbert Buske (ed.), *Die kampflose Übergabe der Stadt Greifswald im April 1945*, Schwerin, 1993, pp. 15–30, 37.

88. Henke, pp. 843–4; Zimmermann, *Pflicht*, pp. 360, 363.

89. Paul Sauer, *Württemberg in der Zeit des Nationalsozialismus*, Ulm, 1975, pp. 492–4; Andreas Förschler, *Stuttgart 1945: Kriegsende und Neubeginn*, Gudensberg-Gleichen, 2004, pp. 8–19; Jill Stephenson, '"Resistance" to "No Surrender": Popular Disobedience in Württemberg in 1945', in Francis R. Nicosia and Lawrence D. Stokes (eds.), *Germans against Nazism*, Oxford and Providence, RI, 1990, pp. 357–8; Jill Stephenson, *Hitler's Home Front: Württemberg under the Nazis*, London, 2006, pp. 324–5.

90. Hildebrand Troll, 'Aktionen zur Kriegsbeendigung im Frühjahr 1945', in Martin Broszat, Elke Fröhlich and Anton Grossmann (eds.), *Bayern in der NS-Zeit*, vol. 4, Munich and Vienna, 1981, pp. 650–54; Fritz, pp. 140–49.

91. Serger, Böttcher and Ueberschär, pp. 255–7, diary entry of Gertrud Neumeister, 17.4.45.

92. See Henke, pp. 844–61; Fritz, ch. 5; Elisabeth Kohlhaas, '"Aus einem Haus, aus dem eine weiße Fahnen erscheint, sind alle männlichen Personen zu erschießen": Durchhalteterror und Gewalt gegen Zivilisten am Kriegsende 1945', in Cord Arendes, Edgar Wolfrum and Jörg Zedler (eds.), *Terror nach Innen: Verbrechen am Ende des Zweiten Weltkrieges*, Göttingen, 2006, pp. 51–79; Egbert Schwarz, 'Die letzten Tage des Dritten Reiches: Untersuchung zu Justiz und NS-Verbrechen in der Kriegsendphase März/April 1945', MA thesis, University of Düsseldorf, 1990, pp. 14–19, 23–7, 35–8 (a regional study of Northern Rhineland-Westphalia); and *DZW*, 6, pp. 652–4, for numerous examples.

93. Troll, p. 652; Fritz, p. 146.

94. *Zeitzeugen berichten . . . Schwäbisch Gmünd*, pp. 43, 49, 77, 83–4; *Justiz und NS-Verbrechen*, vol. 2, ed. Adelheid L. Rüter-Ehlermann and C. F. Rüter, Amsterdam, 1969, pp. 77–101; Albert Deible, *Krieg und Kriegsende in Schwäbisch Gmünd*, Schwäbisch Gmünd, 1954, pp. 26–8, 34–5, 66–8; Kohlhaas, p. 51.

95. *Justiz und NS-Verbrechen*, vol. 1, ed. Adelheid L. Rüter-Ehlermann and C. F. Rüter, Amsterdam, 1968, pp. 505–29; Henke, pp. 848–9; Kohlhaas, p. 51, has fourteen victims, though this figure must include those shot at but not actually hit. As in so many cases, the Kreisleiter had given the order 'to defend the town to the last drop of blood', whereas most people were wholly opposed to such a stance. – Robert Bauer, *Heilbronner Tagebuchblätter*, Heilbronn, 1949, p. 46. Drauz was executed in 1946, his main accomplice sentenced to fifteen years in a penitentiary. For Drauz, notable for his fanaticism, see also Stephenson, *Hitler's Home Front*, pp. 332–3.

96. *Justiz und NS-Verbrechen*, vol. 10, ed. Adelheid L. Rüter-Ehlermann, H. H. Fuchs and C. F. Rüter, Amsterdam, 1973, pp. 205–40; Henke, pp. 851–3.

97. BBC Archives, *The Nazis: A Warning from History* (1997), written and produced for BBC2 by Laurence Rees, interview of Walter Fernau by Detlef Siebert, n.d., *c.* 1997, roll 219, pp. 211, 213; roll 221, pp. 352–3. See also the book of the series: Laurence Rees, *The Nazis: A Warning from History*, London, 1997, pp. 232–4 and 247. Much of the lengthy interview (rolls 217–21, 403pp., in German, with English translation) gives Fernau's own account of the operation of Helm's 'flying court martial' and the trial and execution of Karl Weiglein. Fernau was sentenced in 1952 to six years in a penitentiary for his part in the affair (and in a further case).

98. Jürgen Zarusky, 'Von der Sondergerichtsbarkeit zum Endphasenterror: Loyalitätserzwingung und Rache am Widerstand im Zusammenbruch des NS-Regimes', in Arendes, Wolfrum and Zedler, pp. 116–17; Andreas Heusler, 'Die Eskalation des Terrors: Gewalt gegen ausländische Zwangsarbeiter in der Endphase des Zweiten Weltkrieges', in Arendes, Wolfrum and Zedler, p. 180.

99. Zarusky, p. 113.

100. For numerous cases of mass killing of prisoners in April 1945, see Gerhard Paul, '"Diese Erschießungen haben mich innerlich gar nicht mehr berührt": Die Kriegsendphasenverbrechen der Gestapo 1944/45', in Gerhard Paul and Klaus-Michael Mallmann (eds.), *Die Gestapo im Zweiten Weltkrieg: 'Heimatfront' und besetztes Europa*, Darmstadt, 2000, pp. 554–60.

101. Nikolaus Wachsmann, *Hitler's Prisons: Legal Terror in Nazi Germany*, New Haven and London, 2004, pp. 336–7.

102. Eberhard Kolb, 'Bergen-Belsen: Die Errichtung des Lagers Bergen-Belsen und

seine Funktion als "Aufenthaltslager" (1943/44)', in Martin Broszat (ed.), *Studien zur Geschichte der Konzentrationslager*, Stuttgart, 1970, p. 151; Eberhard Kolb, *Bergen-Belsen 1943 bis 1945*, Göttingen, 1985, pp. 47–51. For Himmler's orders, see Eberhard Kolb, *Bergen-Belsen: Geschichte des 'Aufenthaltslagers' 1943–1945*, Hanover, 1962, pp. 157–60.

103. Kolb, *Bergen-Belsen 1943 bis 1945*, p. 48; Katrin Greiser, *Die Todesmärsche von Buchenwald: Räumung, Befreiung und Spuren der Erinnerung*, Göttingen, 2008, p. 134.

104. Karin Orth, *Das System der nationalsozialistischen Konzentrationslager: Eine politische Organisationsgeschichte*, Hamburg, 1999, pp. 301–5, 308, 311–12; Peter Longerich, *Heinrich Himmler: Biographie*, Munich, 2008, p. 745.

105. Orth, p. 307.

106. Orth, pp. 307–8, 311; *IMT*, vol. 11, p. 450 (testimony of Rudolf Höß). The order to 'secure' the concentration camps in an emergency – presumed to be a prisoners' uprising – had been first issued on 17 June 1944, though this made no explicit mention of what should happen to the prisoners. – IfZ, Nbg-Dok., PS-3683, 'Sicherung der Konzentrationslager' (not in the published trial volumes), by which Himmler gave responsibility for security measures involving the concentration camps to the Higher SS and Police Leaders; Orth, p. 272. According to the testimony of Höß, this left up to them the question of whether a camp should be evacuated or handed over. In early 1945, with the approach of the enemy, the situation changed. In January and February 1945 commandants carried out new instructions to kill 'dangerous' prisoners. Himmler's agreement in March, with the intention of using Jews as pawns in possible negotiations with the western Allies, then temporarily blocked ideas of killing all concentration camp prisoners. – Orth, pp. 296–305. But in April there was another shift. The order indicating that there had been a reversion to the earlier stance was apparently issued on 18 April (not 14 April as often stated) and received in the camp at Flossenbürg the following day. A German text of this order has never surfaced, though its authenticity has been ascertained on the basis of several near contemporary partial translations. – Stanislav Zamecnik, '"Kein Häftling darf lebend in die Hände des Feindes fallen": Zur Existenz des Himmler-Befehls vom 14–18. April 1945', *Dachauer Hefte*, 1 (1985), pp. 219–31. See also *DZW*, 6, pp. 647–8.

107. *IMT*, vol. 11, p. 450 (Höß testimony); Orth, p. 312; Daniel Blatman, 'The Death-Marches and the Final Phase of Nazi Genocide', in Jane Caplan and Nikolaus Wachsmann (eds.), *Concentration Camps in Nazi Germany: The New Histories*, London and New York, 2010, p. 175; *DZW*, 6, pp. 647–8.

108. Orth, p. 307.

109. Orth, pp. 305–9. The conditions in Buchenwald during the final days and the liberation of the camp are vividly described by a prisoner at the time,

Eugen Kogon, *Der SS-Staat: Das System der deutschen Konzentrations-lager*, pb. edn., Munich, 1974, pp. 335–43.

110. Orth, pp. 312–28. The western Allies went to considerable lengths after the war to establish the precise routes of the marches, the numbers killed in each place they passed through, and the exact place of burial of those murdered. The extensive files are housed at the ITS, especially Bestand 'Tote' (83 boxes) and 'Evak' (9 boxes).

111. Greiser, p. 138.

112. Blatman, 'The Death-Marches and the Final Phase of Nazi Genocide', p. 174.

113. Unpublished 'Reminiscences' (1989) of Dr Michael Gero, Hamburg, pp. 111–12, most kindly sent to me by Mr George Burton, the son of one of the prisoners so casually and brutally murdered. What happened to the blond SS murderer is not known.

114. Blatman, 'The Death-Marches and the Final Phase of Nazi Genocide', pp. 176–7, 180–81.

115. Blatman, 'The Death-Marches and the Final Phase of Nazi Genocide', pp. 177–8; Daniel Jonah Goldhagen, *Hitler's Willing Executioners: Ordinary Germans and the Holocaust*, pb. edn., London, 1997, p. 364; Greiser, pp. 136, 140, concludes that, as regards Buchenwald prisoners, non-Jews were no less exposed to the torment than Jews were.

116. ITS, Tote 80, fo. 00044a, Celle, (1946–7), estimates the death toll from the bombing raid at a thousand prisoners. Later estimates have varied wildly, but the most likely assessments seem to be 400–500. – Bernhard Strebel, *Celle April 1945 Revisited*, Bielefeld, 2008, pp. 114–15.

117. Daniel Blatman, *Les Marches de la mort: La dernière étape du génocide nazi, été 1944–printemps 1945*, Paris, 2009, pp. 282–8 (quotation, p. 286). Strebel (whose book offers a careful assessment of the available evidence for the dire events in Celle) estimates (p. 115) around 200 victims of the massacre. See also *'Hasenjagd' in Celle: Das Massaker am 8. April 1945*, Celle, 2005, for eyewitness accounts and an assessment of how the town subsequently dealt with the memory of the massacre.

118. Blatman, *Les Marches de la mort*, pp. 318–61; Joachim Neander, *Das Konzentrationslager 'Mittelbau' in der Endphase der nationalsozialistischen Diktatur*, Clausthal-Zellerfeld, 1997, pp. 466–77; Joachim Neander, *Gardelegen 1945: Das Ende der Häftlingstransporte aus dem Konzentrationslager 'Mittelbau'*, Magdeburg, 1998, pp. 27–35, 40–45; Diana Gring, 'Das Massaker von Gardelegen', *Dachauer Hefte*, 20 (2004), pp. 112–26; Goldhagen, pp. 367–8; Robert Gellately, *Backing Hitler: Consent and Coercion in Nazi Germany*, Oxford, 2001, p. 246; DZW, 6, p. 648.

119. Zentrale Stelle der Landesjustizverwaltungen, Ludwigsburg, IV 409 AR-Z/78/72, fos. 1192, 1234; IV 409 AR-Z/105/72 I fo. 96. I am grateful for these references to Dr Simone Erpel.

120. Both quotations in Greiser, p. 258. A fourteen-year-old boy on the march from Flossenbürg in mid-April recalled that 'most Germans regard us prisoners as criminals'. – Heinrich Demerer, 'Erinnerungen an den Todesmarsch aus dem KZ Flossenbürg', *Dachauer Hefte*, 25 (2009), p. 154.

121. Goldhagen, p. 365, and p. 587 n. 23; Simone Erpel, *Zwischen Vernichtung und Befreiung: Das Frauen-Konzentrationslager Ravensbrück in der letzten Kriegsphase*, Berlin, 2005, pp. 176-7.

122. Cited Blatman, *Les Marches de la mort*, p. 286.

123. ITS, Tote 83, Hütten, fo. 00011a–b (1.4.46, though the evidence is weakened by the fact that the former mayor and Wehrmacht officer were signatories to the report).

124. ITS, Tote 4, Altendorf, fos. 00088a–00099b (July 1947).

125. Some instances are presented in Greiser, pp. 259-75, and in Delia Müller and Madlen Lepschies, *Tage der Angst und der Hoffnung: Erinnerungen an die Todesmärsche aus dem Frauen-Konzentrationslager Ravensbrück Ende April 1945*, Berlin, n.d., pp. 56-7, 87, 89-90. Heinrich Demerer recalled sympathetic faces among civilians watching the marching prisoners and frequently being given bread by civilians, though he thought it was because he was so small, since the other prisoners received virtually nothing as they passed by. – Demerer, pp. 152, 154. Memories of the Ravensbrück death marches provide instances where children at the time recollected their parents putting water and boiled potatoes on the streets for prisoners. The former prisoners themselves, on the other hand, recall, not such instances of aid, but the rejection of the bystanders. – Simone Erpel, 'Machtverhältnisse im Zerfall: Todesmärsche der Häftlinge des Frauen-Konzentrationslagers Ravensbrück im April 1945', in Jörg Hillmann and John Zimmermann (eds.), *Kriegsende 1945 in Deutschland*, Munich, 2002, p. 198.

126. Blatman, 'The Death-Marches and the Final Phase of Nazi Genocide', p. 180; and see Goldhagen, p. 365.

127. Ardsley Microfilms, Irving Collection, Reel 1, R97481, Göring interrogation, 24.5.45.

128. This is the speculation of Rolf-Dieter Müller in *DRZW*, 10/2, pp. 102-4. Speer acknowledged in his post-war trial that he still had conflicting feelings and was after all that had happened even now ready to place himself at Hitler's disposal. – *IMT*, vol. 16, p. 582. Schmidt, pp. 162-3, suggests that Speer sought to influence Hitler to appoint Dönitz as his successor, in the expectation that he himself would play an important role in the administration.

129. Speer, pp. 487-8.

130. BAB, NS19/3118, fo. 3, Himmler's order of 24.1.45, reminding SS men of Hitler's order of 25.11.44 (fo. 2) on required behaviour of officers, NCOs and men 'in an apparently hopeless situation'.

131. Von Oven, pp. 647, 650 (19–20.4.45).
132. Von Oven, pp. 646–7 (18.4.45). Goebbels had also ensured that his diaries had been copied onto glass plates in an early form of microfiche. – *TBJG*, Register, Teil III, Elke Fröhlich, 'Einleitung zur Gesamtedition', pp. 37–47. His posthumous image was much on Goebbels' mind at this time. Speaking to his staff on 17 April and referring to the new colour film *Kolberg*, which had been produced to bolster willingness to hold out and defy the odds, the Propaganda Minister reportedly stated: 'Gentlemen, in a hundred years' time they will be showing another fine colour film describing the terrible days we are living through. Don't you want to play a part in this film, to be brought back to life in a hundred years' time? Everybody now has the chance to choose the part which he will play in the film a hundred years hence. I can assure you it will be a fine and elevating picture. And for the sake of this prospect it is worth standing fast. Hold out now, so that a hundred years hence the audience does not hoot and whistle when you appear on the screen.' The fifty or so men who heard this did not know whether to laugh or swear. – Semmler, p. 194 (17.4.45).
133. Von Oven, pp. 652–4 (22.4.45). See also Semmler, pp. 185–6 (25.2.45). According to the former Gauleiter of Süd-Hannover-Braunschweig, Hartmann Lauterbacher, *Erlebt und mitgestaltet*, Preußisch Oldendorf, 1984, p. 320, Goebbels told him at their last meeting, on 12 April, that all six of the children had cyanide capsules knitted into their clothes so that none of them could fall alive into the hands of the Russians.
134. Ruth Andreas-Friedrich, *Schauplatz Berlin: Ein deutsches Tagebuch*, Munich, 1962, p. 166 (21.4.45).
135. *DZW*, 6, p. 707.
136. BA/MA, NL Heinrici, NL265/108, fos. 11–15, 39–40, 54 (15.5.45).
137. *DZW*, 6, p. 734.
138. BA/MA, NL Heinrici, NL265/108, fos. 52–7 (15.5.45).
139. BA/MA, NL Heinrici, NL265/108, fos. 22–5, 39–41 (15.5.45).
140. BA/MA, NL Heinrici, NL265/108, fo. 29 (15.5.45).
141. *DZW*, 6, pp. 705–26, *DRZW*, 10/1 (Lakowski), pp. 656–73, Erickson, pp. 577–618, and Beevor, ch. 21, provide detailed descriptions of the battle of Berlin.
142. Jodl admitted this to Colonel-General Heinrici on 13 May 1945. – BA/MA, NL Heinrici, N265/108, fos. 57–8 (15.5.45).
143. Steiner had well-warranted reasons for not undertaking the attack and was despairing at being given an order which was, as all with any insight into the position knew, impossible to carry out. See BA/MA, NL Heinrici, N265/108, fos. 19–22 (15.4.45).
144. The uncertainty, also regarding Göring's position, produced by Hitler's breakdown is plainly summarized in the report sent three days later to

Hitler by General Karl Koller, Chief of Staff of the Luftwaffe. – IWM, EDS, F.3, AL 1985 (2), 'An den Führer. Bericht über die wesentlichen Punkte der Vorgänge am 22.4. und meiner Meldung an den Herrn Reichsmarschall am 23.4.' (25.4.45). A brief description of Hitler's remarks, recorded by an eyewitness, Oberleutnant Hans Volck, adjutant to the Luftwaffe Operations Staff, is in IWM, EDS, F.3, AL 1985 (1), 'Meldung über Führerlage am 22.4.1945. Lagebeginn: etwa 15.30 Uhr' (25.4.45). There are minor discrepancies between Koller's report and his subsequent publication, Karl Koller, *Der letzte Monat: Die Tagebuchaufzeichnungen des ehemaligen Chefs des Generalstabes der deutschen Luftwaffe vom 14. April bis zum 27. Mai 1945*, Mannheim, 1949, pp. 28–32.

145. Speer, pp. 479, 484.
146. BA/MA, NL Heinrici, N265/108, fos. 38–9 (15.4.45).
147. BA/MA, NL Heinrici, N265/108, fos. 41–4 (15.4.45).
148. IfZ, ZS 145, Bd. III, Schwerin von Krosigk, fo. 61 (7.12.62).
149. IfZ, ZS 988, Friedrich Wilhelm Kritzinger, interrogation by Dr Robert Kempner, fos. 4, 7, 10 (5.3.47).
150. Krosigk wrote to Speer on 29 March, in the framework of discussions over 'scorched earth', suggesting that intensified Allied bombing had been caused by the desire not to let German industry fall into Soviet hands, and that the more Germany's industrial potential was preserved the greater the bargaining position with the west would be. On 6 April, urgently seeking a meeting with Goebbels, he pressed for action to create the conditions for Britain to break away from the enemy coalition, which he thought was eminently possible. He wrote again to Goebbels on 14 April, describing Roosevelt's death as a 'present from God' that had to be actively exploited, recommending an approach from the Pope to America, which, he claimed, had an interest in German industry as a barrier to a strengthened Soviet state. – All in IWM, EDS, F.3, M.I. 14/369.
151. IfZ, ZS 145, Bd. III, Schwerin von Krosigk, fos. 58–61 (7.12.62).
152. StAA, Gauleitung Schwaben, 1/29, fo. 328836, file note, presumably for Gauleiter Wahl, 20.4.45.
153. StAA, Gauleitung Schwaben, 1/37, unfoliated, note of telephone call from the Kreisleiter of Lindau, n.d., c. 24–6.4.45. Lindau, where reports suggested that up to 60 per cent of the population could be seen as pro-Nazi, remained a trouble spot for the French occupying authorities (in a region that gave them some security headaches) for some weeks after the end of the war. There were some disturbances, cases of apparent arson, and a French officer was shot dead by a fourteen-year-old former member of the Hitler Youth. Much of the town's population was for a short time forcibly evacuated and only allowed to return, two days later, after grovelling pleas for clemency. French troops arriving in the meantime had ransacked much

of the empty town. The whole affair was an embarrassment to the French, and shocked American and Swiss observers. – Perry Biddiscome, *Werwolf! The History of the National Socialist Guerrilla Movement 1944–1946*, Toronto and Buffalo, NY, 1998, pp. 260–63.

154. *Justiz und NS-Verbrechen*, vol. 2, pp. 236–52; IfZ, ED 195, Slg. Schottenheim, vol. 1, pp. 87–91 (written to show the author, Dr Otto Schottenheim, a doctor and the Nazi mayor of Regensburg since 1933, in the best light); Henke, p. 854; Dieter Albrecht, 'Regensburg in der NS-Zeit', in Dieter Albrecht (ed.), *Zwei Jahrtausende Regensburg*, Regensburg, 1979, p. 200, also for Ruckdeschel quotation: 'Regensburg wird verteidigt werden bis zum letzten Stein.' For Schottenheim, who died in 1980 an honoured citizen despite his Nazi past, see Helmut Halter, *Stadt unterm Hakenkreuz: Kommunalpolitik in Regensburg während der NS-Zeit*, Regensburg, 1994, pp. 77–87, and Albrecht, pp. 195–6. Ruckdeschel was sentenced in 1948 for his part in the Regensburg killings to eight years in a penitentiary (a sentence extended to thirteen years in a further trial the following year for ordering the execution of a civilian in Landshut on 29 April 1945). – *Justiz und NS-Verbrechen*, vol. 2, pp. 234–346; *Justiz und NS-Verbrechen*, vol. 3, ed. Adelheid L. Rüter-Ehlermann and C. F. Rüter, Amsterdam, 1969, pp. 763–94. Ruckdeschel died peacefully in Wolfsburg in 1986. – Miller and Schulz, vol. 1.

155. Troll, pp. 660–71; Henke, pp. 854–61; Heike Bretschneider, *Der Widerstand gegen den Nationalsozialismus in München 1933–1945*, Munich, 1968, pp. 218–39; Klaus Tenfelde, 'Proletarische Provinz: Radikalisierung und Widerstand in Penzberg/Oberbayern 1900 bis 1945', in Broszat, Fröhlich and Grossmann, vol. 4, pp. 374–81; Georg Lorenz, *Die Penzberger Mordnacht vom 28. April 1945 vor dem Richter*, Garmisch-Partenkirchen, 1948, pp. 5–11; *Justiz und NS-Verbrechen*, vol. 3, pp. 100–101; *Justiz und NS-Verbrechen*, vol. 13, ed. Irene Sagel-Grande, H. H. Fuchs, and C. F. Rüter, Amsterdam, 1975, pp. 532–40. A sixteenth victim was shot 'while in flight'. – Tenfelde, pp. 378, 380. The post-war trials relating to the murders in Altötting and Munich are in StAM, Staatsanwaltschaften 34876/25 (Altötting) and StAM, Staatsanwaltschaften 6571, 18848/2–3, 'Fall Salisco' (Munich). For an assessment of varied forms of resistance towards the end of the war, see Edgar Wolfrum, 'Widerstand in den letzten Kriegsmonaten', in Peter Steinbach and Johannes Tuchel (eds.), *Widerstand gegen den Nationalsozialismus*, Bonn, 1994, pp. 537–52. The Penzberg mine was not destroyed at the end of the war, and ceased production only in 1966. – Tenfelde, p. 382.

156. *Das letzte halbe Jahr*, p. 334 (10.4.45).

157. BA/MA, N648/1, NL Dethleffsen, Erinnerungen, fo. 39.

158. Ingrid Hammer and Susanne zur Nieden (eds.), *Sehr selten habe ich*

geweint: Briefe und Tagebücher aus dem Zweiten Weltkrieg von Menschen aus Berlin, Zurich, 1992, p. 358 (23.4.45).

159. Anonyma: *Eine Frau in Berlin. Tagebuch-Aufzeichnungen vom 20. April bis 22. Juni 1945*, pb. edn., Munich, 2008, p. 30 (23.4.45).

160. Anonyma, pp. 9–15, 20, 24–5, 34, 39 (20–25.4.45).

161. *VB*, Munich edn., 20, 24, 25.4.45.

162. Anonyma, pp. 19–20 (21.4.45), 30 (23.4.45), 43 (26.4.45); Kronika, pp. 138, 152–3 (23.4.45).

163. Andreas-Friedrich, pp. 166–7 (21.4.45).

164. 'Full of anxiety we went back into the cellar and awaited what might come,' noted one diarist. – Hammer and zur Nieden, p. 364 (26.4.45)

165. Longerich, pp. 750–51; Peter Padfield, *Himmler: Reichsführer-SS*, London, 1990, pp. 593–8.

166. *KTB/SKL*, part A, vol. 68, p. 416A, Beitrag zum Kriegstagebuch Skl. am 2. Mai 1945; Heereslage vom 1.5.45; Anton Joachimsthaler, *Hitlers Ende: Legenden und Dokumente*, Munich, 1999, pp. 282–3.

CHAPTER 9. LIQUIDATION

1. Kathrin Orth, 'Kampfmoral und Einsatzbereitschaft in der Kriegsmarine 1945', in Jörg Hillmann and John Zimmermann (eds.), *Kriegsende 1945 in Deutschland*, Munich, 2002, p. 141.

2. BfZ, Sammlung Sterz, Tagebuch Uffz. Heinrich V., 2.5.45.

3. BA/MA, NL Schörner, N60/18, unfoliated, Tagesbefehl, 3.5.45.

4. Cited in Richard Bessel, *Germany 1945: From War to Peace*, London, 2009, p. 141.

5. BA/MA, N245/3, fo. 88, NL Reinhardt, Kalenderblätter for 1.5.45. The news of Hitler's death also came as no surprise to Colonel-General Lothar Rendulić when he heard it on 1 May in Austria. Discipline among his troops was unaffected, though Hitler's death was seen to improve the prospects of a political way out through cooperation with the west. – Lothar Rendulić, *Gekämpft, Gesiegt, Geschlagen*, Wels, 1952, p. 378.

6. BA/MA, N648/1, NL Dethleffsen, Erinnerungen, fo. 57.

7. Sönke Neitzel, *Abgehört: Deutsche Generäle in britischer Kriegsgefangenschaft 1942–1945*, Berlin, 2005, pp. 210–12 (Eng. language edn., *Tapping Hitler's Generals: Transcripts of Secret Conversations, 1942–45*, Barnsley, 2007, pp. 156–8).

8. Marlis Steinert, *Hitlers Krieg und die Deutschen*, Düsseldorf and Vienna, 1970, p. 582.

9. BfZ, Sammlung Sterz, Tagebuch Eveline B., 6.5.45. Erich Kästner, *Notabene 1945: Ein Tagebuch*, Berlin, 1961, p. 116 (2.5.45), remarked that

people were greeting each other jokingly with 'Heil Dönitz'. The accordion-player had changed, he commented, but the tune was the same.

10. Cited Bessel, p. 141.

11. Ruth Andreas-Friedrich, *Schauplatz Berlin: Ein deutsches Tagebuch*, Munich, 1962, pp. 188–9 (2.5.45).

12. Jörg Echternkamp (ed.), *Kriegsschauplatz Deutschland 1945: Leben in Angst – Hoffnung auf Frieden. Feldpost aus der Heimat und von der Front*, Paderborn, 2006, p. 252, letter from Gerda J., Hamburg/Altona, 7.7.45. This was only an inspired guess at what had happened. Precise details of Hitler's suicide were not known at this time beyond the small circle of those directly involved in the last drama in the bunker.

13. *Anonyma: Eine Frau in Berlin. Tagebuch-Aufzeichnungen vom 20. April bis 22. Juni 1945*, pb. edn., Munich, 2008, p. 143 (5.5.45).

14. *Die Niederlage 1945: Aus dem Kriegstagebuch des Oberkommandos der Wehrmacht*, ed. Percy Ernst Schramm, Munich, 1962, p. 419.

15. Herbert Kraus, 'Karl Dönitz und das Ende des "Dritten Reiches"', in Hans-Erich Volkmann (ed.), *Ende des Dritten Reiches – Ende des Zweiten Weltkriegs: Eine perspektivische Rückschau*, Munich and Zurich, 1995, p. 11.

16. Herbert Kraus, 'Großadmiral Karl Dönitz', in Gerd R. Ueberschär (ed.), *Hitlers militärische Elite*, vol. 2: *Vom Kriegsbeginn bis zum Weltkriegsende*, Darmstadt, 1998, p. 51.

17. *Die Niederlage 1945*, p. 419.

18. *DRZW*, 10/1 (Rahn), p. 61.

19. Jürgen Förster, 'Die Wehrmacht und das Ende des "Dritten Reichs"', in Arnd Bauerkämper, Christoph Kleßmann and Hans Misselwitz (eds.), *Der 8. Mai 1945 als historische Zäsur: Strukturen, Erfahrung, Deutungen*, Potsdam, 1995, p. 57.

20. Kraus, 'Karl Dönitz und das Ende des "Dritten Reiches"', pp. 3–4, 8–11.

21. Heinrich Schwendemann, '"Deutsche Menschen vor der Vernichtung durch den Bolschewismus zu retten": Das Programm der Regierung Dönitz und der Beginn einer Legendenbildung', in Hillmann and Zimmermann, p. 16.

22. BA/MA, N648/1, NL Dethleffsen, Erinnerungen, fo. 57.

23. Quoted in *DRZW*, 10/1 (Rahn), p. 55; see also, for Dönitz's unquestioning loyalty to Hitler and his fanatical exhortations to fight on, pp. 57–60, 67.

24. IfZ, ZS 145, Schwerin von Krosigk, Bd. III, fo. 62, 7.12.62.

25. *KTB/SKL*, part A, vol. 68, pp. 333–4-A, Kriegstagebuch des Ob. d. M., 25.4.45. Dönitz had already a week earlier, at the Soviet breakthrough on the Oder front, provided naval forces for the fight on land. – Schwendemann, pp. 14–15.

26. BA/MA, RM7/851, Seekriegsleitung, fo. 169, Hitler to Dönitz, 29.4.45; Schwendemann, p. 15.

27. *Hitler: Reden und Proklamationen 1932–1945*, ed. Max Domarus, Wiesbaden, 1973, p. 2237.

28. Major-General Dethleffsen recalled shortly after the war his own lack of surprise since he had heard hints earlier in April from the Chief of the General Staff, Hans Krebs, that Dönitz was being viewed by Hitler as his successor. Others, however, according to Dethleffsen, were more taken by surprise at the appointment. – BA/MA, N648/1, NL Dethleffsen, Erinnerungen, fo. 57.

29. IWM, FO645/155, interrogation of Karl Dönitz, 12.9.45, pp. 19–20.

30. Karl Dönitz, *Memoirs: Ten Years and Twenty Days*, Da Capo edn., New York, 1997, p. 442.

31. See Rolf-Dieter Müller and Gerd R. Ueberschär, *Kriegsende 1945: Die Zerstörung des Deutschen Reiches*, Frankfurt am Main, 1994, p. 101 and Kraus, 'Karl Dönitz und das Ende des "Dritten Reiches"', pp. 9, 11. It has, however, been suggested – if without supporting evidence – that Dönitz's presumption that Hitler wanted him to pave the way for a capitulation might have been gleaned before the Grand-Admiral left for Plön, or from conversations with Himmler. – Jörg Hillmann, 'Die "Reichsregierung" in Flensburg', in Hillmann and Zimmermann, p. 41. Hitler's desperate comment, during his temporary breakdown on 22 April, that there was no more fighting to be done – a view he swiftly revised – and that should it come to negotiations Göring would be better than he was, can scarcely be regarded as evidence for a mandate to come to terms with the enemy at his death. See Reimer Hansen, *Das Ende des Dritten Reiches: Die deutsche Kapitulation 1945*, Stuttgart, 1966, pp. 48–50; Walter Lüdde-Neurath, *Regierung Dönitz: Die letzten Tage des Dritten Reiches*, 5th edn., Leoni am Starnberger See, 1981, p. 46; Marlis Steinert, *Die 23 Tage der Regierung Dönitz*, Düsseldorf and Vienna, 1967, p. 45.

32. *DRZW*, 10/1 (Zimmermann), pp. 469–70; *DRZW*, 9/1 (Förster), p. 626; Schwendemann, p. 15.

33. See Hitler's Testament: *Hitler: Reden und Proklamationen*, p. 2237 (not, however, known to Dönitz at the time).

34. Schwendemann, pp. 27–8.

35. IWM, FO645/158, interrogation of Wilhelm Keitel, 10.10.45, p. 27.

36. IfZ, ZS 1810, Großadmiral Karl Dönitz, Bd. II, fo. 55, interview for the *Observer*, 18.11.74.

37. One woman in Berlin wrote as late as 21 May that 'there is still no certain news about Adolf'. – *Anonyma*, p. 221.

38. See Christian Goeschel, 'Suicide at the End of the Third Reich', *Journal of Contemporary History*, 41 (2006), pp. 153–73, and Goeschel's monograph, *Suicide in Nazi Germany*, Oxford, 2009, ch. 5, for extensive analysis of the phenomenon. See also Richard J. Evans, *The Third Reich at War*, London, 2008, pp. 728–33.

39. Goeschel, *Suicide in Nazi Germany*, pp. 153–4.
40. Joseph Goebbels, *Tagebücher 1945: Die letzten Aufzeichnungen*, Hamburg, 1977, pp. 549, 556.
41. *Hitler: Reden und Proklamationen*, p. 2237.
42. Goeschel, 'Suicide at the End of the Third Reich', p. 155.
43. *MadR*, 17, p. 6737.
44. Goeschel, 'Suicide at the End of the Third Reich', p. 158; Jacob Kronika, *Der Untergang Berlins*, Flensburg, 1946, p. 41 (6.3.45): 'Alle Berliner wissen, daß die Russen in Kürze in Berlin eindringen werden – und nun sehen sie keine andere Möglichkeit, als sich Zyankali zu verschaffen.'
45. *Anonyma*, pp. 171, 174 (9.5.45), 207 (17.5.45); Goeschel, 'Suicide at the End of the Third Reich', p. 160; Goeschel, *Suicide in Nazi Germany*, pp. 158–9.
46. Goeschel, 'Suicide at the End of the Third Reich', pp. 162–3 and n. 57.
47. Goeschel, 'Suicide at the End of the Third Reich', p. 169.
48. Klaus-Dietmar Henke, *Die amerikanische Besetzung Deutschlands*, Munich, 1995, pp. 964–5; and see Goeschel, 'Suicide at the End of the Third Reich', pp. 169–70.
49. 'Tief vergraben, nicht dran rühren', *Spiegel Special*, 2 (2005), p. 218. I am most grateful to Klaus Wiegrefe and Michael Kloft for this reference. See also for the atmosphere of panic and numerous suicides, many out of fear of being raped by soldiers of the Red Army, Joachim Schulz-Naumann, *Mecklenburg 1945*, Munich, 1989, pp. 161, 165, 173, 241–2 (accounts given in the 1980s).
50. Based on the recollections of the events in 'Tief vergraben, nicht dran rühren', Norbert Buske, *Das Kriegsende 1945 in Demmin: Berichte, Erinnerungen, Dokumente*, Schwerin, 1995, pp. 9–14, 17–40, 43, 44 n. 3, 48–50, nn. 27–39; and the eyewitness account of Waltraud Reski (née Gülzow), interviewed by Tilman Remme, in BBC Archives, *The Nazis: A Warning from History* (1997), written and produced for BBC2 by Laurence Rees, roll 263, pp. 1–42 (quotation, p. 29). See also Goeschel, 'Suicide at the End of the Third Reich', p. 166.
51. *Die Niederlage 1945*, p. 420.
52. BA/MA, N54/8, NL Keitel, 'Die letzten Tage unter Adolf Hitler', fo. 19.
53. *Die Niederlage 1945*, p. 447 (16.5.45); *1945: Das Jahr der endgültigen Niederlage der faschistischen Wehrmacht. Dokumente*, ed. Gerhard Förster and Richard Lakowski, Berlin, 1975, pp. 422–5.
54. Hillmann, pp. 46–7; *DZW*, 6, p. 770; *Die Niederlage 1945*, pp. 429–30 (5.5.45).
55. BA/MA, N54/8, NL Keitel, 'Die letzten Tage unter Adolf Hitler', fo. 19.
56. IfZ, ZS 145, Schwerin von Krosigk, Bd. I, fo. 24, Eidesstattliche Erklärung, Nuremberg 1.4.49 im Spruchverfahren gegen Ernst Wilhelm Bohle.
57. IfZ, ZS 145, Schwerin von Krosigk, Bd. III, fo. 62, 7.12.62.

58. *Die Niederlage 1945*, pp. 431–2, Dönitz-Tagebuch, Tagesniederschrift 6.5.45; IfZ, ZS 145, Schwerin von Krosigk, Bd. III, fo. 62, 7.12.62.

59. Hillmann, pp. 5–7. Dönitz had initially wanted to change the leadership of the Wehrmacht. He and Krosigk agreed that Keitel and Jodl would be dismissed and replaced by Field-Marshal Erich von Manstein as the new head of the Wehrmacht. But the whereabouts of Manstein (according to one version) could not be located. – Walter Baum, 'Der Zusammenbruch der obersten deutschen militärischen Führung 1945', *Wehrwissenschaftliche Rundschau*, 10 (1960), p. 255. In another account, Manstein said he had been summoned by the OKW to meet Dönitz without being given a reason. He could not attend that day and heard no more about it. Dönitz told Krosigk that Manstein had declined to take over from Keitel, which was not the case. – Lutz Graf Schwerin von Krosigk, *Es geschah in Deutschland*, Tübingen and Stuttgart, 1951, p. 374.

60. IfZ, ZS 145, Schwerin von Krosigk, Bd. III, fo. 62ᵛ, 7.12.62; Schwendemann, p. 18.

61. IfZ, ZS 1810, Großadmiral Karl Dönitz, Bd. II, fos. 60–61, 'Letzte Kriegszeit als Ob.d.M. Zeit als Staatsoberhaupt', no date; Lüdde-Neurath, pp. 81–2.

62. Müller and Ueberschär, p. 103. Major-General Dethleffsen recalled some months later (BA/MA, N648/1, NL Dethleffsen, Erinnerungen, fo. 57) that he had been unable to resist pointing out to the NSFO of Army Group Vistula on hearing the news of Hitler's death that he should think overnight of a new form of greeting since 'Heil Hitler' was now out of date. The thought turned out to be a little premature.

63. *DZW*, 6, p. 776, lists some of the sentences by military courts and the executions that followed.

64. IWM, EDS, H1, 2.5.45. Printed in *1945: Das Jahr der endgültigen Niederlage der faschistischen Wehrmacht*, pp. 361–4. When Dönitz had consulted Ribbentrop about a new Foreign Minister, the latter had been able to think of no one more suitable for the post than himself. – Lüdde-Neurath, p. 82.

65. The 'Tagesniederschriften', taken down by Dönitz's adjutant, Korvettenkapitän Walter Lüdde-Neurath, exist in BA/MA, N374/8, NL Friedeburg with copies in IWM, EDS, F.3, AL2893. They are quoted here from the printed version in *Die Niederlage 1945*, p. 421 (2.5.45). Hillmann sees Dönitz's attempt to work through partial capitulations as continuity rather than 'a new characteristic of policy', since most of Hitler's paladins had at one time or another tried to gain a 'separate peace' or partial capitulation. This overlooks the fact that, before Hitler's death, such actions remained 'unofficial', undertaken behind his back, or were blocked at the outset, whereas once Dönitz became head of state they became overnight official policy. – Hillmann, pp. 48–9. Dönitz repeated in a statement soon after the end of the war that he

regarded an immediate total capitulation as impossible for Germany. The horror at what the Soviets had done was so strong that an immediate general capitulation, abandoning the soldiers in the east and the refugee civilian population to the Red Army, 'would have been a crime against my German people', and the order would not have been followed by German troops, who would have continued to try to fight their way to the west. – IfZ, ZS 1810, Karl Dönitz, Bd. II, 'Kriegsende 1945', 22.7.45, fo. 3.

66. *DZW*, 6, p. 426.
67. NAL, Premier 3/221/12, nos. 3736–7, fos. 413–15, Churchill to Eden, 16.4.45, fos. 392–3, Eisenhower to Combined Chiefs of Staff, 23.4.45, fo. 361, Eisenhower to Combined Chiefs of Staff, 1.5.45. See also Bob Moore, 'The Western Allies and Food Relief to the Occupied Netherlands, 1944–45', *War and Society*, 10 (1992), pp. 106–9. I am grateful to Bob Moore for providing me with these references.
68. *Die Niederlage 1945*, pp. 421 (2.5.45), 425 (3.5.45); BAB, R3/1625, fos. 4–5, Blaskowitz to Lüdde-Neurath, n.d. (30.4.45; the original telex in BA/MA, RM7/854, fo. 177, has no date, though 30.4 is pencilled in the top right-hand corner); Seyß-Inquart 'an den Führer' (i.e. to Dönitz), 2.5.45. For Blaskowitz's stance in the last days of the war, see John Zimmermann, *Pflicht zum Untergang: Die deutsche Kriegführung im Westen des Reiches 1944/45*, Paderborn, 2009, pp. 340–41.
69. Keitel pointed out that the news took Dönitz by surprise but that he supported it. – BA/MA, N54/8, NL Keitel, 'Die letzten Tage unter Adolf Hitler', fo. 20.
70. BA/MA, N574/19, NL Vietinghoff, 'Kriegsende in Italien' (1948), fo. 45; also Förster, p. 56.
71. BA/MA, N574/19, NL Vietinghoff, 'Kriegsende in Italien' (1948), fos. 53–4.
72. IWM, EDS, F.3, M.I. 14/284 (A), Kaltenbrunner to Hitler, 1.5.45.
73. *DZW*, 6, pp. 152–3.
74. BA/MA, N574/19, NL Vietinghoff, 'Kriegsende in Italien', fos. 56–9.
75. IWM, EDS, F.3, M.I. 14/284 (A), Kesselring to Dönitz, Keitel and Deputy Chief, Wehrmacht Operations Staff, General Winter, 2.5.45.
76. BA/MA, N574/19, NL Vietinghoff, 'Kriegsende in Italien' (1948), fos. 60–62. For Kesselring's account, see *The Memoirs of Field-Marshal Kesselring*, Greenhill Books edn., London, 1997, pp. 288–9. See also, for the capitulation in Italy, *DZW*, 6, pp. 749–52; *DRZW*, 10/1 (Zimmermann), p. 472.
77. BA/MA, RW44II/3, fo. 20, Winter to Jodl, 2.5.45.
78. *Die Niederlage 1945*, p. 423 (2.5.45); Schwendemann, p. 18.
79. BA/MA, RM7/854, fo. 13, for Dönitz's order for the capitulation of the city, issued the previous day, 2 May.
80. BA/MA, RM7/854, fos. 33, 36, reports of Kdr. Adm. Deutsche Bucht,

4.5.45. Serious disintegration within the 3rd Panzer Army in Mecklenburg had already been reported on 27 April by General Hasso von Manteuffel, who spoke of scenes which he had not even seen in 1918. – *1945: Das Jahr der endgültigen Niederlage der faschistischen Wehrmacht*, pp. 343–4; *DRZW*, 10/1 (Lakowski), p. 655.

81. *Die Niederlage 1945*, p. 429 (5.5.45); BA/MA, RM7/854, fo. 24, for the earlier confirmation order of 3.5.45 to scuttle ships. A directive had already been issued on 30 April that 'in the event of an unforeseen development of the situation' on the codeword 'Rainbow', all ships, including U-boats, were immediately to be sunk. The demand to hand over all weapons, including U-boats, was seen by Keitel and Jodl as incompatible with German honour. Dönitz accepted the demand only with extreme reluctance. Some 185 U-boats were, in fact, scuttled by their commanders with the Dönitz administration turning a blind eye, before the order to hand them over could take effect. – *KTB/SKL*, part A, vol. 68, p. 421A, Funksprüche der Skl., 3.5.45; Lutz Graf Schwerin von Krosigk, 'Persönliche Erinnerungen', part 2: '25 Jahre Berlin 1920 bis 1945', unpublished typescript, n.d., p. 324; *DRZW*, 10/1 (Rahn), pp. 166–7.

82. *DZW*, 6, p. 742. This figure includes SS and OT members. Howard D. Grier, *Hitler, Dönitz and the Baltic Sea: The Third Reich's Last Hope, 1944–1945*, Annapolis, Md., 2007, p. 218, has a Wehrmacht strength of 350,000 troops.

83. *Die Niederlage 1945*, pp. 423 (3.5.45), 426–7 (4.5.45), 430 (5.5.45); *DRZW*, 10/1 (Zimmermann), pp. 472–4; *DZW*, 6, pp. 773–4; Albert Speer, *Erinnerungen*, Frankfurt am Main and Berlin, 1969, pp. 496–7; Schwendemann, pp. 18–19.

84. BA/MA, RM7/854, fo. 117, Chef OKW, 6.5.45.

85. *Die Niederlage 1945*, p. 425 (3.5.45).

86. *Die Niederlage 1945*, p. 432 (6.5.45); *DRZW*, 10/1 (Zimmermann), pp. 474–5; *DZW*, 6, p. 758; Müller and Ueberschär, pp. 102–3; Schwendemann, p. 23.

87. BA/MA, RM7/854, fo. 71, Keitel telegraph, 5.5.45.

88. BA/MA, RM7/854, fo. 48, FS Chef SKL, 4.5.45.

89. According to the OKW's calculations, 1,850,000 soldiers belonged to the army in the east on 7 May 1945. – *DRZW*, 10/1 (Lakowski), p. 675.

90. *DZW*, 6, pp. 745, 761, 763; Schwendemann, p. 24, for the figures given above, representing the OKW's estimates on 8 May. According to *DRZW*, 10/1 (Lakowski), p. 674, the size of Army Group Centre was estimated at between 600,000 and 650,000 men on 7 May.

91. *DZW*, 6, p. 740; Müller and Ueberschär, p. 108. On Hela, the commander reported on 3 May that, short of men and weapons, the troops there were facing 'certain destruction'. – BA/MA, RW44I/33, fo. 26, KR Blitz von General der Panzertruppe, AOK Ostpreußen an Obkdo. d. WMFStOber

(H) Nordost, 3.5.45. There were some 150,000 soldiers and 50,000 refugees on Hela at the time. – Schwendemann, p. 23.

92. BA/MA, RW44I/86, fo. 5, Bev. Gen. Kurland, gez. Möller, Brigadeführer, an Dönitz, 5.5.45.

93. *Die Niederlage 1945*, pp. 426–7 (4.5.45).

94. *DZW*, 6, p. 758; Rendulić, pp. 378–81; Schwendemann, pp. 25–6.

95. *Die Niederlage 1945*, p. 429 (5.5.45). Löhr's request to be allowed to offer Field-Marshal Alexander his cooperation in an attempt to 'prevent the total Bolshevization of Austria' is printed in *KTB/SKL*, part A. vol. 68, p. 439A.

96. *Die Niederlage 1945*, p. 430 (6.5.45); Schwendemann, p. 20.

97. *Die Niederlage 1945*, p. 425 (3.5.45).

98. *DZW*, 6, p. 761; *Die Niederlage 1945*, pp. 427–8 (4.5.45).

99. *Die Niederlage 1945*, p. 422 (2.5.45).

100. *Die Niederlage 1945*, p. 423 (3.5.45).

101. *Die Niederlage 1945*, p. 431 (6.5.45).

102. *DZW*, 6, pp. 758–67; Müller and Ueberschär, p. 104.

103. *Die Niederlage 1945*, pp. 430–31 (6.5.45).

104. *Die Niederlage 1945*, pp. 432–3 (7.5.45). Eisenhower had given Jodl half an hour to reach a decision, but communications difficulties with Flensburg delayed the arrival of his message and receipt of Dönitz's approval. – *DZW*, 6, p. 774. See also Bodo Scheurig, *Alfred Jodl: Gehorsam und Verhängnis*, Berlin and Frankfurt am Main, 1991, pp. 331–3.

105. Reproduced in facsimile in Müller and Ueberschär, pp. 178–9. Britain had introduced 'double summer time' during the Second World War. This placed Britain one hour ahead of Central European Time.

106. Müller and Ueberschär, pp. 106, 180–81; Schwendemann, p. 30; Baum, p. 261. For a description of the scene, see G. Zhukov, *Reminiscences and Reflections*, vol. 2, Moscow, 1985, pp. 399–400; also Antony Beevor, *Berlin: The Downfall 1945*, pb. edn., London, 2007, pp. 403–5.

107. Speer, pp. 498–9.

108. IWM, EDS, F.3, M.I. 14/284 (A), report on a discussion between Keitel and General Ivan Aleksandrovich Serov, deputy commissar of the NKVD (the Soviet internal security organization, headed by Lavrenty Beria); printed in *KTB/SKL*, part A, vol. 68, pp. 469–71A. Authentication of part of a jawbone which the Soviets had found in the garden of the Reich Chancellery as belonging to Hitler was only made a few days later. Stalin and the Soviet authorities continued for years to disbelieve accounts of Hitler's death.

109. BA/MA, RM7/854, fo. 120, Kriegstagebuch Seekriegsleitung, 7.5.45; *KTB/OKW*, vol. 4/2, pp. 1482–3 (7.5.45); Schwendemann, p. 25.

110. Schwendemann, p. 26.

111. Klaus Granzow, *Tagebuch eines Hitlerjungen 1943–1945*, Bremen, 1965, p. 177 (5.5.45).

112. BA/MA, NL Schörner, N60/18, unfoliated, proclamation by Schörner to soldiers of Army Group Centre, 5.5.45.
113. *Die Niederlage 1945*, p. 431.
114. Schwendemann, p. 25.
115. *DZW*, 6, p. 767.
116. BA/MA, RW44I/54, unfoliated 4pp. 'Aufzeichnung über die Dienstreise des Oberst i.G. Meyer-Detring zu Feldmarschall Schörner am 8.5.45 (p. 3: Unterredung mit Feldmarschall Schörner); *Die Niederlage 1945*, p. 438, for Meyer-Detring's report to Dönitz.
117. BA/MA, NL Schörner, N60/18, unfoliated, proclamation by Schörner to soldiers of Army Group Centre, 5.5.45; printed in Roland Kaltenegger, *Schörner: Feldmarschall der letzten Stunde*, Munich and Berlin, 1994, pp. 297–8.
118. In a case that raised great public interest, with much support for Schörner as well as heated criticism of his actions, the former field-marshal was found guilty in October 1957 of condemning to death without a court, then the hanging, of a corporal said to have fallen asleep, drunk, at the wheel of his lorry in March 1945. He was sentenced to four and a half years imprisonment, of which he served two before being released on health grounds. The Federal Republic refused him a pension. He lived a secluded existence in Munich supported by friends and former military comrades, until his death in 1973 at the age of eighty-one. – Peter Steinkamp, 'Generalfeldmarschall Ferdinand Schörner', in Gerd R. Ueberschär (ed.), *Hitlers militärische Elite*, vol. 2: *Von Kriegsbeginn bis zum Weltkriegsende*, Darmstadt, 1998, pp. 240–42; Klaus Schönherr, 'Ferdinand Schörner – Der idealtypische Nazi-General', in Ronald Smelser and Enrico Syring (eds.), *Die Militärelite des Dritten Reiches*, Berlin, 1995, pp. 506–7. See also, for the controversy around Schörner's trial, Kaltenegger, *Schörner*, pp. 330–54.
119. *DZW*, 6, p. 767; *DRZW*, 10/1 (Lakowski), p. 673; Schwendemann, p. 31; Sebastian Siebel-Achenbach, *Lower Silesia from Nazi Germany to Communist Poland, 1942–49*, London, 1994, pp. 77–8.
120. BA/MA, NL Schörner, N60/74, 'Mein Verhalten bei der Kapitulation im Mai 1945' and 'Zur Vorgeschichte der Kapitulation', both 10.3.58.
121. Steinkamp, p. 238. Kaltenegger, *Schörner*, pp. 306–7, 315, supports Schörner's own account. See also Roland Kaltenegger, *Operation 'Alpenfestung': Das letzte Geheimnis des 'Dritten Reiches'*, Munich, 2005, pp. 336–46.
122. One ordinary soldier in Schörner's army noted in his diary how he and a few comrades were ordered out of the lorry in which they were leaving, desperately trying to reach the Americans after the dissolution of his unit had been determined. The staff officers of his company then climbed in and drove off. 'We are the cheated ones,' the soldier concluded. – Granzow, p. 179 (9.5.45).

123. Schwendemann, p. 27.
124. *DRZW*, 10/1 (Lakowski), p. 677. According to a report for the navy leadership, ships shuttling backwards and forwards across the Baltic ferried out between 11 and 17 May 109,205 soldiers, 6,887 wounded and 5,379 civilian refugees. – BA/MA, RM7/854, fo. 333, Lage Ostsee, 18.5.45.
125. Müller and Ueberschär, pp. 107–8.
126. *DRZW*, 10/2 (Overmans), pp. 502–3.
127. See Schwendemann, p. 27.
128. Neitzel, *Abgehört*, p. 49.
129. *KTB/OKW*, vol. 4/2, pp. 1281–2 (9.5.45); repr. in Müller and Ueberschär, p. 181; *Die Wehrmachtberichte 1939–1945*, vol. 3: *1. Januar 1944 bis 9. Mai 1945*, Munich, 1989, p. 569 (9.5.45).
130. Dönitz, p. 471.
131. *Die Niederlage 1945*, pp. 440, 445 (12.5.45, 15.5.45). Dönitz was still insisting on 18 May that there should be no concession to Allied demands to remove 'emblems of sovereignty' from German military uniforms. – *1945: Das Jahr der endgültigen Niederlage der faschistischen Wehrmacht*, pp. 411–13.
132. *Die Niederlage 1945*, p. 439 (11.5.45).
133. Speer, pp. 499–500, for a description of the continued Dönitz administration; *Die Niederlage 1945*, pp. 433–49, for the entries in Dönitz's diary on the workings of his administration between 8.5.45 and 17.5.45.
134. *Die Niederlage 1945*, p. 446 (16.5.45). For the continuity in Dönitz's political ideas, see Steinert, pp. 283–6, and also Lüdde-Neurath, p. 81.
135. BAB, R3/1624, fos. 10–13, Speer to Krosigk, 15.5.45; Dönitz, p. 471; and see Matthias Schmidt, *Albert Speer: Das Ende eines Mythos*, Berne and Munich, 1982, pp. 167–71.
136. Speer, p. 500.
137. IWM, EDS, F.3., M.I. 14/950, memorandum of Stuckart, 22.5.45; *Die Niederlage 1945*, pp. 433–5, 441–2 (8.5.45, 12.5.45) for discussions of Dönitz's resignation. See also Dönitz, p. 472.
138. Description from David Stafford, *Endgame 1945: Victory, Retribution, Liberation*, London, 2007, pp. 407–8. See also Dönitz, pp. 473–4. For divisions of opinion within the Allied leadership on how to deal with the Dönitz administration, and the steps leading to the arrest of its members, see Marlis Steinert, 'The Allied Decision to Arrest the Dönitz Government', *Historical Journal*, 31 (1988), pp. 651–63.
139. *United States Strategic Bombing Survey*, New York and London, 1976, vol. 4, p. 7. The figure given there for those killed, 305,000 people, has been shown to be too low. See Jörg Friedrich, *Der Brand: Deutschland im Bombenkrieg 1940–1945*, pb. edn., Berlin, 2004, p. 63, who puts the figure at between 420,000 and 570,000, and *DRZW*, 10/1 (Boog), p. 868, which estimates the

civilian dead – not the total number – at 380,000–400,000. Rüdiger Overmans reckons the losses at between 400,000 and 500,000. – 'Die Toten des Zweiten Weltkriegs in Deutschland', in Wolfgang Michalka (ed.), *Der Zweite Weltkrieg: Analysen, Grundzüge, Forschungsbilanz*, Munich and Zurich, 1989, p. 860. See also Rüdiger Overmans, '55 Millionen Opfer des Zweiten Weltkrieges? Zum Stand der Forschung nach mehr als 40 Jahren', *Militärgeschichtliche Mitteilungen*, 48 (1990), pp. 107, 109. Yet a further estimate puts the most likely figure at 406,000, though an upper limit has ranged as high as 635,000. Most were killed in the last phase of the war. – Dietmar Süß, 'Die Endphase des Luftkriegs', in *Kriegsende in Deutschland*, Hamburg, 2005, p. 55. More than half the civilian deaths from bombing occurred in the last eight months of the war. – Nicholas Stargardt, *Witnesses of War: Children's Lives under the Nazis*, London, 2005, pp. 264 and 430 n. 4.

140. Bessel, p. 69. Establishing reliable figures for the number of deaths of refugees fleeing in the last months of the war is extraordinarily difficult. The far higher figures frequently given often extend the categories of refugee and the time and geographical areas covered to include, for instance, the 'resettlement' of Balts of German extraction following the Nazi–Soviet Pact, Soviet Germans deported by Stalin, and Germans expelled from the east after the war. The closest estimate to deaths arising from refugee flight appears to be 473,000. – Overmans, 'Die Toten des Zweiten Weltkriegs in Deutschland', p. 868; Overmans, '55 Millionen Opfer des Zweiten Weltkrieges?', p. 110.

141. Rüdiger Overmans, *Deutsche militärische Verluste im Zweiten Weltkrieg*, Munich, 1999, pp. 238–9, 316, 318, 321. According to Overmans' calculations (p. 265), of the total German military deaths (5,318,000) the eastern front accounted for 51.6 per cent (2,743,000), fighting in the final phase (Jan.–May 1945) 23.1 per cent (1,230,000) and the western theatre 6.4 per cent (340,000).

142. Allied worries about an insurrection never materialized, though Werwolf was still taken seriously in the weeks after the capitulation. – Bessel, pp. 175–6; Perry Biddiscombe, *Werwolf! The History of the National Socialist Guerrilla Movement 1944–1946*, Toronto and Buffalo, NY, 1998, pp. 279–82.

143. See Bessel, ch. 7, 'The Beginning of Occupation', for a good summary of the early stages.

144. *Die Niederlage 1945*, pp. 439, 447 (11.5.45, 16.5.45).

145. Bessel, p. 167.

146. *Anonyma*, p. 183 (11.5.45).

147. StAM, LRA 31391, unfoliated, report of Evang. luth. Pfarramt Berchtesgaden, 25.6.46; report of the Catholic parish of St Andreas, 24.6.46.

148. BA/MA, N648/1, NL Dethleffsen, Erinnerungen, fo. 1.

149. NAL, WO208/5622, C.S.D.I.C. (U.K.) report, 13.5.45, comments of Vice-Admiral Frisius.

150. A. J. and R. L. Merritt (eds.), *Public Opinion in Occupied Germany: The OMGUS Surveys, 1945–1949*, Urbana, Ill., 1970, pp. 32–3. Experiences of occupation and the inevitable hardships of daily life in ruined cities – shortages of food and housing, a valueless currency, and a standard of living frequently lower than it had been before 1944–5 – together with a sense of national humiliation and the creation of denazification trials often seen to be aimed at the 'little man' who, it was felt, had been forced to comply with the demands of the regime, were among the factors that played their part in enhancing a rosy view of the 'good years' of National Socialism, before the disasters of the last phase of the war.

151. See also Peter Fritsche, *Life and Death in the Third Reich*, Cambridge, Mass., and London, 2008, pp. 301–2.

152. 'Tief vergraben, nicht dran rühren', p. 218.

153. Cited in Otto Dov Kulka, 'The German Population and the Jews: State of Research and New Perspectives', in David Bankier (ed.), *Probing the Depths of German Antisemitism: German Society and the Persecution of the Jews, 1933–1941*, New York, Oxford and Jerusalem, 2000, p. 279.

154. For a similar point made about 1918, see Michael Geyer, '*Endkampf* 1918 and 1945: German Nationalism, Annihilation, and Self-Destruction', in Alf Lüdtke and Bernd Weisbrod (eds.), *No Man's Land of Violence: Extreme Wars in the 20th Century*, Göttingen, 2006, pp. 90–91.

CONCLUSION: ANATOMY OF SELF-DESTRUCTION

1. A point well made by Bernd Wegner, 'The Ideology of Self-Destruction: Hitler and the Choreography of Defeat', *Bulletin of the German Historical Institute London*, 26/2 (2004), pp. 19–20. See also Wegner's reflections in *DRZW*, 8, pp. 1185–91.

2. Hans Rothfels, *The German Opposition to Hitler*, pb. edn., London, 1970, p. 146, was adamant 'that Casablanca destroyed any hope of a tolerable peace which might still have been entertained by the German Resistance movement'. Adam von Trott tried in June 1944 to persuade the western Allies to drop the demand, arguing that many in the opposition felt they could not risk an internal rising otherwise. In the event, of course, they did precisely this, despite the demand. Whether in fact the demand for unconditional surrender had any significant impact on the resistance movement remains nevertheless unclear. – Anne Armstrong, *Unconditional Surrender: The Impact of the Casablanca Policy upon World War Two*, New Brunswick, NJ, 1961, pp. 205, 212–13.

3. See *DRZW*, 6 (Boog), p. 85; also Reimer Hansen, *Das Ende des Dritten Reiches: Die deutsche Kapitulation 1945*, Stuttgart, 1966, pp. 20–23, 36–9,

224–5; and Reimer Hansen, *Der 8. Mai 1945: Geschichte und geschicht-liche Bedeutung*, Berlin, 1985, pp. 10–13, 22–3.

4. To mitigate the possibility of their demand for 'unconditional surrender' stimulating resistance, both Churchill and Roosevelt sought in public statements to reassure the German people that the stipulation did not mean that they would be 'enslaved or destroyed'. – Winston S. Churchill, *The Second World War*, vol. 4: *The Hinge of Fate*, London, 1951, pp. 616–18.

5. *MadR*, 17, p. 6734 (late March 1945).

6. See the comments of Rolf-Dieter Müller in *DRZW*, 10/2, pp. 705, 716.

7. See Bernhard R. Kroener, 'Auf dem Weg zu einer "nationalsozialistischen Volksarmee": Die soziale Öffnung des Heeresoffizierkorps im Zweiten Weltkrieg', in Martin Broszat, Klaus-Dietmar Henke and Hans Woller (eds.), *Von Stalingrad zur Währungsreform: Zur Sozialgeschichte des Umbruchs in Deutschland*, Munich, 1988, pp. 653, 658–9, 671–3, 676–7; and MacGregor Knox, '1 October 1942: Adolf Hitler, Wehrmacht Officer Policy, and Social Revolution', *Historical Journal*, 43 (2000), pp. 801–25 (figures on size of the officer corps, p. 810).

8. Klaus-Jürgen Müller, 'The Wehrmacht: Western Front', in David Wingeate Pike (ed.), *The Closing of the Second World War: Twilight of a Totalitarianism*, New York, 2001, pp. 55–6.

9. See the reflections on 'duty', a leitmotiv of the book, in John Zimmermann, *Pflicht zum Untergang: Die deutsche Kriegführung im Westen des Reiches 1944/45*, Paderborn, 2009, pp. 469–70.

10. Sönke Neitzel, *Abgehört: Deutsche Generäle in britischer Kriegsgefangen-schaft 1942–1945*, Berlin, 2005.

11. Albert Speer, *Erinnerungen*, Frankfurt am Main and Berlin, 1969, p. 434.

12. In his testimony at Nuremberg, Speer had explicitly ruled out the possibility of any group being able to confront Hitler with a demand to end the war. – *IMT*, vol. 16, p. 542. Rolf-Dieter Müller, 'Speers Rüstungspolitik im Totalen Krieg', *Militärgeschichtliche Zeitschrift*, 59 (2000), p. 362, points out that, although all Hitler's subordinate leaders played at one time or another with the aim of finding a way out of the war other than total defeat and destruction, there was, in contrast to Italy, no body which could take action against the Dictator. Speer, he adds, 'evidently at no point thought of acting against his mentor'.

List of Archival Sources Cited

Bayerisches Hauptstaatsarchiv, Munich: MInn 72417; Reichsstatthalter 257, 389/4, 644/2, 681/1–8, 686/1, 699, 482/1, 498, 527–8; MA 106695–6.

BBC Archives, London: interviews from the BBC-2 series *The Nazis: A Warning from History* (1997).

Bibliothek für Zeitgeschichte, Stuttgart: Sammlung Sterz – Feldpostbriefe.

Bundesarchiv, Berlin/Lichterfelde: Parteikanzlei der NSDAP, NS6/51, 134–7, 153, 166–7, 169, 277, 353–4, 374, 756, 791–2; Persönlicher Stab Reichsführer-SS, NS19/424, 606, 612, 751, 772, 1022, 1029, 1318, 1793, 1858, 1862, 1864, 2068, 2409, 2454, 2606, 2721, 2864, 2903, 2936, 3034, 3118, 3121, 3271, 3320, 3337, 3652, 3705, 3809, 3833, 3910–12, 3931, 4015–17, Reichskanzlei, R43II/393a, 583a, 648a, 650c, 651d, 664a, 667b, 680a, 684, 692, 692a–b, 1648; Reichspostministerium, R4701 alt R48/11; Reichsministerium für Rüstung und Kriegsproduktion, R3/1511, 1522, 1526, 1528–9, 1531–3, 1535–45, 1583, 1618, 1620–23, 1623a, 1624–6, 1661, 1740; Reichsministerium für Volksaufklärung und Propaganda, R55/601, 603, 608, 610, 612, 620, 793, 21504.

Bundesarchiv/Militärarchiv, Freiburg: Materialsammlung: MSg2/2696–7, 5284; Nachlässe: N6/4, N24/39, N54/8, N60/17–18, 73–4, N245/2–3, 15, N265/26, 108, 112, 118, N374/8, N574/19, 22, N647/12–13, N648/1, N712/15; Heeresgruppen: RH2/319, 2682, 2684–5, RH19/II/204, 213, RH19/III/17, 667, 727, RH19/IV/141, 228, 250, RH20/4/593, 617, RH20/19/196, 245, RH21/3/420, 730, RH21/5/66; Seekriegsleitung: RM7/851, 854; OKW: RW4/57, 494, 881. RW44I/33, 54.

Imperial War Museum, Duxford: EDS [Enemy Documents Section], Collection of Captured German Documents; FO645, Nuremberg Interrogation Files; FIAT interrogation reports on Albert Speer and senior members of his ministry; Memoirs of P. E. von Stemann.

Institut für Zeitgeschichte, Munich: ED 195 (Slg. Schottenheim); Fa-91/2–5 (Parteikanzlei); Fa-93 (Pers. Stab/RFSS); Nbg.-Dok., NS-3501, PS-1787, PS-3683; ZS 145 (Schwerin von Krosigk), 597 (Grohé), 988 (Kritzinger), 1810 (Dönitz), 1953 (Dankwort).

International Tracing Service, Bad Arolsen: Collection Todesmärsche: Tote, Boxes 1–83; Collection Evacuations: Evak 1–9; HNa 68.

Irving Collection: Selected Research Documents Relating to Hermann Göring, Reel 1 (microfilm from Microform Imaging Ltd., East Ardsley, Wakefield).

Liddell Hart Centre for Military Archives, King's College, London: Dempsey Papers, nos. 72–336.

National Archives, London: Foreign Office: FO898/187; War Office: WO204/6384; WO208/4363–5, 5543, 5622; WO219/1587, 4713.

Staatsarchiv Augsburg: Gau Schwaben 1/28–37; Kreisleitung Augsburg-Stadt 1/8, 47, 65, 132; Ortsgruppe Wollmarkt 11/5; Kreisleitung Günzburg 1/42–3, 46–7, 55.

Staatsarchiv München: Gauleitung München, NSDAP 35, 52, 466a, 495, 499; Landratsamt Berchtesgaden, LRA 29656, 29715, 29718, 29728, 31391, 31645, 31908, 31919, 31921, 31936, 156108; Staatsanwaltschaften 6751, 18848/2–3, 34876/25.

List of Works Cited

1945: Das Jahr der endgültigen Niederlage der faschistischen Wehrmacht. Dokumente, ed. Gerhard Förster and Richard Lakowski, Berlin, 1975.

Addison, Paul, and Crang, Jeremy A. (eds.), *Firestorm: The Bombing of Dresden, 1945*, London, 2006.

von Ahlfen, Hans, and Niehoff, Hermann, *So kämpfte Breslau: Verteidigung und Untergang von Schlesiens Hauptstadt*, Munich, 1959.

Akten der Partei-Kanzlei der NSDAP, vol. 1, ed. Helmut Heiber, Munich, 1983; vol. 2, ed. Peter Longerich, Munich, 1989.

Albrecht, Dieter, 'Regensburg in der NS-Zeit', in Dieter Albrecht (ed.), *Zwei Jahrtausende Regensburg*, Regensburg, 1979.

von Alvensleben, Udo, *Lauter Abschiede: Tagebuch im Kriege*, Frankfurt am Main, 1971.

Aly, Götz, *Hitlers Volksstaat: Raub, Rassenkrieg und nationaler Sozialismus*, Frankfurt am Main, 2005.

Andreas-Friedrich, Ruth, *Schauplatz Berlin: Ein deutsches Tagebuch*, Munich, 1962.

Anonyma: Eine Frau in Berlin. Tagebuch-Aufzeichnungen vom 20. April bis 22. Juni 1945, pb. edn., Munich, 2008.

Arbogast, Christine, *Herrschaftsinstanzen der württembergischen NSDAP: Funktion, Sozialprofil und Lebenswege einer regionalen Elite 1920–1960*, Munich, 1998.

Arendes, Cord, Wolfrum, Edgar, and Zedler, Jörg (eds.), *Terror nach Innen: Verbrechen am Ende des Zweiten Weltkrieges*, Göttingen, 2006.

Arendt, Hannah, *The Origins of Totalitarianism*, New York, 1951.

Armstrong, Anne, *Unconditional Surrender: The Impact of the Casablanca Policy upon World War Two*, New Brunswick, NJ, 1961.

Bajohr, Frank, and Wildt, Michael (eds.), *Volksgemeinschaft: Neue Forschungen zur Gesellschaft des Nationalsozialismus*, Frankfurt am Main, 2009.

Balkoski, Joseph, 'Patton's Third Army: The Lorraine Campaign, 19 September–1 December 1944', in Albert A. Nofi (ed.), *The War against Hitler: Military Strategy in the West*, Conshohocken, Pa., 1995.

Barnett, Correlli (ed.), *Hitler's Generals*, London, 1990.

Bartov, Omer, *The Eastern Front, 1941–45: German Troops and the Barbarisation of Warfare*, New York, 1986.

Bauer, Robert, *Heilbronner Tagebuchblätter*, Heilbronn, 1949.

Bauer, Yehuda, *Jews for Sale? Nazi-Jewish Negotiations, 1933–1945*, New Haven, 1994.

Baum, Walter, 'Der Zusammenbruch der obersten deutschen militärischen Führung 1945', *Wehrwissenschaftliche Rundschau*, 10 (1960).

Baumann, Ulrich, and Koch, Markus (eds.), *'Was damals Recht war . . .': Soldaten und Zivilisten vor Gerichten der Wehrmacht*, Berlin-Brandenburg, 2008.

Beevor, Antony, *Berlin: The Downfall 1945*, pb. edn., London, 2007.

—— *D-Day: The Battle for Normandy*, London, 2009.

Behrmann, Günter C., '"Jugend, die meinen Namen trägt": Die letzten Kriegseinsätze der Hitlerjugend', in *Kriegsende in Deutschland*, Hamburg, 2005.

von Below, Nicolaus, *Als Hitlers Adjutant 1937–45*, Mainz, 1980.

Bergander, Götz, *Dresden im Luftkrieg*, Weimar, Cologne and Vienna, 1994.

Bergau, Martin, *Der Junge von der Bernsteinküste: Erlebte Zeitgeschichte 1938–1948*, Heidelberg, 1994.

—— 'Tod an der Bernsteinküste: Ein NS-Verbrechen in Ostpreußen', in Elke Fröhlich (ed.), *Als die Erde brannte: Deutsche Schicksale in den letzten Kriegstagen*, Munich, 2005.

Bergen, Doris L., 'Death Throes and Killing Frenzies: A Response to Hans Mommsen's "The Dissolution of the Third Reich: Crisis Management and Collapse, 1943–1945"', *German Historical Institute, Washington D.C. Bulletin*, 27 (2000).

Berghahn, Volker, 'NSDAP und "geistige Führung" der Wehrmacht 1939–1943', *VfZ*, 17 (1969).

Bernadotte, Folke, *The Fall of the Curtain*, London, 1945.

Bessel, Richard, *Germany 1945: From War to Peace*, London, 2009.

Besson, Waldemar, 'Zur Geschichte des nationalsozialistischen Führungsoffiziers (NSFO)', *VfZ*, 9 (1961).

Biddiscombe, Perry, *Werwolf! The History of the National Socialist Guerrilla Movement 1944–1946*, Toronto and Buffalo, NY, 1998.

Bidwell, Shelford, 'Kesselring', in Correlli Barnett (ed.), *Hitler's Generals*, London, 1990.

Black, Peter R., *Ernst Kaltenbrunner: Ideological Soldier of the Third Reich*, Princeton, 1984.

Blank, Ralf, 'Kriegsalltag und Luftkrieg an der "Heimatfront"', in *DRZW*, vol. 9/1.

—— 'Albert Hoffmann als Reichsverteidigungskommissar im Gau Westfalen-Süd, 1943–1945: Eine biografische Skizze', in Wolf Gruner and Armin Nolzen (eds.), *'Bürokratien': Initiative und Effizienz. Beiträge zur Geschichte des Nationalsozialismus*, vol. 17, Berlin, 2001.

Blatman, Daniel, 'Die Todesmärsche – Entscheidungsträger, Mörder und Opfer', in Ulrich Herbert, Karin Orth and Christoph Dieckmann (eds.), *Die national-sozialistischen Konzentrationslager*, vol. 2, Göttingen, 1998.

—— 'The Death Marches, January–May 1945: Who Was Responsible for What?', *YVS*, 28 (2000).

—— 'Rückzug, Evakuierung und Todesmärsche 1944–1945', in Wolfgang Benz and Barbara Distel (eds.), *Der Ort des Terrors: Geschichte der nationalsozial-istischen Konzentrationslager*, vol. 1, Munich, 2005.

—— *Les Marches de la mort: La dernière étape du génocide nazi, été 1944-printemps 1945*, Paris, 2009.

—— 'The Death-Marches and the Final Phase of Nazi Genocide', in Jane Caplan and Nikolaus Wachsmann (eds.), *Concentration Camps in Nazi Germany: The New Histories*, London and New York, 2010.

Bleyer, Wolfgang, 'Pläne der faschistischen Führung zum totalen Krieg im Sommer 1944', *Zeitschrift für Geschichtswissenschaft*, 17 (1969).

Bloch, Michael, *Ribbentrop*, pb. edn., London, 1994.

Blumentritt, Guenther, *Von Rundstedt: The Soldier and the Man*, London, 1952.

Boog, Horst, 'Die strategische Bomberoffensive der Alliierten gegen Deutschland und die Reichsluftverteidigung in der Schlußphase des Krieges', in *DRZW*, vol. 10/1.

Borejsza, Jerzy W., 'Der 25. Juli 1943 in Italien und der 20. Juli 1944 in Deutschland: Zur Technik des Staatsstreichs im totalitären System', in Jürgen Schmädeke and Peter Steinbach (eds.), *Der Widerstand gegen den National-sozialismus*, Munich and Zurich, 1986.

The Bormann Letters, ed. H. R. Trevor-Roper, London, 1954.

Bosch, Manfred, *Der Neubeginn: Aus deutscher Nachkriegszeit. Südbaden 1945–1950*, Konstanz, 1988.

Breloer, Heinrich (ed.), *Mein Tagebuch: Geschichten vom Überleben 1939–1947*, Cologne, 1984.

Bretschneider, Heike, *Der Widerstand gegen den Nationalsozialismus in München 1933–1945*, Munich, 1968.

Broszat, Martin, 'Nationalsozialistische Konzentrationslager 1933–1945', in Hans Buchheim *et al.*, *Anatomie des SS-Staates*, 2. vols., Olten and Freiburg im Breisgau, 1965.

—— *Der Staat Hitlers*, Munich, 1969.

—— and Fröhlich, Elke, *et al.* (eds.), *Bayern in der NS-Zeit*, 6 vols., Munich, 1977–83.

Buchbender, Ortwin, and Sterz, Reinhold (eds.), *Das andere Gesicht des Krieges: Deutsche Feldpostbriefe 1939–1945*, Munich, 1982.

Buchheim, Hans, *et al.*, *Anatomie des SS-Staates*, 2 vols., Olten and Freiburg im Breisgau, 1965.

Buske, Norbert (ed.), *Die kampflose Übergabe der Stadt Greifswald im April 1945*, Schwerin, 1993.

—— *Das Kriegsende 1945 in Demmin: Berichte, Erinnerungen, Dokumente*, Schwerin, 1995.

Churchill, Winston S., *The Second World War*, vol. 4: *The Hinge of Fate*, London, 1951.

Clark, Christopher, 'Johannes Blaskowitz – der christliche General', in Ronald Smelser and Enrico Syring (eds.), *Die Militärelite des Dritten Reiches*, Berlin, 1995.

Czech, Danuta, *Kalendarium der Ereignisse im Konzentrationslager Auschwitz-Birkenau 1939–1945*, Reinbek bei Hamburg, 1989.

Davies, Norman, *Rising '44: 'The Battle for Warsaw'*, London, 2004.

Deible, Albert, *Krieg und Kriegsende in Schwäbisch Gmünd*, Schwäbisch Gmünd, 1954.

Demerer, Heinrich, 'Erinnerungen an den Todesmarsch aus dem KZ Flossenbürg', *Dachauer Hefte*, 25 (2009).

Denny, Isabel, *The Fall of Hitler's Fortress City: The Battle for Königsberg, 1945*, London, 2007.

D'Este, Carlo, 'Model', in Correlli Barnett (ed.), *Hitler's Generals*, London, 1990.

Das Deutsche Reich und der Zweite Weltkrieg, vols. 7–10, ed. Militärgeschichtliches Forschungsamt, Munich, 2004–8.

Der deutsche Südwesten zur Stunde Null, ed. Generallandesarchiv Karlsruhe, Karlsruhe, 1975.

Deutschland im Zweiten Weltkrieg, vol. 6: *Die Zerschlagung des Hitlerfaschismus und die Befreiung des deutschen Volkes (Juni 1944 bis zum 8. Mai 1945)*, ed. Authors' Collective under the direction of Wolfgang Schumann and Olaf Groehler, with assistance from Wolfgang Bleyer, Berlin, 1985.

Deutschlands Rüstung im Zweiten Weltkrieg: Hitlers Konferenzen mit Albert Speer 1942–1945, ed. Willi A. Boelcke, Frankfurt am Main, 1969.

Dieckert, Kurt, and Grossmann, Horst, *Der Kampf um Ostpreußen: Ein authentischer Dokumentarbericht*, Munich, 1960.

Dönitz, Karl, *Memoirs: Ten Years and Twenty Days*, Da Capo edn., New York, 1997.

Dörr, Margarete, *'Wer die Zeit nicht miterlebt hat . . .': Frauenerfahrungen im Zweiten Weltkrieg und in den Jahren danach*, vol. 3, Frankfurt am Main and New York, 1998.

Downing, David, *The Devil's Virtuosos: German Generals at War 1940–5*, London, 1977.

Echternkamp, Jörg, 'Im Kampf an der inneren und äußeren Front: Grundzüge der deutschen Gesellschaft im Zweiten Weltkrieg', in *DRZW*, vol. 9/1.

—— (ed.), *Kriegsschauplatz Deutschland 1945: Leben in Angst – Hoffnung auf Frieden. Feldpost aus der Heimat und von der Front*, Paderborn, 2006.

Eichholtz, Dietrich, 'Deutschland am Ende des Krieges: Eine kriegswirtschaftliche Bilanz', *Bulletin der Berliner Gesellschaft für Faschismus- und Weltkriegsforschung*, 6 (1996).

—— *Geschichte der deutschen Kriegswirtschaft 1939–1945*, vol. 3: *1943–1945*, Berlin, 1996.

Elliger, Katharina, *Und tief in der Seele das Ferne: Die Geschichte einer Vertreibung aus Schlesien*, Reinbek bei Hamburg, 2006.

Epstein, Catherine, *Model Nazi: Arthur Greiser and the Occupation of Western Poland*, Oxford, 2010.

Erickson, John, *The Road to Berlin*, Cassell edn., London, 2003.

Erpel, Simone, 'Machtverhältnisse im Zerfall: Todesmärsche der Häftlinge des Frauen-Konzentrationslagers Ravensbrück im April 1945', in Jörg Hillmann and John Zimmermann (eds.), *Kriegsende 1945 in Deutschland*, Munich, 2002.

—— *Zwischen Vernichtung und Befreiung: Das Frauen-Konzentrationslager Ravensbrück in der letzten Kriegsphase*, Berlin, 2005.

Eschenburg, Theodor, 'Die Rede Himmlers vor den Gauleitern am 3. August 1944', *VfZ*, 1 (1953).

Evans, Richard, *The Third Reich at War*, London, 2008.

Fest, Joachim C., *The Face of the Third Reich*, Harmondsworth, 1972.

—— *Speer: Eine Biographie*, Berlin, 1999.

Fisch, Bernhard, *Nemmersdorf, Oktober 1944: Was in Ostpreußen tatsächlich geschah*, Berlin, 1997.

—— 'Nemmersdorf 1944 – ein bisher unbekanntes zeitnahes Zeugnis', *Zeitschrift für Ostmitteleuropa-Forschung*, 56 (2007).

Fleischhauer, Ingeborg, *Die Chance des Sonderfriedens: Deutsch-sowjetische Geheimgespräche 1941–1945*, Berlin, 1986.

Förschler, Andreas, *Stuttgart 1945: Kriegsende und Neubeginn*, Gudensberg-Gleichen, 2004.

Förster, Jürgen, 'Geistige Kriegführung in Deutschland 1919 bis 1945', in *DRZW*, vol. 9/1.

—— 'Die Wehrmacht und das Ende des "Dritten Reichs"', in Arnd Bauerkämper, Christoph Kleßmann and Hans Misselwitz (eds.), *Der 8. Mai 1945 als historische Zäsur: Strukturen, Erfahrung, Deutungen*, Potsdam, 1995.

—— 'The Final Hour of the Third Reich: The Capitulation of the Wehrmacht', *Bulletin of the International Committee for the History of the Second World War*, Montreal (1995).

—— *Die Wehrmacht im NS-Staat: Eine strukturgeschichtliche Analyse*, Munich, 2007.

Friedländer, Saul, *The Years of Extermination: Nazi Germany and the Jews, 1939–1945*, London, 2007.

Friedrich, Carl Joachim, and Brzezinski, Zbigniew, *Totalitarian Dictatorship and Autocracy*, Cambridge, Mass., 1956.

Friedrich, Jörg, *Der Brand: Deutschland im Bombenkrieg 1940–1945*, pb. edn., Berlin, 2004.

Frieser, Karl-Heinz, 'Die Schlacht um die Seelower Höhen im April 1945', in Roland G. Foerster (ed.), *Seelower Höhen 1945*, Hamburg, 1998.

—— *et al.*, 'Der Zusammenbruch im Osten: Die Rückzugskämpfe seit Sommer 1944', in *DRZW*, vol. 8.

Fritsche, Peter, *Life and Death in the Third Reich*, Cambridge, Mass., and London, 2008.

Fritz, Stephen G., *Endkampf: Soldiers, Civilians, and the Death of the Third Reich*, Lexington, Ky., 2004.

Fröhlich, Elke, 'Ein junger Märtyrer', in Martin Broszat, Elke Fröhlich *et al.* (eds.), *Bayern in der NS-Zeit*, vol. 6, Munich and Vienna, 1983.

—— 'Hitler und Goebbels im Krisenjahr 1944: Aus den Tagebüchern des Reichspropagandaministers', *VfZ*, 39 (1990).

'Führer-Erlasse' 1939–1945, ed. Martin Moll, Stuttgart, 1997.

Gellately, Robert, *Backing Hitler: Consent and Coercion in Nazi Germany*, Oxford, 2001.

Geyer, Michael, '*Endkampf* 1918 and 1945: German Nationalism, Annihilation, and Self-Destruction', in Alf Lüdtke and Bernd Weisbrod (eds.), *No Man's Land of Violence: Extreme Wars in the 20th Century*, Göttingen, 2006.

Goebbels, Joseph, *Tagebücher 1945: Die letzten Aufzeichnungen*, Hamburg, 1977.

Goeschel, Christian, 'Suicide at the End of the Third Reich', *Journal of Contemporary History*, 41 (2006).

—— *Suicide in Nazi Germany*, Oxford, 2009.

Göhri, Josef F., *Die Franzosen kommen! Kriegsereignisse im Breisgau und in der Ortenau*, Horb am Neckar, 2005.

Goldhagen, Daniel Jonah, *Hitler's Willing Executioners: Ordinary Germans and the Holocaust*, pb. edn., London, 1997.

von der Golz, Anna, *Hindenburg: Power, Myth, and the Rise of the Nazis*, Oxford, 2009.

Görlitz, Walter, *Model: Strategie der Defensive*, Wiesbaden, 1975.

Gotto, Bernhard, *Nationalsozialistische Kommunalpolitik: Administrative Normalität und Systemstabilisierung durch die Augsburger Stadtverwaltung 1933–1945*, Munich, 2006.

Granzow, Klaus, *Tagebuch eines Hitlerjungen 1943–1945*, Bremen, 1965.

Greiser, Katrin, *Die Todesmärsche von Buchenwald: Räumung, Befreiung und Spuren der Erinnerung*, Göttingen, 2008.

Grieger, Friedrich, *Wie Breslau fiel . . .*, Metzingen, 1948.

Grier, Howard D., *Hitler, Dönitz and the Baltic Sea: The Third Reich's Last Hope, 1944–1945*, Annapolis, Md., 2007.

Gring, Diana, 'Das Massaker von Gardelegen', *Dachauer Hefte*, 20 (2004).

Groehler, Olaf, 'Die Schlacht um Aachen (September/Oktober 1944)', *Militärgeschichte* (1979).

—— *Bombenkrieg gegen Deutschland*, Berlin, 1990.

Grosche, Robert, *Kölner Tagebuch 1944–46*, Cologne, 1969.

Gruchmann, Lothar, *Der Zweite Weltkrieg*, pb. edn., Munich, 1975.

Guderian, Heinz, *Panzer Leader*, Da Capo edn., New York, 1996.

Haase, Norbert, 'Justizterror in der Wehrmacht', in Cord Arendes, Edgar Wolfrum and Jörg Zedler (eds.), *Terror nach Innen: Verbrechen am Ende des Zweiten Weltkrieges*, Göttingen, 2006.

Hale, Oron J., *The Captive Press in the Third Reich*, Princeton, 1973.

Halter, Helmut, *Stadt unterm Hakenkreuz: Kommunalpolitik in Regensburg während der NS-Zeit*, Regensburg, 1994.

Hammer, Ingrid, and zur Nieden, Susanne (eds.), *Sehr selten habe ich geweint: Briefe und Tagebücher aus dem Zweiten Weltkrieg von Menschen aus Berlin*, Zurich, 1992.

Hammermann, Gabriele, 'Die Todesmärsche aus den Konzentrationslagern 1944/45', in Cord Arendes, Edgar Wolfrum and Jörg Zedler (eds.), *Terror nach Innen: Verbrechen am Ende des Zweiten Weltkrieges*, Göttingen, 2006.

Hancock, Eleanor, *National Socialist Leadership and Total War 1941–45*, New York, 1991.

Hansen, Reimer, 'Albert Speers Konflikt mit Hitler', *Geschichte in Wissenschaft und Unterricht*, 17 (1966).

—— *Das Ende des Dritten Reiches: Die deutsche Kapitulation 1945*, Stuttgart, 1966.

—— 'Ribbentrops Friedensfühler im Frühjahr 1945', *Geschichte in Wissenschaft und Unterricht*, 18 (1967).

—— *Der 8. Mai 1945: Geschichte und geschichtliche Bedeutung*, Berlin, 1985.

Hartmann, Christian, and Hürter, Johannes, *Die letzten 100 Tage des Zweiten Weltkriegs*, Munich, 2005.

Hartwig, Dieter, *Großadmiral Karl Dönitz: Legende und Wirklichkeit*, Paderborn, 2010.

'Hasenjagd' in Celle: Das Massaker am 8. April 1945, Celle, 2005.

Hastings, Max, *Armageddon: The Battle for Germany 1944–45*, London, 2004.

—— *Finest Years: Churchill as Warlord 1940–45*, London, 2009.

Heinemann, Winfried, 'Der militärische Widerstand und der Krieg', in *DRZW*, vol. 9/1.

Heinrich Himmler: Geheimreden 1933 bis 1945 und andere Aussprachen, ed. Bradley F. Smith and Agnes F. Peterson, Frankfurt am Main, 1974.

Henke, Klaus-Dietmar, *Die amerikanische Besetzung Deutschlands*, Munich, 1995.

Henkys, Reinhard, 'Ein Todesmarsch in Ostpreußen', *Dachauer Hefte*, 20 (2004).

Hennicke, Otto, 'Auszüge aus der Wehrmachtkriminalstatistik', *Zeitschrift für Militärgeschichte*, 5 (1966),

Herbert, Ulrich, *Fremdarbeiter: Politik und Praxis des 'Ausländer-Einsatzes' in der Kriegswirtschaft des Dritten Reiches*, Bonn, 1985.

—— *Hitler's Foreign Workers: Enforced Foreign Labor in Germany under the Third Reich*, Cambridge, 1997.

Herbst, Ludolf, *Der Totale Krieg und die Ordnung der Wirtschaft*, Stuttgart, 1982.

—— *Hitlers Charisma: Die Erfindung eines deutschen Messias*, Frankfurt am Main, 2010.

Herf, Jeffrey, '"Der Krieg und die Juden": Nationalsozialistische Propaganda im Zweiten Weltkrieg', in *DRZW*, vol. 9/2.

—— *The Jewish Enemy: Nazi Propaganda during World War II and the Holocaust*, Cambridge, Mass., 2006.

Herzstein, Robert Edwin, *The War that Hitler Won*, London, 1979.

Hett, Ulrike, and Tuchel, Johannes, 'Die Reaktionen des NS-Staates auf den Umsturzversuch vom 20. July 1944', in Peter Steinbach and Johannes Tuchel (eds.), *Widerstand gegen den Nationalsozialismus*, Bonn, 1994.

Heusler, Andreas, 'Die Eskalation des Terrors: Gewalt gegen ausländische Zwangsarbeiter in der Endphase des Zweiten Weltkrieges', in Cord Arendes, Edgar Wolfrum and Jörg Zedler (eds.), *Terror nach Innen: Verbrechen am Ende des Zweiten Weltkrieges*, Göttingen, 2006.

Hilberg, Raul, *The Destruction of the European Jews*, New Viewpoints edn., New York, 1973.

Hillmann, Jörg, 'Die "Reichsregierung" in Flensburg', in Jörg Hillmann and John Zimmermann (eds.), *Kriegsende 1945 in Deutschland*, Munich, 2002.

—— and Zimmermann, John (eds.), *Kriegsende 1945 in Deutschland*, Munich, 2002.

Hirschfeld, Gerhard, and Renz, Irina, '*Vormittags die ersten Amerikaner*': *Stimmen und Bilder vom Kriegsende 1945*, Stuttgart, 2005.

Hitler and his Generals: Military Conferences 1942–1945, ed. Helmut Heiber and David M. Glantz, London, 2002.

Hitler: Reden und Proklamationen 1932–1945, ed. Max Domarus, Wiesbaden, 1973.

Hitlers Weisungen für die Kriegführung 1939–1945: Dokumente des Oberkommandos der Wehrmacht, ed. Walther Hubatsch, pb. edn., Munich, 1965.

Höffkes, Karl, *Hitlers politische Generale: Die Gauleiter des Dritten Reiches. Ein biographisches Nachschlagewerk*, Tübingen, 1986.

Hoffmann, Peter, *Widerstand, Staatsstreich, Attentat: Der Kampf der Opposition gegen Hitler*, 4th edn., Munich, 1985.

Höhne, Heinz, *The Order of the Death's Head*, London, 1972.

Hornig, Ernst, *Breslau 1945: Erlebnisse in der eingeschlossenen Stadt*, Munich, 1975.

Hoßbach, Friedrich, *Die Schlacht um Ostpreußen*, Überlingen, 1951.

Irving, David, *Hitler's War*, London, 1977.

—— *Göring: A Biography*, London, 1989.

—— *Goebbels: Mastermind of the Third Reich*, London, 1996.

Jaenecke, Heinrich, 'Mythos Hitler: Ein Nachruf', in *Kriegsende in Deutschland*, Hamburg, 2005.

Janssen, Gregor, *Das Ministerium Speer: Deutschlands Rüstung im Krieg*, Berlin, Frankfurt am Main and Vienna, 1968.

Jedlicka, Ludwig, 'Ein unbekannter Bericht Kaltenbrunners über die Lage in Österreich im September 1944', in Ludwig Jedlicka, *Der 20. Juli 1944*, Vienna, 1985.

Jesse, Eckhard (ed.), *Totalitarismus im 20. Jahrhundert*, Bonn, 1999.

Joachimsthaler, Anton, *Hitlers Ende: Legenden und Dokumente*, Munich, 1999.

Johr, Barbara, 'Die Ereignisse in Zahlen', in Helke Sander and Barbara Johr (eds.), *Befreier und Befreite: Krieg, Vergewaltigungen, Kinder*, Munich, 1992.

Jordan, Rudolf, *Erlebt und erlitten: Weg eines Gauleiters von München bis Moskau*, Leoni am Starnberger See, 1971.

Jung, Hermann, *Die Ardennenoffensive 1944/45*, Göttingen, 1971.

Junge, Traudl, *Until the Final Hour: Hitler's Last Secretary*, London, 2002.

Justiz und NS-Verbrechen: Sammlung deutscher Strafurteile wegen nationalsozialistischer Tötungsverbrechen 1945–1966, ed. Adelheid L. Rüter-Ehlermann, C. F. Rüter *et al.*, vols. 1–3, 10 and 13, and *Register*, Amsterdam and Munich, 1968–98.

Kallis, Aristotle A., 'Der Niedergang der Deutungsmacht: Nationalsozialistische Propaganda im Kriegsverlauf', in *DRZW*, vol. 9/2.

Kaltenegger, Roland, *Schörner: Feldmarschall der letzten Stunde*, Munich and Berlin, 1994.

—— *Operation 'Alpenfestung': Das letzte Geheimnis des 'Dritten Reiches'*, Munich, 2005.

von Kardorff, Ursula, *Berliner Aufzeichnungen 1942–1945*, pb. edn., Munich, 1981.

Kästner, Erich, *Notabene 1945: Ein Tagebuch*, Berlin, 1961.

Kater, Michael, *The Nazi Party: A Social Profile of Members and Leaders, 1919–1945*, Oxford, 1983.

Kehrl, Hans, *Krisenmanager im Dritten Reich*, Düsseldorf, 1973.

Kersten, Felix, *The Kersten Memoirs 1940–1945*, London, 1956.

Kilian, Katrin, 'Kriegsstimmungen: Emotionen einfacher Soldaten in Feldpostbriefen', in *DRZW*, vol. 9/2.

Kirk, Timothy, *Nazism and the Working Class in Austria*, Cambridge, 1996.

Kissel, Hans, *Der Deutsche Volkssturm 1944/45*, Frankfurt am Main, 1962.

Klemperer, Victor, *Ich will Zeugnis ablegen bis zum letzten*, vol. 2: *Tagebücher 1942–1945*, ed. Walter Nowojski and Hadwig Klemperer, Darmstadt, 1998.

Knopp, Guido, *Die große Flucht: Das Schicksal der Vertriebenen*, Munich, 2001.

—— *Der Sturm: Kriegsende im Osten*, pb. edn., Berlin, 2006.

—— *Der Untergang der Gustloff*, 2nd edn., pb., Munich, 2008.

Knox, MacGregor, '1 October 1942: Adolf Hitler, Wehrmacht Officer Policy, and Social Revolution', *Historical Journal*, 43 (2000).

Koenig, Ernest, 'Auschwitz III – Blechhammer: Erinnerungen', *Dachauer Hefte*, 15 (1999).

Kogon, Eugen, *Der SS-Staat: Das System der deutschen Konzentrationslager*, pb. edn., Munich, 1974.

Kohlhaas, Elisabeth, '"Aus einem Haus, aus dem eine weiße Fahnen erscheint, sind alle männlichen Personen zu erschießen": Durchhalteterror und Gewalt gegen Zivilisten am Kriegsende 1945', in Cord Arendes, Edgar Wolfrum and Jörg Zedler (eds.), *Terror nach Innen: Verbrechen am Ende des Zweiten Weltkrieges*, Göttingen, 2006.

Kolb, Eberhard, *Bergen-Belsen: Geschichte des 'Aufenthaltslagers' 1943–1945*, Hanover, 1962.

—— 'Bergen-Belsen: Die Errichtung des Lagers Bergen-Belsen und seine Funktion als "Aufenthaltslager" (1943/44)', in Martin Broszat (ed.), *Studien zur Geschichte der Konzentrationslager*, Stuttgart, 1970.

—— *Bergen-Belsen 1943 bis 1945*, Göttingen, 1985.

—— 'Die letzte Kriegsphase: Kommentierende Bemerkungen', in Ulrich Herbert, Karin Orth and Christoph Dieckmann (eds.), *Die nationalsozialistischen Konzentrationslager*, vol. 2, Göttingen, 1998.

Koller, Karl, *Der letzte Monat: Die Tagebuchaufzeichnungen des ehemaligen Chefs des Generalstabes der deutschen Luftwaffe vom 14. April bis zum 27. Mai 1945*, Mannheim, 1949.

Kommandant in Auschwitz: Autobiographische Aufzeichnungen des Rudolf Höss, ed. Martin Broszat, pb. edn., Munich, 1963.

Konrad, Joachim, 'Das Ende von Breslau', *VfZ*, 4 (1956).

Koschorrek, Günter K., *Blood Red Snow: The Memoirs of a German Soldier on the Eastern Front*, London, 2002.

Kossert, Andreas, '"Endlösung on the Amber Shore": The Massacre in January 1945 on the Baltic Seashore – a Repressed Chapter of East Prussian History', *Leo Baeck Year Book*, 40 (2004).

—— *Damals in Ostpreußen: Der Untergang einer deutschen Provinz*, Munich, 2008.

Krakowski, Schmuel, 'Massacre of Jewish Prisoners on the Samland Peninsula – Documents', *YVS*, 24 (1994).

Kramarz, Joachim, *Stauffenberg: The Life and Death of an Officer, November 15th 1907–July 20th 1944*, London, 1967.

Kraus, Herbert, 'Karl Dönitz und das Ende des "Dritten Reiches"', in Hans-Erich Volkmann (ed.), *Ende des Dritten Reiches – Ende des Zweiten Weltkriegs: Eine perspektivische Rückschau*, Munich and Zurich, 1995.

—— 'Großadmiral Karl Dönitz', in Gerd R. Ueberschär (ed.), *Hitlers militärische Elite*, vol. 2: *Vom Kriegsbeginn bis zum Weltkriegsende*, Darmstadt, 1998.

Krautkrämer, Elmar, 'Generalfeldmarschall Albert Kesselring', in Gerd R. Ueberschär (ed.), *Hitlers militärische Elite*, vol. 1: *Von den Anfängen des Regimes bis Kriegsbeginn*, Darmstadt, 1998.

Kriegsende in Deutschland, Hamburg, 2005.

Kriegstagebuch des Oberkommando der Wehrmacht (Wehrmachtsführungsstab), ed. Percy Ernst Schramm, vol. 4, Frankfurt am Main, 1961.

Kriegstagebuch der Seekriegsleitung 1939–1945, part A, ed. Werner Rahn and

Gerhard Schreiber, with Hansjoseph Maierhofer, vols. 63–8, Berlin, Bonn and Hamburg, 1996–7.

Kroener, Bernhard R., '"Menschenbewirtschaftung"', Bevölkerungsverteilung und personelle Rüstung in der zweiten Kriegshälfte (1942–1944)', in *DRZW*, vol. 5/2.

—— 'Auf dem Weg zu einer "nationalsozialistischen Volksarmee": Die soziale Öffnung des Heeresoffizerkorps im Zweiten Weltkrieg', in Martin Broszat, Klaus-Dietmar Henke and Hans Woller (eds.), *Von Stalingrad zur Währungsreform: Zur Sozialgeschichte des Umbruchs in Deutschland*, Munich, 1988.

—— '"Frontochsen" und "Etappenbullen": Zur Ideologisierung militärischer Organisationsstrukturen im Zweiten Weltkrieg', in Rolf-Dieter Müller and Hans-Erich Volkmann (eds.), *Die Wehrmacht: Mythos und Realität*, Munich, 1999.

—— '*Der starke Mann im Heimatkriegsgebiet': Generaloberst Friedrich Fromm. Eine Biographie*, Paderborn, 2005.

Kronika, Jacob, *Der Untergang Berlins*, Flensburg, 1946.

Kulka, Otto Dov, 'The German Population and the Jews: State of Research and New Perspectives', in David Bankier (ed.), *Probing the Depths of German Antisemitism: German Society and the Persecution of the Jews, 1933–1941*, New York, Oxford and Jerusalem, 2000.

—— and Jäckel, Eberhard (eds.), *Die Juden in den geheimen NS-Stimmungsberichten 1933–1945*, Düsseldorf, 2004.

Kunz, Andreas, 'Die Wehrmacht 1944/45: Eine Armee im Untergang', in *DRZW*, vol. 10/2.

—— 'Die Wehrmacht in der Agonie der nationalsozialistischen Herrschaft 1944/45: Eine Gedankenskizze', in Jörg Hillmann and John Zimmermann (eds.), *Kriegsende 1945 in Deutschland*, Munich, 2002.

—— *Wehrmacht und Niederlage: Die bewaffnete Macht in der Endphase der nationalsozialistischen Herrschaft 1944 bis 1945*, Munich, 2007.

Kunze, Karl, *Kriegsende in Franken und der Kampf um Nürnberg im April 1945*, Nuremberg, 1995.

Kurowski, Franz, 'Dietrich and Manteuffel', in Correlli Barnett (ed.), *Hitler's Generals*, London, 1990.

Lagebesprechungen im Führerhauptquartier: Protokollfragmente aus Hitlers militärischen Konferenzen 1942–1945, ed. Helmut Heiber, Berlin, Darmstadt and Vienna, 1963.

Lakowski, Richard, 'Der Zusammenbruch der deutschen Verteidigung zwischen Ostsee und Karpaten', in *DRZW*, vol. 10/1.

—— and Büll, Hans-Joachim, *Lebenszeichen 1945: Feldpost aus den letzten Kriegstagen*, Leipzig, 2002.

von Lang, Jochen, *Der Sekretär: Martin Bormann. Der Mann, der Hitler beherrschte*, Frankfurt am Main, 1980.

Large, David Clay, *Berlin*, New York, 2000.

Lass, Edgar Günther, *Die Flucht: Ostpreußen 1944/45*, Bad Nauheim, 1964.

Latzel, Klaus, 'Wehrmachtsoldaten zwischen "Normalität" und NS-Ideologie, oder: Was sucht die Forschung in der Feldpost?' in Rolf-Dieter Müller and Hans-Erich Volkmann (eds.), *Die Wehrmacht: Mythos und Realität*, Munich, 1999.

Lauterbacher, Hartmann, *Erlebt und mitgestaltet*, Preußisch Oldendorf, 1984.

Lehndorff, Hans Graf von, *Ostpreußisches Tagebuch: Aufzeichnungen eines Arztes aus den Jahren 1945–1947*, pb. edn., Munich, 1967.

Das letzte halbe Jahr: Stimmungsberichte der Wehrmachtpropaganda 1944/45, ed. Wolfram Wette, Ricarda Bremer and Detlef Vogel, Essen, 2001.

Lewis, Sam L., 'Albert Kesselring – der Soldat als Manager', in Ronald Smelser and Enrico Syring (eds.), *Die Militärelite des Dritten Reiches*, Berlin, 1995.

Lilla, Joachim, *Die Stellvertretenden Gauleiter und die Vertretung der Gauleiter der NSDAP im 'Dritten Reich'*, Koblenz, 2003.

Loeffel, Robert, 'Soldiers and Terror: Re-evaluating the Complicity of the Wehrmacht in Nazi Germany', *German History*, 27 (2009).

Longerich, Peter, 'Joseph Goebbels und der totale Krieg: Eine unbekannte Denkschrift des Propagandaministers vom 18. Juli 1944', *VfZ*, 35 (1987).

—— *Hitlers Stellvertreter: Führung der Partei und Kontrolle des Staatsapparates durch den Stab Heß und die Partei-Kanzlei Bormann*, Munich, 1992.

—— *'Davon haben wir nichts gewußt!' Die Deutschen und die Judenverfolgung 1933–1945*, Munich, 2006.

—— *Heinrich Himmler: Biographie*, Munich, 2008.

—— *Holocaust: The Nazi Persecution and Murder of the Jews*, Oxford, 2010.

Lorenz, Georg, *Die Penzberger Mordnacht vom 28. April 1945 vor dem Richter*, Garmisch-Partenkirchen, 1948.

Loth, Wilfried, 'Die deutsche Frage und der Wandel des internationalen Systems', in *DRZW*, vol. 10/2.

Lüdde-Neurath, Walter, *Regierung Dönitz: Die letzten Tage des Dritten Reiches*, 5th edn., Leoni am Starnberger See, 1981.

Ludewig, Joachim, 'Walter Model – Hitlers bester Feldmarschall?' in Ronald Smelser and Enrico Syring (eds.), *Die Militärelite des Dritten Reiches*, Berlin, 1995.

Magenheimer, Heinz, *Hitler's War: German Military Strategy 1940–1945*, London, 1998.

Maier, Reinhold, *Ende und Wende: Das schwäbische Schicksal 1944–1946. Briefe und Tagebuchaufzeichnungen*, Stuttgart and Tübingen, 1948.

Malanowski, Wolfgang (ed.), *1945: Deutschland in der Stunde Null*, Reinbek bei Hamburg, 1985.

Mammach, Klaus, *Der Volkssturm: Bestandteil des totalen Kriegseinsatzes der deutschen Bevölkerung 1944/45*, Berlin, 1981.

Man, John, *The Penguin Atlas of D-Day and the Normandy Campaign*, London, 1994.

von Manstein, Erich, *Lost Victories*, London, 1982.

Mason, Timothy W., *Sozialpolitik im Dritten Reich: Arbeiterklasse und Volksgemeinschaft*, Opladen, 1977.

Mazower, Mark, *Hitler's Empire: Nazi Rule in Occupied Europe*, London, 2008.

Meindl, Ralf, 'Erich Koch – Gauleiter von Ostpreußen', in Christian Pletzing (ed.), *Vorposten des Reichs? Ostpreußen 1933–1945*, Munich, 2006.

—— *Ostpreußens Gauleiter: Erich Koch – eine politische Biographie*, Osnabrück, 2007.

Meldungen aus dem Reich, vol. 17, ed. Heinz Boberach, Herrsching, 1984.

The Memoirs of Field-Marshal Kesselring, Greenhill Books edn., London, 1997.

Merritt, A. J., and Merritt, R. L. (eds.), *Public Opinion in Occupied Germany: The OMGUS Surveys, 1945–1949*, Urbana, Ill., 1970.

Messerschmidt, Manfred, *Die Wehrmacht im NS-Staat: Zeit der Indoktrination*, Hamburg, 1969.

—— 'Krieg in der Trümmerlandschaft: "Pflichterfüllung" wofür?' in Ulrich Borsdorf and Mathilde Jamin (eds.), *Über Leben im Krieg: Kriegserfahrungen in einer Industrieregion 1939–1945*, Reinbek bei Hamburg, 1989.

—— 'Die Wehrmacht in der Endphase: Realität und Perzeption', *Aus Parlament und Zeitgeschichte*, 32–3 (1989).

—— 'Deserteure im Zweiten Weltkrieg', in Wolfgang Wette (ed.), *Deserteure der Wehrmacht*, Essen, 1995.

—— 'Die Wehrmacht: Vom Realitätsverlust zum Selbstbetrug', in Hans-Erich Volkmann (ed.), *Ende des Dritten Reiches - Ende des Zweiten Weltkriegs: Eine perspektivische Rückschau*, Munich and Zurich, 1995.

—— *Die Wehrmachtjustiz 1933–1945*, Paderborn, 2005.

—— and Wullner, Fritz, *Die Wehrmachtjustiz*, Baden-Baden, 1987.

Mierzejewski, Alfred C., *The Collapse of the German War Economy, 1944–1945: Allied Air Power and the German National Railway*, Chapel Hill, NC, 1988.

—— 'When Did Albert Speer Give Up?', *Historical Journal*, 31 (1988).

Miller, Michael D., and Schulz, Andreas (eds.), *Gauleiter: The Regional Leaders of the Nazi Party and their Deputies*, CD ROM (n.d.) (c. 2004).

Mommsen, Hans, 'Social Views and Constitutional Plans of the Resistance', in Hermann Graml et al., *The German Resistance to Hitler*, London, 1970.

—— 'The Dissolution of the Third Reich: Crisis Management and Collapse, 1943–1945', *Bulletin of the German Historical Institute, Washington DC*, 27 (2000).

—— 'The Indian Summer and the Collapse of the Third Reich: The Last Act', in Hans Mommsen (ed.), *The Third Reich between Vision and Reality*, Oxford and New York, 2001.

—— 'The Dissolution of the Third Reich', in Frank Biess, Mark Roseman and Hanna Schissler (eds.), *Conflict, Catastrophe and Continuity: Essays on Modern German History*, Oxford and New York, 2007.

Moore, Bob, 'The Western Allies and Food Relief to the Occupied Netherlands, 1944–45', *War and Society*, 10 (1992).

Moorhouse, Roger, *Berlin at War: Life and Death in Hitler's Capital 1939–45*, London, 2010.

Müller, Delia, and Lepschies, Madlen, *Tage der Angst und der Hoffnung: Erinnerungen an die Todesmärsche aus dem Frauen-Konzentrationslager Ravensbrück Ende April 1945*, Berlin, n.d.

Müller, Klaus-Jürgen, 'The Wehrmacht: Western Front', in David Wingeate Pike (ed.), *The Closing of the Second World War: Twilight of a Totalitarianism*, New York, 2001.

Müller, Rolf-Dieter, 'Albert Speer und die Rüstungspolitik im Totalen Krieg', in *DRZW*, vol. 5/2.

——— 'Der Zusammenbruch des Wirtschaftslebens und die Anfänge des Wiederaufbaus', in *DRZW*, vol. 10/2.

——— 'Das Deutsche Reich und das Jahr 1945: Eine Bilanz', in *DRZW*, vol. 10/2.

——— 'Speers Rüstungspolitik im Totalen Krieg', *Militärgeschichtliche Zeitschrift*, 59 (2000).

——— *Der Bombenkrieg 1939–1945*, Berlin, 2004.

——— 'Der Feuersturm und die unbekannten Toten von Dresden', *Geschichte in Wissenschaft und Unterricht*, 59 (2008).

——— and Ueberschär, Gerd R., *Kriegsende 1945. Die Zerstörung des Deutschen Reiches*, Frankfurt am Main, 1994.

——— and Volkmann, Hans-Erich (eds.), *Die Wehrmacht: Mythos und Realität*, Munich, 1999.

Müller, Sven Oliver, 'Nationalismus in der deutschen Kriegsgesellschaft 1939 bis 1945', in *DRZW*, vol. 9/2.

Münkler, Herfried, *Machtzerfall: Die letzten Tage des Dritten Reiches dargestellt am Beispiel der hessischen Kreisstadt Friedberg*, Berlin, 1985.

Nadler, Fritz, *Eine Stadt im Schatten Streichers*, Nuremberg, 1969.

Neander, Joachim, *Das Konzentrationslager 'Mittelbau' in der Endphase der nationalsozialistischen Diktatur*, Clausthal-Zellerfeld, 1997.

——— *Gardelegen 1945: Das Ende der Häftlingstransporte aus dem Konzentrationslager 'Mittelbau'*, Magdeburg, 1998.

Nebelin, Manfred, 'Nazi Germany: Eastern Front', in David Wingeate Pike (ed.), *The Closing of the Second World War: Twilight of a Totalitarianism*, New York, 2001.

Neitzel, Sönke, 'Der Bedeutungswandel der Kriegsmarine im Zweiten Weltkrieg', in Rolf-Dieter Müller and Hans-Erich Volkmann (eds.), *Die Wehrmacht: Mythos und Realität*, Munich, 1999.

——— *Abgehört: Deutsche Generäle in britischer Kriegsgefangenschaft 1942–1945*, Berlin, 2005.

——— *Tapping Hitler's Generals: Transcripts of Secret Conversations, 1942–45*, Barnsley, 2007.

Die Niederlage 1945: Aus dem Kriegstagebuch des Oberkommandos der Wehrmacht, ed. Percy Ernst Schramm, Munich, 1962.

Noble, Alastair, *Nazi Rule and the Soviet Offensive in Eastern Germany, 1944–1945: The Darkest Hour*, Brighton and Portland, Ore., 2009.

Nofi, Albert A. (ed.), *The War against Hitler: Military Strategy in the West*, Conshohocken, Pa., 1995.

Nolzen, Armin, 'Die NSDAP, der Krieg und die deutsche Gesellschaft', in *DRZW*, vol. 9/1.

—— 'Von der geistigen Assimilation zur institutionellen Kooperation: Das Verhältnis zwischen NSDAP und Wehrmacht, 1943–1945', in Jörg Hillmann and John Zimmermann (eds.), *Kriegsende 1945 in Deutschland*, Munich, 2002.

—— 'Charismatic Legitimation and Bureaucratic Rule: The NSDAP in the Third Reich, 1933–1945', *German History*, 23 (2005).

—— 'Die NSDAP und die deutsche Gesellschaft im Zweiten Weltkrieg', in *Kriegsende in Deutschland*, Hamburg, 2005.

Orlow, Dietrich, *The History of the Nazi Party*, vol. 2: *1933–1945*, Newton Abbot, 1973.

Orth, Karin, *Das System der nationalsozialistischen Konzentrationslager: Eine politische Organisationsgeschichte*, Hamburg, 1999.

Orth, Kathrin, 'Kampfmoral und Einsatzbereitschaft in der Kriegsmarine 1945', in Jörg Hillmann and John Zimmermann (eds.), *Kriegsende 1945 in Deutschland*, Munich, 2002.

von Oven, Wilfred, *Mit Goebbels bis zum Ende*, vol. 2, Buenos Aires, 1950.

—— *Finale Furioso: Mit Goebbels bis zum Ende*, Tübingen, 1974.

Overmans, Rüdiger, 'Das Schicksal der deutschen Kriegsgefangenen des Zweiten Weltkrieges', in *DRZW*, vol. 10/2.

—— 'Die Toten des Zweiten Weltkriegs in Deutschland', in Wolfgang Michalka (ed.), *Der Zweite Weltkrieg: Analysen, Grundzüge, Forschungsbilanz*, Munich and Zurich, 1989.

—— *Deutsche militärische Verluste im Zweiten Weltkrieg*, Munich, 1999.

—— '55 Millionen Opfer des Zweiten Weltkrieges? Zum Stand der Forschung nach mehr als 40 Jahren', *Militärgeschichtliche Mitteilungen*, 48 (1990).

Overy, Richard, *Why the Allies Won*, London, 1995.

The Oxford Companion to the Second World War, ed. I. C. B. Dear and M. R. D. Foot, Oxford, 1995.

Padfield, Peter, *Himmler: Reichsführer-SS*, London, 1990.

Padover, Saul K., *Psychologist in Germany: The Story of an American Intelligence Officer*, London, 1946.

Parker, R. A. C., *Struggle for Survival: The History of the Second World War*, Oxford, 1990.

Patrick, Stephen B., 'The Ardennes Offensive: An Analysis of the Battle of the Bulge', in Albert A. Nofi (ed.), *The War against Hitler: Military Strategy in the West*, Conshohocken, Pa., 1995.

Pätzold, Kurt, and Weißbecker, Manfred, *Geschichte der NSDAP 1920–1945*, Cologne, 1981.

Paul, Gerhard, '"Diese Erschießungen haben mich innerlich gar nicht mehr berührt": Die Kriegsendphasenverbrechen der Gestapo 1944/45', in Gerhard Paul and Klaus-Michael Mallmann (eds.), *Die Gestapo im Zweiten Weltkrieg: 'Heimatfront' und besetztes Europa*, Darmstadt, 2000.

—— and Primavesi, Alexander, 'Die Verfolgung der "Fremdvölkischen": Das Beispiel der Staatspolizeistelle Dortmund', in Gerhard Paul and Klaus-Michael Mallmann (eds.), *Die Gestapo: Mythos und Realität*, Darmstadt, 1995.

Peikert, Paul, *'Festung Breslau' in den Berichten eines Pfarrers 22. Januar bis 6. Mai 1945*, ed. Karol Jonca and Alfred Konieczny, Wrocław, 1993.

Petzold, Heinz, 'Cottbus zwischen Januar und Mai 1945', in Werner Stang und Kurt Arlt (eds.), *Brandenburg im Jahr 1945*, Potsdam, 1995.

Peukert, Detlef, *Die Edelweißpiraten: Protestbewegungen jugendlicher Arbeiter im Dritten Reich*, Cologne, 1980.

Pickholz-Barnitsch, Olga M., 'The Evacuation of the Stutthof Concentration Camp', *Yad Vashem Bulletin*, 16 (1965).

Poll, Bernhard (ed.), *Das Schicksal Aachens im Herbst 1944: Authentische Berichte*, Aachen, 1955.

—— *Das Schicksal Aachens im Herbst 1944: Authentische Berichte II*, Aachen, 1962.

Pöllmann, Guido, 'Rote Armee in Nemmersdorf am 22.10.1944', in Franz W. Seidler and Alfred M. de Zayas (eds.), *Kriegsverbrechen in Europa und im Nahen Osten im 20. Jahrhundert*, Hamburg, 2002.

Pommerin, Reiner, 'The Wehrmacht: Eastern Front', in David Wingeate Pike (ed.), *The Closing of the Second World War: Twilight of a Totalitarianism*, New York, 2001.

Probert, Henry, *Bomber Harris: His Life and Times*, London, 2001.

Rahn, Werner, 'Die deutsche Seekriegsführung 1943 bis 1945', in *DRZW*, vol. 10/1.

Rass, Christoph, 'Das Sozialprofil von Kampfverbänden des deutschen Heeres 1919 bis 1945', in *DRZW*, vol. 9/1.

—— *'Menschenmaterial': Deutsche Soldaten an der Ostfront. Innenansichten einer Infanteriedivision 1939–1945*, Paderborn, 2003.

—— Rohrkamp, René, and Quadflieg, Peter M., *General Graf von Schwerin und das Kriegsende in Aachen: Ereignis, Mythos, Analyse*, Aachen, 2007.

Rauchensteiner, Manfried, *Der Krieg in Österreich 1945*, 2nd edn., Vienna, 1984.

Rebentisch, Dieter, *Führerstaat und Verwaltung im Zweiten Weltkrieg*, Stuttgart, 1989.

—— and Teppe, Karl (eds.), *Verwaltung contra Menschenführung im Staat Hitlers*, Göttingen, 1986.

Rees, Laurence, *Auschwitz: The Nazis and the 'Final Solution'*, London, 2005.

Reibel, Carl-Wilhelm, *Das Fundament der Diktatur: Die NSDAP-Ortsgruppen 1932–1945*, Paderborn, 2002.

Reitlinger, Gerald, *The Final Solution*, Sphere Books edn., London, 1971.

Rendulić, Lothar, *Gekämpft, Gesiegt, Geschlagen*, Wels, 1952.

Reuth, Ralf Georg, *Goebbels*, Munich and Zurich, 1990.

Reynolds, Michael, *The Devil's Adjutant: Jochen Peiper, Panzer Leader*, Staplehurst, 1995.

Richarz, Monika, *Jüdisches Leben in Deutschland: Selbstzeugnisse zur Sozialgeschichte 1918–1945*, Stuttgart, 1982.

Riedel, Hermann, *Halt! Schweizer Grenze!*, Konstanz, 1983.

Rohland, Walter, *Bewegte Zeiten*, Stuttgart, 1978.

Rossiwall, Theo, *Die letzten Tage: Die militärische Besetzung Österreichs 1945*, Vienna, 1969.

Rothfels, Hans, *The German Opposition to Hitler*, pb. edn., London, 1970.

Rudorff, Andrea, 'Blechhammer (Blachownia)', in Wolfgang Benz and Barbara Distel (eds.), *Der Ort des Terrors: Geschichte der nationalsozialistischen Konzentrationslager*, vol. 5, Munich, 2007.

Rusinek, Bernd-A., ' "Wat denkste, wat mir objerümt han": Massenmord und Spurenbeseitigung am Beispiel der Staatspolizeistelle Köln 1944/45', in Gerhard Paul and Klaus-Michael Mallmann (eds.), *Die Gestapo: Mythos und Realität*, Darmstadt, 1995.

Sauer, Paul, *Württemberg in der Zeit des Nationalsozialismus*, Ulm, 1975.

—— *Demokratischer Neubeginn in Not und Elend: Das Land Württemberg-Baden von 1945 bis 1952*, Ulm, 1979.

Schellenberg, Walter, *Schellenberg*, pb. edn., London 1965.

Scheurig, Bodo, *Alfred Jodl: Gehorsam und Verhängnis*, Berlin and Frankfurt am Main, 1991.

Schmidt, Matthias, *Albert Speer: Das Ende eines Mythos*, Berne and Munich, 1982.

Schmiechen-Ackermann, Detlef, 'Der "Blockwart": Die unteren Parteifunktionäre im nationalsozialistischen Terror- und Überwachungsapparat', *VfZ*, 48 (2000).

Schmier, Louis Eugene, 'Martin Bormann and the Nazi Party 1941–1945', Ph.D. thesis, University of North Carolina at Chapel Hill, 1969.

Schönherr, Klaus, 'Der Zusammenbruch im Osten: Die Rückzugskämpfe seit Sommer 1944', in *DRZW*, vol. 8.

—— 'Ferdinand Schörner – Der idealtypische Nazi-General', in Ronald Smelser and Enrico Syring (eds.), *Die Militärelite des Dritten Reiches*, Berlin, 1995.

Schroeder, Christa, *Er war mein Chef: Aus dem Nachlaß der Sekretärin von Adolf Hitler*, Munich and Vienna 1985.

Schulz-Naumann, Joachim, *Mecklenburg 1945*, Munich, 1989.

Schwarz, Egbert, 'Die letzten Tage des Dritten Reiches: Untersuchung zu Justiz und NS-Verbrechen in der Kriegsendphase März/April 1945', MA thesis, University of Düsseldorf, 1990.

Schwarz, Michael, 'Ethnische "Säuberung" als Kriegsfolge: Ursachen und Verlauf der Vertreibung der deutschen Zivilbevölkerung aus Ostdeutschland und Osteuropa 1941 bis 1950', in *DRZW*, vol. 10/2.

Schwendemann, Heinrich, 'Endkampf und Zusammenbruch im deutschen Osten', *Freiburger Universitätsblätter*, 130 (1995).

—— 'Strategie der Selbstvernichtung: Die Wehrmachtführung im "Endkampf" um das "Dritte Reich"', in Rolf-Dieter Müller and Hans-Erich Volkmann (eds.), *Die Wehrmacht: Mythos und Realität*, Munich, 1999.

—— '"Deutsche Menschen vor der Vernichtung durch den Bolschewismus zu retten": Das Programm der Regierung Dönitz und der Beginn einer Legendenbildung', in Jörg Hillmann and John Zimmermann (eds.), *Kriegsende 1945 in Deutschland*, Munich, 2002.

—— 'Tod zwischen den Fronten', in *Spiegel Special 2*, Hamburg, 2002.

—— '"Drastic Measures to Defend the Reich at the Oder and the Rhine . . .": A Forgotten Memorandum of Albert Speer of 18 March 1945', *Journal of Contemporary History*, 38 (2003).

—— '"Verbrannte Erde"? Hitlers "Nero-Befehl" vom 19. März 1945', in *Kriegsende in Deutschland*, Hamburg, 2005.

—— 'Das Kriegsende in Ostpreußen und in Südbaden im Vergleich', in Bernd Martin (ed.), *Der Zweite Weltkrieg und seine Folgen: Ereignisse – Auswirkungen – Reflexionen*, Freiburg, 2006.

—— 'Ein unüberwindlicher Wall gegen den Bolschewismus: Die Vorbereitung der "Reichsverteidigung" im Osten im zweiten Halbjahr 1944', in *Schlüsseljahr 1944*, ed. Bayerische Landeszentrale für Politische Bildungsarbeit, Munich, 2007.

Schwerin von Krosigk, Lutz Graf, *Es geschah in Deutschland*, Tübingen and Stuttgart, 1951.

—— 'Persönliche Erinnerungen', part 2: '25 Jahre Berlin 1920 bis 1945', unpublished typescript, n.d.

Seidler, Franz W., *'Deutscher Volkssturm': Das letzte Aufgebot 1944/45*, Munich and Berlin, 1989.

—— and Zayas, Alfred M. de (eds.), *Kriegsverbrechen in Europa und im Nahen Osten im 20. Jahrhundert*, Hamburg, 2002.

Semmler, Rudolf, *Goebbels – the Man Next to Hitler*, London, 1947.

Sereny, Gitta, *Albert Speer: His Battle with Truth*, London, 1995.

Serger, Bernd, Böttcher, Karin-Anne, and Ueberschär, Gerd R. (eds.), *Südbaden unter Hakenkreuz und Trikolore: Zeitzeugen berichten über das Kriegsende und die französische Besetzung*, Freiburg im Breisgau, Berlin and Vienna, 2006.

Siebel-Achenbach, Sebastian, *Lower Silesia from Nazi Germany to Communist Poland, 1942–49*, London, 1994.

Smelser, Ronald, *Robert Ley: Hitler's Labor Front Leader*, Oxford, New York and Hamburg, 1988.

—— and Syring, Enrico (eds.), *Die Militärelite des Dritten Reiches*, Berlin, 1995.

Speer, Albert, *Erinnerungen*, Frankfurt am Main and Berlin, 1969.

Spiegelbild einer Verschwörung: Die Kaltenbrunner-Berichte an Bormann und Hitler über das Attentat vom 20. Juli 1944. Geheime Dokumente aus dem ehemaligen Reichssicherheitshauptamt, ed. Archiv Peter, Stuttgart, 1961.

'*Spiegelbild einer Verschwörung*': *Die Opposition gegen Hitler und der Staatsstreich vom 20. Juli 1944 in der SD-Berichterstattung*, ed. Hans-Adolf Jacobsen, 2 vols., Stuttgart, 1984.

Sprenger, Isabell, 'Das KZ Groß-Rosen in der letzten Kriegsphase', in Ulrich Herbert, Karin Orth and Christoph Dieckmann (eds.), *Die nationalsozialistischen Konzentrationslager*, vol. 2, Göttingen, 1998.

Stadlbauer, Ferdinand, 'Die letzten Tage des Gauleiters Wächtler', *Waldmünchner Heimatbote*, 12 (1985).

Stadler, Karl, *Österreich 1938–1945 in Spiegel der NS-Akten*, Vienna, 1966.

Stafford, David, *Endgame 1945: Victory, Retribution, Liberation*, London, 2007.

Stahl, Friedrich-Christian, 'Generaloberst Kurt Zeitzler', in Gerd R. Ueberschär (ed.), *Hitlers militärische Elite*, vol. 2: *Vom Kriegsbeginn bis zum Weltkriegsende*, Darmstadt, 1998.

Stargardt, Nicholas, *Witnesses of War: Children's Lives under the Nazis*, London, 2005.

Stehle, Hansjakob, 'Deutsche Friedensfühler bei den Westmächten im Februar/ März 1945', *VfZ*, 30 (1982).

Steinbach, Peter, 'Hans Günther von Kluge – ein Zauderer im Zwielicht', in Ronald Smelser and Enrico Syring (eds.), *Die Militärelite des Dritten Reiches*, Berlin, 1995.

Steinbacher, Sybille, *Auschwitz: A History*, London, 2005.

Steinert, Marlis, *Die 23 Tage der Regierung Dönitz*, Düsseldorf and Vienna, 1967.

—— *Hitlers Krieg und die Deutschen*, Düsseldorf and Vienna, 1970.

—— 'The Allied Decision to Arrest the Dönitz Government', *Historical Journal*, 31 (1988).

Steinkamp, Peter, 'Generalfeldmarschall Ferdinand Schörner', in Gerd R. Ueberschär (ed.), *Hitlers militärische Elite*, vol. 2: *Vom Kriegsbeginn bis zum Weltkriegsende*, Darmstadt, 1998.

Stephenson, Jill, '"Resistance" to "No Surrender": Popular Disobedience in Württemberg in 1945', in Francis R. Nicosia and Lawrence D. Stokes (eds.), *Germans against Nazism*, Oxford and Providence, RI, 1990.

—— *Hitler's Home Front: Württemberg under the Nazis*, London, 2006.

Stettin/Szczecin 1945–1946, Rostock, 1994.

Strebel, Bernhard, *Celle April 1945 Revisited*, Bielefeld, 2008.

Strzelecki, Andrzej, 'Der Todesmarsch der Häftlinge aus dem KL Auschwitz', in Ulrich Herbert, Karin Orth and Christoph Dieckmann (eds.), *Die nationalsozialistischen Konzentrationslager*, vol. 2, Göttingen, 1998.

Sumowski, Hans-Burkhard, '*Jetzt war ich ganz allein auf die Welt*': *Erinnerungen an eine Kindheit in Königsberg 1944–1947*, Munich, 2009.

Süß, Dietmar, 'Die Endphase des Luftkriegs', in *Kriegsende in Deutschland*, Hamburg, 2005.

—— 'Der Kampf um die "Moral" im Bunker: Deutschland, Großbritannien und der Luftkrieg', in Frank Bajohr and Michael Wildt (eds.), *Volksgemeinschaft*:

Neue Forschungen zur Gesellschaft des Nationalsozialismus, Frankfurt am Main, 2009.

Die Tagebücher von Joseph Goebbels, part II, ed. Elke Fröhlich, vols. 12–15, Munich, 1995–6.

Taylor, Brian, *Barbarossa to Berlin: A Chronology of the Campaigns on the Eastern Front 1941 to 1945*, vol. 2, Stroud, 2008.

Taylor, Frederick, *Dresden: Tuesday 13 February 1945*, pb. edn., London, 2005.

Tenfelde Klaus, 'Proletarische Provinz: Radikalisierung und Widerstand in Penzberg/Oberbayern 1900 bis 1945', in Martin Broszat, Elke Fröhlich and Anton Grossmann (eds.), *Bayern in der NS-Zeit*, vol. 4, Munich and Vienna, 1981.

Teppe, Karl, 'Der Reichsverteidigungskommissar: Organisation und Praxis in Westfalen', in Dieter Rebentisch and Karl Teppe (eds.), *Verwaltung contra Menschenführung im Staat Hitlers*, Göttingen, 1986.

Thacker, Toby, *The End of the Third Reich: Defeat, Denazification and Nuremberg, January 1944–November 1946*, pb. edn., Stroud, 2008.

Thorwald, Jürgen, *Es begann an der Weichsel: Flucht und Vertreibung der Deutschen aus dem Osten*, pb. edn., Munich, 1995 (1st edn., 1949).

'Tief vergraben, nicht dran rühren', *Spiegel Special*, 2 (2005).

Tilitzki, Christian, *Alltag in Ostpreußen 1940–1945: Die geheimen Lageberichte der Königsberger Justiz 1940–1945*, Leer, 1991.

Toland, John, *The Last 100 Days*, London, 1965.

Tooze, Adam, *The Wages of Destruction: The Making and Breaking of the Nazi Economy*, London, 2006.

Trevor-Roper, H. R., *The Last Days of Hitler*, pb. edn., London, 1962.

Troll, Hildebrand, 'Aktionen zur Kriegsbeendigung im Frühjahr 1945', in Martin Broszat, Elke Fröhlich and Anton Grossmann (eds.), *Bayern in der NS-Zeit*, vol. 4, Munich and Vienna, 1981.

Ueberschär, Gerd R. (ed.), *Hitlers militärische Elite*, vol. 2: *Vom Kriegsbeginn bis zum Weltkriegsende*, Darmstadt, 1998.

Ungváry, Krisztián, 'Der Zusammenbruch im Osten: Die Rückzugskämpfe seit Sommer 1944', in *DRZW*, vol. 8.

United States Strategic Bombing Survey, New York and London, 1976, vol. 4.

Vagts, Alfred, 'Unconditional Surrender – vor und nach 1943', *VfZ*, 7 (1959).

Die Vertreibung der deutschen Bevölkerung aus den Gebieten östlich der Oder-Neiße, vols. 1–2, ed. Theodor Schieder *et al.*, pb. edn., Munich, 1984.

Vogel, Detlef, 'Deutsche und Alliierte Kriegführung im Westen', in *DRZW*, vol. 7.

Von der Diktatur zur Besatzung: Das Kriegsende 1945 im Gebiet des heutigen Landkreises Sigmaringen, ed. Landkreis Sigmaringen, Sigmaringen, 1995.

Vorländer, Herwart, 'NS-Volkswohlfahrt und Winterhilfswerk des deutschen Volkes', *VfZ*, 34 (1986).

—— *Die NSV: Darstellung und Dokumentation einer NS-Organisation*, Boppard, 1988.

Wachsmann, Nikolaus, *Hitler's Prisons: Legal Terror in Nazi Germany*, New Haven and London, 2004.

Wahl, Karl, *'... es ist das deutsche Herz'*: *Erlebnisse und Erkenntnisse eines ehemaligen Gauleiters*, Augsburg, 1954.

—— *Patrioten oder Verbrecher*, Heusenstamm bei Offenbach am Main, 1973.

Warlimont, Walter, *Inside Hitler's Headquarters 1939–45*, pb. edn., Novato, Calif., n.d. (original Eng. language edn., London, 1964).

Weber, Max, *Wirtschaft und Gesellschaft: Grundriß der verstehenden Soziologie*, 5th rev. edn., Tübingen, 1980.

Wegner, Bernt, 'Deutschland in Abgrund', in *DRZW*, vol. 8.

—— *Hitlers politische Soldaten*, Paderborn, 1982.

—— 'Hitler, der Zweite Weltkrieg und die Choreographie des Untergangs', *Geschichte und Gesellschaft*, 26 (2000).

—— 'The Ideology of Self-Destruction: Hitler and the Choreography of Defeat', *Bulletin of the German Historical Institute London*, 26/2 (2004).

Wehler, Hans-Ulrich, *Deutsche Gesellschaftsgeshichte*, vol. 4: *1914–1919*, 3rd edn., Munich, 2008.

—— *Der Nationalsozialismus: Bewegung, Führerherrschaft, Verbrechen*, Munich, 2009.

Die Wehrmachtberichte 1939–1945, vol. 3: *1. Januar 1944 bis 9. Mai 1945*, Munich, 1989.

Weinberg, Gerhard L., 'Adolf Hitler und der NS-Führungsoffizier (NSFO)', *VfZ*, 12 (1964).

—— *A World at Arms: A Global History of World War II*, Cambridge, 1994.

Welch, David, *Propaganda and the German Cinema 1933–1945*, Oxford, 1983.

Westphal, Siegfried, *Erinnerungen*, Mainz, 1975.

Wette, Wolfram, *Die Wehrmacht: Feindbilder, Vernichtungskrieg, Legenden*, Frankfurt am Main, 2002.

Widerstand und Verfolgung in Köln, ed. Historisches Archiv der Stadt Köln, Cologne, 1974.

Wieck, Michael, *Zeugnis vom Untergang Königsbergs: Ein 'Geltungsjude' berichtet*, Heidelberg, 1988.

Wildt, Michael, *Volksgemeinschaft als Selbstermächtigung*, Hamburg, 2007.

Wilhelm, Hans-Heinrich, 'Hitlers Ansprache vor Generalen und Offizieren am 26. Mai 1944', *Militärgeschichtliche Mitteilungen*, 2 (1976).

—— 'Heinz Guderian – "Panzerpapst" und Generalstabschef', in Ronald Smelser and Enrico Syring (eds.), *Die Militärelite des Dritten Reiches*, Berlin, 1995.

Wolfrum, Edgar, 'Widerstand in den letzten Kriegsmonaten', in Peter Steinbach and Johannes Tuchel (eds.), *Widerstand gegen den Nationalsozialismus*, Bonn, 1994.

Woller, Hans, *Gesellschaft und Politik in der amerikanischen Besatzungszone: Die Region Ansbach und Fürth*, Munich, 1986.

'*Wollt Ihr den totalen Krieg?*' *Die geheimen Goebbels-Konferenzen 1939–1943*, ed. Willi A. Boelcke, Munich, 1969.

Wullner, Fritz, *NS-Militärjustiz und das Elend der Geschichtsschreibung*, Baden-Baden, 1991.

Yelton, David K., *Hitler's Volkssturm: The Nazi Militia and the Fall of Germany, 1944–1945*, Lawrence, Kan., 2002.

Zamecnik, Stanislav, '"Kein Häftling darf lebend in die Hände des Feindes fallen": Zur Existenz des Himmler-Befehls vom 14–18. April 1945', *Dachauer Hefte*, 1 (1985),

Zarusky, Jürgen, 'Von der Sondergerichtsbarkeit zum Endphasenterror: Loyalitätserzwingung und Rache am Widerstand im Zusammenbruch des NS-Regimes', in Cord Arendes, Edgar Wolfrum and Jörg Zedler (eds.), *Terror nach Innen: Verbrechen am Ende des Zweiten Weltkrieges*, Göttingen, 2006.

Zeidler, Manfred, 'Die Rote Armee auf deutschem Boden', in *DRZW*, vol. 10/1.

—— *Kriegsende im Osten: Die Rote Armee und die Besetzung Deutschlands östlich von Oder und Neiße 1944/45*, Munich, 1996.

Zeitzeugen berichten . . . Schwäbisch Gmünd – Erinnerungen an die Zeit von 1930 bis 1945, ed. Stadtarchiv Schwäbisch Gmünd, Schwäbisch Gmünd, 1989.

Zhukov, G., *Reminiscences and Reflections*, vol. 2, Moscow, 1985.

Ziemann, Benjamin, 'Fluchten aus dem Konsens zum Durchhalten: Ergebnisse, Probleme und Perspektiven der Erforschung soldatischer Verweigerungsformen in der Wehrmacht 1939–1945', in Rolf-Dieter Müller and Hans-Erich Volkmann (eds.), *Die Wehrmacht: Mythos und Realität*, Munich, 1999.

Zimmermann, John, 'Die deutsche militärische Kriegführung im Westen 1944–45', in *DRZW*, vol. 10/1.

—— 'Die Kämpfe gegen die Westalliierten 1945 – ein Kampf bis zum Ende oder die Kreierung einer Legende?' in Jörg Hillmann and John Zimmermann (eds.), *Kriegsende 1945 in Deutschland*, Munich, 2002.

—— *Pflicht zum Untergang: Die deutsche Kriegführung im Westen des Reiches 1944/45*, Paderborn, 2009.

Zolling, Peter, 'Was machen wir am Tag nach unserem Sieg?' in Wolfgang Malanowski (ed.), *1945: Deutschland in der Stunde Null*, Reinbek bei Hamburg, 1985.

Index